SOCIAL PSYCHOLOGY

— Soc ψ of org's

— Ethnocent'm

SOCIAL PSYCHOLOGY

Paul F. Secord
QUEENS COLLEGE, C.U.N.Y.

Carl W. Backman
UNIVERSITY OF NEVADA, RENO

Second Edition

McGRAW-HILL BOOK COMPANY

*New York   St. Louis   San Francisco   Düsseldorf   Johannesburg
Kuala Lumpur   London   Mexico   Montreal
New Delhi   Panama   Rio de Janeiro
Singapore   Sydney   Toronto*

SOCIAL PSYCHOLOGY

Copyright © 1964, 1974 by McGraw-Hill, Inc. All rights reserved.
Printed in the United States of America. No part of this
publication may be reproduced, stored in a retrieval system,
or transmitted, in any form or by any means, electronic,
mechanical, photocopying, recording, or otherwise, without
the prior written permission of the publisher.

2 3 4 5 6 7 8 9 0 M A M M 7 9 8 7 6 5 4

This book was set in Times Roman by Rocappi, Inc.
The editors were John Hendry and James R. Belser;
the designer was Ben Kann;
and the production supervisor was Leroy A. Young.
The printer and binder was The Maple Press Company.

Library of Congress Cataloging in Publication Data

Secord, Paul F
    Social psychology.

    Bibliography: p.
    1. Social psychology.   I. Backman, Carl W.,
joint author.   II. Title.   [DNLM: 1. Psychology,
Social.   HM251 S445s 1974]
HM251.S4   1974   301.1   73-12721
ISBN 0-07-055914-7

To my mother
and to
Professor George J. Dudycha
—P.F.S.

To my parents
—C.W.B.

Contents

CHAPTER 16 COGNITIVE CONTROLS AND SOCIAL MOTIVATION

CHAPTER 17 SELF AND PERSONALITY

Preface

This second edition, like the first, is intended to faithfully reflect the active lines of inquiry characterizing contemporary social psychology. It continues the interdisciplinary tradition of the first. Written by a psychologist and a sociologist, the order of authorship does not signify any difference in the relative contributions of the two authors nor of the two disciplines. Some parts of the book stress psychological research and thought; others stress sociological studies and ideas. These varying emphases reflect the empirical literature of the field: certain lines of inquiry have been of greater interest to the psychologically trained researcher and other lines to the sociologically trained. But we have usually presented the viewpoints from both fields on particular topics or problems. Further, we have tried to weave together these contributions into a coherent pattern of explanation.

The text is organized topically rather than in terms of a single theoretical system. But some major topics have been organized in terms of what appears to be the most promising theoretical orientation. This topical treatment should enable instructors to use the book in a highly flexible fashion. They may vary the order of chapters, emphasize some subjects, and omit others. Asking the student to master the entire text in a three-hour semester or a five-hour quarter course might be too great an imposition. Since the book is comprehensive in coverage, many instructors will want to omit or spend less time with certain portions, according to what they think is important or essential. In spite of its range, therefore, the book is suitable for a one-semester course.

Another way to use the entire book has worked out well with the first edition. We have found it practical to offer Parts One and Four (social influence processes and socialization) during the fall semester, and Parts Two and Three (group structure and process and social roles) during the spring semester, with no prerequisite requirement for the second semester. Essentially the second semester then amounts to a course in small group behavior, with the section on social roles tying it to institutional structures.

Two topics often given specific treatment in social psychology texts have been omitted. Collective behavior, which traditionally has included the study of crowds, publics, and social movements, has not been explicitly dealt with—although some topics treated by us, such as the collective resolution of structural strain and social influence processes, do bear on collective behavior. While we believe that collective behavior is an important area, it has been relatively neglected by social psychologists in recent years.

The second topic, culture and personality, has been omitted for a different reason. This area, along with the study of national character, appears to have become a distinctive field in itself rather than an integral part of social psychology. But in discussing topics closely related to culture and personality, such as socialization, we have included some material pertaining to it.

Although we have retained the basic framework of the first edition, we have made extensive changes. Most of the text has been rewritten. The initial chapter in the first edition, on social perception, has been dropped, reflecting the fading interest in this topic. Chapters in the attitude section and in the section on social roles have been rearranged and reorganized.

The substantive changes in topics and treatments naturally reflect current emphases and changes in research in social psychology. Where research has been especially active, greater substantive changes have been made. But even in less active areas the material has been updated and reworked to achieve greater clarity. While we have gone to great lengths to avoid unnecessary jargon, we have provided a glossary of terms that have a use specific to social psychology.

Among the more substantive changes in this edition are the following: a shift in person perception from concern with trait judgments in static situations to attributions made during ongoing interaction, less emphasis on balance and dissonance theory interpretations of attitude change, a shift away from the small laboratory group to processes affecting interaction in a larger societal context, a shift from an emphasis on structure to an emphasis on process—at both the subinstitutional and institutional levels. This shift is illustrated in research on interpersonal attraction, which is now more concerned with the development of relationships between persons than with the properties of the sociometric structure. Similarly, the conception of social roles and role behavior has moved from a static view of role categories with fixed expectations to emphasis on the construction and reconstruction of role expectations through role negotiation and bargaining and the building of role identities. In the area of socialization, social psychologists, at least, are now placing more emphasis on the role of situational determinants of motive states and behavior and less emphasis on intraindividual determinants and childhood antecedents of motives and behaviors.

Our indebtedness to users of the first edition, both instructors and students alike, is very deep. Their helpful suggestions and criticisms have been so numerous that it is impossible to recount them here. We especially thank the psychologists and sociologists who read portions of the manuscript: Richard Curtis, David Goslin, Anthony Greenwald, Bibb Latané, Robert Leik, George Levinger, James Richardson, and Peter Warr. Our most profound indebtedness is to Richard Emerson and Karl Weick, who read and constructively criticized the entire manuscript.

We are indebted to Kim Blau, who has prepared an instructor's manual for this edition of our text. One feature of the manual is its many student exercises, which include experimental and field-study activities as well as classroom demonstrations. It is available from the publisher to teachers of the course.

We also thank Wendy Legge, who helped us with permissions, proofreading, bibliography, and indexing. Above all, we thank our wives, Marcia and Shirley, for their patience, encouragement, and forbearance.

Paul F. Secord
Carl W. Backman

SOCIAL PSYCHOLOGY

1

The Nature of Social Psychology

The most distinctive feature of human life is its social character. People do things in concert; they work together and play together. Moreover, people in interaction share an understanding of their various acts. And they react to one another in terms of these meanings.

The social psychologist studies the behavior of individuals in social contexts. Thus his business differs from that of the general psychologist, who often isolates the individual from his social environment; and it differs from that of the sociologist, who often studies the patterns of social interaction separately from the acting individuals.

Distinctive Characteristics of Interaction

The behavior of an individual in the presence of another person is at once a response and a stimulus to that other person. Because the other person (*O*) reacts to the behavior of a person (*P*), the behavior of *P* is likely to be tempered by the presence of *O*. *P* may consciously or unconsciously behave so as to elicit a particular response from *O*. His subsequent behavior depends upon his success or failure in eliciting certain behaviors from *O*.

But the matter is more complex than a simple sequential patterning of stimulus and response, action and reaction. Under ordinary circumstances, the behavior of people in interaction flows quite smoothly, as in the case of two neighbors chatting over the back fence. This occurs because each party to the interaction has learned to anticipate the response that an action on his part will elicit, as well as to anticipate the responses he will make toward the actions of the other party. Such interactions only flow smoothly, however, when both parties share the same definitions of their own and each other's acts, as well as a common understanding of the structure of their relation to each other. When two men in our society are introduced, each extends his hand and expects the other to extend his hand. But if one of the men is from a society where the handshake is not known as a symbol of greeting, this action is likely to falter. Such *mutual expectations* govern much everyday behavior. If the individual were studied only in isolation from other individuals, many of these controlling features of everyday interpersonal behavior would not be discovered.

Types of Analysis

The behavior of individuals in interaction may be analyzed in terms of three systems: the personality system, the social system, and the cultural system. Analysis in terms of *personality* considers properties of individuals such as attitudes, needs, traits, and feelings, as well as processes like learning or perception. For example, individual members of a delinquent gang might be studied. Such an analysis might reveal that they have stronger aggressive impulses than nondelinquents and that they perceive society as rather difficult and threatening. Analysis in terms of the *social system** focuses on *relations* among persons. Typically, each person is thought of as occupying one or more positions in these relations. Associated with each position are expectations about how a person in that position should think, feel, and act toward other members.

For example, one position in our delinquent gang might be that of gang leader. Closely related to that position might be two others occupied by the gang leader's "lieutenants." Gang members expect a leader to suggest and initiate group activities, to guide the progress of ongoing activities, and to evaluate their success. His lieutenants are expected to provide support and aid to the leader in carrying out the activities. We might think of the remaining gang members as occupying the position of "follower." Thus, much of the behavior of the gang members is a function of the group structure, consisting of

---

* As used in this text, italics serve one or both of the following purposes: (1) they emphasize important words or phrases, and (2) they denote technical words or phrases. Although technical terms and jargon have been kept to a minimum in this text, some terms are indispensable to an understanding of social psychology: these have been included. To aid in making their meanings clear, such terms are usually explained in the text discussion itself, but they have also been included in a glossary at the end of the book. Certain terms have somewhat different meanings in some contexts than in others, and often the glossary entry provides more information than the text proper. It is therefore recommended that the reader refer to the glossary frequently. He should also keep in mind that some perfectly familiar, everyday words have special meanings in social psychology. He should, of course, make sure that he knows how each term is being used in this book. The glossary will help him to do this.

the positions of leader, lieutenants, and followers, and the relations among these positions.

Central to analysis in terms of *culture* are the agreed-upon ideas about the social and nonsocial world. These include complex systems of beliefs as well as the values that members of a society place upon various kinds of activities. The juvenile gang is unknown in some societies, a fact which suggests that certain aspects of our culture are relevant to gang formation. These include belief patterns favoring late marriage, which leave a large number of males unaffiliated, and the complex technological nature of employment in our society, which prevents the early entrance of a sizable number of young males into adult employment.

Psychologists as psychologists are concerned primarily with analysis in terms of individual behavior; sociologists as sociologists are interested primarily in analysis in terms of the social system. Anthropologists are concerned with cultural systems. Social psychologists, however, while using as basic data the behavior and characteristics of individuals, try to understand individual behavior in terms of variables from all three systems. While analysis in each of the systems is kept distinct, individual behavior provides the focal point for relating these systems to each other.

Thus certain aspects of the personality of individuals may result from properties of the social system. When the social system called the family is structured in a certain way, for example, it produces individuals who are strongly motivated to achieve wealth, success, and status in a society, and when structured in other ways, it produces a much weaker need for achievement. Similarly, certain personality variables may affect the functioning of social systems. For example, the personality makeup of members of individual families produces marked variation in the functioning of this social system. Families in a whole society may be structured so as to encourage strong needs for achievement in children, because such behavior is related to the central values of the culture of the group. For the most part, social psychology deals in this fashion with the interplay among personality, social system, and, to a lesser extent, culture.

Approaches to Social Psychology

The mainstream of research in social psychology, especially among social psychologists who are psychologically trained, is experimental. This means that studies are carried out in the laboratory for the most part, although recent years have seen more efforts at experimental work in the field. In addition, however, several important lines of inquiry are found among sociologically trained social psychologists. Besides experimental work in sociology, which differs little from the experimental work of psychologically trained investigators, there are two clearly discernible lines: that of the *symbolic interactionists* and, recently on the scene, that of the *ethnomethodologists.* In addition, many sociologically trained investigators emphasize to a greater extent than psychologists the larger social structure and its functional relations to the behavior of individuals. Thus, sociologically trained social psychologists take more account of the role in individual behavior of such institutions as the family, the school, and the prison, and they have used a variety of methods including participant observation and the survey interview for dealing with such phenomena.

This book, written by a psychologist and a sociologist, attempts to take the best work from both of these fields and to weld them together into a coherent social psychology. While the authors follow the main tradition in emphasizing experimental work where it is available, nonexperimental work is also brought in, to improve both the coverage and the generalizability of the material dealt with. A word about symbolic interactionism and ethnomethodology is in order. Symbolic interactionism, descending from George Herbert Mead, emphasizes the reflexive nature of human interaction—that individuals make indications to themselves about their own actions and those of other persons.[1] These indications are typically linguistic representations which give meaning to human acts. Action is seen as a process of coping with the world instead of reacting to it on the basis of some preexisting psychological structure. As Herbert Blumer puts it,

> In order to act the individual has to identify what he wants, establish an objective or goal, map out a prospective line of behavior, note and interpret the actions of others, size up his situation, check himself at this or that point, figure out what to do at other points, and frequently spur himself on in the face of dragging dispositions or discouraging settings.[2]

In short, the symbolic interactionists emphasize the individual's status as an active agent in the process of constructing his actions as he goes along. Typically, they eschew the experimental method in favor of a procedure called *participant observation.* This method is most often used to study phenomena that cannot be approached by way of an experiment: A traditional investigative approach would destroy or badly distort the phenomena. Further, such phenomena often cannot be studied in retrospect by such means as interviewing. In participant observation, the observer participates actively in the lives of the people he is observing. For example, in studying a medical school, observers went to lectures and frequented laboratories, watching the students and engaging in casual conversation as they went about their activities. They followed the students to their dormitories and sat around while they talked about their experiences as students. In studying the clinical years, they accompanied interns on their rounds, and sat in on discussion groups and oral examinations.[3]

1. MEAD, 1934.   *2.* Reprinted with permission from University of Chicago Press and H. Blumer. Sociological implications of the thought of George Herbert Mead. *American Journal of Sociology,* 1966, **71,** 535–544. *3.* BECKER, 1958.

The newest distinctive approach to social psychology is that of the ethno-methodologists.[4] This is also referred to as *neosymbolic interactionism,* and it has a close relation to what is known as *labeling theory.* Ethnomethodology assumes that the social world has no real meaning apart from the various meanings attributed to it by individuals. This contrasts with traditional sociology, which finds the meaning of human behavior in the structures and processes which determine how people behave (e.g., an individual behaves in a manner appropriate to his social class level). Ethnomethodologists assert that the meanings of behavior are constructed and reconstructed by the ordinary man, as he goes about the activities of his daily life. It is the task of the ethnomethodologist, then, to study human action in a way that takes account of the meanings attributed to it by the ordinary man. This does not mean that all the meaning can be stated by the ordinary man. Certain human actions, for example, might be based upon background factors, upon certain unrecognized premises. The parties to the action behave as if they were acting on these premises even though they are not able to state them. Part of the work of the ethnomethodologist is to discover what the premises are.

Symbolic interactionism and experimental social psychology are somewhat at variance with one another, in that the typical experiment treats the participant as a reacting but noninitiating organism, whereas the interactionists think of the individual as an active, reflective agent who directs his own behavior. The attitude of the experimentalists is reflected in the term they assign to individuals serving in experiments—*subjects*—almost as if they were dealing with objects subjected to forces that change the behavior of the objects, which can then be recorded. The authors have departed from this terminology by adopting the term *participant* instead of *subject.*

At the same time, the great bulk of research in social psychology is experimental in nature and constitutes a substantial contribution to the understanding of human behavior. Throughout the book, the authors have attempted to be sympathetic to both the experimental tradition and the various nonexperimental traditions in social psychology. This approach maximizes the present state of knowledge, and the decision about the merits of particular methodologies is left for the future. The advantages of looking at behavioral phenomena from these several points of view will be repeatedly apparent throughout the book, as it is obvious that a more complete understanding of a particular phenomenon or problem is achieved through this multidisciplinary approach.

The advantages of the experimental method are well known. In natural settings, both persons and situations not only vary in the conditions in which an investigator might be interested, but they also vary simultaneously in other ways not of interest to him, ways that confuse the interpretation of any observations that may be made. The behavior observed in nonmanipulated natural settings may be due to any of the several conditions present, or to the charac-

4. GARFINKEL, 1967.

teristics of the persons involved. The experiment, on the other hand, makes possible setting up only the conditions in which the investigator is interested, so that any observed behavior can be attributed to these conditions. Moreover, assigning persons strictly at random to the various conditions avoids the possibility that the observed behavior might be a function of person characteristics that may in nature be more frequently associated with a particular condition.

An example might help to clarify these arguments. It is often observed in living groups that members like other members who they think like them. From this correlational observation it is not clear whether liking for the other members occurs first, and leads to the perception of being liked, or whether the perception of being liked occurs first and leads to liking for the other person. Further, the correlation might be explained in many ways. Perhaps persons with similar values are attracted to each other, or an individual may perceive other persons who have similar values as liking him. An experiment has resolved these questions.

A series of experimental groups were set up, and controlled information was released to the members before they had an opportunity to interact.[5] The information given each member led him to believe that three designated members in the group were especially apt to like him. Later, after a discussion period, each member was asked to indicate his liking for each of the other members of the group. A clear result was that an individual liked best the other members who he thought liked him.

This experiment establishes that the perception of being liked produces liking for the other person. This goes beyond the mere correlational findings because (1) it establishes the perception of being liked as antecedent to liking the other person, and (2) the three members designated as liking a particular member were selected at *random* by the experimenter, so as to ensure that as a group they would be similar to undesignated members on any characteristic (including actual liking) that might cause them to be liked.

This book covers an enormous amount of research in social psychology, in the attempt to represent a faithful picture of the present state of the field. While there is considerable selectivity in what is included, most major lines of research in social psychology have been represented. Approximately 1,200 studies are cited, selected from the many thousands of investigations in the literature. Because of the broad coverage, and because this is an elementary book on social psychology, the details of experiments are seldom dealt with. Moreover, space is not devoted to discussing the fine points of methodology, or to methodological controversies. Nor are significance levels (statistical estimates of the probability that the same results would be obtained if the experiment were repeated with another sample) reported.

Instead, only studies with adequate significance levels have been included, and investigations with serious methodological defects have been avoided. In

5. BACKMAN & SECORD, 1959.

fact, ideas have been buttressed with a series of studies, wherever available, rather with single investigations. By relying on the judgment of the authors in these matters, readers can focus upon the concepts and principles of social psychology without getting bogged down in the mechanics of validating the findings.

Finally, it should be noted that there is considerable ferment in contemporary social psychology. The overwhelming emphasis on the experimental method has been widely questioned. One of the chief criticisms has been that many research findings might not apply to behavior in natural settings. Another criticism questions the complacency of social psychologists in accepting findings based on group averages, with insufficient attention to the individual characteristics of persons. These criticisms and others are included in a book written by one of the authors in collaboration with a philosopher of science.[6]

That book also raises the fundamental issue of what model of man is most appropriate for behavioral science and social psychology. The choice of a model is a fundamental decision which affects the kinds of research methods used and the sort of theory which is appropriate for explaining observations. Yet, social psychologists have for the most part conducted their investigations without examining the premises implicit in their methods and the model that is implied by them. Little of this ferment is reflected in this textbook, for at this time the issues are highly controversial, and the ultimate direction of the field is unknown.

Plan of the Book

Part One begins with a discussion of how persons are known and evaluated, and the ways in which they constitute the social environment. Several chapters deal with the processes of social influence. Beginning with the elements of the influence process, subsequent chapters examine the operation of this process in mass-communication settings, and its relation to groups and larger structural elements. The part ends with a discussion of how intergroup attitudes originate, are maintained, and are changed.

In Part Two, the focus shifts to group structure and process, stressing features of interaction that lead to regular and stable relations between persons and groups. The observation of small groups enables the investigator to study the emergence of various group structures. Four structures, treated in some detail, pertain to four aspects of relations among group members: liking, social power or influence, status, and communication. Also treated in these chapters is group process: the changing pattern of relations between elements of structure over time. Such processes can best be understood in terms of a theoretical conception that views interaction as an exchange of rewards and costs by individual members.

6. HARRÉ & SECORD, 1972.

Part Three takes up the relation of institutional structures to individual behavior. Institutional structures are analyzed in terms of the concept of social role. Various structured relations that constitute a social system are described. Depending upon the position he occupies in such a system, a person is treated in certain ways and is likely to exhibit behavior appropriate to his position. Special attention is given to sources of strain that disturb the smooth functioning of these systems, as well as to various means of resolving such strains.

Part Four, the final three chapters of the book, is concerned with the processes by which individuals learn the norms and behaviors appropriate to their groups. It begins with the processes by which the child is socialized. Later the shaping of adult behaviors and attitudes is discussed. The closing chapter brings together many of the ideas encountered throughout the book, focusing on the individual and social forces accounting for stability and change in the behaviors of individuals.

PART ONE

Social Influence Processes

Part One begins with a consideration of how we come to know the personal world about us and what the nature of that knowledge is. By far the most important part of that world is the people in it, for most of our lives are spent interacting with other people. An individual's actions are partly shaped by his knowledge of the persons around him and by their expectations concerning his behavior. Thus, Chapter 2 develops the basic aspects of these ideas. In a later part of the book, in the chapters on social roles, some detailed consideration is given to the expectations that people have about each other and how these expectations fit into the scheme of things.

The other chapters in Part One are concerned with the various processes that shape and influence an individual's attitudes toward his environment and that modify his behavior. Chapter 3 deals with the basics of the influence process, focusing on the simpler case of interaction between two people, but considering the effects of influence on personality characteristics and states of individuals, the situational and relational structure in which the influence attempt takes place, and the larger social context or setting surrounding the parties to the interaction. Central to this discussion is the laboratory study in which the influence attempt has generally taken the form of inducing the participants to perform various actions calculated to bring about attitudinal or other behavioral changes. The various consequences of behaving contrary to one's attitudes are considered at some length.

Chapter 4 focuses on a different type of investigation, in which persons are presented with *information* intended to change their attitudes or behavior. This procedure is directly analogous to mass-communication situations, in which communications are presented via television, radio, newspapers, and other media. Characteristics of the communicator, the communication, and the respondent that make for successful or unsuccessful communication are identified. Chapter 5 examines the contribution of group and societal processes to mass communication, as well as some of the by-products of modern mass communication such as the effects of television violence on aggressive behavior. Finally, Chapter 6 takes up intergroup attitudes, which often are a source of social problems. The conditions under which prejudice and discrimination arise and the processes by which they are maintained or reduced are spelled out.

2

Knowing and Evaluating Persons

The everyday world is both familiar and taken for granted. Each of the many objects around us has a meaning, a place, and a function. The most interesting of these objects are other people. Most of our actions are directed toward them or are in concert with them. They, too, are familiar and have a meaning and a place in our daily lives. Indeed, our actions are shaped according to the nature of the people with whom we are in contact, and are further constrained by the situation we are sharing with them. We generally share a common knowledge of the meaning of the situation, which includes expectations on the part of other persons about how we should behave, as well as our own expectations concerning their reactions to our actions. Generally these are taken for granted, and interaction progresses smoothly. But if this knowledge is lacking, our behavior is apt to be unsure, confused, and halting, instead of the smooth-flowing, unhesitating performance that usually characterizes us.

Knowledge of the other person is only a part of the totality that guides our actions, but it is crucial. One has only to imagine being instantly transported to the midst of a group of Martians to appreciate how much our action depends upon our knowledge of persons. Among a group of foreign earthmen we would still act according to certain basic assumptions about the nature of men. But among Martians, even these assumptions could not legitimately provide a framework for action. Since this book is about persons and their interactions with each other, it is fitting that we devote the second chapter to a discussion of our knowledge of other persons and the conditions on which it is based.

The knowledge of persons we will deal with has a dual character. An individual's actions are contingent upon *his* knowledge of the persons who share his life. He has certain views concerning their nature, as well as ideas about their attitude toward the current situation in which he is engaged. And to understand his actions, we need to know what his knowledge and his views of people are. But as social scientists, we can also characterize his knowledge of people in a way that he cannot. We can stand outside his life, so to speak, and see his knowledge of persons and his actions toward them from a broader, more complete perspective. Consequently, the material of this chapter takes these dual perspectives: that of the individual and that of the social scientist.

The Development of Person Concepts

Differentiation of the Individual Person

Knowing persons and anticipating their actions is a skill that develops only slowly. An early step which needs to be taken by the infant is to differentiate persons from the rest of the environment. While identification of a person as a *physical being* different from the inanimate environment probably occurs within months after birth, recent evidence suggests that the process of seeing another individual as an independent and separate *psychological being* takes many years.[1] In younger children, there are two kinds of confusions: (1) those between the person and his social setting or possessions and (2) those between the person and the observer himself. Kindergarten children, for example, when asked to describe their playmate friends, are apt instead to mention the kinds of toys the friends have or the houses they live in, almost as if they do not recognize the independent existence of the playmates themselves. They also are very subjective and self-oriented in describing their playmates, mentioning like or dislike for them, or vice versa, with little reference to their characteristics.

But differentiating another person from his possessions or setting or from oneself is only the first step. The physical behavior of another person, described in objective terms, in itself indicates little about that person. Such behavior takes place in relation to other persons, and in a social context. Through his use of language, man attaches meaning both to the behavior of individuals and to the situation in which they act. The newborn infant enters a world of actions heavily endowed with social meanings. Only gradually, as he takes his place in this world, does he learn these meanings.

Part of this learning, learning about persons, will be discussed in this chapter. Throughout much of the rest of the book we will discuss the structuring and conceptualization of situations. Over the years, by interacting with members of his family, playmates, schoolmates, teachers, and others, the child learns to anticipate how these individuals will behave in various situations. He experiences a wide range of social actions on the part of these individuals, in different social contexts. Gradually he learns how to describe or identify these different social actions and situations in verbal terms, and eventually he is able to characterize particular individuals in such terms. For example, a child learns

---

1. PEEVERS & SECORD, 1973.

that his parents behave differently toward him and toward each other when there are guests present.

The slow development of person concepts may be illustrated in a rough way by examining verbal descriptions of friends given by children of different ages. In one study, the interviewer asked each child to name a number of friends, and then to tell all the things that he could about each of them, about what each friend was like. The school grade and sex of each observer are given below, together with his description of one friend and the comments and questions of the interviewer.

* Male, Kindergarten

He has a swing set in his back yard. And—he has a bike that has training wheels on it. (I see.) His bike has training wheels on it—and that's all. (That's all? Why is he a friend of yours?) I don't know. (Why do you like him?) I don't know. (Okay, well is there anything about him that you don't like?) No.

* Male, 3rd Grade

He's smart and he writes good and he likes me and we play together— and he pays attention in class—and that's all the things I can say. (Why is he a friend of yours?) Well, because we play cars at school and I brought some cars to school and I let him play with some of them so we became friends. And I went to primary with him. (I see. And why do you like him?) Because he plays with me. (Is there anything about him that you don't like especially?) No. (Can you think of anything else to tell me about him?) No.

* Male, 7th Grade

Well, he's nice and he's considerate and thinks about other people—you know, he's not selfish or anything, and he shares things and he's nice to have around—keeps you company—keeps you talking—and well, he's just—you know—just a real good friend to me—because we both really like each other—he lives out at _____ so he can't sleep over too many times, you know—but really, he's got all the—he's got a good personality and he's honest—he's just real good—a real good friend. (Okay. And why do you like him especially—can you kind of summarize?) Well—like I say, he's not the type that likes to fight—he doesn't like to fight a lot, but if he has to he will. And—well because he's nice, he's got a good personality and he's honest and I like people like that—and he's not dirty or anything—know what I mean— he's just really—really you know. (Okay. Well, can you think of anything else to tell me about him?) He was born—you want to know when he was born and where and stuff? (That's all right.) Well, he was born in _____ and I think he moved over here about—oh, maybe about two or three years ago. And he's—unfortunately, he's moving to _____ this summer—so there's one that goes. He's really good. Just a real good friend. (Anything you don't like?) Not that I can think of.

* Male, College (Abridged)

Well, he talks real fast, but not as fast as he used to. There's been a great transition from when I first met him. He used to wear big, thick glasses and he used to be pretty—well, not ugly, but nobody thought he was very attractive. Now he's really pretty good looking. He wears contacts and he's real well liked and goes out on a lot of dates—he's a real good student, real smart, at mathematics. Average in English. And he likes girls and he likes to go out and party with the boys—and I'd say he's kind of oh, a little insecure, but not more so than most college kids at this age. But he's not sure—he wants to be an _____, and he's got the grades, and he'll do it—but he's worried about what direction it will take. And his parents are pretty poor— he's putting himself through school. Is there anything else in particular you want to know about him? (Why a friend?) Oh—because we have a lot of the same interests. He's sensitive to things I want to tell him—problems, you know, if I have any problems, and—I don't know—we just—we have a mutual friendship. We both like each other and we both have mutual interests. You can really talk to him. And so that's what really makes the difference with a real close friend, I think—is that you understand each other's problems and talk about it. (Anything you don't like especially?) Oh, let's see—yeah, probably because of the house, he gets carried away drinking once in a while—I don't mean that he goes out and causes trouble—he never does. I just don't like to see people go out and drink that often. But now he's on a pretty even keel. That's about the only thing, really. (Anything else about him?) Well, let's see. He's—I'd say, with girls now—it's changed a lot. He used to seem to get on a lot of people's nerves, but he's quieted down, he's more sure of himself, he doesn't have to talk as much—say as much, you know. And girls—all girls seem to like him, you know. He likes music, likes to listen to music, likes to dance which I also do. He wants to do some traveling, which he hasn't had any opportunity to do yet, but—he wants to make some money, because he's never had any.[2]

The differences among such descriptions provided by boys of different ages are striking. Among the more obvious differences are the following: The description becomes longer with increasing age. Much more information is given by older boys, and especially by college males. Observations by the youngest boys are superficial, often not saying anything about the friend as an individual. Descriptions by the oldest males not only give such individual particulars, but also deal with transitory characteristics, motivations, and psychological interpretations. It is as if the youngest children have only the vaguest awareness of other persons as individuals—an awareness that is only gradually acquired and articulated in verbal terms as they develop over the long period from kindergarten to college age.

A more formal analysis of 240 such descriptions by sixty males and females, has produced the following generalizations about the nature and development of conceptions of persons.[3]

2. Reprinted with permission of American Psychological Association from B. H. PEEVERS & P. F. SECORD. Developmental changes in attribution of descriptive concepts to persons. *Journal of Personality and Social Psychology*, 1973, in press.   3. PEEVERS & SECORD, 1973.

Descriptiveness

First, conceptualizations of persons vary in *descriptiveness*. Descriptiveness refers to the degree to which an item yields information about the person as an individual. The protocols of young children are very low on this dimension, while those of college students are generally very high. Four degrees of descriptiveness were distinguished in terms of the items that are used to describe persons.

The lowest level consists of *undifferentiating items*. Generally, these do not refer to the individual being described, but either to his material possessions ("He has a swing set in his back yard") or to his social setting ("He has a nice mother").

A second level of descriptiveness consists of *simple differentiating items*. These do refer to the individual being described, but are relatively uninformative about him as a person. They include appearance items ("He has red hair"), behavior items denoting specific acts but which do not imply a disposition or trait ("She had to stay after school"), global dispositions or categories ("He's nice"), expressions of like or dislike ("I like him"), and role category items ("He's a Cub Scout").

Relatively more informative about the individual as a person are *differentiating items,* which constitute a third level of description. These include interests and activities ("He likes to hunt arrowheads"), ability items ("He's a good athlete"), and beliefs and feelings ("He's a conscientious objector").

The fourth and highest level of descriptiveness is illustrated by *dispositional items,* which yield information about an enduring characteristic of the individual being described. These include *implied dispositions,* which tell something about what the individual is like as a person without specifically using a dispositional word ("He's always fighting with people"), and use of *dispositional* or *trait* words ("She's loyal").

Depth

Descriptiveness represents only one of several important dimensions that characterize person concepts. A second dimension is *depth* of descriptiveness, which refers to the extent to which items are qualified by situational conditions or explanations of why the person is as he is. This depth dimension represents a form of variation in the top two levels of descriptiveness—differentiating items and dispositional items.

Level 1 is represented by the simple description of an interest, ability, or belief, or the attribution of traits or implied dispositions ("He's interested in chess"; "He's sincere"). *Level 2* references are those in which contradictory or opposing characteristics are discussed, or in which the circumstances required for manifestation of an attribute of the individual are described ("Probably because of the fraternity house, he gets carried away drinking once in a while").

Level 3 items are those which offer an explanation for the description. The explanation must be one that offers additional insight and knowledge of the individual as a psychological being ("He is very defensive because he is black").

Depth of description does not appear at all in the descriptions given by younger children. But in the oldest observers in the sample studied, Peevers and Secord college males and females, the descriptions at times show considerable depth. Descriptive items are interwoven with explanation of why the person is that way, or with the circumstances under which he behaves that way. A strong temporal dimension also appears: The person is described as he used to be and as he is now, and occasionally, references to his future behavior occur.

Personal Involvement

Another general class of person concepts which seems to vary with age is *personal involvement*. Personal involvement refers to the way in which the observer brings himself into the description of the other person. There are three kinds of stances he may take:

1. Egocentric. The other person is described in subjective, self-oriented terms representing the observer's personal frame of reference. Often this is indicated by the use of "I" or "me" in his description. (Example: "He likes me.")

2. Reciprocal. The other person is seen in a mutual, two-way relationship with the observer. (Example: "We go bike riding together.")

3. Other-oriented. The other person is seen as an entity separate from the self. (Example: "John likes to hunt for arrowheads.")

As might be expected, the descriptions provided by young children are heavily egocentric. Werner has described the egocentrism of the child in a general sense, in terms of his failure to differentiate between the outer world and inner experience: "Outer world and inner experience constitute an undivided unity, of such a kind that the events of the surrounding world appear to be intimately linked with the ego and its needs." This egocentrism is found in young children in the present study in highly subjective and self-oriented descriptions of other persons such as the following:

"He lets me play with his toys."
"I get to play on her tennis court."
"I don't like his house."
"He's always hitting me."
"He likes my toys."

The playmate is seen largely in terms of his effect on the observer, who does not differentiate between the playmate as a person and the playmate's possessions or setting.

Among college students, the proportion of egocentric items is very low. Most of the descriptive material leaves the observer out of the description entirely. Reciprocal items occur infrequently at all age-grade levels, perhaps because the interview focuses on describing the *other person*.

Another finding is that individuals of the same age differ markedly in the level of development of their person concepts. Some show considerable insight into the character of their friends, and are able to give explanatory and motivational material which adds greatly to the description. Other persons of the same age give descriptions that are less differentiated, less deep, and more egocentric. Presumably such skills are not only a function of experience with other persons, but particularly of facilitating experiences. Probably there are both facilitating and inhibiting conditions that prevail during the developmental years, conditions having their locus in parent-child and peer-group relations. Only research on the factors that contribute to the formation of person concepts will firm up these tentative speculations.

Summary: The Development of Person Concepts

A first step taken by the child is the differentiation of other persons from their possessions and their social setting. Preschool children appear to have little appreciation of persons as distinct, unique individuals, and react diffusely to them in terms of their possessions and life settings. The process of differentiation takes a period of years, over which concepts describing persons slowly emerge. These concepts fall into several major categories. One is descriptiveness, which refers to the degree to which an item yields information about the person as an individual. Items range from those that fail to differentiate the person as a separate being to the sophisticated use of dispositional terms. Another category is depth of descriptiveness, which refers to the extent to which items are qualified by situational conditions or explanations of why the person is as he is. The category of personal involvement refers to the way in which the observer brings himself into the description of the other person. In egocentric descriptions, the observer is the frame of reference. At the opposite extreme, the target person is seen as totally separate from the observer.

Sources Contributing to Impression Formation

Person concepts gradually emerge with age. Presumably these reflect increasing understanding of the other person, and increasing ability to anticipate his actions. The functioning of these concepts in knowing and evaluating other persons involves three main sources of information:

1. The situation which provides the setting for the interaction between observer and observed
2. The actions and qualities of the person being observed
3. The nature of the observer himself

The Situation

A number of features of the situation are important. Our evaluation of a person will be affected by knowing who he is. In each encounter with a person, he has a place in a social relation, a place that he recognizes and that is recognized by those who interact with him. Often this is some form of *role category,* with which we associate certain expectations about how he will behave, as well as some personal qualities. For example, if we enter a store, and a person approaches us, we identify him as a salesclerk and expect him to be polite and helpful in locating merchandise or giving us information about it. For those occupational roles that involve frequent contact with the public, we have fairly clear expectations about how persons in those roles will behave. There are also roles associated with social institutions or other types of groups, such as the role of mother, father, small boy, bachelor, mental patient. These, too, have associated with them certain behavioral expectations and personal characteristics.

While it is true that our impression of a person in his role, such as a salesperson, a policeman, a teacher, a physician, may be formed in part from our expectations for that role, in another sense these role expectations may mask his real nature. In his brief contact with us he is performing according to the requirements of his role, perhaps temporarily suppressing some aspects of his more spontaneous nature. For this reason, Jones and Davis have suggested that in-role behavior produces little information about what a person is really like, while behavior that deviates from his role tells us much about him.[4] Some experimental evidence for this idea is available.[5]

But this deviant role behavior would seem to be especially noted when an observer is evaluating a person. If there is, on the other hand, a long history of a relationship between the two parties, out-of-role behavior may simply be discounted as temporary aberration, or even misinterpreted so as to make it more congruent with the familiar image held of the other person.

Placement in a social role of the person being observed does not exhaust the definition of the situation. The situation may be classified in terms of its content. Is it a problem-solving, task-oriented situation, as where an individual is asking directions for finding some location in a city? Or is it a social exchange, as where two strangers on an airplane exchange pleasantries? Is there a status difference between the two persons interacting? Such elements of the situation also have their effects upon how the other person is known and evaluated. Other features of the situation have effects upon certain ideas and feelings that the participants have about each other. For example, we can examine those conditions that enable us to determine whether a person *intentionally* or *unintentionally* acted in a particular way. We would also like to know how we can tell when he is *responsible* for a particular action, or when his action is justified. For example, if an individual is seen as failing because of lack of effort, the responsibility for failure is placed upon him. But if he fails because he is confronted with an impossible task, he is not seen as responsible. Later responsibility and other concepts will be discussed in more detail.

---

4. Jones & Davis, 1965.   5. Jones, Davis, & Gergen, 1961; Alexander & Epstein, 1969; Martin, 1970.

The Stimulus or Target Person

The second source of information stems from the person being observed, commonly referred to as the *stimulus person*. His appearance, his actions, and his qualities contribute to the impression formed. Situations vary markedly in the extent to which these features are important. What determines this importance is the extent of previous interaction between observer and observed, the extent to which the situation is structured in terms of role categories or other specifications, and the "depth" of the interaction itself. For example, if the person observed is a stranger, and if the interaction is a casual, superficial one, the person's appearance and the few actions he performs are apt to strongly determine the impression that is formed. In some situations people disclose intimate information about themselves to strangers because it is clear that they will never interact again with their confidants. Here the revealed information may have a powerful effect and minimize other cues. But if the person being evaluated is a long-time acquaintance, the effect of his appearance and his immediate actions are judged within the context of a whole history of interaction with and knowledge of the person, and thus are apt to have a minimal impact.

The Observer

The third source is the observer himself. Expectations about how another person will behave are colored by the way in which the observer conceives of other persons and how he feels about them. Through long experience with people he develops certain views concerning them. Some individuals develop a deep mistrust of most other persons, and others develop a faith in almost everyone. Some expect others to be helpful and ask for their help; other individuals avoid any form of dependency on other persons. An individual may have special views concerning certain types of persons; for example, some individuals resent persons in authority, and reveal this in their attitudes and behavior toward policemen, supervisors, teachers, parents, and other authority figures.

Research on knowing and evaluating persons has not focused equally on these three sources of information. Most often no attention has been paid to the *characteristics* of *individual* observers and how they contribute to the impression formed. But much of the focus has nevertheless been on observers in general in the attempt to understand the process of inference or judgment or evaluation that underlies the impressions we have of people. In the following sections, we will first show how society provides ready-made views of some people in the form of stereotypes. Next, we will consider the organizational or structural properties of the attributes we give to other people—how the observer organizes and relates this material. Preferences in organization held by individual observers and how such differences are related to observer characteristics will be discussed. Then we move to a discussion of how nonverbal information is used to form impressions, and conclude with a consideration of how evaluations of people are made in daily interaction. Our discussion of these topics is highly selective. More complete coverage can be found in several more general references.[6]

Throughout this chapter, little emphasis will be placed on whether person descriptions represent the person as he really is. We might expect, though, that some persons are better judges of people than others. Also, we are interested in how much discrepancy there is between an impression of a person formed under various conditions and what he is really like. Unfortunately, the assessment of accuracy has raised such difficult methodological problems that the definitive research necessary to provide conclusive answers to these questions has not yet been carried out.[7]

Culturally Provided Categories: The Social Stereotype

In everyday life, we often find ourselves having only categorical information concerning a person. We know only that he is a Jew, a policeman, a teacher, or an old man. Where other information about him is minimal, such knowledge strongly affects our evaluation of him. These person categories occupy a fundamental place in our evaluations of persons and in our interactions with them. If the focus of interest is on evaluation, the person category is generally thought of as a social stereotype; if on interaction, the person category is thought of as a social role. Stereotypes will be discussed in this chapter, and social roles in Chapters 13 and 14.

Schutz has emphasized the importance of person categories in our everyday experience. An individual uses a whole network of *typifications* (categories or types of objects):

> ... typifications of human individuals, of their course-of-action patterns, of their motives and goals, or of the sociocultural products which originated in their actions. These types were formed in the main by others, his predecessors or contemporaries, as appropriate tools for coming to terms with things and men, accepted as such by the group into which he was born. . . .
>
> The sum-total of these various typifications constitutes a frame of reference in terms of which not only sociocultural, but also the physical world has to be interpreted, a frame of reference that, in spite of its inconsistencies and its inherent opaqueness, is nonetheless sufficiently integrated and transparent to be used for solving most of the practical problems at hand.[8]

Thus, typing people is almost inevitable, because of its functional usefulness. No one can respond to other persons in all their unique individuality. That

6. WARR & KNAPPER, 1968; TAGIURI, 1969; TAJFEL, 1969; HASTORF, SCHNEIDER, & POLEFKA, 1970.   7. GAGE & CRONBACH, 1955; CRONBACH, 1955, 1958; SHRAUGER & ALTROCCHI, 1964; McHENRY, 1971.   8. Reprinted with permission from A. Schutz. Equality and the meaning structure of the social world. In A. Schutz (A. Broderson, Ed.), *Collected Papers II: Studies in social theory*. The Hague: Martinus Nijhoff, 1964. P. 232.

form known as stereotyping, however, is generally an exaggerated typing, and has been consistently attacked by social scientists. Stereotyping is a sociocultural phenomenon, in that it is a property characteristic of people sharing a common culture. People do three things in stereotyping: (1) they identify a category of persons (such as policemen or hippies), (2) they agree in attributing sets of traits or characteristics to the category of persons, and (3) they attribute the characteristics to any person belonging to the category.

Identification of a Person Category

Persons have many attributes differing greatly in visibility or distinctiveness. Society selects certain attributes as means of identifying various categories of persons, and ignores others. These attributes may be physical—such as age, sexual, or racial characteristics; they may involve membership in a group, organization, or society—as in occupational, church, or national affiliation; or they may even be based on certain distinctive behavior patterns. Campbell and Levine have suggested that the greater the contrast between two groups on some attribute, the more that attribute is likely to appear in the stereotyped imagery each has of the other.[9] This is as likely to apply to the attributes identifying the group as to the characteristics of the stereotype itself. Thus, having black skin makes a person a target for stereotyping by whites, and white skin becomes a target for blacks.

Consensus on Attributed Traits

The class of persons having some form of common identification is thought to share certain personal attributes. For example, we may group all young people with long hair and shabby clothes into a single class, call them hippies, and believe that they are disillusioned, pacifistic, rebellious against authority, and antimaterialistic. Or Americans may be considered industrious and materialistic; elderly persons may be regarded as old-fashioned, conservative, and cantankerous; blacks may be perceived as happy-go-lucky, lazy, superstitious, and dishonest; and professors may be thought absentminded, impractical, idealistic, and eccentric. By definition it is implied that those who hold the stereotype are in reasonable agreement with each other on the identifying characteristics of the category of stereotyped persons and also on the attributes they possess.

Data collected by Katz and Braly in 1932, by Gilbert in 1951 and by Karlins, Coffman, and Walters in 1967, illustrates this consensus for ethnic stereotypes.[10] A list of ten ethnic groups, together with eighty-four words describing personal attributes (e.g., aggressive, intelligent), was presented to 100 Princeton students. For each ethnic group they checked all the attributes that seemed to

---

9. Cited in Campbell, 1967.   10. Katz & Braly, 1933; Gilbert, 1951; Karlins, Coffman, & Walters, 1969.

be characteristic of the group, and then went back over the checklist to identify the five attributes they thought most characteristic of the group. Tabulations for all three studies appear in Table 2-1.

Table 2-1   Percent of Princeton college students assigning traits to ethnic groups

	YEAR				YEAR		
	1932*	1950†	1967‡		1932*	1950†	1967‡
Americans				**Germans**			
Industrious	48	30	23	Scientifically minded	78	62	47
Intelligent	47	32	20	Industrious	65	50	59
Materialistic	33	37	67	Stolid	44	10	9
Ambitious	33	21	42	Intelligent	32	32	19
Progressive	27	5	17	Methodical	31	20	21
English				**Japanese**			
Sportsmanlike	53	21	22	Intelligent	45	11	20
Intelligent	46	29	23	Industrious	43	12	57
Conventional	34	25	19	Progressive	24	2	17
Tradition-loving	31	42	21	Shrewd	22	13	7
Conservative	30	22	53	Sly	20	21	3
Negroes				**Chinese**			
Superstitious	84	41	13	Superstitious	34	18	8
Lazy	75	31	26	Sly	29	4	6
Happy-go-lucky	38	17	27	Conservative	29	14	15
Ignorant	38	24	11	Tradition-loving	26	26	32
Musical	26	33	47	Loyal to family ties	22	35	50
Jews				**Irish**			
Shrewd	79	47	30	Pugnacious	45	24	13
Mercenary	49	28	15	Quick-tempered	39	35	43
Industrious	48	29	33	Witty	38	16	7
Grasping	34	17	17	Honest	32	11	17
Intelligent	29	37	37	Very religious	29	30	27
Italians				**Turks**			
Artistic	53	28	30	Cruel	47	12	9
Impulsive	44	19	28	Very religious	26	6	7
Passionate	37	25	44	Treacherous	21	3	13
Quick-tempered	35	15	28	Sensual	20	4	9
Musical	32	22	9	Ignorant	15	7	13

* N = 100
† N = 333
‡ N = 150

Source: Reprinted in abridged form by permission from Marvin Karlins, Thomas L. Coffman, and Gary Walters. On the fading of social stereotypes: Studies in three generations of college students. *Journal of Personality and Social Psychology,* 1969, **13**, 1, 1–16.

Consensus among students is striking. If a student were to select five traits *at random,* the chances of assigning any one trait to an ethnic group would be only 5 in 84. For 100 students selecting traits at random, only 5/84 of 100, or approximately six students, would pick any one trait. Thus, for the three generations of students, a figure of 6 percent represents random choice. A mere glance at Table 2-1 reveals immediately that the choice of traits is well above this chance level, and that certain traits are chosen with considerable frequency, indicating agreement among an appreciable number of students. For example, we find that in the years 1932, 1950, and 1967, the percentages of students attributing the trait *industrious* to Americans were 48, 30, and 23, respectively.

Consensus on stereotypes is only partial, even for the most definite stereotypes. That this is true even in the case of a stereotype as definite as that of the Negro may be illustrated by some unpublished data collected by the authors and shown in Table 2-2. People differ even in assigning the physical attributes judged to be characteristic of the race. Thus, while 94 percent of a group of eighty-four students say that dark skin is *very characteristic* of Negroes, 6 per-

Table 2-2   Identifying attributes and trait characteristics of the Negro stereotype

	RESPONSES (IN PERCENT*)		
	Very characteristic	Somewhat characteristic	Not characteristic
Identifying Attribute			
Curly hair	96	2	1
Dark skin	94	6	0
Thick lips	87	13	0
Wide nose	71	27	1
Low eyebrows†	14	51	34
Protruding eyes†	13	49	38
Prominent cheekbones†	14	44	42
Small ears	11	48	42
Personality Trait			
Deeply religious	46	48	6
Superstitious	33	52	14
Happy-go-lucky	26	50	24
Stubborn†	21	49	30
Patient†	18	52	30
Lazy	15	54	31
Boastful†	23	36	42
Moody†	12	54	34

* Percentages are based on an N of 84.

† These traits were included in the list but were not thought to belong to the Negro stereotype.

Source: Authors' unpublished data, collected in 1960.

cent say that it is only *somewhat characteristic.* With respect to the attribute "wide nose," 71 percent say it is *very characteristic,* but 27 percent say it is only *somewhat characteristic.* Much more variation occurs, of course, in the personality traits ascribed to Negroes. No personality trait is considered *very characteristic* by as many as 50 percent of the students.

Particularly notable is the point that attributes included in the checklist but *not* believed by the experimenter to belong to the stereotype were checked in every instance by at least a small minority of the judges as *very* characteristic of Negroes. Thus, with considerable justification, we may speak of a *personal stereotype* as characterizing a single individual's opinions and a *social stereotype* as representing the consensus of the majority of a given population of judges.

Categorical Treatment of Persons

A special property of stereotyping is that membership in a category is sufficient to evoke the judgment that the person possesses all the attributes belonging to that category.

Two studies using photographs varying in "Negroidness" from markedly Negroid to markedly Caucasian tested this notion of categorical response, simply by determining whether the degree of stereotyping was reduced for the more Caucasian photographs.[11] Both studies found that, as long as the individual was recognized as a black, stereotyping did not decrease as the picture became increasingly Caucasoid. This is illustrated in Figure 2-1. Photographs *I* to *K* were almost always perceived as those of blacks. But photographs *J, C,* and *D,* although actually blacks, were perceived as Caucasians.

As indicated by the height of the curve, photographs *I* through *K* were more stereotyped than the Caucasian-appearing black photographs *J* and *D* and than the white photographs. The Caucasian-appearing photograph *C* was, for unknown reasons, perceived as having the personality traits belonging to the black stereotype. Individuals both high and low in prejudice assigned these stereotype traits to photographs *recognized as black* regardless of the extent to which they contained Caucasian features. But persons more highly prejudiced stereotyped all such photographs to a greater degree.

Finally, the responses of the few judges who identified the most Caucasoid of the photographs (*J, C* and *D*) as black were examined. Even these pictures were stereotyped, by these judges only, to an extent at least equal to that of the average black photograph. If these results for stereotyping blacks apply to other groups as well, then it is clear that the assignment of the person to a special category is a critical factor in stereotyping. Assignment to that category results in the attribution of all the traits belonging to it.

In part, this categorical response may be a function of the method used in collecting information on stereotyping. When provided only with an ethnic identification and no other information, as in most studies of stereotyping, an

---

11. SECORD, BEVAN, & KATZ, 1956; SECORD, 1959.

Figure 2-1 Stereotype scores by photograph for judges high and low in prejudice. *(Adapted with permission from P. F. Secord. Stereotyping and favorableness in the perception of Negro faces.* Journal of Abnormal and Social Psychology, *1959, 59, 310.)*

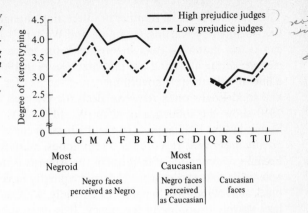

individual is forced to ignore individual differences and to respond to the group as a class of persons. This is illustrated by a study in which three fictitious national groups were invented and college students were asked to rate these "Danerians," "Pirenians," and "Wallonians," along with thirty-two other known ethnic groups.[12] Many students showed no hesitation in rating these groups, and they generally assigned unfavorable traits to them.

In most situations, the observer is confronted with many differences among individuals. Moreover, interaction between the stimulus person and the observer often is a prominent factor affecting how the stimulus person is perceived, so that interaction diminishes categorical responses. The effects of forcing an observer to attribute the same characteristics to all members of a group may be illustrated by contrasting this procedure with one that permitted the judge to recognize subgroups within an ethnic group.[13] When judges were asked to characterize "upper-class Negroes" and "lower-class Negroes," they were found to stereotype only the lower-class blacks.

There is another side to this issue, however. The request to respond to ethnic identification alone does not force *consensus* among observers. Consensus reveals that social forces are shaping the perceptions of a class of persons in a given direction. One might say with considerable justification that a stereotype existed if there were marked consensus among judges on the traits assigned to a category of persons. Moreover, as has been stressed previously, there are many situations in everyday life in which we respond to other persons mainly in terms of their group identification rather than reacting to them as individual persons.

Changes in Stereotypes

The repetition of the Princeton studies over the years provides us with a means of examining changes in stereotypes among samples of Princeton students.

12. HARTLEY, 1946.   *13.* BAYTON, McALISTER, & HAMER, 1956.

These studies reveal a number of interesting changes, as well as some uniformities, as noted by Karlins, Coffman, and Walters.[14] The stereotype of the American is less flattering than before, with the terms *materialistic, ambitious,* and *pleasure-loving* attaining the top three places in 1967. In spite of social reforms, a liberal welfare-state government, and the Beatles, the stereotype of the proper and staid Englishman remains. Both the German and Japanese stereotypes in 1950 show the influence of their World War II encounter with the United States, but by 1967 appreciable shifts have occurred. The Jewish stereotype has greatly improved: Its core traits (ambitious, materialistic, and industrious) have become synonymous with those of the American stereotype, and the less favorable traits that earlier were chosen frequently have dropped considerably. The black stereotype has changed dramatically, with such traits as superstitious and lazy sharply dropping in frequency. It is interesting to note that the image of the militant black and emphasis on black power has not yet affected this stereotype. In fact, a general characteristic of stereotyping seems to be that it lags somewhat behind events that have the potential for changing images.

Further light on the current status of stereotype is found in yet another study of stereotypes of Princeton students conducted in 1969.[15] The same procedures as in the earlier studies were used, except that participants were asked to provide a *public* and a *private stereotype.* The former consisted of the adjectives an individual thought would be attributed to the category by the general American public, and the latter, those which he personally believed to belong to the category. Public stereotypes were found to be similar to those collected under the earlier instructions. But in their private stereotypes, participants less frequently endorsed unfavorable traits and more frequently endorsed favorable ones. These stereotypes continue the trend noted in the earlier studies toward the inclusion of more favorable traits. As noted in this study, individuals probably hold both public and private stereotypes, and the one they use depends upon the situation.

Considering only the 1933 and 1950 studies in the first edition of this book, it appeared that stereotypes were fading in strength. But let us look at a numerical index of *uniformity* which represents the definiteness or strength of a stereotype. This was computed for each ethnic group by counting the *least* number of traits needed to account for one-half of the total selections made by each of the three generations of students. The smaller this value, of course, the greater the uniformity of (or agreement on) the stereotype. This computation resulted in the following average index values for the four years:

YEAR	INDEX
1932	8.5
1950	15.3
1967	10.9
1969	8.6 (12.2)

14. Karlins, Coffman, & Walters, 1969.   *15.* Lewis, Darley, & Glucksberg, 1972.

Although as many as fifteen traits were required to cover one-half of all trait assignments in 1950, this number was reduced to about eleven in 1967, indicating a stronger stereotyping effect. In 1969 we find the public stereotypes fully as strong as those of the original 1932 study, while the private ones are between the uniformity indices of 1950 and 1967.

Stereotypes are not confined to Princeton students. Many students using similar procedures indicate that the general population, not only in this country but in others as well, has similar stereotypes concerning various ethnic groups. For example, one study sponsored by UNESCO carried out an opinion survey in nine countries: Holland, Italy, Australia, France, Germany, England, Russia, Mexico, and the United States. Stereotyping was prevalent in all these countries.[16] Most agreement was obtained on the stereotype of the Russians and the Americans, but some agreement was obtained on the other countries as well.

Processes in Stereotyping

One oversimple view of stereotyping is that it is merely the assignment of a set of traits to a category of persons on the basis of consistency with a positive or negative feeling toward that person category. This is false, because most stereotypes are a composite of favorable and unfavorable traits. Even very negative stereotypes contain some favorable characteristics (e.g., Russians were seen as hardworking, brave, and progressive in the UNESCO study).[17] Rather conclusive evidence that a feeling does not generate a set of stereotyped traits consistently having the same positive (or negative) connotation is found in another study cited earlier.[18] In evaluating photographs of blacks, judges prejudiced against them did not assign unfavorable traits in greater degree than neutral judges, provided these traits *were not part of the stereotype*. Prejudiced judges, moreover, assigned favorable traits in greater degree than neutral judges if the traits were part of the stereotype. This study and data from the Princeton studies suggest that strength of feeling about a group, regardless of its direction, is associated with the definiteness or strength of a stereotype, as measured by the uniformity index. The later Princeton studies showed a strong correlation between the definiteness of a stereotype and favorableness. These *r*'s were: 1933, .16; 1951, .68; 1967, .77. In 1969, the public stereotype correlated only .38 with favorableness, but the private one, .82. Thus, strong emotion is apt to be associated with strong stereotypes, but the emotion is not on a single evaluative dimension.

Campbell and Levine have identified certain links between favorable and unfavorable traits lying in the processes which are associated with stereotyping.[19] For example, they suggest that traits unfavorably evaluated in one's own

16. Buchanan, 1951.   *17.* Buchanan, 1951.   *18.* Secord, 1959.   *19.* Cited in Campbell, 1967.

group are apt to be attributed to the outgroup. Moreover, the outgroup accept these traits in themselves, but couch them in language that makes them favorable. Thus, the English describe themselves as *reserved* and *respecting the privacy of others* and describe Americans as *intrusive, forward,* and *pushy.* But the Americans describe the English as *snobbish, cold,* and *unfriendly* and describe themselves as *friendly, outgoing,* and *openhearted.*

Two groups may also have the *same* traits, but use unfavorable language for the outgroup. *Loyalty* in the ingroup becomes *clannishness* in the outgroup: *pride* becomes *egotism; standing up for one's rights* becomes *belligerence.* Lewis, Darley, and Glucksberg in the 1969 Princeton study also point out that the shift toward favorableness over the years in many of the stereotypes was accomplished by retaining the same trait, but changing the connotations of the language in a manner similar to the above examples.[20]

These investigators also call attention to another process. Given a few bits of information about a category of persons, individuals can readily generate additional related terms to fill out a stereotype. If a person is reserved, he is also quiet. If a person is ambitious, he is also likely to be shrewd; if he is grasping, he is apt to be sly. They demonstrate that stereotypes contain clusters of traits which, while not synonymous, are strongly associated with one another.

Truth or Falsity of Stereotypes

Social psychologists have emphasized the falsity of stereotypes. In one sense, it would seem that the inaccuracy of a social stereotype follows from one of the elements of its definition—namely, that all persons in a given class possess the traits assigned to that class. Since real individuals universally vary in the kinds of traits which make up a social stereotype, it is obvious that the stereotype traits do not apply in the same degree to each member of the class. If an individual makes known what traits he believes are possessed by the average member of a class of persons, and at the same time recognizes the existence of individual differences, there is nothing necessarily inaccurate about his judgments. On the other hand, if he attributes exactly the same characteristics to each individual member of the class, his stereotype is necessarily a departure from reality.

That an individual readily assigns traits to a class of persons in a laboratory setting does not mean that he will do so to the same degree when confronted with an individual representative of that class in a face-to-face setting. For example, if an American is confronted with another American in a setting that does not contrast Americans with foreigners, neither one is likely to assign to the other stereotype traits that might belong to that nationality. On the other hand, if an American enters a room containing a Frenchman, a German, and an Italian, his ethnic stereotypes may well affect how he perceives them. As

---

20. LEWIS, DARLEY, & GLUCKSBERG, 1972.

Bruner and Perlmutter put it, "If objects that are alike in all respects save one are considered together, their difference in this one respect will be more critical in the impression one forms of the objects."[21] Thus, if our Frenchman, German, and Italian are all businessmen and appear to be alike in all respects *except* their nationality, the latter is apt to become more important in evaluating them. But if one of them is a professor, another a circus star, and the third an artist, ethnic identification will have much less influence on how they are evaluated.

Most stereotypes are undoubtedly gross exaggerations or are completely false. But occasionally they may have a kernel of truth, twisted and distorted by the flexibility of our language. We have already seen examples of how two groups may have the same characteristics, each describing their own in flattering terms and those of the outgroup in unflattering terms. In such cases, there is apt to be some truth in the attribution of the underlying traits, apart from the connotations. An outgroup can be hated as too lazy or too industrious, too dumb or too shrewd, too forward or too reclusive, too emotional or too cold, too generous or too thrifty.[22] They are easily damned, even if they have the same traits as oneself.

But there are also certain sociological facts, to be discussed in more detail in Chapter 6, which suggest that some stereotypes have some truth in them. An ethnic group may actually have attributes associated with a lower social class because society keeps the members of the group in that status. Prejudice against a group can produce some of the characteristics that make it the object of prejudice (e.g., clannishness, oversensitivity, belligerence). Anthropological studies suggest many stereotypes that are based on actual characteristics.[23] For example, the Luo in Kenya are primarily farmers, overpopulated on poor land. Some have become manual laborers on the railroad and elsewhere, spreading throughout the country. The stereotype of the Luo is based upon these migrant laborers. They are perceived as physically strong, lazy, spendthrifty, and dressy. In fact, they are physically strong, and they describe themselves as spendthrifty.

Summary: The Social Stereotype

Typing people and other entities is a common and necessary practice for living in the everyday world. We could not possibly respond to the full individuality of the persons we encounter in our daily lives. Stereotyping is an exaggerated form of typification that has three characteristics: (1) People identify a category of persons according to certain attributes. (2) People agree in attributing sets of traits or characteristics to the category of persons. (3) People attribute the characteristics to any person belonging to the category.

For most familiar minority groups, consensus among observers is very much above the level that would be achieved if traits were chosen at random. Some

21. BRUNER & PERLMUTTER, 1957, p. 259. *22.* MERTON, 1957*b*. *23.* CAMPBELL, 1967.

stereotypes are more definite than others, judging by the varying amount of consensus. Stereotyping is not simply the assignment of favorable or unfavorable traits to a class of persons as a function of whether the observer has a positive or negative attitude toward the person category. Most stereotypes have both favorable and unfavorable traits, and more prejudiced individuals assign both in greater degree. Often, traits unfavorably evaluated in one's own group are attributed to the outgroup. On the other hand, two groups may have the same traits but use favorable language for describing their own group, and unfavorable language for the outgroup.

Social psychologists have emphasized the falsity of stereotypes. To some extent, the inaccuracy of a social stereotype follows from one of its properties; namely, that membership in a category is sufficient for the traits to be attributed. When an observer is provided with nothing more than an ethnic identification of a person, he is forced to ignore individual differences in judging him. Occasionally, however, stereotypes have a kernel of truth, twisted and distorted by the flexibility of our language. The attributes assigned may be present in some degree because society creates the conditions that produce the stereotyped traits.

Organizational Processes in Person Descriptions

Most of the descriptions of people introduced at the beginning of this chapter were highly organized. They were not simply strings of adjectives or phrases. Often they had one or more central themes relating to some outstanding characteristic. Stereotyping, too, focused upon a set of related traits. At this time we turn our attention to such organizational or structural properties. Insofar as a description consists of a variety of discrete elements, we can ask a number of questions about these elements and their relation to one another. For example, do some elements occur much more frequently than others in the description of persons? What properties of the stimulus person affect these frequencies? In what way are the elements related to one another? Do certain elements occur together; that is, when one of the pair is found in a person, does the other also tend to be attributed? Can the elements used in describing persons be organized into some structural scheme which reveals a small number of basic dimensions that are used in describing persons? Are the elements organized differently in different observers? Although conclusive answers to all these questions are not available, research has contributed fairly solid answers to some questions and tentative answers to others.

Some situations in everyday life provide us with verbal information about another person about whom we have little other information. On the basis of the verbal information alone, we make inferences about other aspects of his personality. This occurs in reading about people in the news media, in reading novels, or in receiving verbal descriptions of persons from acquaintances. This situation is analogous to at least two kinds of laboratory procedures. In one, verbal information about a *hypothetical person* is presented, and the observer is asked to form an impression of him by writing a sketch, by filling out checklists, or by rating traits. The other procedure places more systematic emphasis upon the inferences that the observer makes. He might be told, for example, that a person is *intelligent,* and asked to estimate on a numerical scale how probable it is that he is also *educated.* The purpose of those studies is to gain some under-standing of the connections or links among various descriptive terms—some idea of how inferences about a person are made.

Impression Formation Based on Inferences

The first series of investigations to be discussed involve presentations of from five to seven traits describing a hypothetical person and asking observers to write down their impressions or to fill out *trait-rating scales* or *checklists.* Gen-erally the analyses of the results are relatively informal, focusing on the consis-tency of the impressions and a number of other features. In a now classic study performed by Asch in 1946, groups of college students were told that a list of characteristics belonging to a particular person would be read to them and that they should try to form an impression of the kind of person described. A sample *cue-trait* list representing a *stimulus person* is as follows: "energetic, assured, talkative, cold, ironical, inquisitive, and persuasive." The subjects were then asked to write a characterization of the person in a few sentences. Asch found that his observers readily accepted the task, in spite of the sparsity of information about the hypothetical person.

Written impressions obtained in this manner differed greatly, in spite of the fact that all individuals were exposed to an identical list of traits. Asch found that many persons organized the list of traits into a relatively integrated, consis-tent picture of a person; the traits went together. In this process, certain traits were made *central* aspects of the person's character, while others were relegated to a minor role—or even ignored entirely, suggesting a process of simplifica-tion. For example, when the cue traits *warm* and *cold* were used, they usually dominated the impression formed. In some instances, the impression formed included new qualities not in the original stimulus list. Occasionally the per-ceiver went so far as to give a physical description of the person. Those new qualities, physical or otherwise, were usually compatible with other elements of the written sketch.

The original experiment by Asch has been repeated with the same proce-dure, and comparable results have been obtained.[24] It has also been repeated using an actual person, a stranger to the subjects, as the stimulus person. In one experimental variation the class instructor introduced a guest speaker by de-scribing him before his entrance with the stimulus words from Asch's experi-

---

24. MENSH & WISHNER, 1947; VENESS & BRIERLEY, 1963.

ment, using *warm* or *cold* to describe the central trait to different groups of subjects.[25] In another variation a person representing himself as a veterinarian described his activities in terms calculated to fit the *peripheral* terms from Asch's list.[26] *Warm* and *cold,* the central traits, were represented in two different groups by the tonal qualities of the voice of the speaker, who was a speech expert. Both these experiments were successful in replicating the essential results of Asch's study.

Luchins and others have noted that not all people respond by elaborating upon the word list presented.[27] Some merely repeat the list or give synonyms of words in the list. A few do not even think of the traits as belonging to a single person. In general, however, the various repetitions of Asch's experiment have confirmed his original results, and it appears that most people, at least, form impressions that go well beyond the stimulus information presented.

Warr and Knapper have taken pains to demonstrate that findings using the rather artificial stimulus "person" represented by seven trait words in Asch's study nevertheless hold up in a more natural situation.[28] They composed two rather lengthy versions of a realistic-appearing newspaper report about the manager of a football team, differing only in the words *warm* and *cold.* Different groups of college students read each version and rated the manager on thirteen personality characteristics. Appreciable differences were found on almost half the scales, supporting the earlier findings. An additional study applying the central words *humane* and *ruthless* to a police chief yielded comparable results. Moreover, in two additional investigations the investigators increased the length of the descriptions from 250 to 450 words and obtained weaker but still significant results supporting the original findings. Considering that these descriptions differed only in a single short phrase containing the words *warm* and *cold* or *humane* and *ruthless,* these results are striking.

IMPLICIT PERSONALITY THEORIES   Bruner and Taguiri have suggested that observers have an *implicit personality theory* which guides the inferences they make about people from the information they receive.[29] In the previous section, such a "theory" is suggested by the inferences that judges make from such traits as *warm* and *cold.* They refer to the connections between traits or bits of information about people, ideas of what goes with what. Thus, a warm person was apt to be seen as sociable, friendly, and kind. Because most research on this concept has analyzed data from groups of observers, the results pertain to observers in general rather than to individuals, or at least to the kinds of people used in the studies (mostly college students). And so findings probably reflect common properties of language usage, although they go beyond mere semantics.

Cronbach extended the meaning of implicit personality theory in two directions.[30] He emphasized the implicit personality theory of a *single observer.* He

---

25. KELLEY, 1950.   26. VENESS & BRIERLEY, 1963.   27. LUCHINS, 1948; DINNERSTEIN, 1951; GOLLIN, 1958.   28. WARR & KNAPPER, 1968.   29. BRUNER & TAGIURI, 1954.   30. CRONBACH, 1958.

also emphasized features other than linkages between trait words. Observers have biases toward rating other persons higher on some dimensions and lower on others, and they also vary in their use of extremes on a dimension. Similarly, single individuals might have their own peculiar associations between descriptive terms for persons. Unfortunately, most investigators have continued to analyze group data, primarily in terms of trait linkages, and few have studied the single observer. This section will review the findings for data based on group averages. The next major section will describe studies of single observers or types of observers, focusing on the individual observer.

INFERENCES FROM CUE TRAITS   While the studies of impression formation reported in the previous section deal with the extent to which various traits are inferred from the stimulus or cue trait, the method used does not lend itself to sophisticated statistical analysis, primarily because the stimulus person is described in terms of a cluster of cue traits presented simultaneously. Thus it is not possible to calculate the implication of each cue trait taken separately. The most popular procedure for intensive statistical analysis is the *if . . . then* or *implication* model: "If a person is *intelligent,* how likely is it that he is also *wise?* " Probability estimates are usually made on a numerical scale, or sometimes adjectives such as *nearly always* and *fairly often* are used. The data from such judgments can be analyzed to discover the associations between the cue traits and inferred traits and to calculate other statistical properties.

Bruner, Shapiro, and Taguiri were the first to apply this procedure to judgments about persons.[31] They demonstrated that many of the inferences were not at all obvious, nor were they based on mere semantics. For example, more than half the participants indicated that *intelligence* implies that a person is active, deliberate, enterprising, efficient, conscientious, honest, independent, reliable, and responsible. Nonobvious inferences of this kind are common in judgments of people.

Many other investigations of this sort have since been conducted. But one question often raised is whether such isolated judgments are representative of the kinds of inferences that would be drawn in the more complex, nonlaboratory situations. One study not only presenting cue traits but also specifying the person as either white or Negro produced similar inferences for the two classes of stimulus persons.[32]

Warr and Knapper carried the matter further by using several treatments: six cue traits presented for people in general, three cue traits for men or women, and three cue traits for men students and bank managers.[33] Thus, the first item in each treatment in effect asked one of the following questions: "How likely is it that cynical people in general are ambitious?" "How likely is it that cynical men are ambitious?" "How likely is it that cynical women are ambitious?" "How likely is it that cynical men students are ambitious?" "How likely is it

31. BRUNER, SHAPIRO, & TAGIURI, 1958.   *32.* SECORD & BERSCHEID, 1963.   *33.* WARR & KNAPPER, 1968.

that cynical men bank managers are ambitious?" Inferences were made from each cue trait presentation to a list of twenty-five traits. Of course cue-trait presentations were appropriately spaced, so that different treatments were not presented at the same time. Warr and Knapper found that there were few differences between inferences made from people in general and those made from men or from women. But inferences from the same cue trait were quite different for bank managers and male students. The cue trait *impulsive* produced seventeen differences in the twenty-five scales, *practical* produced thirteen, and *precise* produced six. Apparently the stimulus value of the role label overrode the cue trait in many instances (e.g., *impulsive* implied *careless* for people and for male students, but not for the bank manager). Thus, inference rules appear to be stable across general categories of persons, but not across more specific ones.

ROLE OF EVALUATIVE CONTENT IN INFERENCES   Examining the degree of association between cue trait and inferred trait is not the only approach. We can ask why certain traits are linked. Are the impressions we form of other persons mainly a reflection of our liking for the persons—our evaluation of them as good or bad? Or are our impressions based primarily on the descriptive qualities of what we know about the traits? In terms of the inferences we have been discussing, we could ask, for example, whether a person who judges an individual known to be generous as also cheerful does so because both are *favorable* traits or because both have a similar *content*. Everyday phenomena such as the tendency to assign favorable traits to a friend and unfavorable ones to an enemy would seem to favor the evaluation principle. Peabody has selected sets of traits such that the relative effects of the evaluative aspect and the descriptive content could be assessed.[34] The procedure involved finding pairs of terms that were alike in evaluation but different in descriptive content (e.g., thrifty and extravagant) and terms alike in descriptive content but different in evaluation (e.g., thrifty and stingy). Persons were provided with a trait and asked to infer the likelihood that a person would have one or the other member of the pair. This may be illustrated by an example:

CAUTIOUS

bold: _____ : _____ : _____ : _____ : _____ : _____ : timid

If the judge responds to the positive connotation of the term *cautious,* he will lean toward the trait *bold,* also positive. But if he pays more attention to the descriptive content of the term *cautious,* he will lean toward *timid,* discounting the positive connotation.

Several studies provide information about making inferences from traits where the evaluative and descriptive aspects have been controlled in this manner.[35] Both evaluative and descriptive consistency were found to be important

34. PEABODY, 1967, 1970.   35. ROSENBERG & OLSHAN, 1970; FELIPE, 1970; PEABODY, 1970.

in making judgments. When descriptive relations are strong, inferences are mostly based on description. In combining traits, descriptive inferences are enhanced.

COMBINING INFORMATION   From a practical standpoint, in life situations we are often interested in the overall impression, judgment, or evaluation of a person, rather than the individual bits of information. Some investigators have therefore turned their attention to how inferences are combined to form judgments. This process may be conceptualized according to various mathematical models. One model, for example, is based on *averaging.* Suppose we make inferences about *competence* from the cue traits *intelligent, capable,* and *fair-minded.* Is our judgment of the person's competence determined by averaging these three ratings? Or by adding them to get a total—the so-called *additive* model? A weighted averaging model is also possible. In this example it would seem that the inference from *capable* would receive the most weight, *intelligent* the second highest weight, and *fair-minded* a low weight.

Even more complex models would be required if bits of trait information *interacted*—by augmenting or negating each other. For example, it might be that a person described as honest and trustworthy would be judged to be *more honest* than a person described as honest and helpful. That is, the presence of the trait *trustworthy* leads the observer to assume greater honesty. The general approach has been not to try to deal with such complex models, but rather to see whether the simpler ones provide an adequate explanation of the judgments obtained. Moreover, most of the work on finding appropriate models for combining information has been limited to the single overall impression of liking for the stimulus person.

Norman Anderson has produced a good deal of data in support of a weighted averaging model, working not only with inferences about persons, but with a considerable variety of other judgments and with processes of attitude change.[36] We will not deal further with these models here, except to note that Warr and Smith have attempted an evaluation of six different models for combining information.[37]

Multidimensional Analysis

Instead of using inferences to analyze impressions of persons, it is possible to use *direct ratings* of them. For example, an individual may be asked to estimate on a scale like that on page 34 the degree of boldness or timidity of a person he knows, without being provided with any information, such as the cue trait *cautious.* Another procedure is *trait sorting,* in which an individual is asked to describe several persons by selecting from a set of traits a subset best suited for each person. Various complex statistical procedures available for application to such ratings (*factor analysis* and *multidimensional scaling*) provide information about basic dimensions that underlie a set of judgments concerning a person.

36. ANDERSON, 1971.   *37.* WARR & SMITH, 1970.

Rosenberg and Sedlak have reviewed studies using trait sorting and check-lists.[38] They found that judgments of persons are organized around three dimensions, *evaluation, potency,* and *activity.* The first, *evaluation,* is typically the strongest and suggests that many judgments are organized according to a *good-bad* continuum. Associated with the *potency* dimension are such characteristics as *strong-weak, hard-soft, stern-gentle, dominating-submissive.* The third basic dimension, *activity,* is represented by such traits as *active-passive, energetic-slow, industrious-lazy.* In the studies where the investigator provided the trait list on which judgments were made, these three dimensions appeared to be relatively independent. A quite different picture emerged when individuals made their own selections of traits to be judged. Here the three dimensions were also found, but were weaker and no longer independent of each other. The standing of a person on one was related to his standing on the others. For example, a person extreme on evaluation would be above average on potency and activity.

Results from the hundreds of studies using ratings, as opposed to checklists or trait sorting, can hardly be summarized in any simple way. But one finding is pertinent here. We can ask whether the dimensions discovered are characteristic of the persons rated, or whether they represent the way in which the judges use the trait words. Several studies using factor analysis show quite conclusively that the organization lies in the judgments, rather than in the stimulus persons' actual characteristics.[39] What these studies show is that the underlying structure of the judgments remains unchanged whether friends or total strangers are rated. Thus, ratings take form from the judges' own organization of trait concepts, rather than from some organization that exists in the stimulus persons they are rating. While the dimensions that emerge from these studies of ratings appear to be quite different from the previously discussed ones of evaluation, activity, and potency, these three dimensions have been shown to be inherent in dimensions based on trait ratings.[40]

Summary: Organizational Processes in Person Evaluations

Descriptions of people are typically highly organized, and judgments of people that might appear to involve different traits are nevertheless highly related. Typically, research on this organizational property has used a hypothetical target person, a kind of nonexistent Everyman, rather than specific categories of persons specified in terms of age, sex, occupational role, or other criteria. Thus the focus has been on the general properties of judgments of people.

Impressions formed from verbal descriptions of people show that some cue traits are more central than others: They have a strong impact on the impression formed. This occurs even when descriptions are lengthened and given some realistic form, such as a news report. The links between cue traits and inferred traits have been thought of as constituting an implicit personality theory of what people are like. This section has dealt with the implicit theory

38. Rosenberg & Sedlak, 1972.   39. Norman & Goldberg, 1966; Passini & Norman, 1966.
40. Kuusinen, 1969.

pertaining to observers in general, based on averaging of group data. Both the evaluative and the descriptive connotations of the cue traits contribute to the impression formed. The overall impression formed from cue traits appears most often to be based on a process of averaging the various inferences. Multidimensional analysis has revealed that a prominent set of dimensions underlying the evaluation of people consists of evaluation (*good-bad*), potency (*strong-weak*), and activity (*active-passive*). Many other dimensional interpretations are possible, however.

The Observer in Person Evaluations

The discussion to this point has dealt largely with a variety of principles characterizing the person descriptions given by observers in general, without regard to individual differences among observers. This section will first illustrate some ways in which observers' judgments differ and then identify some characteristics of observers who differ in the judgments they make. Essentially we are here dealing with the implicit personality theories of *individual* observers or *types* of observers, as opposed to observers in general.

Differences in Observer Judgments

One of the most common characteristics varying among observers is a consistent bias in certain judgments. All of us are familiar with the perpetual grouch, who has little good to say about any person or even most events. The trusting soul is biased in a different direction. In comparison with other observers, he should rate persons higher in honesty, sincerity, and similar traits. This type of bias is illustrated in a study which shows that college students give traits that are important to them extreme ratings in judging other people.[41] The importance of a personality characteristic to an observer apparently leads to a number of other judgmental differences. For example, observers have been shown to have a greater liking for persons who possess traits that are important to the observers.[42]

This "weighting" of traits is a major difference in observers' judgments of people. The other major difference is in the use of dimensions or traits. Where the observer is given some freedom in choosing descriptive terms, some observers may use many traits, and others, few. Several studies illustrate both the weighting process and the different use of dimensions by different observers. For example, when well-known political figures were judged on the basis of similarity or dissimilarity to one another, one type of observer judged politicians along a single *good-bad* dimension, another type used a *good-bad* dimension but also a *Republican-Democratic* distinction, and a third type made many subtle distinctions, presumably reflecting a complex set of dimensions.[43]

Another investigation[44] presented observers with a variety of information

41. TAJFEL & WILKES, 1964.   *42*. ROMMETVEIT, 1960.   *43*. JACKSON & MESSICK, 1963.   *44*. WIGGINS & HOFFMAN, 1969.

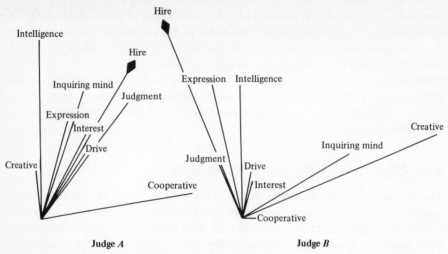

Figure 2-2   *Organization of traits as perceived by two interviewers.* *[Reprinted by permission from L. J. Cronbach. Proposals leading to analytic treatment of social perception scores. In R. Tagiuri and L. Petrullo (Eds.),* Person perception and interpersonal behavior. *Stanford, Calif.: Stanford University Press, 1958. P. 364.]*

about persons, such as their high school rating, social status, degree of self-support, effectiveness in use of English, and mother's level of education, and asked them to estimate the intelligence of each person from this information. Statistical analysis enabled the investigators to determine the weight that each observer put on each item of information in judging intelligence. Observers were found to fall into eight groups or types, each of which used a different weighting system. For example, one group of forty-five observers judged intelligence almost exclusively on the basis of high school performance and number of credit hours taken. A second group emphasized effectiveness in English as a principal criterion and high school rating as a secondary one, but virtually ignored other information. A third group assigned most of the weight to high school rating, effectiveness in English, responsibility, and study habits. Such information about the underlying bases of judgments of intelligence is extracted by factor analysis and does not imply that the observers are aware of the way they weight information items.

The weighting of attributes in judgment is further illustrated in Figure 2-2.[45] Two industrial interviewers rated the same applicant on a set of traits and then rated his potential as an executive. In Figure 2-2, the degree of association between two rated traits or between a trait and the decision to hire is represented by the angle between the lines, with an angle of 0° representing perfect correlation, and 90°, zero correlation. The relation of the *hire* vector to a trait indicates the extent to which the judge thinks that the trait is related to potential job performance of the interviewee: the smaller the angle between the *hire*

45. CRONBACH, 1958.

vector and the trait, the more that trait is perceived as important for job performance. The *length* of the line represents the extent to which the judge varies his ratings of different interviewees: short lines indicate that he does not vary them much, and thus they are not too important to the decision to hire, because most people have those qualities in the same degree. Thus, we can see that judge A has made his decision on the basis of a combination of two independent attributes, *intelligence* and *cooperativeness. Inquiring mind* (related to *intelligence*) and *judgment* also contribute. But judge B has made his decision on the basis of *intelligence* and *expression,* which in his thinking are closely related. *Cooperativeness* and *inquiring mind* play no part in his evaluation, and *creativity* actually makes a slight *negative* contribution to the decision (the angle is more than 90°). As the investigator puts it, the two interviewers look at applicants through different spectacles.

Differences in Observer Characteristics

Our discussion so far has been limited to showing that different observers make evaluations of people or describe them in quite different ways, without making any attempt to identify the *observer* characteristics associated with different views of people. Unfortunately, research attempting to identify such characteristics has been less successful, although some findings are available.

Some observer characteristics associated with evaluations of people are quite obvious. We saw at the beginning of this chapter that older children differ from both adults and younger children in the way they describe people. Generally speaking, older adults describe people in a more varied and more complex way than do younger adults or children.[46] While we might also expect that male and female observers would show wide differences in the way they evaluate people, a review of studies in this area indicates relatively few differences.[47]

A natural place to look for observer characteristics that relate to ways in which people are evaluated is in the observer's general handling of cognitive materials. The way in which an individual views his world and the objects in it should be related to his views of people. Harvey, Hunt, and Schroder have interpreted the conceptual systems that observers use for viewing their world in terms of *concreteness-abstractness.*[48] Concreteness in a person is manifested in many ways, including: He makes more extreme distinctions (good-bad, right-wrong, black-white, etc.); he depends more on authority, precedent, and other extrapersonal guidelines for action; he is intolerant of ambiguous situations; he has a low capacity to act "as if" and to take the role of the other person. The abstract person behaves in the opposite of these ways. Clearly, abstract observers should be better able to integrate diverse information about another person. Judges were presented with two sets of adjectives having opposite meanings and asked to form an impression of the persons represented by each set.[49] Later

46. WERTHEIMER, 1960; BEACH & WERTHEIMER, 1961; KOHN & FIEDLER, 1961; FIEDLER & HOFFMAN, 1962.
47. WARR & KNAPPER, 1968.   48. HARVEY, HUNT, & SCHRODER, 1961.

they were asked to combine these impressions into those of a single person. The more abstract judges were better able to do so.

In another study, behavioral information about a person was presented successively in three pairs, all three pairs consisting of desirable items or undesirable items.[50] For example, an unfavorable stimulus item was "picked up tips for the waitress left by other patrons," and a favorable item was "frequently sent flowers and get-well wishes to hospitalized friends." Participants known to be either concrete or abstract made estimates of how plausible it was that the described person would have other behavioral characteristics (which also were either desirable or undesirable). Where the estimated item was consistent with the stimulus items in favorability or unfavorability, plausibility was high, but concrete individuals judged it more plausible than did abstract individuals. The reverse was true for abstract judges, who were more willing than concrete individuals to consider it plausible that an inconsistent item could be attributed to the stimulus person. These effects were most pronounced when all six items of stimulus information had been presented (as compared with the first two or the first four). Thus, it appears that concrete persons are more disposed to see the "good" person as all good and the "bad" person as all bad.

These results are not unlike those for the cognitively complex observer, who uses more dimensions in evaluating people.[51] In a tape recording, different speakers described a person as possessing the positive traits *considerate, intelligent, humorous,* and *well-liked* and the negative traits *immature, bad-tempered, dishonest,* and *sarcastic.*[52] For some groups of observers, positive traits were presented last, and for others, negative traits. The impression of the person formed by observers low in complexity was dominated by the traits presented last, but perceivers high in complexity achieved an ambivalent impression, making use of both positive and negative traits.

Evaluations of persons are affected by the "authoritarian" traits of the observer. An individual with an authoritarian personality rigidly adheres to conventional middle-class values and has an exaggerated concern with such values, is submissive toward the moral authorities of his ingroup, condemns and rejects people who violate conventional values, is preoccupied with power and status considerations, tends to identify with powerful figures, and is generally hostile toward members of outgroups. These traits are thought of as belonging together. A person high in some of them tends to be high in the remaining ones; similarly, a person average in some of them tends to be average in the remaining ones; and so forth. The extent to which an individual is authoritarian is assessed by a questionnaire known as the *F-scale,* originally developed in 1950 by Adorno, Frenkel-Brunswik, Levinson, and Sanford. Sample items which an authoritarian individual would agree with are: "Every person should have complete faith in some supernatural power whose decisions he obeys without question"; "The wild sex life of the old Greeks and Romans was tame com-

49. HARVEY & SCHRODER, 1963.   50. WARE & HARVEY, 1967.   51. BIERI, 1955.   52. MAYO & CROCKETT, 1964.

pared to some of the goings-on in this country, even in places where people might least expect it."

Several investigations placed observers in two-person groups for approximately a twenty-minute period, instructing them to discuss radio, television, and the movies with each other.[53] This was done in order to provide each observer with information about the other. In some instances, two persons high in authoritarianism were paired, in others, two persons low in authoritarianism, and finally, pairs consisting of one high-authoritarian and one low-authoritarian person. The investigators were interested in the impressions formed of the other person in the dyad and wanted to find out how these would vary with the individual's own authoritarian traits. After completing the discussion period, each observer filled out a questionnaire as he thought the other person would fill it out. Items on the questionnaire were from the F scale, which is used for assessing the extent to which a person possesses authoritarian traits. In later studies, instead of having the individual actually interact with another participant, recordings of mock interviews with high-authoritarian and low-authoritarian persons were presented.[54] The latter technique has the advantage of presenting more precisely controlled and structured information to the observer. The results of these various studies were consistent with the following generalizations:

1. The observer usually assumes that the other person is a peer; that is, he is not thought of as having any especially significant characteristics that might set him apart from others.

2. The high-authoritarian observers assume that the other person has values like their own, and consequently they place him high on most of the authoritarian traits.

3. The low-authoritarian observers do not rate the other person as low-authoritarian but usually rate him as average on authoritarian traits.

These results provide adequate evidence to the effect that the observer's own characteristics will affect the manner in which he describes others. Such descriptions would presumably be quite different, however, if the observer did not regard the other person as belonging to the ingroup. Moreover, these findings are subject to various interpretations. Several investigators interpret them as supporting the view that the low-authoritarian observer perceives others more accurately (the high-authoritarian observer even evaluates low-authoritarian persons as high).[55] Others have suggested that the high-authoritarian and the low-authoritarian people are simply reflecting their experience with other persons in everyday life and are little influenced by the stimulus information.[56] This view is based on the assumption that the high-authoritarian person will mostly associate with others like himself, but the low-authoritarian person will

53. Scodel & Mussen, 1953; Scodel & Freedman, 1956; Crockett & Meidinger, 1956.   *54.* Jones, 1954; Kates, 1959; Lipetz, 1960.   *55.* Scodel & Mussen, 1953; Scodel & Freedman, 1956; Lipetz, 1960. *56.* Crockett & Meidinger, 1956; Rabinowitz, 1956.

frequently encounter persons having high-authoritarian traits. Thus, each could be regarded as making a kind of probability judgment about the traits of a complete stranger.

This explanation is made especially plausible by a study in which subjects were given no stimulus materials but were asked to estimate how the "typical college student" would respond to F-scale items.[57] Results closely parallel those of the previously cited investigations using stimulus materials.

The most successful attempt to relate the characteristics of an observer to his descriptions of people is found in a study of a single observer. Rosenberg and Jones analyzed the descriptions written by Theodore Dreiser in *A Gallery of Women,* using several forms of multidimensional analysis.[58] Three major dimensions underlying his use of ninety-nine descriptive traits were *conforms— does not conform; male-female;* and *hard-soft.* The last two dimensions were closely related. Dreiser was deeply involved with women in two ways: as sexual partners and as intellectual companions. His sexual involvement with women shows up in the traits he associated with femaleness: attractive, beautiful, graceful, lovely, physically alluring, and sensual. But he liked his attractive, unconventional women to be clever and he employed them as literary agents. This aspect shows up in traits he assigned to females such as reads, defiant, intelligent, cold, and clever. Conformity relates to a second theme in Dreiser's life. Throughout his literary career, he fought against social convention. He had to fight to get his works published and he was contemptuous of beliefs held by the common man. The analysis of his descriptions of women reflects this theme, in that *conforms—does not conform* appears repeatedly as a major dimension.

Summary: The Observer in Person Evaluations

Individuals differ in the complexity of their grasp of language and in their implicit theories of what people are like. One of the most common characteristics varying among observers is a consistent bias in certain judgments: They overestimate or underestimate the amount of a trait that people possess. Observers also weight information differently in their assessments of people: The contribution of some bits of information, including cue traits, is greater than that of others.

Less progress has been made in identifying the characteristics of observers that are associated with differing forms of judgment or implicit personality theories. Although observers differing in age and sex evaluate people differently, the nature of these evaluations is poorly specified. Another characteristic of observers associated with different styles of evaluating people is concreteness-abstractness. Concreteness is reflected in extreme distinctions between good and bad, right and wrong; in dependence on authority and precedent; and in refusal to recognize differing points of view. Abstractness is char-

---

57. Rabinowitz, 1956.   58. Rosenberg & Jones, 1972.

acterized by opposite qualities. Concreteness-abstractness is closely related to another concept, the complexity of observers. More complex or abstract observers use a larger number of dimensions or concepts in describing persons than do less complex observers, and are better able to attribute incongruous traits to the same person. Finally, observers characterized as having an authoritarian personality assume that others have values like their own and are high on authoritarian traits. Those low in authoritarianism do not make this assumption, but judge other persons to be average in authoritarianism.

Forming Impressions from Nonverbal Information

In many life situations a person is observed although he does not speak. And in some situations where verbal information is available, it is so ritualized that it is valueless for forming an impression of the person (e.g., as in a social introduction where two persons exchange formal greetings or acknowledgments). Then there are cases where verbal information has clear implications for evaluating the person, but the observer wishes to check out his impression against more indirect information. For example, an observer may have inadvertently performed an action that would normally make another person angry. That person says he is not angry, but the observer also uses indirect information such as tone of voice, posture, and facial expression to determine the sincerity of the statement. Thus, research on forming impressions from nonverbal information has potential applicability to many life situations.

Nonverbal information as a basis for forming impressions of a person can be divided into two large categories: *structural* and *kinetic*. Structural information includes such relatively unmodifiable elements as physiognomy (the shape of the face and its various features) and body build or type. Kinetic information includes gestures, expressive movements, posture, observable tension or relaxation, and similar items. Our discussion will treat these two categories separately.

Structural Nonverbal Information

Facial features, body build, and general appearance play an important role in interactions among persons. They create expectations about the kind of person one is and determine how he is treated. Thus, the well-dressed, athletic-looking man is apt to be treated with greater deference than the sloppily dressed, weak-looking man. The extent to which a person is physically attractive in part determines how other persons behave toward him. A study of nursery school children found them to hold quite different beliefs about attractive and unattractive children.[59] Aggressive, antisocial behavior was believed more charac-

59. Unpublished study by DION & BERSCHEID, 1971. Cited in BERSCHEID & WALSTER, 1972.

teristic of unattractive boys than attractive ones, whereas attractive children were seen as more independent. Whether or not these beliefs reflect real differences is less important than that such beliefs are apt to affect how these children are interacted with, to the great advantage of the attractive ones. A review of research on physical attractiveness by Berscheid and Walster indicated that physically attractive adults have similar advantages.[60] The discussion that follows will show that more specific impressions may also be drawn from various structural features of persons.

FACIAL FEATURES AS STIMULUS INFORMATION   Human physiognomy has fascinated man throughout recorded history. The literature of all ages includes references to physiognomy as if it were an integral part of human character. Paintings and sculpture often use the head alone as subject matter, as if this portion of the person represented him in essence. Physiognomy pertains to relatively unmodifiable structural features: the width and length of the face, the shape of the nose, the configuration of the mouth, the size and shape of the eyes, the arrangement of the facial planes. Often included as well are relatively permanent expressions (e.g., those of a consistently anxious, tense person, perhaps expressed in wrinkles or skin folds).

It would seem that in situations where an observer had little other information and yet needed to form an impression of a person, he would base it to some degree on facial features. The evaluation might, of course, be quite wrong; but if such evaluations are frequently made, it is of interest to know how they are arrived at. Thus, the focus is not upon the accuracy of judgments about persons, but upon the nature of the information used and the manner in which it is used to form the judgment.

Studies of physiognomy by Secord and his colleagues have demonstrated beyond doubt that observers can readily form impressions of persons from their photographs.[61] Further, that these observers use somewhat similar processes to arrive at essentially the same impressions is suggested by the high degree of agreement among judges working independently. This does not mean, of course, that their impression is correct, nor does it mean that they would form the same impression if they had additional information about the person. But it does suggest that, in the starkly limited situation where the only information provided is a photograph of the face, individuals generate judgments through processes that they share in common.

What apparently happens is that individuals make inferences from the facial information available according to various rules. Sometimes these inferences draw upon communitywide prejudices. For example, photographs of dark-skinned faces evoke unfavorable impressions—hostile, conceited, dishonest, and unfriendly.[62] Similarly, inferences may be based upon socially standardized or conventional meanings. Thus, if a photograph of a young woman portrays

60. BERSCHEID & WALSTER, 1972.   *61.* SECORD, 1958.   *62.* SECORD, DUKES, & BEVAN, 1954.

the appropriate use of cosmetics along with well-groomed hair, she is seen as sexually attractive.[63]

Often structural features of the face may suggest facial expressions that have a standard meaning. For example, persons with a slight but permanent upward curve at the corner of the mouth, which might suggest the makings of a voluntary smile, were rated as friendly, easygoing, and good-tempered. Vertical or horizontal wrinkles in the brow, suggesting tension, caused attribution of such attributes as quick-tempered and hostile.

Sometimes the inferences made about people are based upon metaphor or analogy. A person with a coarse *skin* may be viewed as a coarse or insensitive *person.* The analogy is often founded on the *function* of some facial feature. For example, the mouth is used for talking. Thus, persons with thin, compressed lips are rated low on the trait of *talkativeness.*[64] Further examples readily come to mind: A woman with a full mouth is seen as sensual; a high forehead may suggest intelligence; etc.

A word of caution is in order. On the whole, the impressions formed from viewing facial features cannot be fully understood by identifying specific features. While some specific features were related to a specifiable aspect of the personality impression formed, many aspects of the impression that were agreed upon by observers could not be related to specific facial features. Several of our studies suggested that the observer forms a total impression which is based upon some complex, patterned view of the face as a whole.[65] The observers were not able to tell us how they arrived at their impressions, and these studies were not entirely successful in identifying precisely those aspects of the face that account for the overall impression.

APPEARANCE AND BODY BUILD   We mentioned earlier the importance of a person's identity in determining how he is known and evaluated. One cue to identity is appearance and clothing. For example, whether a person is male or female is ascertained instantly from his bodily appearance, and usually from his clothing as well. The significance of this particular identity is illustrated by the annoyance expressed by many members of the older generation about the trend toward obscuring sexual identity—young men by wearing their hair long and young women by wearing blue jeans and other masculine clothing—that started in the late 1960s.

Uniforms are one of the most obvious and deliberate uses of clothing to fix identity: One can identify a policeman instantly. But interviews with people about the clothing that they and other persons wear testify to its significance in establishing identity in less direct ways. For example, one informant was asked whether he would rather wear a greater or a smaller variety of clothes on the job. He replied, "A smaller variety so you will look the same every day. So people will identify you. They look for the same old landmark."[66]

63. SECORD & MUTHARD, 1955.   64. SECORD & MUTHARD, 1955.   65. SECORD, DUKES, & BEVAN, 1954; SECORD & MUTHARD, 1955; STRITCH & SECORD, 1956.   66. STONE, 1962, p. 95.

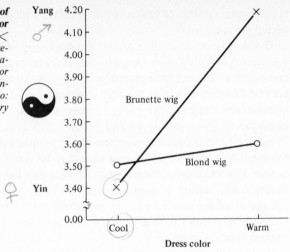

Figure 2-3 Combined effect of blond or brunette wig and warm or cool dress. *(N = 88, F = 5.7, < 0.05, for wig by dress color.) (Prepared from data provided by L. Mahannah. Influence of clothing color on the perception of personality. Unpublished master's thesis, Reno: University of Nevada, January 1968.)*

A study of dress and wig color by Mahannah yielded dramatically differing impressions.[67] A college woman serving as a model wore a dress in a "cool" color (blue) in one condition, and a "warm" color (red-orange) in another. She also wore either a brunette or a blond wig. Impressions of judges were measured by rating scales representing a *yin-yang* dimension. These terms are from the Chinese. *Yin* refers to feminine qualities such as delicate, sensitive, introverted, dependent, while *yang* refers to masculine ones such as bold, aggressive, self-sufficient. The results for male judges are shown in Figure 2-3. We can see that with a blond wig, the model was judged to be toward the feminine side wearing either a cool or a warm dress. Similarly judged was the model in a brunette wig and cool dress. With the warm dress, however, she was judged appreciably less feminine. Mahannah suggests that the strength of the stereotype for blond women overrides the effect of the warm dress, so that the model is still judged feminine. But since most people are brunette, there is no stereotype for brunettes, and dress color plays a more important role. Although studies using additional models and judges are needed to confirm these generalizations, it seems clear that clothes and hair color can have dramatic effects upon impressions.

The idea that personality and temperament are related to physique has a long history extending back to the ancient Greeks. A frequently quoted passage from Shakespeare's *Julius Caesar* (Act I, Scene 2) illustrates the point:

> Let me have men about me that are fat,
> Sleek-headed men, and such as sleep o' nights.
> Yond Cassius has a lean and hungry look.
> He thinks too much. Such men are dangerous.

67. Mahannah, 1968.

In modern times, extensive studies of the relation between personality and physique have been conducted. Although these studies focus upon the accuracy of judgments of personality from physique alone, they also contribute information about the formation of personality impressions that are not necessarily valid. Kretschmer observed that schizophrenics tend to be tall and thin, and manic-depressives, short and fat.[68] He generalized this observation to normal persons differing in body build, and suggested that tall, thin persons were usually sensitive, withdrawn, and reserved, and short, fat persons, sociable and forceful. He continued to refine his early ideas for many years, and the above statement is a considerable oversimplification of his typology. In a general sense, however, it does accord with what appear to be widespread lay notions concerning thin and fat persons.

Sheldon and his colleagues offered a somewhat different system of describing body build and relating it to personality.[69] The interesting point about their ideas for our purpose is that evaluations of temperament (or personality) were based upon ratings made by themselves or by others who themselves were thoroughly familiar with their system of body typology. It is generally accepted that the correlations which Sheldon and his colleagues found between physique and personality were somewhat inflated because of failure to rate personality independently of knowledge of the stimulus persons' body build. But the presence of this "error" suggests the potency of body build in contributing to personality "impressions," whether correct or incorrect. Instead of explaining this relation as an error, we suggest that the very choice of traits for describing personality produced relations between physique and personality through reasoning by analogy.

For example, heavy, fat persons were characterized as loving physical comfort, slow to react, and relaxed. Persons of athletic build were described as energetic, assertive of posture and movement, needing and enjoying exercise, and loving physical adventure. Thus, these "personality traits" may be arrived at by using analogy to make inferences from body structure.

Kinetic Nonverbal Information

The posture and movement of persons often convey useful information to others. Argyle and his coworkers arranged videotapes so that previously equated verbal and nonverbal information was systematically presented in different ways to assess its relative impact on the impressions formed.[70] They found that nonverbal information shifted judges' ratings 4½ times as much as verbal information. Argyle has suggested three broad classes of communicative function served by such kinetic information.

First, nonverbal communication aids in managing the immediate situation by providing cues to interpersonal attitudes that help to structure the interac-

68. Kretschmer, 1925.   *69.* Sheldon, Stevens, & Tucker, 1940; Sheldon & Stevens, 1942.   *70.* Argyle, Salter, Nicholson, Williams, & Burgess, 1970.

tion between persons. Cues to attraction and relative status are conveyed non-verbally. To illustrate, a superior attitude toward another person may be indicated by an erect posture and a haughty and unsmiling facial expression, by adopting a loud, resonant, commanding tone of voice, and by staring the other person down. Or liking and receptiveness may be conveyed by what Scheflen has called quasi-courtship behavior in psychotherapy.[71] Women may stroke their hair, rearrange their clothing, cock their heads, roll their hips. Male therapists stroke their hair, adjust their coats, pull up their socks. The whole serves to communicate in a subtle way the actor's liking for the other person and his readiness for an intimate but not necessarily sexual relationship.

Second, nonverbal information serves in the immediate situation as a powerful indicator of the emotional state of persons. Most persons have difficulty controlling nonverbal signs of emotional arousal; thus, such signs are often given more credence than what the person says about his feelings.

Third, nonverbal information plays a major role in self-presentation. By his clothes, his manner of speaking, the kinds of words he uses, and his general style of interaction, one gives the impression of being a certain type of person. Stone has offered a similar argument to the effect that nonverbal information establishes the other person's role.[72] Upon entering a store, for example, one discovers the salesperson by his distinctive dress, as well as his postural attitude toward the customer. At the very least, the sex of the other person is established by his appearance, laying the groundwork for an appropriate interaction.

Since the first edition of this book, research by Ekman and his colleagues has made considerable progress in unraveling the difficult mystery of how information is conveyed through nonverbal means.[73] Except where otherwise indicated, the remainder of this section is based upon their work. They have noted that to fully understand nonverbal communication, we must discover how a particular behavior became part of the individual's repertoire, the circumstances of its use, and the rules which explain how the behavior conveys information.

They have demonstrated that accurate inferences about emotions, attitudes, interpersonal roles, and severity of pathology can be made by observers who have had no specialized training.[74] Different body areas convey somewhat different information.[75] The *face* conveys information about the nature of an emotion (sadness, anger, fear). Bodily *actions* provide information about both the intensity and the nature of the emotion. *Static positions* of the body provide information about intensity of emotion, and sometimes about the gross emotional state—whether the person feels pleasant or unpleasant.

Certain acts have been found to have fairly specific meanings. For example, covering or partly covering the eyes is often associated with shame or embarrassment. The meaning of specific acts must be judged in context, however; it may vary with age, physical setting, social role, and different verbal behaviors.

---

71. Scheflen, 1965.   *72.* Stone, 1962.   *73.* Ekman & Friesen, 1969.   *74.* Ekman, 1964; Ekman, 1965a; Ekman & Friesen, 1965.   *75.* Ekman, 1965b; Ekman & Friesen, 1967.

Research has also focused on the extent to which nonverbal behavior can reveal information that is not perceptible in verbal behavior.

Movements called *illustrators* serve to show what is being communicated verbally. Generally they are used intentionally and with awareness, although somewhat less so than are gestures. In research with psychiatric patients, use of illustrators was found to be greater as the patients recovered, and least in the acute phases. Particular types of hand-to-face movements (grooming, auto-erotic motions, attacking actions) were found to be associated with the breaking of interocular contact between patient and interviewer.

More revealing of the person is another category of movement, *affect dis-plays*, in which feelings or emotions are conveyed by facial expressions. Primary emotions which are readily distinguished by observers in our culture and probably in other cultures are: happiness, surprise, fear, sadness, anger, disgust, and interest. The expression of these emotions is complicated by several *display rules*, probably learned quite early in life, and taking different forms in different societies. These are deintensification (e.g., a fearful person attempts to look less afraid), overintensification (e.g., a person expresses more pleasure than he feels), neutralization (e.g., an agitated person tries to appear unperturbed), and masking, where the person conceals his feeling by giving the appearance of experiencing some other contrary feeling (e.g., a person feeling sad tries to look happy).

Undoubtedly each society has norms for the use of these rules governing the display of affect. A hostess whose guest has just dumped a cup of coffee on her new rug hides her feeling of annoyance; a professor deintensifies his puzzlement when a student asks him a difficult question; a person receiving a gift of little value overintensifies his pleasurable display. These norms also vary in different cultures: For example, in some cultures sadness is overintensified at funerals; in others, it is deintensified; and in some, it is masked. Complications in decoding display of affect arise in a number of ways, perhaps most notably because in any given display, two or more affects may be blended. Although we are usually aware of our affect displays, they may or may not be intentionally communicated. Similarly, the application of a display rule may or may not be intentional.

Vocal Cues to Personality Impressions

Another form of nonverbal information consists of the vocal qualities of a person's voice and his manner of speaking: These may sometimes contribute to forming impressions of a person. Such features as speed, loudness, pitch, tuning, accent, and speech errors may have a critical effect.[76] Anxious people speak rapidly and make a relatively large number of speech errors.[77] A dominant person speaks loudly and slowly.[78] In a study where trained speakers of

---

76. ARGYLE, 1970.   77. DAVITZ, 1964.   78. ELDRED & PRICE, 1958.

both sexes simulated certain voice qualities, impressions were affected as follows[79]: Breathiness (speaking accompanied by the passage of unvocalized breath) in males made them seem young and artistic; female speakers with this voice characteristic were seen as feminine and pretty. Flatness (absence of pitch modulation) made both male and female speakers seem cold, masculine, sluggish, and withdrawn. Throatiness (a hard quality associated with sound from the throat rather than mouth) led male speakers to appear mature, sophisticated, and well-adjusted, but the same qualities in females produced impressions containing a considerable number of undesirable characteristics. Orotundity (fullness and strength of voice) in both males and females generally produced a desirable impression of energy and liveliness. A difficult problem in research on voice quality as stimulus information is that voice quality is difficult to characterize in an objective fashion. One promising approach to this problem is the use of a voice spectrograph, a machine which analyzes the voice in terms of a mix of a fundamental pitch and a variety of overtones, which can be given different emphases in speaking. In one study, the voice spectrum of depressed patients was shown generally to be lacking in the higher overtones, yielding an impression of dullness, a lifeless quality with diminished inflection.[80]

Summary: Impressions from Nonverbal Information

Various studies show clearly that certain types of structural nonverbal information (facial features, body build, etc.) can be readily used by observers to form impressions about other persons. The readiness with which they perform this task and the degree of agreement they achieve suggests that, in those life situations where they have primarily this kind of information, they do form impressions based upon it.

Kinetic nonverbal information includes gestures, expressive movements, posture, and observable tension or relaxation. A growing body of research details the ways in which such information produces certain judgments about the target person. Such information appears to provide cues to interpersonal attitudes that help to structure the interaction between persons, to serve as an indicator of the emotional state of persons, and to play a role in self-presentation. Among the more important categories of nonverbal behavior are *illustrators* which graphically display what is being communicated verbally and *affect or emotional displays* involving mainly facial expressions. These are complicated by *display rules* which specify the situation for which the various displays are appropriate. Different societies have differing *norms* for the use of these various means of communication.

Less progress has been made in the study of vocal cues to personality impressions. Yet it seems established that vocal cues can occasionally be used to form impressions and even to make effective judgments of other persons.

79. ADDINGTON, 1968.   80. HARGRAVES, STARKWEATHER, & BLACKER, 1965.

Person Evaluations in Ongoing Interaction

It is obvious that in everyday situations, the behavior of another person toward us markedly affects our evaluation of him. Less obvious, perhaps, is that an individual can treat another person in ways that are apt to bring out some of that person's qualities. Yet the previous discussion has been primarily of studies in which there was no opportunity for such interaction. Such studies permit the assessment of other determinants of impression formation by eliminating the confounding effects of interactions on the evaluation of the stimulus person. But a thorough understanding of how people develop their ideas and feelings about others requires that we consider the effects of interaction. Fortunately, more research is being carried out today in which interaction between the observer and the target person is permitted and analyzed. These studies are too few to yield conclusive results, but they do at least constitute a beginning. We should hasten to say that these studies necessarily place *some* restrictions on interaction, in order to assess its effects. With complete freedom it would, under most circumstances, be impossible to describe what influences a person to form the impression that he does.

Effects of the Observer's Behavior

What a person is like and how he is evaluated depends in part on whom he is interacting with. Just as an observer on earth can see only one side of the moon, any individual's view of another person is based on the behavior that occurs in his presence. And that behavior is partly a function of the observer's own behavior toward the other person. Each observer elicits certain behaviors from those around him. For example, a hostile observer is apt to believe other persons are more hostile than they are, simply because his own aggressive behavior draws hostility in return.

A series of laboratory studies using the prisoner's dilemma game demonstrate this phenomenon nicely.[81] In this game a player can play cooperatively, being concerned with both his own score and that of the other player, or he can play competitively, in his own interest and against his opponent. (See Chapter 8 for a more complete explanation of this game.) Most players can be described as either the cooperative type or the competitive type. When a normally cooperative player is matched against a competitive one, he adopts a competitive strategy. He is aware that this departs from his usual behavior, but the competitive opponent is not. The cooperator's view of other persons is that they may be either cooperative or competitive. But the competitive type thinks that all persons are competitive, because his own competitive behavior elicits competitive behavior from his opponent. This general phenomenon has also been demonstrated in bargaining games, and is found in survey data pertaining to

81. KELLEY & STAHELSKI, 1970.

student-administration conflict in universities.[82] Thus, certain attitudes toward other people take the form of self-fulfilling prophecies—the actor behaves so as to elicit from others behavior that confirms his beliefs.

Impression Management

To some degree, all of us manage the impression we present to other persons. We behave so as to create a certain image of ourselves. This process is not necessarily deceptive or calculating, for there are situations in which the other party expects us to behave according to a particular image. An example is a boy and a girl on a date. He presents himself and she presents herself as attractively as possible, which adds to their enjoyment of each other.

One motive for managing the impression one presents is the desire to obtain the support or approval of other persons. A set of behaviors for accomplishing this has been termed *ingratiation tactics.*[83] Such tactics include giving compliments, behaving in a pleasing manner, and agreeing with or conforming to the expressed opinions of the other person. As is suggested by the use of the word *tactics,* these actions are performed to gain favor. Such flattery is only successful where the intention of the flatterer is concealed, and success is most likely where the flatterer would seem to have nothing to gain. Jones has also noted that flattery shows diminishing returns; if continued beyond a certain point, it may produce an effect on the target person opposite to that intended.[84]

The employee who "yesses" the boss to gain approval is proverbial. In experiments, however, an individual who consistently agrees with another person on whom he is dependent is less liked by an observer than an individual who is dependent but less consistently agrees or than an individual who agrees but who is not dependent.[85] A more subtle form of ingratiation tactic involves deliberate disagreement with a person who is being obnoxious in order to avoid being cast with him by a third party who is present.[86]

Laboratory studies have suggested some conditions under which ingratiation tactics are effective, and others under which they fail. As might be expected, the social context in which ingratiation occurs is critical. First, the effectiveness of ingratiation varies with the status of the ingratiator. If he has high status, it seems *legitimate* for him to praise the other person, and there is little suspicion of his intentions. When a low-status person praises a superior, however, his intentions are apt to be suspect. In one study, a confederate of the experimenter enacted several flattery treatments in interview situations: valid praise, invalid praise, and no praise.[87] In one condition the confederate was given an introduction providing her with high status, and in the other, low status. The findings were that she was positively evaluated under all the high-status conditions. Her superior position had the same effect whether she used valid or invalid flattery

82. K. WEICK, personal communication, 1971.   83. JONES, JONES, & GERGEN, 1963.   84. JONES, 1964.
85. JONES, JONES, & GERGEN, 1963.   86. COOPER & JONES, 1969.   87. IVERSON, 1968.

or no flattery at all. In the low-status condition, however, invalid flattery produced extremely low liking ratings, as compared with more moderate ratings for valid flattery or none at all.

Another investigation dealt with doing another person a favor under different conditions.[88] Pairs of individuals participated in a word game, under either a competitive or a cooperative set. In each game one individual perceived that the other won most of the money. The favor took the form of the winner's sharing his winnings with the loser. It was found that players who shared in the cooperative condition and who did *not* share in the competitive condition were liked better than those who offered to share in the inappropriate competitive condition. Thus, even though in an objective sense a favor benefits the recipient, it does not increase his liking for the performer of the favor unless the behavior of the latter is appropriate to his role. This experiment demonstrates the point emphasized by Jones that ingratiation is a form of impression management that *departs from normative expectations.*[89]

This notion of violation of expectations is an important but subtle one. Any interaction between two persons has underlying it certain shared expectations, a kind of implicit contract. The ingratiator *acts as if he accepts these expectations, but in fact does not.* Consider, for example, the seduction of a naïve woman. The seducer plays the part of a man falling in love with her—he is especially attentive, considerate, appreciative, and complimentary—and she accepts his actions as appropriate to a romantic, potentially enduring relation. But his real purpose is seduction and, once accomplished, the relation is ended. If the woman were experienced instead of naïve and actually shared his goal, however, the behavior of the man would not be considered ingratiating, for both parties would implicitly share the expectation that the relation was only transitory and that it would culminate only in sexual intercourse.

Several investigations by Jones and his students have made clear that if the ingratiator is dependent upon the goodwill of or subject to the control of the person he is trying to influence, he is more negatively evaluated than if he behaves in the same way but is not dependent upon the goodwill of the target person.[90] This documents the point that any condition that leads outside observers or the target person himself to suspect the motives or intentions of the ingratiator will render his actions less effective. An interesting additional finding was that the person who behaved autonomously was liked better when he was dependent on the target person than when he was not. This suggests that a person who stands to gain by altering his self-presentation but who resists the temptation is granted some "extra credit." Further, it was found that persons who were themselves the target of ingratiation did not judge the ingratiator as harshly as did uninvolved observers. Apparently it is more difficult for a person who is a target of such tactics to see through them.

88. KIESLER, 1966.   89. JONES, 1964.   90. JONES, 1964.

Responsibility and Locus of Cause

One fundamental idea popularized by Heider which pertains to inferences about persons in interaction is that the cause of a person's action may be seen to lie in himself or in external circumstances.[91] Two things contribute to how the locus of cause is perceived. One is the extent to which the individual is seen to engage in the act of his own volition—how hard he tries, whether he goes out of his way to perform the act. The other lies in the actor's situation: Circumstances may compel him to act, or they may leave him completely free not to perform if he so chooses. Where the situation leaves him free to choose or where he is seen as engaging in the act of his own volition, the cause of his act is ordinarily seen as lying within him, and he is seen as responsible for his act. But where circumstances are compelling, the cause of his act is viewed as external, and he is seen as having minimal responsibility for it. We shall discuss a number of experiments where the volition of the actor is systematically varied and other investigations where the situations vary in the constraints they place upon the actor, and will take particular note of the way in which he is perceived in these differing situations.

In one experiment, a problem-solving situation was arranged so that the perceiver was deprived of a reward as a result of the actions of the stimulus person, who was a confederate of the experimenter.[92] The situation was arranged so that the confederate was seen either as not trying or as being confronted with an impossible situation. Under the special circumstance where the actor was seen as failing the problem due to lack of effort and thus depriving the perceiver of a reward, he was evaluated less favorably on a variety of traits. This is a situation where the "cause" of deprivation was seen as lying in the actor: He didn't try to solve the problem, though he could have. In another condition, where he was perceived as unable to solve the problem even if he tried, he was *not* evaluated unfavorably. Here the "cause" was seen as external to the stimulus person.

Another experimental situation involved acceptance by the stimulus person of an attempt by the perceiver to influence him.[93] Under one condition, the actor had high status and power relative to the perceiver (he was presented as a university instructor or a Harvard law student with a superior background). Under another, the actor had low status (he was presented as a college freshman with an inferior background).

This situation again involves internal and external loci of cause. If a person has high status and power relative to you, he does not have to accept your attempt to influence him. If he nevertheless accepts it, you are likely to believe that he does so voluntarily because he is a "nice guy." On the other hand, if a person has an inferior status relative to yours, he may accept your influence simply because of the pressure he feels. The general hypothesis tested by this

---

91. HEIDER, 1958.   *92.* JONES & deCHARMS, 1958.   *93.* THIBAUT & RIECKEN, 1955.

experiment, then, was that if a person seemed to accept influence of his own volition, the perceiver who influenced him would experience an increase in liking for him. If, on the other hand, the cause of his acceptance was perceived as external to him—was perceived as lying in the status relations between him and the perceiver—the perceiver would not like him more than he did before the influence attempt. This hypothesis was confirmed: A large majority of the subjects who influenced the high-status person increased their liking of him to a greater extent than those who influenced the low-status person.

In another experimental situation, an individual who talked a great deal during a group discussion was perceived as having good ideas and as the group leader by persons who heard a tape recording of the discussion.[94] But he was not perceived as having good ideas or as a group leader by persons who heard the tape recording and who were also shown that the experimenter had rewarded this individual for talking and discouraged the other group members from making contributions to the discussion. The latter group saw his behavior as externally caused rather than springing spontaneously from his good ideas and leadership qualities.

Whether or not an individual has surveillance over the behavior of another is also important. In one investigation, each participant served as a supervisor of the work of two other individuals who, unknown to him, were confederates of the experimenter.[95] The situation was arranged so that the participant supervised the work of one confederate more closely than that of the other. In time, he came to believe that the work of the less closely supervised individual sprang from an internal cause: interest in the work. When later given an opportunity to exercise equal supervision over both confederates, he continued to maintain a closer watch over the individual he had been supervising all along and regarded him as less trustworthy, suggesting an assumption of external cause: the supervision itself. Thus, the investigator concluded that a supervisor cannot be assured of the loyalty of his subordinates unless they have the opportunity to be disloyal. In terms of attribution theory, for an individual to form a definite impression of another person, the stimulus person has to have a chance to display the behavior relevant to that impression.[96] He cannot be in a constrained situation where he is prevented from displaying the behavior.

We may inquire further into the reasons for this. Kruglanski has suggested several possible explanations.[97] First, because in continually monitoring the behavior of the subordinate the supervisor has been behaving in a distrustful manner, he may justify his behavior by forming the impression that the subordinate cannot be trusted. Second, the supervisor might think that the subordinate would resent monitoring of his behavior and would retaliate unless closely watched. Third, the subordinate again might react in a hostile way toward the supervisor, but for a different reason, to wit, that he is being discriminated

94. Hastorf, Kite, Gross, & Wolfe, 1965.   *95.* Strickland, 1958.   *96.* Kelley, 1967.   *97.* Kruglanski, 1970.

against in being monitored more than the other subordinate. Experiments were conducted to check out these reasons.

To test the first idea, that the more frequently monitored subordinate was seen as less trustworthy because the supervisor needed to justify his monitoring action, a supervisory situation was set up in which the supervisor had the power either to reward or to punish the subordinate. The idea behind this was that, where the supervisor could reward the subordinate, his monitoring would be favorably received, because it would be associated with giving the subordinate a reward. In this situation the supervisor could readily justify his behavior to himself. Thus there should be no need for him to perceive the subordinate as untrustworthy. Where the supervisor could punish the subordinate, however, monitoring for this purpose should be quite negative and need strong justification. Here the monitored subordinate should be perceived as less trustworthy. But the results did not bear out this reasoning. The less frequently monitored subordinate was seen as more trustworthy both in the situation where the supervisor had reward power and in the one where he had coercive power. Thus, it seems that the need for justification does not explain the perception of trustworthiness.

The second and third ideas were not supported either. An examination of supervisors' views of the more frequently monitored subordinate yielded no evidence that he was seen as resenting surveillance. Nor was he seen as having feelings of being discriminated against.

These findings, then, support the original view—that the supervisor is reluctant to attribute trustworthiness when the actor has not really had an opportunity to display it. That this is the case is further suggested by a variant of the experiment where the situation is structured as cooperative or competitive. Where the situation is competitive, participants may be expected to ingratiate themselves with the opposing side for possible gain; thus, their behavior may not be trustworthy since it has an ulterior motive. In that competitive condition, both subordinates were seen as less trustworthy, thus minimizing the effect of monitoring their behavior. These experiments on monitoring, then, reveal some of the subtleties of the social context and the pressures it exerts on the behaviors of the actors which lead to their being perceived in different ways.

Although they have somewhat different shades of meaning, the responsibility and justifiability of actions may also be interpreted in terms of loci of cause. If a person is seen as the cause of an action he performs, he is assumed to be responsible for it. If his action is not within his control, he is not assumed to be responsible. An action performed because of powerful external pressures is likely to be seen as justifiable. Here the locus of cause lies outside the person. Heider's idea that less responsibility for an act will be attributed to the performer when circumstances justify the act has found support in experimental work.[98] Intentionality is also related to loci of cause; here, however, both loci

98. HEIDER, 1958; SHAW & SULTZNER, 1964.

are often found within the person. An individual may injure another person maliciously, or he may do it by accident. In one case the cause lies in his malicious intent, in the other case it may lie in his clumsiness or inattention to what he was doing.

Pepitone has summarized a series of experiments investigating these variables.[99] In one study, by presenting recordings of supposedly authentic conversations among students like those serving in the experiment, intentionality was varied experimentally.[100] Participants were asked to put themselves in the place of one of the individuals in the conversation and to judge the other as if he had behaved toward them in that way. In these "overheard" conversations, O insulted S by disparaging his intelligence. Under one condition, O had good intentions: trying to get S to study. In the other, he had bad intentions: trying to impress his instructor. The experimenters found that O was less disliked when he had good intentions than when he had bad ones. An attempt to vary responsibility in a similar fashion was unsuccessful.

Justifiability may be illustrated by common experience. The extent to which another person's actions toward you are justified has much to do with your feelings toward him. For example, a boy might be angry with a girl who broke a date for no apparent reason, whereas if she broke it because of illness, he would be unlikely to feel angry. Justifiability was successfully varied in another experiment, and O's attractiveness to S was shown to vary with the degree of justifiability of O's actions: The more justifiable the action, the more the person was liked.[101] In further experiments, Pepitone also investigated the conditions which govern the attribution of such variables as responsibility and intentionality to other persons.[102] He found that the higher the status of the other person, the more likely he was to be seen as having responsibility for his actions, as possessing good intentions, and as performing justified actions.

Quite a variety of factors may affect the attribution of responsibility for an act to another person. This is illustrated by a series of studies in which individuals were asked to indicate the extent to which they felt persons were responsible for the accidents they had. At first it appeared that the more severe the accident, the more the responsibility attributed to the victim.[103] Walster suggested that this occurred because of a process of *defensive attribution:* The more severe the accident, the more threatening it was for the observer to consider that it might happen to him, and therefore, he blamed the victim (as careless, negligent, etc.) rather than chance. Replications of this study, however, have failed to show these effects of severity on the attribution of responsibility.[104] Shaver suggested and provided some evidence for a somewhat different view: that the observer was more interested in avoiding blame.[105] Thus the more similar the victim was to the observer, the less responsibility was attributed to him, and the more he was seen as careful.

99. PEPITONE, 1958.   100. PEPITONE & SHERBERG, 1957.   101. PEPITONE, 1958.   102. PEPITONE, 1958.   103. WALSTER, 1966.   104. WALSTER, 1967.   105. SHAVER, 1970.

Summary: Person Evaluations in Ongoing Interaction

Each observer elicits certain behaviors from persons around him, and thus biases what he is able to observe. Conversely, all of us are active in creating the impression that others form of us. We have an interest in being seen in a certain way, depending upon our values as well as the situation in question. Studies in ingratiation tactics have shown the effects on the impression formed of status, praise, doing favors, agreeing with another person, and departures from normative expectations.

Inferences about persons in interaction are often classified in terms of locus of cause—whether the cause of a person's action is seen to lie within him or in external circumstances. Two major determinants of causal locus are the extent to which the individual is seen to engage in the act of his own volition—Did he try?—and the degree to which external circumstances compel him to act. Closely tied to locus of cause is the attribution of responsibility and justifiability of the act. A series of investigations have documented the various conditions of interaction that affect such perceptions. Among the more general findings are the idea that an individual must have an opportunity to perform or not perform an act if it is to be used to form judgments about him. Research has turned up a variety of conditions that affect the degree to which responsibility and justifiability are attributed to the other person for his acts.

3

Processes of Social Influence

Processes by which people are influenced to change their behavior or beliefs are at the core of social psychology. Most topics in social psychology depend upon our understanding of these processes. Somewhat paradoxically, our grasp of influence processes also depends upon our understanding of social psychology. Presenting an adequate discussion of social influence at the outset, before other social psychological topics have been introduced, therefore poses something of a problem. Yet, this topic is so central to almost any area in social psychology that introducing it at an early stage is logical.

The complex linkage between social influence and the rest of social psychology is suggested by the way in which we define *influence*. Social influence may be said to have occurred when *the actions of one person are conditions for the actions of another*. Defined in this way, direct attempts to persuade constitute only a part of the social influence process.

We usually think of persuasion as emphasizing in some manner the *advantages* of complying with the persuasive attempt. But social influence may also involve ingratiation (see Chapter 2), threats, punishment, bribes, studied indifference, and many other tactics. Further, social influence need not be intentional. Often, actions performed by an individual with no intent to influence nevertheless bring about appreciable change in the beliefs or behavior of other persons. The most notable of these is the process of *imitation* or *modeling* (see Chapter 15). Individuals choose other persons as models and copy their behavior, sometimes without either party being especially aware that imitation is taking place. Most commonly, this takes place in children's imitations of their parents' behavior or that of characters in movies or television scenes. An adequate treatment of social influence therefore requires a thorough consideration of many facets of interaction between two or more persons.

The topic is further complicated by the fact that the success of an influence attempt depends heavily on many conditions that extend beyond the interaction process itself. For example, certain characteristics and temporary states of each party to the interaction affect the degree of influence. An angry parent is more apt to influence his child than a placid one. The past history of their relation also bears on the influence process. Repeated displays of anger may build up resistance to compliance. Moreover, the place of the parties in the social network together with the implied formal relation between them is important. A parent has far more influence on his own child than the child's teacher does. In sum, a full understanding of social influence requires a thorough acquaintance with the nature of interaction between people, with related personality characteristics and states of individuals, with the situational and relational structure in which the event takes place, and with the larger social context or setting surrounding the actors.

The *paradigm* case of social influence is represented by an episode occurring between two persons which results in a change in the attitudes or behavior of one or both parties. While we can also discuss other types of influence situations, such as the effect of a television program upon a solitary listener, or the effect of a small group of persons upon one of their members, our understanding of these other cases depends upon a thorough analysis of the paradigm case where one person influences another. As we will see later, the effects of television and other mass media are heavily contingent upon the relation between the target person and other persons, even though these other persons may not be immediately present at the time of exposure to a communication.

Through life experiences, everyone acquires considerable practical knowledge of processes of social influence. Parents learn how to make their children behave according to standards which they establish. People in many occupations, such as sales work, the law, the ministry, and teaching, learn various techniques for persuading other persons to adopt certain beliefs or to act in certain ways. Each of us, in fact, has some skill in such matters as getting a friend or acquaintance to accompany us in some recreational pursuit, or obtaining some help in solving a problem requiring the assistance of another person.

We also have some acquaintance with the considerable variety of social contexts within which influence episodes occur. The influence process is quite different in different social contexts. For example, in parental control of children, the discrepancy between the *social power* of the parent and that of the child is important. Both the power to reward and the power to punish may be operating here. In work situations, influence depends upon persuasion and argument, as well as upon social power. Military personnel follow orders out of a healthy respect for the sheer power of their superiors.

Although practical knowledge is essential for getting along in the world, one cannot systematically describe this knowledge to other persons. Much of it is intuitive. An individual *knows how* to influence another person, but he cannot necessarily describe how he does it. For example, parents are generally unaware of much of their influence on their children. This becomes especially clear when the child persists in objectionable behavior and the parents feel powerless to control it. Often they are maintaining or supporting the child's objectionable actions without realizing it.

Perhaps we can gain some insight into social influence if we consider an everyday example at some length. Later the theories and empirical research conducted by behavioral scientists will be examined to gain a more systematic understanding of social influence.

Consider a parent who wishes his ten-year-old son to perform a household chore. There are a variety of possibilities that entail quite different factors. If the household chore is one that the child regularly performs, then there is apt to be an explicit agreement between parent and child about the task. Cutting the lawn, for example, may have been mutually defined by both parties as a part of the regular duties of the boy. This might be based on the idea that each member of the family has certain obligations which stem from their membership in the family group, and that cutting the lawn is the boy's obligation. In American families, there is apt to be a somewhat different basis for this task assignment: The chore is performed in exchange for some reward or privilege. For example, the agreement that the boy would regularly cut the lawn might be part of a bargain involving a raise in his weekly allowance. At a later age, when the boy is old enough to drive, he might be given the privilege of using the car for recreational purposes if he also agrees to run errands with it and to act as a chauffeur for younger members of the family. This notion of *exchange* is usually involved in situations where there is a regular performance of obligations, and it will be discussed more fully in other parts of the book (see particularly Chapters 7 to 11).

In the present discussion we are interested in single episodes where one person influences another and where the episode is not part of a regular "bargain" or "contract" between the parties. Another type of parent-child influence situation has this character. For example, a parent may wish his child to eat a vegetable that the child dislikes and frequently does not eat. The parent may use his control over *resources* to influence the child: no vegetable, no dessert. He may also use persuasive arguments, even though they are generally ineffective in a case of this kind. He may tell the child that the vegetable is necessary for his health. He may point to models: The parents themselves eat it and enjoy it, older siblings eat it, or Popeye eats his spinach. He may also threaten punishment for not eating the vegetable.

Another less obvious but effective technique is to require him to eat only one spoonful on that particular occasion, gradually raising the amount eaten on later occasions. We will see later in this chapter that certain important principles are involved here, that of *commitment* (agreeing to eat the spoonful), and *consistency* (having eaten it on one occasion, it is consistent to eat it again).

Although this can be regarded as a single influence episode, it is important to recognize that the kind of enduring relation that prevails between parent and child is an important background condition affecting the parent's success in any particular episode. If the parent's general handling of the child has been especially repressive and has created some rebellious feelings in him, the child may use the meal situation to express his rebellion by refusing to eat the vegetable, no matter what kinds of persuasive or coercive acts the parent performs. On the other hand, if a cooperative, warm relation exists between parent and child, persuasion may be easily effective.

The introductory discussion has emphasized the complexity of the influence process and the large number of conditions, states, or contexts that modify what happens. To deal with these complexities, the social psychologist develops systematic theory which explains with some precision how influence takes place. The present chapter will focus on two-person interaction as a form of influence, without forgetting that the presence of the experimenter and the institutional context in which studies are conducted have their effects on the nature of the interaction. Chapters 4 and 5 will extend this basic analysis to social influence as it occurs in society, under the heading of mass communication.

It will be impossible, however, to deal thoroughly here with every facet of the influence process, because that would require presenting virtually all of social psychology in this chapter. Thus, many other chapters will elaborate on some facet of the influence process. Chapter 7, for example, deals with what factors influence one individual to like another. Chapter 8 deals with the social power relations between persons that make influence possible. The bearing of an individual's status on his ability to influence people is brought out in Chapter 9. How a group keeps its members in line is discussed in Chapter 10. Chapter 11 shows how leaders emerge and how they move their groups toward their goals. Parts of Chapters 11, 12, 13, and 14 deal with the structure of the relationship between the parties and the type of "social contract" that has been negotiated. The process of modeling or imitation is treated in Chapter 15. Finally, in Chapter 17, the role of self and personality in the influence process is brought out.

The goal of the social psychologist is *systematic* description of the influence process. At the core of this description is a *theory* of influence. This theory consists of the concepts used to describe the process and an explication of the way in which the process works. The theory may contain one or more *models* of the influence process.

The advantages of a systematic approach lie in the possibility of testing and refining the ideas, and in the deeper understanding achieved. Through such systematic formulations, we come to see relations among various kinds of social influence that were not previously apparent. We discover that some kinds of behaviors which, on the surface, did not look at all like influence processes are indeed just that. We become able to identify and describe many more subtle types of influence than would be the case if we had only practical knowledge.

Unfortunately, no comprehensive theory of social influence is currently available, although theories dealing with a part of the process have been developed (e.g., *dissonance theory*). Hence the discussion will reflect the partial information available, plus some modest theoretical contributions by the authors.

Elements of the Influence Process

Besides the communication itself, which will be treated in Chapter 4, there are four major categories that need attention in any discussion of the influence process:

1. The *target act.* This is the act which is to be performed by the recipient of the influence attempt (e.g., a confession, a purchase, a favor, an opinion change).

2. The *target person.* The target person is the recipient of the influence attempt.

3. The relation between the target person and other persons.

4. The social context surrounding the target act.

An overview of these four elements may be seen in Figure 3-1. We may think of the target act as nested within the other elements of the communication process, each larger circle embracing a more extended area of the social context within which the target act is embedded. These elements of the communication process are not independent, and will be discussed in relation to each other to gain a better understanding of what happens when a person is influenced.

The Target Act

The target act may be not only an overt act, such as a purchase made as a result of a sales pitch or a confession following interrogation, but also a change in attitude. In customary usage, an attitude has two components: an *evaluative* component and a *belief* component. Sometimes a *behavioral* component is included—say, a *behavioral intention,* stating what the individual intends to do.[1] But behavior can also be treated separately from the attitude, a practice we will follow here.

Evaluative component refers to the positive or negative character of an individual's orientation toward an aspect of his world. This evaluation may be

---

1. Ajzen & Fishbein, 1970.

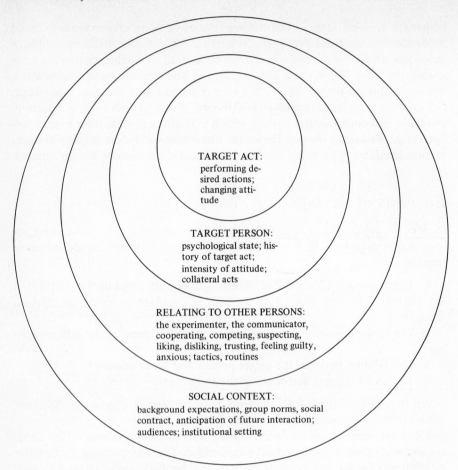

Figure 3-1   The target act and its setting.

affect

identified through observing an individual express his feelings, state his beliefs, convey his intentions, or perform certain actions. It is generally thought of as having a given degree of intensity: weak or strong.

The belief component is the content of the attitude, typically expressed in verbal statements. Thus, one individual might say, "War is not essential to the defense of our country." Another person might say, "War brings out the worst qualities in men." Both statements are fairly strong negative evaluations of war. But their content is radically different.

In most studies, investigators assess the evaluation component of an attitude by having a participant endorse or rate several belief statements concerning the attitude object. While there are formal, carefully worked-out scales (questionnaires) for measuring attitudes, these are seldom used in experimental investigation. Thus, we will not discuss here the extensive technology that has been developed for assessing attitudes. Such discussions are available elsewhere.[2]

Relation between Target Person and Target Act

What the target act means to the person and how it relates to his personality and his psychological state at the time of influence has much to do with the success of the influence attempt. For example, the target act might well fit a strong need of the target person. He may, for example, have decided to buy a new car; salesmen then exert influence on him to choose a particular make and model. Needs take an endless variety of forms. A person may like to impress his neighbors and friends; this may influence him to buy an expensive house or car. Or a person will be especially susceptible to confidence games if he has a need to make a quick and huge profit.

How the target act relates to other acts of the target person is also of considerable importance. Is it a novel act, or has he performed it before? If so, perhaps the act is supported by habit (e.g., cigarette smoking). Also, he may feel a need to be consistent with his own previous actions.[3] The process of *commitment* generated by having decided to act or having actually performed the act will be treated later in connection with our discussion of *dissonance theory*.[4] Dissonance is a state of discomfort that arises if an individual has committed himself to perform an act that is contrary to his beliefs or values or that is inconsistent with his other acts. Note that in this section we have talked only of private acts of commitment, resulting from a decision or choice not yet made public.

Relation between Target Person and Other Persons

In a two-person situation, one of the most important conditions for influence is the dependence of the target person on the communicator. Essentially this can be discussed in terms of the amount of social power that the communicator has over the target person. Social power is discussed at length in Chapter 8, and so we will mention only its rudiments here.

Certain conditions give one person power over another. A communicator may be in a position to reward or to punish the target person (e.g., give him a raise in pay; provide him with special privileges; fine him; fire him). He may be able to give such resources as love, warmth, amusement, companionship. Or a person may have expert knowledge that the target person does not possess but needs. A different source of power that may even lead to unintentional influence exists when the communicator is viewed as a model to emulate. When the

---

2. McNemar, 1946; Edwards, 1957; Fishbein, 1967; Scott, 1968.   3. Abelson, Aronson, McGuire, Newcomb, Rosenberg, & Tannenbaum, 1968.   4. Festinger, 1957.

target person admires another, he may be influenced to adopt some of the other's characteristics or actions. Another person may also have legitimate power based upon the acceptance by the target person of *norms* which require that he accede to influence attempts by another person because of that person's status. Thus, a soldier executes the command of an officer, a child obeys his parent, a driver stops at the signal of a policeman, or a person lends money to a friend.

The amount of power possessed by the communicator is not a direct function of his resources, but also depends on the extent to which the target person is dependent on the communicator or needs his resources. This dependency is essentially a function of the target person's *comparison level.* His comparison level is what he would ordinarily expect to get from this relation. It is influenced by his past experiences in this type of relation and his judgment of what others like himself are receiving. The power of the communicator is a function of his resources relative to the target person's comparison level. The greater the resources relative to the level, the greater his power.

Finally, the dependency of the target person on the communicator and thus the power of the communicator depends on the alternatives open to the target person. If alternative sources are more rewarding or less costly, for example, the communicator has less power. Expert knowledge is itself based upon scarcity of alternatives: Only the expert possesses the information. In an affectionate relationship, the partner may be the only current source of certain psychological resources, such as love. In general, then, the fewer or weaker the alternatives, the more power the communicator has over the target person.

Besides the relative power of the parties to an influence attempt, a variety of other aspects of the relation may be important. The situation may be one where a cooperative relation prevails. There might be trust or distrust (the credibility of the communicator will be discussed in the next chapter). Various *tactics* and *routines* used in influence deserve analysis. Tactics are strategies deliberately adopted to influence another person. Routines are ways of behaving that influence another person without the parties being especially aware of the influence process. For example, in repeatedly punishing a child, a parent may intend to eliminate some undesirable act, teasing a younger sister or brother, for example; but he may, at the same time, unintentionally be causing the child to become resistant to his influence attempts and may even be influencing the child to continue the undesirable behavior. Ingratiation has already been discussed in Chapter 2. Other tactics and routines will be discussed mainly in other parts of the book (see especially Chapters 8, 10, and 17).

The communicator is not the only person affecting the success of the influence attempt. If one or more other persons are present during the attempt, they can have a profound influence on acceptance or rejection. Moreover, many studies by social psychologists of two-person groups where one attempts to influence the other involve a third person whose part may have a significant impact: the experimenter himself. As we will see, some findings can only be understood when the experimenter's role is accounted for.

Social Context Surrounding Target Act

Making public a decision to perform a target act strengthens the commitment of the target person.[5] In its strongest form, commitment may take the form of an *obligation* to another person or group, as well as to oneself.

The target act may have social or moral sanctions. Is it a *legitimate* or an illegitimate act? (See Legitimate Power in Chapter 8.) Whether or not the target person performs the act depends in part on how it is related to these sanctions. Social or moral sanctions also enter into preventive influence attempts. Thus, attempts may be made to stop a person from smoking cigarettes or taking drugs. In preventive influence attempts, the personal or social consequences of performing the act may be important, as may habit, mentioned previously.

Also pertinent here are *expectations* about what types of influence attempts are appropriate to the situation. Under ordinary circumstances other persons have certain expectations about how we should behave in given situations, and we hold these same expectations for our own behavior. One relevant set of expectations is those that pertain to what types of requests from other persons we consider acceptable. If an influence attempt is to be successful, it must be in accord with these expectations; otherwise it is regarded as illegitimate.* For example, if a teacher asks a student to do a routine assignment the request is within the bounds of legitimacy and would not be rejected on that ground. But if a teacher asks a student to cut his hair short, the student may feel strongly that the request is illegitimate.

Violation of *background expectations,* on the other hand, sometimes produces compliance with a bizarre situation.[6] Background expectations are taken for granted by everyone, and are so well accepted that their violation often produces incredulity and bewilderment. The individual is at a complete loss about how to handle the situation, and may succumb to the influence attempt because there is no clear guide to how he should behave. It is violation of these expectations that accounts for the success of the television program *Candid Camera,* which has repeatedly shown individuals complying to a remarkable degree. For example, in a restaurant counter, a television actor was shown repeatedly asking permission to sample the food of the stranger next to him, receiving it, and then eating considerable quantities of the food. The successful requests appear to be totally outside normal expectations. In this example, the

* Expectations and their limits are discussed in Chapter 13.

5. Deutsch & Gerard, 1955.   6. Garfinkel, 1967.

actor displays incredible audacity. Having no standard behavior pattern for such requests, the bewildered victim simply complies.

We have already mentioned the *social contract,* to be dealt with in more detail in Chapters 10, 13, and 14. The target person and the communicator may have an unwritten pact which takes the form of a rule or norm on which both parties have agreed. A salesman who handles letterheads and envelopes, for example, may have accounts with companies who agree to give him all their business in his line. In informal social situations, more tacit, less specified agreements may also prevail. Close friends, if they live in reasonable proximity, expect to see each other a certain proportion of the time. If one becomes unavailable, the other may be disturbed by this violation of a tacit, unspoken agreement.

Aside from the research on mass communication to be discussed in Chapters 4 and 5, experimental research directly concerned with the social influence process has been surprisingly parochial. In terms of our discussion of elements of the influence process, most of this effort has been focused on the relation between the target act and the target person, with little attention given to other important aspects of social influence. More time has been spent on attitude change than on changes in behavior. What research there is that bears on these other aspects has often been done in other contexts, such as the study of the process by which children and adults are socialized into groups, and the normative processes by which groups control their members. These topics will be discussed in other chapters. Some attention will be given in the chapters on mass communication to the effects on attitude change brought about by persons other than the communicator. Much of Chapter 8, dealing with social power, relates to elements of social influence not dealt with in this chapter.

The remainder of the present chapter will therefore be confined primarily to discussing the large body of research directly concerned with social influence, but which has been focused largely on the effects of the relation between the target person and the target act. This means essentially that social psychologists have been content to look at influence largely in terms of the individual person and his actions and beliefs, giving relatively less attention to the role of other persons and the social context.

This emphasis on only the individual component of the communication process is well illustrated by the following section, which deals with the intensive research effort that has been put into how acts of an individual contrary to his attitude bring about a change in attitude. In this paradigm, the change in attitude is the target act. The contrary action is a factor leading to the change, and is often a form of commitment. The concepts traditionally used here to explain attitude change mainly refer to processes occurring within the individual: concepts representing private, nonsocial events. In terms of Figure 3-1, they deal primarily with the target act and the target person. As we will see, however, the most recent theory and research do go beyond these two elements and use concepts involving relations to other persons and the social context.

Behaving Contrary to Attitude

One of the common experiences of everyday life is to have to do things that one dislikes doing. These include some acts that are fatiguing, require a lot of effort, or run contrary to our feelings. Every employee has to do his work in a manner prescribed by his superiors, a manner sometimes different from what he would choose if left to his own devices. Often in the course of his work he is required to carry out a variety of tasks which are disagreeable to him because they run counter to his attitudes. Students sometimes find assignments disagreeable and studying for examinations painful. In the family, each individual member cannot do as he pleases and must show some regard for the wishes of the other members: This produces much behavior that is discrepant from attitudes. The housewife and mother, for example, often resents some aspects of her role, particularly if she has a strong inclination to follow some occupational career.

These acts are of special interest to social psychologists because sometimes, as a consequence of behaving contrary to his attitude, an individual changes his attitude to conform to the new behavior. For example, a student may become interested in some of the subjects that he has studied. Or a politician urged by his constituents to foster legislation against air pollution may eventually come to believe in a cause that he was at first neutral toward. Psychologists have attempted to develop theories which explain such attitude changes and to discover the conditions under which they take place. These efforts have led to considerable controversy which is as yet unresolved. Yet, through continued experimentation and attempts at explanation, some insights into the effects of behaving contrary to attitudes have been gained.

It has already been stressed that two factors are important in any influence process: the social context of the act which is the target of influence and the relation between the communicator and the target person. Indeed, as shown below, much of the confusion in the experimental literature has occurred as a result of ignoring these two factors. Laboratory experiments are too often interpreted within a narrow framework in which the participant is considered in isolation from the experimenter, and in which the target act is focused on, whereas other acts or individual characteristics of the participant are neglected. The discussion will begin with a narrow focus of this sort, and the view will be gradually expanded until the contrary act is seen in a full social and relational context.

Induced-Compliance Paradigm

Experimentation on acts contrary to attitudes has centered around what we will call the *induced-compliance paradigm.* This is an experimental setting where a participant is induced to behave in a manner contrary to his attitude. (The term which has come into common usage is *forced compliance.* This term, however, is unfortunate, as the participant is not really *forced* but complies because of his desire to cooperate with the experimenter—or, alternatively, because he does not want to appear a fool.) In this paradigm, the conditions under which the participant performs are varied in order to identify those which lead to a change in attitude as a result of the contrary behavior. This line of research developed out of two separate lines of thought: dissonance theory and playing the role of an advocate. Before introducing an example of this type of experiment, we will discuss dissonance theory, introduced in 1957 by Festinger.

DISSONANCE THEORY   The term *dissonance* refers to an inconsistency between two or more elements. Two elements are in a dissonant relation if, considering these two alone, the *opposite of one element would follow from the other.* For example, the following two elements are dissonant:

"I do not need a car."
"I have just bought a car."

Central to dissonance theory is the concept of *cognitive element.* A cognitive element is a single unit of knowledge, a single belief, or an evaluation held by a person about some object in his environment, about his behavior, or about himself. The following are examples of cognitive elements:

I smoke one pack of cigarettes every day.
Smoking causes lung cancer.
I am engaged to marry Jane.
Students should have a voice in governing colleges and universities.
Black Americans deserve the same rights and privileges as any other American.
I like John.

In practical or experimental situations, more than two elements are almost always involved. The dissonance experienced is a joint function of two sets of elements. In the context of the present topic, one set is associated with the contrary behavior, and the other with the attitude.

The amount of dissonance created by behaving contrary to one's attitude may be expressed in the following formula:

$$\text{Dissonance} = \frac{\text{cognitive elements dissonant with engaging in the act}}{\text{cognitive elements consonant with engaging in the act}}$$

In the original formulation, elements were weighted by importance. Almost no work has been done along these lines, however, and so the ratio cannot be used to obtain a precise quantitative measure of dissonance. But it is a useful heuristic device for determining the *relative* strength of dissonance in two or more situations. As we will see shortly, in a typical experiment, the elements representing the experimental treatments are typically identical, except that one situation contains either one additional element or one element which is more important than the other.

Dissonance theory presumes that a state of dissonance is uncomfortable and gives rise to pressures to reduce dissonance. Reduction of dissonance may occur through a change in one's attitude or behavior or by addition of a new cognitive element. In these cases, the cognitive elements associated with these changes are thought to change accordingly. Thus, a smoker worried about lung cancer may stop smoking, change to filter cigarettes, get a physical examination, start a health routine, or decide that the evidence against smoking is insufficient. To represent reduction of dissonance in the ratio just presented, we could either add cognitive elements to the denominator (which would produce a smaller fraction), or remove elements from the numerator. Another possibility is that one element may be substituted for another element of different importance.

This conceptualization allows us to set up various conditions and to predict which set will bring about the most attitude change. For example, our formula shows the nonobvious fact that, the greater the pressure to engage in the contrary act, the *less* the dissonance aroused. In the formula, pressure to engage in the behavior is an element consonant with the behavior, and so it would enter the denominator. Thus the more the pressure, the less the dissonance. Suppose, for example, an individual having a strong preference for Democratic candidates were paid $100 to go out and persuade other persons to vote for Republican candidates, and that this amount were just barely sufficient to persuade him. This would represent the maximum dissonance, much more than if he were paid $5,000. In terms of ratios, the magnitude of dissonance would look like this:

GREATER DISSONANCE

$$\frac{\text{Elements of Democratic attitude}}{\text{Being paid \$100 for urging people to vote Republican}} < 1$$

LESSER DISSONANCE

$$\frac{\text{Elements of Democratic attitude}}{\text{Being paid \$5,000 for urging people to vote Republican}} \ll 1$$

The maximum dissonance possible is reached when the ratio approaches 1.00. (As an exercise, the student may figure out why dissonance cannot be greater than 1.00.)

If the only way of reducing dissonance in this example were for the Democrat to modify in a Republican direction some elements of his political attitude, we would predict that the Democrat paid $100 would experience greater change than the Democrat paid $5,000. This occurs simply because he would be more strongly motivated to reduce dissonance.

This line of thinking produces the paradoxical generalization that, the more we reward an individual for engaging in an act contrary to his attitude, the less likely he is to change that attitude. But if the amount of reward is just barely sufficient to get him to engage in the discrepant act, we should obtain maximum change. In other words, dissonance theory predicts that there will be an inverse or opposite relation between the amount of reward and the amount of attitude change. This is illustrated in a well-known experiment, which has become a classic example of the *induced compliance paradigm.*[7]

After completing a dull "experimental" task, participants were informed that a student helper usually brought in the next experimental subject and told him how enjoyable the experiment was. It was implied that this helper had failed to show up, and each student, as he completed the task, was asked to serve in this capacity. Two magnitudes of reward were used for different groups of students: $1 and $20.

Here, then, is an experimental situation where the subject forms a strong private opinion that the task he has just engaged in is dull, but where for a price (and presumably other considerations, such as his desire to cooperate with the experimenter), he agrees to tell a new subject that it is an enjoyable task. After they had served as helpers, participants were interviewed and asked to rate their opinions concerning the experiment on an 11-point scale from maximum negative opinion to maximum positive opinion. As predicted, those who had received a reward of only $1 rated the experiment higher in terms of its enjoyability than those who had received $20.

The formula for this experiment would take the following form:

$$\text{GREATER DISSONANCE} \quad \frac{\text{Feeling that the task is dull}}{\text{Pressure by E plus \$1}} \qquad \text{LESSER DISSONANCE} \quad \frac{\text{Feeling that the task is dull}}{\text{Pressure by E plus \$20}}$$

In other words, if monetary reward is used as the pressure to win such compliance from a person, the prediction is that the more money he receives for complying, the less his attitude will change. The key to understanding this is the point that dissonance is at its maximum when the opposing cognitive elements are equal in strength and importance. Since the amount of attitude change is a function of the amount of dissonance, the greatest attitude change will occur at the point where these opposing elements are equal. If opposing elements are made unequal by appreciably strengthening the set of elements in the denominator, dissonance will be somewhat less, and attitude change will be smaller.

The most common explanation for this dissonance effect is in terms of *justification.* After making his decision and engaging in the contrary behavior, the individual experiences uncomfortable dissonance. But he can reduce this discomfort by *justifying* his behavior. If he adopts some elements of Republican views, then urging other persons to vote Republican is not as disturbing as it might be, especially when he has been paid $100 for this effort. If he is paid $5,000, his behavior is even easier to justify, if he needs money and does not feel strongly about politics; and so in that instance, it is unnecessary for him to

7. FESTINGER & CARLSMITH, 1958.

adopt Republican views to justify his behavior: The $5,000 is sufficient justification.

ADVOCATING A CONTRARY POSITION   For the moment, we will leave the dissonance paradigm and take up another line of research, *advocating a contrary position.* In some studies using dissonance theory, individuals were asked to advocate a position contrary to their own attitude. Thus, in the famous $1 and $20 experiment just discussed, participants did tell a person assumed to be the next participant that the experiment was interesting and enjoyable (when in fact they knew it was dull and boring). In some other studies, the participant wrote a brief essay in favor of a position that the experimenter knew was objectionable to the writer.

Janis, Elms, and others have argued that it is not the arousal of dissonance but *advocating* a position contrary to one's own attitude that accounts for a change in attitude.[8] They reason that when an individual actively supports a position he does not agree with, he does two things: (1) he scans his memory and experience for information that supports the advocated position, and (2) he constructs or invents arguments and reasons supporting that position. In a sense, he convinces himself that the position has at least some validity, and changes his attitude toward it. Moreover, if this interpretation is correct, the amount of reward should be directly proportionate to the amount of change, unlike dissonance theory predictions. This should occur because the participant receiving greater rewards should produce more and better arguments and reasons, and thus, change his attitude more in their direction.

An early experiment on advocacy of a contrary position used participants in turn both as speakers and as audience, each time on a different topic.[9] While acting as speakers, they were provided an outline and asked to improvise a talk on a position with which they disagreed. As a member of the audience they simply listened. The degree to which an individual changed his attitude as a speaker was compared with his change as a member of the audience: He changed his attitude more when he was a speaker. This result occurred for two of the three topics. It is consistent with the reasoning just presented: Improvising a talk should produce more arguments and reasons favoring the new position and should also be more satisfying.

To determine conclusively whether improvisation and satisfaction were important to attitude change, a second experiment was conducted. Participants were assigned to one of three treatments: One group made an impromptu presentation after reading a magazine article, another simply read the script aloud, and a third merely read the script silently. The individuals who had to improvise a presentation showed more attitude change than those who read aloud or who read silently. Among those who improvised, satisfaction appeared to make little difference in the amount of attitude change.

8. JANIS & GILMORE, 1965; ELMS, 1967.   9. JANIS & KING, 1954.

That the change in attitude is due to the development of new arguments is suggested indirectly by another study.[10] When participants were given an opportunity to consider and reject arguments *before* advocating the position supported by the arguments, little attitude change occurred after the contrary position was advocated. This suggests that it is the new arguments that arise through actively advocating the new position which bring about the change in attitude. In this study, this could not happen as readily, because the participant was given the arguments in advance and rejected them.

Two additional investigations using advocacy explored further the reasons for attitude change. These were intended to bear on the issue of whether attitude change would occur in inverse proportion to the amount of reward (as predicted by dissonance theory), or whether change would be in proportion to the amount of reward (predicted by advocacy theory).

In both studies, college students were asked to write a few paragraphs in favor of the proposition that a year of mathematics and a year of physics be required of all college students (an assignment presumed to be contrary to their attitudes). This was done in return for either a high or a low monetary reward. They were told that their activity had a sponsor; the sponsor was chosen so as to create positive attitudes for some (a national research organization), negative attitudes for others (an exploitative commercial sponsor).

In the first study, positive sponsorship yielded significantly more attitude change, but there was no variation in attitude with the amount of incentive, with either positive or negative sponsorship.[11]

In the second study, the positive sponsorship condition (which was more positive than in the first study) yielded more attitude change in *direct proportion* to the amount of incentive.[12] No systematic change with incentive occurred for the negative sponsor.

So far, then, the results of advocacy studies are only partially supportive of advocacy theory and only partially contradict dissonance theory. Proponents of advocacy theory have attempted to explain the inconsistency of their results by the idea of *interfering factors*. For example, Elms has suggested that the usual operation of scanning one's memory and experience and inventing new arguments is disrupted if the reward is so large as to arouse suspicion.[13] While this might help to explain the obtained results, it also makes clear that advocacy theory by itself cannot handle all the findings. Essentially this occurs because, like dissonance theory, advocacy theory focuses almost exclusively on nonsocial processes that occur within the individual participant, ignoring his relation to the experimenter (with large rewards, the participant is apt to be suspicious of the experimenter and his motives).

CONFRONTATION AND PRIVACY   Carlsmith, Collins, and Helmreich conducted an experiment in which they attempted to reconcile these various conflicting

10. GREENWALD, 1970.   *11.* JANIS & GILMORE, 1965.   *12.* ELMS & JANIS, 1965.   *13.* ELMS, 1967.

results.[14] They focused particularly on the point that in previous studies, participants advocating contrary positions had always had an audience (the experimenter or sometimes a hypothetical audience) who *knew* that they were not expressing their *own* attitude. They set up a situation similar to the $1 and $20 experiment where the participant was asked to tell a female (who was a confederate of the experimenter) that a dull experiment was interesting and exciting. The maximum reward used, however, was only $5. Other participants were asked to write an essay for the experimenter, who *knew* that the opinions expressed were not their *own*. The essay was to consist of a positive description of the experiment.

Under these conditions, the dissonance-predicted inverse relation was obtained between incentive and attitude for the face-to-face situation, while a positive relation was obtained for the essay situation.

The face-to-face situation and the essay situation used here differ in more ways than one. The face-to-face situation is public, with an audience whose opinion might be of some concern to the participant. The essay situation is private, and may be regarded as a mere intellectual exercise. Collins therefore conducted a series of experiments to determine whether the public-private dimension was the critical factor.[15]

He found that, on the whole, this dimension was unimportant. What seems to be the critical difference here is the *personal commitment* in the two conditions. The face-to-face role player is making a strong commitment in espousing a position that he does not believe in, without any opportunity to explain to his audience, a coed. The essay writer is not espousing views that appear to be his own, but helping the experimenter in a writing exercise. Thus, these findings again emphasize a social factor: commitment to an audience. This is a form of *social* commitment, extending beyond commitment occurring in a private, anonymous condition.

Limitations of Dissonance Theory and Some New Leads

At present writing it seems that some investigations have obtained results supporting each of the various interpretations of attitude change, and that the reasons for inconsistencies among these studies are still not entirely known. Collins and his colleagues have conducted over twenty experiments attempting to find a dependable induced-compliance paradigm.[16] Not only have the original $1 and $20 experiment and its variants proven difficult to replicate, but not even the essay design has yielded consistent results.

If we look back over the research on induced compliance (only a fraction of which has been presented here), certain patterns emerge. First, it is obvious that dissonance theory specifies too little. It does not even make clear when two elements are dissonant.

14. CARLSMITH, COLLINS, & HELMREICH, 1966.   15. COLLINS, 1969.   16. COLLINS, ASHMORE, HORNBECK, & WHITNEY, 1970.

The elements of dissonance theory are somewhat more ambiguous than certain other consistency theories (e.g., Heider).[17] For example, in several theories, the object itself is an element (e.g., John, lung cancer, etc.), and the evaluation of the object is another separate element (e.g., *liking* John, the *negative implications* of lung cancer). But in dissonance theory, a single element sometimes contains both an object *and* an evaluation of the object (e.g., I like John), and sometimes is simply a statement of fact or a statement about one's behavior. This imprecision of dissonance theory is perhaps one reason why it does not always make clear when two elements are dissonant with one another.

Some further discussion of what it means for the opposite of one element to *follow from* another is desirable. This has never been made entirely clear, although certain additional points can be made. In the first place, *follow from* is meant in a psychological sense, not a logical one. In logic, *not A* would certainly be the opposite of *A*. But it is clear that this logical sense would not fit all cases of dissonance. Consider as an example the following pair of items:

"I smoke one pack of cigarettes per day."
"I believe that smoking causes lung cancer."

Clearly, the second item is not the *negation* of the first item. (Negation would be: "I do not smoke cigarettes.") Yet, intuitively or naïvely these two cognitive elements are clearly jarring or inconsistent.

In the authors' opinion, one ambiguity concerning the implication that one cognitive element has for another is caused by the fact that elements typically used in dissonance theory studies contain to a mixed degree evaluated objects and relations that are not made as explicit as they might be. If we consider the pair of elements just cited, we see that the second element, "I believe that smoking causes lung cancer," implies a negative evaluation of smoking. This occurs because lung cancer is associated with pain and death and is represented as an effect caused by smoking. The first element, "I smoke one pack of cigarettes per day," implies a positive evaluation of smoking. Thus, when these two elements are put into juxtaposition, the opposing positive and negative evaluations arouse dissonance.

But there is another route to dissonance, starting with these same items. The second item clearly implies: "I should not smoke." And the first clearly implies: "I will continue to smoke." Now we have dissonance between two behavioral intentions rather than two evaluations. Which is the correct interpretation? The answer, of course, is neither. Dissonance theory simply does not specify precisely how dissonance arises.

Abelson has suggested that we discover empirically when two items follow from one another.[18] His procedure follows from the fact that we are dealing with *psychological,* not *logical,* implications. His suggestion is that we simply present an item to a person, and ask him what it follows from. An illustration

17. Heider, 1958.   *18.* Abelson, 1968.

is: "Joe dislikes Bill. How come?" Some reasonable answers are: "Bill offended Joe," "Bill dislikes Joe," and "Bill is obnoxious." Each of these possible answers contains the *implication* that Joe dislikes Bill. That is, from the fact that Bill is obnoxious it follows that Joe dislikes him, etc.

As Abelson himself recognizes, this does not solve all the problems. A major difficulty in resorting to an empirical procedure for determining implication, or what follows from what, is that it does not provide a system for knowing in advance what elements will produce dissonance. Considered more broadly, then, we can say that dissonance theory does not provide a set of propositions that enable the experimenter to determine which situations will produce dissonance and which will not. Moreover, it is silent about the individual who experiences the dissonance, and the effects that his various psychological states might have on dissonance arousal and attitude change. It has little to say about the experimental setting, illustrated in Figure 3-1. Acts collateral to the counterattitudinal act and to the target act may well be important, as are the relation to the experimenter and an audience. Serving in an experiment and anticipation of future interaction need to be included in any theory that is to be adequate for conducting social psychological experiments.

Some efforts are being made to meet these objections to dissonance theory. Recent studies have emphasized several ideas in extending dissonance theory. One stresses the importance of involvement of self in the contrary action. This has been emphasized by Bramel:

> The theoretical relevance of the self in this view of dissonance theory now becomes clearer. I am arguing that dissonance is a feeling of personal unworthiness (a type of anxiety) traceable to rejection of oneself by other people either in the present or in the past. Any information which implies that one is incompetent or immoral arouses dissonance. The reason dissonance is greatest when the person feels personally responsible for his behavior is that rejection by other people is usually greatest when they believe the person voluntarily acted in an inappropriate way. Further, a person's expectations about his own behavior should be aroused most clearly when he perceives his behavior as emanating primarily from himself rather than from environmental pressure. Most dissonance experiments have induced the subjects to behave in ways that lead both to disconfirmation of expectations about oneself and to the arousal of implications that one's behavior has been incompetent or immoral.[19]

Rosenberg has also argued that active involvement is important.[20] The participant who is paid $20 does not have to involve himself; the $20 justifies acting contrary to his attitudes. But the person paid only $1 has to justify it; the act has to be his responsibility. In Rosenberg's experiment, one group worked

19. Reprinted with permission from BRAMEL, D. Dissonance, expectation, and the self. In R. P. ABELSON, et al. (Eds.), *Theories of cognitive consistency: A sourcebook.* Chicago: Rand McNally & Company, 1968. P. 365. *20.* ROSENBERG, 1970.

for six minutes actively promoting and elaborating a position counter to their attitude. For this group, the greater the reward, the more the attitude change. Another group role-played for only 1½ minutes, without active advocacy, and their attitude changed inversely in proportion to the reward. Thus, he sees the dissonance interpretation as applicable only in rather superficial situations where individuals are not actively involved.

Another emphasis on the individual comes from attribution theory.[21] Instead of attributing the effects to cognitive dissonance, an internal state, the argument is that the individual observes how he has behaved. He analyzes the stimulus conditions that were associated with his behavior, and deduces what his attitude must have been. This would, of course, explain an inverse incentive effect. If a participant were paid $20 for advocating an attitude contrary to his own, he could attribute his behavior to the high payment. But if he were paid only $1, then his behavior would imply that he really held the attitude that he advocated.

Although the experimental evidence is sketchy at the present time, it does seem reasonable to assume that the different conditions of the many experiments on attitude change create different degrees of engagement of self on the part of the participant. The evidence suggests that this is one of the conditions accounting for conflicting results.

The consequences of one's act have also been shown to be important, and it is likely that this is related to engagement of self. In one study, participants learned either that they had succeeded in convincing their supposedly naïve colleague that a dull task was interesting and enjoyable, or that they had failed. Only those who thought they succeeded changed their attitude in inverse proportion to the amount of incentive.[22] Several other experiments also support the view that the consequences of one's acts for the audience are a critical condition for bringing about attitude change.[23]

Aronson has also suggested that the crucial determinant in induced compliance studies is whether or not the counterattitudinal behavior threatens to diminish the individual's self concept, by virtue of its consequences for the audience.[24] Dissonance, he argues, is between a cognition about the self and a cognition about a behavior which violated this self concept (e.g., "I am a good and decent person; I have committed an indecent act: misleading another person").

In an experiment using incentives of 50 cents and $5, different groups of participants made a video recording of an argument favoring legalization of marijuana, and were told that their recording was to be addressed to one of three groups: (1) a group in favor of the legalization of marijuana, (2) a group opposed to the legalization of marijuana, and (3) a group which had no opinion.[25] A dissonance effect (inverse relation between attitude change and incen-

21. BEM, 1967; KELLEY, 1967.   *22.* COOPER & WORCHEL, 1970.   *23.* COLLINS et al., 1970.   *24.* ARONSON, 1968, 1969.   *25.* NEL, HELMREICH, & ARONSON, 1969.

tive) was obtained for the participants whose audience had no opinion. Obviously this was the group that might be most easily influenced, and the one where the moral consequences would be greatest. But we might add that an alternate interpretation is available here. This undecided audience is also the condition where the advocate would feel most uncomfortable, and thus taking a high reward for persuading them would be particularly distasteful.

These recent interpretations of dissonance effects move away from viewing participants in experiments as passive objects manipulated by the experimenter, and toward the idea that participants are agents who can make choices for which they feel responsible. With this in mind, it is possible to use these ideas of self-involvement and the consequences of one's actions for other persons to form a theory that resolves some of the contradictory findings and helps to specify the conditions for various experimental outcomes. Tedeschi, Schlenker, and Bonoma have suggested a theory of impression management that accomplishes these objectives.[26] They propose that it is not some internal state of "dissonance" that accounts for a person's change in attitude or behavior, but rather his desire to *behave consistently toward other persons.*

First, they call attention to the point made in Chapter 2 that observers cannot infer the true intentions of an actor as long as his behavior is controlled by external factors: For intention to be attributed, it has to be seen as internal to him—that he is the locus of cause. Therefore, if pairs of *acts* are considered rather than cognitive elements, the actor will feel a contradiction only if *both* of his acts are likely to be seen by other persons as internal to him. If one of them is externally caused (as when he is paid $20 for performing a simple act), he should not experience much contradiction. Such a contradiction is apt to be felt, for example, when he is paid only $1 for telling a lie to another participant about the nature of the experiment. And to resolve the contradiction, he changes his attitude toward the experiment to make his act less deceptive. But if he is paid $20, his act is seen as externally caused, and he should not experience much contradiction.

We may note further that the crucial point is not so much whether the actor experiences a contradiction but, rather, whether he believes that his audience sees the contradiction. Only in the latter instance would he change his attitude to resolve the contradiction. Therefore, if his behavior is anonymous (as in some of the essay-writing experiments), he should not change his attitude in inverse proportion to incentive. He is more likely to do so when his behavior is public and has significant consequences for the persons who are affected by his act. Moreover, this thinking stresses the participant's knowledge that he is performing under the critical eye of the experimenter. How he thinks his performance is viewed by the experimenter is critical in determining the direction that his actions take. While this theory is too new to be evaluated with certainty, it does take into account more fully the social nature and setting of the

26. TEDESCHI, SCHLENKER, & BONOMA, 1971.

influence process, and with sufficient development, may be able to encompass more of the empirical findings than dissonance and advocacy theory are at present able to cover.

The most recent move toward regarding participants in experiments as active agents is that of Collins and Hoyt.[27] They have identified two critical conditions for obtaining dissonance effects: (1) the assumption by participants of personal responsibility for their choices, and (2) making choices that have important consequences for other persons. The chief dissonance effect under consideration here is a negative relationship between incentive and attitude change like that obtained in the $1 and $20 experiment discussed earlier: the smaller the incentive, the greater the attitude change (presumably because more dissonance is aroused with the low incentive). Collins has emphasized that it is not retaliation or ridicule from their audiences that participants are concerned about, but that they are bothered by the possibility of persuading their audience in the wrong direction, the possible immoral connotations of their action, or the possible consequences for policy implementation.[28] In their review of the research on induced compliance and related experiments, Collins and Hoyt found that experiments that manipulate choice typically yield dissonance effects when participants feel that they have freely chosen to perform the action contrary to their attitudes. Similarly, experiments that manipulate consequences typically yielded dissonance effects when participants believed that their acts had significant consequences for other persons. Thus, Collins and Hoyt argue that in order to produce a negative relationship, a participant must feel personally responsible for an act which appears to have significant consequences. Experiments which include variations in both these conditions simultaneously supported this proposition.[29] Thus, the conflicting findings of earlier experiments have been at least partially resolved by taking into consideration the social setting in which the participants' contrary actions occur as well as the implications of their actions in terms of personal and social responsibility.

Summary: Behaving Contrary to Attitude

Being required to behave contrary to one's attitude is a common experience in everyday life. Psychologists have tried to develop a theoretical explanation of the fact that such experiences are often accompanied by a change in the attitude to make it more consistent with the new behavior. The bulk of the research on such behavior has been oriented largely in terms of either counteradvocacy or dissonance theory. Within these more general rubrics are a variety of more specific explanatory mechanisms. These explanations focus on events occurring within the individual's private, nonsocial events.

Two cognitive elements are in a dissonant relation if, considering these two alone, the opposite of one element would follow from the other. In experimen-

27. Collins & Hoyt, 1972.   28. Collins, 1969.   29. Collins & Hoyt, 1972; Hoyt, Henley, & Collins, 1972.

tal situations the relative amount of dissonance aroused can be assessed by determining the ratio of dissonant to consonant elements. The situation in which these elements are more closely balanced arouses greater dissonance. Thus, in induced-compliance situations, the amount of force just sufficient to persuade the individual to engage in behavior contrary to his attitude will arouse the greatest dissonance and produce the most attitude change. Where the pressure to engage in the contrary behavior takes the form of an incentive or reward, the theory predicts an inverse relation between the amount of incentive and the amount of attitude change. Thus a large incentive outweighs the contrary behavior. Dissonance predictions have been supported by many experiments, and are only occasionally contradicted. Often, however, alternative interpretations of the phenomena are available.

Advocacy interpretations of the attitude change that takes place have pointed to several other explanatory mechanisms. They note that if a person espouses a contrary attitude either in an essay-writing exercise or in an attempt to persuade some one else, he often has to improvise arguments favoring the new position. He also scans his own memory and experience for arguments supporting the new position. These actions, it is argued, may well bring about attitude change. To the extent that the actions are encouraged by incentives, we would expect that attitude change would be in direct proportion to the amount of incentive. Advocacy theorists and others have also pointed to interfering factors especially associated with the high incentive. These factors interfere with or prevent attitude change from occurring. For example, an individual paid $20 for espousing a view that he knows perfectly well is not true may consider himself bribed or at least may be suspicious of the experimenter's motives, and thus hold fast to his original attitude, rather than change.

Although the face-to-face persuasive condition and the essay-writing situation differ in that the former is more public and the latter private, this does not seem to be the crucial factor accounting for the different results obtained from these two actions. The more personal commitment of the face-to-face situation is a better candidate for explaining the difference.

An overview of the voluminous research literature clearly reveals that dissonance theory specifies much too little to provide an adequate explanation of behavior contrary to attitude. Advocacy theory has fared well in some situations, but a lot of evidence is not entirely consistent with it, either. More recently, a number of dissonance theorists have suggested that self-involvement, often not controlled in earlier experiments, is critical to attitude change. Dissonance has here been reinterpreted as a feeling of personal unworthiness or a concern about having performed a morally undesirable act. Also important are the consequences of the contrary behavior for other persons who are present. Quite possibly an internal state of "dissonance" arising from acts contrary to one's attitude is not the critical factor, but rather the actor's concern that he might appear inconsistent or irresponsible to observers.

Both on theoretical grounds and in terms of hindsight it is clear that much of the research has neglected the social nature of the contrary act and the larger setting in which it is performed, and that this neglect is in large part responsible for the fact that a prodigious amount of experimentation has failed to produce a sufficiently precise theory and an adequate body of knowledge concerning the effects of behaving contrary to one's attitude.

The more recent explanations of the effects of contrary behavior have the merit of moving somewhat in the direction of the setting and the social context of such experiments. They give at least some consideration to the relation of the participant to other persons, including the experimenter, and to the social context within which the experiments are conducted. While the experiments still focus on events occurring within the individual, they are events related to his looking outward at other persons and to the social implications of his behavior. Thus, indirectly, they bring in other persons and the social context. The next logical step in this whole line of research is to produce more variations in the behavior of the experimenter and the other persons involved, and to conduct the research in varying social contexts.

Beyond the Laboratory: Processes of Change

Most of the discussion in these changes has treated attitudinal and behavior change as if it were a simple, relatively isolated, one-shot event. Nothing could be farther from the truth for most naturally occurring changes. At its very best, experimentation on the induced-compliance paradigm is confined to a very narrow segment of time and of the participant's life. Moreover, the behavior contrary to one's attitude, which is the chief mediating source of the attitude change, is produced through the powerful influence that the experimenter has over students in institutions of higher learning.

The remarkable acquiescence of participants in experiments has been repeatedly demonstrated. At the experimenter's instruction, they have, without complaint, performed such tasks as: (1) adding all adjacent numbers on sheets containing random digits, tearing each sheet into thirty-two pieces after completing it, then doing the next sheet, and continuing for 5½ hours until the *experimenter* gave up trying to exhaust the subjects' patience,[30] (2) dumping cans of garbage on the floor and sorting it into piles of like material,[31] and (3) a large assortment of various other tasks all designed to be as obnoxious, boring, and meaningless as a psychologist could make them.[32]

It is easy to see that the experimenter is in an unusually powerful position for effecting change, a position quite unlike that of most influence agents outside the laboratory. Thus, such research considered alone is unlikely to give us a clear view of the process of change as it occurs in natural situations. Chapter 5 will deal in part with social influence as it occurs outside the laboratory. At

30. ORNE, 1962.   *31.* PEPITONE, 1958.   *32.* ORNE, 1962.

this point, however, we can discuss one type of situation for which the laboratory experiment in contrary or advocating behavior is an analogue: situations where captors have attempted to change the attitudes of their prisoners.

Coercive Persuasion

The most publicized and intensively studied situations where captors attempted to indoctrinate prisoners are the efforts of the Chinese Communists to brainwash American prisoners taken during the Korean war and Chinese political prisoners taken during the revolution in China. Although brainwashing in POW camps was generally ineffective in bringing about genuine changes in attitudes (contrary to reports in the popular press), brainwashing of Americans in civilian prisons on the Chinese mainland was sometimes successful, as was brainwashing of Chinese forced to attend the revolutionary war colleges.[33]

Schein, Schneier, and Barker have adopted a term that aptly describes the influence process occurring in these situations: *coercive persuasion.*[34] It is a term preferable to *brainwashing*, for it emphasizes the complete control that the communicators have over the respondents with respect to both communication and the administration of rewards and punishment. Processes of control discussed by Schein, Schneier, and Barker include the following: (1) The captors exercised virtually complete control over reward and punishment. In the case of civilians imprisoned in Communist China, eating, sleeping, urination, defecation, and even free movement in cramped cells were controlled by the captors. (2) Communications were controlled in a variety of ways. In the Communist POW camps, letters from home detrimental to morale were permitted to reach the captive; other letters were withheld. No access to mass media from the home country was permitted; in general, only Communist publications were available. An atmosphere of distrust was created by the establishment of an informer system among the prisoners and a spy system among the prison personnel. (3) The individual was separated from his normal social contacts and daily routine and was thus deprived of sources that normally provide anchorage for one's beliefs. In civilian prisons in China and in POW camps in Korea, interpersonal liaisons that might have interfered with institutional goals were discouraged and blocked. Such potential sources of stubborn resistance to change were handled by physical relocation of the members, by assignment of leaders calculated to create norms congenial to the prison authorities, and in POW camps, by encouraging mistrust and informing among fellow prisoners.

Both the laboratory analogue and these life situations use powerful controls to produce behavior contrary to attitudes. Civilians in prison and at the revolutionary war colleges in Communist China were required to make confessions of "guilt." These were extorted through a process of deprivation, badgering, and interrogation, and consisted of the admission of "thinking wrong thoughts."

---

33. SCHEIN, SCHNEIER, & BARKER, 1961; LIFTON, 1957.   34. SCHEIN et al., 1961.

Statements of the "correct" way of thinking were extorted. This process was repeated endlessly, for hours and hours, days and days, weeks and weeks. In POW camps, in the early stages, prisoners would be interrogated singly. When they became accustomed to saying what they were forced to say, they could be managed in small groups. "Study" groups were organized for this purpose in prisons, camps, and the revolutionary colleges. The colleges had a liberal sprinkling of cadre devoted to communism, who were members of these groups. Confession of wrong thinking and profession of proper attitudes in these group settings amounted to a *public commitment* to the new beliefs (even if the individual privately retained his old ideas).

Although many American POWs cooperated with their captors in various ways, few of the many thousands of prisoners accepted communism on a permanent basis. On the other hand, many Chinese in the revolutionary war colleges who had previously been anti-Communist converted to communism and entered the new society as such. Some American civilians imprisoned for many years in Communist China eventually identified with a cellmate or with their interrogator, gradually adopting his communist ideology and in particular his belief that they had been guilty of "crimes against the people" and of "bourgeois thinking."

From these studies it seems clear that inducing behavior contrary to an individual's attitude, or having him advocate new attitudes contrary to his own, is unlikely to bring about any significant changes in his attitudes unless it is continued for a long period of time. Even then, unless social supports are created for the new attitude, it is unlikely to last. Certainly, if the individual returns to old friends and associates who still hold the old attitudes, he is apt to revert quickly. On the other hand, if the new attitude becomes functional—if it aids him in making an adjustment to his life situation—he is likely to adopt it as his own, as in the case of many Chinese who went through the revolutionary war colleges. By adopting communism, they were able to assume a rewarding place in the new society.

We should not overlook the fact that induced compliance occurs in many other natural situations. In some of these, induced compliance is only one part of a larger influence process that is pervasive and compelling. For example, in monasteries, medical and graduate schools, and the military services various behaviors and attitudes are adopted because of the pressures of the training program. Since these behaviors and attitudes are essential to effective functioning in the new role to be adopted, they are likely to be accepted by the individual and to become a part of his life. They are maintained by strong social support not only from the training agent, but also from one's peers. This socialization process will be discussed in more detail in Chapters 15 to 17. It could be argued that these voluntary (except the military) situations are better analogues of laboratory experiments in contrary behavior than the POW situation because of the demonstration that the appearance of freedom is important to attitude change in the laboratory. Yet it is clear that participants in experiments are under powerful pressures to comply. This whole question of generalization from the laboratory needs more analysis and empirical study.

Flux of Influence Processes

Few situations involve such total control as those just discussed. Thus it is not surprising that change outside the laboratory often involves moving back and forth, trying out new ways and abandoning them, getting advice and other information, and putting up initial resistance to change, as well as resisting temptation after the change has been made. Consider the New Year's resolution, mostly a joke because of the short duration of the resolve. Or more seriously, consider attempts to stop smoking or to diet. These are on-and-off, start-and-stop processes, with many ramifications. A review of 87 studies attempting to help smokers quit indicated that three months after they stopped smoking two-thirds of them had resumed smoking.[35] The total process and the context of change need more consideration than they have received in focused experimental study of contrary behavior.

From his studies of people deciding whether to undergo a major surgical operation and of people trying to give up smoking or to reduce their weight, Janis has developed a description of stages that enter into change.[36] We will discuss here some of the major aspects of this process, elaborating freely with our own ideas and those from other sources.

If there is to be a change, what must occur first is a challenge or threat to the individual's present attitude and behavior. A crisis of some kind arises: A heavy smoker is hit with the threat of lung cancer, or a person finds that he must face a major surgical operation. This stage is concluded when the person accepts the challenge; he then moves to the next.

If the challenge is accepted, action recommended in the persuasive attempt is evaluated. The advice of other persons or reference sources may be sought. Alternative actions may be imagined or sought out. In the consideration of these various alternatives, arguments and counterarguments are apt to be generated in their support or refutation. This stage is resolved when the individual either returns to his initial attitude of equilibrium, or accepts the recommendation and decides to act upon it. If the challenge is a really serious one, this stage may last for a long time and involve considerable vacillation, as in the case of the decision to stop smoking.

Once the recommendation is accepted and the individual is committed to the new line of action, new processes enter in. He reveals his decision to other persons important to him: His commitment becomes a public one. Kelman has noted how a new line of action initiates a serial process.[37] The action may

35. Hunt & Matarazzo, 1973.    36. Janis, 1968.   37. Kelman, 1962.

provide the occasion for new experiences in relation to the object (e.g., the alcoholic who stops drinking finds that he feels much better, has more energy, is more effective, etc.).

Or action may create a new psychological situation. If the initial situation is thought of as one in which the tendency to approach the goal is weaker than the tendency to avoid it, the commitment to move ahead will bring the person in actual contact with a goal which has hitherto been avoided. This new engagement with the goal may now permanently reduce avoidance tendencies. A simple illustration is found in the initial resistance to performing some anxiety-arousing action for the first time, such as diving from a height or making a public speech. Usually such initial actions are followed by a considerable drop in resistance to further enactment. Thus, the commitment to a line of action, even though only an initial step, may lead to permanent change. If the influence agent is a friend or associate, the commitment to the recommended action may produce a change in the relation to him that further supports the new line.

Janis has also called attention to the role of negative feedback in this final stage.[38] Typically, adopting the new line will arouse various counterpressures. Friends or other significant persons may disapprove. Subjective experiences accompanying the new line may be unpleasant, such as hunger in dieting, or feelings of deprivation by an alcoholic who attempts to stop drinking. The actor must cope with these negative feedbacks and manage them; otherwise he may revert to an earlier stage.

On an overall basis, these stages of making a decision to change represent increasing commitment to the change. Janis finds that in order for the change to be successful, the individual must have worked through each stage. If he has not carried out the actions involved in a particular earlier stage, he may be vulnerable to negative feedback in the final stage. For example, if he has not adequately evaluated the alternatives, a sudden confrontation with one of these alternatives later may cause him to revert to his earlier behavior.

Janis also notes that an individual's reaction to information is very much a function of the stage he happens to be in. For example, antismoking information is met with indifference or resistance before the first stage is completed. At later stages it elicits great interest and will be carefully evaluated. In the final stage it is welcome and will be uncritically accepted. But information favoring continuing smoking is handled very differently. There is considerable interest during the early stages, with unbiased evaluation. Near the final stage, such information is avoided or actively refuted.

We have said little here about the role of internal processes in fixing or upsetting attitudinal or behavioral change. But most beliefs and actions are embedded in a complex of attitudes, values, and actions. Whether they will change and how persistent the change will be depend upon changes in the structure of this complex. Attitudes toward the self, for example, are integrated

---

38. Janis, 1968.

with the way one behaves and also with the treatment that an individual receives from other persons.[39] Some of the processes that contribute to stability
and change with respect to beliefs about the self and in relation to other people
will be discussed in Chapter 17.

Summary: Beyond the Laboratory

Laboratory experimentation on induced behavior contrary to attitude is confined to a very narrow segment of time and of the participant's life. Even if it is
effective in the laboratory, its effects may fade rapidly. In life situations such as
prison camps where it has been possible to maintain the contrary behavior for
long periods of time through the use of coercion, both the contrary behavior
and associated attitudes seem usually to disappear when the coercion is removed. Thus, considered by itself, contrary behavior seems insufficient to engender real change.

But there are some life situations where the induced contrary behavior is
only the first step in a sequential influence process ultimately leading to permanent change. In such a context, it might well be an effective means of changing
attitudes. This appeared to be the case for the indoctrination of Chinese political prisoners during the revolution in China. Many of these individuals ultimately embraced communism and took their place in the new society. Induced
compliance also occurs in monasteries, medical and graduate schools, and the
military service. In many instances it is a part of the larger process leading to
the socialization of individuals into a profession. It seems that the key to permanence lies in the social supports that are provided for the new behaviors or
attitudes.

Study has begun of attitudinal and behavioral change of individuals in their
daily lives, over a longer time period. From preliminary work, it seems evident
that change outside the laboratory often involves moving back and forth, trying
out new ways and abandoning them, getting advice and other information, and
putting up initial resistance to change, as well as resisting temptation after the
change has been made. Five stages have been proposed as composing the process of change: (1) challenge to existing attitude and behavior, (2) appraisal of
the challenge, (3) selection of a favored alternative, (4) commitment to the
alternative, and (5) adherence despite negative feedback. Very different processes operate at these various stages.

39. Secord & Backman, 1961, 1965.

4

Persuasive Communication and Influence

As noted in the introduction to Part One, different ways of treating social influence will be discussed in several places in this book. Chapter 3 dealt with the effects of behaving contrary to one's attitude. The setting for this discussion was mainly laboratory experimentation, where generally the influence attempt took the form of inducing the participants to perform various actions calculated to bring about attitudinal or other behavioral changes. This chapter and Chapter 5 use a different *paradigm:* Persons are presented with *information* calculated to change their attitudes or behavior. This procedure is more directly analogous to mass-communication situations, where communications are presented via television, radio, newspapers, and other media.

This chapter deals primarily with characteristics of the communicator, the communication, and the respondent that make for successful or unsuccessful communication. Chapter 5 examines the contribution of group and societal processes to mass communication, as well as some of the by-products of modern mass communication such as the effects of television violence on aggressive behavior. Separation of material in this way is somewhat arbitrary, for the insight gained into psychological influence processes from both of these approaches increases our understanding of influence in general, regardless of the setting in which it occurs.

The Communicator

Long before behavioral science developed, the importance of the communicator was recognized. Aristotle, in *Rhetoric,* emphasized the communicator and suggested that listeners evaluate speakers in terms of their intelligence, character, and intentions.[1] History calls attention to the many public figures who were notable for their skill in persuading the masses—sometimes in inflaming them to riot and other forms of violence, sometimes in calming them and preventing hasty action. In contemporary politics we speak of a politician's image: Certain politicians are consistently good vote getters, sometimes in part because of the personal qualities they project. And anyone who has had experience in groups has observed that some members are listened to and followed more than others. Thus we must give some attention to what makes communicators credible, and perhaps to other attributes as well, such as likability.

Credibility of the Communicator

The familiar way in which we think of an orator, for example, leads us to focus solely on his personal characteristics. But his persuasiveness is not only a function of his personal characteristics, but also of his position or status, the nature of the communication, the context in which it is delivered, his relation to the listener, and even the listener's characteristics.

Hovland, Janis, and Kelley have suggested that two main characteristics of communicator credibility are expertness and trustworthiness.[2] Expertness may be a personal characteristic, deriving from special training or education, experience, social background, or even age. But it may also be more of a nominal characteristic, stemming from position or status. A related but somewhat distinct attribute is the legitimate power held by the communicator. Legitimate power is based on the acceptance by the recipient of the idea that the position or status of the communicator gives him the authority to influence people—by making decisions, determining policy, or giving orders. (See Chapter 8 for a more extended discussion of this concept.) Thus, messages to the people from the President of the United States are likely to receive acceptance in part because of the high prestige of his office.

Trustworthiness is also a property attributed to a highly credible communicator. The characteristics of a communicator that lead people to trust him may be widely varied. He may be trusted because he is in a position of authority. Certain personality characteristics, physical appearance, ways of expressing oneself, and style or mannerisms may be associated with trustworthiness.

Another factor in trustworthiness is the perceived intent of the communicator, as gleaned from what he says or what is known about him. If he stands to gain through acceptance of his message by other persons, he is usually considered untrustworthy. Many people therefore are skeptical of the communications of publicity agents, salesmen, politicians, and purveyors of products advertised in radio and television commercials.

A good example of how the communicator's apparent motives may determine his credibility is found in an experiment where the communicator

1. COOPER, 1932.   *2.* HOVLAND, JANIS, & KELLEY, 1953.

Self-int

argued for a position opposed to his own best interest.[3] The issue was whether prosecutors should have more or less power than at present. A "criminal" (ordinarily of low credibility) arguing for more power for the *prosecutor* was found to be more credible and more effective than a "prosecutor" (ordinarily of high credibility) making the same argument. The reverse was true when the communicator argued for less power.

Some understanding of how a credible communicator is perceived may be gained through an examination of studies in which communicators were rated and the ratings analyzed by means of various statistical procedures. Public figures and media sources such as the New York *Times* were rated on a large list of attributes.[4] These ratings were *factor-analyzed,* a procedure in which psychologically related attributes are grouped together so that the groups or clusters may be identified as basic dimensions underlying the ratings. Similar factors were found to emerge for the different sources of communication.

factor analysis

The first of these, although labeled *safety* by the investigators, consisted of the attributes safe-unsafe, just-unjust, kind-cruel, friendly-unfriendly, honest-dishonest, and could equally well be labeled *trustworthiness.* The second factor was equivalent to *expertness,* and the attributes were trained-untrained, experienced-inexperienced, skilled-unskilled, qualified-unqualified, informed-uninformed. In this respect, this study is consistent with earlier ideas that two main components of credibility are trustworthiness and expertness.

(1)

(2)

A third factor was also found, however, labeled *dynamism* by the investigators, with the attributes aggressive-meek, emphatic-weak, bold-timid, active-passive, energetic-tired. This essentially relates to style of presentation. Among a sample of the adult population of Lansing, Michigan, trustworthiness was twice as important as expertness and dynamism. In a college student sample, trustworthiness and expertness were equally important, and dynamism was of relatively minor importance. These three dimensions of credibility are by no means exhaustive; individual studies reviewed by Giffin include quite a number of other attributes.[5]

(3)

?

Two other studies reveal, moreover, that the structure of the characteristics attributed to the communicator varies markedly depending upon whether he has high or low credibility. Highly credible communicators are seen as having a greater number of independent dimensions, each contributing only in small degree to the image, whereas communicators of low credibility are seen in terms of a smaller number of dimensions contributing more heavily to the overall picture.[6]

That credibility of the communicator is associated with successful persuasion has been repeatedly documented in research spanning several decades. The literature has been reviewed by Hovland, Janis, and Kelley in 1953 and discussed further in 1969 by McGuire.[7] In simulated mass-communication situ-

3. WALSTER, ARONSON, & ABRAHAMS, 1966.   *4.* BERLO, LEMERT, & MERTZ, 1969-1970.   *5.* GIFFIN, 1967.   *6.* SCHWEITZER & GINSBURG, 1966; SCHWEITZER, 1967.   *7.* HOVLAND, JANIS, & KELLEY, 1953; McGUIRE, 1969.

ations, elevating the communicator's status by attributing to him knowledge, education, intelligence, and various forms of status is generally effective in changing attitudes. In naturally occurring situations that have been studied, however, peers exert considerably more influence than persons of superior status.[8] Apparently this is due to the ubiquitous contact with peers as compared with authorities or experts. Where there is considerable communication across different levels of status, superiors have a greater impact.[9]

In spite of the extensive support for the effectiveness of highly credible communicators in changing attitudes, some recent evidence qualifies this conclusion. Most studies of communicator credibility have been carried out under circumstances where the participants have not been strongly involved in the issue. Generally the topic has been one not particularly exciting to the usual college participant, or the experimental context has not made the recipients feel that their attitudes on the topic are especially important. The term *ego involvement* has come to be used to refer to the extent to which the topic and the attitude-change issue are important to the participant. Several recent studies have examined the effects of high and low credibility under conditions of high and low ego involvement. They found that the degree of credibility makes a difference only when the participant's ego involvement is low.[10] One possible explanation for this is that high ego involvement leads to greater scrutiny of the message itself, washing out the differences between the communicators. Thus, it appears that high credibility has its effects largely through facilitating uncritical acceptance of the message when the recipient is uninterested in it.[11]

The dynamic quality or style of the communicator's presentation has been less studied, and its effect on persuasion is not always consistent. One study varied style of presentation, having a speech expert present on tape identical communications in a dynamic, forceful style, and in a dull, passive style.[12] The dynamic style enhanced the credibility of the communicator in a manner independent of his other attributes. Several studies suggest the possibility that the dull, passive style leads to a perception of the communicator as less credible or perhaps results in poorer comprehension of the communication.[13] But still other research shows that an overly dynamic, hard-sell style may generate suspicion of the communicator's intent, and consequently, less opinion change, while a soft-sell style is slightly more effective.[14] What is needed to resolve these inconsistencies is a more precise characterization of style of presentation.

More extensively researched is the communicator's intent in delivering a persuasive message. If he is judged to be unbiased, as not having a personal

8. KATZ & LAZARSFELD, 1955.   9. STRODTBECK, JAMES, & HAWKINS, 1958.   10. JOHNSON & SCILEPPI, 1969; RHINE & SEVERANCE, 1970.   11. JOHNSON & SCILEPPI, 1969.   12. SCHWEITZER, 1967.   13. BEIGHLEY, 1952; THISTLETHWAITE, DE HAAN, & KAMENETZKY, 1955; IRWIN & BROCKHAUS, 1963; MILLER & HEWGILL, 1964; BOWERS, 1965; BOWERS & OSBORN, 1966.   14. DIETRICH, 1946; BETTINGHAUS, 1961; BOWERS, 1963; CARMICHAEL & CRONKHITE, 1965.

motive in attempting to bring about change, as objective and fair, he presumably will appear more credible and will be more successful in persuasion. Early studies did not always indicate that an unbiased communicator was more effective in persuading his target persons.[15] Later research developments suggest that these inconsistent results occurred because of the effects on perceived intent of a rather complex set of factors.

One line of research used *forewarning* in an attempt to accentuate the effects of intent. In spite of the fact that participants were warned of the communicator's intent to persuade, in many of the studies there was no effect of the warning on attitude change. In others, attitudes changed slightly less, especially if the warning was delivered before the communication itself.[16] But in some instances, warning of persuasive intent actually increased attitude change.[17] This is easily explained: Where the participants are inclined to cooperate with the communicator (or experimenter), alerting them to his persuasive intent simply makes their line of action clearer. McGuire notes that the obvious idea that hiding persuasive intent enhances opinion change is not always supported by the findings.[18] One reason for this is that when the respondent desires to cooperate with the communicator, knowing his intent makes it easier for him to do so: He learns his message more readily.

Liking for a Communicator and Persuasibility

It is reasonable to suppose that a person who likes a communicator will be readily influenced by him. This is predicted both by consistency theory and by exchange theory. Consistency theory, discussed in more detail in Chapter 7, asserts that a state of balance prevails when all three relations among two persons and an object are positive and also when one is positive and two are negative.[19] Thus, if a person P likes a communicator O, and O positively evaluates an attitude object X, then P will be positive toward X, producing a balanced state. Therefore if P is initially negative toward X, his liking for O and O's positive evaluation of X will produce a stress toward resolving the imbalance, resulting in P's adoption of a positive attitude toward X. Thus a person will experience a strain toward positively valuing the objects that a friend or loved one values. Moreover, if P dislikes O, he will be positively inclined toward objects that O evaluates negatively. We are apt to like those who attack our enemies.

We can also think of liking for a communicator as having a positive influence in terms of exchange theory, explained in Chapter 7. This theory asserts that liking between two people is based upon an exchange of rewards and minimization of costs. Thus, by agreeing or complying with a liked person's

15. McGuire, 1969.   *16.* Kiesler & Kiesler, 1964; Freedman & Sears, 1965; Greenberg & Miller, 1966.   *17.* Sears, 1965.   *18.* McGuire, 1969.   *19.* Heider, 1958.

request, one might gain his approval and be liked in return. This application, however, requires two-way interaction—the communicator must receive feedback.

While some studies support the idea that a liked communicator is more persuasive, under some conditions liked communicators are not more persuasive; moreover, in some situations *disliked* communicators are more persuasive than *liked* ones.[20] We would expect these exceptions to occur where gaining approval of the liked communicator by agreeing with him is not rewarding.

For example, in one experiment conducted in a college setting and in a situation using Army reserves, a disliked communicator persuaded more participants to eat fried grasshoppers than did a liked communicator.[21] Exchange theory would predict that participants would eat grasshoppers as a favor to a liked communicator. But dissonance theory (see Chapter 3) suggests that participants who initially dislike but who voluntarily commit themselves to eat grasshoppers in response to persuasion from a disliked communicator would be less able to justify their action than those who commit themselves in response to a liked communicator. To reduce dissonance and increase justification, they increase their liking for and eat more grasshoppers.

As McGuire notes, just the act of agreeing to listen to a disliked communicator might, in some instances, make the listener more receptive to his message, in order to avoid dissonance.[22] McGuire also points out that a stranger can be more persuasive than a liked person because the communication from the stranger is less redundant and thus more novel and meaningful. Many parents have repeatedly urged their child to take some line of action without success, only to see him perform it with alacrity upon a single request from a comparative stranger.

On the other hand, a disliked communicator may not only be ineffective, but may cause a "boomerang effect"—the recipient may move in a direction opposite to the communicator's message. One experiment demonstrated this effect in a field experiment conducted on park benches.[23] A confederate of the experimenter, who appeared to be simply another inhabitant of the park, became involved in a debate with the naïve participant at the instigation of a "roving reporter" (the experimenter). According to a systematic plan he made disparaging remarks about the opinions expressed by selected participants. Measures obtained before and after the interview session indicated that, unlike most laboratory studies, the insulted participants shifted their attitudes in a direction opposite to that of the persuasive attempt.

A considerable variety of other attributes of the communicator have been investigated, but few generalizations are supported by sufficient and consistent research data.

20. McGuire, 1969.   *21.* Zimbardo, Weisenberg, Firestone, & Levy, 1965.   *22.* McGuire, 1969. *23.* Abelson & Miller, 1967.

Summary: The Communicator

The characteristics of the communicator that have been most intensively studied are his credibility and his likability. Both of these characteristics have been found to affect the degree of attitude change. Attributes that contribute to the impression of credibility are the communicator's expertness, trustworthiness, legitimate power, and dynamic quality. Intentions attributed to the communicator are an important component of his trustworthiness. His dynamic quality refers to such personal characteristics as boldness, activity, decisiveness, and effective style of presentation. The credibility of the communicator is more effective in bringing about change in attitudes which are not too important to the recipient. If the attitude topic is one in which the recipient is highly ego-involved, the credibility of the communicator may make little difference, apparently because more attention is paid to the content of the message than to the communicator.

According to balance theory, liking for a communicator will produce more acceptance where acceptance leads to a balanced cognitive structure. For example, when a liked communicator positively recommends adopting an attitude which itself easily generates positive feeling, the structure is balanced. It is also balanced when an individual is negatively inclined toward an attitude object which has been recommended by a disliked communicator. Empirical studies only partly support balance theory. Under certain conditions, a disliked communicator has been shown to produce more attitude change (e.g., when he arouses more dissonance than a liked communicator).

The Message

In considering persuasion through communication, one's attention is often focused on the message itself. It is as natural to think of the message as a primary source of attitude change as it is to think of the communicator. If one thinks the message is effective, the desired persuasive effect will take place. In line with this view, many students of the communication process have presented messages in various forms in order to assess their relative effectiveness. As we will see, however, the message cannot be considered in complete isolation from other elements of the communication process.

Many aspects of the message may be considered as potentially affecting persuasion. Among these are emotional versus rational appeals and such organizational characteristics of the message as the ordering of elements within it, the presence of reinforcing elements, the extent to which conclusions or recommendations are made explicit, and the mention and refutation of counterarguments to the message theme. Most of these factors will be only briefly considered here. More attention will be given to the use of fear appeals, because of the extensive research available on this topic.

Persuasiveness of Fear-arousing Appeals

Since appeals that arouse fear are one form of emotional appeal, we shall introduce fear appeals by considering the more general question of the relative merits of emotional versus rational appeals. Can the orator skilled at playing upon the emotions of his audience sway it more effectively than the statesman who appeals to the intelligence and good sense of the audience? Behavioral scientists have subjected to controlled experimentation the question of emotional versus rational appeals. The early approaches to this topic have been reviewed by Hovland, Janis, and Kelley.[24] Experimental findings are quite contradictory; some support rational appeals and others, emotional appeals.

Unfortunately, as Hovland and his colleagues note, the problem was not clearly defined in these early experiments. For one thing, the identification of a communication as having a rational or an emotional appeal is not always clear-cut. A rational appeal may arouse certain emotions; an emotional appeal may make a person think. One experiment has demonstrated quite clearly that both naïve and expert judges were unable to agree on the classification of materials intended by the experimenter to have either a rational or an emotional appeal.[25] Even more serious is that the aspects of a communication which account for its effectiveness or ineffectiveness could not be identified in the early types of experiments conducted. Finally, these early approaches did not clarify why and how emotional or rational appeals lead to an audience response, although such knowledge is necessary for complete understanding of the problem.

In recent years the fear appeal has received intensive study attempting to pin down the means by which it succeeds or fails to persuade. Many mass communications use fear appeals. Government officials, for example, may try to gain support for national defense activities by stressing the dangers inherent in failure to prepare for emergency situations. Health organizations, both public and private, may emphasize disease and pain in an attempt to promote better health. Advertisers sometimes employ fear appeals: Witness the widespread use by toothpaste and deodorant advertisers of the threat of being unpopular because of failure to practice oral or body hygiene by using their products. All these influence attempts consist essentially of information describing a danger and recommendations for action that would avoid the danger. They "threaten" the individual with unfortunate consequences unless he follows the advice of the communicator. Thus, the terms *threat appeal* and *fear appeal* are commonly used to refer to them. Such threat appeals deserve study because of their widespread use and because of the theoretical problems they raise in connection with understanding persuasive communications.

PERSUASION AND THE DEGREE OF FEAR AROUSED   One question asked early in research on fear appeals was simply: "Are strong fear appeals more persuasive

24. HOVLAND, JANIS, & KELLEY, 1953.   25. RUECHELLE, 1958.

than weak fear appeals?" If fear is thought of as a drive, a motivating force, then one might expect that the greater the fear, the stronger the influence. Several early studies suggested that the reverse was true: Mild fear led to a change in attitudes and behavior, but strong fear produced little change.[26] In these studies, strong fear was aroused by vivid and realistic presentations, such as threatening smokers with lung cancer by showing color photographs of diseased lungs. Milder effects were produced by using x-rays or other more impersonal illustrations in the communication.

Explanations of these results were offered which did not abandon the hypothesis that fear acted as a drive. The basic idea was that fear acts as a motivating force leading the person to accept the recommendations offered in order to reduce his fear, but that when fear was too strong, other processes entered in. For example, strong fear appeals may be seen as offensive and exaggerated—deliberate attempts to scare the listeners—thus producing discounting of the communication and resistance to change. Or when the listener actually becomes afraid, he may generate defenses against his fear—such as arguments counter to those of the communicator.

But we shall have to abandon these neatly plausible explanations. More recent studies find that mild fear is associated with *less* persuasion.[27] At the same time, contrary to the early findings, a considerable number of these studies indicate *greater* persuasion when more intense fear is aroused. (Higbee cites twenty-two such studies.[28]) Explanations for this more current finding are also ready at hand. Indeed, the problem is an abundance of interpretations, some of them mutually incompatible. Thus, it has become necessary to postulate more precisely the means by which fear facilitates or inhibits persuasion, and to specify the conditions under which it does so. In the process of designing experiments to discover this information, investigators have been led to elaborate more complex models of the fear-persuasion process. The work of Howard Leventhal is a major contribution to this topic, and our discussion leans heavily on it.[29]

THE PARALLEL MODEL EXPLANATION   Leventhal has proposed that a fear-arousing communication produces two parallel and independent reactions.[30] One reaction is to *control the fears aroused by the threat.* While fear control may take place by means of actions that cope with the danger, many other actions that control fear are either irrelevant to or interfere with coping behavior. For example, defenses against fear would include withdrawing from the situation, thinking up counterarguments against the threat, stopping thinking about the danger, obtaining reassurance, and developing rationalizations for not worrying.

The other reaction is to *cope with the danger.* This would include facing and

26. JANIS & FESHBACH, 1953; HOVLAND, JANIS, & KELLEY, 1953; NUNNALLY & BOBREW, 1959.   27. LEVENTHAL, 1970.   28. HIGBEE, 1969.   29. LEVENTHAL, 1970.   30. LEVENTHAL, 1970.

"Diff counter — flavors in the mind"

acknowledging the danger, accepting the recommendation of the communication, adopting other adequate means of avoiding the danger, and obtaining additional information on how to cope with it.

Leventhal notes that, typically, there is some correlation between the fear and coping reactions.[31] More serious threats elicit stronger coping responses *and* stronger emotional reactions. But this occurs because of the nature of the communication; there is no *necessary* connection between fear arousal and coping behavior—one does not cause the other. This model of independent but interacting reactions to fear arousal suggests explanations for some familiar phenomena. For example, fear is often strongest *after* one has successfully coped with a dangerous situation. Leventhal gives the example of controlling a car which had started skidding dangerously, and only experiencing fear after it had been brought to a stop. In this instance, coping with the danger also controls or inhibits the fear, but when coping behavior ceases, the fear reaction occurs.

In other instances, however, a fear response may interfere with coping behavior (e.g., as when the danger has to be faced: taking an x-ray, going to the hospital). Obviously, fear often generates avoidance responses that interfere with coping with the danger. Thus, because these two reactions are independent and interact in different ways, a wide variety of ways of handling fear-arousing communications becomes possible.

We can, for example, consider situations involving delayed responses. When persuasive fear communications are presented under conditions where it is *not* possible to act immediately, the normal dissipation of fear over time permits coping with the danger by taking positive action at a later time. Where the recommendation may be acted upon immediately, and strong fear is aroused, defenses against fear may be dominant.

Leventhal contrasts this explanation of delayed response to fear-arousing communications based on his parallel model with the quite commonly accepted explanation which treats fear as a drive or motive.[32] This model postulates a serial process with later behaviors mediated by the emotional responses in the chain. It predicts that messages arousing high fear will produce greater persuasion than those arousing low fear, provided the recommendations presented are fear-reducing. This assumes that mentally rehearsing the communicator's recommendations reduces the fear, which in turn reinforces the recommendations. The fear-drive model also recognizes situations where, instead, fear is reduced by denying or ignoring the danger: This reinforces resistance against the communication so that at a later time individuals who had experienced high fear will be even less accepting of the recommendation.

For delayed-response situations, the fear-drive model makes opposite predictions from the parallel response model: Messages arousing high fear will be more effective than those arousing low fear when action is taken immediately

31. LEVENTHAL, 1970.   32. LEVENTHAL, 1970.

after the communication.[33] The relation will be reversed if action is delayed. The reason for the prediction is that an immediate reaction will be more strongly reinforced by the fear reduction than a delayed reaction, where defenses against fear arise. Leventhal cites several experiments providing little support for the fear-drive model predictions.[34]

Two other experiments support the parallel-response model prediction that communications arousing high fear will be more effective if the response is delayed (contrary to the fear-drive model). In the first experiment, different films on lung cancer were presented to three groups of individuals.[35] The films were designed to arouse low, medium, and high degrees of fear. The film arousing high fear presented an actual lung cancer operation in color, showing the initial incision, the forcing apart of the ribs, the removal of the black and diseased lung, and the open cavity with beating heart. It was very effective in arousing fear. The film arousing moderate fear omitted the operation scenes but told the same story of how the editor of a small-town newspaper discovered that he had lung cancer. The treatment arousing low fear presented the same story but in pamphlet form instead of film. The films all included advice to stop smoking and to get an x-ray at a mobile unit near at hand.

The outcome was that fewer smokers took x-rays immediately after the communication arousing high fear than after the messages arousing low or medium fear. Nonsmokers were equally willing to take x-rays, regardless of the level of threat. This reduced persuasibility for smokers immediately after a communication arousing high fear is inconsistent with the fear-drive model, which predicts that such a message will be effective immediately, but not later. The alternative explanation, based on the parallel model, is that when fear is intense immediately after the communication, it disrupts attempts to cope with the danger. After the fear subsides, the danger can be coped with. This is consistent with a follow-up conducted five months later, which revealed that *smoking reduction was greatest among smokers who had been exposed to the condition inspiring high fear.*

Another study comparing immediate and later reactions complicated the model by introducing a personal characteristic, *self-esteem*, that affects the way in which a person reacts to or handles fear.[36] It was hypothesized that participants with high self-esteem could handle fear better than those with low self-esteem. Participants were given the opportunity to take antitetanus shots either immediately after the communication or not until a day later. When shots were available immediately, the more threatening the communication, the more shots were taken by participants with high self-esteem, but the fewer shots were taken by those with low self-esteem. This is consistent with the idea that the coping responses of participants with low self-esteem were temporarily disrupted by their inability to handle the fear aroused.

33. Leventhal, 1970.   34. Haefner, 1965; Leventhal & Niles, 1965; Singer, 1965.   35. Leventhal & Watts, 1966.   36. Kornzweig, 1967.

An alternative explanation is quite plausible, but wrong: Perhaps the participants with low self-esteem took fewer shots because they expect bad things to happen to them no matter what they do. But this is negated by the fact that in a control group where no fear was aroused, all participants with low self-esteem took shots and few individuals with high self-esteem did.

While the fear-drive model cannot explain why communications arousing high degrees of fear are more effective after the passage of time, the model does allow for less effectiveness of communications arousing high fear than those arousing low fear. Under certain conditions the communications arousing high fear are presumed to produce defenses against the fear or denial and avoidance of the threat. Some of the older studies were consistent with this view, including a classic study of the effects of fear appeals on dental hygiene, where the minimum fear appeal was most effective.[37] But the parallel response model suggests an alternative explanation which is consistent with more recent investigations—that high fear arousal prevents one from coping with the actual danger.

We can test this idea by varying the effectiveness of the recommendations. The fear-drive model predicts that highly effective recommendations will reduce fear and be accepted, but ineffective recommendations will fail to reduce fear, which will generate defenses and resistance to the recommendations. In an experiment manipulating the perceived effectiveness of a drug for roundworms (from 90 to 30 percent), the willingness to use the drug was greater at the level of high fear arousal than at the level of low fear arousal, *regardless of the effectiveness of the drug*.[38]

We can safely reject the idea that in this instance high fear arousal interferes with persuasion by generating defenses, for if this were the case, high fear arousal combined with ineffective recommendations would produce less persuasion than high fear arousal combined with effective recommendations that make defense unnecessary. Several other investigations are consistent with this view.[39] Thus, it seems that high fear arousal, when it does interfere with persuasion, operates by interfering with coping responses.

FACTORS AFFECTING COPING WITH DANGER   There are several factors that might affect coping with the threat presented in a persuasive communication: (1) personality traits that interfere with or facilitate coping actions, (2) other characteristics of participants unrelated to personality but associated with coping actions, and (3) situational conditions that affect coping. In one study, participants were classified by means of a word-association test as avoiders or copers.[40] The avoiders were less accepting of the recommendation contained in a communication arousing strong fear than in one arousing low fear. Copers, on the other hand, reacted equally to high-fear and low-fear communications.

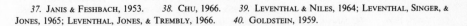

37. Janis & Feshbach, 1953.   38. Chu, 1966.   39. Leventhal & Niles, 1964; Leventhal, Singer, & Jones, 1965; Leventhal, Jones, & Trembly, 1966.   40. Goldstein, 1959.

Several studies indicate that participants with low self-esteem are less likely to accept the recommendations of high-fear messages than are those with high self-esteem.[41]

Another condition that should affect a person's reactions to a threatening health communication is his feeling of vulnerability to illnesses. He may feel immune or he may feel especially vulnerable. When a person in one of these states hears a fear-arousing communication, his present state should affect his reaction to it, including his coping response. We should expect that the participant who feels vulnerable will be less likely to act on the recommendations in a strong fear-arousing communication for several possible reasons, such as: (1) his feeling of vulnerability might lead him to grapple with his fear rather than the danger or (2) his feeling of vulnerability might make him think that the threat is uncontrollable. Several experiments are consistent with these ideas, but do not result in a clear choice among the possible alternative explanations.[42]

An experimental manipulation of the feeling of being vulnerable to lung cancer helps to clarify this issue.[43] Four conditions were used: (1) a control group not exposed to a communication, (2) a group exposed to a communication that created feelings of vulnerability to cancer, (3) a group exposed to a communication that created strong fear of cancer, and (4) a group exposed to communications that made them feel both vulnerable and fearful of cancer. One week later and again one month later, the two groups either exposed to the fear condition or made to feel vulnerable were smoking less than the controls. But participants made to feel both vulnerable and fearful continued to smoke as much as the controls. Thus, these participants rejected the recommended action, presumably because feeling both vulnerable and fearful interferes with realistic coping and causes the respondent to deal only with his fears, even after a month has passed.

EMOTIONAL ROLE PLAYING   The fear-drive model and the parallel-response model are relevant to the interpretation of role-playing studies conducted in an effort to change attitudes or behavior. Janis and Mann performed a role-playing experiment with women smokers. Each woman in turn played the part of patient and was told by her "doctor" (the experimenter) that she had lung cancer and should follow a certain recommendation for treatment.[44] Control participants heard the sessions on tape but did not play a role.

In this investigation, the women who played the part of patients reported stronger feelings of vulnerability and stronger intentions to quit smoking than the control women. An eighteen-month follow-up showed an appreciable reduction in smoking among those who had played the part of patients, in comparison with the control participants.[45] Janis and Mann interpret this form of

41. DABBS, 1964; DABBS & LEVENTHAL, 1966; KORNZWEIG, 1967; LEVENTHAL & TREMBLY, 1968.   *42.* BERKOWITZ & COTTINGHAM, 1960; LEVENTHAL, et al., 1965; LEVENTHAL & WATTS, 1966; LEVENTHAL, et al., 1966. *43.* WATTS, 1966.   *44.* JANIS & MANN, 1965; MANN & JANIS, 1968.   *45.* MANN & JANIS, 1968.

role playing which arouses considerable fear as successful because it breaks through the defensive facade that prevents people from recognizing their vulnerability and acting on it.

But this interpretation would not be consistent with the parallel-response model, which would require that people continue to feel *invulnerable* so that they can cope with the danger. Reexamining the earlier experiments, Leventhal found that a correct statistical analysis would have shown the effects of emotional role playing to be so small as to be insignificant.[46] More recent role-playing studies, moreover, support the parallel-response model interpretation that participants made to feel most vulnerable would show the least acceptance of the recommendations.

In one study, four groups were used: (1) participants who played the role of a patient with lung cancer, (2) participants who played the part of a physician informing his patient that he had lung cancer, (3) participants who observed the interaction between physician and patient, and (4) a control group.[47] The vulnerability interpretation suggests that the participants who played the role of patient would show the least reduction in smoking because they would be made to feel most vulnerable and highly threatened. Results were in accord with this interpretation: The patient group changed smoking habits no more than the controls, while the doctor group and the observer group showed a substantial reduction in the mean number of cigarettes smoked.

COPING AND ACTION INSTRUCTIONS   Leventhal has stressed the individual's manner of coping with the actual danger.[48] He points out that motivation is not enough, but that the individual also needs to perform a series of actions in order to cope with the danger. These actions need to bridge the gap all the way from the receipt of the communication to the final act (e.g., finding out where to go for a tetanus shot, making an appointment to get one, and keeping the appointment). This provides the possibility of experimenting with various action instructions to discover the most effective form in which they can be delivered.

In one experiment about influencing students to have tetanus shots, five groups were given the following conditions: (1) high fear arousal plus action instructions, (2) low fear arousal plus action instructions, (3) high fear arousal with no action instructions, (4) low fear arousal with no action instructions, and (5) no fear arousal with action instructions.[49] The action instructions were as follows: a map of the local campus was provided with the health service building circled, several examples were given of how one could pass the health service building while changing classes or en route to various buildings, and the student was asked to review his daily schedule and to choose an appropriate time for the tetanus shot.

46. LEVENTHAL, 1970.   *47.* MAUSNER & PLATT, 1968.   *48.* LEVENTHAL, 1970.   *49.* LEVENTHAL, SINGER, & JONES, 1965.

High fear arousal produced favorable attitudes toward getting the tetanus shot, but action instructions had no effect upon attitudes. Favorable attitudes, however, were not enough to induce action; only 3 percent of those not receiving action instructions took the tetanus shots, while 29 percent of those in the high-fear-arousal and low-fear-arousal conditions who also received action instructions took tetanus shots. But action instructions alone were not sufficient to persuade the participants to take tetanus shots: No one who received action instructions without fear arousal took tetanus shots. Thus, while some degree of fear arousal is necessary for action instructions to be effective, compliance does not increase with an increase in fear.

This experiment has important implications for planning influence on behavior. The students who did not receive action instructions nevertheless knew the location of the health center and were capable of getting there. Moreover, those in the high-fear-arousal groups were motivated to get tetanus shots, according to their expression of intention. But few of them did so. The students whose fear was aroused and who were provided with a specific plan which fitted the action into the larger pattern of actions performed during the course of the day, however, did get tetanus shots.

The experiment described above introduced a new action into the student's normal activities. Another study was done to determine the effect of action instructions on an established habit.[50] Its design resembled the previous investigation, but the action instructions consisted of detailed techniques for avoiding the purchase and the smoking of cigarettes. A week after exposure to the fear-arousing communication there were no differences among the groups. But one month later and three months later, appreciably more participants experiencing high or low fear arousal and also receiving action instructions had cut down on smoking. A national survey of smoking behavior complements these results.[51] Neither seeing smoking as a threat nor seeing oneself as a smoker was related to cutting down smoking. But believing that one could control the habit *was* related to a reduction in smoking.

SUMMARY: PERSUASIVENESS OF FEAR-AROUSING APPEALS   Early experimentation reported in the research journals and in the first edition of this book which led to the conclusion that mild fear appeals were more persuasive than strong fear appeals has not been supported by more recent investigations. Later work more often supports the reverse idea: The stronger the fear appeal, the greater the persuasion. Moreover, the idea that fear acts as a drive motivating the respondent to accept the influence attempt is not supported by more recent data.

We have given considerable attention to Leventhal's parallel-response model explanation, which is that there are two independent but interacting reactions to the communication situation. One reaction is to control the fears aroused by

50. LEVENTHAL, WATTS, & PAGANO, 1967.   *51.* HORN, 1968.

the threat: for example, by withdrawing from the situation or by thinking of counterarguments. The other reaction is to cope with the danger: for example, by accepting the effective recommendation of the communication. Either may occur independently of the other: A person may control the fear but not the danger, or vice versa.

A considerable amount of evidence is consistent with the parallel-response model. Where strong fear is aroused and an immediate response is required, the communication is ineffective, presumably because the respondent is busy dealing with the fear. Where it is possible to react at a later time, after the fear has dissipated somewhat, strong fear appeals are more effective. A personality characteristic, self-esteem, enters into this situation. Persons with high self-esteem, apparently able to handle strong fear, do accept the recommendations under the strong fear condition, while those with low self-esteem do not. Another factor that has an effect is that strong fear may be shown to disrupt actions that would otherwise cope with the danger.

Coping with the danger implied by the communication (by such actions as quitting smoking, getting a chest x-ray, or taking a tetanus shot) is affected by several different factors: (1) personality traits of the listeners, (2) other characteristics of participants associated with coping actions, and (3) situational conditions that affect coping. Some persons seem to have a habitual problem-solving or coping orientation to stress or danger, while others avoid or withdraw in the face of danger. These two types of individuals react differently to fear-arousing communications. Persons may also vary in their state of vulnerability to danger; for various reasons some may feel invulnerable to lung cancer, and others, highly vulnerable. Such differences lead them to respond differently to fear communications.

Earlier studies of emotional role playing suggested that smoking behavior was reduced by breaking down the feeling of invulnerability while inducing fear. Recent findings suggest an opposite result: that fear combined with vulnerability inhibits change by focusing on the reduction of fear and thus disrupting coping responses.

Instruction in coping actions has been shown to increase the likelihood of acting on recommendations under certain conditions. These instructions take the form of fitting the recommended actions into the individual's daily routine by tying them in at an appropriate point in sequences or episodes that are regularly enacted in life situations. Action instructions are not usually effective in the absence of any fear arousal or threat, but given some minimal level of arousal, they have a significant impact which is not increased when the intensity of arousal is raised.

Organization of the Message

Persuasiveness is also determined by the way in which a communication is organized. Many aspects of organization have been studied. One question concerns the effect of ignoring the arguments of the opposition as compared with the effect of actively refuting them: Should a communicator present just the arguments in favor of the conclusion he wants the audience to adopt, or should he acknowledge and elaborate some of the counterarguments? Another question is: Should the message draw its own conclusion, or should drawing a conclusion be left to the audience? The *primacy-recency* problem asks the question: Is information presented first or information presented last more effective? Another aspect of message structure is the sequential arrangement of two kinds of elements: (1) those that arouse a need or motive and (2) those that offer a means of satisfying the need. Many communications must include both pro and con arguments; the most effective ways of arranging these have also been studied. Finally, the effects of the individual's desire for knowledge and its relation to the structure of the communication have been investigated. Each of these topics will be considered in this section.

IGNORING COUNTERARGUMENTS VERSUS REFUTING THEM   Everyone is familiar with the high-pressure salesman who presents a wealth of overextended arguments in favor of his product and who will not accept any suggestion that the product might have its limitations. Such a communicator represents the extreme of the one-sided case. To what extent is a one-sided presentation effective? Can the introduction of some arguments opposed to the communicator's position improve his effectiveness in persuading others to accept his influence attempt?

One of the best-known experiments on this topic was conducted during World War II.[52] When Germany surrendered, the military command feared that soldiers in general would fail to appreciate the extensive efforts yet to be expended in defeating Japan.* Most soldiers, they thought, might expect to go home long before they actually could be discharged.

In the process of preparing an information program designed to convince soldiers that a long and hard war with Japan was yet to be fought, social psychologists devised an experiment to compare a one-sided message in which counterarguments are not even mentioned with a message in which arguments on both sides are brought up. The one-sided message mentioned such arguments as the great length of supply lines to allied forces in the Pacific, the resources and stockpiles of Japan, the size and quality of the Japanese army, and the determination of the Japanese people. The two-sided communication discussed these same points, but also acknowledged some factors which would favor a short war, such as allied naval victories and superiority, the previous progress made in a two-front war, Japanese shipping losses, and future damage from air war. Such arguments for the other side were merely acknowledged;

---

* The sudden capitulation of Japan resulting from the atomic bombing was not anticipated at that time.

52. HOVLAND, LUMSDAINE, & SHEFFIELD, 1949.

both messages still predicted a long war of at least two years' duration. These communications were presented in recorded form to different groups of soldiers, whose opinions were determined before and after the communication. A control group received no communication but took the initial and final questionnaires.

The result was that neither the one-sided nor the two-sided message had any overall superiority in changing the attitudes of the soldiers. Both messages lengthened the estimate that soldiers generally made of the duration of the war.

More important was the discovery that the two communications had different effects on soldiers of different levels of education. Among soldiers who had not completed high school, a larger proportion was influenced by the one-sided communication than by the communication acknowledging arguments favoring a long war. Conversely, of those who had been graduated from high school, a larger proportion was influenced by the message acknowledging such arguments. Differences were also apparent according to the initial opinions of the soldiers before exposure to the communication. Those who had originally thought the war would be a short one were more effectively influenced by the two-sided communication, and those who had thought the war would last at least two years were more effectively influenced by the one-sided communication.

Advertising is typically one-sided and rarely contains a negative comment on even a minor aspect of the product. This suggests that it is minimally effective with people who are informed or educated. The inclusion of some negative material in an overall favorable context might well produce higher credibility. One example was found in the caption in an advertisement for the English Ford: "Here's the car with 'the inside door handle too far back—but everything else is wonderful.'"[53] In an experimental attempt to apply the two-sided approach to advertising, Faison prepared one-sided and two-sided commercials on automobiles, gas ranges, and floor wax. These were tested on approximately 500 high school, vocational school, and college students, and it was found that the two-sided commercials produced significantly more attitude change in favor of the product. This change was still present when tested six weeks later. Quite possibly, Volkswagen's use in its advertising of such appellations as "beetle," "bug," "box," and "ugly" represents acknowledgement of a negative side in an attempt to enhance the virtues of that automobile.

One-sided and two-sided communications also differ in their ability to "inoculate" the respondent against later counterpropaganda. In one experiment, the two-sided communication was shown to be dramatically effective in inoculating the audience.[54] Different groups who had heard the argument that Russia would not be able to produce atomic bombs in quantity for at least five years were exposed to a countercommunication at a later date. They differed radically in their receptiveness to the countercommunication, depending upon

53. Faison, 1961.   *54.* Lumsdaine & Janis, 1953.

whether or not the initial message acknowledged counterarguments. Only 2 percent of those who had initially been exposed to a one-sided communication retained the position advocated by that communication, whereas 67 percent of those who had initially been exposed to a communication containing counterarguments retained that communication's position in spite of the subsequent countercommunication.

In other words, the effect of the one-sided communication was entirely wiped out by the countercommunication, but the two-sided communication including counterarguments retained its effect. This is demonstrated by the fact that the acceptance of the initial communication by a control group not exposed to the countercommunication was roughly equal to that for the group exposed to the two-sided communication followed by the countercommunication, namely, 69 percent. The investigators suggest that the presentation of opposing arguments in a context that rejects them weakens their future effectiveness.

Another question concerns the manner in which opposing arguments should be handled. Such arguments may merely be acknowledged, as in the experiments already described; or they may be both acknowledged and actively refuted; or they may be acknowledged and actively refuted, with evidence offered to support the refutation. It is not surprising that attempts to test these different communications experimentally have yielded contradictory results.[55] As McGuire notes, whether to acknowledge or refute counterarguments has rather complex contingencies.[56] Explicitly mentioning opposing arguments might simply suggest reservations that the listener might not otherwise have had, especially if he is less informed and less educated. Or mentioning opposition arguments might suggest that the issue is controversial, and might cast doubts on what the communicator's position really is. We will return to this topic later in our discussion of resistance to persuasion.

ORDER OF PRESENTATION OF SEPARATE COMMUNICATIONS   Besides the question of presenting, acknowledging, and refuting counterarguments, two other questions concerning organization of the communication are: (1) What is the most effective order of presentation of separate communications? (2) What is the most effective ordering of the elements in a communication? A typical example of the first question is whether the first or the second of two political candidates appearing on the same television program has the advantage. The second question has many ramifications. To illustrate one, if a single communication has arguments the audience wants to hear (e.g., taxes can be reduced) and also arguments they are less receptive to (e.g., national defense is weak), in what order should they be arranged.?

An entire volume has been published on order of presentation, and many

55. JANIS, LUMSDAINE, & GLADSTONE, 1951; LUMSDAINE & JANIS, 1953; PAULSON, 1954; THISTLETHWAITE & KAMENETSKY, 1955; THISTLETHWAITE, KAMENETSKY, & SCHMIDT, 1956; LUDLUM, 1958.   56. McGUIRE, 1969.

individual experiments are scattered throughout the research literature. Only the highlights of this topic will be discussed here.[57] A more detailed discussion has been provided by McGuire.[58] In this section we are interested in the primacy-recency question as it applies to successive persuasive communications, as well as to the elements of a single communication.

The question has been raised whether a "law of primacy" applies to persuasive processes. Do initial communications, like first impressions, have a stronger impact than later ones? In 1957 Hovland and Mandell found that although some experiments have yielded significant results in favor of primacy, others have failed to confirm these results and in some instances have favored recency. They suggest that primacy is more likely to occur in an experiment where the classroom instructor is the experimenter. Students may receive the first communication as something to be learned, and the prestige of the instructor is likely to command its acceptance. In this context, the second communication, having a content opposite to the first, is likely to be confusing and therefore is less likely to be accepted. A review by Lana points out that primacy occurs only under certain conditions and that with the present incomplete knowledge, primacy-recency is not entirely predictable from experimental conditions.[59]

Several discussions suggest another reason why primacy-recency investigations of communication often do not yield consistent results.[60] The temporal arrangement of the communications and of the tests measuring the subject's knowledge of the communications is likely to have marked effects upon recall and acceptance of the messages. From extensive experimentation on forgetting, we know that if two communications are equally well learned, the more recent of them will be better remembered. But this difference varies with the interval between presentations and with the interval between the last presentation and the test of recall. As every student studying for his final examinations knows, material learned well early in the term is not recalled as easily as material learned well at the end of the term. He also knows that at the end of the term, there is little difference in recall of material learned in the second and third weeks of the term, even though the latter was more recently learned. Two factors, then, favor recency: (1) a longer interval between successive communications and (2) presentation of a test for retention of the materials immediately after the last communication.

As far as recall is concerned, learning theory predicts a recency effect in the typical experiment on successive persuasive communications. Communications are typically presented in immediate succession, followed by an immediate recall test. Although the successive presentation does not favor either primacy or recency, the immediate recall test favors recency. Thus it is surprising that primacy effects have been attained at all. It is possible that if these experiments had used delayed tests of acceptance and recall, results would have favored

57. HOVLAND, 1957.   58. McGUIRE, 1969.   59. LANA, 1964.   60. BATEMAN & REMMERS, 1941; HOVLAND et al., 1953; MILLER & CAMPBELL, 1959.

primacy to a greater extent than they have. One experiment with persuasive communication confirms a maximum interval between communications and immediacy of the *recall* test as favoring recency.[61] It further demonstrates that a primacy effect occurs on *acceptance* (not recall) of the communication under conditions that minimize recency. Several later investigations provide additional support,[62] although one other study fails to confirm this reasoning.[63]

A final caution should be added. Under nonexperimental conditions, many other factors can enter to affect the relative advantages of being first or last. For example, in a courtroom or in a debate, the second party can modify his presentation to take into account the earlier communication.

Where individuals are not a captive audience, communications that reach them initially may be more effective because they may elect not to attend to later communications that oppose those already accepted. This points up the desirability of being the first to get a message across in a practical situation, but it does not, of course, mean that later communications are "weaker." A possible reason why initial communications may have more effect in a nonexperimental situation is that individuals may make public commitments to a given position after hearing the communication and thus may feel compelled to reject contrary communications.

However, three studies specifically concerned with commitment in the context of primacy and recency provide no support for this suggestion.[64]

ORDERING OF ELEMENTS WITHIN A COMMUNICATION   Many questions arise concerning the arrangements of elements within a communication, but most of these have been little studied. Moreover, findings on this topic are not very consistent, and so we will summarize them very briefly. A more detailed report may be found elsewhere.[65] The communication in which the conclusion is explicitly drawn is usually more effective than the one in which the conclusion is left for the listener to draw. For some individuals, however, and under some conditions, a less explicit communication is more effective. This is likely to occur with highly intelligent recipients who draw the conclusion for themselves.

More relevant to ordering elements within a communication is the question whether drawing the conclusion early or late is more effective. Presenting the conclusion before presenting arguments or supporting evidence could alienate the listener, especially if he is in initial disagreement with it. On the other hand, presenting the conclusion first makes the message clearer and more comprehensible, and indirect evidence favors this path of action.

Where a communication contains some elements that are agreeable to an audience and others that are disagreeable, what order should be used? The communicator could create an initial favorable impression by presenting the agreeable elements first, or he could present them last so that the audience is

61. MILLER & CAMPBELL, 1959.   *62.* INSKO, 1964; ANDERSON, 1972; ANDERSON & HUBERT, 1963.   *63.* SCHULTZ, 1963.   *64.* HOVLAND, CAMPBELL, & BROCK, 1957; LUCHINS, 1957*b*; ANDERSON, 1959.   *65.* MCGUIRE,)969.

left with a favorable feeling. Presentation of the favorable material first is suggested by the idea that the audience would thus be reinforced for listening and paying attention. If the initial material is unpleasant, the audience may develop a set of not attending, so that the later favorable material is not fully picked up. Although the evidence is not entirely consistent, most of it supports presenting the agreeable material first.

Various other considerations involve: (1) presentation of material that arouses a need, followed by other content that satisfies the need, (2) whether to refute counterarguments before or after giving one's own, (3) whether or not to start with the strongest argument, and (4) the degree to which elements should be repeated. Experimentation on these issues is too scanty to produce definite conclusions.

SUMMARY: ORGANIZATION OF THE MESSAGE   Many aspects of the organization of the communication have been studied. One question is whether one-sided or two-sided messages are more effective. No general answer to this has been provided: The relative effectiveness of the two types of communications varies with different conditions. One-sided communications appear to be more effective than two-sided messages if the audience is already in substantial agreement with the communicator or if the audience lacks knowledge concerning the issues and arguments. Two-sided communications also appear to inoculate the person against later counterpropaganda to which he may be exposed. Although communications that draw the conclusion for the audience have been compared with messages that allow the audience to draw its own conclusion, no clear-cut findings in favor of either have emerged.

Two additional questions concerning organization of the communication are: (1) What is the most effective order of presentation of separate communications? (2) What is the most effective order of elements in a communication? The first question has led to a number of experiments to determine whether a message was more effective when it was presented before or after another communication. This is commonly referred to as the primacy-recency question: If the first communication is more effective, the result is referred to as a primacy effect; if the last is more effective, as a recency effect.

A number of methodological problems in this experimentation have made it difficult to determine whether primacy or recency of communication had the advantage. In the typical experiment, the two communications are presented in immediate succession and are followed by an immediate test of recall and of attitude change. Presenting the communications in immediate succession provides little advantage to recency; presenting the test immediately after the last communication clearly favors recency. These effects hold true with respect to the amount of learning of the communication that takes place. They also apply to attitude change resulting from acceptance of the communication, although for acceptance, primacy may be somewhat stronger than recency. Under nonexperimental conditions, primacy is likely to have advantages over recency.

When a communication contains two kinds of elements, one tending to arouse a need and the other tending to satisfy the need, the most effective arrangement presents the need-arousing elements first and the elements providing need satisfaction last.

Communications often contain some arguments (called pro arguments) that favor the communicator's position and other arguments (called con arguments) that are opposed to his position. If the con arguments are nonsalient (not likely to be thought of by the respondent), the most effective sequence in which they may be presented is pro arguments first, con arguments last. This finding is consistent with approach-avoidance concepts derived from learning theory. One experiment viewed arguments as reinforcing for the respondent if they led to favorable consequences, and as punishing for him if they produced unfavorable consequences. Presentation of the favorable arguments first was found to be more effective, a result consistent with the hypothesis that a "habit" of acceptance or rejection is built up, depending upon the order in which arguments are presented.

The Target Person

Last to be considered in the persuasive process but certainly not the least important is the individual who is the target of persuasion. We can think of his role in two partially separate senses: first, his situation vis-à-vis the communicator and, second, the individual characteristics that make him more or less persuasible. The major topics discussed under the first of these views are: (1) the process by which he voluntarily exposes himself to different communicators and topics, (2) the effects of his having an attitude position at a distance from that of the communicator, and (3) the dynamics of resistance to persuasive influence. The extent to which the persuasibility of people is an individual characteristic which is fairly general under different conditions and topics will then be discussed.

Voluntary Exposure to Information

A problem faced by individuals desiring to influence substantial numbers of people is how to reach them. Politicians, educators, and proponents of numerous causes strive to get their message across to people who might give them significant support. But the persons whom the communicator most desperately wishes to reach are the very ones who are most likely not to receive his message. For example, studies of the behavior of voters in election campaigns demonstrate clearly that voters who are already heavily committed to a partisan position are the ones most likely to hear and read campaign speeches.[66]

66. Lazarsfeld, Berelson, & Gaudet, 1948; Berelson, Lazarsfeld, & McPhee, 1954; Campbell et al., 1960; Trenaman & McQuail, 1961.

The process by which an individual exposes himself selectively to communications that are consonant with his attitudes is known as *selective exposure*. This is by no means as straightforward or as simple as it looks. Loyal party voters may pay considerable attention to the opposition. One study, for example, obtained quantitative measures of the number of items read or heard that were favorable to each of the presidential candidates in the 1948 election.[67] Although 54 percent of the Republicans heard or read more items favorable to Dewey, the Republican candidate, 46 percent of them heard or read more items favorable to Truman. That almost one-half of the Republicans were exposed to more items favorable to Truman and to Dewey is more striking when it is considered that total media information disproportionately favored Dewey. These figures suggest that by and large partisans are likely to expose themselves to opposition arguments as well as to partisan ones.

A study of the Nixon-Kennedy television debates conducted during the 1960 election also indicates surprisingly little avoidance of opposing arguments.[68] Since both candidates appeared on the same program, of course, opposing arguments might be somewhat more difficult to avoid than in the case of a program presented by a single candidate. Nevertheless, it would be possible for viewers to attend closely to their candidate and turn their attention to other matters when the opposition candidate appeared. Selective exposure may take place even when the communicator and respondent are in close communication—as every college professor knows through his classroom experience with students. A comparison of the extent to which arguments presented by opposing candidates in the television debates were recalled, however, suggested a minimum of selective exposure, since viewers recalled arguments from both sides equally well. This was true for viewers who said that both candidates made effective arguments and for those who said that only their own candidate made effective arguments. Only viewers who said neither candidate presented effective arguments recalled appreciably more of the arguments of their own candidate than of the opposition.

That the motives underlying voluntary exposure are not merely based on seeking consonant information is well illustrated by a study of participants in the draft-resistance movement.[69] Yale students who opposed signing a pledge that they would go to Vietnam showed little interest in reading antipledge arguments consonant with their position, apparently because they were already very familiar with the arguments. Men favoring signing the pledge were strongly interested in reading antipledge arguments contrary to their position. A series of interviews suggested that the interest of both groups in information contrary to their position was based largely on their desire to be thoroughly familiar with the possible consequences of signing or not signing the pledge.

The data discussed so far have been collected by survey methods. In such studies it is extraordinarily difficult to determine the reasons why people expose

---

67. BERELSON et al., 1954.   *68.* CARTER, 1962.   *69.* JANIS & RAUSCH, 1970.

themselves to some information and not other information. An early assumption was that people chose to listen to or read material that agreed with their beliefs and values, and actively avoided contrary information. As we have just noted, this is not well borne out by all the studies we have cited. Even in those instances where it might appear obvious that people exposed themselves to a communication because they were supporters of it, other interpretations remain possible. For example, groups differ in level of education, social class, and income, all characteristics that may produce the same effects as selective exposure, but which have not always been controlled.

Because of these difficulties in interpreting field studies, social psychologists turned to the laboratory in an attempt to understand better the factors controlling voluntary exposure. At about the time of this move, dissonance theory emerged as a popular framework for conducting laboratory experiments. This led to what has in retrospect turned out to be an undue emphasis upon the idea of *selective avoidance* of persuasive communications that are dissonant with the position one has committed oneself to. A few early studies supported the idea that individuals avoid material that is dissonant with a position they have just committed themselves to, and expose themselves to material consonant with that position. As additional laboratory evidence accumulated, however, the opposite conclusions were often supported by the data, and the total data are highly inconsistent and inconclusive. (Several reviews of these investigations have been made.[70])

The search for the factors that govern exposure to persuasive communications has thus been broadened to examine motives other than seeking consonant information and avoiding dissonant material. Sears has noted that in life situations, supportive or consonant information is much more abundant than dissonant material, so that even random choice would mostly select supportive information.[71] Another factor that does seem important in some situations is the utility of the information: People do sometimes seek information that is useful to them. This information may agree or disagree with their own position, depending upon circumstances.

Research supports the importance of utility. Women were offered a choice between a talk dealing with environmental factors and one on hereditary factors in child behavior. The former is more usable, and was preferred by a three-to-one margin.[72] Another study, in which housewives were offered a pamphlet on toilet training, demonstrated that those who had an infant in the pertinent age bracket most often requested it and actually read it.[73]

Several more recent studies create conditions that make information useful and demonstrate that useful information is preferred. Two investigations told participants either that they would have to present reasons for choosing a

70. Freedman & Sears, 1965; Rhine, 1967; Mills, 1968; Sears, 1968; Katz, 1968; McGuire, 1968; McGuire, 1969; Sears & Abeles, 1969; Fishbein & Ajzen, 1972.   *71.* Sears, 1968.   *72.* Adams, 1961. *73.* Maccoby, Maccoby, Romney, & Adams, 1961.

particular article (thus making supportive information more useful) or that they would have to engage in a debate to rebut arguments on the opposing side (favoring nonsupportive information).[74] Participants were found to choose the articles that were more useful to them, independently of whether they were supportive of or opposed to their own position. Another investigation varied utility by having different participants (1) choose to receive information by mail, (2) anticipate joining a discussion group after receiving information, or (3) anticipate engaging in a debate after receiving information.[75] Interest in supportive information was greatest when the participant expected to debate. We may expect that information on both sides will have less utility if a person's decision is irreversible than if he is still able to change his mind. This has also been demonstrated experimentally.[76]

Not all the evidence for utility is positive.[77] Various studies support the idea that novelty is important; moreover, the overall context in which the information is to be received has been given some attention. Presentation of strong one-sided information followed by the opportunity to obtain additional information resulted in a strong preference for information on the other side.[78] For example, the information that made a person seem clearly guilty (or clearly innocent) of a murder was followed by a preference for additional available information that countered the initial evaluation. To some degree, however, choice of material depends upon the amount of information a person has. Informed participants prefer communications opposite to their position and naïve ones favor communications supportive of their stand.[79]

In sum, the view that voluntary exposure to persuasive communication is based primarily upon the desire to find material supportive of one's attitudes and to avoid contrary information has little basis in fact and is a gross oversimplification of the motivations that people have in seeking information. The tenacity of this view in the face of accumulating negative evidence in part reflects the desire of research investigators to find simplifying principles supported by hard evidence. But inevitably this approach does not do justice to the nature of man; it postulates a rather mechanical response to a single characteristic of the stimulus situation.

More recent experimentation has recognized to a greater extent the complexity of information exposure and has identified a variety of factors that operate under some circumstances. Supportive material is more abundant in life situations than in the laboratory, and thus people are more exposed to it for that reason alone. The degree to which information fits some purpose of the recipient appears to be important. This usefulness outweighs considerations of consonance or dissonance as where, for example, a person needs material for purposes of argument or debate, or where he has made a tentative decision that

---

74. CANON, 1964; FREEDMAN, 1965.   75. CLARKE & JAMES, 1967.   76. LOWE & STEINER, 1968.   77. BROCK & BALLOUN, 1967; BROCK, ALBERT, & BECKER, 1970.   78. FREEDMAN, 1965; SEARS, 1965, 1966; ROSNOW, GITTER, & HOLZ, 1969.   79. SEARS & ABELES, 1969.

can still be reversed. One's store of information affects future choice in several ways. Material that is familiar is less interesting and less sought. Novel information is often preferred. Moreover, if a person is in possession of markedly one-sided information, he may often be receptive to receiving material counter to his present knowledge. A suggestive general notion for future research is that the use to which information will be put is the guiding principle in its reception or rejection.

Distance between Source and Target Person

The discussion of one-sided communication noted that individuals who were initially opposed to the position taken by the communicator were more influenced by a message that acknowledged counterarguments. Conversely, those who were in essential agreement with the position of the communicator were more influenced by a one-sided message. Thus, the reaction of the recipient is markedly affected by the discrepancy (or correspondence) between the communicator's position and his own.

Sherif and his colleagues have systematically analyzed effects of discrepancies between the position of the communicator and that of the recipient.[80] In the first place, the position of the communicator as perceived by the respondent is not necessarily the same as his position as determined by social consensus. The experiments reported demonstrate the operation of systematic biases or distortions. Two major processes are *assimilation* and *contrast*.

A respondent whose own position is relatively close to that of the communicator is likely to perceive the communicator's position as even closer than it is: This is the *assimilation* effect. But a respondent having a position rather distant from that of the communicator is likely to see the communicator's position as even more distant: This is the *contrast* effect. Experimental work has confirmed these effects. Thus the respondent's *perception* of the position of the communicator must be taken into account in determining the potential effect of the communication upon the respondent.

Whether a communication is seen as fair and unbiased is related to the distance between the position of the communicator and that of the respondent. For each respondent and each issue, there is a range within which the position of the communicator can differ from that of the respondent and still be evaluated as fair and unbiased. Positions outside that range will not be favorably evaluated by the recipient. A similar range exists for rejection of the communication.

This is illustrated by an experiment in which a nonauthoritarian communication intended to reduce prejudice slightly increased prejudice of individuals high in authoritarianism, and an authoritarian communication intended to increase prejudice slightly reduced prejudice of individuals extremely low in au-

---

80. Sherif & Hovland, 1961; Sherif, Sherif, & Nebergall, 1965; Sherif & Sherif, 1967.

thoritarianism. This reverse outcome has been termed the *boomerang effect*. (Authoritarianism is highly correlated with prejudice.) In both cases where the respondent moved in a direction *opposite* to the communication, his own initial position and that of the communicator were at a considerable distance from each other.

The relation between an individual's own stand and his evaluation of a communication is also well illustrated by an experiment conducted in a region where prohibition was a lively topic of discussion.[81] It had recently been submitted in a referendum to the voters of Oklahoma, where legal prohibition of alcoholic beverages was optional for each county. The term *dry* will be used to refer to a stand favoring prohibition and the term *wet* to a stand favoring unrestricted sale of alcoholic beverages. The sample of persons tested included some with extremely dry positions, such as the members of the Woman's Christian Temperance Union. Comparable extremes at the wet end of the attitude continuum were more difficult to obtain, but the investigators selected some individuals, mostly college students, through personal acquaintance.

Each individual's own position was assessed by means of a set of attitude statements ranging from extremely dry positions to extremely wet positions. Then a five-item scale was used to determine each respondent's evaluation of the fairness and impartiality of communications having three different positions. A very close relation was found between the evaluation of a statement and its distance from the position of the respondent. For example, the extremely wet statement was evaluated most favorably by the respondents who themselves favored an extremely wet position. As the stand of the respondent deviated from an extremely wet position, he evaluated the extremely wet statement less favorably. Those having extremely dry positions, for example, regarded the extremely wet statement as completely unfair and biased. Similar results were obtained for an extremely dry statement: The closer the respondent's own stand to that of the statement, the more favorably he evaluated it. Finally, a statement having a moderately wet position was most favorably evaluated by respondents holding a similar position.

To review, then: Latitudes of acceptance and rejection vary depending upon whether the issue is a familiar or an unfamiliar one, whether the issue is one in which the respondents are especially interested and involved, whether the communicator has high or low credibility, and whether the facts on the issue are ambiguous or clear. In the study just discussed, ranges of acceptance were relatively narrow because of high involvement and familiarity. These same factors *broaden* the range of *rejection*.

So far we have focused on the evaluation of the communication. While a favorable evaluation implies that more attitude change will occur, the relation of attitude change to the degree of discrepancy between source and target person must be examined directly. Several studies indicate that where credibil-

81. Hovland, Harvey, & Sherif, 1957.

ity is high, the amount of attitude change is a direct function of the discrepancy, over a wide range.[82] At quite extreme ranges, less persuasion occurs, under certain conditions.[83]

One other important condition affecting the relation between discrepancy and attitude change is the degree of involvement that the target person feels in the issue. The voting studies referred to earlier (under Voluntary Exposure to Information) illustrate the effect of high involvement. Most voters feel very strongly on the issue of party affiliation and vote accordingly. Because of this high involvement, the latitude of acceptance of political communications that deviate from one's own position is very narrow and the latitude of rejection is broad. These concepts are consistent with the findings of voting studies that political communications produce very little change in the positions of the voters.

The implications of these ideas are that on issues of great personal concern to individuals, and where the credibility of the communicator is not great, the communicator's message must not deviate very far from the position held by his respondents if he is to be successful at all. If he wishes to change their position markedly, he apparently will be able to do so only in a series of communications, each moving the respondent a small distance at a time. On the other hand, if an issue is of little concern to a recipient, and the communicator is highly credible, a communicator is likely to induce change more effectively if his position is more distant from that of the respondent.

A laboratory experiment was designed to test this notion.[84] Because of the laboratory setup, the communicator was highly credible, and issues such as the desirability of compulsory voting and the adequacy of five hours of sleep per night were chosen so that subjects would not feel high personal involvement. It was found that the greater the discrepancy between the position of the communicator and that of the recipient, the more the recipient was influenced. In other words, the greater the amount of change advocated by the communicator, the greater the change in the respondent's attitude. This conclusion applies only where all conditions favor a very wide latitude of acceptance, as in this experiment.

The effects of discrepancy are complicated by factors which reduce the latitude of acceptance. If the issue is one in which the participant is ego-involved, the discrepant attitude positions that he will accept fall within a much narrower range than if he does not care about the issue. Under conditions of low ego involvement, the prediction is that moderate discrepancy between the position of the communicator and that of the respondent will produce more change than low discrepancy, but large discrepancies will produce less change than

82. BERGIN, 1962; ARONSON, TURNER, & CARLSMITH, 1963; BOCHNER & INSKO, 1966.   *83.* HOVLAND, HARVEY, & SHERIF, 1957; FISHER & LUBIN, 1958; WHITTAKER, 1964a, 1964b; INSKO, MURASHIMA, & SAIYADAIN, 1966.   *84.* HOVLAND & PRITZKER, 1957.

moderate ones.[85] Although complicating circumstances produce inconsistent results, by and large this prediction is supported by experimental data.[86]

As compared with high credibility, medium or low credibility of the communicator is also likely to have an effect similar to high ego involvement: The discrepancy increases attitude change only up to a point.[87]

In sum, the evaluation of a communication is related to the perceived distance between the positions of the communicator and the respondent. For each respondent and each issue, there is a range within which the position of the communicator can differ from that of the respondent and still be evaluated as fair and unbiased. These latitudes of acceptance and rejection vary depending upon whether the issue is a familiar or an unfamiliar one, whether it is one in which respondents are especially interested and involved, whether the communicator has high or low credibility, and whether the facts on the issue are ambiguous or clear. Thus, if a communicator is to be successful he must make sure that his position is within the respondent's range of acceptance.

The need for being within the range of acceptance creates something of a dilemma for the communicator whose position is quite distant from that of the respondent. How is he to avoid being rejected? One suggestion comes from a field study using a "foot-in-the-door" technique.[88] The investigators precede a large request, likely to be refused, by a small request to see if this later produces more acceptance of the large request. While not concerned with attitude change, the study suggests that a series of small influence attempts might move a person by degrees to an appreciable change from his initial position.

In this investigation, the main objective of the interviewer was to convince women that he interviewed in their homes to allow large safe-driving signs to be installed on their lawns for a week or more. He showed the women a picture of a rather poorly lettered sign installed in front of an attractive house so that it obscured much of the house and the front entrance. Depending upon the treatment to which they were assigned, some women had been previously visited by a different interviewer and asked either to install a small safe-driving sign (3 inches square) in the window, or to sign a petition to "keep California beautiful." Of a control group that had no previous contact, 17 percent agreed to accept the large safe-driving sign. But 76 percent of the women who had accepted the small sign later accepted the large sign, and 49 percent of those who had signed the (unrelated) petition accepted the sign.

Thus, having acceded previously to a request by an interviewer greatly increased acceptance of a later, larger request. This does not seem to be due to becoming involved in the issue (at least not wholly) because accepting an unrelated influence attempt also increases later acceptance. The investigators sug-

85. SHERIF, SHERIF, & NEBERGALL, 1965.   86. ZIMBARDO, 1960; FREEDMAN, 1964; JOHNSON & SCILEPPI, 1969; RHINE & SEVERANCE, 1970.   87. BOCHNER & INSKO, 1966; JOHNSON & SCILEPPI, 1969; RHINE & SEVERANCE, 1970.   88. FREEDMAN & FRASER, 1966.

gest that what may occur is a more general change in the person's feeling about taking action on things he believes in, about cooperating with good causes. More research is needed to identify the precise mechanisms, but the trend is clear.

Susceptibility to Persuasion

Persons differ markedly in their susceptibility to persuasive communications. That some people, but not all, are "pushovers" for sales pitches is common knowledge. Advertising is more likely to be believed by some people than by others. In interpersonal situations, some persons may be readily persuaded to go along with the suggestions of their friends or associates, while others stubbornly "stick to their guns." Many students accept uncritically much that their professor tells them; others critically examine his ideas.

Or *are* people as consistently resistant or persuasible as we ordinarily assume? Perhaps we observe only selected instances where a person yields, and fail to notice those where he resists, and vice versa. By persuasibility, we mean the tendency of an individual to accept or reject persuasive communications. One of the questions we must answer is whether the persuasibility of an individual on different topics and situations is general. Is his persuasibility relative to other persons for these different occasions roughly the same?

Several studies have examined the extent to which persuasibility is consistent, not only on different topics, but for different types of appeals as well (e.g., rational versus emotional).[89] In general, these studies imply that the degree to which a person is persuasible is somewhat consistent for different topics and appeals, including those that agree with or run counter to his attitudes and those on which he has considerable knowledge or little knowledge.

At the same time, these studies also reveal considerable individual variability in response to these different aspects of communication situations. Even though a person's *average* level of persuasibility in many situations may be appreciably higher than the average level of most persons, he may show a fairly wide range of responsiveness to communication situations differing in the respects that have been enumerated. Because of this variability, measures intended to represent individual levels of persuasibility should consist of a composite score for each person based on a variety of topics and appeals. The vast inconsistencies among studies of the relation between personality and persuasibility suggest that the effects of personality on persuasibility are usually mediated by a host of situational and other conditions that must be considered in any adequate account. Most of the discussion below will follow McGuire's excellent analysis calling attention to these factors.[90]

---

89. JANIS & HOVLAND, 1959; JANIS & FIELD, 1956; ABELSON & LESSER, 1959; LINTON & GRAHAM, 1959.
90. MCGUIRE, 1968.

INTELLIGENCE AND SUSCEPTIBILITY TO PERSUASION   Common sense suggests that the more intelligent person would be less susceptible to persuasive communications than the less intelligent person. Presumably the more intelligent person would be more critical of a propaganda message, for example, because he is usually more informed and because he has a superior understanding of the logic of arguments and an ability to weigh evidence. Yet, early studies reported up to 1937 showed almost no correlation between resistance to persuasive communications and intelligence level.[91]

A review by Hovland and his colleagues of more recent studies indicates, however, that intelligence is positively associated with resistance to some types of communications and negatively associated with resistance to other types.[92] These reviewers suggest that studies are contradictory or inconclusive because the various components of intelligence have different implications for reaction to persuasive communications.

Extending this view, McGuire has identified several components occurring in response to a persuasive communication.[93] If we consider only two components—*yielding* to the persuasive attempt, and the extent to which the message is *attended to and grasped*—we can easily see that intelligence can have opposite effects for these components. The more intelligent a person, the more confidence he would have in his beliefs, the more critical he would be, and the better able he would be to develop counterarguments. Thus, in terms of yielding, more intelligent people would appear to be less susceptible than less intelligent people.

But in terms of ability to attend to and comprehend a set of arguments, the intelligent individual would also be superior. In terms of this component, the intelligent person might be more readily influenced because he comprehends the persuasive message better. McGuire notes that in experiments where the communication is simple to grasp, intelligent people are more apt to be resistant. Where the message is complex, they may well be more susceptible. Whether intelligence is positively or negatively related to persuasibility therefore depends on the extent to which the communication situation emphasizes yielding or comprehension.

PERSUASIBILITY AND OTHER PERSONALITY CORRELATES   Investigators have attempted to demonstrate a relation between persuasibility and a host of personality characteristics, some relatively enduring and others fairly temporary (e.g., chronic anxiety versus situational anxiety). Among the characteristics studied have been self-esteem, aggressiveness, neurotic defensiveness, perceptual dependence, inner-directedness and other-directedness, authoritarianism, dogmatism, social isolation, richness of fantasy, and sex. Virtually without exception,

91. MURPHY, MURPHY, & NEWCOMB, 1937.   *92.* HOVLAND, JANIS, & KELLEY, 1953; HOVLAND & JANIS, 1959.   *93.* McGUIRE, 1968.

no strong and consistently substantiated relations between these characteristics and persuasibility have been found.

Paradoxically, this does not mean that personality plays no part in whether people may be successfully persuaded. What it does mean is that we should not look for simple relations between personality and persuasibility. Instead, persuasibility is complicated by a host of conditional factors in which personality probably does often play an important role. This section is an explanation in nontechnical language of some of the complicating factors that have been noted by McGuire and by others.[94] Many of these explanations represent compelling logical possibilities although they have not yet been demonstrated by empirical study.

We have already noted the yielding and comprehension components of the persuasive process that potentially operate in the case of intelligence. These can also cause complications in the case of some personality characteristics. For example, we might expect people with high self-esteem to learn a message more readily than people with low self-esteem, since low self-esteem is associated with distractibility, lack of intelligence, and social withdrawal. But because people with high self-esteem are also more independent, they are less likely to yield to persuasive arguments. Thus the relation would vary with messages of differing complexity. Moreover, persuasive situations that vary in compulsion may complicate the issue further. Where the situation is highly compelling, individual variations in the tendency to yield are less important, and learning the message is more important.

Situational (temporary) and chronic (enduring) personality characteristics may also be confused. Some studies induce varying levels of self-esteem by manipulating success or failure experiences, and then measure persuasibility. While one might expect situational and chronic characteristics to complement each other and yield similar results, McGuire has noted a number of reasons why the results might instead be inconsistent.[95] The situational condition, for example, may be considerably weaker than the chronic one (the hyperanxiety of some individuals is difficult to reproduce in the laboratory and is contraindicated for ethical reasons as well).

Chronic personality attributes are almost always correlated with other attributes that may be responsible for the results instead of the trait focused on. Situational attributes do not have this shortcoming, if good experimental design is used. Another related factor is the possibility that personality states produced in the laboratory may be less than authentic, differing in important ways from the chronic trait. McGuire's review of the empirical findings about the relation of persuasibility to situational and to chronic self-esteem supports the hypothesis that these factors may be important sources of confusion.[96]

Various other situational complications can have an effect. Some personality attributes relate more to the communicator or source than to the yielding or

94. McGuire, 1968.   95. McGuire, 1968.   96. McGuire, 1968.

comprehension component of persuasion. The level of self-esteem of the recipient may render him differently susceptible to communicators varying in status (e.g., an individual with low self-esteem is apt to be considerably affected by a high-status communicator). The authoritarianism of the recipient is also apt to have complex interrelations with the status and authority of the communicator.

Factors in the message itself have an effect on some personality characteristics. The best example of this was brought out above in describing the extensive research on variation in the amounts of fear aroused by communications. Self-esteem, chronic anxiety level, coping ability, and feelings of vulnerability, to name a few attributes, all moderate the effects of fear on persuasion.

Little is known of the effects of media factors. But it is even possible that different relations between persuasibility and personality would be found using different media of communication—with a special contrast between face-to-face communication and impersonal media. Finally, there are a host of technical problems in studying the relation between persuasibility and personality that might produce misleading results. One example is that although one might expect a negative relation between persuasibility and the aggressiveness of the recipient, Janis and Rife point out that the usual measures of aggressiveness are self-inventories, and on such instruments, aggressive people, because they are also apt to be defensive, may refrain from endorsing items that reveal their aggressiveness.[97]

SUMMARY: SUSCEPTIBILITY TO PERSUASION   The discussion has made clear that individual susceptibility to persuasion depends upon complex factors that make it difficult to draw generalizations. The empirical fact is that people who are consistently persuasible or consistently resistant to different communications and in different situations have been hard to find. A speculative analysis by McGuire suggests that, in part, this is due to the multiple components involved in reactions to communications. For example, it has been possible to demonstrate that only three components—yielding to the persuasive communication, comprehending the communication, and the complexity of the communication—are sufficient to predict both positive and negative associations between the intelligence of the recipient and his acceptance of the communication. Similar complications are demonstrated for personality characteristics. A further complication lies in the different effects of situational (temporary) and chronic (enduring) attributes upon persuasibility.

Processes of Resistance to Change

In the twentieth century a tremendous number of communications barrages the average person from every side; some authorities have expressed serious doubts that he will be able to retain his identity and independence. Both classic and

97. JANIS & RIFE, 1959.

contemporary science fiction have repeatedly pictured a future world in which communication systems are used to conduct surveillance and control the citizens. Although it is undoubtedly true that modern technology has scored considerable gains in both distributing and monitoring information, and also that modern man is subjected to many more influence attempts than his predecessor, the individual today still has many resources at his command for resisting influence in all but the most rigid, totalitarian societies.

The opposite of selective exposure may be a source of resistance: The individual can often selectively *avoid* communications. Often people can tune to another channel or turn to another page. Even in the immediate presence of visual or audio information, they can be nonattentive, fail to absorb the message, or learn it in a distorted form. Moreover, certain group processes, discussed in Chapter 5, can be used to resist influence. This section discusses various cognitive and motivational processes that often result in failure of a message to persuade the receiver.

COGNITIVE BALANCING AS A DEFENSIVE PROCESS   Resistance to attitude change may be conceptualized in terms of the need of the organism to retain a state of consonance, cognitive balance, congruity, or consistency. In this view, any persuasive communication that is dissonant with existing attitudes will arouse defensive reactions. Most of the psychologists who have a theory based on consistency have dealt with this problem of defensive reactions. A number of processes suggested by Abelson may be used for illustrative purposes.[98] Rosenberg and Abelson have further elaborated and formalized these processes.[99]

Essentially, their system states that cognitive elements have either a positive or a negative value and that, in addition, the relation between elements may be either positive or negative. Thus, such concepts as *mother, money,* and *God* have positive values for most persons, and *death, injury,* and *imprisonment* have negative values. Positive relations between elements are illustrated by such terms as *likes, helps, is consistent with;* while negative relations are depicted by such terms as *dislikes, fights, opposes, is inconsistent with.* A *balanced* state exists under the following conditions:

1. Two positive elements have a positive relation. Example: My best friend (+) won (+) a prize (+).

2. Two negative elements have a positive relation. Example: A corrupt judge (−) has been indicted (+) for accepting bribes (−).

3. A positive element and a negative element have a negative relation. Example: The district attorney (+) has been fighting (−) corruption by unscrupulous city officials (−).

An *unbalanced* state exists under the following conditions:

1. A positive element is negatively related to another positive element. Ex-

98. ABELSON, 1959.   *99.* ROSENBERG & ABELSON, 1960.

ample: My best friend (+) has received only rejection slips (−) for his latest novel which is excellent (+).

2. Two negative elements have a negative relation. Example: My worst enemy (−) was robbed (−) by some burglars (−).

3. A positive element and a negative element have a positive relation. Example: My best friend (+) likes (+) my worst enemy (−).

States of imbalance are regarded as disturbing and are likely to be resolved by various means. They are referred to as *belief dilemmas* because of the lack of balance. In the examples given, this view seems intuitively correct except for the second unbalanced example, which does not seem disturbing or to require resolution. This example indicates that imbalance is not always clear for the case having three negative signs. Abelson has suggested some modes of resolving belief dilemmas, including the following[100]:

1. Denial. Denial is the simplest mode of resolving a belief dilemma. The value of an object is denied or declared to be opposite, or the sign of the relation is explained away, as illustrated in Figure 4-1. For example, the heavy cigarette smoker values smoking positively but lung cancer negatively. A communication linking smoking with lung cancer is likely to be resisted because it creates imbalance. Denial can be used to explain away the positive relation between lung cancer and smoking by suggesting that this correlational finding does not demonstrate cause and effect, or that the evidence for the relation is insufficient. Another less likely mode of resolution through denial shifts the value of smoking from positive to negative.

2. Bolstering. One of the two objects involved in a particular case may be additionally supported by relating it to other cognitive objects in a balanced way, as illustrated in Figure 4-2. For example, the smoker who is anxious about lung cancer may tell himself that smoking is extremely enjoyable, soothes his nerves, and adds to his social life. The imbalance between lung cancer and smoking is not eliminated, but the total balance in the system of related elements is improved. This mechanism is very similar to Festinger's notion, discussed in Chapter 3, of adding new cognitive elements to reduce dissonance.

100. ABELSON, 1959.

Figure 4-1   Achievement of balance through denial. *An imbalanced structure may be converted to a balanced one by changing one of the elements or the relation between them. (Adapted with permission from R. P. Abelson. Modes of resolution of belief dilemmas.* Journal of Conflict Resolution, *1959, 3, 343–352.)*

Original imbalanced structures   Balanced structures

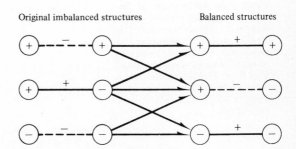

Figure 4-2 Reduction of imbalance through bolstering. *In the bolstered structure the units AC, AD, and AE are all balanced. The relative effect of the imbalanced unit AB is thus reduced. (Adapted with permission from R. P. Abelson. Modes of resolution of belief dilemmas. Journal of Conflict Resolution, 1959, **3**, 343–352.)*

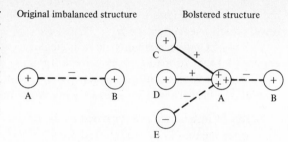

Original imbalanced structure   Bolstered structure

3. *Differentiation.* Denial and bolstering are defenses that preserve the identity of the elements. Differentiation restores balance by splitting an element into two parts that have a negative relation to each other, as illustrated in Figure 4-3. For example, construction of nuclear power plants is positively valued by many people as desirable for alleviating a severe power shortage, but negatively valued because of the dangers of radiation and pollution. For people with both these values, there is imbalance in the proposition that nuclear power plants be constructed. This imbalance could be resolved by differentiating the attitude object into two parts: constructing nonpolluting power plants, and constructing polluting power plants. The lung cancer problem provides a similar example: Smoking can be differentiated into smoking ordinary cigarettes and smoking filter cigarettes. If a person believes that filter cigarettes protect against lung cancer, he can restore balance by smoking them.

Thus, when cognitive balance or consistency is threatened by a persuasive communication, the individual has a variety of resources for restoring balance without yielding to the pressure exerted by the communication.

IMMUNIZATION AGAINST COUNTERPROPAGANDA   Some early work suggested that when a communication is anxiety-arousing, it may produce defenses that cause future exposure to similar communications to result in less anxiety and little attitude change. In one experiment, conducted before there was any public knowledge that the Soviet Union had produced an atomic bomb, an experi-

Figure 4-3 Achievement of balance through differentiation. *One element is split into two which have opposite signs, both possessing balanced relations with the remaining element. (Adapted with permission from R. P. Abelson. Modes of resolution of belief dilemmas. Journal of Conflict Resolution, 1959, **3**, 343–352.)*

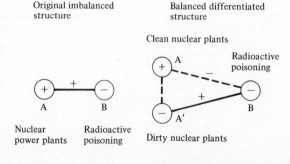

Original imbalanced structure   Balanced differentiated structure

mental group was given a pessimistic communication about the atomic bomb—
that Russia already had an atomic bomb, had atomic factories, etc.[101] Control
groups did not receive this communication. Some months later, President Truman announced that Russia did in fact have an atomic bomb. The reactions of
the experimental and the control groups to this announcement were immediately studied and compared. The group that had already been told Russia had
the atomic bomb reacted to Truman's message with less concern and worry
than the groups whose first knowledge came from the President's message.

The investigators suggested that a form of "emotional inoculation" takes
place when a fear-arousing communication is first presented and that later
communications become less effective as a result. Apparently, various defensive
reactions of the individual come into play as a result of the arousal of fear.
Studies of the intensive and persistent bombing raids in Britain, Germany, and
Japan during World War II similarly suggest that, although at first the average
citizen is greatly frightened, he later becomes relatively inured to subsequent
raids.[102]

A more systematic series of experiments examines a quite different but related idea: Defenses developed for a belief may serve as inoculation against
counterpropaganda. When a belief is widespread in a society, so that the individual is unlikely to encounter contradictory evidence or opinions, the belief
will yield readily to a strong persuasive attack. The reasoning behind this is
that under such circumstances the individual has had no occasion for developing resistance to countercommunications or for thinking of arguments in support of his belief. But if, before an attack upon the belief, arguments against it
are presented in weakened form, he should develop some resistance to future
attacks. The more such arguments lead to active formulation of defenses
against them, the better the individual will be immunized against further attacks.

In the first study designed to examine these ideas, four beliefs about health
were chosen, including "The effects of penicillin have been, almost without
exception, of great benefit to mankind," and "Most forms of mental illness are
not contagious."[103] Each person was put through two experimental sessions—
first, an immunizing session, and second, a test session. In the first session,
persons in the control group received no treatment; others received various
forms of treatment intended to immunize them against later attack. Immunization procedures included active defenses such as writing an essay providing
arguments in support of or refuting arguments against the belief, and passive
defenses such as reading an essay provided by the experimenter which either
defended or supplied weak arguments refuting the belief.

In the test session, strong arguments against the belief were presented. The
results were in accord with the predictions. When the initial beliefs had not
received any immunization treatment, they were appreciably weakened by the

101. JANIS, LUMSDAINE, & GLADSTONE, 1951.   *102.* JANIS, 1951.   *103.* MCGUIRE & PAPAGEORGIS,
1961.

strong counterarguments in the test session. Initial beliefs that had received *supportive* arguments in the immunizing session were further strengthened by these arguments; but when they were subsequently exposed to counterarguments, the initial beliefs were weakened virtually as much as if they had received no supportive treatment. In contrast, initial beliefs that had been immunized by exposure to weak counterarguments were less influenced by subsequent strong counterarguments—demonstrating that the beliefs had acquired some immunity to countercommunications.

A further experiment determined that exposure to weak counterarguments created resistance not only to the specific counterarguments later presented in a stronger form, but also to alternative arguments not introduced as a part of the immunization procedure.[104] This effect occurs presumably because exposure to *any* counterarguments is likely to lead the recipient to think up a variety of supporting arguments for his belief, including some which will enable him to resist counterarguments he has not yet heard. This defensive process is probably effective also because it produces lower credibility toward later countercommunications—that is, it produces a larger number of cognitive elements dissonant with the later communication.

That active defense produces the most general immunization is indicated by another condition varied in this and a subsequent experiment.[105] When a recipient exposed to weak counterarguments was required to compose an essay actively defending his belief, the immunization process applied to novel counterarguments as well as to the original ones. But when the individual was required only to read an essay defending his beliefs, the immunization effect did not generalize to new arguments. Finally, a study by McGuire demonstrated that active refutation also establishes resistance that persists over a longer period of time than resistance established by mere exposure to supporting arguments, and that this persistence also applies to counterarguments other than the ones explicitly refuted.[106] Thus exposure that generates an active process of defense rather than a passive one is likely to provide the most general form of immunity to counterarguments. Resistance to the counterarguments is equally strong immediately after and two days after the initial communication is delivered. Seven days later, resistance has weakened somewhat, but is still appreciable. A later study demonstrated that active participation in the communication process, although not immediately effective, produced more attitude change six weeks later.[107] Further, presenting a communication discrepant with the recipient's position and including at least one counterargument stimulates the production by the recipient of more counterarguments; moreover, high communicator competence inhibits the production of counterarguments.[108]

A qualification must be entered here. While it is absolutely clear that the presentation of information contrary to attitude results in more resistance to

---

104. Papageorgis & McGuire, 1961.   *105.* McGuire, 1961.   *106.* McGuire, 1962.   *107.* Watts, 1967.   *108.* Cook, 1969.

contrary information presented later, the mechanism of counterargument has not been definitely identified. A review of these studies and consideration of other possible mechanisms makes clear that some means of detecting the presence of counterarguing must be found if this explanation is to be convincing.[109] The difficulty arises from the fact that thinking of counterarguments is ordinarily a covert, unobservable process, and that certain types of attempts to measure it may well produce it, even though it was not present before the measurement attempt. Nevertheless, the idea of inoculation appears to be strongly supported, and the development of counterarguments appears to be the best available explanation at the moment.

If we may assume that these findings hold generally, they have very important implications. The central values of American culture might be readily susceptible to change if forcible exposure to counterarguments occurred, simply because no defenses have been developed against attacks on these values. Thus, belief in a democratic government, virtually universal among Americans, may well be susceptible to change in a situation where an American is isolated from his fellow believers and exposed to counterarguments—as in Korean prison camps where the Chinese Communists used intensive brainwashing procedures. The experimental work on inoculation suggests that challenging the concepts and principles of democracy will force the individual to develop defenses and will thus build resistance to such attacks.

109. MILLER & BARON, 1973.

5

Mass Communication and the Social Structure

Previous chapters have focused primarily upon the individual, discussing his persuasibility, its relation to his personality, and internal processes such as dissonance and consistency. This treatment may have created a picture of persuasive communication as a process that occurs between a single communicator and a single recipient. Such indeed was the conception of mass communication held by many observers in the decades before World War II, a conception well characterized by Katz and Lazarsfeld:

> Their image, first of all, was of an atomistic mass of millions of readers, listeners and movie-goers prepared to receive the Message; and secondly, they pictured every Message as a direct and powerful stimulus to action which would elicit immediate response. In short, the media of communication were looked upon as a new kind of unifying force—a simple kind of nervous system—reaching out to every eye and ear, in a society characterized by an amorphous social organization and a paucity of interpersonal relations.[1]

Thus each individual was visualized as sitting before his television set or reading his newspaper and responding to the message in a manner having little to do with the rest of his life or his relations to other persons and groups. This is a false image of the communication process. Research has made abundantly clear that the effects of a communication depend upon the respective places of

---

1. Reprinted by permission from E. KATZ & P. F. LAZARSFELD, *Personal influence.* Chicago: The Free Press of Glencoe, Ill., 1955. P. 16.

Figure 5-1 Two views of mass communication.

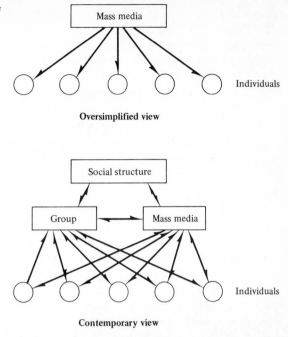

the communicator and the respondent in the structure of society and upon their immediate relations to other persons and groups. These two views of mass communication are presented schematically in Figure 5-1.

Survey versus Laboratory Studies

A comparison of survey studies of the effects of mass media such as radio and television with investigations of the communication process in the experimental laboratory illustrates the importance of the social structure in the communication process. Laboratory studies have several characteristics: They use communications constructed to suit the experiment; the issues they cover are not of vital concern to the respondents and sometimes are not current; and the audience is a captive one, frequently consisting of college or high school students.

Survey studies, on the other hand, attempt to determine the effects of actual communications in the mass media, such as the effects of a political campaign upon voter preferences, and they use a representative sample of the population. For example, one common procedure used in survey studies of voting is the *panel technique*.[2] A sample of voters is chosen as a "panel." They are interviewed a number of times during and just after an election campaign. This

2. LAZARSFELD, BERELSON, & GAUDET, 1948; BERELSON, LAZARSFELD, & McPHEE, 1954.

procedure allows the investigators to discover how voters make up their minds to vote one way or the other and how a wide variety of factors—including the mass media—influence the decision process.

The differences in the survey and laboratory methodologies have resulted in widely divergent effects of persuasive communications in the two settings. While one-third to one-half of the respondents in the typical laboratory experiment change their attitudes in the direction advocated by the communicator, only about 5 percent of the respondents in survey studies shift in the desired direction. The limitations of mass campaigns have been well documented. One experiment, conducted in Allentown, Pennsylvania, used leaflets to influence the citizen to vote for the Socialist party (in the 1930s the Socialist party was much stronger than it is today).[3] Although the propaganda leaflets were judged to be above average in their appeal, it was estimated that it took approximately 10,000 of them to win only seventy-two additional votes for the Socialist party. The experimenter estimated further that about half of these seventy-two votes would probably have been obtained without the aid of the leaflets, because of certain other factors having nothing to do with the experiment.

A later study covered a six-month educational campaign designed to acquaint the people of Cincinnati with the United Nations.[4] Hundreds of movies were shown, radio stations carried 150 spot broadcasts per week, newspapers played up the United Nations, 2,800 clubs were reached by speakers, and 59,588 pieces of literature were distributed. Yet the percentage of citizens who had heard of the veto power of the United Nations Security Council increased only 3 percent, from 34 percent to 37 percent. The percentage of those who could explain how the veto power worked (7 percent) did not change at all.

A number of plausible reasons for the marked discrepancy between the effectiveness of persuasive communication in the laboratory and in survey studies are discussed below. Most of them have been suggested by Hovland.[5]

Selective exposure might account for a part of the difference obtained in the two approaches. High school or college students in a classroom make a compact audience forcibly exposed to the experimental communications. But when a communication is distributed to the general population through television, radio, leaflets, or some other mass medium, the individual has freedom of choice about listening to or reading it. Those opposed to the position of the communicator and those who are neutral may choose to ignore the communication and thus not be influenced by it. Evidence that this process occurs is equivocal, as shown in the previous chapter, although people are more likely to expose themselves to information that will be useful to them.

In the survey method respondents are not segregated from communications that may conflict with the communication under study. In assessing the effectiveness of an advertisement channeled through the regular mass media, for

3. Hartman, 1936.   *4.* Star & Hughes, 1950.   *5.* Hovland, 1959.

example, it is impossible to isolate the respondent from all other competing advertisements before the survey interviewer reaches him to obtain his reactions. But in experimental studies where opinion is assessed before the respondent leaves the laboratory, he has had no opportunity to be exposed to subsequent countercommunications. Of course, in many laboratory experiments there is an interval of a week or more between the communication and the test of opinion change, during which the respondent may well be subjected to various countercommunications. Even here, however, if the topic of the laboratory communication is quite unlike those appearing in the mass media, the respondent may not be exposed to countercommunications.

Often the communicator in the laboratory or classroom is more credible than the communicator in everyday communication situations. He is usually implicitly sponsored by the instructor of the class and by the educational institution in which the experiment takes place. We noted in the previous chapter that the *demand characteristics* of an experiment often have powerful effects upon participants. Since in studies on attitude change the purpose or "demand" can often be fathomed, participants are likely to change in the direction consistent with the experimental treatment.

On the other hand, the communicator in mass media is frequently anonymous, as he is in most newspaper articles, and sometimes he is definitely suspect. Influence attempts often come from advertisers, politicians, salesmen, and many others who are likely to gain personally from acceptance of their message; hence the respondent may heavily discount the influence attempt.

Still another difference is that communications in survey studies are frequently of considerable interest to the respondent. He may become personally involved in such matters as the election of local, state, or federal officials, and he may have strong feelings about national or international issues. As a result, he often has a vested interest in not changing. Topics used in laboratory studies have less often aroused strong feelings, although there are some exceptions. By its very nature, the laboratory experiment makes the communication one in which the student is less involved—it is often not a communication that he can go out and act upon.

Finally, the laboratory audience is relatively isolated, and conditions are such that interaction among its members is highly restricted. In contrast, communication via the mass media may be talked over with friends, relatives, and other associates, who are likely to share the same opinions as the respondent himself and to help him resist attempts to change his attitudes. When interaction is restricted in the laboratory, acceptance or rejection is more likely to be an individual decision.

The many differences between the laboratory setting and communication in everyday life necessitate consideration of the role of the social structure in mediating communications. The rest of this chapter will be devoted to that role. It should be noted that even though results obtained in the laboratory often differ from those obtained in survey studies, laboratory studies have their merits. They have provided a useful framework for conceptualizing attitude organization and change in the individual, and they have pointed to the various sources of resistance that may arise. The general principles discussed in Chapter 3 pertaining to dissonance, consistency, contrary behavior, and resistance to change also apply to communication in the social structure.

Functions of Groups in the Communication Process

It has been previously noted that groups may reinforce or interfere with the effectiveness of a communication. This section discusses the ways in which such processes operate. Because investigations in this area have studied the relationship of small groups to the communication process in two different contexts, discussion will be divided into two overlapping parts. One part is concerned primarily with the functioning of the groups themselves and is based to a great extent on research with laboratory groups. The other has a somewhat broader framework encompassing the associations of the respondent with other persons and his place in larger social structures and is usually studied by survey methods. Small groups in the persuasion process are discussed as (1) agents for resistance to change and (2) agents of change. The place of the individual in larger social structures and the effects of this place upon his reception of communications are discussed later in the chapter.

Groups as Agents for Resistance to Change

Groups may reinforce or interfere with the effect of a communication from a media source in three general ways: (1) through the effects of group structure on exposure, (2) by determining the credibility of various communicators, and (3) by providing social support for attitudes.

EFFECTS OF GROUP STRUCTURE ON EXPOSURE   The group structure may affect the manner in which a communication is filtered as it passes from one person to another. This filtering process determines the degree to which group members are exposed to the various elements of the communication. As shown in Chapter 9, groups have a communication structure. It is of particular relevance here that some members are more active than others in spreading messages through the group, usually these active members reflect the value structure of the group. Thus, they may block or distort messages that are dissonant with group values, and facilitate messages that are consonant.

To illustrate, studies of voting, for example, have shown that people talk politics primarily with friends and family members. Since these persons usually have similar political attitudes, the chances of encountering dissonant views through interpersonal channels are low. The degree to which family members have similar political attitudes is emphasized by a study of a panel of voters in one county where only 4 percent of the voters had relatives who voted differ-ently from themselves.[6] Moreover, discussion with those who disagree with one's opinions is likely to be actively avoided; thus one Republican says, "All of my neighbors are Democrats, so there's no use talking with them about it [politics]."[7]

Brodbeck attempted to demonstrate a form of selective exposure within the group.[8] She reasoned that members of a group whose confidence in their own beliefs had been shaken by an exposure to a countercommunication would seek discussion partners who agreed with their beliefs. A number of small groups of participants were offered the choice between listening, over a one way tele-phone, to a partner who agreed with their position or to one who disagreed. After comparing participants who disagreed with a communication but whose confidence had been shaken with participants who agreed with the communica-tion, she concluded that her hypothesis was confirmed. Steiner, however, has pointed out that the number of disagreeing individuals with shaken confidence who chose a discussion partner with the same attitude did not exceed chance: Only nine of the twenty-seven subjects made such a choice, whereas eleven would have been expected to do so if all members had chosen purely at ran-dom.[9] Considerably more than eleven members would have chosen partners with the same attitude if Brodbeck's hypothesis were correct.

Unwillingness to listen to people who disagree should not be confused with having no interest in talking to them. Under certain circumstances, consider-able communication is directed toward a person who deviates from group opin-ion, discussed later in this chapter and in Chapter 10.

CREDIBILITY OF COMMUNICATORS   The members of a group are likely to have not only similar opinions on a variety of issues but also similar opinions about the credibility of various communicators. For a highly religious group, for example, a minister of their faith has high credibility and an atheist has low credibility. For a group of physicians, a surgeon has high credibility but an athletic coach talking about health has much lower credibility. In general, communicators likely to transmit messages consonant with group attitudes and values are assigned high credibility and those with dissonant communications are assigned low credibility. A factor multiplying the effectiveness of highly credible communications directed toward groups is that key positions in the group's communication structure are held by members who personify group values: They are apt to relay communications consonant with their values and to filter out dissonant communications.

GROUP SUPPORT FOR ATTITUDES   Groups are not so homogeneous, nor are the communication channels so uniform, that people are never exposed to contrary

6. LAZARSFELD et al., 1948.   *7.* BERELSON, LAZARSFELD, & MCPHEE, 1954, p. 102.   *8.* BRODBECK, 1956, 1960.   *9.* STEINER, 1962.

communications. A person in a modern society is continually bombarded with a great variety of messages, many of them contrary to his attitudes. Perhaps the most dramatic source of resistance to continual pressure is found in the social support provided by a group with whom the individual identifies. This support is one of the most important reasons why one's attitudes do not constantly shift in the direction of each new barrage of communications. Essentially, the support of the group may be characterized in the following terms.

Persons are attracted to others who have attitudes similar to their own. When confronted with a person whose attitudes are at variance with theirs, they exert pressure on him to change. Festinger has suggested that these tendencies arise out of a need to validate one's attitudes—to find support for them in *social reality*.[10] The concept of *social reality*, discussed in more detail in Chapter 10, is based on the scarcity in the physical world of evidence that could be used to affirm or deny the truth of many of our attitudes. What people do in the absence of conclusive proof is to rely upon agreement with other persons as a source of support for their attitudes. This dependence on other persons begins in the small child whose parents define for him what is safe and what is dangerous, what is good and what is bad, and countless other beliefs.

These pressures toward uniformity arising out of the need to validate attitudes are particularly effective in small, intimate groups, because persons in such groups are normally highly dependent on each other for the satisfaction of their emotional needs, such as the needs for affection, companionship, and encouragement. Such groups have been traditionally referred to as *primary groups*. The processes by which group members exert influence on each other to bring about conformity will be treated in more detail in Chapter 10.

An excellent example of how membership in a primary group may produce strong resistance to persuasive communications is provided by an analysis of the German Wehrmacht in World War II.[11] According to this study, the most important factor accounting for the strong resistance of German troops to Allied propaganda, in spite of the hopelessness of their situation toward the end of the war, was the loyalty of a soldier to his own unit. The unit met his physical needs, providing him with food, clothing, shelter, and protection, and also offered him affection, esteem, and support. Allied propaganda disseminated among German troops in the form of leaflets urging surrender had little effect upon soldiers belonging to these units. Asking a soldier to surrender had small chance of success if it meant that he must desert his comrades. Even less effective were Allied communications attempting to cast doubt on the Nazi ideology: Most soldiers did not concern themselves with politics, and devotion to Nazism was not a basis for their resistance to Allied propaganda.

On the other hand, once the primary group was broken up, or its functions were disrupted by lack of food or ammunition, the need for physical survival became so strong that persuasive communications urging surrender and guar-

10. Festinger, 1954.   11. Shils & Janowitz, 1948.

anteeing safe-conduct were frequently effective. Thus, either the virtual dissolution of the primary group or the agreement of the entire group to surrender was a necessary condition for effectiveness of Allied persuasive communications. Similar feelings of loyalty to the primary group existed among American soldiers, who, when asked what factors enabled them to keep going when things were tough, stressed that they couldn't let their outfit down, that "buddies" depended upon them, etc.[12]

Other examples of how the group helps the individual to resist influence come from the study of prisons and of delinquent gangs. Although prisons are supposed to rehabilitate the criminal, influences in that direction are usually effectively blocked by the formation of strong informal groups among prisoners. These groups support and perpetuate attitudes that are favorable to continuation of criminal activity after release. Similarly, members of delinquent gangs are strongly resistant to reform efforts of police, social workers, and other community workers.

According to several authorities, attempts of Chinese Communists to brainwash American prisoners captured in the Korean conflict were successful in destroying resistance and obtaining minor cooperation in part because primary groups were deliberately broken apart.[13] The Chinese captors segregated leaders and resistors, instituted an informer system, gave special privileges to those who cooperated, and removed all recognition of military rank. As a result, the average American stood alone against his captors, although he was physically in the midst of his fellow prisoners.

On the other hand, virtually all the Turkish prisoners captured in the same war successfully resisted attempts by their captors to obtain cooperation. They were probably kept together for the convenience of their captors because of the lack of Turkish-speaking Chinese. They took advantage of being together by maintaining a high level of discipline and organization, the highest-ranking Turk remaining in charge of the unit and receiving full support from other Turkish prisoners.

A laboratory experiment has shown that placing a high value on one's group is associated with resistance to communications running counter to the group's values.[14] The experiment was performed with Boy Scout troops, using a communicator who suggested that boys in the modern world would profit more from learning about their cities and from various activities in town than they would from the typical Boy Scout activities. Measures of attitude before and after the communication revealed that those who strongly valued their membership in the group reacted against the communicator's critical message and took an even more favorable position on scout activities. Boys who valued the group less highly either were not influenced by the communicator or were influenced to adopt slightly less favorable attitudes toward scout activities.

12. SHILS, 1950.   *13.* COMMITTEE ON GOVERNMENT OPERATIONS, 1956; SCHEIN, 1958.   *14.* KELLEY & VOLKART, 1952.

The discussion so far has shown that the group supports members in resisting communications that run counter to shared attitudes representing the central values of the group and strongly sanctioned by it. It would also be interesting to know whether attitudes that are shared by the members but are not particularly relevant to the goals of the group are also resistant to change because of group support. Several studies show that, even on issues of low relevance, the group does exert some pressure on persons who deviate.

One experiment established laboratory groups that varied in two ways: (1) in the power of the group to hold its members and (2) in the relevance or importance of the activities over which the power of the group extended.[15] By prearrangement with the experimenter, certain paid participants deviated from established group attitudes. When the activities performed by the deviate were not particularly important to the group, it exerted some pressure on him to conform, but not as much as it exerted for more relevant activities. In a study of friendship associations, attitudes having little relevance to friendship (opinions about big business) were nevertheless frequently adopted because individuals perceived their friends as exerting pressure for adoption.[16]

One study appears to provide direct evidence for group support of judgments that have no particular relevance to the group as such.[17] It dealt with seemingly countable beats produced by a pulse generator in three situations: (1) a group context, (2) a temporary "togetherness" with another person with whom there were no personal ties, and (3) a single individual in a solitary situation with the experimenter. Pairs of participants in the group situation belonged to the same clique in college. The togetherness situation simply assigned to the task two college students unacquainted with one another. During the initial situation, all three groups formed *normative judgments* of the number of beats produced. [A social *norm* (see Chapter 10) is an expectation shared by group members which specifies behavior that is considered appropriate for a given situation.] In the ambiguous situation with the pulse generator, participants in a group agreed upon a narrow range of judgments as "correct"—a range that varied from group to group. Later each individual was placed with another who had a norm different from his own. As anticipated, those who had formed their normative judgments in the group context were most resistant to change, and those who had formed norms in the solitary context, least resistant.

SUMMARY: GROUPS AS AGENTS FOR RESISTANCE TO CHANGE   Groups may interfere with the effect of a communication from some media source in several ways. One of these is through the communication structure existing in the group, which serves to filter out dissonant communications. Another is by determining the level of credibility of communicators according to the degree of consonance or dissonance between their attitudes and those of the group. Fi-

---

15. SCHACHTER, 1951.   *16.* STEINER, 1954.   *17.* An unpublished study by Pollis described in SHERIF, SHERIF, & NEBERGALL, 1965.

nally, groups furnish social support for the attitudes of their members by providing rewards for conformity and sanctions for deviation. The degree to which sanctions are exercised against deviators varies directly with the power of the group and with the relevance of the attitude to the group's central values. Primary groups are especially effective in providing resistance to change.

Groups as Agents of Change

The group may facilitate change in several ways, each of which will be discussed in turn: (1) indirectly, by removal of support for an attitude, (2) by generating discussion that leads to clearer and somewhat different conceptions of what attitudes are shared by group members, and (3) through group-decision processes.

REMOVAL OF SUPPORT FOR AN OPINION   If the group is weakened by external or internal stresses, it may abandon its shared attitudes and accept new ones that would otherwise have been strongly resisted. The role of the small combat unit in maintaining the fighting spirit of the German army in World War II has already been noted. At first Allied propaganda urging surrender had little effect upon German troops. Near the end of the war, however, when the primary groups were disorganized and scattered by Allied forces, the soldiers surrendered readily. Many of them mentioned that the safe-conduct leaflet urging surrender which was distributed as propaganda warfare played a significant role in bringing about their decision.[18] Similarly, North Koreans who were separated from their military units were readily influenced by United Nations propaganda which, before separation, had little effect upon them.[19]

Another experiment illustrates that perceived support for a contrary opinion leads to change.[20] College students who listened to a recorded communication contrary to their norms and who heard applause from an audience supposedly like themselves were more likely to accept the counternorm communication than students who believed that the applause came from anonymous outsiders.

DISCUSSION   Klapper calls attention to the role of communication and discussion among group members in bringing about change.[21] Various problems or crises confronting the group may stimulate intensive discussion that clarifies group attitudes. Members who previously had perceived the group attitudes incorrectly may not agree with them once the misunderstanding is cleared up; the attitudes become targets for change. According to Katz and Lazarsfeld, such discussion may also reveal the presence of hitherto unsuspected minority group support for opinions contrary to the norms.[22] Thus individuals who had privately held dissident opinions are encouraged to bring them into the open.

18. Herz, 1954.   *19.* Riley, Schramm, & Williams, 1951.   *20.* Kelley & Woodruff, 1956.   *21.* Klapper, 1961.   *22.* Katz & Lazarsfeld, 1955.

THE GROUP-DECISION PROCESS   A somewhat more direct use of the group as an agent of change involves a process commonly known as *group decision*. It was first studied in a series of experiments conducted during World War II by Lewin and his colleagues.[23] In the light of present knowledge, the term group decision is not really appropriate, for the process includes quite a number of elements in addition to the making of a decision by the group.

The steps commonly taken in bringing about change by group decision include the following: (1) The group leader presents an issue which involves a course of action that can be associated with existing motivations of the audience. (2) He asks members of the audience to discuss their feelings about cooperating with the actions described, and to include in the discussion any objections that they might have. (3) The leader recognizes and accepts objections without disapproval, supporting the rights of members to raise objections. (4) He complies with requests for information. (5) He encourages discussion among the members that will answer as many of the objections as possible. (6) At the end of the discussion, the leader asks members to make a decision about whether or not they will carry out the desired actions (a procedure referred to as *individual commitment*). (7) He then gives members the opportunity to see how many others agree to try out the new actions (a procedure known as *perceived group consensus*).

Many elements of the group-decision process have been familiar for a long time in other contexts as practical means of influencing a person. Requiring someone to take a pledge or an oath or to swear on the Bible is a method of eliciting individual commitment which has been practiced since ancient civilization. Newer forms involve encouraging people to sign a pledge card to donate a certain amount to charity, to respond to an advertisement by clipping a coupon and sending it in, to sign a preliminary sales contract, etc. The techniques used by Alcoholics Anonymous are good examples of the combined use of individual commitment and group consensus. The new member pledges not to drink again, and he also gains support by becoming acquainted with other members of the chapter who have made similar commitments; thus the force of group consensus is placed solidly behind his new resolve to stop drinking.

In the experiments reviewed by Lewin, the objective was to persuade housewives to make more use of certain unpopular meats—sweetbreads, beef hearts, and kidneys—in order to alleviate the meat shortage and help the war effort. Three groups used as controls were exposed to conventional techniques of persuasion, consisting of attractive lectures that linked the problem of nutrition with the war effort, emphasized the vitamin and mineral value of the three meats, and stressed health and economic values. Recipes were also distributed. Three other groups were handled by the group-decision process, which consisted of the seven steps listed above. At a later time, women from the two kinds of groups were asked whether or not they were using the meats. Among

23. LEWIN, 1958.

Table 5-1   Possible effective factors in group decision as compared with lecture

GROUP DECISION	LECTURE
Audience actively participates and is likely to become personally involved.	Audience is passive; does not participate.
Members perceive willingness of some other members to unfreeze attitudes.	Audience is silent; members cannot perceive inclinations of others.
Leader's permissive attitude toward objections may strengthen desire to help him by behaving in the manner suggested.	Audience does not participate; hence leader cannot win support by being permissive.
Members are required to commit themselves on the desired action.	Audience is not required to make decision on desired action.
Members perceive others committing themselves to desired action.	Audience is unable to perceive private decisions of others.

women who had never before used them, only 3 percent of those who had heard the lectures were using them, but 32 percent of those who had participated in the group-decision process were using them. Similar experiments aimed at increasing the home consumption of fresh and evaporated milk and encouraging the feeding of orange juice and cod-liver oil to infants also yielded results in favor of the group-decision process.[24]

Lewin interpreted group-decision procedures as a three-step process: "unfreezing" the group attitudes that ordinarily serve to resist change, establishing a new set of attitudes, and "freezing" the new attitudes. This appears to be a reasonable interpretation of what happens. What is not clear, however, is which elements of the group-decision process are responsible for the changes. A glance at Table 5-1 indicates that quite a variety of factors might account for the difference in the relative effectiveness of the propaganda lecture and the group-decision procedure.

Fortunately, one experimenter later undertook to determine the relative effectiveness of the various aspects of the group-decision process.[25] She used a large number of groups so that the effects of each factor could be separately assessed and the remaining factors controlled. The experiment investigated the importance of the following conditions: decision versus no decision, discussion versus no discussion, public commitment versus private commitment, and high perceived group consensus versus low perceived consensus. The experimenter attempted to influence college students to volunteer for participation in various psychological experiments which were to be conducted during the semester. The criterion of effectiveness was the number of students in each experimental condition who did volunteer.

The investigation led to the following conclusions: Group discussion was not

---

24. LEWIN, 1958.   *25.* BENNETT, 1955.

a more effective inducement to action than a lecture. Also, a decision involving public commitment was not more effective than one made less publicly or made anonymously. On the positive side, a decision regarding future action was more effective in bringing about that action than no decision on it. Also effective was a high degree of actual or perceived group agreement on performing the desired action.

An earlier experiment suggested that additional conditions affecting the group-decision process need to be identified.[26] Although it also demonstrated that more subjects volunteered when they perceived that others were willing to volunteer, its results were unlike Bennett's in that the opportunity to make a private decision led to more volunteering than a decision requiring public commitment. In still another experiment, where the decision concerned the behavior of the group as a whole, rather than individual actions, group discussion did play an important role in bringing about change.[27]

Another experiment took into account the type of relation the leader has to his members.[28] Kipnis's investigation compared participatory leadership with a lecture style of leadership under three conditions: (1) where the leader offered to reward subjects for compliance, (2) where the leader threatened to punish those who did not comply, and (3) where no sanctions were exercised by the leader. One result was that, when the leader either had reward power or exercised no sanctions, participatory leadership induced more private attitude change than lecture leadership. Threat of punishment resulted in more change under lecture leadership than under participatory leadership: Group discussion in the participatory condition reinforced resistance to change.

PEOPLE-CHANGING GROUPS   If some change can be brought about in groups of strangers through group decision processes, it follows that powerful changes might be wrought by so-called living groups organized for that purpose. Let us consider a type of group to which members are admitted only if they agree to change themselves radically; a group, moreover, whose members eat together, work together, play together, and reside in the same building; a group which endures over a long period of time. Not many groups meet these qualifications, for most such groups quickly stabilize and enforce conformity rather than change, and accept new members who are like older members, rather than different from them. One such set of organized groups, however, is those of the Synanon Foundation.[29] Members of these groups are former drug addicts, and the new members are individuals who, generally in desperation, come to Synanon to get rid of their addiction.

Prospective new members are intensively questioned and the depth of their motivation to join is assessed. If they are not willing to submit to the rules of the house, they are not allowed to join. A Synanon house constitutes a primary

26. Schachter & Hall, 1952.   27. Pennington, Haravey, & Bass, 1958.   28. Kipnis, 1958.   29. Yablonsky, 1965.

group. Members develop close attachments and experience intense emotions under house conditions. Once a member has joined, he becomes totally dependent on Synanon for every basic life function: living, eating, sleeping, working, and playing. This strong dependency, with Synanon controlling all the resources, gives the house enormous power over the member. (See Chapter 8 for an analysis of sources of power.)

Although there has been no carefully designed evaluative study of Synanon, it is clearly often effective in rehabilitating people addicted to drugs. Central to the change process are group sessions called *synanons,* held three times per week, with about ten to fifteen persons participating. An older, experienced member of the house serves loosely as a leader. The emphasis is on extreme candor and honesty, and expression of opinions and emotions is encouraged. Typically, an individual with an addiction has built up certain delusions about himself and his behavior, and exhibits negative behavior both in house living and in the group. All evasive behavior and pretenses are savagely attacked by members of the synanon. The aim is to force the individual to adopt a more realistic view of himself and to start shaping up his behavior. In the background, however, underlying these powerful attacks by group members, is strong acceptance and emotional support of the individual. The house is his only home; and the other members are the only friends he has and are also his family. He has no alternatives. The "outside" is hopeless; he must succeed in his new setting or fail altogether. The following excerpt gives some of the flavor of a synanon session in which the theme was antiprejudice. (The chief characters are Don, who is Jewish, and two blacks, Pete and Wilbur. The other members are white.)

Nancy: Don, you can do the right thing in here by spewing your prejudice garbage in a synanon, where more people can look at it with you. Get it out here and now. Then maybe you won't be spreading it all over the house.

Pete: You gutless mother-fucker, you won't call him [Wilbur] anything to his face. You'd rather go behind his back and call him something. Why don't you call it to his face?

Don: We've spoken about my prejudice already in synanons.

Pete: Tell him now.

Don: I'm not going to tell it to him again. I told him how I feel about him.

Pete: How do you feel about him, then?

Don (in a ludicrous understatement of his feelings): I can't see a colored guy doing executive work or in charge of me.

Jack: What did you tell Sherry [a black woman] the other night? You know, all colored broads ain't supposed to do nothing but clean up, you know?

Don: When did I tell her this?

Jack: In synanon the other—

Don: Oh, you say a lot of things to trigger the group.

Jack: That's how you feel. Man, why not admit it? Get it out. You might feel better!

George: This is how you feel. You know you've had this all your life. All colored women coming and cleaning your house and so forth, once a week or every other week, you know? And this is the condition you've had.

Pete: You fat, ignorant slob. That's exactly what you are. And you don't have any guts, man—not a gut in your whole fuckin' body. You're the biggest asshole in the house and biggest coward.

Don (trying to act unprovoked): Right.

Pete: I could probably get up and spit in your face right now and all you'd do is wipe it off.

Don: Go ahead and try it.

Pete: You fuckin' coward.

Don: Go ahead and try it.

(A strict house rule against physical violence permits expression of real feelings without retaliation.)

Pete: What do you think of me now?

Don: What am I supposed to do, get mad at you now?

Pete: I'm mad at your crazy ass right now. You know what you are to me right now?

Don: What?

Pete: You're exactly like the suckers down in Birmingham last week that turned dogs loose on people to do what they couldn't do. . . .

Don: That's good; that means you respect me, you're afraid of me.

Pete (sarcastically): Yeah, I respect you all right.

Don: Definitely.

Herb: Do you think anybody in here respects you, Don?

Don: No.[30]

While Synanon living groups appear to be powerful agents for change, many others types of groups function at times to produce change. As shown in Chapters 15 to 17, families socialize children by means of group processes. Therapy groups that meet for psychotherapeutic purposes over long periods of time are common. A more recent phenomenon is the encounter or sensitivity group. All these groups appear to effect change at times, although encounter groups appear to have little lasting positive effect upon the individual, and sometimes do serious harm.[31]

SUMMARY: GROUPS AS AGENTS OF CHANGE   A group may facilitate attitude change in indirect ways. Any actions or processes that weaken the group open the way for change. Also, extensive discussion may clarify group attitudes so that they become targets for change. Discussion may also reveal minority

---

30. Reprinted with permission from L. YABLONSKY. *Synanon: The tunnel back.* New York: The Macmillan Company, 1965. Pp. 144-145.   31. BACK, 1972.

group support for attitudes that vary from the group norms and may thereby strengthen the deviant attitudes of members who hold them secretly.

The process of group decision has frequently been used as a deliberate means of bringing about change. A leader encourages discussion of an issue involving a course of action that can be associated with existing motivations of the group members. He recognizes objections to the proposed action and complies with requests for information, but allows the group to make its own decision about adopting the action. At the present time, the elements in this process which effect change appear to be (1) the making of a decision or commitment by the members, (2) the perception that a large proportion of the other members have committed themselves to change, and (3) group discussion in situations where the leader either has reward power or does not exercise any form of sanction.

Living groups are more powerful forces for change, because they provide members with deeper gratifications and create strong dependency. To the extent that the member lacks alternative sources of gratification, the power of these groups is intensified.

Position in the Social Structure

Reference Groups and the Communication Process

So far discussion has been primarily about the effect of small, intimate groups on communication processes. The place of the individual in the larger social structure is also relevant to his acceptance or rejection of a communication. A person need not even be a member of a group in order for it to influence him; if he merely aspires to become a member, the attitudes held by the group may serve as a guide to his opinions and behavior. The same is true when a person has just joined a group and is not yet accepted as a member in the fullest sense.

Thus, in World War II, "green" replacements assigned to veteran combat units which had been temporarily removed from the battlefront rapidly shifted their initial attitude of eagerness for combat to acceptance of the attitude that "combat is hell." Veteran replacements assigned to inexperienced units did not undergo a shift in attitude toward combat.[32] Presumably, the replacements assigned to veteran units wanted to be accepted by the veterans and thus shifted their opinions to conform.

THE CONCEPT OF REFERENCE GROUP   The influence of a group on the attitudes of an individual is often treated in terms of the concept of *reference group*.[33] A reference group is a social unit which the individual sees as holding interests, attitudes, and values in common with his own, and which he takes as a basis for

32. MERTON & KITT, 1950.   *33.* HYMAN, 1942, 1960.

self-evaluation and attitude formation.[34] Such a group may have one or both of two functions: (1) the *normative function,* setting and enforcing standards of conduct and belief; and (2) the *comparison function,* serving as a standard or comparison point against which persons measure themselves and others.[35]

The comparison function may be illustrated by some studies of men drafted in World War II. Nearly half of the married men felt that they should not have been drafted, but only 10 percent of the unmarried men held this attitude. Married men had these feelings of injustice because, compared with unmarried men, they were making a greater sacrifice, and their married civilian friends were escaping altogether from the sacrifice.[36] Comparison processes will be treated in more detail in the discussion of status in Chapters 9 and 12. The discussion here is mainly limited to the normative function of reference groups.

One further restriction will be placed on the present treatment. Originally the term *reference* was applied to both the single individual and the group, but reference individuals have been more recently referred to as *opinion leaders.* Much of the discussion of reference groups here applies also to opinion leaders, but the leaders will be discussed separately in a later section.

A reference group may be a membership or a nonmembership group. Usually, of course, groups to which a person belongs are reference groups for him. Although a reference group is usually a group whose acceptance and approval is desired, in some instances an individual may be influenced by a group that he dislikes or is rebelling against. In this case he is motivated to adopt attitudes opposite to those of the group, and the group is termed a *negative reference group.* For example, while the family is normally a positive reference group, two studies of political attitudes demonstrate that it can be a negative reference group in that those who rebel against it often adopt a political position opposite to that of their parents.[37]

REFERENCE GROUPS AS SOCIAL SUPPORT   Reference groups often play a role in the communication process similar to that already discussed for primary groups. They may establish various levels of credibility for the communicator, thereby creating selective exposure, and they may provide social support for the individual's attitudes. This social support often takes the form of providing a frame of reference or a context within which the communication is received and interpreted. An example is the finding that persons moving up the socio-economic ladder are more likely to be Republican than Democratic, a phenomenon which suggests that they are using groups to which they aspire to belong as a frame of reference for their political attitudes.[38] Several studies indicate that where the values of one's reference groups change, the individual changes his judgments in the same direction.[39]

Many communications in everyday life call up an anticipated audience—

34. MERTON, 1957*a.*   *35.* KELLEY, 1952.   *36.* STOUFFER, SUCHMAN, DeVINNEY, STAR, & WILLIAMS, 1949.   *37.* NEWCOMB, 1943; MACCOBY, 1954.   *38.* MACCOBY, 1954.   *39.* Cited in SHERIF et al., 1965, p. 65.

some individual or reference group to whom we might relay the message, or with whom we might talk it over. One experiment demonstrates clearly that such anticipated audiences may affect the manner in which the communication is received.[40] The experimenter gave two groups two sets of arguments, for and against lowering the voting age to eighteen years, and told them to prepare speeches in competition for a prize. For one group, the prize was to be given by the "The Society for Constitutional Government—dedicated to preserving the U.S. Constitution unchanged"; for the other, it would be awarded by "The Association for Lowering the Voting Age to 18—if they can fight, they can vote." These groups, together with a control group that received no communication, were given attitude tests before and after the communication. Each group was found to remember more arguments consonant with the aims of the organization giving the prize. A related experiment obtained similar results.[41] Thus, it seems that people are likely to interpret a message in a direction consonant with the attitudes of positive reference groups or persons associated with the communication.

Several studies make clear that voting preferences are strongly influenced by reference groups.[42] For example, the individual who early in an election campaign favors a candidate not preferred by his family or by his close associates frequently casts his final vote for their candidate, not his. Since most of a voter's discussion of politics takes place with his friends, coworkers, and family, the implication is that the shift is probably due to actual pressures from the group. An illustration is the famous Nixon-Kennedy television debates. Most people viewed the debates in group settings (usually family) and talked mainly with persons who agreed with their own opinions, which reinforced their voting inclinations.[43] On the other hand, those who talked with people who favored the opposite candidate often changed their voting intention.

A more precise demonstration of how voting is associated with the political affiliation of friends is seen in a study of voting in Elmira County, N.Y.[44] Eighty percent of Protestants and 36 percent of Catholics voted Republican. But Catholics or Protestants who had close friends with a political affiliation different from that of their religious group voted like their friends instead of like their religious group. This effect may be seen in Table 5-2, which shows that the more Republican friends they had, the more both Catholics and Protestants voted Republican. The effect is especially strong for Catholics, who normally voted Democratic.

The use of reference groups is not always apparent. In one study, white students classified as prejudiced or unprejudiced toward blacks were asked in a laboratory situation to agree to have their picture taken with a black of the opposite sex for use in further sessions of the experiment.[45] They were requested to sign a release to permit the use of the photograph in a series of

40. SCHRAMM & DANIELSON, 1958.   *41.* ZIMMERMAN & BAUER, 1956.   *42.* LAZARSFELD et al., 1948; BERELSON et al., 1954.   *43.* KATZ & FELDMAN, 1962.   *44.* KAPLAN, 1968.   *45.* DE FLEUR & WESTIE, 1958.

Table 5-2   *Close friends as a reference group for voting*

PERCENT VOTING REPUBLICAN

Friends	Catholics	Protestants
RRR	61	93
RRD	42	84
DDR	36	*
DDD	10	21

Note: Each R stands for a Republican friend and each D for a democratic friend.

*The number of Protestants having as close friends two Democrats and one Republican was too small to calculate a reliable percentage. *Source:* Adapted with permission from Norman Kaplan. Reference groups and interest group theories of voting. In Herbert H. Hyman and Eleanor Singer (Eds.), *Readings in reference group theory and research.* New York: Free Press, 1968. Pp. 461-472.

future situations of varying public exposure (e.g., use in experiments, use in the student newspaper, or use in a nationwide campaign). In a subsequent interview, three-quarters of the participants reported that in considering whether or not to sign, they thought of some reference group which influenced their decision, most often a peer group.

SALIENCE OF REFERENCE GROUPS   Everyone has many reference groups, but not every group is relevant to each communication. For example, the church group to which a person belongs is unlikely to be a salient group when he is watching a sports broadcast on television. Several experiments have stressed the point that a reference group must be made salient before it can affect attitudes.[46] This has also been recognized by groups in a practical sense and has stimulated the development of devices likely to make the group salient—for example, uniforms, badges, pins, insignia, and certain rituals such as the salute. More study is needed to define the conditions under which a reference group is salient to a communication situation.

For example, there is some evidence that the individual need not be clearly aware of the influence of the group on his attitudes. At the end of their freshman year, sophomore women were asked to indicate their preference concerning which college houses they wished to live in.[47] Houses on the "Row," formerly sorority houses, had the highest status, and girls who were more status-oriented especially preferred them. Not all girls received their choice, however, and those who were assigned to less status-oriented houses and who lived in them during their sophomore year shifted their attitudes to place less emphasis on status. This occurred even for women who again expressed a preference for

46. FESTINGER, 1950; KELLEY, 1955; CHARTERS & NEWCOMB, 1958.   47. SIEGEL & SIEGEL, 1957.

a Row house at the end of their sophomore year. Thus, they were influenced by their membership group to place less emphasis on status even though they retained the Row house as a reference group. The greatest change occurred among women who desired to remain in a non-Row house at the end of their sophomore year.

On the other hand, people may often be quite aware of their reference groups with respect to some action or intention. When Kennedy, a Catholic, ran for President, according to one study Protestants in the Southwest were strongly aware of his religious affiliation and considered it an important factor in how they would vote.[48] For Protestants in the Northwest, however, his affiliation was much less important. Another investigation has shown that his affiliation had most effect on the voting of voters who were active churchgoers.[49]

A good example of how making a reference group salient contributes to change of attitudes and behavior is found in the efforts of the Chinese Communists to reform the intellectuals of their country (scholars, teachers, writers, artists, and other professional people).[50] Thought reform was viewed as a struggle each individual goes through, a struggle between his old and his new ideologies. In the process, as members of special groups or schools, individuals were prodded again and again to review their life and their thoughts *in the light of the Communist ideology*. A process of comparison of their specific behaviors and thoughts against the new ideology was required. This was actively pursued in study groups and other settings. "Confessions" were encouraged, consisting of admissions of guilt about having behaved or thought in bourgeois ways. Individuals who refused to confess were attacked vigorously, their every word and act criticized in ideological terms. This was a method par excellence for making the Communist ideology a salient reference point for all their thoughts and actions.

KINDS OF REFERENCE GROUPS   Many investigations provide definite evidence that the effects of a communication on the respondent vary with the kinds of reference groups he has, although the exact nature of the process is not always clear. One study, for example, assesses the effects of the mass media on preadolescents and adolescents in terms of two reference groups: their parents and their friends or peers.[51] The subjects were classified according to whether their family was their only reference group, or whether they also had peers as reference groups. Definite differences were discovered between the two classifications in preferences for certain types of comics, radio programs, and television programs. Young children who had only the family as a reference group liked the "Bugs Bunny" type of comic and action programs such as Westerns to a greater extent than children who had both family and peer reference groups. Among adolescents, those who had only the family reference group had stronger preferences for action and violence programs. To some extent, differences

48. SHERIF et al., 1965.   *49.* CONVERSE, 1961.   *50.* CHEN, 1960.   *51.* RILEY & RILEY, 1951.

in preference for various mass media may directly reflect peer-group values. Young children and adolescents who, in addition to having the family as a reference group, emphasized peer group values also had the strongest preferences for media reflecting such values as sports, popular music, popularity with the opposite sex, and association with the gang. The data appear to support the view that the type of group membership may influence the impact of the mass media on individuals. An alternative interpretation, however, is that program preferences reflect individual personality characteristics which also determine the individual's group memberships.

SUMMARY: REFERENCE GROUPS   A reference group may have two functions: a normative function and a comparison function. The normative function is setting and enforcing standards of conduct and belief. The comparison function is establishing a standard or comparison point against which persons may compare themselves and others. This discussion has been mainly limited to the normative function; the comparison function will be discussed in Chapters 9 and 12.

A person need not be an actual member of a group to use it as a reference group. Reference groups establish various levels of credibility for communicators, support selective exposure to different communications, and provide social support for a person's attitudes. A person who accepts the position taken by his reference group will readily accept communications that advocate a similar position, but will be likely to reject those that run counter to it. The effects of a reference group depend on its salience to a particular communication. Some evidence shows that the kinds of reference groups a person has affect his response to various communications.

Interpersonal Communication Networks

It has already been stressed that the group plays the role of a comparatively stable structure or system of channels through which communications move. Communications that are counter to group opinions may never travel through the entire network to reach all members of the group, whereas those that are in agreement with group attitudes are likely to be freely transmitted. Communication channels also extend beyond the group, as has been implied in mentioning the role of the group in establishing the levels of credibility of various communicators. The larger communication process is one in which messages travel from the mass media or other general sources to ultimately reach the respondent.

THE TWO-STEP FLOW OF COMMUNICATIONS   Much of what has been said emphasizes the function of groups in the influence process as they affect both exposure to and acceptance or rejection of a communication. Such emphases suggest that influence attempts through secondary sources like the mass media are relatively ineffective. Yet communications through the mass media apparently do modify or reinforce opinions, although often in an indirect manner known as the *two-step flow of communications.*[52] This means that not all persons in a group receive information directly from the media. Some receive it second-hand, relayed by an opinion leader; thus, opinion leaders are thought to play an important role in mass communication.

In their analysis of the 1940 presidential election, Lazarsfeld, Berelson, and Gaudet observed that personal contacts were more effective than the mass media in influencing voter decisions.[53] They suggested that ideas flow from the mass media to certain key persons and from these opinion leaders to less active individuals. Thus, they visualized the mass media as exerting influence mainly through the opinion leader. Other studies have also stressed the importance of interpersonal channels of communication. Klapper notes that in totalitarian countries, the contents of such radio programs as Voice of America and Radio Free Europe spread freely by means of person-to-person contact among certain segments of the population.[54] Additional studies, described later, have shown the importance of interpersonal channels in contexts including public affairs, moviegoing, marketing, fashions, and the adoption of a new drug by physicians or of changes in agricultural practices by farmers.

Actually it appears that the flow of communications is patterned differently in developed and developing countries. In the United States, the mass media are the first source of information about news events for most people. Other people are initial sources of news for only a relatively small number of people, even for important news events.[55] An exception was the assassination of President Kennedy, when apparently a very large number of people first learned the news from another person—an exception accounted for largely by the tremendous emotional impact of the event. Generally speaking, even relatively important events are first communicated through mass media. Television is typically the most important carrier, with newspapers second, and magazines and radio far behind.[56]

By way of contrast, in the developing countries oral communication and face-to-face contact are predominant. The most frequent channel cited by the people studied in India and China was personal communication.[57] In part, of course, this reflects the much smaller distribution of radios and newspapers, to say nothing of television sets. Another factor is illiteracy, so that even the availability of printed material would not guarantee its reception.

Media are not wholly insignificant in such countries, however, nor does the number of newspapers or radios reflect the true audience. Such sources are not only transmitted to their owners but relayed to many additional people. For example, in India, a common practice is for one paper to be read by several people in a village and to be read aloud to many more who are illiterate.[58] Thus, the circulation figures of newspapers do not reflect their true audience.

52. Lazarsfeld et al., 1948.   *53.* Lazarsfeld et al., 1948; Katz, 1957.   *54.* Klapper, 1961.   *55.* Weiss, 1971.   *56.* Weiss, 1971.   *57.* Weiss, 1971.   *58.* Eapen, 1967.

Other studies suggest that the conception of the two-step flow of communications as merely a relay function is an oversimplification.[59] In particular, investigations of the process of diffusion or spread of new elements through a population have added considerable detail to the notion of a two-step flow. They have provided a better understanding of the conditions under which mass communications are disseminated through interpersonal channels, as well as of the conditions under which mass communications reach the respondent directly. First, more than two steps may sometimes be involved. Opinion leaders may pass a message along to their own opinion leaders, who in turn may pass it along to theirs. Thus, a chain of interpersonal links rather than a single link may connect the original source with its recipients. Second, the flow is not necessarily from the mass media through interpersonal contacts to the persons ultimately affected. The flow may be reversed: Interpersonal communication channels may stimulate persons to consult the mass media. In a study of the diffusion of information in an industrial firm, many employees who received word of an impending reorganization from personal contacts turned to such media as the company newspaper for further information.[60]

Whether a person obtains information directly from the mass media or indirectly from other persons depends in part on his position in the social structure. Doctors who were well integrated into the medical community—as measured by the number of other doctors who considered them friends and persons whose advice was valuable—were more influenced by interpersonal channels of communication than were less integrated doctors.[61] In a group like the medical community where norms and values favor innovations, such highly integrated doctors are apt to lead the way in the adoption of a new drug. But in groups where the norms are unfavorable to innovation, as in certain agricultural communities, highly integrated persons are not likely to lead in the adoption of an innovation.[62] The degree to which a new practice is diffused through interpersonal channels and the speed of diffusion are largely dependent on whether integrated persons or isolated ones adopt the practice. When a practice is taken up by integrated persons and norms are favorable to innovation, the innovation is likely to spread rapidly through the group.[63]

Whether persons are more apt to be influenced directly through the mass media or indirectly through interpersonal communications depends on the stage of the adoption process, as well as on whether persons are early adopters or late adopters. Rural sociologists studying the adoption of new farming practices have postulated a process consisting of the following five stages[64]:

1. Awareness stage. The individual is initially exposed to the new practice but lacks details about it.

2. Information stage. He secures more information about the new practice.

59. Rogers & Beal, 1958.   60. Wager, 1962.   61. Menzel & Katz, 1965.   62. Marsh & Coleman, 1956.   63. Becker, 1970.   64. Rogers & Beal, 1958.

3. *Application stage.* He considers the advantages and disadvantages of the new practice and makes a decision about whether or not to try it.

4. *Trial stage.* He tries out the innovation on a limited and temporary basis.

5. *Adoption stage.* He makes the decision either to continue or discontinue the new practice on a permanent basis.

In a study of the adoption of a new type of agricultural spray, it was found that the mass media were more important than interpersonal influences in the early phase of making persons aware of the product.[65] In the later phases of acquiring additional information and deciding whether to use the product for a trial period, interpersonal influences predominated. Also, persons who adopted the product relatively late were more influenced by interpersonal communications than were early adopters. These findings add support to the distinction emphasized by Katz between obtaining information and legitimation, or sanction by the group in favor of the innovation.[66]

Katz arrives at this conclusion from a comparison of two diffusion studies. In both cases commercial or formal sources played an important role in disseminating information about the innovation; but in its trial and adoption, personal communications with friends, neighbors, and colleagues played the crucial role of legitimizing its use. Farmers gained information about a new hybrid corn primarily from salesmen and agricultural bulletins; doctors gained information about a new drug from salesmen or medical journals. Farmers were most influenced to try out or adopt the product by their neighbors; doctors by their colleagues and by medical journals.

OPINION LEADERS AND THE FLOW OF INFORMATION   A number of studies have shown that opinion leaders are specialized: They are leaders in one content area and not in another.[67] Depending on the content area, both the opinion leaders and the persons they influence have certain characteristics. For example, in fashions, young and gregarious women are likely to be leaders, but in public affairs, the opinion leader is likely to be mature, of high status, and well educated.

Although opinion leadership varies with content, Katz has noted some consistent characteristics of opinion leaders: (1) They personify certain values, (2) they are competent, and (3) they have a strategic social location.[68] A fourth characteristic suggested by Weiss is that they are not necessarily active proselytizers, but may be passive sources of information.[69] With respect to the first characteristic, opinion leaders often represent the values and attitudes of their group more closely than anyone else. Thus, for the members, an opinion leader personifies their values, and they identify with him and support him. In a study of boys' camps, for example, it was shown that the leaders represented the

65. ROGERS & BEAL, 1958.   66. KATZ, 1961.   67. MERTON, 1949; KATZ & LAZARSFELD, 1955.   68. KATZ, 1957.   69. WEISS, 1969.

important group values—fighting ability and campcraft.[70] Boys imitated these leaders even when the leaders had made no attempt to influence them.

The second characteristic, competence, often means that the leader has more expert knowledge than others. Thus the leaders in the boys' camps were the most competent at fighting and campcraft. Physicians who led in the adoption of new drugs were more in touch with the professional literature and with research information disseminated at medical conventions.[71] Similarly, the farmers who made more trips to the city were leaders in adopting a new hybrid corn seed.[72]

As for the third characteristic, location in the communication structure, opinion leaders have a wider range of acquaintance than nonleaders, and they are "centrally located."[73] For example, the doctors who had the largest number of social contacts with other physicians were almost always those who influenced other physicians in the friendship group to adopt a new drug. Similar findings were obtained for the doctors who were most often turned to for advice and for those with whom cases were most often discussed. Another aspect of social location characterizing opinion leaders is that they often form a link between outside media or agencies and the smaller communication system in which they are influential. Men are often opinion leaders in politics because they circulate outside the home to a greater extent than women. Opinion leaders in politics also belong to a greater number of organizations than do nonleaders.[74] Another study has identified some personality characteristics of innovators in sports: venturesomeness, imaginativeness, dominance, sociability, and self-sufficiency.[75]

Except for governmental and commercial agents of change, the opinion leaders identified through the usual research methods are apt to be resource persons whom others seek out for information, rather than active proselytizers for change.[76] The methods of study used merely identify persons from whom individuals got information; they do not examine the *process* of influence itself.

Klapper has called attention to a neglected function of the opinion leader, that of resisting change.[77] Since the leader is likely to conform most closely to the group norms, it would appear that most of his communications with others would be in the direction of the norms and he would be likely to resist outside communications reaching him that are counter to the norms. This pull in the direction of the norm is illustrated by the finding reported earlier, that voters who early in the campaign intended to vote differently from their family and associates more often than not finally changed their minds and voted with their primary group.[78] That discussion of politics in such groups waxed strong in the later phases of the campaign suggests that opinion leaders played a part in the

70. Lippitt, Polanski, Redl, & Rosen, 1952.   71. Coleman, Katz, & Menzel, 1957.   72. Katz, 1961.   73. Menzel & Katz, 1956.   74. Katz & Lazarsfeld, 1955.   75. Loy, 1969.   76. Weiss, 1969.   77. Klapper, 1961.   78. Lazarsfeld et al., 1948.

vote changes. This role of opinion leaders in stabilizing norms and resisting influence deserves further study.

THE MARGINAL PERSON: CROSS-PRESSURES   Some persons occupy a position in the social structure that subjects them to opposing points of view. In an election, for example, the members of a person's family may support one candidate and his close friends another. An early study of voting revealed that these "marginal" persons were more likely than others to make up their minds later in the campaign, to change their vote intentions, and to make frequent changes.[79] Such marginal persons have often been considered especially susceptible to persuasive communications. Indeed, political strategists argue that mass campaigns might well direct themselves primarily to undecided persons, since it has been repeatedly demonstrated that individuals with entrenched positions are unlikely to be readily influenced by the mass media. One problem in this connection, however, is that marginal persons often escape from their dilemma by turning away from the issue. Voters subjected to cross-pressures, for example, have less interest than other voters in the election, and mass campaigns are therefore unlikely to reach them.[80]

CONDITIONS AFFECTING IMPORTANCE OF PERSONAL INFLUENCE   A note of caution should be given concerning the two-step flow hypothesis. Opinion leaders are not a necessary link between the mass media and the respondent. Some target persons receive information directly from the media. Moreover, it has already been mentioned that the role of personal influence varies considerably depending upon the topic of influence. A study of the Kennedy-Nixon television debates before the 1960 election, for example, suggests that at least a minority of voters were influenced directly by the television program.[81] An experimental study of leaflet communications is consistent with this finding: It demonstrated that as the volume of information increased, interpersonal channels of communication assumed proportionately less importance.[82]

Several studies of the spread of major news items also support the view that important news in the mass media reaches persons directly, although a majority of these persons then talk it over with others.[83] In other words, when a mass campaign is not very intensive and does not pertain to an important issue, its effectiveness might be amplified by dissemination through personal channels; but when a campaign concerns an important issue and has the massive coverage achieved by the television debates, personal communications assume somewhat less importance.

In contrast to the television debates, the magnification of personal influence with diminished information flow is dramatized by a study of the small Greek village of Kalos, where the town's opinion leader was one of the only two

79. LAZARSFELD et al., 1948.   80. LAZARSFELD et al., 1948.   81. GOEKE, 1961.   82. DE FLEUR & LARSEN, 1958.   83. LARSEN & HILL, 1954; DANIELSON, 1956; DEUTSCHMANN & DANIELSON, 1960.

villagers who could read.[84] He received a newspaper and relayed the contents that he felt worth conveying; obviously his function was of tremendous importance. An opinion leader in a strategic position like this is called a gatekeeper because he controls the flow of information.[85]

SUMMARY: INTERPERSONAL NETWORKS. Person-to-person communications play a very important role in dissemination of messages from the mass media. Communications sometimes follow a two-step flow pattern, from the media to the opinion leader and from the opinion leader to other respondents. In this process the opinion leader serves not only to relay the information but also as an influence agent. The flow pattern may sometimes comprise a chain of several opinion leaders. Opinion leaders may also function in another way: They may stimulate persons to consult the mass media.

People's positions in the social structure in terms of the frequency of their communication with others determine both followership and leadership in the adoption of innovations. The process by which innovations are adopted has several stages, ranging from awareness of information about a new practice to a final decision to adopt the practice permanently. Information received directly from the mass media plays an important role in the early stages, whereas in the later stages interpersonal influences predominate.

Opinion leaders are likely to be specialized; their leadership is often confined to a particular content area. Three general characteristics of opinion leaders that have been identified, however, are: (1) opinion leaders personify the values of the group, (2) they are competent, and (3) they have a strategic social location. As representatives of the group norms, opinion leaders may also serve to resist change.

A particular kind of respondent is the marginal person, who is subjected to cross-pressures because he has membership in groups with opposing attitudes. Although he might be considered an easy target for change, he often lacks interest in or actively avoids issues related to the conflict between the groups.

Society and Mass Communication

For the most part, the discussion so far has concentrated upon the effects of the respondent's primary groups and immediate associates upon his acceptance of communications. This aspect of the social structure has received the most emphasis in research, and it is undoubtedly paramount in the influence process. The larger society in which communication takes place, however, may also affect the communication process in various ways.

84. STYCOS, 1952.   *85.* LEWIN, 1958.

The Primary Group and the Larger Social Structure

The function of primary groups in helping the individual to resist influence is often buttressed by the larger social systems to which they are related. For example, aspects of the larger German military system augmented the previously mentioned role of the small combat units of the Wehrmacht in helping individual soldiers to resist Allied propaganda.[86] A small but dedicated core of Nazi officers served as links between the armed forces and the leaders of the Nazi party, and controlled the German military. Certain policies of this larger system strengthened the primary groups in their resistance to propaganda. Solidarity was fostered by maintaining men in the same small units over a long period of time. The Nazi officers warned soldiers of severe sanctions for desertion. In addition, letters from home which encouraged military efforts were approved, but strict controls were placed upon letters which mentioned deprivations at home and which might draw the loyalty of the soldier from his combat unit to his family.

Opinion Leaders as Links between Society and the Individual

The larger social structure also influences the effectiveness of the opinion leader. In a study of the process of absorbing new immigrants into Israel, the opinion leaders who were initially most effective were community leaders such as rabbis, teachers, or local businessmen.[87] One of their main functions was determining what economic, political, and occupational activities were most desirable for the immigrant—in general, interpreting the new society to the immigrant. The following quotation from an immigrant illustrates this role of the opinion leader in linking the individual to the larger society.

> Whenever we do not know what to do, we come and ask them. . . . They are able to tell us what we have to do, how we can best get the work, to what schools to send our children. These parties and elections are also so confusing, and we do not know what they are for and how one should behave there. . . . They explain it to us and advise what to do. If it were not for this, we would probably get lost and suffer a lot. . . .[88]

At a later stage in the assimilation of the immigrants, however, the community leaders lost favor with those immigrants who gained a good understanding of the new country and its values. They came to regard their former leaders as overly conservative and not completely representative of the new society. The shift in attitude was accompanied by a greater dependence on communications from the mass media. This study demonstrates that much of the strength of the

86. SHILS & JANOWITZ, 1948.   87. EISENSTADT, 1951, 1952.   88. Reprinted with permission of The University of Chicago Press. From S. N. EISENSTADT. The place of elites and primary groups in the process of absorption of new immigrants in Israel. *American Journal of Sociology*, 1951, **57**, 222-231.

opinion leader is dependent upon his relation to and his place in the larger social structure, as well as upon his relation to the persons he influences.

The Value Structure and the Communicator

The values prevailing in a society affect the degree to which communicators are motivated and permitted to structure the situation in order to facilitate persuasion. An extreme example, referred to earlier, is the efforts of the Chinese Communists to reform the intellectuals.[89] After the Communists gained full control of the government of China, the government would not tolerate expressions of opinion in conflict with the Communist ideology. Individuals who attempted to criticize the regime or who refused to accept the party line were savagely attacked in public on repeated occasions. The regime used arrests and other forms of punishment to bring intellectuals in line. Such efforts were unrelenting for many years, and most rebels eventually gave in.

Actually, all societies place certain limits on expression of opinion, but they differ with respect to the range of values that may be expressed and with respect to certain structural features that make such restriction effective. In a democratic society, where the range of expression is apt to be broad and restrictions are less effectively implemented, some views receive wider expression than others. In the United States, a citizen cannot advocate the overthrow of government without incurring penalties, although he may freely criticize the government in many ways. As shown below, the narrower the range of values which are permitted expression, the more effective communication based on those values is likely to be.

The contrast between totalitarian and democratic societies, however, is not so wide as it may appear; communication is controlled and channeled in democratic societies to a larger extent than is widely realized. In the United States communication is affected by such factors as the continually decreasing number of newspapers that manage to avoid bankruptcy, the frequency of newspaper mergers, the growth of newspaper chains, the dominant position of the news wire services, and the power of the radio and TV networks. These circumstances inevitably put the responsibility for presenting undistorted pictures of events into the hands of a relatively small number of people.

In the first place, the sheer volume of news is so large that only a small fraction of it can be widely disseminated. The gatekeepers of the mass media make the decisions about which items shall receive national coverage. One study of the flow of news from the Associated Press to four nonmetropolitan dailies in Wisconsin documents this point very clearly.[90] About 100,000 to 125,000 words of news copy flow into the Associated Press in one daily cycle. Editors select approximately half the copy for transmission over trunk lines. From this half, the Wisconsin AP bureau selects only one-fourth for transmis-

89. CHEN, 1960.   90. CUTLIP, 1954.

sion to Wisconsin dailies, adding, however, additional Wisconsin news. Four typical dailies printed from 55 percent to 87 percent of the copy they received. Thus only a small fraction of all the news is ultimately printed in these papers.

Second, and perhaps most important, is that because of their nationwide audiences, the people who control the mass media present material that in overwhelming proportion is consistent with the audience's dominant values and attitudes. Divergent views as a rule cannot attain a widespread sympathetic hearing even though there is freedom to speak. People whose views are not in accord with dominant values are limited to media having very small and specialized audiences. Thus the mass media in a free society, as in a totalitarian society, function largely to preserve the status quo.

Informal communication channels in a free society, however, are more divergent from those in a totalitarian society. Groups that have deviant attitudes and values within a rather wide range can communicate freely and relay their views to others. A free society usually contains a great many groups and organizations with all sorts of aims and purposes that deviate from the society's central values. Some such informal channels exist in totalitarian societies as well, but they are necessarily clandestine and are greatly restricted in scope.

The Effectiveness of Mass Communications

No doubt most persons interested in the influence process would like to know exactly how effective the mass media are in disseminating information and obtaining desired actions. As this chapter has indicated, however, a general answer to this question is not very helpful. Effectiveness varies with the nature of the communication, the situation, the communication channels, and the prevailing attitudes and behaviors of respondents.

Mass communications may be thought of as having several kinds of effects. One effect is to expose persons to information about various aspects of reality ranging from the latest happenings on the international scene to the recent trends in food preparation. A second effect is to persuade people to vote, to buy, or to behave in other ways in accordance with the communicator's wishes. A third class of effects, which has little to do with persuasive intent, includes the many kinds of reactions to the entertainment content of the mass media.

Acquaintance and Persuasive Functions of the Mass Media

There seems little doubt that the mass media, through repeated exposure, can acquaint large numbers of people with a commercial product. Many persons can readily repeat some radio and television advertisements from memory, for example. Whether or not such exposure leads to acceptance of the product depends upon many other factors, including the person's attitude toward the use of the product, the degree to which his habits are already established, and the number of competing communications. If the individual's attitude is relatively neutral, if he does not have established preferences, and if competing communications are few, an intensive advertising campaign may be highly effective. This is particularly true of products that are readily accessible and that are bought on impulse, such as items on the shelves of a supermarket. Faced with a variety of labels for the same product, the consumer is likely to select the familiar one if such other matters as accessibility and price are relatively equal. But sometimes the desire for novelty and curiosity about the unfamiliar may lead him to try a new product.

Where communications run counter to important attitudes, however, quite a different result may be expected. The most intensive studies of the mass media have been in the area of elections, where the individual usually holds firmly established attitudes highly resistant to change and where he is strongly supported by group attitudes.[91] Despite the popular belief held by news commentators, politicians, and journalists that the political campaign, especially as conducted through the mass media, has a decisive influence on elections, the evidence suggests that media influences affect a very small proportion of the voters. If an election is very close, a campaign may well be decisive; but if there is a large gap between the candidates, a campaign is unlikely to close it.

An election campaign does not convert large numbers of people to new political preferences.[92] Campaigning seems primarily to intensify existing preferences, to strengthen weak ones, and to provide minimal information to voters concerning the candidates and their platforms. One study reported that there was no relation between the total amount of money spent on radio and television programs and the election of senatorial, gubernatorial, and presidential candidates.[93] However, a certain minimal exposure seems required. Free television time in England produced gains for the Liberal party, which had been previously underpublicized.[94] Another study indicated that expenditures for broadcasts had a significant effect on the *margin* of victory in both congressional houses.[95] But this effect was five times greater in the Senate, and only there was it sufficient to affect election outcomes. The study also indicated that a minimum expenditure seemed important for little-known candidates. A candidate who was an incumbent was generally known, and expenditures were less important.

Another popular belief is that television is capable of building a favorable "image" of a candidate—even an image that will enable him to win the election. Of course, television does reveal a candidate's appearance and manner, and does suggest various personal characteristics. But a review of research on images by Weiss concludes that different viewers form different impressions of a candidate from the same presentation, and that even when some definite image characteristics are created, they usually have little effect on voting be-

91. KATZ & FELDMAN, 1962.   *92.* BLUMLER & MCQUAIL, 1969; WEISS, 1971.   *93.* ALEXANDER, 1966.
94. ROSE, 1967.   *95.* DAWSON & ZINSER, 1971.

havior.[96] Numerous studies of the television debates between Nixon and Kennedy also concluded that, although the debates reached a sizable proportion of the electorate, their overall effect was to reinforce prior voting inclinations rather than to change them.[97]

Nonpersuasive Effects of the Mass Media

So far, the discussion in these chapters on social influence and attitude change has ignored a variety of effects which might result from mass communications, but which have little relation to the intent of the communicator. Some of these nonpersuasive effects are: (1) the effects on human values of crime and violence in the mass media, (2) the effects of escapist media material, and (3) the effects of audience passivity in media attendance.

CRIME AND VIOLENCE   Parents, educators, and others have often expressed concern about the high proportion of crime and violence in mass media and about its effects on children, particularly the possibility that it may contribute to juvenile delinquency. Periodically, leading public figures question its impact, and Congress has conducted a number of inquiries over the years. Contemporary discussions parallel earlier ones indicting older media such as movies and comic books. All three sources have frequently been charged with contributing to a rise in crime and violence. Content analyses have confirmed that the mass media do, in fact, devote much of their content to crime and violence in fictional form. A 1969 study estimated that 64 percent of the leading characters in television programs used violence.[98] Moreover, over 90 percent of the cartoon programs which children watch contained some violence, and 88 percent of their leading characters used violence. During the years of the Vietnam war, moreover, depiction of violence in fictional media has been paralleled by extensive coverage of real-life violence—shooting, bombing, burning—and much display of the injured, maimed, or dead victims. It is also clear that children are heavy users of television;[99] thus, especial concern has been expressed over possible effects upon them.

But that children are exposed to scenes of violence on television does not by itself allow the conclusion that such scenes cause them to become more apt to engage in violent behavior. The behavior of any individual is a complex function of many factors, and viewing television violence by itself is likely to have an inconsequential effect upon the behavior of most people. Most aggressive actions are subject to intensive shaping by socialization agents in society (e.g., parents and other significant persons). It is explained in more detail in Chapters 15 to 17 that as a result of this process children develop moral values—internal standards of right and wrong which guide their behavior to some degree. Cer-

96. WEISS, 1971.   *97.* KATZ & FELDMAN, 1962.   *98.* GERBNER, 1971.   *99.* TANNENBAUM & GREENBERG, 1968.

tain actions displayed on television would not be performed by most viewers because of their built-in internal controls or moral standards. For example, most children and adults will not intentionally kill another person or seriously injure him.

Whether or not aggressive actions occur in life situations also depends upon the nature of the situation. Most situations have normative controls with respect to various behaviors, including violence. For example, violence is the exception rather than the rule in interactions among family members or among friends or work associates, but it is expected behavior for military personnel in time of war. Even in war, however, only the enemy is the approved target.

Several reviews of research on aggression and on television are available, including the first of six volumes on research on television and violence sponsored by the National Institute of Mental Health.[100] Though some clear findings have emerged, there is also much that we do not yet know. At least two basic processes operate in the sequence of viewing violence and then behaving aggressively: first, imitation, and second, instigation. Many laboratory studies have demonstrated quite clearly that children are capable of imitating acts performed by fictional characters or live persons. The process of imitation will be discussed at much greater length in Chapter 15.

But demonstrating that children or adults can learn to perform violent acts that they have observed does not necessarily mean that they *will* perform them. What is crucial is the factors or conditions that instigate the violence. Berkowitz and others have conducted considerable research on conditions that help to instigate aggression.[101] In the laboratory media presentations designed to instigate aggression are effective only when a number of conditions are met. An individual who has viewed media violence will aggress against a frustrating agent only where: (1) the media violence is justified by the context, (2) the viewer is subsequently frustrated by an agent, (3) the agent of this later frustration is associated in some way with the previously witnessed victim in the media presentation, (4) both external and internal barriers to aggression are minimal.[102] One weakness of even this qualified generalization is that in all the studies, the experimental context was contrived to give participants the impression that aggression was not only permissible but possibly encouraged. In studies where the participant was required to deliver an electric shock to a frustrating agent after having viewed filmed aggression, for example, he was not given the choice of delivering no shock, but only a choice of how much.

As in much other social psychological research, emphasis on measurable behavior has somewhat obscured the dependent variable under investigation: Questions have been raised about whether the behavior investigated is indeed aggressive. Is, for example, hitting a rubber doll or popping an inflated balloon

---

100. GORANSON, 1970; WEISS, 1969, 1971; SURGEON GENERAL'S SCIENTIFIC ADVISORY COMMITTEE ON TELEVISION AND SOCIAL BEHAVIOR, 1971.   101. BERKOWITZ, 1964, 1965, 1969, 1970.   102. BERKOWITZ, 1965; BERKOWITZ & GEEN, 1966.

aggressive? Usually aggression is defined as behavior that injures another person, but in research the definition has been extended to behavior that, *if* it were directed at another person, would injure; by this standard, hitting a doll is aggressive. But an act can only be aggressive if its *intention* is to injure. An accidental harm to another person is not aggressive. Most researchers have paid little attention to this element of intent, or indeed to any of the logical properties of the concept of aggressive action. In most studies, for example, whether the participants who performed some "aggressive" action *felt* angry is not even investigated. Weiss underscores this failure to study the meanings of the actions performed:

> More generally, there is a total lack of information concerning the subjects' definitions of the experimental situations and the meanings or interpretations they give to the movie or the behavior of the models, or concerning their reactions during the observation of the model or the movie. In the absence of such knowledge, and in view of the fact that the fight scenes are out of their normal context and the disordered behavior of the adult model was given no rationale, any facile assumption about the viewers' reactions and interpretations should be viewed with considerable caution.[103]

More recent studies have turned to the question of the extent to which television programs actually instigate aggressive actions on the part of the children and adolescents.[104] In these investigations, television programs or films containing violent episodes were shown to one group of children, and relatively nonviolent material was shown to another group. The programs in these studies were actual programs used on television or were similar to them, unlike the brief film clips used in earlier studies. After the showing, the children were observed for a wide variety of aggressive actions, not simply the imitation of the acts they saw in the programs. Potentially, at least, these types of studies are more likely to generalize to the child viewing television at home.

None of these studies produced dramatic differences between the group exposed to media violence and the control children, but the general trend was toward increased aggressive behavior by children exposed to violence. This effect, however, was not uniform; indeed, only a minority of children accounted for the differences in aggression found. Further, these children were initially (before viewing) more aggressive than the other children. Little else is known of the characteristics of children who are affected by television violence and those who are not. Correlational studies of television viewing by adolescents and their aggressive actions also yielded positive but low relationships between television violence and aggressive behavior.[105] These findings are more

103. Reprinted with permission from W. WEISS. Effects of the mass media on communication. In G. Lindzey & E. Aronson (Eds.), *The handbook of social psychology.* (2d ed.) Vol. 5. Reading, Mass.: Addison-Wesley Publishing Company, Inc., 1969. Pp. 77–195.   *104.* EKMAN, LIEBERT, FRIESEN, HARRISON, ZLATCHIN, MALMSTROM, & BARON, 1971; FESHBACH, 1971; LEIFER & ROBERTS, 1971; LIEBERT & BARON, 1971; STEIN & FRIEDRICH, 1971.   *105.* SURGEON GENERAL'S SCIENTIFIC ADVISORY COMMITTEE, 1971.

difficult to interpret, because of the possibility that those who behave more aggressively watch more violent programs (correlation does not demonstrate a causal relation), and also because low relations of this kind can be due to association of television viewing and aggressive behavior with some unknown third factor (e.g., parental emphasis on nonaggressive behavior might produce less aggressive behavior and also less viewing of violent programs).

A once popular hypothesis was that viewing aggressive behavior has a *cathartic effect*. The assumption was that an individual builds up a need to perform aggressive acts, and that this need is satisfied or reduced in strength when the person carries out such actions. Catharsis is an alternative way of reducing this need. Because the viewer identifies himself with the aggressor, he experiences some release through viewing aggressive actions, as if he were carrying them out himself. Early experiments aimed at testing the hypothesis that viewing aggression reduces an individual's aggressive behavior yielded contradictory and meager results.

But a recent television study indicated that boys from eight to eighteen years old assigned to a heavy diet of televised violence for six weeks showed *reduced* aggressiveness in their values and in their ordinary behavior toward peers, as compared with boys given a diet of nonviolent television entertainment.[106] The investigators argue that these results suggest a cathartic effect. Unfortunately, however, a replication of this study has failed to confirm the findings.[107]

In sum, research on violence in the mass media clearly indicates that at least some children are encouraged or influenced to behave aggressively as a result of having viewed media violence. But so far it is not possible to specify precisely how many children are so affected, nor can the degree to which they are influenced be spelled out. Moreover, not enough is known about the characteristics of these children. Those who are already inclined toward violence are more affected by viewing violent programs, but other attributes that might be important are unknown. Similarly, conditions that either facilitate or inhibit the effects of television violence have not been clearly identified. Some evidence suggests, for example, that strong family norms against aggressive behavior mitigate the effects of television violence, but the findings are not entirely consistent, and little is known of other conditions that might be important.[108] Research currently under way should help to resolve these issues.

ESCAPIST CONTENT OF THE MASS MEDIA   Another criticism directed against the mass media is that much of it is escapist or fantasy material. This includes television family comedy, much light fiction, daytime serials, and often even the very material considered serious drama by television officials. Claims and counterclaims about such escapist content are widely heard. Some critics maintain that viewers turn into television addicts, become apathetic, and no longer "face

106. FESHBACH, 1971.   *107.* WELLS, 1971.   *108.* SURGEON GENERAL'S SCIENTIFIC ADVISORY COMMITTEE, 1971.

the real world." Supporters, on the other hand, argue that such material provides relaxation. Klapper notes that much content of the mass media is in fact escapist in nature, but concludes that such material does not cause any particular life pattern.[109] It does, however, serve certain psychological needs and reinforce patterns already characteristic of the audience.

PASSIVITY IN RECEIVING MASS COMMUNICATIONS   A widespread criticism of the mass media, particularly of its fictional material, has been that consuming this material is a passive occupation which is substituted for more spontaneous and creative activities the individual might otherwise engage in. There appears to be little doubt that television in particular has preempted a considerable portion of the average child's day. One extensive study has estimated that the average school child in the early grades spends two hours a day watching television and by the sixth or seventh grade spends three to four hours—a peak that falls slowly through the high school years.[110] Ten years later, another study confirmed an average viewing time of two hours per day.[111] The earlier investigation also notes the dramatic changes that such extensive viewing has produced in leisure-time activities. It has cut deeply into time spent in movie theaters, listening to the radio, and reading comic books and pulp magazines, and it has reduced the time for play. In general, television dominates the child's leisure time. On the whole, however, these data suggest that television has not been substituted for active pursuits, but has displaced other passive outlets. The most elaborate study relevant to this topic, conducted in Britain, also indicates that television does not produce passivity.[112]

The most general conclusion that can be drawn at the present time concerning the various nonpersuasive effects of the mass media is that such media are selectively used by different individuals according to predispositions and already existing attitudes. For most children, their effect, if any, consists of reinforcement of existing characteristics rather than induction of new ones. But it is also likely that a small number of children are directly influenced to adopt behaviors that are widely depicted on television, such as violence and other forms of physical aggression, and that they adopt a more accepting attitude toward such actions.

109. KLAPPER, 1961.   *110.* SCHRAMM, LYLE, & PARKER, 1961.   *111.* GERBNER, 1971.   *112.* HIMMELWEIT, OPPENHEIM, & VINCE, 1958.

6

Intergroup Attitudes

Perhaps the most intensively investigated attitudes have been those toward ethnic minorities. A vast literature is devoted to prejudice against minority groups of all types in a great variety of countries around the world. In recent years, attention has been increasingly focused upon intergroup conflict and its resolution, with topics ranging all the way from factional disputes within tribes to wars between nations. Three basic questions may be asked about intergroup attitudes: (1) What are the conditions under which unfavorable attitudes arise toward groups? (2) Through what means are unfavorable attitudes maintained? (3) How can unfavorable attitudes be changed in a more favorable direction? Although the answers overlap to some extent, each question is relatively independent of the other.

In spite of the voluminous research literature, theory on intergroup attitudes is rather poorly developed. In early research the need for theoretical guidance on intergroup attitudes, as on social psychology generally, was not clearly recognized. Research on prejudice suffers also from the focus of most past empirical work on cognitions and feelings, with less attention given to intergroup *behavior*. Recently, interest in intergroup theory and behavior has markedly increased. Especially important in raising interest has been the new self-consciousness and pride that have arisen among ethnic minorities. Led by the "black power" movement, ethnic and other minorities have taken active steps to increase their awareness of themselves as a people with a history and a destiny. The idea of America as a melting pot, which places emphasis upon

1. KATZ, 1970.

accommodation and assimilation of the minority group, has been abandoned by some groups. Instead of focusing on fitting into and modeling themselves according to a majority pattern, many ethnic groups are emphasizing their uniqueness and distinctiveness and are thus building an identity of their own. Blacks are most outstanding in this respect, with their emphasis on African studies, black literature, and other cultural achievements, along with a distinctive style of dress and the slogan "Black is beautiful." This new emphasis should lead to more research on the attitudes of minorities toward majority groups, an area that has been much neglected.

During the past two decades, social psychological theory has developed more rapidly than hitherto, and has assumed a more central role in social psychology. The attempt in this chapter is to take advantage of this development to organize a more coherent body of knowledge about prejudice and discrimination.

Prejudice, Discrimination, and Conflict

Prejudice is an attitude that predisposes a person to think, perceive, feel, and act in favorable or unfavorable ways toward a group or its individual members. Whether or not a prejudiced individual will actually behave in accordance with his attitude depends upon situational and other factors. Thus the term prejudice stresses the perceptual, cognitive, and emotional content of the individual's internal predispositions and experience. It does not necessarily imply that behavior is congruent with such experience.

The perceptual-cognitive or belief content of prejudice has already been discussed at length in Chapter 2 in the section on stereotypes. Members of a group or category of persons are seen as having certain traits or qualities that are different from those of the general population. Such stereotyping has three characteristics: (1) Persons are categorized according to certain identifying characteristics, (2) people in general agree on the attributes that the persons in the category possess, and (3) a discrepancy exists between attributed traits and actual traits. Although some stereotypes are more definite than others, for most familiar minority groups consensus among observers is very much above the level that would be achieved if traits were assigned to the group at random.

Social psychologists usually think of the emotional strength of prejudice in a particular individual as a point on a continuum ranging from extremely unfavorable to extremely favorable. Thus, an individual's prejudice may be strongly unfavorable, moderately unfavorable, etc. Other emotional aspects of prejudice may be studied, such as the actual content of emotions as expressed verbally by the individual, or the consistency with which he expresses such feelings in a wide variety of situations. The most common measure of prejudice used in research, however, is the individual's degree of positive (or negative) feeling toward the ethnic group.

Discrimination is the inequitable treatment of individuals considered to belong to a particular social group.[2] As Simpson and Yinger note, discrimination is ordinarily the overt or behavioral expression of prejudice; it is the categorical treatment of a person because of his membership in a particular group.[3] In general, the individual so treated is denied privileges or rights that are accorded to other members of society who do not belong to the minority group. Simpson and Yinger also note, however, that discrimination may occur without the accompanying feeling of prejudice—for example, when a proprietor refuses to accept as patrons members of a minority group because he feels it would injure his business. He may not be prejudiced but may feel that he must place his business before other considerations; or he may actually be prejudiced and simply use his business as vehicle for expressing his prejudice.

Origins of Prejudice and Discrimination

This section identifies the conditions under which prejudice and discrimination against a particular group arise. It is addressed to the question of why one group rather than another is singled out as an object of prejudice and discrimination. The factors responsible for the maintenance of such prejudice and discrimination will be discussed later.

It is convenient to use the terms *ingroup* and *outgroup*. An *ingroup* consists of persons who experience a sense of belonging, a sense of having a like identity. An *outgroup,* considered from the point of view of ingroup members, is a group of persons who have distinctive characteristics that set them apart from the ingroup.

Origins of Prejudice

A first principle is: The character of the existing relations between ingroup and outgroup generates attitudes toward each other that are consonant with these relations. In other words, unequal status and power between two groups produce feelings of prejudice. For example, when a dominant group holds another group in a condition of slavery, slaves are likely to be considered lazy, irresponsible, and lacking in initiative. These beliefs emerge because slaves act upon orders from their masters and are denied opportunity to demonstrate initiative or responsibility. Thus the beliefs about them are consonant with their behavior, which is controlled by the structure of the relation.

Another example comes from the historical development of prejudice against Jews. An image of Jews as rich, grasping, and shrewd grew out of their occupational role as moneylenders.[4] In the tenth and eleventh centuries the development of cities led to a sharply increased demand for capital in the form of money. The Catholic Church prohibited Christians from lending money at

2. WILLIAMS, 1947.   3. SIMPSON & YINGER, 1965.   4. SIMPSON & YINGER, 1965.

interest, but did permit Christians to borrow from Jews. Thus Jews became bankers at a time when this occupation was extremely profitable, and the cognitive images commensurate with the role became firmly established. In addition, no doubt, competitive circumstances produced hostility toward Jews: they refused to lend money to some would-be borrowers, they charged more interest than borrowers thought fair, and they were envied for their wealth.

Data collected during the dispute between India and China over the borderline between their countries provide another illustration of the marked change in the perception of an outgroup which occurs because of a change in the structure of intergroup relations.[5] Stereotypes of the Chinese held by Indians were measured before the state of conflict arose and again when tensions were strong. College students at Patna University in India were asked in February 1959 and again in December to select the five attributes from a list of eighty that most characterized members of nine countries, including China. A dramatic change occurred in characteristics assigned to the Chinese. Only three of the ten traits originally most often assigned to the Chinese were attributed to them during the dispute. The Chinese had been looked upon as friendly, progressive, honest, nationalistic, brave, cultured, and active before the dispute, but were subsequently considered to be aggressive, cheaters, selfish, warmongers, cruel, shrewd, and stupid. Only minor changes occurred in the stereotypes of the other countries. A number of other studies have shown similar changes in national stereotypes as a result of world events.[6]

Origins of Discrimination

Unequal status between groups, then, generates prejudice. In attempting to determine how unequal status arises in the first place, a basic principle from exchange theory is relevant: Where the reward-cost outcomes of two separately bounded groups are perceived to be mutually exclusive, so that each group can improve its outcomes only at the expense of the other, the members of each group strive to protect or to increase their outcomes. In other words, the effort of the more powerful ingroup to maintain outcomes of the outgroup at a low level and their own at a high level is at the base of discrimination and conflict. If the two groups are unequal in power, they will establish different outcomes unless prevented by norms that restrain exploitation of the weaker by the more powerful. These different outcomes create differences in the status of the two groups.

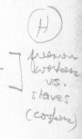

The extent to which the members of the outgroup feel discriminated against and dislike or feel hostile toward the ingroup is a function of the relation between their own *comparison level* and that of the ingroup, as well as the relative outcomes of each. In the discussion of exchange theory in Chapter 7 the comparison level is defined as the outcome an individual believes he de-

5. Sinha & Upadhyaya, 1960.   6. Dodd, 1935; Dudycha, 1942; Seago, 1947; Buchanan, 1951.

serves to attain. If the outgroup has the same comparison level as the ingroup but is receiving an appreciably lower outcome, it is likely to be dissatisfied and hostile. But if its comparison level is sufficiently low relative to that of the ingroup, no such feelings may be experienced. Whether the outgroup uses the comparison level of the ingroup in determining its own comparison level depends upon the past experiences of the outgroup, the outcomes available in alternative relations, and structural and cultural factors. For example, differential outcomes would be more likely to create dissatisfaction in a society with strong equalitarian values than in a society where a caste system is the accepted way of life.

Outgroups with rising comparison levels not matched by increasing outcomes are likely to be very dissatisfied. For example, as long as the comparison level of the American black was kept very low, he did not express much overt dissatisfaction. Since World War II, however, the gains made by the black in partially breaking down segregation and other forms of discriminatory practices have contributed to a rising comparison level but only slight gains in outcome, resulting in much greater dissatisfaction. In the first edition of this book it was predicted that mass demonstrations, organized protests, and more violent forms of rebellion would increase with a rising comparison level.[7] A decade later it is apparent that history has borne out the prediction. Since there remains today a considerable gap between expectations and outcomes for such ethnic groups as blacks, Puerto Ricans, and Mexican-Americans, continued conflict may be anticipated.

The subjective judgment of the individual who is the target of prejudice and discrimination is crucial. It is not the *realities* of a situation that determine behavior, but the *judgment* that outcomes are mutually exclusive, the *judgment* of one's own outcomes as compared with those of the other group, and the *judgment* of possible threats to the present level of outcomes.

Thus, discrimination and conflict arise from competitive situations, particularly those where one side has greater power and status than the other and where the comparison levels of the two groups are determined by the same considerations. An illustration is a laboratory experiment in which the experimenter established two levels of status for two groups of boys. They played several games in which one group was always assigned a lower status by the experimenter. The game of "human croquet" is described by the experimenter as follows:

> In this game the members of one team stand side by side in a line and each member bends over to form an arch or "wicket." The members of the other team then are formed in a single file and, on a signal from the experimenter, the first member crawls through the wickets and back again, at which time he touches the second member who then crawls through and back, and so on. The goodness of a team's performance depends on how long it takes all of its members to complete this procedure.[8]

7. Secord & Backman, 1964a, p. 415.   8. Thibaut, 1950, p. 257.

The point is that the team assigned to the passive role of wicket was not allowed to assume the other role of showing how it could perform in the game. Similarly, the high-status team in another game was allowed to throw beanbags at a target held by the low-status team, who also retrieved the beanbags. The low-status team was not given an opportunity to toss bags at the target.

Throughout the investigation, the experimenter consistently favored the high-status group. These conditions produced a good deal of hostility, particularly by the low-status team toward the high-status team, expressed by such taunts as "My little sister can throw better than that" and by name calling, kicking, pushing, slapping, and hitting. The high-status team appeared to experience some triumph but also some guilt feelings arising from the norms of fair play, which restrict exploitation. In this experiment, however, most of the hostile feeling was expressed toward the high-status team by the deprived low-status unit. Some hostility was probably also aroused toward the experimenter, but displaced toward the high status team because of the experimenter's status and authority.

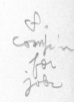

In a more elaborate experiment conducted in a field setting, two groups were put in competition with each other under such conditions that both sides experienced losses.[9] Considerable hostility developed in both groups. Two separate groups of boys were set up in a camp situation. For the first two days neither group knew the other was there, and no interaction took place between them. During this period, stable group structures became established, as well as ingroup feelings. In the next stage various competitive situations were set up between the groups, such as a tug of war which was won by the "Rattlers." The "Eagles" retaliated by burning the Rattlers' flag. Such incidents multiplied, producing extreme social distance between the groups. In addition, stereotyped images arose. The boys applied such terms as *brave, tough,* and *friendly* to members of their own group, and *sneaky, smart alecks,* and *stinkers* to members of the outgroup. Bias was illustrated by the fact that the performance of outgroup members was underestimated, whereas ingroup performance was overestimated.

The principle that actions of an outgroup which lower the reward-cost outcomes of the ingroup lead to discrimination and conflict is supported by other field studies. In a study of neighborhoods in Chicago near areas that had recently been occupied by blacks, the investigator found that low-income whites in the area closest to the new black neighborhoods were more hostile than low-income whites whose neighborhoods were a little farther away.[10] After evaluating interview responses, the investigator concluded that the hostility was based on competition for dwelling units in the midst of a severe housing shortage. The white residents believed, with some justification, that they would be driven out because of the desire of their landlords to rent to blacks who would be willing to pay a higher rent.

9. SHERIF, HARVEY, WHITE, HOOD, & SHERIF, 1961.   *10.* WINDER, 1955.

Summary: Origins of prejudice and discrimination

A basic principle underlying the origins of prejudice and discrimination against minority groups is: The character of the existing relations between ingroup and outgroup generates attitudes toward each other that are consonant with these relations. In other words, the structure of the relation between two groups in terms of relative status and power produces cognitions and feelings which are appropriate to that structure. Attributes and beliefs not directly relevant to the intergroup relation may also be perceived: If an outgroup has a status different from that of the ingroup with respect to certain attributes, its members are likely to be perceived as having other attributes and beliefs congruent with that status.

Discrimination and hostility arise from a relation in which two groups have unequal status. The unequal status between groups is explained in terms of exchange theory. Members of groups engaged in interaction with each other behave so as to maximize the reward-cost outcomes accruing to themselves. If two groups are unequal in power, members of the more powerful group are likely to establish more favorable reward-cost outcomes than those in the less powerful group. To the extent that the comparison levels of the two groups are determined by the same conditions, the group having lower status is likely to feel discriminated against and to experience dislike and hostility toward the majority group.

Maintenance of Prejudice and Discrimination

Some of the conditions that create prejudice and discrimination are rather obvious. The factors that maintain prejudice and discrimination over a period of time are perhaps more subtle. We may view these factors as operating on three levels: the social structure, individual personality dynamics, and the culture.

Factors in the Social Structure

CONFORMITY TO THE NORM OF PREJUDICE   Once prejudice and discrimination against an outgroup are well established, the accompanying cognitions, feelings, and ways of treating the outgroup become *social norms*. Social norms are attitudes that are *shared* by members of the ingroup; members *expect* each other to hold such attitudes. A good illustration comes from a housing study.[11] It was anticipated that white and black housewives in an integrated housing project would have more contacts with each other than would white and black husbands, and thus the white housewives were expected to be less prejudiced than their husbands. This hypothesis was not substantiated. The experimenter

11. WORKS, 1961.

suggested that the explanation was that wives influenced their husbands to change their attitudes in the direction of less prejudice. Interviews with husbands provided some support for this view.

Pettigrew's study of prejudice against blacks in the southern and the northern United States and in the Union of South Africa may have presented the best evidence that conformity to social norms is an important factor in prejudice.[12] It is important to note that this study was done in the mid-1950s, when prejudice toward blacks was a widely shared social norm in the regions studied. The investigation demonstrated that the persons who were most likely to conform to the norms of their society were also the most prejudiced. The degree of prejudice against Africans by white South African students was determined by an attitude scale, and two groups were formed: those higher than average in prejudice and those lower than average. Another questionnaire was scaled to measure conformity to social norms that were independent of prejudice (e.g., attendance at church). The more highly prejudiced group endorsed every item of the scale to a greater extent, demonstrating a direct association between conformity and prejudice. Other characteristics likely to be associated with acceptance of the social norms of prejudice were then studied. Students were found to be more antiblack if they were born in South Africa, if they identified with the Nationalist party, if they were upwardly mobile, and if their fathers were employed in a manual occupation.

In studying the southern United States, Pettigrew thought that six sociocultural dimensions would be associated with greater conformity to social norms and thus would be likely to identify persons who were more prejudiced. These six dimensions were all found to be associated with higher prejudice. Females were more prejudiced than males, churchgoers more than nonchurchgoers, the upwardly mobile more than the nonmobile, Democrats or Republicans more than independents, the nonveteran more than the veteran, and the less educated to a greater degree than the more educated. The most crucial factor in interpreting these data is that in the northern United States, on the other hand, these sociocultural dimensions were either not associated with prejudice or were associated to a lesser extent. This is as expected, since prejudice against the black is less pervasive as a social norm in the North. There it tends to be more covert and not quite socially acceptable. In conclusion, the study indicated that both in South Africa and in the southern United States, where prejudice is an important social norm, persons who show more conformity to norms are also more prejudiced. A possible alternative interpretation—that the conformers were more prejudiced because they were more authoritarian in personality—was ruled out by a statistical analysis of the measures of authoritarianism obtained from the South Africans and from Americans in the Southern and Northern states.

The factors underlying conformity to the norms of prejudice may be ex-

12. PETTIGREW, 1958.

plained in terms of the varying reward-cost outcomes ensuing from conformity or noncomformity. If prejudice and discrimination against another group are the norm, then the overt expression of prejudice and the performance of acts of discrimination are likely to elicit approval from other members.[13] Conversely, expression of a friendly attitude toward members of the outgroup or failure to discriminate against them violates the norm of prejudice and is likely to be costly in bringing forth disapproval and other sanctions from group members. This is consistent with the observation that people in some Southern communities who dared to speak out in favor of integration often had to bear slanderous letters and telephone calls, burned crosses, and bomb threats.[14]

One illustration of the rewards for conformity is the success of Southern politicians who have risen to power on the issue of maintaining segregation and white supremacy. For example, one study of Arkansas voting patterns has shown that before the Little Rock racial crisis involving integration in public schools, the more the voters of a county favored segregation, the less likely they were to vote for Governor Faubus.[15] After he assumed his dramatic role as a defender of segregation, however, this condition was reversed: The counties most strongly supporting segregation cast proportionately more votes for him. Another investigation of voting patterns for J. Strom Thurmond, the Dixiecrat candidate for President in 1956, indicated that he received much support because of his emphasis on white supremacy.[16]

The perceived costs of nonconformity to norms are widely varied and act in many ways to reinforce prejudice against ethnic groups. For example, officials of some universities which once used quota systems to exclude all but a small proportion of ethnic group members pleaded that if their institutions did not conform to the prejudices of the students and faculty, morale of the campus community would be greatly damaged.[17] Fortunately this attitude has changed greatly and most colleges and universities are actively recruiting more ethnic and minority group students. Another example is a business executive who argues that since Jews are not accepted as members in various exclusive clubs in which important business deals are transacted, he cannot hire them as executives in his business:

> It is important for our business . . . that our plant managers maintain a certain status in their communities. They must join the country club and the leading city club. Today, that's where the big deals are discussed and made. They must be socially acceptable to the banking and business leaders of the town. They must be able to maintain a free and easy association with the people who count. If we promote Jewish personnel into key, sensitive positions, we run a risk of social non-acceptability. We avoid this by picking someone else.[18]

13. HYMAN & SHEATSLEY, 1954.   *14.* PETTIGREW, 1961.   *15.* PETTIGREW & CAMPBELL, 1960.   *16.* HEER, 1959.   *17.* EPSTEIN & FORSTER, 1958.   *18.* Reprinted with permission from N. C. BELTH. Discrimination and the power structure. In N. C. Belth (Ed.), *Barriers: Patterns of discrimination against Jews.* New York: Anti-Defamation League of B'Nai B'rith, 1958. P. 11.

The costs of nonconformity may also be illustrated by the dilemma which confronted Protestant ministers in the Little Rock crisis. National Protestant leadership had come out strongly in favor of integration. Various opinion polls, however, showed that only one out of six Southerners favored desegregation. Thus, a minister who followed his church leaders and spoke out vigorously in favor of school integration was in danger of lowering both attendance and contributions to his church—and of losing members outright. A study of the behavior of Little Rock ministers faced with this dilemma showed that, although initially their public statements had favored integration, after rioting occurred at Central High School they did not take a clear position on the integration issue, but simply denounced violence and stressed peace and prayer.[19]

In all these instances, it is the *perceived* costs of conformity that determine behavior. For example, discrimination against ethnic groups in business transactions is probably in the long run more costly than nondiscrimination; but actual long-run costs do not affect behavior unless they are perceived.

INTERACTION PATTERNS   Prejudice and discrimination create certain interaction patterns that contribute to maintenance of the status quo. Several interaction patterns increase cohesion and thus strengthen the power of the group to enforce conformity to norms of prejudice and discrimination. Any factor that makes members more dependent on the ingroup is likely to increase cohesion. For example, members of the ingroup interact more frequently with each other and reduce interaction with members of the outgroup. Such interaction produces positive affect and greater cohesion among members of the ingroup, giving them more power to enforce conformity.

Interaction within the ingroup may also increase the economic dependence of members upon each other. Businessmen or professionals who deal exclusively with members of the ingroup face loss of investments and income if they refuse to side with the ingroup in any issue involving prejudice or discrimination. Also, to the extent that a group member looks to other members for validation of his attitudes and beliefs, he is more subject to conformity pressures. Finally, if interaction within each group predominates over interaction across group lines, the development of patterns of thinking, feeling, and behaving unique to each group is fostered. Such interaction patterns extend the cultural gulf that separates the two groups. For example, the segregation of the American black increases interactions among blacks and among whites but reduces interaction across these racial groups. Lack of interaction contributes to differences in attitudes and values between the two groups.

LEADERSHIP SUPPORT   Still another maintenance process is the emergence of leaders who support norms of prejudice and discrimination. Political leaders, as noted earlier, are likely to rise to power to the extent that they represent the

19. CAMPBELL & PETTIGREW, 1959.

norms characteristic of the voting populace. Persons who hold attitudes at variance with the norms are not likely to be successful in elections. Thus, as leaders acquire power, they exert further influence in support of the status quo. In the past this process was probably extremely important in the South in maintaining prejudice against the black. More recently, however, there has been some replacement of segregationist leaders by more moderate ones in some Southern states and local areas. This change has been brought on in part by an approach to resolution of the conflict between Southern values and national values of equality, in part by respect for the implementation by courts of the Supreme Court desegregation decision of the 1950s, and also in part by industrialization of the South, which moves the area toward national instead of regional social norms.

ENVIRONMENTAL SUPPORTS FOR PREJUDICE   Krech and Crutchfield have observed that where prejudice is widespread, the discrimination arising from it creates social conditions and individual characteristics that support the prejudiced attitudes.[20] It was noted above that prejudice and discrimination arise out of a specific type of relation between an ingroup and an outgroup and that eventually attitudes toward the outgroup acquire a normative character. Ultimately these attitudes are built into the social institutions of the society in which they prevail. For example, until after World War II, attitudes toward blacks were reflected in the practices of the military services, which assigned black soldiers and sailors to segregated units, thus helping to perpetuate prejudiced attitudes. In Southern states, segregation in parks, schools, restaurants, terminals, and other public facilities had been legitimatized by municipal and state laws for more than a century until declared unconstitutional by the U.S. Supreme Court. Segregating blacks in this way emphasized their differences and made it easier to attribute unfavorable characteristics to them.

In literature, movies, and television, ethnic group members have often been cast in roles appropriate to minority group stereotypes.[21] A study conducted in 1969 indicates that this practice has become relatively rare.[22] In addition, the black movement has led to the production of films and other media in which blacks are favorably portrayed, although some films are an exception to this shift. Other institutions such as the church and the educational system have also contributed to the support of prejudice and discrimination; only recently, as a result of the Supreme Court decision in 1954 outlawing segregation in educational institutions, have there been widespread attempts to erase the reflection of the norm of prejudice from public schools and colleges.

Finally, because of discrimination, certain objective qualities of some minority groups, such as blacks, are in fact consistent with prejudiced attitudes. There are two categories of qualities created by discrimination. First, since most blacks receive poor educations, have low incomes, work in menial occu-

20. KRECH & CRUTCHFIELD, 1948.   *21.* BERELSON & SALTER, 1946.   *22.* COX, 1969.

pations, and live in substandard housing, they are in fact different from many members of the majority white group. These differences provide the prejudiced person with evidence of the "validity" of his beliefs and feelings about the black. Because they are strongly discriminated against, blacks well illustrate the importance of such environmental supports.

Another category of difference stems from the ethnic group member's reaction to discrimination. Allport has cited a number of such reactions that serve as environmental supports.[23] For example, because of the constant anxiety over meeting a prejudiced reaction in an interpersonal situation, a member of an ethnic group may become oversensitized to possible prejudice. His attitude may be used against him by prejudiced persons, who complain that he goes around with a "chip on his shoulder." An opposite mechanism may also be used as an illustration. In reaction to prejudice, members of minority groups may withdraw from contact with majority group members: They are then accused of being clannish.

Individual Processes

The social structure has much to do with determining the particular groups that become objects of prejudice and discrimination, and it also establishes various conditions that help to maintain prejudice toward these groups. Certain processes operating at the level of the individual personality should not be ignored, however. Prejudice is established and maintained in each individual through learning and other individual processes.

FRUSTRATION AND AGGRESSION: SCAPEGOATING   Freud was one of the first to emphasize and analyze in great detail the point that when a person is prevented from satisfying his needs, he is likely to engage in aggressive behavior.[24] Early experimental work on this hypothesis provided some support for it.[25] Often the frustrating agent is not a suitable target for hostility because of his great power. In such instances the hostility may be directed against a "scapegoat," an innocent party. Simpson and Yinger describe this process and note that ethnic group members may often be selected as targets:

> There is much evidence to indicate that the blocking of goal-directed behavior frequently creates hostile impulses in the individual. In many instances this hostility cannot be directed toward the source of the frustration; there may be no human agent, or the agent may be unknown, or too powerful to strike. . . . The hostility under such circumstances may be stored up, or it may be directed toward oneself or toward some substitute target that is more accessible or less able to strike back. In other words, a "free-floating," undirected hostility may result from frustration when the actual frustrating agent

23. ALLPORT, 1958.   *24.* FREUD, 1915.   *25.* DOLLARD, DOOB, MILLER, MOWRER, & SEARS, 1939.

cannot be attacked; and the social context often favors displacement of this hostility onto minority-group members.[26]

In the process of scapegoating, the true basis of the frustration is not removed. Thus the hostility is continually generated, and continually expressed toward the outgroup. A study of feuding between clans in Morocco suggests that this social conflict is quite functional.[27] Under the harsh conditions of life there, enemy clans provide an outlet for a person's aggressions; moreover, the continual feuding with these clans strengthens the feeling of security that the individual experiences through membership in his own clan.

Quite a number of studies have been conducted in the attempt to test the scapegoating hypothesis experimentally.[28] Although not all the studies have supported the hypothesis, some investigations have.[29] These have also identified some of the limitations of the experiments that failed to substantiate the notion of scapegoating.[30] Studies of scapegoating generally set up a situation in which the participants are made to fail in a task, are insulted by the experimenter, or are blocked from attaining some goal in which they are interested. Such frustration is presumed to create aggression, some of which should result in an increase in prejudice on scales administered after the frustrating experience. The investigations vary considerably, however, in the methods by which people are frustrated, the measures of prejudice used, and the overall situations that define the experimental context.

One of the more adequate of these studies is Weatherley's.[31] He administered an anti-Semitism scale to a large number of male non-Jewish college students and chose two groups high and two groups low in anti-Semitism. One group in each category was subjected to an aggression-arousing situation: The experimenter made highly insulting remarks while the participants were filling out a brief questionnaire. The controls, also consisting of one group high and one group low in anti-Semitism, filled out the same questionnaire in a friendly, nonprovoking atmosphere.

A different experimenter, who ostensibly had nothing to do with the earlier sessions, then gave both groups picture-story tests. The pictures were eight pencil sketches, two each of four different males, to whom were assigned names, ages, and occupations. Two of the names sounded Jewish and two did not. The experimenter asked the subjects to tell a story about each picture. When the stories were analyzed to determine the number of aggressive acts described toward each character depicted, the most significant findings were (1) that the stories by the highly anti-Semitic subjects directed more aggressive acts

26. SIMPSON & YINGER, 1958, p. 76.   *27.* LEWIS, 1961.   *28.* MILLER & BUGELSKI, 1948; ROSENBLITH, 1949; LINDZEY, 1950; STAGNER & CONGDON, 1955; COWEN, LANDES, & SCHAET, 1958; BERKOWITZ, 1961; WEATHERLEY, 1961; BERKOWITZ & GREEN, 1962.   *29.* COWEN et al., 1958; BERKOWITZ, 1959, 1961; WEATHERLEY, 1961; BERKOWITZ & GREEN, 1962.   *30.* ZAWADSKI, 1948; LINDZEY, 1950; STAGNER & CONGDON, 1955.   *31.* WEATHERLEY, 1961.

toward the Jewish characters than the subjects low in anti-Semitism did, and (2) that there was no difference between high and low groups in the number of responses they assigned to non-Jewish characters.

Although many other studies have tested the scapegoating hypothesis, that prejudiced persons have a generalized tendency to displace aggression, this study tests the more specific hypothesis that a highly anti-Semitic person may have a strong tendency to displace aggression toward Jews, but not necessarily toward other objects. One limitation of this study, however, is that most of the differences between participants high and low in anti-Semitism can be attributed to a bias toward Jews by participants low in anti-Semitism, rather than to a bias against Jews by persons high in anti-Semitism. The experimental group low in anti-Semitism differed from the control group low in anti-Semitism by directing appreciably fewer aggressive actions against the Jewish characters than against the non-Jewish characters. Similarly, the experimental group low in anti-Semitism directed fewer aggressive actions against the Jewish characters than against the non-Jewish characters.

Two other studies also emphasize the stimulus qualities of the scapegoat. In the first, participants who worked in pairs were induced to like or dislike their partners.[32] Subsequently, the experimenter frustrated half of the pairs and gave the other half more pleasant treatment. In the last part of the study, the two members of each pair and a neutral peer, a confederate of the experimenter, were put to work on a cooperative task. According to scapegoating theory, when the persons were later asked to evaluate their work partners, the hostility aroused by the experimenter should have been displaced to the disliked partner rather than the neutral partner. This hypothesis was confirmed.

Another investigation compared hostility directed against two frustrating agents, one who had the same name as a victim of aggression in a film shown to the participants and one who had a different name.[33] More hostility was directed against the former than the latter. Such studies demonstrate that a person who is disliked or who has been a victim of aggression is apt to be an object of scapegoating. By implication, persons who are objects of prejudice are also probable candidates for scapegoating.

ECONOMIC AND STATUS GAINS   One might expect scapegoating to occur most frequently when competition is most severe and status is threatened. There is no direct evidence on this point, but prejudice does seem to be greatest under such conditions. A study made in a Southern county in the United States identified a "hard core" of white men who said they would use force to oppose desegregation if necessary.[34] These men as a group were at the bottom of the status hierarchy in education, income, and occupation; of all the white men in the county, they had the poorest chances for improving their own position and

32. BERKOWITZ & GREEN, 1962.   *33.* BERKOWITZ & GEEN, 1967.   *34.* TUMIN, 1958.

were the most threatened by the rise in status of blacks. People in such a condition are likely to believe that they have much to gain by maintaining prejudice and discrimination against the black.

Simpson and Yinger note shifting attitudes toward the black in concert with changing economic periods.[35] During the early years of the United States, a time of expansion when work for skilled persons such as carpenters and brick-layers was ample, the proportion of blacks doing these types of labor was relatively high. As the amount of work available diminished, the proportion of blacks in these trades was gradually reduced; from 1910 to 1940 it fell from 26 percent to 15 percent in the South. Presumably this fall made room for lower-class whites in these occupations, resulting in an economic gain for them.

PERSONALITY NEEDS   A variety of personality needs may support prejudice. One need that has been intensively studied is intolerance for ambiguity. Persons differ in the extent to which they are disturbed by confusing or ambiguous situations. At one extreme, some people like to have everything clearly defined in terms of good and bad, and at the other, some are not in the least disturbed by confusing or uncertain situations. In general, persons who are intolerant of ambiguity are also likely to be prejudiced.[36] Prejudice may serve the needs of such people because it clarifies ambiguous and confusing situations. A white laborer who has lost his job and who is having a difficult time finding another may, for example, decide that the cause of his troubles is the influx of blacks into his city.

Likewise, a need to achieve superior status may be supported by prejudice, which classifies a group of persons as lower in status than oneself. A person may also feel a sense of identification with his own kind through prejudice. Allport describes clearly how a person may bolster his self-esteem by turning his attention to outgroups:

> The easiest idea to sell anyone is that he is better than someone else. The appeal of the Ku Klux Klan and racist agitators rests on this type of sales-manship. Snobbery is a way of clutching at one's status, and it is as common, perhaps more common, among those who are low in the ladder. By turning their attention to unfavored out-groups, they are able to derive from the comparison a modicum of self-esteem. Out-groups, as status builders, have the special advantage of being near at hand, visible (or at least name-able), and occupying a lower position by common agreement, thus providing social support for one's own sense of status enhancement.[37]

The need for security may be satisfied through rejection of an outgroup. Many writers have noted that conflict between an ingroup and an outgroup leads to increased solidarity among members of the ingroup.[38] Such friction

---

35. SIMPSON & YINGER, 1965.   *36.* ADORNO, FRENKEL-BRUNSWICK, LEVINSON, & SANFORD, 1950.   *37.* ALLPORT, 1958.   *38.* COSER, 1956.

sharpens the boundaries between groups and reaffirms the identity of the in-group. Two experiments previously cited support these ideas.[39] Thus, we may expect that discrimination and conflict with an outgroup are likely to make an individual feel more secure in his ingroup membership—to give him a greater sense of belonging.

The comparatively recent movement toward developing pride in ethnic identity, typified for blacks in the slogan "Black is beautiful," is relevant here.[40] This trend toward emphasizing the distinctiveness and uniqueness of an ethnic group, its identity as a people, is apt to have a number of consequences. One is to increase the degree to which the members of the group are perceived as different from the ingroup; they are then seen as more of an outgroup, which is apt to increase prejudice and discrimination against them. At the same time their comparison levels are apt to rise and their dissatisfaction with their status will become more acute if their outcomes do not rise sufficiently rapidly. Pettigrew has viewed this trend toward separateness from society as a whole and cohesiveness within the ethnic group with alarm, noting that it prevents learning of values common to all and develops values that are distinctive to the ethnic group, reducing contact and communication between it and other groups.[41]

Guttentag, on the other hand, has emphasized the positive values of ethnic identity.[42] The conflict produced by it between the ethnic group and the larger society is apt to increase the cohesiveness of the ethnic group and to strengthen its position and its motivation to improve outcomes. Ethnic group members who have been unable to identify either with their own group or the larger society can find a place among their "brothers and sisters" with the aid of a sense of ethnic identity. Self-hate, a phenomenon common to oppressed groups, is apt to be reduced. Reviewing the history of many different groups, Guttentag observes that the ethnic groups that have survived poverty have been those with an ideology that stressed their superiority vis-à-vis other groups or the larger society. Lewin's 1936 review of the history of the Jewish people in previous centuries led him to the same conclusion.[43]

THE AUTHORITARIAN PERSONALITY   Chapter 2 described a type of person with an *authoritarian personality,* a pattern of traits which shows an important relation to prejudice. This pattern, found in the adult person, appears to relate to certain aspects of family structure and discipline experienced as a child. His parents are thought to have exercised rigid discipline, affection being conditional upon approval of his behavior. Dominance, submission, and differential status were emphasized. Expression of hostility, particularly toward his parents or other family members, was strictly prohibited. The theory is that a child who grows up in such an atmosphere develops repressive mechanisms for disguising

39. THIBAUT, 1950; SHERIF et al., 1961.   40. CAPLAN, 1970.   41. PETTIGREW, 1969.   42. GUTTEN-TAG, 1970.   43. LEWIN, 1948.

his own hostility and controlling his impulses. These mechanisms lead to some lack of insight into his own functioning and to rigid attitudes toward interaction with other persons. The values of the authoritarian person and the manner in which he functions appear to be especially suited to forming prejudice toward outgroups. He emphasizes power, status, and dominance. His hostilities are repressed, and the prejudice toward outgroups sanctioned by his society provides an outlet for these hostilities. His rigidity and inflexibility lead him to make strict discriminations among other groups of persons.

ATTITUDINAL CONSISTENCY   Chapter 3 discussed the tendency of various attitudinal components to be consistent with one another. The individual strives for a state of consistency among affect, cognitions, and behavioral dispositions. Thus, forces toward changing any one of these components are resisted so long as the other components remain unchanged. This principle produces some distortion or misperception of the behavior of the outgroup. A person who has a set of cognitions and a given level of affect toward an outgroup is likely to misperceive actions of the outgroup that are at variance with his preconceptions, and to classify them as consistent with his preconceptions. Similarly, he will avoid friendly behavior toward the outgroup because such behavior would be inconsistent with his hostile affect and cognitions.

An anecdote reported by Allport illustrates distortion of cognition in the direction of prejudice:

> At a session of summer school an irate lady of middle age approached the instructor saying, "I think there is a girl of Negro blood in this class." To the instructor's noncommittal reply, the lady persisted, "But you wouldn't want a nigger in the class, would you." Next day she returned and firmly insisted, "I know she's a nigger because I dropped a paper on the floor and said to her, 'Pick that up.' She did so, and that proves she's just a darky servant trying to get above her station."[44]

Although some support for the principle of consistency was cited in Chapter 3, sufficient empirical evidence is not yet available in support of consistency among evaluative, cognitive, and behavioral components of *prejudice*. Moreover, where consistency requires that the individual change the evaluative component of his attitude, the strong anchorage of emotions in physiological functions is apt to produce resistance to change. Evaluative components of prejudice are often gut feelings, presumably produced through extensive conditioning.

Several different investigations have shown that participants have a large *galvanic skin response* (GSR—a measure of emotional response associated with the autonomic nervous system) to the reading of a complimentary statement

---

44. Reprinted with permission from G. W. ALLPORT. *The Nature of prejudice.* Garden City, N.Y.: Doubleday & Company, Inc., 1958.

about a group against whom they are strongly prejudiced.[45] The most recent of these studies indicated that such responses did not occur for groups toward whom the individual had less strong feelings. Another investigation reported that prejudiced white individuals had larger GSRs to pictures of blacks than did unprejudiced white individuals, although results varied considerably with the sex of the participant and the sex of the person in the stimulus picture.[46] These studies provide support for the view that prejudice toward a minority group is likely to have a strong emotional component that makes it resistant to change.

Another form of consistency pertains to consistency among different attitudes. For example, prejudice against minority groups would seem to be incompatible with belief in democracy, which stresses equal rights and justice for all. Prejudiced attitudes, more than any other kind of attitudes, appear to be especially associated with such individual processes as misperception, compartmentalization, and rationalization and also with the group process of developing collective beliefs such as the ideology of race relations. These mechanisms may be interpreted as devices for alleviating inconsistency between prejudice and other attitudes. They suggest further the importance of the consistency principle. Finally, Scott has noted that not all attitudes have a rational structure: The individual is not always able to state the values that are linked to the attitude and its objects and events.[47] Presumably, prejudice has a large degree of such nonrationality, which isolates it to some extent from other attitudes.

PREJUDICE AND BELIEF DISSIMILARITY   Rokeach, Smith, and Evans have proposed that dissimilarity in religious belief is more important than ethnic or racial membership as a determinant of prejudice and discrimination.[48] In other words, one person will be more apt to dislike another if he thinks the other has dissimilar beliefs than he will if he thinks the other is of a different race. This proposal is consistent with the theory of interpersonal attraction outlined in Chapter 7.

In order to test their hypothesis, Rokeach and his colleagues prepared a set of hypothetical descriptions of persons. In a given pair of descriptions, race was varied while belief was held constant, belief was varied while race was held constant, or both were varied simultaneously. For example, the following pair varies race, but holds belief constant:

A white person who believes in God
A black person who believes in God

And this pair varies belief, but holds race constant:

A white person who believes in God
A white person who is an atheist

45. COOPER & SINGER, 1956; COOPER & SIEGEL, 1956; COOPER & POLLOCK, 1959; COOPER, 1959.   *46.* WESTIE & DE FLEUR, 1959.   *47.* SCOTT, 1958.   *48.* ROKEACH, SMITH, & EVANS, 1960.

The investigators had white participants indicate for each description the extent to which they felt that they *could be friends with such a person.* A statistical analysis of the various responses indicated clearly that similarity of belief was more important than similarity of race in the feeling of friendship expressed by the participants. Triandis, however, has criticized this study on the grounds that the measure used is one of friendship, not prejudice.[49] His analysis of his own data, using social distance measures, finds race to be far more important.[50] Two recent studies of belief similarity also show that race is more important for more intimate situations (e.g., marriage and dating), while belief similarity weighs heavier in nonintimate circumstances.[51]

Several other studies, however, suggest that assumed dissimilarity of beliefs may well play some role in prejudice. One study demonstrates that prejudiced white people do assume that blacks have beliefs dissimilar to their own while unprejudiced people do not.[52] It also shows that similarity of attitudes produces positive ratings of the other person and dissimilarity of attitudes produces negative ratings, regardless of the race of the other person.

In an experimental conformity situation, one experimenter asked groups of people to make judgments about their perceptions.[53] In each group, (by prearrangement with the experimenter) the majority had been previously instructed to make a judgment different from that which the participants were led to perceive as correct. The experimenter anticipated that prejudiced white individuals would not be swayed by the judgments of a black majority, but in fact, they did conform to a black majority as often as to a white majority. This experiment also suggests the greater importance of similarity of belief as compared with dissimilarity of race. Unfortunately, the experiments did not determine whether a reduction in prejudice took place.

In these various studies showing an association between dislike or prejudice, on the one hand, and dissimilarity, on the other, the causal sequence is not clear. As support for a theory of prejudice, these studies suffer from the possibility that the prejudice may cause the perception of dissimilarity. Dienstbier has made this clear through further study.[54] He has shown that the beliefs attributed to a person who is an object of prejudice must be relevant to the stereotype of him. Under some circumstances prejudice may influence beliefs; under others, beliefs may influence prejudice. Both processes may operate simultaneously, having complex influences on each other.

Cultural Factors

Prejudice in a society maintains itself by contributing to the development of ideologies supporting prejudice and by guaranteeing that children will be appropriately indoctrinated.

---

49. TRIANDIS, 1961.   50. See also ROKEACH, 1961.   51. TAN & DE VERA, 1970; MEZEI, 1971.   52. BYRNE & WONG, 1962.   53. LONG, 1970.   54. DIENSTBIER, 1972.

VALUES AND PREJUDICE   Ultimately, attitudes toward minority groups may become part of a cultural ideology—a complex system of ideas, attitudes, and beliefs that are closely associated with cultural values. For example, whites may think that blacks are more apelike and more primitive than whites, and are biologically inferior to them in a number of other ways. Associated with these beliefs are others: that mixture of races is biologically undesirable, and that such traits as sexuality, irresponsibility, and violence are related to race. The widespread acceptance of such ideologies helps to support prejudice and discrimination. One of the most important ways the ideologies help maintain prejudice is that they provide a means of working attitudes and values that are actually inconsistent with each other into a seemingly consistent system. For example, if one believes blacks to be "subhuman," then discrimination against them is not inconsistent with a belief in equal rights for all *human* beings.

Ideologies are often developed about groups that do not even constitute races, as in the myth in Nazi Germany that the alleged undesirable characteristics of the Jews were qualities to be expected of those not belonging to the "Aryan race." In addition, there is no conclusive evidence that the kinds of attributes generally assigned to members of various races are in any way associated with the morphological and physiological properties of race. In spite of these well-known facts, such ideologies persist and provide additional support for prejudice and discrimination.

An analysis of prejudice toward three groups in three different cultures has shown how differences in values may or may not support prejudice. The Jews, the Armenians, and the Parsis each occupied the role of middleman or trader in their countries.[55] The Jews and the Armenians were objects of prejudice, but the Parsis in India were not objects of prejudice, even though they occupied a role that was considered low in status. The investigator attributed this difference to a difference in the political values of India. The other countries valued an emerging nationalism which stressed the importance of having groups conform to a national pattern; hence, groups that were "different" were penalized. But in India internal differences among groups were not a threat to an important value; thus there was no need for prejudice against the Parsis.

A study of race relations in Panama and the Canal Zone also shows the importance of the central values of the society.[56] In the Canal Zone, controlled by the United States, segregation and differential status between American whites and Panamanians were practiced, while outside the Zone, in Panama, integration and equal-status interaction prevailed. The investigators suggest that this condition was in part reinforced by the difference in values between the two societies. In the Canal Zone, a premium was placed upon high technological rationality and highly developed occupational roles, whereas in Panama, life was much more casual. Because the Panamanians were ill prepared to meet the formal requirements of life in the Canal Zone, the formalism

55. STRYKER, 1959.   *56.* BIESANZ & SMITH, 1951.

and discipline of the area supported the pattern of discrimination against them, but the informal character of life in Panama had the reverse effect.

SOCIALIZATION OF THE CHILD   The child is born without any prejudice. But he is usually born into a family that reflects the prevailing attitudes of society. He is dependent upon the adult members of the family for the satisfaction of his needs, and he is ultimately expected to take over their attitudes and values. Socialization processes will be discussed in detail in Chapters 15 to 17; here the concern is only with the development of prejudice and discrimination in the child.

Prejudice develops in children at a relatively early age, in the preschool or early school years. When tested by means of pictures or hypothetical situations, they indicate some preference for associating with other members of the majority group and avoiding members of minority groups.[57] The particular groups that are objects of prejudice are determined by the prevailing prejudices in the society. Such prejudice is mild at first but becomes stronger throughout the childhood years. At an early age children are not aware of their prejudice; adults estimate that they first became prejudiced at around twelve or thirteen years of age.[58] Small children are also unable to give the usual reasons for prejudice; as they grow older, however, they learn the supporting ideology and recite traditional cultural reasons for prejudice.[59]

That prejudice is a direct function of socialization is demonstrated clearly in a 1936 study that compares the development of prejudice against blacks among several groups of white Tennessee schoolchildren and several groups of white children in New York City.[60] Prejudice was apparent in the first grade and increased throughout the primary grades. There was no difference in prejudice between Northern and Southern children, nor was there any difference between New York children from an all-white school and New York children from a mixed school. This similarity in attitudes was anticipated, for both the Tennessee and the New York children were widely exposed to prejudice against the blacks. A striking difference was found, however, between the children living in a cooperative housing project sponsored by a Communist organization and all the other children. An element in Communist ideology which was particularly strong in the 1930s when the study was conducted is a belief in the equality of all races. Children of Communist parents are likely to learn this belief from their parents—an expectation consistent with the data.

In sum, attitudes toward minority groups are ultimately woven into a complex pattern of ideas, attitudes, and beliefs closely associated with cultural values. The widespread existence of such ideologies helps to support prejudice and discrimination. When prejudice and discrimination are extensive through-

57. HOROWITZ, 1936; CRISWELL, 1937.   58. ALLPORT & KRAMER, 1946.   59. SIMPSON & YINGER, 1958.
60. HOROWITZ, 1936.

out a society, the socialization of the child toward acceptance of prevailing ideologies and behavior concerning minority groups is assured.

Summary: Maintenance of Prejudice and Discrimination

Factors that maintain prejudice and discrimination have been discussed on three levels: the social structure, individual personality dynamics, and the culture. Several structural processes contribute to maintenance of prejudice and discrimination. Once cognitions and feelings accompanying prejudice and discrimination are well established, they acquire a normative quality. Group members are expected to hold them, and positive and negative sanctions are applied by the group to individual members who conform or fail to conform. Increased interaction among ingroup members increases mutual affect and dependency, and interaction between ingroup and outgroup on the basis of unequal status supports prejudice and discrimination. Interaction within the group also leads to the development and maintenance of distinctive subcultural patterns of thought and behavior which may be used to justify discrimination. The persons who conform most closely to norms that include prejudice and discrimination are likely to rise to positions of leadership and to further support prejudice and discrimination.

Certain individual processes support prejudice: Individual aggression aroused by frustration may be displaced to minority groups. Such personality needs as intolerance of ambiguity and the need for status and security are likely to contribute. A person with an authoritarian personality is likely to be quite prejudiced because prejudice is consistent with his dominant values, which include emphasis on status and power and adherence to conventional social norms. Prejudice and discrimination are likely to be perceived as contributing to economic gain. The tendency of an individual to maintain consistency among the affective, cognitive, and behavior components of prejudiced attitudes produces resistance to change, and in particular, is likely to lead to misperception of the minority group. The emotional component of prejudice makes it likely that affective-cognitive consistency will work in the direction of maintaining prejudice. This explains the wide use by prejudiced persons of a variety of mechanisms that seemingly resolve or gloss over actual inconsistencies.

The prevalence of prejudice in a society contributes to its own maintenance. Persons are enabled to observe features of their environment that support prejudiced attitudes. Such features appear in institutional practices, in the mass media, and even in the objective characteristics of the minority group members themselves, characteristics that are created by the way they are treated. Attitudes toward minority groups are woven into a complex pattern of ideas, attitudes, and beliefs closely associated with cultural values. These ideologies appear to be self-consistent, and thus they help the individual to resolve actual inconsistencies in his attitudes and values. The widespread existence of prejudice and discrimination in a society also ensures that children will be socialized in the direction of these prevailing attitudes.

Changing Intergroup Prejudice

An examination of the numerous studies of conditions that bring about a reduction—or an increase—of prejudice and discrimination provides additional material which is consistent with the principles outlined so far. In addition, it gives some further insights into the nature of prejudice and discrimination.

Early studies raised the hypothesis that the greater the contact between groups, the more likely prejudice is to be reduced. It soon became apparent, however, that the kind of relation between the two groups is important. As we have already seen, certain types of competitive contacts may increase prejudice. Likewise, frequent contact between master and servant or between persons in other unequal-status relations would do little to reduce prejudice. The previous discussion, which indicated that prejudice emerges from relations where statuses are unequal, would lead to the belief that *reduction* of prejudice would occur as a result of relations on an equal-status basis.

The equal-status hypothesis appears to be fairly consistent with various studies on the reduction of prejudice and has been widely accepted by students of intergroup relations. A precise, two-part explanation and a review of the pertinent evidence are given below. Much of this evidence is taken from studies conducted in the 1940s and 1950s, with good reason. At that time egalitarianism was not as pervasive a social norm as it is today. So it was easier to find people who would admit to prejudice and to find control situations involving segregation which could be used for comparative purposes. The authors' two principles for the reduction of prejudice may be stated as follows:

> *1. Incongruent roles.* Interaction with a person who occupies a role category that is incompatible or incongruent with the ethnic stereotype ordinarily attributed to him will lead to the reduction of prejudice.
> *2. Interdependent behavior and common fate.* Interaction between two people under circumstances in which both will experience the same outcome or fate, and in which the outcome is dependent on both working cooperatively toward a shared goal, will reduce prejudice.

Incongruent Roles and Prejudice Reduction

Each instance of intergroup contact that has been studied occurs in a particular type of situation: integrated housing, military combat, crews on shipboard, and various work situations. So that intergroup contact may be described more accurately, two concepts to be discussed in more detail in Chapters 13 and 14 will be introduced here: (1) position or role category and (2) role expectations. A *position* is a category of persons occupying a place in a social relation. Examples of positions which are important to this discussion are combat infantryman, sailor, neighbor, work associate, black, Jew. Associated with each position or role category are *expectations* of how a person occupying that category should behave and the personal characteristics he should possess.

From the point of view of these concepts, any contact situation may be represented as follows: Because of a person's position or role category as a member of an ethnic group, certain stereotyped characteristics are likely to be attributed to him and certain behaviors are likely to be expected of him. When he occupies another role, however, such as coworker or neighbor, conflicting expectations about his behavior and characteristics are likely to be aroused. On the one hand is the tendency to attribute to him the characteristics that are considered appropriate to members of his ethnic group; on the other is the tendency to attribute to him the characteristics that belong to a coworker or neighbor. Contrasted to situations in which a member of an ethnic group clearly occupies an additional role are situations of merely casual contact in which he is likely to be perceived and behaved toward in terms of his ethnic group role. Also, as noted earlier, in the discussion of environmental supports, prejudice is reinforced when the ethnic group role is compatible with other roles. For example, the black stereotype is supported as long as the black is restricted to menial occupations.

Continued interaction with an ethnic group member who occupies two roles has certain logical consequences. To the extent that the behavior of an ethnic group member is compatible with expectations for the role category of coworker rather than that of the ethnic group, expectations associated with the ethnic group category are likely to be gradually modified or abandoned. Thus if the expectation for a coworker is that he be energetic rather than lazy, and the expectation for an ethnic group member is that he be lazy rather than energetic, energetic behavior over a period of time by an ethnic group member who is a coworker is likely to lead to abandonment of the idea that he is lazy.

More generally, when contacts with ethnic group members involve a role that is incompatible with their ethnic group status, the expectations associated with the incompatible role are likely to lead to new behavior toward them and to appropriate changes in the corresponding perceptions of their characteristics. But it is important to note that the new perceptions of these individuals are associated with their occupation of a particular role category. It might be expected that the modified perceptions would be confined to situations in which the individuals occupy the role category in question, and that under many circumstances such perceptions would not be generalized to other situations.

Incongruent roles are apt to be especially effective in changing stereotyped conceptions of the role partner as contrasted with changing feelings toward him. This point will be further discussed after a description of research that bears on incongruent roles and prejudice reduction.

The importance of *active* role involvement with the ethnic group member must be emphasized here. If an ethnic group member merely occupies a role that has expectations incompatible with our stereotype of him, and we have little interaction with him, our feelings toward him may remain the same. Contrast, for example, simply knowing that a black neighbor is a skilled surgeon with another situation: being his patient and having him successfully perform a dangerous operation on yourself. An investigation of contacts between American students and Israelis over a period of several months supports the importance of active participation rather than mere presence, although the observations were reported informally.[61]

The effects of occupying other role categories in addition to ethnic group status are illustrated by an investigation showing the amount of social distance felt toward blacks in various occupational roles.[62] The investigator chose white respondents at random in Indianapolis and interviewed them in their homes. Lower-class whites indicated that they felt socially distant from blacks and made little discrimination among blacks in different occupations, but middle-class and upper-class whites indicated less social distance and showed much more variation in feeling toward blacks in such different occupations as medicine, banking, machine operating, and ditchdigging. This study illustrates the point that some people's feelings toward an ethnic group member are associated with other positions that he occupies.

One of the clearest illustrations of the importance of role categories comes from a study by Minard of black and white miners in the Pocahontas coalfields of West Virginia.[63] He describes a situation in which the mines are completely integrated, with blacks and whites working side by side, but community life is almost completely segregated:

> The boundary line between the two communities is usually the mine's mouth. Management assists the miners in recognizing their entrance into the outside community with its distinctions in status by providing separate baths and locker rooms. The color line, that is, becomes immediately visible as soon as the miner's eyes accustomed to the inner darkness of the mine have accommodated themselves to the light of the outside world. . . .
>
> The white miner adjusts to these conflicting influences by adoption of a dual role. Within the mine he assumes a role toward his fellow workers posited upon acceptance of practical equality of status. Outside his role as member of the white community involves an elevation of status in which he becomes a member of a superior caste group.[64]

If the role interpretation of reduction in prejudice and discrimination is correct, quantitative data on attitudes toward ethnic group members should show change for attributes relevant to the role but not for those irrelevant to the role. That is, if the ethnic group member is a coworker, perception of his

61. Schild, 1962.   *62.* Westie, 1952.   *63.* Minard, 1952.   *64.* Minard, 1952, p. 30.

attributes that are relevant to his work should be adjusted, but perception of his attributes that are relevant to personal friendship, for example, should not change. Although the data from various studies are often not complete and are sometimes subject to alternative interpretations, taken together they weave a fairly convincing pattern consistent with this viewpoint.

A study was made of two department stores where black workers had been introduced.[65] For purposes of the study, white workers were divided into three groups. The equal-status group consisted of whites who were working or had previously worked in departments where there was at least one black with status equal to or higher than their own. The unequal-status group consisted of white persons who were working or had previously worked in departments where all the black persons were of lower status than themselves. A third group consisted of whites who had never worked with blacks. The investigator asked each member of all three groups the questions shown in Table 6-1. These questions were not asked successively, but were interspersed with other questions not pertaining to blacks.

The percentages of persons in each group who gave favorable responses to each question are listed in Table 6-1. Workers in the equal-status group showed favorable attitudes toward blacks on job-related items, but not on items related to public transportation, restaurant facilities, housing, or friendship. Thus, on questions which are not job-related, employees who work with blacks on either an equal or an unequal basis are not more favorable toward blacks than those having no work contacts. But on questions pertaining to work relations, those who work with blacks on an equal basis have the most favorable attitudes. This strongly suggests that the impact of the role situation has changed role-related attitudes, but has not generalized to other situations. Although blacks had been employed in one store for four years and in the other for less than one year, there was no difference between the two stores in the prevailing attitudes toward blacks.

The importance of the demands of the role situation in bringing about acceptance is nicely illustrated by a case study of the introduction of black workers into a Chicago meat-packing plant. One black with considerable seniority was transferred to the machine shop, which hitherto had been barred to blacks. His own report shows how pressures of the job requirements brought about limited acceptance during the first two weeks:

> Monday morning I punched in and there was a lot of whispering and looking over at me, you know. Everybody would walk by and look me over like they'd never seen a man like me before. So I waited and a man would come up to the foreman to ask for a helper, and the foreman would look over at me and say, "he's the only helper left." So the man would decide that he didn't need a helper after all and walk away. So this went on for two days. Nobody would work with me. They put me to work by myself dismantling

65. Harding & Hogrefe, 1952.

Table 6-1   *Percentage favorable to blacks for different groups and items*

QUESTIONS	EQUAL-STATUS CONTACT	UNEQUAL-STATUS CONTACT	NO CONTACT
Job-related Items			
How would you feel about taking a new job in which there were both Negroes and white people doing the same kind of work as you?	73	61	48
How would you feel about working under a Negro supervisor?	37	29	33
Do you think Negroes should have the same chance as white people to get any kind of job, or do you think white people should have the first chance at any kind of job?	65	51	57
Items Not Related to Job			
How do you feel about sitting next to Negroes in buses or trains?	73	71	70
How would you feel about sitting down at the same table with a Negro in a lunchroom or cafeteria?	51	53	51
How would you feel about living in a new apartment building or housing project which contained both white and Negro families?	13	22	18
How would you feel about having a Negro for a personal friend?	12	16	20
Number of respondents	82	49	79

Source: Reprinted by permission from J. Harding & R. Hogrefe. Attitudes of white department store employees toward Negro co-workers. *Journal of Social Issues,* 1952, **8,** (1), 22.

pumps and stuff and cleaning up around. I would go up to a man at a lathe and ask him a question and he would answer me with only a word if he'd answer at all. Finally, on the third day, they had a job that needed two men and I was the only helper available so the man accepted me and we worked together. The next day I worked with another man. Now there are five men there who I've worked with and who will come over and start a conversation with me on their own. The rest still won't talk to me unless I talk to them first.[66]

In spite of their acceptance of this black man on the job, the five white men who worked with him would not eat or take coffee breaks with him—another illustration of the specificity of the role relation.

66. PALMORE, 1955, p. 28.

A study of employees of a trade union with militant antidiscrimination policies showed that whites held highly favorable attitudes toward black coworkers.[67] Unfortunately, no matched control group was used; the results were compared only with other studies which had used somewhat different attitude items as well as samples of persons who were likely to differ in characteristics relevant to attitudes. Almost all the questions concerned work relations. It may be noteworthy that these workers responded less favorably to a question about having blacks for neighbors than did persons living in an integrated government housing project. Again, this suggests that shifts in the work role do not extend to the neighbor role.

In an investigation of integrated children's camps, white children formed friendships largely with black children who shared their living cabins.[68] In larger situations, such as swimming, games, and other recreations, small segregated groups appeared more frequently.

Changes which were appropriate to role relations but which did not generalize are also reported in a postwar study of attitudes toward Japanese-Americans who had been brought to the University of Colorado in Boulder to teach Japanese to naval personnel during World War II.[69] Attitudes of neighbors and nonneighbors of the Japanese-Americans were compared. On questions pertaining to the neighbor role, such as whether they would rent to Japanese-Americans or whether they would be unhappy if Japanese-Americans bought homes in the neighborhood, neighbors were more favorable than nonneighbors. In replying to question about national policy on the Oriental Exclusion Act, however, neighbors showed no greater desire for modification of the act than nonneighbors.

Another study, conducted during World War II, examined the degree of contact between black and white infantrymen in combat situations and the amount of prejudice of the whites toward the blacks. In the most integrated instances, black platoons (about 50 men) were assigned to white companies (about 200 men). In other cases, black platoons were part of a regiment (3,000 men), a division (13,000 men), or even larger field forces varying considerably in size. The assignments caused progressively less contact between black and white soldiers. Less favorable attitudes toward blacks were held in the less integrated units. Evidence indicated that the favorable attitudes in more integrated units were to some degree confined to black soldiers as *combat* companions. The investigators make the following comment on this point:

[Many soldiers] took occasion to note that relationships were better in combat than they were in the garrison situation. Not that there was serious overt friction between Negro and white soldiers. Such instances were, as far as is known, confined to isolated cases and involved white soldiers from other units who did not know the combat record of the Negro men. There were,

67. GUNDLACH, 1956.   68. CAMPBELL & YARROW, 1958.   69. IRISH, 1952.

however, some tensions in companies stationed where friendly contact with liberated populations was possible, and there was some expression of preference for separation in garrison. . . .

Relationships in combat could be regarded as working relationships rather than social relationships. More precisely, they could be confined more narrowly to a functionally specific basis than could the contacts involved in community living. In particular, the combat situation was exclusively masculine, and issues of social relationships between men and women did not appear as they did in garrison. Far from being a "test case" in ordinary Negro-white relations, the combat setting may be regarded as a special case making for good relationships, for the sense of common danger and common obligation was high, the need for unity was at a maximum, and there was great consciousness of shared experience of an intensely emotional kind.[70]

Some studies made in the early 1950s, before development of the movement toward black identity and pride, compared the attitudes of whites living in housing projects with blacks under different degrees of integration, a condition over which the tenants had no control.[71] The conclusions of these studies were quite consistent: Whites in integrated projects showed less prejudice and had more favorable attitudes toward blacks than those in segregated projects. Furthermore, whites who lived in closer proximity with blacks, either because they lived in one of the more highly integrated projects, or because they lived in an apartment close to one occupied by blacks, were less prejudiced than whites who had fewer contacts with blacks.

These studies more than any others appear to show an association between favorable attitudes and close personal contact. The explanation lies in the definition of the neighbor role. One should be friendly and sociable toward one's neighbor, should respect him, and should help him and expect help in return. The role of neighbor differs from that of coworker in containing a strong element of sociability and friendliness. When circumstances place an ethnic group member in a neighbor role, appropriate role expectations should lead to friendly feelings and behavior toward him. The various studies document the point that this role is important. For example, they show that in integrated projects a sizable proportion of residents indicated that they had blacks as friends; in segregated projects no one claimed blacks as friends.

Little attention has been given in neighbor studies to the crucial question whether changes in attitudes generalize to other roles. One investigation did present a five-item ethnocentrism scale to white tenants in four buildings of a housing project.[72] Unfortunately, results were not reported separately for each

70. STAR, WILLIAMS, & STOUFFER, 1958, pp. 598-600.   71. WILNER, WALKLEY, & COOK, 1955.   72. WILNER et al., 1955, p. 69.

item. One item pertained to a work situation: "It would be a mistake ever to have Negroes as foremen and leaders over whites." Another pertained to schools but also to general contact: "Negroes have their rights but it is best to keep them in their own districts and schools and to prevent too much contact with whites." The remaining three items, however, were general statements about blacks.

It is interesting to note that when tenants who had more contacts with blacks are compared with those who had fewer contacts, only one of the four buildings showed a significantly different proportion of persons agreeing with the various items. This was an integrated project in which white attitudes toward blacks were favorable. The other integrated project and the two segregated ones showed no significant differences. The published information is not detailed enough to indicate whether the failure to get an appreciable difference was due to the presence of the nonrole items mentioned above, but the investigators drew a conclusion consistent with the above interpretation in that they indicated only slight generalization to nonhousing situations:

> It appears, then, that proximity is related to favorableness of attitude toward the *specific Negroes in the contact situation and to acceptance of the particular inter-racial experience* [italics supplied]. Moreover, the more favorable attitudes of the "nears" toward the specific Negroes are generalized to some extent, but by no means completely, to Negroes as a group. There is a slight tendency, too, for the greater acceptance of the particular inter-racial experience on the part of the "nears" to be generalized to acceptance of Negroes in other social situations.[73]

Another more recent study supports this conclusion: Attitudes about *interracial living* changed favorably as a result of intergroup contact on an equal-status basis, but no such changes occurred in other aspects of the ethnic attitude.[74]

Housing and other life situations are complicated by many factors that do not arise in the laboratory. Studies of villages and towns with large numbers of immigrants indicate that receptivity toward immigrant groups varies markedly with initial attitudes and different living patterns. Europeans are less satisfied with their neighbors in a heterogeneous neighborhood than are the North Africans and Near Easterners in the same neighborhood.[75] But an investigation of immigrant towns in Israel found that most people were indifferent to the ethnic backgrounds of their neighbors, and that the more heterogeneous the neighborhood, the more receptive were its inhabitants to members of other ethnic groups.[76] Finally, a study in England found that attitudes toward Italians were a function of the degree of contact experienced with the group. People who

73. WILNER et al., 1955, p. 69.   *74.* MEER & FREEDMAN, 1966.   *75.* SHUVAL, 1962.   *76.* SOEN & TISHLER, 1968.

were relatively isolated from Italians expressed indifference; those who had contact in public situations had unfavorable attitudes; and those who had continuous or frequent face-to-face relations had positive attitudes.[77]

Further illustration of the complicated network of factors affecting prejudice in life situations is found in studies of desegregation in schools.[78] To say that desegregated schools reduce prejudice would be too simplistic. In an organization as large as a school, various groups and cliques coalesce around a variety of values and goals. In many desegregated schools, particularly in the higher grades and at the college level, whites, blacks, and other ethnic group members largely associate with others whom they perceive as similar to themselves, maintaining cleavage along ethnic lines. Moreover, intergroup action often takes forms that raise rather than lower prejudice. In other schools there is considerable intermixing, and prejudice is sometimes reduced.

The emphasis in this section on the role relations among ethnic and societal groups should not obscure the importance of personality factors in prejudice. The earlier discussion of individual processes in prejudice still applies: In the kinds of contact situations described, not all individuals respond in the same way. For example, in Minard's study of black and white miners in the Pocahontas coalfields, about 60 percent of the white miners switched their role relation to blacks upon entering and leaving the mine, behaving on an equal-status basis in the mine and a superior-status basis outside.[79] Another 20 percent of the men remained strongly prejudiced both in and out of the mine. The remaining 20 percent maintained friendly, nonprejudiced attitudes outside the mine as well as in. In other words, 20 percent of the miners were so strongly prejudiced that they discriminated against blacks in the mine and out of it, and another 20 percent were sufficiently favorable toward blacks that they behaved in a friendly manner in the community as well as in the mine. The middle 60 percent had a moderate degree of prejudice which yielded in the face of the powerful forces of the work situation but was operative where community support was provided. Similar individual differences which occur in many of the other contact situations may also be attributed to the personality factors discussed earlier.

Changes in prejudice through interacting with people who occupy roles incongruent with their ethnic stereotype are apt to occur through a cognitive mechanism. The role expectations and the beliefs associated with the stereotype are inconsistent, and continued emphasis on the role expectations should weaken the stereotype beliefs. This change in turn should reduce prejudice. An individual moves from a negative evaluation to a positive one, consistent with the positive role expectations. But this change in *feeling* or *affect* occurs by way of the conflict between cognitive elements.

77. CHADWICK-JONES, 1962.   78. CARITHERS, 1970.   79. MINARD, 1952.

Interdependent Behavior and Common Fate

The implication of the above discussion is that role incongruency results in cognitive change which in turn reduces prejudice. The second principle stated early in this section suggested that some circumstances will result directly in a change of affect. In Chapter 7 a variety of forms of interaction that are likely to produce an increase in interpersonal attraction will be reviewed. At first we might expect that any form of interaction that would ordinarily lead people to like each other would lead to a reduction in prejudice. But a closer look reveals that in prejudice the initial relation is one of dislike and mistrust, which is quite different from starting with a neutral position, the approach taken in many attraction studies. When we interact with a person toward whom we feel prejudiced, we are apt to perceive his actions in a distorted way so as to make them consistent with our existing prejudice. Moreover, when circumstances permit, our behavior is apt to be cautious, mistrustful, and divisive.

It follows that effective reduction of prejudice occurs only in a situation structured so as to *induce* or *force* interaction appropriate to increased attraction. If misperception or inappropriate interaction is possible, reduction of prejudice will not occur. One situation that clearly fits this criterion involves behavior that is interdependent and that leads to a common fate or outcome. When two individuals are held in a situation by strong forces, and when they both desire the same outcome but can only achieve it by working together cooperatively, their behavior is said to be interdependent and to be subject to a common fate (failing or succeeding). Both experimental and field observations support the idea that interdependent behavior leading to a common fate causes the participants to feel more positively toward one another. This increase in attraction is apt to be intensified if the participants are subjected to some external threat or danger.

Some housing situations and some work situations are apt to partially meet this criterion of interdependent behavior and common fate, especially if the occupants form an organization to fight the landlord or the workers go on a strike. White soldiers fighting side by side with black ones against a common enemy appeared to adopt more favorable attitudes toward blacks.[80] White merchant seamen who had been under enemy fire with blacks were less prejudiced than those who had not.[81] In the experiment with boys' camps described early in this chapter, in which hostilities between the Eagles and the Rattlers were deliberately produced in intergroup competition, a series of threatening situations created an interdependent situation which required cooperation between the groups.[82] For example, the water supply was cut off, and all the boys had to work together to handle the emergency. Another time a truck stalled and could only be started if the two groups of boys pulled together on the tow rope. Such

---

80. Star et al., 1958.   *81.* Brophy, 1946.   *82.* Sherif et al., 1961.

enforced cooperative situations in the face of threat created a single goal that both groups desired to achieve, and that could only be achieved through cooperation. These situations led to a marked reduction in hostility between the groups.

Several laboratory experiments lend further support to the efficacy of interdependent behavior in a common-fate situation as a means of reducing prejudice. One study found that shared threat produced a decrease in prejudice toward blacks, but that personal, nonshared threat did not.[83] In another investigation, white participants who varied in degree of prejudice toward blacks were placed, under conditions of shared threat or nonthreat, in groups requiring cooperation to solve the task imposed by the experimenter.[84] One member of each group was a black who was a confederate of the experimenter and was already familiar with the problem-solving task. Threat was created for members of the experimental group by informing them that the psychology department and the university were embarking on a program of evaluating students through these experimental situations, and that complete records of their performances would be placed on permanent file. The black confederate behaved in a standard way in the threat and nonthreat situations. As anticipated, measures of prejudice taken before and after the experimental situation revealed a significant drop in prejudice for the experimental group but not for the control group who had not been exposed to threat. Finally, a more recent experimental investigation found that white participants working cooperatively with a black person had a more favorable attitude toward him than participants who worked in his presence but independently.[85]

In sum, interaction with a person under circumstances where both will experience the same outcome or fate, and where the outcome is dependent on both parties working cooperatively toward a shared goal, will reduce prejudice. Unlike the incongruent role, which probably changes negative feelings indirectly through a change in the beliefs associated with the ethnic group stereotype, the interdependent behavior and shared goal apparently produce a change in feeling by more direct means. Many kinds of interaction that ordinarily lead to increased attraction will not reduce prejudice, because the initial state of prejudice allows distortion and mistrust to operate, and sometimes changes the character of the interaction. Interdependent behavior with a common fate for the participants is effective because they are locked into a situation which forces them to work cooperatively and to achieve a positive outcome through shared efforts.

Prejudice Reduction through Personality Dynamics

Certain internal needs may be served by prejudice. It may allow the expression of pent-up hostility, it may lead to economic gains, it may give one a feeling of superiority. Among the techniques that might be used in reducing the prejudice

83. Feshbach & Singer, 1957.   *84.* Burnstein & McRae, 1962.   *85.* Ashmore, 1969.

of the individual are: psychotherapy, reeducation, catharsis, and changing the individual's life circumstances so that frustration, hostility, and other prejudice-serving needs are reduced or eliminated. While various experiments at times have had limited success with such procedures, often they have not worked at all. Moreover, changing the individual is a very expensive, time-consuming process—to say nothing of the fact that many people do not want to be changed. Finally, changing individuals is relatively fruitless if the social conditions that produce prejudice are themselves left unchanged.

Dissonance Arousal and Attitude Change

It has been stressed that active involvement with a role partner is important in change of attitudes due to interaction with ethnic group members who occupy roles incompatible with their stereotypes. The purpose of this section is to examine the behavior of the prejudiced in such situations and its consequences for attitude change. In Chapter 3, the arousal of dissonance as a result of engaging in attitude-discrepant behavior and the manner in which dissonance led to attitude change was discussed at length. Such concepts appear to be relevant to the present situation.

A prejudiced person who has made a decision to move into a public housing project finds himself committed to a situation where he is to some extent required to behave in a manner contrary to his attitudes. Housewives in the project, for example, come into frequent contact with neighbors of different ethnic backgrounds at the laundry facilities, in the backyards, in the play areas with their children, and in many other places. The force of the neighbor role leads them to behave in a friendly and cordial manner. If a housewife is prejudiced, her friendly behavior should arouse internal dissonance. Ultimately the dissonance may be resolved by modification of the aspects of her attitudes toward these ethnic minorities that are dissonant with the neighbor role. On the other hand, a working woman or man living in the project might remain in relative isolation from the neighbors and experience little dissonance about them.

In dissonance situations, only the aspects of attitudes relevant to the role situation need change; these are the only elements that are likely to be dissonant. A rule for creating more general changes, however, is that any conditions that make nonrole elements of the attitude relevant to behavior in the role situation are likely to facilitate change in these nonrole elements as well. In a work situation, for example, relevant elements involve competence and cooperation. But if members of different ethnic groups bowl together on the company team and win a trophy they may develop mutual team spirit and emotional support, extending the attitude change beyond the work situation.

Intergroup-contact situations need more explicit study from the point of view of dissonance concepts before any firm conclusions may be drawn, however. In the general discussion of attitude change the role of commitment in contributing to dissonance was stressed. The part played by commitment in the various contact situations is not at all clear. Personal decision to move into a housing project appears to be clearly voluntary, but a person who is assigned by authorities to an integrated or a segregated project is not acting voluntarily. In work situations, moreover, employees of different ethnic backgrounds are hired by the employer, and the employee ordinarily has no part in the decision. On the other hand, some form of personal commitment may operate in such work situations. The individual worker may feel that he has a choice about whether to behave in a prejudiced or an unprejudiced manner toward his fellow worker. The workers who exhibit reduced prejudice may well be those who made a conscious decision to treat their minority group coworkers on equal terms. Further investigation of intergroup-contact situations is needed to verify these possibilities.

Sanctions for Certain Roles

In reporting on studies of public housing, investigators have suggested that the official policy of the housing authority was important in creating acceptance of the situation and indirectly bringing about a reduction in prejudice. That each family unit was in a government housing project gave official sanction to the pattern of integrated or segregated housing established by the authority. Assignment to a particular unit was made by the authority; the individual family was not able to choose the location.

Similarly, in some of the work situations studied, an active nondiscriminatory policy on the part of either the employers or the union sanctioned equal-status role relations. The authoritarian structure of the military, where personnel are accustomed to taking orders from higher authorities, would also seem to foster workable integrated patterns of interaction. Such official sanctions help to establish social norms which favor interaction on an equal-status basis.

On the other hand, sanctions from authorities or important reference persons or groups may also maintain or increase prejudice. In studies of white residential areas which blacks began moving into, the areas rather rapidly become wholly black. The rapid movement of whites out of an area is accelerated by a variety of pressures from "authoritative" groups or persons. When blacks move into an area, property owners fear a reduction in property values. Because of the lack of adequate black housing, many black buyers become interested once an area is no longer segregated. Real estate agents thus pressure white residents to sell to blacks, from whom they can get a better price. Lending agencies and government insuring agencies discourage prospective white buyers from buying into the area. Similar pressures arise from public school staffs, religious institutions, and property owners' associations. Thus, without some form of control it is difficult to maintain a mixed residential area. In some instances, biracial organizations have been formed in the attempt to maintain the existing integrated pattern.

The sanctions of authority need not always bring about change in the direction advocated. Under some circumstances an attempt by officials to change norms may lead to the development of counternorms. For example, the series of Supreme Court decisions on school desegregation of blacks led to the formation of various groups that were opposed to desegregation and were active in promoting resistance to it, such as the White Citizens' Councils throughout the South. The conditions under which norms are likely to be formed or changed will be discussed at length in Chapter 10 in the discussion of emerging norms and conformity. The principles outlined there are applicable to the present discussion.

Summary: Changing Intergroup Prejudice

At least two important principles are at work in the reduction of intergroup prejudice. First, interaction with a person who occupies a role category that is incompatible or incongruent with the ethnic stereotype ordinarily attributed to him will lead to the reduction of prejudice. The negative feeling is probably changed through changes in the beliefs associated with the stereotype. Since these beliefs are inconsistent with the role expectations and the actual behavior of the role partner, they weaken and are replaced by new beliefs compatible with the other person's role. It is worth emphasizing that the participants must be actively engaged in interaction in order for this effect to occur.

A second principle is that interaction with a person under circumstances where both will experience the same outcome or fate, and where the outcome is dependent upon both parties working cooperatively toward a shared goal, will reduce prejudice. Interdependent behavior and common fate apparently produce a change in feeling by more direct means than do incongruent roles. Many interactions lead to increased attraction among people who are not prejudiced against each other, but will not reduce prejudice among those who are prejudiced because the initial state allows distortion and mistrust to operate and sometimes changes the character of the interaction. Interdependent behavior with a common fate for the participants does reduce prejudice because the participants are locked into a situation which forces them to work cooperatively and to achieve a positive outcome through shared efforts.

The arousal of dissonance as a result of engaging in behavior discrepant with a prejudiced attitude might reduce prejudice in some circumstances, including the situation involving interdependent behavior and common fate. But since few experiments have been carried out in which dissonance theory has been used to reduce prejudice, its application to prejudice reduction must remain an open question. Several factors may increase the likelihood of prejudice reduction in incongruent role situations or common-fate situations. These include the sanction of nonprejudice by authoritative sources, pressure on the interacting partners in the form of external threats or dangers, and the juxtaposition of interaction situations with egalitarian values of society.

PART TWO

Group Structure and Process

This part and the following one examine the emergence, maintenance, and change of regularities in interaction. In part, such regularities of thought, feeling, and behavior can be explained in terms of expectations, norms, or rules of conduct that guide behavior in social situations. This source of regularity, the institutional structure, will be treated in Part Three, using the concept of social role.

Part Two focuses on regularities whose source is subinstitutional: the direct exchange of primary rewards. Primary rewards are inherent in the interaction itself and not contrived to elicit certain behaviors. Examples are the pleasures of companionship experienced by friends and the enjoyment of social conversation between fellow workers. In contrast, institutional regularities are supported by secondary reinforcers, such as money or social approval. A worker is formally rewarded for his productivity through a complex payroll system.

Subinstitutional regularities, termed *elementary social behavior* by Homans, are better highlighted by some situations than others. For example, the behavior of a group of strangers in the small-group laboratory is less influenced by institutional controls than the behavior of a well-established, formally organized group. Similarly, interaction in informal situations, such as association between two friends or among a group of children at play, is more likely to illustrate elementary social behavior. By studying such situations, principles underlying elementary social behavior may be more readily identified.

Elementary social behavior is not confined to newly formed groups; moreover, these units are not free from institutional controls. The exchange of affection between two persons, an example of elementary social behavior, may occur between two children whose play is relatively free from institutional controls, but in other instances, such an exchange may be tightly interwoven with a host of institutional processes. An example of the latter is love between husband and wife, where the institution of the family is relevant. Thus, elementary social behavior and institutional behavior are separate largely in an analytical sense; most concrete behaviors illustrate both.

The concept of *structure* refers to patterned regularities in feelings, perceptions, and actions that characterize aspects of the interactions among members of a group. For example, the pattern of liking among group members has been called the *affect* or *sociometric* structure. This is portrayed graphically by a *sociogram*, where points representing each member are connected by arrows indicating the direction of liking from member to member. The organization and patterning of such sociograms portrays the idea of structure in a concrete fashion.

The term *process* refers to the changing pattern of relations between elements of structure over time. For example, in a newly formed group of strangers, the process by which friendships develop may be traced. The various stages of this process may be illustrated by showing the affect structures existing in the different periods of development. Such processes may best be understood in terms of a theoretical conception that views interaction as an exchange of rewards and costs by individual members. While it is difficult to isolate and measure the rewards and costs that persons exchange in interaction and thus directly test this theory, exchange theory admirably performs one function of theory—that of organizing in a coherent framework many diverse empirical findings.

These chapters on group structure and process make abundantly clear that the relation between two people is a function of more than their characteristics as individuals. Even when the characteristics of both are taken into consideration, their behavior cannot be predicted without knowing something of the history of the relation between them and of their relations with other persons.

Chapter 7, a discussion of interpersonal attraction, has as its major topic the sources of attraction between people. Much of this discussion deals with liking and friendship between two persons. Also examined is the attraction structure of groups—often called the *sociometric structure*. This kind of structure was one of the first forms of elementary social behavior to be studied, and a great deal of research literature is available. The chapter also treats processes that lead to progressive modification of attraction. In contrast, social power, treated in Chapter 8, has not been intensively studied, and the discussion is more speculative. Social power pertains to the relative ability of persons to influence other members of the group. As will be seen, power is dependent upon a variety of factors and takes several different forms. The exercise of different types of power over a period of time also has different consequences depending upon the type of power that is used. While *legitimate power,* a form stemming from the institutional structure, is given some attention, more discussion is devoted to the forms of power that are based upon a more direct exchange of rewards and costs.

One topic in Chapter 9 is status, which refers to patterns of differential evaluation or estimated worth of group members as judged by each other. As in the case of power, a variety of criteria may underlie status. The basis of such status rankings and the processes that maintain or underlie change in these rankings are considered. Since the relation between status and various patterns of communication in groups has frequently been a focus of empirical study, the other topic in this chapter is the communication structure of the group.

Chapter 10 deals with a phenomenon basic to the functioning of all groups: the emergence of norms. Continued interaction results not only in regularities of feeling and behavior, but also in perceptions and cognitions of the conduct of group members. Group members arrive at consensus on what feelings, perceptions, and behaviors are appropriate or inappropriate. A theory is presented offering an explanation of how and where such consensus occurs and the degree to which members conform to these norms. Chapter 10 is concerned primarily with how such normative structures emerge. Later, in Part Three, more attention will be given to the effects of well-established norms on the behavior of the individual.

Leadership, the focus of Chapter 11, has long been a popular topic with behavioral scientists. Their research has gradually led to abandonment of the lay view that leadership is an attribute of an individual. Leadership is currently conceived of by the behavioral scientist as a role or function that arises in a group and that is filled or met in varying degrees by a number of group members, according to the demands of the situation and the members' characteristics.

The chapters previewed so far have emphasized the determinants rather than the consequences of structures and processes emerging from interaction among groups of persons. Chapter 12 shifts to the most frequently explored consequences of variations in group structure and process: the effectiveness with which a group performs its tasks and its efficiency in providing satisfaction to its members. The effects of various structural and other variables, such as size of the group, on effectiveness and satisfaction are discussed.

7

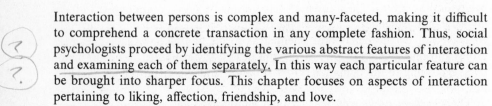

Interpersonal Attraction

Interaction between persons is complex and many-faceted, making it difficult to comprehend a concrete transaction in any complete fashion. Thus, social psychologists proceed by identifying the various abstract features of interaction and examining each of them separately. In this way each particular feature can be brought into sharper focus. This chapter focuses on aspects of interaction pertaining to liking, affection, friendship, and love.

Such interaction ranges from the exchange of small talk to the deep involvement of romantic love. Participation in social behavior is essential to a feeling of well-being, a point reflected in the familiar proverb, "All work and no play makes Jack a dull boy." Social interchange is rewarding, and has the effect of producing attraction between the participants. Such attraction produces increased association, and ultimately may lead to friendship or love. In addition, attraction contributes to the way in which groups are structured and the manner in which they function. Even in large, formal organizations, attraction determines to some extent the patterns of association, communication, and influence that occur among individuals. How and why attraction contributes to friendship and various group structures is the concern of this chapter.

The chapter is divided into two main sections, the first dealing with *dyadic attraction,* and the second with the *affect structure* of small groups of persons. *Dyadic* pertains to two persons: a *dyad* is a two-person group. The *affect structure* of a group is identified by ascertaining the pattern of liking and disliking that group members have for each other.

Dyadic Attraction

Although much early research on attraction was not guided by systematic theory, in more recent years the accumulation of empirical findings has led to more systematic conceptualizations of interpersonal attraction. Explanations of attraction fall into two broad, not entirely exclusive classes: those that consider attraction as an effect resulting from the characteristics of the persons making up the dyad, and those that focus on the rewards and costs experienced in the interactional process. Each of these classes will be discussed separately.

Explanations Based on Characteristics of Persons

Three approaches to explaining attraction between people postulate similarity between them as a basic condition, but differ in their explanation of why this similarity leads to attraction. One argues that attraction develops because similarity produces a *balanced* state, another that similar persons provide *rewards* for each other, and a third that similarity produces an *anticipation* of being liked, which in turn produces liking for the would-be friend. Each of these approaches will be discussed in some detail.

SIMILARITY AND BALANCE THEORY   Newcomb, following Heider, has developed a theory that relates attraction between persons to the attitudes that they hold in common toward objects.[1] This theory is frequently referred to as the *ABX theory of attraction,* for reasons to be explained shortly. The elements of the theory are as follows. Persons who interact live in a world of common objects *(including other persons)*. Through their experience with these objects, they develop certain attitudes toward them. These attitudes may be negative or positive. A state of balance prevails if the two persons like each other and have similar attitudes toward the objects. If they like each other but have dissimilar attitudes or dislike each other and have the same attitudes a state of strain or imbalance exists. In states of imbalance, one or more components are likely to change to restore balance.

Newcomb's *ABX* theory is more formally precisely depicted in Figure 7-1. A state of balance or strain is always seen from the point of view of a single person in the system. In Figure 7-1, *A* represents this person. Under consideration are his attitude toward an object, *X,* and the attitudes he believes person *B* holds toward *X* and toward him. Thus, in Figure 7-1, the solid directional lines represent *A*'s attitude toward *B* and toward *X,* and the dashed directional lines indicate *A*'s perception of *B*'s attitude toward him and toward object *X*. At top left, since all the attitudes are positive (indicated by +), the system is balanced. Note that *B*'s actual attitudes do not enter into the system, except insofar as they form the basis for *A*'s perception of them. Of course, by consid-

1. NEWCOMB, 1961.

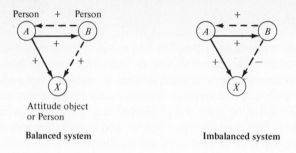

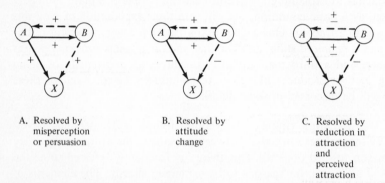

Figure 7-1   *The* **ABX system of person** A. *Solid lines represent* A's *attitudes; dashed lines represent the attitudes that* A *attributes to person* B.

ering the system state of *A and* that of *B,* these attitudes can be taken into account and, indeed, must enter into any thorough study of attraction between persons.

Suppose we now consider an imbalanced system by changing one element: At top right, *B* is seen as disliking *X.* This imbalanced system could be returned to balance in several ways. First, a shift could occur in *A*'s perception of *B*'s attitude: *A* might decide that he was mistaken in attributing to *B* a negative attitude (indicated by −). This form of resolution, shown in part A, would be labeled *misperception.* Second, *A* might successfully convince *B* that he is mistaken about *X,* also resulting in the system depicted in part A. Third, *A* might change his own attitude in the direction of *B*'s attitude and develop a similarly negative attitude toward *X,* as illustrated in part B. Fourth, as shown in part C, *A* might reduce the strain of imbalance somewhat by reducing his attraction toward *B* and perceiving that *B* is less attracted to him.*

* In order not to complicate this illustration further, two other changes have been omitted. Since the degree of strain is in part a function of the importance and perceived common relevance of person *X* to person *A,* changes might be made with regard to those two variables in order to reduce strain.

Certain additional factors influence the system state. The greater the *importance* and *common relevance* of the attitude object to the persons in a dyad, the stronger the attraction. The *importance* of the object is reflected in the amount of feeling, intensity of belief, or degree of behavior involvement with it. *Common relevance* means the degree to which the object is perceived as having mutual consequences for the persons in question. For example, for most married couples agreement on whether or not they like children is of more relevance than whether or not they like a particular make of automobile. Agreement on the former will lead to more attraction than will agreement on the latter.

From his theory Newcomb predicted that, as strangers in a new group begin to interact and thus to gain information concerning each other's attitudes, the bonds of attraction form most strongly between those persons who hold similar attitudes toward objects of importance and common relevance.[2] This prediction was tested in a study of two groups. Both were composed of male college students who were initially strangers and who lived together in a house provided by the experimenter. Their orientations toward a variety of objects, including each other, and the patterns of attraction that developed were measured at various points during a sixteen-week period.

The observations and the changes that occurred over the period observed were in accord with the theory. Preacquaintance similarities, measured from the students' responses to questionnaires on a variety of specific topics and from their rankings of certain values, led to the development of patterns of attraction between persons at a late stage in the sixteen-week period, but not at an early stage. Since attitudinal values did not change to any extent over the period studied, it would appear that as persons became acquainted with each other's values, attraction formed between those who were similar. When two persons held similar orientations toward themselves and toward other house occupants, they were especially likely to be attracted to each other. As acquaintance increased, consensus in attitudes between members of a pair toward other house members increased, and there was a parallel increase in their attraction to each other.

If the assumption is made that persons positively value themselves, the theory would predict that a close association would be found between liking other persons and believing that they like oneself in turn. Such was the case: A person liked others who had the same feeling toward him as he had toward himself. The association between attraction to a person and perceiving him as having similar attitudes was true for cognitive elements as well. Each individual described himself by checking a series of adjectives and then used the same adjective checklist to describe himself as he thought each of the others in the group would. A close association was found between attraction and perceived agreement on such a self-description.[3] This appeared to hold for unfavorable as

2. NEWCOMB, 1956.   3. NEWCOMB, 1956.

well as favorable items: An individual was attracted to persons whom he perceived as seeing him in the way he saw himself, in terms of both faults and virtues. These findings with regard to the self as an object have been confirmed by others.[4] Also, a study conducted in another theoretical context, described below, showed that attraction was affected not only by perceived similarity but by actual similarity as well.[5] A recent replication of the Newcomb study similarly found that individuals liked other persons who had favorable attitudes toward them.[6] But individuals were only weakly attracted to persons who ascribed to them characteristics that they ascribed to themselves.

Finally, another study, while not concerned with attraction as the dependent variable, provides experimental evidence for strain toward balance.[7] Two balanced and two imbalanced conditions in a perceptual task situation were created: (1) a liked partner was perceived as making judgments similar to one's own, (2) a disliked partner was perceived as making judgments dissimilar to one's own, (3) a liked partner was seen as making judgments dissimilar to one's own, and (4) a disliked partner was seen as making judgments similar to one's own. The prediction that persons would change their judgment more frequently in the imbalanced situations (3 and 4 above) was confirmed. In another similar situation, however, where judgments of the outcome of jury trials were made, the prediction that persons would respond so as to be different from a disliked partner and similar to a liked partner received less conclusive support.

A number of studies, including a partial replication of the dormitory study by Newcomb, but with individuals who were members of the successful American Mount Everest expedition, suggested that the importance of these balancing tendencies depends on both the type of group and the temporal phase of its existence.[8] Balancing tendencies appear to be more important determinants of attraction in groups whose primary function is the satisfaction of social-emotional needs, and less important in task-oriented groups, such as the Mount Everest team or in problem-solving groups in the laboratory. They are also more important in the early phases of group development than in the later phases, where perhaps other sources of attraction are sufficiently powerful to overcome the strain arising from attitude dissimilarity.

Balance theory is not borne out as well in situations involving feelings toward another person that are negative instead of positive. In a study of a living group of disabled veterans, sociometric triads were seldom balanced in the instances where negative feelings were involved.[9] However, in an experimental study involving negative feelings, results were in accord with balance theory.[10] Individuals first experienced pleasant or harsh treatment from an experimenter and later were allowed to overhear a supervisor of the experimenter treat him in either a harsh or a pleasant manner. At a still later point and in a different context they were given an opportunity to help the supervisor. Those who had been dealt with harshly by the experimenter offered more help to the supervisor

4. DOHERTY & SECORD, 1971.   *5.* BACKMAN & SECORD, 1962.   *6.* CURRY & EMERSON, 1970.   *7.* SAMPSON & INSKO, 1964.   *8.* LESTER, 1965.   *9.* DAVOL, 1959.   *10.* ARONSON & COPE, 1968.

who had dealt harshly with the experimenter, thus validating the saying, "My enemy's enemy is my friend."

Differences in the methodology employed as well as the populations studied may account for differences among these various studies, but at this point at least, the evidence of the applicability of balance theory to instances of negative affect is equivocal.

Finally, the importance of an attitude and its relevance in the situation appears to modify the effects of similarity. In studies where the expected relations between similarity and attraction have not been obtained, either the attitudes employed were unimportant to the participants, or similarity in them was of little value or perhaps even interfered with the functioning of the group.[11] In task-oriented groups, for instance, differences in attitudes and values might facilitate performance by providing useful criticism. Forces of attraction arising from this condition may counterbalance the forces arising from the lack of agreement.

SIMILARITY AS A SOURCE OF REINFORCEMENT   In one series of experiments, Byrne and his colleagues demonstrate that similarity is associated with attraction. In a second series, they attempt to demonstrate that similar attitudes can have reinforcing value.

In an experimental situation that largely eliminates the influence of other variables, Byrne and his associates have demonstrated that an individual is attracted to a hypothetical other person in proportion to the extent that he perceives the other person to hold attitudes similar to his own.[12] Their basic method is as follows: Participants fill out an attitude scale. At a later time, in the context of a study which they are told is designed to explore how individuals judge other persons under conditions of limited information, they are asked to read an attitude scale supposedly filled out by another person. The proportion of statements agreeing with those previously endorsed by the participant is varied for different participants. Embedded in a questionnaire requiring the individual to make judgments of the other person on the basis of this limited information are two items that allow attraction to be measured.

In a number of experimental variations of this procedure, the attraction scores were found to vary directly with the proportion of similar items: The more similar in attitude the other person appeared to be, the more he was liked. Attitude statements presented on tape recordings and in color sound movies had the same effect on attraction as those presented in the form of the other person's responses to a questionnaire.[13] These findings have been obtained not only with college students, but also with children and adolescents in the fourth through twelfth grades, members of the Job Corps, hospitalized alcoholics, and schizophrenics.[14]

Dimensions of similarity other than attitude have also been used, including

11. MORAN, 1966.   *12.* BYRNE & NELSON, 1965.   *13.* BYRNE & CLORE, 1966.   *14.* BYRNE & GRIFFITT, 1966; BYRNE, GRIFFITT, HUDGINS, & REEVES, 1969.

items from personality inventories and questions about personal finances.[15] Differences in similarity were also created by varying the proportion of positive and negative evaluations of the participants made by the other person[16] For each of these dimensions, the proportion of similar items was directly related to attraction. Items that pertained to the evaluation of the participant had especially strong effects on attraction, approximately three times that of attitudinal items.

An assumption widely accepted by social psychologists is that persons have a need to assess social reality correctly. Although aspects of the physical world can frequently be checked through the visual and other senses, social beliefs can only be validated by other persons. Thus, it is assumed that everyone is dependent upon other persons for checking out his version of social reality. This process in which other persons confirm our views has been called *consensual validation*. Along similar lines, Byrne has suggested that persons have a learned drive to be logical and to interpret correctly their stimulus world. He proposes that similar attitudes held by another person are satisfying because of the anticipation that a person with similar attitudes will share one's view of the world and not threaten it.

Byrne and Clore tested this idea by increasing in varying degree the need of an individual for consensual support in interpreting the current situation.[17] This was done in three ways by having persons: (1) view specially prepared films whose content was meaningless and confused, (2) experience disconfirmation of their expectations about their performance on an intelligence test, and (3) confront the attitude responses of a stranger different from their own. These manipulations were followed by their model procedure which tested attraction in persons varying in attitude similarity. Presumably, the stronger the need for consensual support, the greater the attraction. Contrary to the hypothesis, the overall results of these investigations suggested that moderate arousal of the need for support increased the effects of similarity on attraction, whereas high states of arousal dampened this effect.

A different experiment attempted to determine directly whether similar attitude statements could be used as reinforcements in learning a simple discrimination task.[18] Analysis showed that attitude statements did operate like rewards and punishments. But a later study suggested that this effect was due not to the similarity or dissimilarity of the statements, but to their positive or negative connotations.[19] This was demonstrated by showing that the attractiveness of nonsense syllables could be conditioned by pairing them with adjectives that were regarded by the participants as either pleasant or unpleasant, but not by adjectives that were either descriptive or not descriptive of the participants. Thus, it is possible that the attitude statements used by Byrne and his associates as well as other indicators of similarity such as personality traits have the

15. Byrne, Griffitt, & Stefaniak, 1967; Byrne, Clore, & Worchel, 1966.   *16.* Byrne & Rhamey, 1965.   *17.* Byrne & Clore, 1967.   *18.* Byrne, Young, & Griffitt, 1966.   *19.* Stalling, 1970.

effects they do because they are positively valued rather than because they are similar. As others have suggested, this study casts some doubt on the role of similarity per se as a cause of liking.[20]

A critical examination of many of these experiments on attitude similarity points up some rather serious restrictions on generalizing these results to non-laboratory settings. In the model experiment employed by Byrne and his colleagues, individuals were supplied with extremely limited information about a hypothetical stimulus person. Typically this consisted of a set of twelve attitude items which, for different stimulus persons, varied in similarity to the individual's own attitude. Under these severe constraints, the only information the participants could use to rate the attraction items was similarity-dissimilarity, since they were told nothing else about the stimulus person. That an appreciable majority chose similarity as a basis may only reflect some type of personal logic rather than a genuine empirical association between liking and similarity.

Moreover, individuals were given a judgmental set which implicitly emphasized accuracy, and were asked to endorse, among others, two items pertaining to attraction. In addition, the arousal of the need for consensual validation would lead the judges to be especially logical and rational in judging attraction. Yet, outside the laboratory, attraction is spontaneously experienced rather than judged. Further, it is not entirely clear how similarity in *personality* or *social background* rather than *attitudes* would satisfy the consensual needs producing greater attraction. But the positive or negative connotations of personality and background could account for attraction.

Finally, recent studies using different experimental procedures have found only very weak or inconsistent associations between attraction and similarity. We have previously noted that a replication of Newcomb's dormitory study found much weaker support for attitude similarity except where the object of the attitude was the self.[21] Two field studies of changes in attraction over time, one between roommates and the other between courting couples, similarly failed to support the attitude-similarity attraction hypothesis.[22] A questionnaire study of the characteristics of male friends in an urban area found little if any support for the relation between attitude similarity and friendship.[23] Studies of same-sexed friends using a more elaborate measure of attraction and various measures of similarity suggest that the effects of similarity depend both on the type of similarity and the sex of the individual.[24] While perceived or actual agreement on specific issues did not lead to attraction, men who liked the same activities were mutually attracted, and women who agreed on abstract values liked each other.

ATTRACTION AND ANTICIPATION OF BEING LIKED Attraction to a person with similar attitudes has also been explained as resulting from an anticipation of

20. LEVINGER, 1972; FISHBEIN & AIZEN, 1972.   21. LEVINGER, 1972.   22. LESTER, 1965; CURRY & EMERSON, 1970.   23. LAUMANN, 1969.   24. WRIGHT & CRAWFORD, 1971.

being liked.[25] Perceiving another person as having similar attitudes might lead an individual to conclude that *the other person would like him*. Being liked in turn would produce liking for the would-be friend.

In one study, individuals were asked to predict whether a stranger would like them. Almost invariably, if they thought the other person would like them, they liked the stranger.[26] Liking for the stranger was related to the similarity of his attitudes, and this might produce the inference of being liked. The investigators point out that their study leaves either interpretation open: Similarity might independently affect attraction, or it might be mediated by an anticipation of being liked. The studies by Byrne and his colleagues are also open to this alternative interpretation: Similarities in attitudes and personality could function as cues to potential favorable evaluation by another person.

Anticipation of being liked by similar persons seems especially important to people who are insecure or are concerned about being liked. An experimenter caused one group of participants to think they would not be liked when introduced to a group of strangers, caused another group to think they would be liked, and gave a control group no preliminary treatment.[27] In comparison with the control group, the first group more frequently chose to associate with strangers who seemed similar to them and the second group more frequently chose dissimilar people. In another experiment, it was found that similarity in personality traits was associated with friendship among high school seniors and among college freshmen but not among college seniors.[28] If it can be assumed that adolescents are more insecure than college seniors, this finding is consistent with the hypothesis that insecure people choose similar friends in anticipation of being liked.

SUMMARY: SIMILARITY AS A SOURCE OF ATTRACTION   There are three explanations of the general finding that interpersonal attraction is associated with similarity. In checking these explanations against the experimental literature, it was found that the first of these, a variant of balance theory called Newcomb's *ABX* theory, received partial support. The theory appears to hold best for liking rather than disliking, for social-emotional relations rather than task relations, for attitudes toward the self, and for the early rather than later phase of friendship.

Byrne's idea that similarity reduces the need for consensual validation and thus produces attraction, while generally consistent with his research findings, is not the only way of interpreting the data. A person may be attracted to another with similar attitudes, personality traits, or other characteristics because the attribute of the other person is positively valued rather than because it is similar. The experimental model underlying much of this research, in order to achieve control of extraneous variables and to obtain clear-cut relations

25. ARONSON & WORCHEL, 1966; NELSON, 1966; McWHIRTER & JECKER, 1967.   26. McWHIRTER & JECKER, 1967.   27. WALSTER & WALSTER, 1963.   28. IZARD, 1963.

between similarity and attraction, sacrifices external validity—the ability to generalize easily to situations outside the laboratory.

The view receiving the strongest empirical support is that similarity produces an anticipation of being liked, which in turn attracts the individual to his would-be friend. This interpretation is consistent with studies that vary the person's concern for being liked, or his general insecurity, and it is also compatible with the general finding that similarity is more often associated with attraction in the earlier stages of friendship.

Explanation Based on Complementary Needs

Perhaps the most widely known approach that stresses *differences* rather than *similarities* between two partners is the idea that *complementary needs* produce attraction between persons.[29] This idea, developed and tested largely in the context of mate selection, has been offered as a general principle of dyad formation, of which mate selection is a special case. While not denying that persons who fall in love and marry are usually similar in a number of respects such as social-background characteristics, Winch suggested that the need structure of persons attracted to each other is different or complementary rather than similar.

Winch proposed two basically different reasons why persons whose needs are complementary are attracted to each other: (1) *mutual need gratification* and (2) *attraction to an ego ideal.* The first of these has been commonly associated with need complementarity, and has led to some research; the second has been little studied. In mutual need gratification, each member of the dyad find interaction mutually or reciprocally rewarding because his needs are expressed in behavior that is rewarding to the other member. For example, a person with strong needs to nurture behaves in a protective, nurturing manner toward another person who has strong needs to be dependent. In this way, each individual satisfies his needs and is in turn satisfied.

Attraction to an ego ideal takes the following form. Persons are attracted to others who have characteristics they once aspired to but were prevented by circumstances from developing. Instead, they have modeled themselves after the image of a person with the opposite traits. But they still retain a wistful admiration for individuals who possess the once-coveted traits.

Need complementarity may take either of two forms. Persons *A* and *B* may be regarded as complementary in needs because *A* is high and *B* is low on the same needs, or because *A* is high on one or more needs and *B* is high or low on certain different needs. In the first form, called *Type I complementarity,* a person who is very high in the need to dominate others and a person who is very low in this need are mutually attracted. *Type II complementarity* is illustrated by the

29. WINCH, 1958.

previous description of a nurturer and a dependent person attracted to each other.

Evidence for need complementarity is far from conclusive. Winch and his associates studied the need structures of twenty-five married couples and concluded that the bulk of the evidence supported his general hypothesis of complementarity. Most subsequent studies, however, have failed to confirm Winch's conclusions,[30] although a few have provided some support.[31]

The plausible hypothesis of need complementarity may fail to be confirmed because of conceptual weaknesses or because of methodological shortcomings in studies designed to test it. Both Rosow and Levinger have suggested that the theory does not adequately specify those combinations of needs that are complementary, and further, that some complementary needs are similar instead of opposite.[32] For example, two persons high in the need for affiliation might be expected to enjoy each other's company. Rosow has also pointed out that a methodological problem arises because need complementarity may sometimes function at a covert or even unconscious level, rather than an overt one.[33]

Both Levinger and Tharp have questioned the assumption that need expression and satisfaction can be considered apart from particular role relations.[34] Tharp, in particular, argues that a given personality need is related to attraction and compatibility only to the degree that it facilitates meeting the role expectations of persons in a specific relationship, such as friendship or marriage. Most studies that have failed to confirm the need-complementarity hypothesis have used paper-and-pencil tests, in which persons describe their needs in general and not in a role relationship. Testing in such a manner is consistent with the traditional view of personality in which traits are thought to represent general characteristics of the individual which he displays in all situations and relationships. However, there is increasing evidence that such a view of personality is incorrect: that much of the stability observed in an individual's behavior is specific to particular situations and relationships. Thus a man may be dominant in his relation with his wife or children but quite submissive in his relation with his boss.

Evidence suggests that need satisfaction and expression may indeed be specific to roles. Preferences for interaction have been shown to vary for different roles: In one study, they were based on similarity for the role of boss but on complementarity for the role of neighbor.[35] Another study using a scale modified to measure need satisfaction specifically in the marriage relation provided some further support for nurturer-dependent complementarity in marital pairs.[36] Moreover, even the marital relation may have within it several types of role relations, not all of which display need complementarity. One investigation

30. Bowerman & Day, 1956; Schellenberg & Bee, 1960; Murstein, 1961; Hobart & Lindholm, 1963; Levinger, Senn, & Jorgensen, 1970.   *31.* Kerckhoff & Davis, 1962; Katz, Cohen, & Castiglione, 1963; Rychlak, 1965.   *32.* Rosow, 1957; Levinger, 1964.   *33.* Rosow, 1957.   *34.* Tharp, 1963, 1964; Levinger, 1964.   *35.* Rychlak, 1965.   *36.* Katz et al., 1963.

studied twenty-five couples who advocated a traditional husband-wife role and twenty-four couples who advocated a companion relation.[37] Only the former displayed need complementarity; the latter were similar in needs.

On the other hand, Rosow has pointed out that to focus on a particular relation such as the marital role overlooks the possibility that needs may often be gratified through complementarity outside this role relation, making the data obtained for the marital role appear to falsify the idea of need complementarity.[38] Also, one study indicated that the stability of student nurse roommate dyads was independently contributed to both by need complementarity and by similarity in conformity to normative roles for student nurses.[39]

Explanations Based on Interaction Process

Four approaches derive interpersonal attraction from the interaction process. First, consensual validation of an individual's experience by another person is held to produce liking for that person, especially if the other validates the individual's self concept. Second, situations where an individual can reduce dissonance by changing his feelings toward another person have been found to produce liking and disliking. A third explanation is based on conditioning: Attraction is thought to occur when the interaction process generates stimulus-response sequences that are followed by reinforcement. Finally, a more comprehensive explanation is offered in terms of exchange theory, which has been developed in some detail by Homans, by Thibaut and Kelley, and by Blau.[40] This approach analyzes the rewards and costs exchanged in interaction, and regards attraction as a function of the relation of these *outcomes* (rewards minus costs) to the expectations held by the individual. The first three approaches are discussed in this section; a more extensive treatment of exchange theory is given in a subsequent section.

ATTRACTION AS A FUNCTION OF CONSENSUAL VALIDATION   The concept of consensual validation has already been mentioned in connection with Byrne's idea that perceiving another person as similar satisfies an individual's drive to assess social reality correctly, producing liking. But consensual validation may also occur in other ways.

Two studies relate to the general notion of consensual validation. In one study, first-born individuals liked those with whom they shared the stressful experience of receiving an electric shock.[41] The investigators interpreted these findings to mean that people needed to compare their reactions with those of others who had experienced similar stress. Satisfaction of this need led to increased liking.

The second study showed that persons who behave in a manner contrary to

37. HOLZ, 1969.   *38.* ROSOW, 1957.   *39.* BERMANN, 1966.   *40.* THIBAUT & KELLEY, 1959; HOMANS, 1961; BLAU, 1964.   *41.* LATANÉ, ECKMAN, & JOY, 1966.

what would be expected on the basis of the social situation are less liked than those whose behavior is appropriate and predictable.[42] Partners who appropriately shared their rewards for task achievement in a condition defined as cooperative and who did not share them in a competitive condition were liked better than those who inappropriately did not share in a cooperative condition and did share in a competitive one.

Secord and Backman have outlined a theory of stability and change in behavior that bears on the present discussion (see Chapter 17 for a more extended treatment of the theory).[43] They proposed that individuals are attracted to other persons whose characteristics, behavioral and otherwise, aid them in maintaining *congruency*. Such a perceptual-cognitive state is achieved by an individual in a relation with another person when the other's characteristics or behavior contain implications congruent with elements of his own behavior and self concept. Two forms of congruency especially relevant to attraction are *congruency by implication,* where an individual perceives the other person's behavior as directly confirming a component of self, and (2) *congruency by validation,* where the other person's behavior leads an individual to behave in ways that confirm an aspect of self. An illustration of the first is an individual who regards himself as mature and responsible, and perceives that other persons notice and respect these characteristics. An illustration of the second is an individual who regards himself as nurturant and encounters a person in need of help; this allows him to behave toward the person in a manner that supports his nurturant aspect of self.

These are forms of consensual validation of the self concept. A variety of studies support the view that persons who consensually validate the self are liked and those who invalidate it are disliked. A study of a sorority demonstrated that members were most attracted to those other girls whom they believed to have and who actually had congruent views of them.[44] Another study of pairs of friends suggested that friendship was associated with congruency by validation.[45] On a number of needs, individuals who perceived themselves as high on a particular need perceived their friends as high on a congruent need. For example, persons who were high on dependence viewed their friends as high on nurturance. Friends were not found to be high on needs that could not be conceived to produce congruency by validation. The similarity of these effects to need complementarity is obvious; however, it must be emphasized that while congruency theory makes some predictions similar to those of need complementarity, it also produces some predictions involving needs that would not be paired by the need-complementarity principle.

Positive or negative evaluations by other persons may be congruent or incongruent with an individual's self concept, leading to like or dislike. One study induced success in some individuals and failure in others on an experimental

42. KIESLER, 1966.   43. SECORD & BACKMAN, 1961, 1965.   44. BACKMAN & SECORD, 1962.   45. SECORD & BACKMAN, 1964*b*.

task, and arranged for evaluations supposedly by other persons serving in the experiment.[46] In the following summary of results, order of treatments is arranged from the one in which the other person O was most liked by person P to the one in which O was least liked by P: (1) P succeeded and O evaluated him favorably; (2) P failed and O evaluated him unfavorably; P failed and O evaluated him favorably; and (3) P succeeded and O evaluated him unfavorably. These results yield partial support for congruency theory: notably that P's who failed and were unfavorably evaluated by O liked O better than did P's who succeeded and were unfavorably evaluated by O. But positive evaluation, whether congruent or incongruent, also led to liking of the other person.

Another investigation used five different degrees of discrepancy between an individual's own evaluation and the other person's *negative* evaluation.[47] When the other person's evaluation was congruent or nearly so, he was rated more favorably. But increasing incongruency led to increasingly unfavorable ratings of the other person. Another study demonstrated that individuals who decide not to attempt a task because of doubts about their ability are attracted to those persons who affirm their own opinion of their inability to succeed at the task.[48] Two studies of roommate choice and congruency also support the idea that consensual validation leads to attraction.[49]

In conclusion, actions by another person that either directly or indirectly validate an individual's experience, especially his self concept, have been shown to produce liking for that person. Evidence is most conclusive when a positive self concept is validated by a positive evaluation; negative evaluations that are congruent do not always produce liking.

ATTRACTION AS A MEANS OF RESOLVING DISSONANCE   Dissonance theory (see Chapter 3) has been used to explain changes in attraction following various experiences. In general, where one of the elements contributing to a state of dissonance is liking or disliking, one way of reducing the dissonance is to change this feeling. Several experiments have been designed to test this means of resolving dissonance. Individuals who believed themselves responsible for an electric shock received by another experimental subject made his suffering more consonant by attributing to him less desirable characteristics.[50] In a similar experimental situation, participants whose self-esteem had been momentarily raised by an experimental manipulation lowered their attraction toward the person whom they thought they had shocked, thus reducing the dissonance arising from their aggressive behavior and their favorable self-image.[51]

Individuals also reduce dissonance by liking a person less upon learning that they have misjudged him unfavorably.[52] Stuck with their unfavorable judgment, they try to justify it by liking him less. Two other studies have shown that

46. DEUTSCH & SOLOMON, 1959.   47. HARVEY, 1962.   48. WILSON, 1962.   49. BROXTON, 1963; DOHERTY & SECORD, 1971.   50. LERNER & MATTHEWS, 1967.   51. GLASS, 1964.   52. WALSTER & PRESTHOLDT, 1966.

persons who suffered considerable discomfort in order to become members of a group increased their liking for other group members.[53] Increased liking justified the unpleasantness endured in order to become group members, reducing the dissonance originally aroused. A similar effect has been reported in another investigation.[54] People who anticipated being paired with an undesirable person exaggerated in a favorable direction the traits of the partner and voluntarily chose that partner when later given the opportunity. Persons who anticipated that they would be forced to associate with either a positive or a negative partner did not exhibit these behaviors to the same degree.

The conclusion is that in a variety of situations that may be interpreted as dissonance-arousing, liking or disliking occurs in a manner that reduces the dissonance.

ATTRACTION AS A FUNCTION OF REINFORCEMENT   Lott and Lott have derived from learning theory principles a variety of explanations of the development of liking and have tested their ideas in experiments with children.[55] Their explanations range from classical conditioning to vicarious reinforcement.

The essence of conditioning is that an organism producing certain responses which are followed by reinforcement learns to give these responses to stimuli which have been repeatedly present. Thus, Pavlov's dog learned to salivate in response to a buzzer which had been repeatedly sounded just before the presentation of food. Lott and Lott apply the idea of conditioning to the development of liking in the following way:

1. Assume that an individual receives various rewards while in the presence of another person; for example, smiles of approval, praise, enjoyment of a shared activity.

2. The individual reacts in some fashion to these rewards; for example, a child who is praised may smile and experience a feeling of pleasure.

3. Such responses, like any response, will become conditioned to all discriminable stimuli (including the other person) that are present at the time of reinforcement.

4. The person who is repeatedly present during such response-reinforcement sequences becomes able eventually to evoke the responses by his mere presence.

In short, liking for a person is the set of responses (or variants of responses) that an individual makes in the presence of another person because these have been previously reinforced in his presence. These include not only overt responses such as smiling or talking, but also covert responses such as feelings. This conditioning interpretation of liking and its origins requires only that the other person be present during the response-reinforcement sequence, not that

---

53. ARONSON & MILLS, 1959; GERARD & MATHEWSON, 1966.   54. BERSCHEID, BOYE, & DARLEY, 1968.
55. LOTT & LOTT, 1968.

the other person be the source of the reinforcement. Thus, from this viewpoint, an infant fed mechanically by means of specially devised equipment would nevertheless come to like his mother (or any other person) if she were consistently present during the feeding situation.

Various experiments conducted by Lott and his associates have yielded results consistent with a conditioning explanation of liking. These experiments have used children as participants, generally in game-playing contexts.[56] Some of the investigations reported in the contexts of other explanations of liking are also consistent with a conditioning interpretation. As these investigators recognize, however, some of their findings suggest that one must go beyond the simple conditioning explanation of liking. This point will be elaborated upon shortly in our discussion of exhange theory.

Another principle from learning theory is that delayed reinforcement is less effective than immediate reward. This was tested in an experiment with children.[57] The children experienced immediate reward in the presence of one adult helper and a ten-second delayed reward in the presence of a second helper. The experimenters expected that they would like the former helper better, because of the lesser efficacy of delayed reward. Liking was measured in five different ways, and while the results were in the predicted direction in all cases, only three of the five were statistically significant. The investigators suggested that results for the two nonsignificant measures might have been attenuated by the children's trying to be fair and to give each helper an equal chance to assist them.

Lott, Lott, and Matthews extended their learning-theory interpretation of liking to imitation and modeling behavior.[58] They hypothesized that reward need not be actually experienced, but the person need merely observe someone else being rewarded, for liking to increase. They suggested that the observer who sees another person rewarded may observe or infer certain liking responses occurring in that person, and that the observer consequently produces similar responses in himself, through empathy. But these ideas extend reinforcement theory so far as to make it unrecognizable.

SUMMARY: INTERACTIONS THAT PRODUCE ATTRACTION   Several forms of interaction that lead one person to like another have been reviewed. Actions or evaluations by another person that validate an individual's experience or his self concept produce liking. This effect occurs most consistently when the evaluations are positive. Liking and disliking have also been shown to occur as a result of dissonance reduction. The explanation of attraction in terms of conditioning, while consistent with much experimental data, often needs amplification in terms of cognitive variables such as the individual's conceptions of what is rewarding and what is not, as discussed in the next section.

56. LOTT & LOTT, 1960; JAMES & LOTT, 1964; LOTT, LOTT, & MATTHEWS, 1969.   57. LOTT et al., 1969.
58. LOTT et al., 1969.

Exchange Theories of Attraction

A number of theorists during the past decade have conceptualized interaction in terms of exchange processes. [59] While such reinforcement concepts as reward and punishment have figured prominently in these theories, this approach has differed from learning interpretations of behavior in two ways. First, the focus of exchange theory has been on the *relation between individuals* rather than on the individuals themselves. Emphasis is on how various characteristics of a relation emerge, and on how this process changes as a result of the reciprocal process of reinforcement between individuals. Second, cognitive elements play a much more central role in these theories than in traditional reinforcement theory. Rewards and punishments are thought to have effects only as they are mediated by the expectations and perceived intentions of persons in interaction. These expectations are thought to be influenced by such normative cognitions as rules of justice and ideas about what constitutes equivalence in exchange. For example, a mild but unjust punishment may be felt more severely than a strong but just punishment. Central to all these theories has been interpersonal attraction, since this constitutes one of the most potent rewards exchanged in interaction.

Four concepts are basic to exchange theory: reward, cost, outcome, and comparison level. The term *reward* is a familiar one. The preceding review of other theories has taken note of rather important rewards that are achieved in interaction. These have included actions that validate one's attitude toward other persons or toward oneself, as well as actions that resolve dissonance or reduce negative drive states. Any activity by one person that contributes to the gratification of another person's need can be considered a reward from the standpoint of the latter person. The term *cost,* similarly, covers a broad concept. The costs of engaging in any activity not only include "punishment" incurred in carrying out the activity, such as fatigue or anxiety, but also, as Homans argues, include the value of rewards foregone to engage in this activity rather than alternative activities.

The term *outcome* refers to rewards minus costs. If the outcome of an interaction is positive, it may be said to yield a profit; if it is negative, a loss. That a person profits from an interaction with another, however, does not necessarily mean that he likes that person. For attraction to occur, the outcome must be above some minimum level of expectation, called the *comparison level.* This level is influenced by his past experiences in this relation, his past experiences in comparable relations, his judgment of what outcomes others like himself are receiving, and his perceptions of outcomes available to him in alternative relations.

Evidence also suggests that comparison level varies from person to person because of individual differences in the characteristic saliences of costs and of

59. THIBAUT & KELLEY, 1959; HOMANS, 1961; BLAU, 1964.

rewards.[60] Some persons appear to be more oriented to reward and others, to costs.

That the development of attraction in a particular dyad is influenced by outcomes available in alternative relations is nicely illustrated by a study comparing the effects of interaction in isolated and nonisolated groups.[61] Each of nine pairs of persons worked and lived in a small room for ten days, with all outside contact denied (i.e., no alternative relationships were permitted). Control dyads followed a similar schedule, but had access to other people and outside facilities. The interaction for the isolated dyads was strikingly different from that for the control pairs. There was much more self-disclosure, including some intimate items; depth of disclosure resembled that achieved with close friends. Observers noted much more friendly and sociable behavior among the isolated dyads, as compared with the control dyads.

SIMILARITY, MUTUAL ATTRACTION, AND EXCHANGE THEORY   Exchange theory can further explain the relations between similarity and interpersonal attractions, discussed in the previous section, by analyzing the implications of similarity between persons in terms of rewards and costs. The similarities observed between friends on a variety of social-background and demographic characteristics, such as religion, rural or urban background, class in college, and age, may well be a product of two processes involving exchange.

First, many such characteristics are related through the social structure to frequency of interaction. Other things being equal, persons in the same college class or in the same age category would be expected to interact more frequently because of the greater opportunity for interaction. Opportunity to interact is related to attraction. Thus the similarity of friends to each other may result simply from the fact that similar persons have more opportunities to interact and consequently to become friends. Second, similarity in background characteristics[62] is associated with similarity in values. Similarity in values is rewarding because each person, at low cost to himself, provides consensual validation to the other.

Similarity in abilities and personality traits is a more complex matter, since rewards and costs depend in part on the particular ability or trait. With certain traits or abilities, the attraction between similar persons may rest on the fact that the trait or ability allows them to engage in an activity which is mutually rewarding. This is most obvious in the case of abilities and skills. In the game of bridge, for instance, the possession of similar skills allows partners to take pleasure in competitive teamwork; the annoyance and anger experienced when one's partner is markedly inferior is notorious. Further, Festinger has presented a theory, and has cited considerable evidence consistent with it, involving the assumption that individuals have a need to compare their abilities with others who have similar abilities.[63] Since interaction with those who are similar would

60. UPSHAW, 1967.   61. ALTMAN & HAYTHORN, 1965.   62. LAZARSFELD & MERTON, 1954.   63. FESTINGER, 1964.

generally lead to satisfaction of this need for comparison, attraction should occur as a consequence.

Exchange theory also explains the contradictory findings about personality traits. Persons who are similar in such traits as the need for order would be likely to find interaction most profitable. On some other traits, persons with different but complementary traits would probably provide each other with maximum reward at minimum cost. Again the combination of a nurturant and a dependent person may be cited as an illustration.

EXCHANGE THEORY AND OPPORTUNITY TO INTERACT   One of the most interesting questions is why propinquity and other factors that affect opportunity to interact are associated with liking. Although individual characteristics have been emphasized as important determinants of attraction, the mere ease and volume of interaction also has rather strong effects on attraction. As Homans has noted, "You can get to like some pretty queer customers if you go around with them long enough."[64]

Thibaut and Kelley have suggested a number of ways in which physical proximity may be related to attraction.[65] First, those who are located close to each other are more likely to interact because of the low cost of initiating such interaction. This in turn heightens the possibility that they will discover behaviors that are rewarding to both.

Second, persons who are physically close are often more similar than those who are physically distant. For instance, people who live in the same neighborhood usually have the same socioeconomic background and are often of similar ethnic and religious backgrounds. Their shared similarities in values provide consensual validation.

Third, when two people interact continuously, each becomes able to predict the behavior of the other, and predictability is related to attraction.[66] Such predictability reduces the costs of interaction and increases the level of rewards exchanged. Such costs as the effort exerted in learning how the other person will respond to various behaviors or the anxiety generated over doing or saying the wrong thing are reduced as one gets to know another person well enough to predict his responses. Such predictability also allows one to elicit rewarding behavior more effectively from the other person. The net result is a more favorable reward-cost outcome.

A fourth factor, noted by Homans and by Thibaut and Kelley, is that continued interaction with those who are physically close costs less in time and effect than interaction with those more distant.[67] Other things being equal, then, the profit experienced in relations with more accessible persons is higher. Thibaut and Kelley suggest that in view of this, relations maintained over some distance must be more rewarding than relations between persons who are

---

64. HOMANS, 1950, p. 115.   65. THIBAUT & KELLEY, 1959.   66. KIESLER, 1966.   67. HOMANS, 1961; THIBAUT & KELLEY, 1959.

physically close. They cite a study by Williams that provides some support for this supposition.[68] Residents of a suburban housing development who had friends residing outside the immediate community had greater agreement on values with these friends than with persons residing in the same area. As observed earlier, an important reward that individuals gain in their interaction with others is support for their values.

A fifth way in which interaction may be related to liking has been suggested by Newcomb.[69] As persons interact, or to use Newcomb's term, engage in communicative behavior, they exchange information. This in itself increases the degree to which they are similar and contributes further to attraction.

Other findings cited previously fall conveniently into this framework of rewards and costs intrinsic or extrinsic to the relation.[70] Liking other persons who like us in turn, who see us in a favorable light, and who recognize both our virtues and our faults is consistent with a reward-cost viewpoint. Support for one's self concept is an important reward gained in interaction with other persons. If the effects of rewards experienced in a given situation generalize to other aspects of the situation including persons, then the finding that people who are present in rewarding situations are liked is also understandable within this framework.[71]

EXCHANGE THEORY, FRIENDSHIP, AND LOVE   A major advantage of exchange theory is that it reveals unifying principles underlying the various empirical generalizations about interpersonal attraction. Even more important, however, is that such a unifying framework provides an explanation for the exceptions to these generalizations. Even a cursory examination of one's own friendships reveals exceptions. You may not like the person next door or someone with whom you have had considerable interaction. Your best friend and you may differ not only on some social-background characteristics but on a number of attitudes. He may on occasion criticize your faults or, even worse, your virtues. Exchange theory treats these problems effectively by means of a *process* analysis of friendship formation.

Such an analysis focuses upon the sequential events and stages leading to the development of friendship. These processes may be examined by describing them in terms of an imaginary group. Suppose that a group of students from various universities, all initially strangers to each other, meet for a weekend conference. The formation of dyads characterized by a relatively high rate of interaction and positive affect may be described in terms of the following sequence.

At the first meeting of the hypothetical group, beneath the hum of polite conversation a process termed *sampling and estimation* occurs. Each person explores, at varying degrees of cost to himself, the rewards available in poten-

68. WILLIAMS, 1959.   *69.* NEWCOMB, 1956.   *70.* SIDOWSKI, WYCKOFF & TABORY, 1956; SIDOWSKI, 1957; KELLEY, THIBAUT, RADLOFF, & MUNDY, 1962.   *71.* KELLEY et al., 1962.

tial relations with other persons around him. Consider, for example, a man named Gary and a woman named Sandra. Although accidental factors operate at this phase, an important determinant of whether Gary will approach Sandra is his estimate of potential costs and rewards.

His estimate of cost will be affected by factors ranging from sheer distance—it takes less effort to talk to the girl standing close to him than to Sandra, who is across the room—to his estimate of how likely it would be that he could strike up a conversation with her. If she already is earnestly conversing with several others, he may be discouraged by the costs of breaking into the conversational circle and the likelihood that he would have to share with others the available rewards. These perceived costs and rewards are always weighed against estimates of reward-cost outcomes in other relations available at that time. As for estimation of rewards, a variety of cues might suggest to Gary that Sandra has possibilities in that direction. Perhaps her face, perceived via processes discussed in Chapter 2, suggests that she has certain personality characteristics that Gary finds rewarding in other persons. She may, by her clothes or her manner, suggest that she would have the same interests as Gary, or perhaps she strikingly conforms to his ideas of beauty.

Assume that the approach is made and that Gary strikes up a conversation with Sandra. The conversation, initially at least, may be governed by the dictates of politeness, but a certain amount of exploration may also be noted. For instance, one feature frequently characteristic of opening conversations is that each person attempts to discover what he has in common with the other. Inquiries are made about where the other comes from, whether he knows a mutual acquaintance, what his college major is, and perhaps what he thinks about the purpose of the student conference. What each person encounters in the other depends in large part on what aspects of himself each discloses. This is in part determined by the strength of his desire to continue interacting, which in turn depends on the costs and rewards being exchanged and his estimates of future costs and rewards relative to those anticipated in alternative relations. It also depends on his estimate of the effects of various disclosures.

At this point there begins another process, which for want of a better term we have labeled bargaining. The term *bargaining* may suggest a highly conscious and rational process, and in this respect the word is inappropriate. The process is not highly conscious; yet actions occur that have the character of the marketplace. Each person attempts to negotiate a definition of the situation and the resultant relationship that will maximize his outcomes.

In part, such attempts take the form of certain strategies whose common aim is to manage the other person's perception of what he is giving and receiving and what he may expect in the future. One may exaggerate one's value to others and the costs to oneself of what one is offering. Upon learning of Sandra's interest in skiing, for example, Gary may exaggerate his own interest in this activity. Or both persons may indicate that other alternative relations are open to them and that they are incurring some costs in continuing to talk with each other. One function of name-dropping is to indicate to the other person the number and high value of one's alternative relations.

In part, however, attempts to elicit rewards from the other person take the form of giving progressively greater rewards that prompt the other to return in kind. For Gary and Sandra these may be especially warm smiles and a special attentiveness to each other. At the same time, each person may also attempt to lower the costs of the other so as to improve the other's profit position and ensure the continuation of the exchange. Both may, for instance, discover a difference in views on some subject and tacitly agree to avoid the subject. Each recognizes that the costs of an argument might reduce the profit of the other person to the point where the rewards being currently received from him would be eliminated by termination of the relation. Where the bargaining process progresses in this fashion, a spiral effect can be observed. As each person is increasingly rewarded, he in turn is motivated to increase the profit of the other. This process can be expected to stabilize at the point where the costs of increasing the profit of the other person become so large that more can be gained from some alternative relation.

Although this discussion has focused only on the dyad, the interaction of Gary and Sandra goes on against a background of alternatives. In fact, during the course of the evening each person may sample alternatives and estimate possibilities in other relations. If the relationship develops during the evening, Gary and Sandra are less likely to do this. Other persons have also been forming subgroups, and such grouping progressively increases the costs of interaction with alternative persons. Gary might well have reaped a higher rate of profit with Alma, but her involvement with other persons discouraged the processes of sampling and bargaining that might have resulted in attraction between them.

Another process is called *commitment*. Members of a pair progressively reduce sampling and bargaining with other persons. They commit themselves to a particular other person. Gary and Sandra each stop casting a roving eye and settle down to an evening together. Should this association endure beyond the evening, and should the couple continue to associate on an increasingly exclusive basis, a final stage termed *institutionalization* is reached.

In institutionalization, shared expectations emerge recognizing the rightness or *legitimacy* of the exclusiveness of the relation and patterns of exchange that have developed. These expectations will be shared not only by members of the dyad but by other group members as well. Perhaps by the end of the conference Gary and Sandra are "going steady," a relation that has become institutionalized in American society.

This treatment of exchange theory is not intended to imply that the decisions and procedures engaged in by persons in the process of friendship formation are calculated and deliberate, in the same way that one might shop for an automobile. Such conscious rational processes are indeed suggested by the terms *sampling, estimation,* and *bargaining.* But the authors' view is that a person learns to behave without conscious deliberation through long experience in social situations; his actions are spontaneous, not calculated. If anything, they are guided more by feeling than by a reasoning process. The person has learned to behave so that his feelings guide him in maximizing his outcomes in social situations. Indeed, when he has not adequately learned this, he is often characterized as emotionally disturbed or neurotic; his feelings interfere with rational action, instead of facilitating it.

The discussion so far has made little reference to the more intense forms of attraction, such as infatuation and romantic love. Falling in love is often an intense, relatively rapid experience. Theories of attraction in terms of conditioning, similarity, or complementarity seem quite inadequate to explain it, although exchange theory is of some use. To explain this intense form of attraction, physiological contributions to a state of excitement or emotional arousal, and also the vital role of social definitions of love and romance in giving meaning to this emotional state, must be emphasized.

Walster and Berscheid have developed a theory of passionate love which emphasizes both physiological and social determinants of love.[72] Citing Schachter, they note that the subjective experience of an emotional state created by a physiological change is determined by the situational factors that lead the person to define this state as he does. For example, the same physiological state may be experienced as fear or anger, depending on the social situation prevailing. Through social learning, emotional arousal comes to be associated with certain types of experiences. The child is impulsive and relatively uncontrolled in becoming emotionally aroused and in expressing his emotions. Gradually he learns to control or moderate some of his feelings—to manage them so that they become less intense or more socially acceptable. He may also learn to become aroused under circumstances that initially had no emotional impact. And most important of all, with increased experience, he learns to give these states social meanings.

According to Walster and Berscheid, the emotion of love, then, is a state of physical arousal which is socially or cognitively defined as love.[73] The implication is not that this arousal state is the same as that for other emotions. No doubt the physiology of sexual arousal is an important component. But we should not make the mistake of thinking that sexual arousal by itself explains love. Other aspects of interaction with the opposite sex may also arouse powerful emotions. For example, a strong boost in an individual's self-esteem may generate euphoric feelings that contribute to the experience of being in love.

Romantic love is largely a product of and is largely confined to Western society and to other societies influenced by Western culture. This means that the nature of the feeling of being in love, the thoughts and attitudes one has toward the person who is the object of love, and the appropriate behavior toward that person are all socially defined. In the process of growing up, a child

72. WALSTER, 1971; SCHACHTER, 1964.   73. WALSTER, 1971.

has to learn what being in love means; otherwise he will not have the experience. Cultural norms also specify who shall be partners in love and set some of the conditions facilitating or inhibiting being in love. The dating situation in adolescence contributes to falling in love. The incest taboo prevents members of the same family from loving each other romantically, except for the husband and wife. A widespread norm seems also to limit the age gap between partners unidirectionally—females are expected to be of the same age as or younger than the male, or at least not much older than him.

The nature of the interaction between love partners, particularly as it occurs over time, contributes some further understanding. Among the factors that seem of especial significance are mutuality of attraction, the exclusiveness of the relation, and readiness to fall in love. These conditions can all be discussed in terms of exchange theory.

In a love relation, *mutual attraction* contributes in a special way to emotional arousal and gratification. Mutual attraction produces a sense of personal worth, being liked leads to liking in turn, rewards in the presence of the other person are repeatedly obtained through shared experiences, and self-disclosure is followed by consensual validation. In addition, mutual attraction is a state in which psychological costs of interaction are minimized. One-way attraction always runs the risk of rebuff. An individual initially attracted to another person without reciprocation is apt to make efforts to attract him, efforts that are psychologically costly. Similarly, inadvertent self-disclosures in ordinary interactions are always a risk; when there is mutual attraction, this cost is removed by assurance that confidence will be accepted. Thus, a part of the explanation of a love relation lies in its mutuality.

Blau has noted that this delicate balance of mutuality is crucial for the growth or decline of the relationship.[74] If one party becomes more deeply involved than the other, continuance of the relation is threatened. Blau explains how the emergence of a deeper involvement by one party raises the psychological costs of the less involved party, reducing his outcomes in the relation. These costs consist of such factors as unwillingness to spend the time desired by the other party and unwillingness to commit himself to the same deep extent. This lowering of his outcomes changes his behavior in a way visible to his partner and in turn further upsets the imbalance.

 A factor that further intensifies rewards in a love relation is the development of the idea that the other person is an exclusive source of rewards.[75] The feeling that the other person is unique is commonplace among individuals in love. Just why this occurs is not entirely clear. In part, this may result from the wide variety of activities that the lovers have experienced together, and can dwell upon in memory or fantasy. Moreover, some of these activities may actually be unique because of the exceptional nature of the relation.

In part this may also derive from the support received for self through

74. BLAU, 1964a.   75. SIMMEL, 1950.

congruency and consensual validation. Being loved is apt to induce a strong feeling of personal worth, which may well generalize to aspects of self not previously supported or formerly negatively evaluated. The lover thus is uniquely valued in order to retain this special source of self-support. The total commitment to the relation, excluding alternative sources of satisfaction, is also a probable contributor to this feeling of exclusiveness. Dissonance theory suggests that commitment to an exclusive source of satisfaction enhances the value of this source.

If we look at a developing romance sequentially we can see factors over and above the effect of mutuality. In the early stages of a romance, exchanges are quite subtle. They may consist of a special attentiveness to the other person, a sensitivity to his actions and feelings, maintenance of a minimum distance from him, and a slowness or unwillingness to leave his company. Several studies support the view that the desire for affiliation and feelings of attraction are associated with greater frequency of eye contact.[76] There is also a suggestion that frequency of eye contact between opposite-sex pairs, especially long looks, is associated with intimacy.[77]

While these are all nonverbal behaviors, they are likely to communicate very clearly a feeling of strong attraction. In the initial stages of romance, these and other actions with similar meaning can be engaged in without cost, in the sense that no overt, explicit commitment is made to the other person, a commitment that would be costly if the other person failed to reciprocate. Later, of course, exchanges symbolic of commitment may occur, such as hand-holding. Ultimately, the rewarding nature of the association may be greatly intensified by engaging in sexual behavior.

The development of a romance between two persons requires a certain state of readiness, one that can be described in terms of exchange theory. According to exchange theory, experiences that lower a person's comparison level should make him particularly susceptible to becoming attracted to another person. Exchange theory suggests that readiness for a new relationship would be produced by a low comparison level for rewards having to do with self-evaluation and emotional support. If a man has not been receiving much support from his female companions, his expectations of support in his present circumstances (his comparison level) will be low, and a new source of support will affect him more strongly than it would another individual with a higher comparison level.

This idea is consistent with experimental findings.[78] Some, but not all, participants liked more those who first evaluated them negatively and then positively. Presumably the effect of the negative evaluation was to reduce their comparison level, and that of a preceding positive evaluation was to raise it. The self-esteem of individuals was temporarily manipulated upward or downward by exposing them to the results of a personality test that had been prepared in a manner that was either favorable or unfavorable. Women whose

76. EXLINE & WINTERS, 1965; EXLINE, GRAY, & SCHUETTE, 1965; RUBIN, 1970.   77. ARGYLE & DEAN, 1965; RUBIN, 1970.   78. ARONSON & LINDER, 1965; WALSTER, 1965.

comparison level had been lowered responded with greater liking for a handsome male confederate who asked them for a date than those whose comparison level had been raised. The support this experiment provides for the susceptibility to romance of people with a low comparison level is somewhat weakened by the fact that this study has not been successfully replicated.

In certain well-known life situations, exchange processes operate to raise or lower the level of attraction, or lead to leaving the relationship and forming a new attachment. These include adolescent crushes, broken love affairs, and divorce. The processes may be detailed as follows.

Adolescence is a period in which the youth has partially emancipated himself from the emotional support of his parents: He no longer wants to be "mothered." Although the peer group substitutes for this parental support, it often does not provide the close, intimate support that was enjoyed in the family. In adolescence and young adulthood an individual may compare himself with friends who have steady girl friends or wives, and find himself at a disadvantage. Thus, his comparison level for emotional support is low. In addition, new aspects of self are emerging for which he needs emotional support. If he encounters a girl who behaves as if she is strongly attracted to him, he may find her positive behavior intensely rewarding. If she in turn has a low comparison level, his positive behavior toward her will be intensely rewarding for her. These very high outcomes in relation to a low comparison level intensify their attraction further. Thus what occurs is a rapid process of rising outcomes, and the couple will define themselves as in love. Mutual rewards are further intensified by engaging in rewarding sexual behavior.

Whether the relation endures or not depends on its further progress. As the couple continue to interact, types of rewards and costs other than mutual attraction will enter the relation. If they find that they share values, interests, and activities in common, rewards are apt to be maximized and costs minimized. If, on the other hand, they find they do not share the same values, interests, and activities, the costs of interacting will become more and more apparent with time, and rewarding interaction will diminish.

After a broken love affair or after divorce there may be a temporary period of disillusionment with the opposite sex, and a certain wariness in interaction. But, like the adolescent, the rejected lover or the divorced person has a very low comparison level for emotional support. Thus, a divorced man, for example, will easily fall in love if he encounters a woman who behaves as if she is attracted to him. This phenomenon is so common that the English language has a phrase for it: falling in love on the rebound.

The case of the middle-aged married man or woman who has an extramarital love affair is analogous. In many marriages, emotional outcomes suffer a slow decline from youth to middle age, probably for a great variety of reasons.[79] For example, each spouse may develop independent interests (the man in his profession or work, the wife in the children and the home, for example)

---

79. BLOOD & WOLFE, 1960.

which lead them to give insufficient emotional support to each other. The comparison level for emotional support gradually drops to keep pace with outcomes. Thus, a middle-aged wife often has a comparison level similar to that of the adolescent or the divorced person. If she encounters someone who provides outcomes considerably in excess of her depressed comparison level, her attraction toward this new source of emotional support is apt to be intense. Moreover, increased outcomes from this new relation should have the effect of raising her comparison level to the point that it approaches or exceeds the level of outcomes that she is experiencing in her relationship with her husband, resulting in a decline in attraction within the marriage and eventually its termination.

The case of the middle-aged husband sometimes involves an additional exchange process. Not only may he be receiving a relatively low level of emotional support from his wife, but in some instances, he has advanced to a position of relatively high status (in his profession or work, his income, and possessions). This is apt to raise his comparison level for alternatives, leading him to desire a woman of beauty, charm, youth, or other high-status attributes.

The exchange processes operating in the emergence of friendship and romance may be summarized as follows. When a group of strangers meet, each person experiences different outcomes in interaction with various other persons. After sampling various interactions and estimating outcomes, he generally commits himself to the interaction yielding the highest outcomes. In a dyad he engages in a process of bargaining, by means of which he elicits rewards from the other person in exchange for his own rewarding behavior toward the person. Bargaining is characterized by an attempt to obtain maximum rewards at minimum cost. In part, the process may include some misrepresentation of one's own resources in order to encourage rewarding responses from the other person. As a whole, bargaining tends toward maximizing the rewards and minimizing the costs of both members of the dyad. The terms *sampling, estimation,* and *bargaining* are not meant to imply a conscious deliberate process, but refer to spontaneous choices based on experience.

As a relation develops, a stage called *commitment* is arrived at. In this stage, interactions with alternative persons are minimized or stopped altogether, and the members of the dyad focus on their interaction with each other. An eventual stage may be reached in which the relation becomes institutionalized, as in engagement, living together, or getting married.

In this whole process, the special gratification provided by interactions under conditions of mutual attraction plays an important part. This type of reward is especially essential for the formation of intense relations between persons. An important factor that sets the stage for intense attractions in a new relation is a low comparison level for emotional support.

Some details of the longer, ongoing process of exchange in more enduring relations, such as long-term friendships or marriages, have not yet been considered. Changes occur in rewards and costs, and in comparison level, in these enduring dyads.

CHANGES IN COSTS AND REWARDS   As mentioned earlier, exchange theories view attraction as a function of the reward-cost outcomes that persons experience in relation to some level of expectation of what these outcomes should be (the *comparison level*). From this standpoint any change in affect in a positive or negative direction can be analyzed in terms of either a change in costs and rewards or a change in comparison levels. Thus, an individual may be less attracted to another person if his cost rises rapidly relative to his reward and his comparison level remains constant, or if his outcomes are constant while his comparison level rises.

Changes in the costs and rewards that persons experience in relations with others may stem from any of five sources. First, simply as a function of past exchanges, outcomes may either decline or increase. As each person continues to exchange rewards, the behavior rewarding to the other may become increasingly costly to produce due to fatigue, embarrassment, or loss of alternative rewards. At the same time, the value of the reward may decrease as the relevant needs of each person become satiated. Or changes in the direction of an increase in rewards and a reduction in costs might occur similarly as a function of past exchanges. Dependencies may be established, and the needs created may be satisfied by behavior that, as a result of practice, is both more effective and produced at less cost.

To illustrate a decline in outcome, consider a hypothetical marital relation in which one partner makes continual demands for support of a precarious self conception. Such demands may be met by his partner at increasing costs in terms of feelings of loss of integrity, increasing disgust, loss of opportunities to engage in rewarding interaction with others, etc. To illustrate an increase in outcome, consider a dyad in which both partners share participation in some rewarding activity (a sport, a hobby, a business enterprise) and become increasingly skilled at it, raising each other's outcomes. A related point is that the experience gained as a function of past exchanges makes the behavior of the other person more predictable. This in turn lowers costs stemming from uncertainty and increases the ability of each to elicit rewarding behavior from the other person.

A second source of change in costs and rewards arises from shifts in the characteristics of the dyad members. Although this may occur as a result of previous exchanges in the relation, frequently such changes come about in other ways. As a result of experiences in other relations and with the nonsocial environment, new opinions, attitudes, and self conceptions are developed that require consensual validation. In addition, other kinds of needs emerge and new goals are embraced. These changes alter both the reward value and the costs of a person's behavior to others and theirs to him. Such changes may lead to increased attraction between two persons, as when one adopts a new attitude and finds that the other person, whose previous views were of little account, is now a valuable ally because he holds a similar view. A decline in attraction may also occur. Behavior of the other person which formerly had high reward value may now carry less value, or perhaps the behavior demanded by the other which at one time was expressed with little cost now comes at considerable sacrifice.

A third source of change is modification of the external situation so that the behavior of persons in the relation acquires different reward-cost values. The sudden increase in the attraction toward the expert when a new situation demands his skills or knowledge is a case in point. Another is the case of the successful executive whose wife was frugal and thus helpful during his struggling early days, but whose behavior is inappropriate and actually costly now that success has been achieved.

A fourth source of change lies within the relation itself. A person experiencing profitable interactions becomes increasingly motivated to ensure the continuation of such interaction by increasing the profit of the other. Such a cycle, in which each person motivates the other and is similarly motivated in turn, can also work in the reverse direction. A person whose reward-cost outcome is adversely affected may be motivated to reduce the profits experienced by the other, who retaliates and thereby continues the cycle.

A fifth form of change occurs through the association of behaviors having certain reward-cost values with behaviors having quite different values. One way in which this happens is that behaviors of each person which were initially neutral will, through association with an exchange of behaviors which are rewarding or costly, become rewarding or costly in themselves. A person may come to enjoy playing bridge because such play has been associated with other rewards exchanged during the game. Another way in which this association occurs is that the behavior of each person, which was initially rewarding to the other, may in time become rewarding to the actor himself because it has been regularly associated with rewarding responses of the other. A person may enjoy playing bridge because playing has been previously associated with appreciative responses from his partner. By a similar process of association, behavior that is costly to oneself or the other person may gradually become inhibited.

CHANGES IN COMPARISON LEVEL   Rewards and costs might remain the same, yet affect in a relation might change through a lowering or raising of the persons' comparison level. The comparison level may be affected by a number of factors, including reward-cost experiences in the dyad, the perception of the experiences of others in relations like one's own, and what each of the participants estimates he might legitimately expect in alternative relations.

Thibaut and Kelley suggest that the comparison level will gradually rise as the outcomes of the dyad members become progressively better or decline as they become worse.[80] This rise in comparison level relative to the profits received may underlie the generally experienced decline in noticeable satisfaction after the initial glow that characterizes many relations in their early stages, such as an infatuation with a member of the opposite sex. Similarly, the decline in comparison level when outcomes are reduced may well explain how persons

80. Thibaut & Kelley, 1959.

find satisfaction in situations that they never thought they would. The common emotion of envy when another person's outcomes are improved relative to one's own may be seen as a rise in comparison level on perceiving the improved outcomes of the other. In particular, where the other is one's partner in an exchange, such envy may contain a strong element of feelings of injustice. *equity*

This discussion has identified factors that influence the level of affect, but has not specifically referred to the determinants of the permanence of a relation. Obviously, affect is important to permanence. In most relations, positive affect and permanence are associated, but in some this is not so. Persons may remain in them even though the outcomes they receive are below their comparison level and they are repelled rather than attracted to the other person.

The loveless marriage is a case in point. The couple stay together even though the satisfactions received are below the level that would result in positive attraction. They do so because they perceive that in the alternatives available, the costs are greater or the rewards are less. A wife whose outcomes are below her comparison level may feel that she has no chance of getting a better husband and that without one, the prospects for adequate support for her and her children are dim. Other costs that function to preserve such relations include guilt over depriving children of a loved parent, religious sanctions, and fear of loneliness. Thibaut and Kelley explain such conditions in terms of the *comparison level for alternatives.*[81] As long as a relation provides outcomes above the comparison level for alternatives, it will endure even though such outcomes are below the comparison level in the relationship and the persons are not attracted to each other.

SUMMARY: EXCHANGE THEORY AND ATTRACTION   Exchange theory focuses on the relation between individuals rather than on the individuals themselves, and on process rather than on structural aspects of a relation. Exchange theory views attraction as a function of the degree to which persons achieve in their interaction with others a reward-cost outcome in excess of some minimum level. Any activity on the part of one person that contributes to the gratification of the needs of another is considered a reward. Costs include punishments incurred and deterrents in interacting with another person, such as fatigue, anxiety, and fear of embarrassment, as well as rewards foregone because of the interaction. The reward-cost outcome must be at least slightly above some minimum level of what the person feels is his due. This *comparison level* is *equity* influenced by past experiences in the relation and in comparable relations, perceptions of what others like oneself are obtaining, and perceptions of rewards and costs obtainable in alternative relations.

Exchange theory offers an explanation of why similarity between persons leads to mutual attraction. Similarity in social background and in values provides high rewards at low cost to both members of the dyad. Similarity in abilities, and to a lesser extent in personality traits, has comparable effects. In

81. THIBAUT & KELLEY, 1959.

not only rewards are explored but costs!

some instances different or complementary traits may be the basis of a high reward-cost outcome in interaction. Exchange theory also explains the relation between attraction and opportunity to interact: The greater the opportunity, the lower the cost.

In the initial stages of friendship formation, each person samples interaction with various other persons and estimates outcomes. Generally he commits himself to those interactions yielding the highest outcomes. In a dyad he engages in a process of bargaining by means of which he elicits rewards from the other person in exchange for his own rewarding behavior toward the person, a process for maximizing rewards and minimizing costs. Sampling interactions and estimating outcomes is sharply reduced with commitment to a relation. An end stage is reached when the relation becomes institutionalized.

In intense attachments, such as romantic love, the thoughts and feelings one has are socially defined. In romantic love, the special gratification provided by interactions under conditions of mutual attraction are important. Ultimately the rewards provided by the partner take on a quality of exclusiveness.

Certain conditions produce a susceptibility to involvement in a romantic attachment. A low comparison level for emotional support is apt to increase a person's readiness to fall in love. Such levels may be created by temporary setbacks of various kinds, by a general state of insecurity, by a broken love affair or a divorce, or by gradual declines in outcomes due to a host of factors.

Rewards and costs may change as a function of (1) past exchanges which shift reward-cost values of current behaviors, (2) changes in the characteristics of the dyad members occurring through training, education, or other experiences, (3) changes in external circumstances that introduce new rewards and costs or modify the values of old ones, (4) sequential factors in the relation itself, such as the augmentation of satisfaction in current relations as a result of previously rewarding experiences in the dyad, and (5) associations with other behaviors having different reward-cost values. Comparison levels change in various ways. They rise when outcomes rise, or fall as outcomes are lowered. The permanence of a relation is a joint function of outcomes in the relation and the comparison level for alternative relations. As long as a relation provides outcomes above the comparison level for alternatives, it will endure even though such outcomes are below the comparison level in the relation and the persons are not attracted to each other.

The Affect Structure of the Group

The discussion to this point has focused mainly on the dyad. The remainder of this chapter deals with larger groups, and examines the patterns of likes and dislikes that form the *affect structures* of such groups. *Sociometric measurement,* a method of studying affect structures, is considered first, and then some of the processes that pertain to these structures are taken up.

Sociometric measurement

Any group of persons observed over a period of time exhibits regularities in patterns of association. Where members can choose whom to associate with in a given activity, some persons are chosen more frequently than others. Each individual, moreover, regularly chooses certain persons and ignores others. Where the interaction takes the form of social-emotional behavior, choices are based upon liking or positive affect toward the other person. We may conceive of these attractions among group members as forming a pattern or structure. It is useful to describe or display such a structure, for such a description tells us much about the group. Sociometric measurement is a procedure for obtaining a view of this structure, which has been termed the *affect structure* or *sociometric structure.* The sociometric method and some of the early techniques of analyzing data obtained from it were developed by Moreno.[82] His followers and other behavioral scientists elaborated upon the procedure and used it to study various group phenomena.

The Sociometric Test

Essentially, a sociometric test is a means of obtaining quantitative data on the preferences of group members for associating with other members. In a sociometric test, persons indicate their choices or rejections of other group members for association in some specified activity or context. Since people are sensitive to being liked or disliked, administration of sociometric tests is arranged so as to protect the privacy of the individual's choices, lest he be afraid to reveal his true feelings. Almost any criterion for choice may be specified. Individuals may indicate which persons they prefer as *friends,* or simply whom they *like* or *dislike.* More often some more specific criterion is used, such as choice of a roommate by college students, choice of a flying partner by Air Force pilots, choice of a group leader in a fraternity, or choice of a work partner by employees.

Analysis of Sociometric Data

Responses to a sociometric questionnaire may be summarized in a number of ways. Perhaps the best-known method is a graphic presentation called a *sociogram.* A sociogram consists of circles connected by lines or arrows, as in Figure 7-2. Each circle represents a person. The solid lines in this particular sociogram represent choices, and the broken lines, rejections. Arrows indicate the direction of choice.

The circles in a sociogram are arranged so that the distances between them represent the degrees of positive attraction between the persons in the group.

82. MORENO, 1953.

Figure 7-2 A sample sociogram.
Each circle represents a group mem-
ber. Solid arrows represent choices;
broken arrows, rejection. (Adapted
with permission from M. Jahoda, M.
Deutsch, and S. W. Cook (Eds.),
Research methods in social relations. *Vol. 2. (New York: Holt,*
Rinehart and Winston, Inc., 1951.)

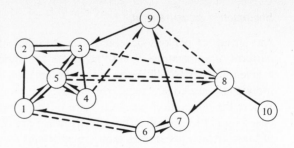

For instance, the circles representing two persons who choose each other will be placed closer together than circles representing two persons only one of whom chooses the other. Those circles in turn will be closer together than circles representing two persons neither of whom choose each other. In Figure 7-2, the pair consisting of persons 2 and 3, where attraction is mutual, is closer together than the pair consisting of persons 3 and 9, where attraction is only one-way. Similarly, the pair 5 and 8, who reject each other, are placed a greater distance apart than the pair 8 and 9, involving one-way rejection.

The sociogram presents in easily discernible form a number of features of the sociometric structure. Some individuals are the focus of many solid lines. Such highly chosen persons are frequently referred to as sociometric *stars* (see person 5). Others, such as person 10, are relative *isolates,* receiving few choices and making few. *Cliques* or subgroups can be identified from the clustering of points located closely together and having lines indicating mutual choice. See, for instance, the clique composed of persons 1, 2, 3, 4, and 5. Cleavages between subgroups are represented by the distance between groups, reflecting the absence of choices between them, or by broken lines indicating rejection that connect members of two groups.

While a sociogram may readily convey a sense of structure, the construction of such a diagram is often a result of a trial-and-error process in which certain features may be missed in the attempt to achieve a simple structure. Moreover, if the number of persons in the group is large, and if they are permitted to make many choices, such diagrams are unwieldy. For these reasons a variety of statistical procedures have been developed for the treatment of sociometric data, methods too complicated for presentation here.[83]

In sum, sociometric analysis is a means of representing quantitatively and objectively the feelings of a group toward its own members and toward other groups. Such analysis makes possible objective identification of persons in the group who are generally liked, disliked, or ignored. Using criteria more specific than liking or disliking, may make possible discovery of other kinds of key

---

83. See Forsyth & Katz, 1946; Festinger, 1949; Proctor & Loomis, 1951; Lindzey & Borgatta, 1954; Coleman & McRae, 1960; MacRae, 1960; Alexander, 1963; Lindzey & Byrne, 1968.

persons, such as leaders or followers, or persons who are important communication links in the group. Such analysis also makes possible the identification of cliques within a group and the kind of feeling existing between the clique and other subgroups or between the clique and the group as a whole.

Correlates of Choice Status

The previous discussion of theories of attraction as well as numerous studies of the sociometric structure of groups suggest a variety of factors which determine the sociometric choices of group members. These can be summarized as follows: A person is likely to choose the following individuals: (1) those with whom he has a greater opportunity to interact, (2) those who have characteristics most desirable in terms of the norms and values of the group, (3) those who are most similar to him in attitudes, values, and social-background characteristics, (4) those whom he perceives as choosing him or assigning favorable characteristics to him, (5) those who see him as he sees himself, and (6) those in whose company he has achieved gratification of his needs.

Exchange Theory and Sociometric Choice

Exchange theory helps to explain why persons receiving many sociometric choices have the characteristics they do. Such persons must have characteristics that have considerable reward value to an appreciable number of group members; similarly, it must be possible to interact with these preferred members at low cost. The following analysis shows why this is the case.

First, the preferred member facilitates rewarding interaction for others. Jennings notes that girls in a training school who are frequently chosen by other members of their groups help others, protect others, and increase the rewards and reduce the costs that other girls, particularly the less popular, experience in interaction with them as well as with others in the group. Referring to preferred members as leaders, Jennings notes the following:

> Each leader "improves" from the point of view of the membership, through one method or another, the social milieu. Each widens the social field for participation of others (and indirectly her own social space) by ingratiating them into activities, introducing new activities, and by fostering tolerance on the part of one member towards another. Each leader shows a feeling for when to censure and when to praise and apparently is intellectually and emotionally "uncomfortable" when others are "unhappy" or "leftout."[84]

Second, the ability of the preferred member to handle his own emotional

---

84. Reprinted by permission from H. H. JENNINGS. *Leadership and isolation.* (2d ed.) New York: Longmans, Green & Co., Inc., 1950. P. 203. Copyright by David McKay Company, Inc.

problems minimizes the cost to others of interaction with him. Jennings notes further:

> Moreover, each leader appears to succeed in controlling her own moods, at least to the extent of not inflicting negative feelings of depression or anxiety upon others. Each appears to hold her own counsel and not to confide her personal worries except to a selected friend or two; even among leaders between each other this very careful reticence is usual. Each appears able to establish rapport quickly and effectively with a wide range of other personalities and to win their confidence. Each appears to possess to a greater or less degree unusual capacity to identify with others to the extent of feeling solicitude for them and to act in their behalf. By one manner of behaving or another, each leader lightens the "burdens" of other members of the group.[85]

For a quite different population, male college undergraduates, a similar picture of preferred members emerges: They possess traits that increase the rewards and decrease the costs of others.[86] A study of characteristics of people who are rejected sociometrically is also consistent with exchange theory.[87] Such persons have been shown to display domineering, belligerent, inconsiderate behaviors which raise the costs to other persons of interacting with them.

Choice, Group Factors, and Exchange Theory

Characteristics of preferred members may account for the fact that often individuals have a similar choice status in several groups; for example, if they are high in one group, they also are high in several others. This occurs because the same characteristics will facilitate favorable reward-cost outcomes in virtually any group. In particular where the person possesses an attribute valued similarly by several groups his choice status in these groups is apt to be similar. This occurs not only because of the reward-cost implications of the attribute or behavior in question, but also because he is apt to be seen as possessing other highly valued traits as well. Physical attractiveness provides a good example of this. It should come as no surprise that a number of investigations have shown that physical attractiveness is an important determinant of liking.[88] Persons whose physical features conform to the norms for physical attractiveness in a particular culture provide aesthetic rewards to others. But beyond that, individuals perceive attractive other persons as having other desirable traits as well, whereas undesirable characteristics are attributed to unattractive persons.[89] Three factors determine what individual characteristics are related to choice status: (1) special characteristics of other group members, (2) properties of the group, and (3) the general situation in which interaction occurs.[90]

85. Reprinted by permission from H. H. Jennings. *Leadership and isolation.* (2nd ed.) New York: Longmans, Green & Co., Inc. 1950. Pp. 203-204. Copyright by David McKay Company, Inc.   86. Bonney, Hoblit, & Dreyer, 1953.   87. Kidd, 1951.   88. Walster, Aronson, & Abrahams, 1966; Byrne, Lendon, & Reeves, 1968; Stroebe, Insko, Thompson, & Layton, 1971.   89. Berscheid & Walster, 1972a, 1972b. 90. Jennings, 1950; Bonney et al., 1953.

That the character of the group affects choice status is illustrated by Homans's analysis of some of Jenning's findings in which he makes the point that the desirability of traits depends upon who judges them.[91] During the study of these girls, housemothers were interviewed and the behaviors that they approved and disapproved in the various girls were noted. A comparison of the persons chosen frequently, rarely, and an average number of times suggested that, in *most* instances, both the housemothers and the girls found the same characteristics rewarding. The housemothers saw the preferred girls as possessing approved traits and those who were least preferred as possessing disapproved traits. As Homans notes, the *exceptions* were consistent with exchange theory:

> The few kinds of behavior that the housemothers disapproved of but mentioned the overchosen (preferred members) most often as displaying were just the kinds of behavior that the girls themselves were apt to have looked on much more favorably. Their rebellious behavior, described as "refusing to do what is requested by a person in authority," initiatory behavior ("behavior considered as too self-directive and too self-confident"), and reticent behavior ("does not bring personal problems to the housemother") were surely characteristic of independent girls, ready to lead and support their fellows in standing up to the housemother on occasion. If, in short, the housemothers found rewarding most of the activities provided by the overchosen, the girls themselves probably found all of their activities rewarding. And the more valuable to the other members of her group were the activities that a girl performed, the higher was the esteem in which they held her.[92]

A trait may also be associated with choice status because its possession may facilitate the achievement of some goal which members share. Characteristics popularly associated with leadership, such as intelligence, knowledge, and aggressiveness, might lead to popularity in a situation where the accomplishment of some task was highly rewarding to the group.

When the individual characteristics are attitudes, those individuals whose attitudes correspond to group norms have high choice status. One of the rewards people achieve in interaction is consensual validation. The person whose attitudes and behavior correspond to the norms provides rewards to many others in the group at very low costs to himself. He does so since norms are by definition widely shared with respect to objects of importance to group members.

Elements of Structure

THE CHOICE CRITERION AND STRUCTURE   The affect structure revealed by a sociometric test as well as the correlates of choice depend in part on the choice criterion used in the sociometric questionnaire. In her early work, Jennings

91. HOMANS, 1961.   *92.* HOMANS, 1961, p. 160.

found that the choice pattern differed depending upon whether the choice was of persons to spend leisure time with or persons to work or live with.[93] Her analysis of the reasons her subjects gave for choosing or rejecting persons suggested two bases for choice. On the criterion of spending leisure time, subjects chose a person on the basis of her ability to satisfy their social-emotional needs, such as the need for support for one's self conception, for consensual validation about the world, etc. Choices made according to the criterion of living or working together appeared to be based on the person's group role, her contributions to the smooth functioning of the group, her conformity to group standards, etc.

Jennings refers to the structure revealed by the use of a leisure-time criterion as a *psychegroup* and that revealed by the use of a working or living criterion as a *sociogroup.* These two terms are simply analytic devices to emphasize two different bases of choice. A given choice in any situation reflects both to some degree. The distinction is nevertheless useful to keep in mind, because the basis of choice affects certain features of the structure.

Jennings found, for instance, that in contrast to a sociogroup, a psychegroup is characterized by higher mutuality; each person makes fewer choices, but choices are more frequently reciprocated. Among over 400 girls in a state institution about 70 percent of the choices on a leisure-time criterion were mutual. In contrast, on a living-working group criterion, only 35 percent of the choices were mutual. In addition, choices were more evenly distributed when a leisure-time criterion was used: Fewer persons received a large number of choices, and more persons received at least one choice.

These findings might be expected from the above discussions of interpersonal attraction and the nature of the difference between the bases of attraction in a psychegroup and a sociogroup. When the criterion is a sociogroup one, choices of all members should be concentrated on a few persons whose group role is crucial. When the choice of another person is in terms of a psychegroup criterion, choices should be more widely distributed over the membership, since needs of members differ markedly. Mutuality would be higher also in a psychegroup since reciprocity of choice would be associated with the satisfaction of social-emotional needs.

MEMBER CHARACTERISTICS AND GROUP STRUCTURE   Given a particular criterion, the affect structure will be influenced by the distribution of the needs and resources of the persons involved. What characteristics will become relevant depends in part on the particular personalities and other characteristics of the individuals involved, and the alternatives open to them for obtaining satisfaction, as well as the demands of the situation. The situation affects the resultant structure by determining the relevance of individual characteristics and the frequency and ease of interaction. In addition, what characteristics will become

93. JENNINGS, 1950.

relevant depends in part on the past history of the group and values that have emerged in this historical process. One of Newcomb's living groups very early began to separate into two groups along the lines of urban-rural background.[94] This separation was accompanied by the development of stereotypes in terms of which members of each group saw the other. The stereotypes hastened the process of further separation from the outgroup and attraction for the ingroup by providing the members with perceptions of the similarities and differences which influence attraction.

No analysis based on the characteristics of its members will provide a complete explanation of choice. One reason is that persons may not accurately assess the characteristics of others, and another is that the final structure which emerges is always a compromise. The group structure moves toward an equilibrium in which each person's position in the affect structure is the best he can obtain in terms of his reward-cost outcomes. Two individual features of the sociometric structure, the development of mutuality and the tendency to choose persons equal to oneself in choice status, are a result of this *compromise process* or tendency toward equilibrium.

Over time, the attraction between persons becomes increasingly mutual. Newcomb, in the living-group study described previously, found that mutuality increased with increasing acquaintance, particularly among persons who were not excessively popular or unpopular.

Newcomb suggests that these findings are consistent with the principle that systems tend toward a balanced state. Assuming that the common focus of orientation in this case is the self and, further, that persons usually evaluate themselves positively, the perception that another person who is liked does not return the feeling would be strain-inducing. Such strain would be reduced by decreasing one's feeling of attraction toward this person. An individual would similarly experience strain if he perceived that another person toward whom he had little feeling had a warm regard for him. A more balanced state would be achieved by developing warm feelings toward that person.

A related tendency is for persons to choose others who are equal to themselves in choice status. According to Homans, the findings of Jennings that girls chose as leisure-time companions other girls who were equal to them in their work-living status reflects this tendency.[95] Homans's reasoning is based on the relation between positions in two different sociometric structures, one representing personal liking or attraction and the other representing evaluations of contributions to the group. But the work of Newcomb, as well as that of Backman and Secord, who have also published evidence showing that pairs of mutually attracted persons in a group tend toward equality of choice status, suggests that on the undifferentiated criterion of liking, those who are equal in attraction status are preferred.[96] Mutuality and the choice of persons who are

94. NEWCOMB, 1961.   *95.* HOMANS, 1961; JENNINGS, 1950.   *96.* NEWCOMB, 1961; BACKMAN & SECORD, 1964.

similar in choice status to the chooser may be thought of as an outcome of the stabilization of relations, where each person is obtaining his best available reward-cost outcomes. Another study demonstrated that judgments of friendship for hypothetical persons are strongest for those stimulus persons closest in status to the individual making the judgments.[97] Some investigations have found that persons of lower status direct their choices upward rather than toward status equals.[98] However, such choices generally reflect an unreciprocated desire to associate with a person rather than the stable friendship structure that emerges in a group.

An examination of certain departures from this state of equilibrium should identify the forces toward balance. Two assumptions are made. One is that the order of persons by choice status represents the order of value attached to their behavior and to their other characteristics. A second assumption, true by definition, is that the order of choice status reflects the quantity of alternative relations available to each member. The greater the number who choose a given person, the greater the number who are willing to establish a relation with him.

Consider first the case where person A of low status is attracted to person B of high status. The chance for the development of a mutually satisfactory relation is low, because both are apt to experience outcomes that are lower than in some alternative relation. B's profit in such a relation is apt to be relatively low because of the low value of A's behavior. In this instance we would expect him not to continue the relation.

Under certain circumstances, B might be able to exact from A behavior that is of high value to him. But since A has low choice status, such valuable behavior is not typical of him and would normally be produced only at high cost to A. Were this the case, the outcomes to A would be low, and he would withdraw from the relation. Such a relation would be maintained only in instances where the initial assumptions stated above did not hold, as where some aspects of A's behavior are of particular value to B but not to others, where this behavior can be produced by A at low cost, or finally, where B is prevented either through inaccurate assessment of his alternatives or by some force of circumstances from establishing more valuable alternative relations.

That movements toward mutuality and equality of choice status between choosers are observable fairly early in the formation of a group, particularly at high levels of attraction, suggests that persons become relatively adept at gauging their chances of satisfactory outcomes in a relation. This undoubtedly stems from previous experiences in relations with persons of markedly different status that led to poor outcomes. Probably "crushes" in adolescence, characterized by lack of mutuality and equality, provide useful training, leading persons in the courtship process to select and fall in love with those whose value in the marriage market is roughly the same.

97. TRIANDIS, VASSILIOU, & THOMANEK, 1966.   98. HURWITZ, ZANDER, & HYMOVITCH, 1960; TAGIURI, KOGAN, & LONG, 1958.

Some experimental evidence is consistent with these speculations. In the choice of work partners in a laboratory experiment, and in the choice of roommates, subjects' choices appeared to reflect a compromise between the desirability of the other person and an estimate of his availability.[99] Presumably individuals had learned that to aim too high leads to rejection or an unsatisfactory relation. One study did not provide evidence in support of a compromise process.[100] College students who attended an arranged dance in which they were randomly paired did not display this tendency. They desired and liked those persons who were more physically attractive, but, contrary to expectations, their own attractiveness did not influence their choice. Perhaps the novelty of the situation and the fact that the situation did not involve serious commitment dampened the tendency to temper choice by reality considerations. In a more recent study individuals were asked to rate pictures of persons varying in attractiveness in terms of their desirability on a number of grounds including choice as a date.[101] Compared with subjects who rated themselves as attractive, those rating themselves as unattractive were more likely to consider unattractive others and less likely to consider attractive others as dates.

The compromise process, then, consists of adjustments in relations among group members in the direction of a state of equilibrium in which each person's reward-cost outcomes are maximized. This state of balance is characterized by many mutual choices, especially between persons equal in choice status.

COHESIVENESS   As previously noted, members of a dyad are attracted to each other to the extent that their reward-cost outcomes exceed their comparison levels. However, persons may remain in a relation even where the outcomes experienced drop below the comparison level and they are no longer attracted. They remain as long as the outcomes are above the comparison level for alternatives. In this instance, the binding force is not attraction but the awareness that the outcomes in the relation are better than can be obtained outside. With groups larger than a dyad, the term *cohesiveness* is employed to refer to the forces acting on group members to remain in the group. While cohesiveness is generally equated with attraction to the group, our previous analysis suggests that in some instances this interpretation may be inappropriate. A variety of bases of attraction to a group have been suggested, falling into three categories:[102]

1. The basis of attraction to the group may lie in the interaction itself. Interaction results in high reward-cost outcomes to participants because the needs of various members are complementary, their interests and attitudes are similar, or the organization of the group and the situation in which interaction takes place are conducive to cooperative, friendly interaction. For example, members of a political action group may enjoy exchanging ideas with each other because of their similar values.

99. Rosenfeld, 1964; Bechtel & Rosenfeld, 1966.   *100.* Walster et al., 1966.   *101.* Stroebe et al., 1971.   *102.* Thibaut, 1950; Festinger & Kelley, 1951; Libo, 1953; Cartwright & Zander, 1960.

2. Members may be attracted to the group because each individual finds the group activities *inherently* rewarding. Groups formed to pursue a particular recreation or hobby, such as golf, tennis, or chess, are examples. In such a group each individual enjoys the activity itself.

3. Members may be attracted to a group because membership is a means to achieving other ends. They may perceive that only through group action can they achieve a goal, such as getting a particular piece of legislation enacted. Or perhaps membership may be a source of favorable reward-cost outcomes in terms of the status one can achieve among persons outside the group.

These bases of cohesion have been incorporated into a theory of cohesion designed to explain a person's attraction to the group as a function of four interacting sets of variables:[103] (1) the person's motive base for attraction, i.e., his needs and values that can be satisfied by group membership, (2) the incentive properties of the group, including goals, programs, activities, and characteristics of group members, that are relevant to the persons' motive base, (3) his expectancy that actual membership will have favorable or unfavorable consequences, and (4) his comparison level. While much research has been devoted to the first two sets of variables, less attention has been paid to the last two. The discussion of exchange theory should underscore the importance of the comparison level of group members. A consideration of a related concept, the comparison level for alternatives, suggests that the total force operating on group members is a function not only of attraction to the group but also of the *outcomes available in alternative relations outside the group.*

Some groups are highly cohesive even though their members are experiencing low reward-cost outcomes. For example, a baseball team in fifth place may nevertheless have a good team spirit. The level of attraction among members may be higher than might be expected on the basis of outcome experiences. This occurs because outcome must be considered in relation to comparison level. If the team has customarily been in last place, both the low level of outcomes previously experienced and perceptions of what other players like oneself are obtaining suggest a low comparison level. Since attraction to the group is a function of the degree to which outcomes are above the comparison level, attraction among members of the team in fifth place may well be higher than would be expected from their standing alone.

For similar reasons, persons may remain in a relation even when attraction is absent and their outcomes fall below their comparison level. This occurs, however, only if their outcomes remain above their comparison level for alternatives. They are held in the group by the realization that leaving it would result in even lower outcomes. The inclusion in the above theory of the variable of expectancy also helps explain changes in group cohesion that might otherwise be puzzling. Thus, often group cohesion may change not because the

103. Cartwright, 1968.

groups' ability to satisfy member needs changes, but because group members' expectations change. In the early phases of a group's existence, members may have unrealistically high expectations and thus may maintain a higher level of cohesion than that which formally obtains when expectations become more realistic through experience.

Summary: The Affect Structure of the Group

This section has focused on the pattern of liking and disliking among members. By asking members of a group to indicate their preferences for association with other members, various graphical or quantitative descriptions of the affect structure of a group may be obtained. This technique is useful in identifying persons who are highly popular and who are relatively isolated. It is also useful in identifying cliques and other aspects of the group, such as its state of morale. Because of the importance of the affect structure, many investigators have studied the factors that determine choice. Empirical evidence indicates that members are likely to choose (1) those with whom they have a greater opportunity to interact, (2) those who have the most desirable characteristics in terms of the norms and values of the group, (3) those who are most similar to themselves in attitudes, values, and social-background characteristics, (4) those who are perceived as choosing them or assigning favorable characteristics to them, (5) those who see them as they see themselves, and (6) those in whose company their needs are best gratified. These empirical findings are consistent with predictions from exchange theory.

Variation in sociometric structure is based on a number of factors. When choice is based on a leisure-time criterion, structure is characterized more by mutual choice and an even distribution of choice. When choice is based upon a work criterion, choices are more concentrated on the few persons who play a crucial role in carrying out the task. The compromise process contributes to the group structure that emerges. This process consists of adjustments in relations among group members in the direction of a state of equilibrium in which each person's reward-cost outcomes are maximized. This state of balance is characterized by many mutual choices, especially between persons equal in choice status.

Cohesiveness is related to the affect structure of the group. The term refers to the forces acting on group members to remain in the group. In part, they may be represented by attractions having three different bases: (1) high reward-cost outcomes stemming directly from interaction between members, (2) group activities that are rewarding for their own sake, and (3) membership in the group as a means to attaining other ends. Attraction is also based upon the comparison levels of group members, and the total force operating on group members to remain in the group is a function not only of attraction to the group, but also of the outcomes available in alternative relations outside the group.

8

Social Power

It was shown in the last chapter that one can look at the totality of social interaction and select some particular attribute, such as affect or feeling. In this chapter the focus is on *social power*. Consider the relations between the following dyads: supervisor and employee, officer and soldier, parent and child, politician and voter, doctor and patient, teacher and student. All these dyads have a common feature: One member has more social power than the other. The same can be said for members of almost any group, for social power is rarely distributed evenly among members. One can also speak of the relative social power of two groups; however, this discussion will deal primarily with social power as it is manifested in interaction between two persons or among the members of small groups, because the focus of social psychology is at this level, and because research on larger units in terms of social power is scarce.

Social power is a property of a relationship between two or more persons, and is best understood in terms of exchange theory. A tentative definition of social power is that the power of person *P* over person *O* is a joint function of his capacity for affecting the outcomes of person *O* relative to his own outcomes. Thus, the more control *P* has over *O*'s outcomes and the less adverse the effects of such control on his own outcomes, the more power he has over *O*. Put more simply, if *P* can give *O* a great deal at minimum cost to himself, or can use strong coercion with little cost, he is apt to have considerable power over *O*. This is a tentative and partial statement, for social power is a complex function of certain additional factors.

Social power is most often used to influence the behavior of other persons, but is conceptually distinct from influence. A person might have considerable social power but rarely exercise it. Social power does not arise directly from the personal characteristics of the individual wielding power, but is dependent on the relation between individuals and the place of that relation in the context of the larger social structure. The power of a corporation president, for example, stems primarily from the authority vested in his position which enables him to make decisions that radically affect the employees of the corporation and its functioning.

But even at a less formal level, say in interaction between two friends, the social power of each stems from certain properties of the relation between them and their relation to other persons. In a continuing relationship, each exercise of power involves an expenditure of rewards and costs by both parties, and results in specific outcomes for each. A child who gets his way with his parents by throwing a temper tantrum receives the reward he wants, but only at the cost of an emotional upheaval. The parents are relieved at resolving the emotional crisis, but incur some cost in letting the child do something they oppose. Underlying this transaction is the mutual dependency of the child on the parents (who control rewards and punishments), and the parents on the child (who want him to behave according to certain standards). This mutual dependency is at the base of the power that each has over the other. Each exercise of power involves an exchange. The more powerful person may exact compliance from the less powerful, but in return he is expected to give his good will, his approval, or some other resource.

Determinants of Social Power

Either explicitly or implicitly, most contemporary discussions of social power recognize three interdependent properties of a relation that determine the amount of power that individuals are able to exert in a given situation: resources, dependencies, and alternatives. A *resource* is a property or conditional state of an individual—a possession, an attribute of appearance or personality, a position he holds, or a certain way of behaving—which enables him to modify the rewards and costs experienced by another person. The value of such resources is determined primarily by the *dependency* of the other person on him. For example, the beauty of a woman is a resource only in relation to those men who are attracted by feminine beauty. The value of a resource also varies with the situation: Beauty is more likely to be a resource on a date than in work as a laboratory technician where competence is at a premium. Some situations create temporary dependencies: In an emergency a group may desperately need an expert to solve a problem.

The potentialities for influence in a relation between two persons are, however, dependent on more than just the characteristics of each person and the situation. They extend beyond the dyad itself and are a function of the availability of *alternative sources* of reward and alternative means of reducing costs outside the dyad. The power of an expert, for example, depends upon the scarcity of persons with his expertise and the scarcity of sources of expert knowledge. This simple description does not exhaust the determinants of resources, dependencies, and alternatives. The following discussion identifies them in more detail.

Resources

French and Raven have delineated types of social powers, mainly according to the resources on which they are based.[1] Each type has associated with it certain rewards and costs. In addition, these investigators have shown how types of powers vary in such matters as the range of behavior subject to influence and the degree to which the exercise of power changes the balance of power between persons. These types of powers are not entirely independent and are rarely found in pure form in actual situations. Most acts of influence involve a combination of several types. Nevertheless, identifying those pure forms is a useful aid to understanding power in social relations.

REWARD AND COERCIVE POWER   The first type of power is *reward power*. This type, exerted by person P on another person O, is based on the perception by O that P has the ability to provide rewards for him. A supervisor has power over an employee because the worker knows that his supervisor can recommend wage increases or perhaps even get him promoted. Similarly, a second type of power is called *coercive power*, and is based on O's perception that P has the ability to punish him. A supervisor is perceived as capable of withholding a raise or getting a worker fired.

These two types of power are similar in a number of respects. In both, the power is limited to that range of behaviors for which P can reward or punish O. The strength of both appears to be a joint function of the magnitude of the rewards or punishments involved and the perceived probabilities that these will be incurred, if one yields or does not yield to P's influence attempts. These perceived probabilities are a function of two factors. One is the extent to which O thinks he is being observed by P. The greater the surveillance by P, the more likely O is to believe that his behavior will be rewarded or punished. The other is the past history of O's relation to P. If a supervisor has seldom rewarded or punished an employee, either directly or indirectly, his reward and coercive power is likely to be weak. The effectiveness of rewards and punishments will also depend on how accurately P gauges what behaviors are rewarding or costly to O.[2] Finally, one difference between reward and coercive power should be mentioned. Thibaut and Kelley have suggested that surveillance is apt to be more difficult in the case of coercive power. Whereas persons display behavior that is apt to be rewarded, they hide behavior that leads to punishment.[3] Thus,

---

1. FRENCH & RAVEN, 1959.   *2.* COLLINS & RAVEN, 1969.   *3.* THIBAUT & KELLEY, 1959.

the use of coercion by *P* will be more costly to him than the use of reward, since he must divert his energies from other activities to carry on the necessary surveillance.

REFERENT POWER   Reward power has a property which coercive power lacks: It may gradually be transformed into *referent power*. Referent power is based on identification. The various determinants of identification, one of which is attraction, will be discussed in more detail in Chapter 15. To the degree that *O* is attracted to *P*, he will model himself after *P* and in that way be influenced by *P*'s behavior. A possible explanation of this transformation of reward into referent power is that, first, the exercise of reward power by *P* makes him attractive to *O*, and second, *P*'s attractiveness makes him an object for identification. That reward power makes *P* attractive is suggested by an experiment demonstrating that individuals whose power was based solely on reward were rated more favorably than those having no power or those whose power was based solely on punishment.[4] French and Raven suggest that the strength of the referent power of *P* over *O*, as well as the range of behaviors to which it applies, will vary with the attractiveness of *P* to *O*.

Another determinant of identification is the need for consensual validation. It has been previously noted that in the absence of some physical basis for assessing the validity of his opinions and feelings, a person compares his experiences with those of other persons, particularly persons similar to himself. Thus, *P* may influence *O* by providing him with a model on which to pattern his behavior and interpret his experiences. This form of power appears to be particularly effective to the degree that *P* is similar to *O* and the situation is ambiguous. Under these conditions *O* is especially apt to find identification with *P* rewarding.

While behaviors that *O* adopts as a result of *P*'s referent power are initially dependent on *O*'s relation to *P*, some of them may in time become independent of *P*. Unlike the case of reward or coercive power, the persistence of such behavior is not dependent on *P*'s ability to observe it. In fact, unlike reward or coercive power, *O* may be influenced by referent power even when neither he nor *P* is aware of the influence, or even when they are aware and opposed to any exertion of influence. Herein lies a distinction between the powers of parents and police officers: Parental power is largely referent power, but police power is based mainly on coercion. Thus, children eventually behave well in the absence of their parents, but traffic laws are frequently broken when no policemen are around. The question of surveillance as a necessary condition for control will be treated in more detail in Chapter 10.

The comments so far have been relevant to positive referent power. *P* may influence *O* to behave oppositely to *P*. This phenomenon has been termed *negative referent power*.[5] Although evidence suggests that the strength of this

4. BRIGANTE, 1958.   5. COLLINS & RAVEN, 1969.

type of power varies with the degree to which P is unattractive to O,[6] whether this form of power is analogous in other respects to its positive form is yet to be adequately demonstrated.

EXPERT POWER   *Expert power* is based on O's perception that P has some special knowledge in a given situation, as in the case of a patient who is influenced by his physician to follow a particular regimen. (A more extended discussion of the determinants of expert power is given by Thibaut and Kelley.[7]) The rewards obtained by O from recognition of P's expert power involve feelings of confidence and assurance that the course of action is a correct one. Costs that can be avoided by consulting an expert are feelings of uncertainty and fear of doing the wrong thing. The strength of this type of power varies with the degree of expertness attributed by O to P. Though the power of the expert is usually limited to behavior relevant to his area of expertise, expertise in one area may give rise to expectations of proficiency in other areas as well.[8] Whether behavior induced in O by his perception of P's proficiency will persist depends upon its continued association with the advice of the expert. Continuation of P's expert power over O is not dependent, however, on the degree to which O's behavior is subject to surveillance by P. Expert power may also be lost if the expert transmits his knowledge or skill.

LEGITIMATE POWER   *Legitimate power* is based on the acceptance by O of internalized norms and values which prescribe behaving in a particular fashion. This may include accepting the authority of P by virtue of certain characteristics such as age, social class, or caste; by virtue of his position in some recognized hierarchy; or because he has been designated by some authority as having a legitimate right to prescribe O's behavior in one or more areas. The nature of the exchange in the exercise of legitimate power is that individuals feel satisfied when their behavior conforms to their values and norms; when their behavior does not conform, they incur costs in the form of guilt feelings. Both parties may receive rewards or punishments from outside sources.

Examples of legitimate power abound. The power held by military officers, corporation executives, governmental officials, and parents rests, in part, on legitimate power. Somewhat surprising, however, is the extent of legitimate power that resides in the experimenter-subject relation. Though it has been known for some time that college students would perform extremely boring and seemingly irrelevant tasks at the request of an experimenter, the strength of the power stemming from the experimenter's institutionalized position has been dramatically demonstrated by Milgram.[9] In his experiments, each participant administered electric shocks to another person at the request of the experimenter. Participants willingly increased the level of shocks to levels that appar-

6. OSGOOD & TANNENBAUM, 1955.   7. THIBAUT & KELLEY, 1959.   8. ALLEN & CRUTCHFIELD, 1963.
9. MILGRAM, 1963; MIXON, 1972.

ently were dangerously high, even though the victim, a confederate of the experimenter, convincingly portrayed severe and increasing discomfort. The legitimacy in this situation stemmed from the position of the experimenter as a scientist from a high-prestige university, from the voluntary status of both the participant and his victim, and from various comments of the experimenter made whenever the shock giver objected to continuing, such as: "Please go on." "The experiment must go on." "It is absolutely essential that you continue."

The exercise of legitimate power may also include evoking norms which, while not explicitly requiring O to accept the influence of P, nevertheless require O to behave in a manner that favors P. A powerful norm governing the exchange process among persons is the *norm of reciprocity*.[10] This is the generally accepted idea that when a person does a favor for you, you are obligated to return it in some fashion. Where P evokes this norm requiring O to repay some past social debt, he exerts influence on O. Also widely held is the *norm of social responsibility*, which dictates that one should help other persons in need. A series of investigations has demonstrated the force of this norm.[11] To the degree that O is seen to be dependent on P, P is motivated to exert himself on O's behalf.

The continuation of behavior induced by the exercise of legitimate power depends not on its observability but on the persistence of the underlying values and norms involved. The strength of legitimate power depends upon the degree of O's adherence to the underlying norms and values. Although legitimate power may on occasion cover a broad area of behavior, more frequently it is narrow in scope. For example, while a mother may exert legitimate power over a wide range of her child's behavior, a department head in a business firm must restrict his legitimate power to job-related behavior.

Not much studied, but obviously important, is the extent to which these various powers are associated in everyday situations. Parents, for example, typically possess all five types of power over their young children. But as the children grow older, the expert, reward, and coercive powers of the parents dwindle. Ultimately, especially in adolescence, their referent power may disappear or even become negative, and their legitimate power may be vigorously challenged. Teachers have legitimate power only with respect to classroom discipline and school requirements, and are narrowly limited in their use of reward and coercive power. (As an exercise, the student might work out for himself the types of power held by policemen, judges, baby-sitters, and corporation executives.)

CONTINUED EXERCISE OF POWER   An important contribution from exchange theory is that in a continuing relationship a person uses his resources to influence another only at some cost.[12] Thus, the strength of his power over another

10. GOULDNER, 1960; BLAU, 1964*b*.   *11.* BERKOWITZ & DANIELS, 1963; BERKOWITZ & DANIELS, 1964; BERKOWITZ, KLANDERMAN, & HARRIS, 1964; SCHOPLER & BATESON, 1965; GORANSON & BERKOWITZ, 1966. *12.* HARSANYI, 1962.

person is a function not only of his resources, but also of the cost of using them. A parent who spanks his child to get him to behave incurs the emotional cost of inflicting pain on his child. The more costly the resource is, the less the net strength of *P*'s power over *O*. A lover who threatens to commit suicide if his loved one deserts him is using a very costly resource, his own life, and is not likely to be effective. A legislator may have a number of favors owed to him by various other legislators, and these debts provide him with some power over their votes. But use of this power is costly; once the favors are returned, his power is lost. Thus he is likely to use them only for issues very important to him on which he expects a close vote.

The types of power differ in the extent to which they may be continually exercised and still remain effective. A change in the power relation resulting from exercise of it may occur in two ways: (1) through its effects on rewards and costs, and (2) through creation of conditions that alter the bases of power.

The first of these changes occurs because continued use of power by *P* over *O* directly affects the rewards or costs experienced. Repeated use of the same rewards by *P* may make them less satisfying to *O* as his needs become satiated. For example, as an executive's salary continues to rise, his major needs become relatively satiated, and other costs in terms of responsibility and demands upon his time continue to rise. The promise of a further salary increase is likely to be less effective as a means of control over his behavior. In contrast are other rewards which increase dependency and thus increase power. The executive may develop a strong personal tie to his superior as well as a deep involvement in the company's success.

It was noted earlier that reward power may be transformed into referent power; this transformation is an example of a change in power base resulting from the continued exercise of power. Similarly, the continued use of coercive power is likely to diminish *O*'s feeling for *P* and decrease identification with him, thereby reducing *P*'s positive referent power, or perhaps engendering negative referent power. In the latter, *O* would be motivated to do the opposite of what *P* wants. In contrast to reward and coercive power, the continued exercise of legitimate power is not apt to lead to an increase or diminution of power except where it might lead to further affirmation or to questioning of norms and values.

Blau has emphasized that the exchange of resources for compliance is governed by norms of justice which discourage exploitation on the part of the more powerful person.[13] Only when legitimate power is justly exercised does it maintain its strength or become enhanced. Expert power is not apt to be affected by continued use except where its continuation increases or decreases *P*'s stature as an expert or results in *O*'s picking up the knowledge upon which *P*'s expert power is based. The use of reward or coercive power to extract public compliance without initial changes in private attitudes may, in time, bring about

13. BLAU, 1964*a*.

change of private attitudes independently of future reward or punishment contingencies (see Chapter 3).[14]

STATUS AS A RESOURCE   Though the preceding discussion of resources suggests that the power of *P* over *O* always rests on some attribute of *P* which is objectively related to *O*'s satisfaction, this is not always the case. Resources that make *P* powerful in one situation may maintain his power even in another situation where they are irrelevant.[15] Thus, a wealthy businessman or a distinguished statesman may find that people accede readily to his requests in non-business or nonpolitical situations. Similarly, a person may acquire superior power because of such characteristics as age or beauty, which manifestly are unrelated to performance in many situations.

SUMMARY: RESOURCES   A resource is a property or conditional state of an individual—a possession, an aspect of his behavior, or merely his presence—which enables him to affect the rewards and costs experienced by another person. The value of a resource is not determined by the individual alone, but also by the dependency of the other person on him.

Five types of powers have been distinguished, each based on somewhat different resources. The first is *reward power,* based upon the perception by *O* that *P* can directly or indirectly reward him. The second, *coercive power,* is the counterpart of reward power and is based on *O*'s perception that *P* can directly or indirectly punish him. Both of these kinds of power apply only to the behavior that *P* can reward or punish, and their strength is a joint function of the strength of the reward or punishment and the probability that it will be incurred. Reward power, however, has a property which coercive power lacks: It may gradually be transformed into a third type of power, referent power. *Referent power* is based on the mechanism of identification. Unlike reward and coercive power, it does not require continued surveillance of *O* by *P* in order to ensure conformity of *O*'s behavior to *P*'s wishes. A fourth type of power, *expert power,* stems from special knowledge *P* has which *O* needs. Fifth, *legitimate power* is based on the acceptance by *O* of internalized norms and values which dictate that he accept influence from *P*.

These types of power differ in the extent to which they may be continually exercised and still remain effective. They also interact in their effects; one form may augment or reduce the effects of another. A change in the power relation resulting from continued exercise may occur in two ways: (1) through its direct effects on rewards and costs and (2) through creation of conditions that alter the bases of power. Thus, the continual use of certain kinds of rewards may lead to satiation or, conversely, to increased dependency. The continued exercise of power may produce changes in identification, in norms and values, or in expert knowledge, similarly altering the power bases.

14. COLLINS & RAVEN, 1969.   *15.* BERGER, COHEN, & ZELDITCH, 1966.

From the viewpoint of exchange theory, each exercise of power is in exchange of rewards and costs. Resources may be interpreted in such terms, and exchange theory will be useful in the treatment of power processes later in the chapter.

Dependencies

The behavior or other characteristics of a person constitute a resource only if they satisfy another person. An understanding of why person *P* is able to influence *O* requires as much knowledge of *O*'s dependencies as of *P*'s resources. Such dependencies may have their source in characteristics of the individual or the situation, or in some combination of both. Characteristics of a person take the form of social needs or other attributes that make the resources of *P* especially valuable to him. For example, a person with a strong need for approval and emotional support will be dependent on those persons who can provide it.

Children are apparently dependent on the friendliness and helpfulness of other children. A study of power in children's groups suggests that children whose behavior facilitates the gratification of the social-emotional needs of other children have high power in a group. The investigator summarizes his results as follows:

> The data show that the higher power children are in fact more friendly as a group, more likely to be helpful to their peers, and more able in terms of their psychological adjustments to be outgoing in social relationships, while the low power children as a group are quite different, and are, for example, more likely to use physical force as a method of attempting to influence their peers and more likely to manifest behavior symptoms of deeper lying disturbances.[16]

That this principle is not restricted to children's groups is suggested by another study.[17] The investigators found that characteristics associated with high power in a group of boys aged twelve to fourteen were also generally found among adult women. For boys, the order in which characteristics were associated with high power was: helpfulness, fairness, sociability, expertness, fearlessness, and physical strength. For the women, the order of the items was the same except that fairness was placed before helpfulness.

The more frequently situations call for a particular resource, the more dependent on that resource an individual is apt to be. The finding that fearlessness and physical strength were not attributed to power figures by boys or women was explained by the fact that relatively few situations call for these resources. Ability to satisfy social-emotional needs is a much more important

---

16. Reprinted by permission of the American Sociological Association. From M. Gold. Power in the classroom. *Sociometry,* 1958, **21,** 59.   *17.* Rosen, Levinger, & Lippitt, 1961.

resource, as noted in the previous chapter in the discussion of characteristics of individuals with high sociometric choice status. The discussion revealed a high correlation between popularity and social power, particularly in small, informal groups, where satisfaction of social-emotional needs is dominant.

Alternatives

Power is determined not only by the resources of *P* and the dependency of *O* on *P*, but also by the consequence of not complying. *O* compares his reward-cost outcome for compliance with that for noncompliance. The greater the disparity between these outcomes, the greater *P*'s power over *O*. Essentially this disparity is a function of the alternatives available to *O*. If *O* has a resource in sufficient quantity himself, or if he may gain the resource at lower cost in relations with persons other than *P*, it will be relatively ineffective as a source of *P*'s power over *O*. This is most obvious in the case of expert power: The expert influences others by his possession of scarce knowledge. If everyone were an expert (a contradiction in terms), the expert would be powerless.

The consequences of not complying have a special significance when *P*'s influence attempt is based upon threats. One possibility is that *P* will not carry out his threat anyhow. Thus, the extent to which *P*'s threat is convincing affects the power that *P* has over *O*. One of the most interesting forms of threats, that which is based on the promise of mutual harm, has been analyzed intensively by Schelling.[18] A union may threaten a strike costly to itself if management does not raise wages a few cents. A furious driver may threaten to smash another car with his own if the right of way is not yielded. The mutual dependence of each person on the other's actions is nicely illustrated in the game of

18. SCHELLING, 1960.

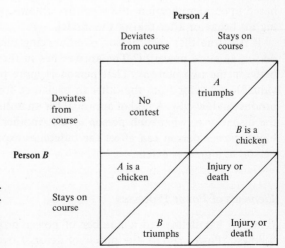

Figure 8-1 *Exchange outcomes of two persons playing the game of "chicken."* *The four possible outcomes for* A *and for* B *are shown to be a joint function of their choices.*

"chicken," shown in matrix form in Figure 8-1. Such matrices are very useful in clarifying exchange-theory application. Schelling notes that in these instances *P* really does not have much incentive to carry out the threat, because of its cost to himself. In the case of such threats, power appears to vary with the extent to which *P* can make *O* believe that he is committed to carry out the threat. A driver may speed up so that a collision cannot be avoided unless the other party yields the right of way. Any means by which *P* gives up his control over the exercise of the threat is a strategy likely to secure his power. A favorite of crime writers is the blackmailer who deposits a damaging secret paper with another person unknown to *O*, with instructions to release it in the event of his death.

Power Processes

The previous discussion emphasized that we must not think of power as an attribute of a person. The exercise of power is a function of characteristics of both the influencer and the influencee, as well as of other people in the situation. But the analysis must be carried still further: Power must be examined in the context of ongoing interaction processes.

From the point of view of exchange theory, a conception of power as a process whereby one person causes changes in the behavior of another is inadequate because it ignores the symmetry implied by the notion of exchange. Not one but both persons are influencing and being influenced. They are exchanging behaviors that result in their experiencing certain costs and certain rewards. What is exchanged differs depending upon the type of power exercised. When an employee complies with his supervisor's legitimate requests, he receives continued approval in exchange. Behind this approval, of course, lies the power of the supervisor to facilitate or retard the employee's advancement. If power is based upon identification, the identifier obtains psychic satisfaction in modeling his behavior after that of the model.

If it is true that each person is influencing the other, why do we view one person as more powerful? The answer lies in the nature of the *bargain* made between the two persons. That person is more powerful who receives rather valuable behavior from the other in exchange for behavior that he is able to produce at low cost. A nod of approval for an arduous task well done illustrates the disparity in what each person gives. Another way of stating it is that the higher-power person can affect the outcomes experienced by the lower-power person to a greater extent.

Elements of Power Processes

Emerson has delineated a number of power processes. He defines power as follows: "Power *(PAB)*, the power of actor *A* over actor *B*, is the amount of resistance on the part of B which can be potentially overcome by *A*." This power lies in *B*'s dependency on *A*, which is determined by the variables in the following proposition: "Dependency *(DBA)*, the dependency of actor *B* upon actor *A* is *(a)* directly proportional to *B*'s *motivational investment* in goals mediated by *A*, and *(b)* inversely proportional to the *availability* of these goals to *B* outside of the *A-B* relation."[19] Thus, as previously emphasized, power is a function not only of *A*'s resources, but also of *B*'s dependencies and alternatives.

Since both parties in a relation have varying degrees of power over the other, Emerson demonstrates that a power-dependence relation between *A* and *B* can be described as a pair of equations:

$$PAB = DBA$$

$$PBA = DAB$$

These may be translated as follows: The power that *A* has over *B* is equal to the dependency of *B* on *A*. Similarly, the power that *B* is capable of exercising over *A* is equal to *A*'s dependency on *B*.

Power relations described in this manner may vary in two independent ways. First, they may vary in the degree to which each person is capable of exercising power relative to the other. This depends on the strength of the dependencies that exist between the two persons. They may be relatively independent, as in the case of two casual acquaintances neither of whom has much influence over the other, or highly dependent, as in the case of lovers each of whom has the power to strongly affect the outcomes of the other. A second manner in which power relations may vary is in the degree of equality that exists between the two persons. Emerson characterizes a relation as balanced where, regardless of the degree or level of dependency, the parties hold equal power over each other. In terms of his equations this is represented as follows:

$$PAB = DBA$$
$$\parallel \qquad \parallel$$
$$PBA = DAB$$

A relation is described as unbalanced when one actor has greater power than the other. Symbolically this could be represented as:

$$PAB = DBA$$
$$\lor \qquad \lor$$
$$PBA = DAB$$

In this instance, the power of *A* over *B* *(PAB)* is greater than the power of *B* over *A* *(PBA)* because the dependency of *B* on *A* *(DBA)* is greater than *A*'s dependency on *B* *(DAB)*.

19. EMERSON, 1962.

Consequences of High but Equal Power: Balanced Relations

Where both members of a pair have high power over each other, each person's power might appear to be balanced by the counterpower of the other, thereby producing a minimum of mutual influence. It would seem that each person, being highly dependent on the other, would be reluctant to make demands, since the other could impose equally costly counterdemands or interfere with his gratification by breaking off the relation. One might further suppose that the potentiality for conflict in such a situation would be great. Yet everyday observation, as well as more systematic evidence, suggests that persons who are close friends exercise considerable influence on each other and at the same time maintain amicable relations.[20] This occurs because certain arrangements emerge to facilitate influence without conflict.

In one such arrangement, the two parties assign different values to various activities. Norms are established dictating that in one situation, one party will give way, and in another situation, the other will give way. For example, a pair of friends whose preferences differ may agree to go ice-skating one week and to play tennis the next. In a second type of arrangement, norms dictate some alternation of advantage, as when two children equally powerful and equally motivated to play with a particular toy agree to take turns. Many of the rules of "fairness" have as their function the avoidance of costs arising out of power struggles. Third, since two persons are unlikely to be precisely equal in power, conflict may be avoided by the regular acquiescence of the less powerful member. The parties themselves may not be aware of a condition of slight inequality, and hence the stronger of the two is unlikely to get his way all the time.

Modes of Resolving Imbalance

Emerson has argued that an unbalanced relation is unstable since it encourages the use of power, which in turn sets into motion processes that he has called cost-reduction and balancing operations.[21] These are illustrated in the following hypothetical example.

Consider a man and a woman who have been having a love affair. Suppose that, in its current stage, the interest of one party (designated *P*) has lessened somewhat, while the interest of the other party *(O)* remains sustained. In that case, the power of *P* over *O* is greater than that of *O* over *P*. If *P* uses this power differential, *P* may be less punctual for appointments, may have more conflicting engagements and more unaccounted-for weekends, and may occasionally see someone else.

These actions greatly raise the psychological costs of *O*. But *O* may reduce these costs somewhat by making excuses for *P*'s behavior or by attributing the causes of it to inadvertent failings in *O*'s own actions. This resolution does not reduce *O*'s power disadvantage. A second solution helps to restore balance: *O*

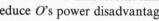

20. BACK, 1951.   *21.* EMERSON, 1962.

may redefine the relation as a nonserious, temporary one, and occasionally date other persons. This *partial withdrawal* from the relation reduces *O*'s dependency on *P,* possibly to the point where it is equal to that of *P* on *O.*

Complete withdrawal from a relation occurs when the costs incurred by the less powerful member result in a reward-cost outcome that is below some alternative, including the alternative of no relation at all. In a voluntary relation, this places a limit on the degree to which the more powerful member of a pair may exploit the less powerful.

The process of partial withdrawal is one of four balancing operations in which inequality can be corrected. In the second balancing operation, *forming alternative relations* (termed by Emerson *extending the power network*), the dependency of one party is also decreased so that it is equal to that of the other. In the case cited above, for example, *O* might develop a satisfying relation with someone other than *P.*

The third and fourth balancing operations require more discussion, since they are related to a number of features of process and structure in interaction. Emerson derives the phenomenon of *status* or *differential evaluation* from the third balancing operation. The status given to the more powerful member is a source of satisfaction to him *which is provided by the less powerful person.* As the more powerful member becomes increasingly motivated to achieve positive evaluation from the less powerful, his dependency on the latter is increased and the power discrepancy between the two is decreased. Abuse of power on the part of the more powerful is discouraged by the prospect that such behavior will lead to loss of status.

The fourth balancing operation involves a process that has received considerable attention: *coalition formation.*[22] Ever since the observations of Georg Simmel in this regard, investigators have been intrigued with the tendency in three-person groups for a pattern to emerge which consists of a pair and a third party.[23] Emerson views this as a model of the process leading to the emergence of norms which ensure group functioning against the disruptive effects of abuse of power. The power of each member is restricted by the potential combination of other members that constrains him to behave in conformity to a norm.

It is difficult to illustrate this point, since such norms are an integral part of every group situation. They only become visible when they are violated. Even in newly formed groups, members are guided by norms (such as those of courtesy) which control unrestricted use of power and which have been developed in other group contexts. Yet during a crisis created by an overuse of power, this process of coalition formation may be readily observed, as when workers combine and demand that a boss agree to rules restricting the requests that he can make of them. Perhaps a clearer illustration is the instance where two children threaten not to play with a third unless he stops being so bossy. In situations

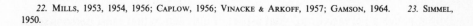

22. MILLS, 1953, 1954, 1956; CAPLOW, 1956; VINACKE & ARKOFF, 1957; GAMSON, 1964.   *23.* SIMMEL, 1950.

where the male has a dominant role in relation to subordinate females, and where he might thereby exploit the relation for sexual purposes, norms placing limits on his power hold him in check. This is illustrated by norms against dating and other forms of association between a male supervisor and a female worker or between a male teacher and a female student. A more complete discussion of norm development in such situations will be offered in Chapter 10.

One final point not made by Emerson might be included. In general, continued interaction between two persons will increase the motivational investment of each in the goals mediated by the other *in the direction of greater equality* unless there are certain safeguards against this process. This might occur for a number of reasons. Outcomes of each member of a dyad increase with continued interaction because each person becomes increasingly adept at providing and motivated to provide rewards to the other, and they provide them with less cost. But because the higher-power member is able to exact more from the relation, his dependency increases at a more rapid rate. The lower-power member provides rewards at greater cost, and ultimately may feel the burden too onerous. Accordingly, the balance of power moves toward equality. In addition, increased interaction between members of a pair decreases both the degree of dependency on and the availability of relations with other persons. These processes, together with the inertia inherent in human relations, go far to explain the continuation of a relation which appears, to the outsider at least, to be an exploitative one.

Maintenance of Power Differences

Where it is essential for power differences to be maintained, various features of the social structure operate to discourage the development of mutual dependency. In the military, officers and enlisted men are segregated to some extent and a degree of formality is maintained in their relations, as illustrated by the salute and the use of titles and last names. Similarly, in business organizations, high executives erect a variety of barriers between themselves and their underlings, such as separate lunchrooms and rest rooms. The most common form of dependency that threatens to develop between superiors and subordinates is friendship, which would upset the power differential required if the organization is to function properly. Other mechanisms with a similar function arise in other relations requiring a power differential, such as the teacher-student relation and the officer-soldier relation. In all these situations it is essential for the achievement of organizational goals that the more powerful person retain the power of decision and control of the relation.

Perception of Power

Power is such a pervasive and vital aspect of interaction that most persons seem to be quite sensitive to the facts about power. There is some systematic evidence that most people perceive fairly accurately the power structure in a group and their own relative position in the structure, and further, that their behavior toward other persons is consistent with such perceptions. In a study of power in two boys' camps, boys were found to perceive accurately the relative power of group members, including their own.[24] Furthermore, the frequency and character of the attempts of each boy to influence another person were consistent with these perceptions. Boys who perceived themselves as high in power made more attempts to influence others and in one camp were more directive in these attempts. A study of Air Force enlisted men solving laboratory problems provides similar evidence.[25] The amount of influence attempted by an airman was proportional to the extent that he was liked and accepted by the person he influenced.

Perhaps more striking are the results of another study.[26] The perception of the relative power of partners working together on a task was experimentally varied over a series of joint decision-making trials. Individuals were given different initial perceptions of their own resources and of their task ability relative to the partner, and the partner (who actually was the experimenter's assistant) varied the degree to which he accepted or rejected the naïve participant's attempts to influence him. Variations in initial information and in the feedback of information from the partner were expected to produce corresponding variations in the participant's perceived power, and he was expected to behave in accordance with his perceived power. For example, if he believed his power was low, he was expected to reduce his influence attempts, to decrease his refusals to concede to his partner, and to reveal less confidence when speaking to him. These hypotheses were confirmed. In particular, whether the partner acquiesced to or resisted influence attempts appeared to be the most important determinant of the perception of power and of power-relevant behavior.

Summary: Power Processes

When the exercise of power is examined in the context of interaction, a number of features are seen to be associated with it. Each exercise is an exchange between persons, often an asymmetrical exchange of behavior varying in value to each party. Power is seen to be a direct function of the dependency of *O* upon *P*. The greater *O*'s dependency, the stronger *P*'s power over *O*. Dependencies may be mutual or balanced, or they may be disparate and unbalanced, with one member of the pair being considerably more dependent. This type of imbalanced situation often leads to efforts to redress the balance. Such balancing operations include withdrawing from the relation, forming an alternative relation, increasing the status and resultant dependency of the higher-power person, and forming a coalition. Balancing does not always occur: Elements of the social structure operate to maintain differences in power.

24. LIPPITT, POLANSKY, REDL, & ROSEN, 1952.   *25.* FRENCH & SNYDER, 1959.   *26.* LEVINGER, 1959.

Interpersonal Strategies

In recent years behavioral scientists have studied the ways in which persons exert power as forms of *strategy*. First, some research has examined the strategies that persons employ in everyday interaction to get others to behave in a desired manner. Second, the behavior of persons in situations requiring negotiations has been studied. These negotiations range from games played in laboratory settings to simulated or actual bargaining situations between labor and management or between nations. Various strategies include the direct offering or withholding of one's own resources, the invocation of various norms believed to restrict or control the other party's behavior, and the use of promises or threats intended to change the beliefs of the other party concerning his or one's own past or future actions. Important to the whole process is the nature of the relationship between the two parties. It may be cooperative or competitive, or a mixture of both; it may involve trust or mistrust.

Strategies in Everyday Interaction

That everyday strategies can be readily classified according to the various bases of power has been demonstrated.[27] In a variety of hypothetical situations in which the object was to obtain a desired response from another person, individuals were presented with a list of sixteen strategies, such as making a promise or threat, a moral appeal, or a claim of obligation, and were asked to rate the likelihood that they would use each strategy. Their ratings were analyzed statistically to discover how the strategies grouped themselves into the same or different categories.

They fell into classes that, for the most part, related closely to the bases of power discussed earlier. For example, one cluster of strategies apparently involved reward power, and another, coercive power. Another class involved the use of expertise, thus relating to expert power, and still another, influencing the person by reminding him of obligations, involved a use of referent power if the obligation was a personal one, and legitimate power if it was impersonal. In another study of hypothetical situations, this one between clients and bureaucratic officials, the persuasive attempts again grouped themselves according to the same bases of power.[28]

DIRECT USE OF OWN RESOURCES   One very direct, simple strategy is to offer a resource to the other party in exchange for a desired behavior on his part. A salesman may cut his commission to make the sale. In labor negotiations, the company's firm offer of a wage increase or other benefits may be such a strategy. In everyday situations, doing a favor may be another illustration. One general strategy under this heading involves attempts to increase one's attrac-

27. Marwell & Schmitt, 1967.   28. Katz & Danet, 1966.

tiveness to the other person. Jones and his colleagues have identified a set of techniques under the heading of ingratiation (see Chapter 2).[29] These include flattery; enhancement of the other person's self; conformity in opinion, judgment, and behavior; and tactics of self-presentation that either advertise the ingratiator's strengths or virtues or by implication enhance the strength and virtues of the person who is the target of such tactics.

INVOKING NORMS   An individual may use legitimate power as a strategic base by invoking norms. In presenting a particular identity—presenting himself as a certain kind of person—an individual often makes salient those norms which require other persons to behave toward him in an advantageous manner. The individual who presents himself as a martyr makes salient powerful norms of justice which constrain other persons to make amends to him.[30] Similarly, various techniques of *altercasting* involve the use of both reward and legitimate power. Weinstein and Deutschberger use this term to refer to the process by which another person (an alter) is placed in an identity or a role that requires him to behave in a manner advantageous to the manipulator.[31] For example, students may ask a teacher a series of questions in order to keep him from presenting too much new material in class. He falls into the trap because he is called on to enact his role of teacher. Some identities and roles (e.g., honest person or friend) have positively valued attributes, and being cast in them is rewarding. In this sense, altercasting would be a form of other-enhancement.

More generally, however, altercasting is used to evoke normative constraints over other persons. Where altercasting is used to exert legitimate power in this fashion one of several norms is likely to be invoked. First is the *norm of fairness or justice.* Here, the exchange process is governed by expectations about what is a just or fair exchange. On some occasions justice calls for each individual to receive equivalent outcomes. An example would be two partners who put an equal amount of work into a task: each would expect a 50-50 split of the profits. In other situations, equity may prescribe that one person receive more because he has contributed more. Second is the *norm of altruism.* To the extent that an individual presents himself as helpless or dependent on other persons, those with whom he interacts will feel obligated to come to his aid.[32]

Finally, the *norm of reciprocity* is a pervasive expectation governing the exchange process.[33] Individuals in interaction are expected to pay back benefits received from other persons and thus to keep their social debts to a minimum. Individuals invited to a dinner party are ordinarily expected to extend an equivalent social invitation or, where that is impossible, to bring a gift. Thus, presenting oneself as a creditor or casting the other in the identity of a debtor because of past favors that have gone unreciprocated is a way of exercising legitimate power.

29. JONES, 1964.   *30.* LEVENTHAL, 1967.   *31.* WEINSTEIN & DEUTSCHBERGER, 1963.   *32.* BERKOWITZ & DANIELS, 1963.   *33.* GOULDNER, 1960.

DEBT MANAGEMENT AS A COUNTERSTRATEGY   The pervasiveness of the norm of reciprocity in the exchange process has led Blau to argue that this is the basic psychological mechanism underlying status and power differentiation in groups.[34] To the extent that persons do not have the resources to return benefits in kind to those who command resources on which they are dependent, they must repay their benefactors in esteem and future compliance. Leaving oneself open to future demands is costly. Because giving esteem to other persons reduces one's own status, it too is costly. Thus, certain strategies are used to keep obligations to a minimum and to ensure that other persons will not make excessive use of their advantageous position.

In part, management of such social obligations or debts involves cognitive restructuring of the situation.[35] The magnitude of the social debt depends not only on the rewards and costs experienced by both donor and recipient but also on the degree to which the donor's acts are perceived by the recipient as voluntary, intentional, and without ulterior or sinister motives.[36] To the extent that the recipient perceives that the donor's acts were required of him by his role or were unintentional or insincere, any debt incurred is reduced. Where the situation is ambiguous, cognitive restructuring frequently occurs.

Several studies support these ideas. In one, judgments of the amount of gratitude due a favor doer in a series of hypothetical situations were directly related to the extent to which the favor was intentional, what it cost the donor to do it, and the value of the favor to the recipient.[37] In another, both the amount of help and the giver's intentions were directly related to the willingness of the players to reciprocate.[38] Similarly, the amount of reward provided by one individual to another person in another experimental gaming situation was directly related to the amount of past rewards received from that individual.[39] It was also greater when the other person's past resources were small and future resources large. These findings with respect to the size of the other person's past resources suggest that the amount of debt is determined in part by the degree of sacrifice made by the other person. The investigator suggests further that the effect of the size of the person's future resources may support one interpretation of the norm of reciprocity: People feel compelled to return favors so that they can look for future favors. When persons will have large resources in the future, individuals wish to be in a position to request favors from them.

People also avoid incurring too great an obligation to reciprocate by accepting favors only under appropriate conditions. An unsolicited favor or one that is inappropriate to the role occupied by the donor may be seen as incurring less of an obligation. In one experiment, participants received an unsolicited favor from another person and were then asked to rate him accurately. Those participants led to believe that the ratings were very important were less inclined to

34. BLAU, 1964a.   *35.* SCOTT & LYMAN, 1968.   *36.* GREENBERG, 1968.   *37.* TESSER, GATEWOOD, & RIVER, 1968.   *38.* FRISCH & GREENBERG, 1968.   *39.* PRUITT, 1968.

return the favor on a later occasion. The investigators argued that incurring the obligation where the ratings were important would curtail the recipient's freedom more severely; thus, they asserted their freedom by not returning the favor.[40] Another investigation had interviewers give a flower to a female interviewee in a situation where the interview was conducted formally, and in another where it was done informally.[41] The formal situation was the less appropriate one for this act, and girls interviewed in that situation were less inclined to return the favor when given an opportunity. Here the interpretation is that, where the favor is inappropriate, the recipient attributes selfish motives to the donor, such as the desire to manipulate him, and thus does not return the favor. If this is true, we would also expect that the recipient would not like the donor of the inappropriate favor. This suggestion is consistent with a study indicating that individuals are less attracted to donors who give favors inappropriate to their role (sharing winnings in a competitive game situation).[42]

Studies of how individuals react to having harmed another person reveal actions that reduce obligations. Just as an obligation can be incurred by accepting a favor, so one can be incurred by harming another person. The common use of "Excuse me" or "Pardon me" for jostling another person is a means of denying intentionality and thus responsibility or obligation. Two common reactions found in studies of harm doing were that the harm doer reduces the worthiness of the victim or blames him for his own fate, thereby absolving himself. Outside the laboratory, in those instances where adequate compensation is available and other responses such as justification or self-punishment are ineffective or too costly, the victim may be compensated, following the norm of reciprocity.

Sometimes reciprocation is impossible or can only be made at high cost, such as a loss of status or an overburdening obligation. In these instances, resentment is apt to accompany gratitude. This may well be an explanation for the ambivalence that many poor people feel toward charity: They cannot reciprocate the aid they have received. On the other hand, they may feel comfortable in accepting unemployment compensation because they have previously paid taxes to the government.

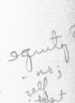

THREATS AND PROMISES   The effectiveness of threats and promises has also received some attention. What is crucial is the credibility of the threat or promise. To the extent that the other party believes that the promised or threatened outcome will necessarily occur as a consequence of his acts, he will be induced or deterred from acting. The empirical evidence, however, is far from conclusive. Based on one set of experiments involving a laboratory game, Deutsch has argued that the use of threat interferes with achieving a cooperative solution in a conflict situation. The use of threat enhances the competitive interests of the

40. Brehm & Cole, 1966.   *41.* Schopler & Thompson, 1965.   *42.* Kiesler, 1966.

players and turns the game into a competitive struggle for self-esteem in which each views backing down as a loss of self-esteem.[43]

Others have failed to find evidence for the deleterious effects of threat.[44] The threats may, as a form of communication, facilitate coordination and improved outcomes, and may deter competitive or exploitive responses.[45] Perhaps threat can have both types of consequences depending on the situation. A recent study suggests that where persons experience a need to save face they will engage in retaliatory behavior even where this leads to a reduction in their own outcomes, and they will do this to an even greater degree when the other party to the negotiations is unaware of the costs of retaliation.[46] This implies that a hostile reaction to threat occurs with adverse consequences to the person reacting in this manner if it provides a way of saving face, supporting Deutsch's argument that threat can lead to counterthreat and a spiral of animosity which interferes with maximizing outcomes.

Another study suggests that the amount of reward at stake affects the probability that threats will be used.[47] Where rewards were either high or low, threats were less often used. One interpretation of this is that, where little is at stake, threats may not be used because they are perceived as ineffective, while under conditions of high reward they may not be used because their use is perceived as too costly.[48]

Negotiation and Games of Strategy

The process of negotiation for advantage has been studied in the laboratory using games of strategy and make-believe negotiations. In most negotiation situations and games of strategy, both cooperation and competition are involved. Persons cooperate because the outcomes of each participant are dependent upon the behavior of the other participants. At the same time, they are motivated to compete, since the interdependence of the outcomes allows one person to gain at the expense of another. Because these situations involve both the motive of cooperation and the motive of competition, they have been referred to as *mixed motive* situations.[49]

A model situation involving negotiation may be described as follows. We may consider two persons negotiating a single issue, such as the adjustment of tariff levies between states or the withdrawal of troops between nations at war. The choices of each party can be represented in terms of a decision matrix, similar to the one presented earlier for the game of "chicken." The alternatives faced by two nations negotiating tariff reduction are shown in Figure 8-2.[50] Each can either hold out for the present high tariffs or lower his tariffs.

The resulting outcomes dictated by their joint decisions are portrayed in the

---

43. Deutsch & Krauss, 1960, 1962; Hornstein, 1965.   *44.* Schomer, Davis, & Kelley, 1966; Geivitz, 1967.   *45.* Geivitz, 1967; Meeker, Shure, & Moore, 1964.   *46.* Brown, 1968.   *47.* Swingli, 1967. *48.* Vinacke, 1969.   *49.* Schelling, 1960.   *50.* Sawyer & Guetzkow, 1965.

	HOLD OUT for present high tariff	lower tariff to a COMPROMISE level
HOLD OUT for present high tariff	Outcome Status quo: both tariffs remain high Utility 0 for A 0 for B	Outcome A's tariff remains high B's tariff lowered Utility +10 for A −5 for B
Lower Tariff to a COMPROMISE level	Outcome A's tariff lowered B's tariff remains high Utility −5 for A +10 for B	Outcome Both tariffs are lowered Utility +5 for A +5 for B

(Top-left diagonal cell: Alternatives for nation B / Alternatives for nation A)

Figure 8-2 *Illustrative matrix of outcomes and utilities when each of two nations may alternatively "hold out" at the present high level or lower its tariff to a "compromise" level. [Reprinted with permission from J. Sawyer and H. Guetzkow. Bargaining and negotiation in international relations. In H. C. Kelman (Ed.),* International *behavior. New York: Holt, Rinehart and Winston, Inc., 1965. P. 474.]*

four cells of the figure in terms of numbers representing the utility of each of the four possible joint decisions. If both choose to hold out, the status quo is retained, and the utility to each is represented in the upper left-hand cell as zero since neither gains anything. If, however, one party lowers his tariff while the other retains a high tariff, the latter gains and the former loses, represented by the +10 and −5 in the lower left-hand and upper right-hand cells. Finally, if they compromise and both lower their tariffs, both gain, although the amount shown in the lower right-hand cell is less than each would have gained had he held out and the other had lowered his tariffs. Such a situation presents a dilemma. The dilemma arises because if each tries to gain his maximum outcome, each gains nothing. But if one party lowers his aim, and the other does not, he loses, while his opponent gains. Only when both parties are willing to compromise do both gain, and neither has a guarantee that the other will cooperate.

The situation confronting two nations at war can be similarly represented if the alternatives are simply to continue fighting or to withdraw troops. While mutual withdrawal might end the war, if one nation can induce the other to withdraw unilaterally the resulting political settlement can be fashioned to the advantage of the party that maintains its troop strength in the disputed area.

The prisoner's dilemma, which provides the paradigm for a widely used laboratory game in studies of negotiations and the determination of trust, has essentially the same matrix structure. This game has been described as follows:

> Two suspects are taken into custody and separated. The district attorney is certain that they are guilty of a specific crime, but he does not have adequate evidence to convict them at a trial. He points out to each prisoner that each has two alternatives: to confess to the crime the police are sure they have done, or not to confess. If they both do not confess, then the district attorney states he will book them on some very minor trumped-up charge such as petty larceny and illegal possession of a weapon, and they will both receive minor punishment; if they both confess they will be prosecuted, but he will recommend less than the most severe sentence; but if one confesses and the other does not, then the confessor will receive lenient treatment for turning state's evidence whereas the latter will get "the book" slapped at him.[51]

As in the negotiation situation previously described, each person is faced with a choice between two alternatives, in this case to confess or to remain silent. His outcome depends on his decision as well as on the decision of the other party. This situation can be represented as a decision matrix with the outcomes for each party in terms of the length of prison sentence to be expected. It can be seen from Figure 8-3 that the best outcome for the pair if neither confesses is not as good as what might be experienced by either person if he confesses and his partner does not.

In research on strategies the payoffs are monetary rewards rather than prison terms. Further, the relation of the values placed in the various cells

---

51. Reprinted with permission from R. D. Luce and H. Raiffa. *Games and decisions.* New York: John Wiley & Sons, Inc., 1957, p. 95.

Figure 8-3 The prisoner's dilemma. *(Reprinted with permission from L. Ofshe and R. Ofshe. Utility and choice in social interaction. Englewood Cliffs, N.J.: Prentice-Hall, Inc., 1970. P. 139.)*

		Prisoner Y	
		Not confess	Confess
Prisoner X	Not confess	1 year each	X gets 10 years Y gets 3 months
	Confess	Y gets 10 years X gets 3 months	8 years each

		Player Y	
		1	2
Player X	1	X Y +5, +5	X Y −5, +10
	2	X Y +10, −5	X Y +1, +1

tempts persons to depart from a cooperative alliance. Thus, in a typical payoff matrix such as that in Figure 8-4, where the first entry in each cell represents the payoff for player X and the second entry that of player Y, if both choose alternative 1 each receives $5. If, however, player X chooses 1 and player Y chooses 2 the former will lose $5 and the latter will gain $10. Certain important restrictions on this situation should be noted. Frequently no direct communication between participants is permitted. Each party must evaluate the other's intentions only through observing his choices, as they are made. Moreover, the values in the cells are fixed and are known by both parties. This precludes the use of most strategies other than those designed to alter the other party's perceptions of what each is likely to do on each trial. However, in most situations requiring negotiations, the values are not fixed or known and thus it is to the advantage of each person to convince the other that the values of the expected outcomes favor a decision on the part of the latter which in reality would favor the former.

An important condition in bargaining and negotiation is *trust*. An individual trusts another person if he behaves in a way that would allow the other person to take advantage of him. In the prisoner's dilemma game, the choice of the first matrix alternative by each player can be considered a cooperative or trust-ing response. Such a choice is consistent with defining the situation as one in which the other person will also choose the first alternative, despite the tempta-tion to maximize his gains by choosing the second. In each trial of the game, each individual is placed in a dilemma: He can make a trusting response by choosing the first alternative and exposing himself to the possibility that his partner will exploit him, or he can choose the second alternative, hoping that his partner will make a cooperative response which will yield him maximum outcomes. In the latter case, he takes the risk that his partner will also try the same tactic, choosing the second alternative, which would yield minimum out-comes to both.

If both players choose the first alternative, each gains five points. By cooper-ating on such a choice, each player could maximize his net gain, since neither would have any losses. But this cooperative choice is not the most popular.

Depending on experimental conditions, the percentage of cooperative choices ranges from 10 percent to 90 percent, with 45 percent being representative.[52] A wide variety of task, situational, and personality variables have been related to the proportion of cooperative responses.[53] In general, the obtained relationships appear understandable in terms of how a given variable affects each player's definition of the situation, including his perceptions of the objective of the games, the values and intentions of his partner,[54] and the purposes of the experiment.

These relationships are most obvious for variations in the experimenter's instructions to players. Where instructions emphasize that players are partners and that both can win, they choose the cooperative alternative more often. Where the instructions define their relationship as a competitive one, they make the competitive choice.[55] Where communication is possible, and particularly where persons can indicate their own intentions and their expectations about how each other will behave, a cooperative, mutually advantageous relation emerges.[56]

In one study, the responses of accomplices were prearranged by the experimenter in a game situation where players could behave in either a cooperative or a competitive manner.[57] Some accomplices adopted a "turn-the-other-cheek" strategy, responding to attacks or threats with rewarding behavior and otherwise making cooperative responses. In a second experimental condition, the accomplices adopted a nonpunitive strategy, responding self-protectively to attack but otherwise reciprocating the partner's behavior. A third group of accomplices adopted a deterrent strategy: counterattacking in the case of attack and cooperating when partners made cooperative responses. Two additional groups of accomplices suddenly shifted their behavior halfway through the game, with one group adopting a nonpunitive strategy after having behaved aggressively and threateningly, and the other switching to the turn-the-other-cheek strategy.

Both the responses of the players and their perceptions of the accomplices were clearly affected by the type of strategy used. Players cooperated more with the nonpunitive partners, took advantage of those who adopted the turn-the-other-cheek strategy, and competed more with those adopting the deterrent strategy. As the investigators suggest, the relative ineffectiveness of the pacifist strategy may in part be attributed to a special feature of the experimental situation. Persons might think such behavior foolish and inappropriate in a competitive game situation. In other studies, where experimental conditions made salient the competitive norms that normally operate in social games, competition increased. For example, where a cumulative score allows players to check their standing against that of their partner, competitive responses are

52. SCHEFF & CHEWNING, 1968.   53. SCHEFF & CHEWNING, 1968; VINACKE, 1969.   54. SCHEFF, 1967.
55. DEUTSCH & KRAUSS, 1960.   56. LOOMIS, 1959; SCHEFF, 1967.   57. DEUTSCH, EPSTEIN, CANAVAN, & GUMPUT, 1967.

markedly increased.[58] At the same time, features of the gaming situation that highlight the costs of competition through lowered outcomes will serve to dampen competitive responses. Thus, increasing the amount of rewards at stake generally increases cooperation.[59]

The role of trust in nonlaboratory negotiations has also been considered. Osgood has argued that making concessions is apt to create trust, but Siegel and Fouraker contend that making concessions is apt to encourage the other party to drive a harder bargain.[60] Osgood's model of negotiation leading to a state of peaceful coexistence between nations is based on the notion that mutual distrust and tension prevent negotiators from making concessions. He argues that the only way negotiations can proceed is for one party to take the initiative and unilaterally make a concession. This, he argues, will have the effects of reducing tension and distrust, leading the other party to make a concession. The result is a spiral of mutual concessions of increasing size until agreement is reached.

Evidence on making concessions to gain trust is somewhat mixed. Two studies find that the adoption of a firm bargaining position by a negotiator (making only small concessions) gains the most advantageous terms.[61] However, both note that this occurs at the risk of not obtaining an agreement. A moderately stiff position may be advantageous; however, an extreme position may so drastically reduce any chance of agreement that negotiations fail, with costly results for both sides. This would be particularly the case where costs of not obtaining an agreement would be high, as in a lengthy strike over a labor-management dispute, nuclear war, or a major conflict between nations. Unfortunately, in laboratory studies of negotiation it has not been possible to introduce costs of a comparable magnitude for failing to agree, so that the effects of a firm bargaining position has not had the same consequence in the laboratory that it has in a life situation.

Another feature of the typical laboratory situation that makes it difficult to set up an adequate test of the relative merits of these two positions is that the attitudes of the participants in a laboratory may be quite different both in content and origin than the attitudes prevailing in conflicts outside the laboratory. Osgood's model assumes a high state of tension and distrust between the parties, as in a cold war having a history of mutually escalated conflict. Persons in a laboratory game or simulated bargaining situation may simply be motivated to play the game well in order to maximize their advantage irrespective of cost. Whereas unilateral concessions may have the results envisioned by Osgood in the case of hostile nations on the brink of nuclear conflict, they might well be viewed as weakness or at least as silly or inappropriate behavior in a game. At any rate, considerably more research is necessary before any firm conclusions can be drawn.

58. McClintock & McNeel, 1966.   *59.* Gallo, 1966.   *60.* Osgood, 1959, 1962; Siegel & Fouraker, 1960.   *61.* Bartos, 1965; Komorita & Brenner, 1968.

Summary: Interpersonal Strategies

Various interpersonal strategies for obtaining more power in a given situation are available. One's own resources may be offered or withheld, in a kind of direct, obvious strategy to gain power. These include attempts to increase one's own attractiveness to the other person through ingratiation, as well as advertising one's own good qualities. Certain resources are inherent in the normative social structure governing many social interactions. In presenting a particular identity—presenting himself as a certain kind of person—an individual often makes salient those norms which require other persons to behave toward him in an advantageous way. Or, in altercasting, the other person is cast into an identity, with similar effect. This process often invokes the norm of justice or fair play, the norm of altruism, or the norm of reciprocity. The person feels pressure to honor the norm, and under some conditions may feel resentment at being put in a position of indebtedness to the other person. This depends on many factors, such as the intentions of the other party, the degree of sacrifice he is making, and the ability of the recipient to repay the debt.

Everyday situations and laboratory ones where both cooperation and competition are involved have been characterized as mixed-motive situations: The participants are motivated both to cooperate and to compete. Basic to such relations between persons is trust, which is present when an individual perceives the other person as behaving or likely to behave in a helpful manner. The trusting person is more likely to cooperate; distrust leads to competition and attempts to achieve maximum gain for oneself at the expense of the opponent. Cooperation may be used as a strategy, to gain the other person's trust. Or one may behave nonpunitively in response to the opponent's ploys, in the hope of gaining his trust and cooperation. The effectiveness of such strategies varies markedly with the conditions of the laboratory game or the negotiation under way. Making concessions in negotiation has been considered a way of gaining trust. But it has also been argued that making concessions may only lead one's opponent to drive a still harder bargain. As might be expected, the effects of such strategies vary tremendously from laboratory game situations to actual negotiation between nations.

9

Status and Communication

The previous two chapters have dealt with the affectional and the power aspects of relations between persons. Still another dimension of interpersonal relations is *status*. Star athletes are idolized by sports fans; the successful business executive is admired by the average citizen; scientists, professors, and physicians are respected by most people; beautiful women are admired by men; distinguished statesmen command deference from many; and heroes are honored by all. In small groups, the worth of each member is evaluated in an agreed-upon way by all the other members. The form that these evaluations take is known as the *status structure* of the group. The first half of this chapter will discuss the nature of status, identify characteristics of status structures found in groups, and describe processes associated with status.

In addition to affect, power, and status structures, a fourth kind of structuring in groups may be observed. Systematic observation reveals that some members of a group initiate communications more frequently than others. Also, communications are not addressed equally to all; some members receive communications more frequently. Thus, the group may be thought of as having a communication structure. The last half of the chapter will describe a variety of processes associated with that structure. Status and communication structures are related: status is one determinant of the patterns that communications form.

Status

Nature of Status

Status is the worth of a person as estimated by a group or a class of persons. Most often, but not always, the status accorded a person derives from the social category or position that he occupies, such as his occupation or his role as leader of a group. Underlying this estimate of worth is the extent to which his attributes, characteristics, possessions, or role are perceived to contribute to the shared values and needs of the group or class of persons who accord the status to him.

Which attributes contribute to status depends upon the persons making the status evaluation. Status attributes may relate to values and needs shared by only a small group or by a whole society. In our own society, examples of attributes widely regarded as signs of status are beauty, especially in a woman, and the possession of wealth. Examples of attributes whose contribution to status varies from group to group include the following. Among physicians, being a surgeon carries high status; among adolescents, the possession of a car confers status; and among professors, the publication of significant research contributes to status. Attributes are sometimes rather broad, such as beauty in women. These attributes may be broken down into more specific characteristics, in this instance perceptual ones, such as the shape and configuration of facial and bodily features.

Only those attributes that are similarly valued by group members contribute to status. Possession of a unique characteristic which is of value only to one or two other members of a large group does not contribute to a person's status. Suppose, for example, that only two members of a tennis club know how to play chess. Although this skill might be mutually valued by the two members, and each of them might value the other, possession of the skill would not confer any status upon them. On the other hand, the best tennis players in the club would have very high status.

Determinants of Status

Status attributes, like affect and power, may be understood in terms of exchange theory. Among the several bases for status are the capacity of a person for rewarding those with whom he interacts, the scarcity of the capacity, the extent to which he is seen as receiving rewards, the types of costs he incurs, and his investments.

REWARD VALUE OF HIGH-STATUS PERSONS   Persons are accorded high status to the degree that their attributes and behavior are rewarding to an appreciable proportion of group members. The attribute that provides the greatest reward to the greatest number is associated with maximum social approval and thus with maximum status. But an additional element is that these rewarding attributes must also be relatively rare. Certain activities contributing to highly important values of the group are engaged in by all members, and thus no one member gains an advantage in terms of status. Only the attributes in scarce supply confer status. Members of a football team who are average in ability may confer high status on the one man who can save the game through his superior skill at kicking a field goal or completing a forward pass leading to a touchdown. Similarly, on a scientific research team the man with deep insight and brilliance is likely to have very high status because of his ability to solve difficult research problems regarded as insoluble by other members of the team.

Following exchange theory, Blau has suggested that status evaluations arise out of the inability of group members to reciprocate in kind the valuable contributions of those persons with rare but important resources.[1] Receiving these resources leaves members indebted to these persons. The members pay off the debt by being deferential toward the persons with rare resources—awarding them status. This motivates these valuable group members to continue in the group. Davis and Moore have offered a similar theory to explain status levels (also referred to as *social stratification*) in whole societies: Inequalities in prestige and esteem evolve unconsciously in all human societies to ensure that the most important positions are filled by the best-qualified persons.[2]

REWARDS RECEIVED AND COST ABSORBED   Persons are also accorded status depending on the extent to which they are seen as receiving rewards. To the extent that a person is a recipient of things valued by our society, such as high income, he is likely to be accorded status. This appears to stem from the tendency of individuals to evaluate persons in a consistent, holistic fashion: persons having one good attribute are accorded others. Esteem is another type of reward, and to the extent that a person is perceived as esteemed by other persons, he is ranked high in status. Thus, an individual who learns only that another person has received popular acclaim is likely to attribute high status to him.

Persons may be similarly ranked in terms of costs which they experience. The great distinction conferred on a soldier who receives the Congressional Medal of Honor is in direct proportion to his personal sacrifice and disregard for his own safety; often the award is posthumous. Unlike rewards, not all costs contribute to status. Only those costs that assist in the realization of the values of the group and that are not incurred by almost everyone are associated with high status. The soldier who exposes himself to the enemy needlessly, without achieving an objective, is likely to be reprimanded instead of being given a medal. Similarly, such features of an occupation as responsibility and drudgery are both costs, but only the former contributes to high status.

INVESTMENTS   Another feature associated with status is a person's *investments*.[3] Whereas attributes previously discussed have reward value, investments may or may not have intrinsic value. Investments that do not have intrinsic value may acquire value through consensus of opinion. They confer upon a person a right to be accorded a certain status. Examples of investments of this type are race, ethnic background, family, and sex. An investment that is apt to have at least

1. BLAU, 1964*a*.   *2.* DAVIS & MOORE, 1945.   *3.* HOMANS, 1961.

some intrinsic value is *seniority.* Regardless of their intrinsic value, however, it is the value that people attribute to investments that counts. A factory worker who has been on the job a long time expects certain privileges not accorded to relatively new employees. For example, he expects to be paid a higher salary, to receive certain vacation privileges, and in the event of a slowdown in production, to be retained while newer employees are laid off. Similarly, seniority on a faculty carries with it certain privileges. Faculty members with the rank of full professor are more likely to be able to specify the hours during which they will teach, to choose the more interesting courses, and to have larger, more private offices, as well as to be paid higher salaries.

In sum, status arises out of interaction. Persons are accorded high status to the degree that their attributes are rewarding to group members. To contribute to status, however, such attributes must be relatively rare: Only those characteristics in scarce supply confer status. The more a person is perceived as receiving rewards, the higher his status is likely to be. Similarly, high status is associated with absorbing relatively rare costs that contribute to the realization of the values of the group. A person's investments—his past history or background—also contribute to status.

Comparison Processes and Status

Basic to the phenomenon of status is the process of comparison. Persons compare themselves and others with respect to rewards received, costs incurred, and investments accumulated, and they are in varying degrees satisfied or dissatisfied with the comparisons. Homans has suggested that reactions to such comparisons can be understood in terms of two principles: *distributive justice* and *status congruence.*[4]

DISTRIBUTIVE JUSTICE   *Distributive justice* is obtained when the outcomes or profit of each person—his rewards minus his costs—are directly proportional to his investments. Realizing that persons do not generally measure and compare outcomes in such an exacting manner, Homans suggests that in practice a person merely compares his standing relative to another person on these variables, thinking of himself as higher than, lower than, or equal to the other person.

This principle could be stated in terms of the following equation:[5]

$$\frac{\text{My investments}}{\text{His investments}} = \frac{\text{my rewards minus costs}}{\text{his rewards minus costs}}$$

When equality prevails, distributive justice is achieved. Marked inequalities are perceived as unjust.

4. HOMANS, 1961.   5. HOMANS, 1961.

Homans provides from his own research an illustration of how feelings of injustice arise when investments are not proportional to outcomes.[6] Two groups of female employees in a utility company were the ledger clerks and the "cash posters." The groups were equal in pay and in independence, but the ledger clerks were superior in such investments as seniority and knowledge, and their costs in terms of responsibility were also greater. Although their work had more intrinsic interest and more variety, this apparently was not in proportion to their superior investments and costs in accordance with the principle of distributive justice, and they complained about the injustice of being underpaid and not having more independence.

Another investigation of workers in an oil refinery also supports the principle of distributive justice.[7] For example, it was reported that if a comparison person who earned more than the respondent was superior in such investments and costs as seniority and education, only 14 percent of the respondents were dissatisfied when they compared their own wage with his. But if they regarded themselves as equal or superior to the comparison person in investments and costs, 75 percent were dissatisfied with the fact that he earned more.

STATUS CONGRUENCE   That individuals compare their standing relative to that of other persons suggests that a condition Homans calls *status congruence* would prevail in groups. Status congruence is that condition in which *all* the status attributes of a person rank higher than, equal to, or lower than the corresponding attributes of another person. That is, their rankings are consistent with one another. Thus, a faculty member of professional rank expects himself to be not only a better teacher than a young instructor, but also a wiser committee member and a more accomplished scholar. Homans gives an example of a person who is established as another's superior in most status attributes, but who, when in danger of losing his superiority in one of them, exerts himself to maintain his superiority. He notes that in certain supermarkets, full-time workers were paid more and held higher seniority than part-time workers. The attempt to maintain status congruence occurred when a full-time and a part-time worker were assigned the same job. It was well expressed by one of the full-timers: "A full-timer has got to show the part-timers that he can work faster than they can. It's better to work with them than against them, but he's got to show he's a better man."[8]

Status congruence also explains *status symbols.* Characteristics which initially have no status value but which are regularly associated with certain status levels eventually come to be perceived as symbols of status. In an American business corporation, the status of an executive is often associated with such features as the privacy and size of his office, the cost of his office furnishings, and the number of secretaries and telephones assigned to him. The importance of status symbols is illustrated by the report that in one corpora-

6. HOMANS, 1954.   7. PATCHEN, 1961.   8. HOMANS, 1961.

tion, when an executive of lesser rank moved into an office formerly occupied by an assistant vice-president, a maintenance man was sent to the office to remove 1 foot of carpeting from the borders of the room so that the office would no longer have wall-to-wall carpeting, a status symbol reserved for higher-ranking officials.[9]

As in the case of distributive justice, status congruence follows from exchange theory. Individuals have learned that when the various statuses they present to other persons are not consistent, others will behave toward them in an unpredictable manner—sometimes in a rewarding fashion and other times not. For example, a business executive without a college degree may hide or misrepresent his educational background out of concern that others will treat him in accordance with his educational level rather than his level of income and occupation. Thus, Homans' view of status congruence is that persons strive toward a state in which they will be ranked uniformly in all respects because such a state is associated with the rewarding certainty that others will behave consistently toward them.[10]

Much of the research on the effects of status inconsistency or incongruence has been based on the view that status incongruency creates uncertainty and problems in interaction. Undoubtedly, however, some of the findings may also be a product of the reaction of persons to violations of the principle of distributive justice. In an early study, the degree of status congruence among the dimensions of income, occupation, education, and ethnic position was determined for each individual in the group.[11] Persons having low status congruence were found to be politically liberal, which suggests that they were dissatisfied with the present state of affairs, felt frustrated, and sought social change. Persons high in status congruence were less frustrated and more satisfied, and they were more conservative in their politics. Consistent with this is another report of an inverse relation between status congruence and a preference for a change in the distribution of power in society.[12] The lower the status congruence of an individual, the more he desired change.

But more recent research and theorizing has raised some doubts about these conclusions. While some further evidence for the relation between status incongruence and liberalism has been found,[13] other reports yield only a very weak or no relation between liberalism and status incongruence.[14] Such conflicting results are difficult to reconcile and have led to a number of methodological critiques of this literature.[15] A major problem appears to be separating the effects of status congruence from the effects of other associated conditions. For instance, Treiman has suggested that the findings previously cited of a relation between status incongruence and political liberalism can be explained by the tendency of those with low ethnic status to be politically liberal irrespective of positions on other status dimensions.[16]

9. HARTLEY & HARTLEY, 1952.   10. HOMANS, 1961.   11. LENSKI, 1954.   12. GOFFMAN, 1957.
13. LENSKI, 1967.   14. KENKEL, 1956; KELLY & CHAMBLISS, 1966.   15. JACKSON & CURTIS, 1968.   16.
TREIMAN, 1966.

Investigators have attempted to determine the conditions under which status incongruence will have effects. One suggestion is that status inconsistency will prevail only if the dimensions involved are related in such a manner that holding different positions will expose the individual to conflicting expectations; there is some evidence to support this idea.[17] Further, where one dimension of status is made more important or salient, the effects of inconsistency are reduced.[18] Finally, where the resolution of status incongruence would result in an increased inconsistency between one's self and one's role, or would interfere with achieving maximum reward-cost outcomes, status incongruence will be preferred, and the status incongruence will not be disturbing to the individual.[19]

INTERPERSONAL COMPARISON   Basic to the phenomenon of status is the process of interpersonal comparison. It is through periodic comparison with others that an individual eventually develops a clear idea of his status. A person frequently compares himself with others with respect to income, possessions, skills, or other attributes. He does not, however, compare himself with just anyone. He may feel angry or embarrassed if certain persons make more money than he does, but the income of some other persons are of no interest to him. The people with whom a person compares himself and the degree to which he makes comparisons are determined by the principle of distributive justice, the person's perception of his own power, and the conditions allowing for ease of comparison.

Thibaut and Kelley have noted several conditions under which status comparisons are likely to be made.[20] First, each person must be able to observe the rewards, costs, and investments of others so that he can compare them with his own. Second, with respect to a more powerful authority, each person must have approximately the same power to obtain rewards or avoid costs, since this creates a rivalrous condition. Third, a person is likely to compare himself with another whose rewards and costs are not too different from his own. The principle of distributive justice suggests a fourth condition: Comparisons are likely to be made with persons having similar investments, because of the belief that such persons should experience similar costs and rewards. Many small face-to-face groups meet these conditions. Examples include men in prison, minority groups living in ghetto conditions, graduate students in an academic department, pledges in a fraternity, and various work groups in industry. These conditions are also usually met in a family where there is sibling rivalry. Thibaut and Kelley note that sibling rivalry occurs where children require and receive essentially the same treatment from a parent. Any difference in the quantity of rewards received under such circumstances will be highly visible. Sibling rivalry can only be avoided if the parent is scrupulously equitable or if some sort of noncomparability prevails between the children. Such noncomparability is readily accomplished when the age gap between the children is large.

17. SAMPSON, 1963, 1969; BRANDON, 1965.   *18.* SAMPSON, 1969.   *19.* SAMPSON, 1969; KIMBERLY & CROSBIE, 1967.   *20.* THIBAUT & KELLEY, 1959.

People compare costs as well as rewards. This is well illustrated by the child who becomes extremely indignant when his brother is not punished for something for which he himself has been punished. Similar reactions occur in adults, although they may be clothed with pious declarations. If we assume that people incur costs in resisting temptations to commit crimes, a similar comparison of costs may underlie the public reaction of indignation over "easy" treatment of a criminal.

SUMMARY: COMPARISON PROCESSES AND STATUS   Status arises out of comparisons of people's rewards, costs, and investments, through the principles of distributive justice and status congruence. Distributive justice is obtained when the outcomes of each person are directly proportional to his investments. The theory is that if one person's investments are more extensive than those of another, his reward should be greater and his costs higher. Status congruence is a condition in which all the statuses presented by an individual rank higher than, equal to, or lower than all the statuses presented by another person. When these statuses are out of line, other people will behave toward the individual in an unpredictable manner, sometimes in a rewarding fashion and sometimes not.

Some experimental results support the idea that status incongruence and distributive injustice are accompanied by tension, dissatisfaction, and the desire for change, while other results fail to provide evidence of these reactions. This suggests that status incongruence is disturbing only under certain conditions. Studies have shown that when one of the conflicting dimensions is made more salient, or when status incongruence is accompanied by *consistency* between self and behavior, dissatisfaction is not present and the incongruence is not resolved.

Status comparisons are likely to be made when individuals can observe the rewards received and costs incurred by other persons, when everyone has relatively equal power to obtain rewards or avoid costs, and when the rewards and costs of different individuals do not cover too wide a range.

Stability in the Status Structure

Most status structures are quite stable: Each member remains at the same relative level over an appreciable period of time. Stability is a product of a number of sets of processes. One set consists of those processes that ensure status congruence and distributive justice. Forces toward incongruence or injustice are resisted, lending stability to the system. A second set of processes contributes to stability by increasing the value consensus in a group. Since status attributes depend on group values, the greater the consensus with respect to group values, the greater the stability of the system. Third, a person's position in the status structure allows and encourages him to behave in a manner that validates his status.

In addition Benoit-Smullyan and others have called attention to *status conversion* processes, which lead to status congruency.[21] In part such processes involve behaving so that others will judge one similarly on various dimensions of status. An individual may use resources associated with a position on one continuum to advance himself on another, as when a wealthy person uses his money to obtain power, or a teacher uses his disciplinary authority to silence a student who is asking questions he cannot answer. Or a person may carefully monitor his behavior and appearance so as not to behave incongruently. One such instance revolves around the exchange of help among workers. Workers avoid asking help from others whom they regard as their equals, since such requests would imply that they were less competent and deserved a lower status. This phenomenon has been noted among a group of employees in a governmental agency and among employees of a machine shop.[22]

Status congruence is aided by the tendency of perceptual processes to be balanced. Status is likely to be perceived in a global fashion; people who are high in one dimension are seen to be also high on others. Persons presented favorably in terms of one aspect are judged favorably in terms of other aspects. The general idealization of heroes is a more commonplace example: They are not expected to have traits or attributes for which they cannot be admired. These phenomena are consistent with balance theory as proposed by Heider and others (see Chapter 3).[23] Another tendency is to perceive persons who are seen together as having equal status. Benoit-Smullyan notes that servants of a king assume a superior demeanor toward nonroyalty, as if they share the royal blood.[24] Perhaps closer to everyday experience is the nurse who, when dealing with patients, assumes the superior status of her physician-employer.

So far, various internal processes contributing to status congruence have been noted, and it has been suggested that the desire to maintain status provides internal resistance to change. Stability of the system is also in part a function of external factors that produce value consensus. The determinants of value consensus will be more fully discussed in Chapter 10, but their relation to the status structure should be noted here. Obviously those persons high on the various dimensions of status support values related to these dimensions. Not so obvious, however, is that low-status persons support the same values, even though the values are related to dimensions on which these persons are ranked low. The impoverished person who ranks others in terms of wealth is a case in point.

Thibaut and Kelley have suggested a number of reasons for this consensus on values.[25] In part, those who are disadvantageously ranked perceive some prospect of achieving high status in terms of these values. Another support for the values, however, is that they are of functional importance in everyday life. Even though a poor person may maintain that money isn't everything, he

21. Benoit-Smullyan, 1944; Blau, 1955; Homans, 1961.   *22.* Blau, 1955; Zaleznik, Christensen, & Roethlisberger, 1956.   *23.* Heider, 1958.   *24.* Benoit-Smullyan, 1944.   *25.* Thibaut & Kelley, 1959.

knows full well that he would have difficulty getting along with less than he has.

Perhaps a more subtle reason, noted in the previous chapter, is that when the low-status person acknowledges the superior attributes of the high-status person, he reduces the power of that person to some degree.[26] The high status of a person is dependent upon the assent of the low-status persons to the values supporting his high status. Only if they recognize his status does he really have it. Thus the high-status person cannot abuse his position by misusing his power, for he may thereby lose his status. The dignitary given the best table and attentive service in a fine restaurant is in no position to register complaints; in fact, he must recognize that he has been accorded high status by generous tipping. This example illustrates another reason why low-status persons often support the high status of others; they may make direct gains from it. For example, high-status persons in a community must contribute much of their time and money to charity. High-status persons in a business organization are expected to work overtime without extra pay if the work is needed. Thus, the low-status person often escapes many responsibilities and obligations that go with high status.

Several studies suggest that individuals behave so as to validate their status, thus helping to maintain the status structure of the group, as well as their own position. Whyte, in his classic study of a street corner gang, noted that the bowling scores of the members consistently reflected their status when they were bowling with the group but deviated markedly in some cases when they were not bowling with the group.[27] Whyte explained this consistency as a function of the correspondence between a member's confidence and his group status and also as a result of group pressures. When the scores of low-status persons momentarily rose out of line, they were often mercilessly heckled until their confidence was shaken and their performance suffered.

That confidence and status are associated is also suggested by another study which demonstrated that a subject's expectations concerning future performance in a dart-throwing game corresponded to his group status.[28] Finally, a study of a group of boys revealed that members overestimated the performance of high-status boys in a baseball-throwing contest and underestimated the performance of low-ranking members.[29]

A person's ideas of his performance in specific areas are related to more general aspects of self and also to evaluations of him by others. Substantial correlations have been found between a person's performance in several areas of study and his self conceptions of his abilities in general and in specific areas.[30] These conceptions of ability also correlate with the ideas individuals had concerning what other persons thought of their abilities.

26. Blau, 1964*a*.   27. Whyte, 1943.   28. Harvey, 1953.   29. Sherif, White, & Harvey, 1955.
30. Brookover, Thomas, & Paterson, 1964.

SUMMARY: STABILITY OF STRUCTURE   Since status congruence and distributive justice are rewarding conditions, people resist changes that disrupt these conditions, and by doing so they contribute to stability of the status structure. Status conversion processes contribute to status congruency: A person presents himself to others so that they judge him similarly on various dimensions of status, or he uses a resource from one status dimension to advance himself on another. Balance theory suggests that status is perceived in a global fashion: There is a tendency to see all its dimensions in a favorable or an unfavorable light. Association between a person of low status and one of high status is likely to raise the status of the former.

Certain external processes contributing to value consensus among group members also contribute to stability of the status structure. Obviously persons high on the various dimensions of status support values related to these dimensions. But low-status persons also support these values. In part this is because they perceive some prospect of achieving these values. The values are also functionally important in everyday life: They bring rewards and reduce costs. A more subtle factor is that, by acknowledging superior attributes of the high-status person, the low-status person reduces the power of that person. Finally, persons are allowed and encouraged to behave in a manner appropriate to their position in the status structure.

Change in the Status Structure

Status congruence, distributive justice, and value consensus have been discussed from the standpoint of stability, but these same variables together with a fourth, the need for self-enhancement, also have implications for an analysis of change. The need for self-enhancement, which is discussed in more detail in Chapter 17, is expressed in the use of various individual processes to maximize status. A person may present himself so as to increase his status on a particular dimension. He may also misperceive his own characteristics and those of other persons in order to convince himself that he occupies a higher status. Even though such actions may alter an individual's position, they do not interfere with the stability of the status system in a group unless competition for position becomes too disruptive.

Another type of reaction does upset stability, however, since it reduces value consensus. Of the dimensions upon which people are judged, some are more crucial than others. One way in which a person can increase his estimate of his own status relative to others is to place a high value on attributes he possesses, and devalue those that he lacks. The findings from a number of studies suggest that persons do engage in this process. The older worker in industry emphasizes seniority more than education. Persons who have recently become upper middle class emphasize the role of wealth in determining overall class position and deprecate the importance of coming from a family that has been middle class for several generations. When group members emphasize different values in this manner, the status structure becomes less stable.

Value consensus within a group may also be weakened during a period when objective conditions are changing the value structure of the group. Attributes that at one time were important determinants of status, because they were associated with attaining important values and goals and were relatively rare, may no longer carry as much weight. In the early period of a group's existence, for example, the abilities of a "promoter" may lead to high status, but after the group becomes established, administrative abilities may become more important.

Status congruence has been emphasized as a source of stability in the group structure, in that departures from such a state encounter resistance. At the same time, however, status congruence can spread the effects of changes in one dimension to other dimensions. As a new dimension emerges or becomes more important, the ranking on this dimension will exert pressure toward realignment of persons on other dimensions and will thus reestablish congruence at a new level. Similar effects occur as a result of the failure of distributive justice.

Distinctions between Status and Affect Structures

Unfortunately, affect and status have not been clearly separated in studies involving sociometric measurement. Particularly where findings based on different criteria of choice have been lumped together, it is difficult to know whether conclusions drawn apply to the affect structure or the status structure, or both. Yet affect and status involve different sentiments and represent different group structures. There is a subtle but very real distinction between affection and admiration, which the disappointed swain well knows when told, "I admire you immensely but I do not love you."

One distinction between affect and status was established in the discussion of psychegroups and sociogroups. Choices on a psychegroup criterion reflect the relatively idiosyncratic needs of the individual; those involving a sociogroup criterion reflect the shared needs of group members as influenced by task, group, and situational factors. As a result, the psychegroup structure is characterized by a more even distribution of choices and the sociogroup structure by a concentration of choices directed toward certain persons.[31] A study of popularity among adolescents found a much greater concentration of choice on a few persons where the criterion of choice reflected status, and a more even distribution where it reflected liking.[32] This difference between the two structures reflects a difference in the shared bases of evaluation. People accord status to others on the basis of values and needs that are *jointly held* by group members, but they like each other on the basis of relatively unique values and needs.

31. Jennings, 1950.   *32.* Coleman, 1961.

This is not to say that affect is based on completely unique values. Certain persons are widely liked because their behavior meets common needs and coincides with widely held values. But liking includes a sizable component of uniqueness and status does not.

Because of this difference, the status structure is more hierarchical than the affect structure and this, in turn, helps explain why persons are so concerned about their status. Whatever an individual's needs and values, he is apt to find someone who likes him. But if his needs and values are not important to the group, no one will accord him high status. This is true because status is based on agreed-upon criteria, and liking is not. The shared nature of status criteria is crucial here. The moral element peculiar to status, as well as its importance to the individual, follows from this. Status comparisons always involve relative worth. Each person is judged in comparison with his peers. He is evaluated on how well he measures up to widely shared, important values. That the values are widely shared means that other persons will react uniformly to an individual in terms of the degree to which his behavior is consistent with them. Whereas an individual may find some persons but not others whose relatively unique needs and values result in their liking him, he will be accorded higher or lower status uniformly by all persons. Since persons are rewarded to the degree that their behavior coincides with the values of others, status becomes strongly associated with the rewards individuals experience in interaction. Consequently, people learn to become crucially concerned about their status.

Communication Structure and Process

The communication structure is related in certain ways to status. More communication is apt to be directed toward persons of higher or equal status than toward those of lower status. Where the equality of status of two persons is in doubt, they are likely to avoid communicating with each other. As shown below, these relations follow from the processes inherent in the communication and status structures and from factors that simultaneously determine the communication, status, affect, and power structures.

A commonplace observation is that some people talk more than others. Moreover, they address themselves more to some people than to others. Underlying such phenomena is the communication structure of the group. In the past, most social psychological investigations of communication have focused on the determinants and consequences of the communication structure, and its relation to the status structure. Few investigations have focused on the ongoing process of communication, in the attempt to identify the more subtle forms that communication takes. Fortunately, research interest has shifted toward an interest in ongoing process.

Nonverbal Elements in the Communication Process

Recent years have seen an upsurge of interest in the process of nonverbal communication. Birdwhistell has estimated that no more than 30 or 35 percent of the social meaning of a conversation is carried by words.[33] A variety of paralinguistic features of speech, such as tone of voice, inflection, rate of speaking, duration, and pauses, also serve to convey meaning. Similarly, a variety of meanings are conveyed by bodily gesture, dress, and other aspects of the person's appearance. Argyle, in a recent review of the literature, distinguishes many kinds of nonverbal symbols in the communication process.[34] The use of these symbols varies from situation to situation, from group to group, and in various cultures. They include the following:

1. Bodily contact.   Bodily contact includes hitting, pushing, holding, striking, shaking hands, embracing, kissing, touching, and a variety of other activities. Their use varies with the type of relation and situation: compare same-sex and opposite-sex contacts, in public and in private. Bodily contact seems to be somewhat less common in northwestern Europe than in Arabic or Latin cultures.

2. Proximity.   The distance persons maintain in interacting with others serves, among other things, to signal the beginning and end of an encounter. It also appears to reveal the degree to which persons are attracted to each other. Again, there are situational and cultural differences. Conversational distances appear to be maintained at approximately 5.5 feet between two persons placed in a large lounge. In private homes, however, the range is greater, from 8 to 10 feet between chairs.[35] Latins and persons from Arab countries stand much closer when conversing than do northern Europeans.

3. Orientation.   Orientation refers to the angle at which persons sit or stand in relation to each other. People may sit or stand face to face, side by side, or at some other angle. Such positioning appears to reflect the kind of relation between persons. Cooperating persons are apt to sit at a table, side by side. Competing persons face each other, and those conversing prefer to sit at right angles to one another.[36] Again, cross-cultural influences appear, with Arabs preferring the face-to-face or head-on position[37] and Swedes avoiding the right-angle position.

4. Odor.   Odor in the form of perfume or toilet water may be used by women in the Western world, at least, as a sexual attraction signal. Argyle also reports that in some countries the odor of the breath may be used as a signal to invite closer proximity.

5. Posture.   The different ways of standing, sitting, and lying convey a variety of meanings. Conventions governing different situations require particular

33. Birdwhistell, 1952.   *34.* Argyle, 1972.   *35.* Argyle, 1972.   *36.* Argyle, 1972.   *37.* Argyle, 1972.

postural forms. The expected posture for sitting in church or in school differs from postures expected in a more informal context. Posture is often used to convey a superior or subordinate status or to show emotional and affective states such as tension or hostility. Since posture is less well controlled than voice, it may serve as a clue to emotional states which otherwise might be successfully disguised.[38] While to some extent posture, like facial experssion, appears to have universal meaning, there are cross-cultural variations in meaning, particularly as these meanings are affected by conventions governing particular social situations.

6. Head nods. Argyle notes that head nods play an important role both as a reinforcer to another person in a conversation, signifying attentiveness or agreement, and to give the other person permission to carry on speaking.[39] He observes that head nods, like certain other bodily movements, are coordinated between two interactors so that they appear to be engaged in a "gestural dance."

7. Facial expressions. Chapter 2 discussed the ways in which facial expressions contribute to an impression of a person. Argyle observes that facial expressions are used in close combination with speech to emphasize or modify meanings and to provide feedback.[40] Vine has observed that a listener signals his responses to what is being said by small movements of the eyebrows and mouth, expressing surprise, pleasure, puzzlement, disagreement, and other reactions. Similarly, a speaker signals through appropriate expressions the context within which his speech is to be interpreted—whether it is serious, funny, friendly, or cold.[41]

8. Gestures. Hand movements may be another form of speech, as in the sign language used by the deaf. Ordinarily, however, they express emotion or describe objects of special shape, and appear to be closely coordinated with speech. However, in line with Ekman and Friesen, Argyle concludes that such hand movements appear highly idiosyncratic and that they communicate little to the listener.[42]

9. Looking. Visual interaction in the form of intermittent looks, changes in the angle of regard, and direct eye contact play an important part in communication. Not only may eye contact reflect attraction as well as other emotional states, but it appears to contribute to regulating the flow of communication. Kendon has suggested that as conversationalists take turns talking, they signal the end of each turn through eye contact. His research indicated that, as the speaker concluded, he looked directly at the listener as if to transfer the lead. As the listener began to speak, he momentarily diverted his gaze away from the former speaker.[43] Further research by Duncan, however, has revealed that "turns" in conversation are much more complicated. Head direction was more reliably recorded than gaze. And turn signals were displayed not only through

38. ARGYLE, 1972.   *39.* ARGYLE, 1972.   *40.* ARGYLE, 1972.   *41.* VINE, 1970.   *42.* EKMAN & FRIESEN, 1967; ARGYLE, 1972.   *43.* KENDON, 1967.

head direction but also through intonation, extension or shortening of individual syllables, and deviations in intensity or pitch as well as through such body motions as gestures, shoulder movements, facial expressions, foot and leg movements, posture changes, and the use of artifacts such as pipes, papers, clipboard, etc.[44]

Differences between the sexes in their patterns of visual interaction have been reported.[45] Women looked more at a speaker than men, and both looked less when the content of a conversation was embarrassing. In general, one person looks at another considerably more when listening than when speaking. Research also suggests that proximity and mutual eye contact are interchangeable cues to intimacy. As persons come closer to each other, the frequency of their mutual eye contact decreases. Finally, it should be noted that persons appear to be quite sensitive to cues indicating that they are being observed.[46]

10. *Nonverbal aspects of speech.*   A variety of nonverbal or paralinguistic characteristics of speech, including voice tone, loudness, timing, pitch, speech errors, and pauses or hesitations have been studied in terms of how they may serve to convey meanings as well as how they govern the exchange of communication between persons in interaction. Such features of speech as voice intonation add differential emphasis to key words in an experimenter's instructions and serve as one way of conveying his expectations concerning the outcome of the experiment.[47] Voice tone, tempo, hesitancies, and speech errors also appear to convey emotional states.

Finally, the social context should be kept in mind as a source of communication and meaning. Various features of the social context both convey meanings by themselves and also modify and transform the meanings of other elements. Thus, verbal insults traded by persons in the context of friendship or in a situation of friendly rivalry will have quite different meanings from those exchanged by strangers or persons engaged in a serious conversation. That one set of cues may modify another has been emphasized by Haley as well as by Watzlowich, Beavin, and Jackson.[48] They distinguish between communication and metacommunication, the latter referring to communications concerning how a message is to be interpreted. Such messages as "This is an order" and "I am only joking" conveyed verbally or by tone of voice or perhaps by a wink of the eye serve to modify the content of the communication that accompanies them. Unexpected or situationally inappropriate behaviors, including those typically defined as symptomatic of underlying neurotic or psychotic states, are also regarded by Watzlowich and his colleagues as forms of communication, particularly as they convey messages which help define the relation between a person and the others about him.

44. Duncan, 1969, 1972, 1973.   45. Exline, Gray, & Schuette, 1965.   46. Argyle & Dean, 1965; Wardwell, 1963.   47. Duncan & Rosenthal, 1968.   48. Haley, 1963; Watzlowich, Beavin, & Jackson, 1967.

FUNCTIONS OF NONVERBAL ELEMENTS IN COMMUNICATION   One function of nonverbal elements, as pointed out in Chapter 2, is to provide cues to a person's attitudes and traits and to his identity as a person. A second function of nonverbal cues is to help sustain and regulate the communication process.[49] It has already been noted that nonverbal cues play an important role in the regulation of alterations in the flow of conversation between persons. Nods of the head, grunts, and shifts of gaze or tone of voice are crucial. Goffman's description of an encounter illustrates this process:

> An encounter is initiated by someone making an opening move typically by means of a special expression of the eyes but sometimes by a statement or a special tone of voice at the beginning of a statement. The engagement proper begins when this overture is acknowledged by the other, who signals back with his eyes, voice, or stance that he has placed himself at the disposal of the other for purposes of a mutual eye-to-eye activity—even if only to ask the initiator to postpone his request for an audience.
>
> There is a tendency for the initial move and the responding "clearance" sign to be exchanged almost simultaneously with all participants employing both signs, perhaps in order to prevent an initiator from placing himself in a position of being denied by others. Glances, in particular, make possible this effective simultaneity. In fact, when eyes are joined, the initiator's first glance can be sufficiently tentative and ambiguous to allow him to act as if no initiation has been intended, if it appears that his overture is not desired.[50]

Once a conversation is started, nonverbal cues help sustain it by providing a steady stream of feedback information concerning the other person's responses—whether he continues to attend to the message being conveyed through such devices as positive orientation and gaze, reactions of belief or disbelief, and smiles. Nonverbal cues from posture and gestures may also help sustain communication by emphasizing or illustrating points made in the verbal message. Argyle suggests that in the absence of such nonverbal cues, as in a telephone conversation, persons must rely on verbalized *listening behavior* to help sustain the conversation.[51] Thus, we typically hear persons on the phone using such expressions as "I see," "really," and "how interesting."

Finally, under circumstances where verbal communication breaks down, nonverbal communication may serve as a substitute. When high levels of noise interfere with verbal communication or where silence is required, nonverbal systems of communication are apt to arise. In fact, Argyle notes that in some countries, such as Greece, a gestural language has developed which is frequently used for everyday discourse even when speech is possible.[52]

---

49. ARGYLE & DEAN, 1965.   *50.* Reprinted with permission from E. GOFFMAN. *Behavior in public places: Notes on the social organization of gatherings.* New York: The Free Press of Glencoe, 1963. Pp. 91-92.   *51.* ARGYLE, 1972.   *52.* ARGYLE, 1972.

Observation and Analysis of the Communication Structure

Underlying the ongoing communication processes discussed above are various communication structures, considered below.

If over a period of time one were to make a systematic observation of groups such as residents of a dormitory casually discussing campus events, a committee focusing on a neighborhood problem, or housewives talking together during intervals in the day's work, he would note certain regularities in communication among group members. Such regularities constitute the communication structure. If each person's communicative acts were counted, a fair degree of consistency in their frequency would be discovered over time. If in addition to his initiation of communications, the number of times each person received a communication were recorded, certain persons would be observed to receive many more communications than others. The same persons would be likely to address various members and the group as a whole more frequently than the others. If the content of communications were also taken into account, certain systematic differences would be perceived. Some group members would express opinions more often, and others would more frequently request opinions or express agreement or disagreement with the opinions stated.

Bales has provided a method called *interaction process analysis* for observing communication in a systematic fashion.[53] The heart of the method is a system of categories which is presented in Figure 9-1. The system is used to classify the interaction that takes place in a group. Each item of behavior, whether a verbal comment or merely a shrug or laugh, is classified in one of the categories shown in Figure 9-1 and tallied. For each item, the person initiating it and the person (or persons) toward whom he directs it are identified. Bales provides a hypothetical running account of this recording procedure. Here is the first portion of his account:

> Let us imagine we are observing a group of five persons who are meeting together to come to a decision about a point of policy in a project they are doing together. Three or four of the members have arrived, and while they wait they are laughing and joking together, exchanging pleasantries and "small talk" before getting down to business. The missing members arrive, and after a little more scattered conversation the chairman calls the meeting to order. Usually, though not necessarily, this is where the observer begins his scoring. . . .
>
> The chairman brings the meeting up to date with a few informal remarks. He says, "At the end of our last meeting we decided that we would consider our budget before laying out plans in greater detail." The observer, sitting with the observation form in front of him, looks over the list of twelve categories and decides that this remark . . . takes the form of an "attempted answer" to this problem, and so he classifies it in Category 6, "Gives . . . information.". . . The observer has already decided that he will designate the

53. BALES, 1970.

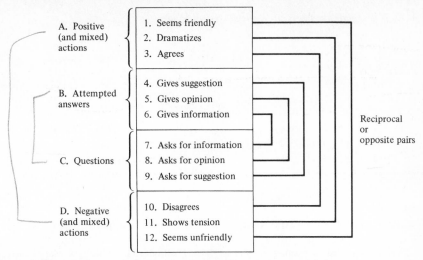

Figure 9-1 *Categories for interaction process analysis. Note: Category 1 was formerly* "shows solidarity," *category 12 was* "shows antagonism," *and category 2 was* "shows tension release." *(Reprinted with permission from R. F. Bales.* Personality and interpersonal behavior. *New York: Holt, Rinehart and Winston, Inc., 1970. P. 92.)*

chairman by the number 1, and each person around the table in turn by the numbers 2, 3, 4, and 5. The group as a whole will be designated by the symbol 0. This remark was made by the chairman and was apparently addressed to the group as a whole, so the observer writes down the symbols 1-0 in one of the spaces following Category 6 on the observation form.

In this one operation, the observer has thus isolated a unit of speech or identified the number who performed the act, and the person or persons to whom it was directed. If he were writing on a moving tape instead of a paper form, as we do for some purposes, he would also have identified the exact position of the act in sequence with all others.[54]

Observations recorded in this manner may be analyzed in a number of ways. One is to construct a "who-to-whom" matrix. In this matrix, shown in Table 9-1, persons are arranged on one axis as initiators and on the other as the recipients of a communication. Many of the empirical studies discussed in the following sections make use of this type of matrix to analyze data.

The Communication Structure and Its Correlates

One investigation combined observations made on a number of groups in a variety of face-to-face situations and put them into one matrix.[55] When partici-

54. Reprinted with permission from American Sociological Association. From R. F. BALES. A set of categories for the analysis of small group interaction. *American Sociological Review*, 1950, **15**, 259-260.   55. BALES, 1952.

Table 9-1   Aggregate matrix for eighteen six-man groups

PERSON ORIGINATING ACTS			INDIVIDUAL RECEIVING ACTS				TOTAL TO INDI- VIDUALS	TO GROUP AS A WHOLE	TOTAL INI- TIATED
	1	2	3	4	5	6			
1		1238	961	545	445	317	3506	5661	9167
2	1748		443	310	175	102	2778	1211	3989
3	1371	415		305	125	69	2285	742	3027
4	952	310	282		83	49	1676	676	2352
5	662	224	144	83		28	1141	443	1584
6	470	126	114	65	44		819	373	1192
Total received	5203	2313	1944	1308	872	565	12205	9106	21311

Source: Reprinted by permission from R. Bales, F. Strodtbeck, T. Mills, & Mary E. Roseborough. Channels of communication in small groups. *American Sociological Review,* 1951, **16,** 463.

pants were ranked according to the total number of acts they initiated, it was found that they ranked similarly on the number of communications they received, the number they directed toward other individuals, and the number they addressed to the group as a whole. Not only did high initiators differ from others in the volume and direction of their communications, but the content of their communications also differed. Those who most frequently initiated acts gave out more information and opinions to other persons than they received, while the remarks of the low communicators more frequently fell in the categories of agreement-disagreement and requests for information.

These features of communication appear to be related to the task facing the group, the conditions under which it functions, the size of the group, the physical arrangements of its members, the members' personalities, the group's normative structure, certain features of the communication process, and the affect, power, and status structures of the group. These factors are discussed below.

SIZE AND PHYSICAL ARRANGEMENT   Group size has been related to several features of the communication structure and to several other communication variables.[56] Two studies suggest that, as size increases, the most active communicators become increasingly active relative to the other group members.[57] In a different task situation this result was not obtained, however, which casts some doubt on the generality of these findings.[58]

The content of the communication also appears to vary with group size. One study found that, as size increased, the frequency of communication increased

56. THOMAS & FINK, 1963.   57. STEPHAN & MISHLER, 1952; BALES & BORGATTA, 1956.   58. MILLER, 1951.

in the categories showing tension release and giving suggestions, and decreased in showing tension, showing agreement, and asking for opinion.[59] Other studies show that smaller groups inhibit the expression of disagreement and dissatisfaction.[60]

As to physical arrangement, a number of studies suggest that proximity or nearness, as well as other physical features which increase the probability of contact, also affects the frequency of communication between members and the amount of interpersonal attraction.[61] Presumably this occurs because of the lowered cost of communicating under these circumstances.

INDIVIDUAL DIFFERENCES IN COMMUNICATION   Individual differences in the rate and length of communication acts appear to be a function both of personality characteristics and of features of the relations among the persons involved. Indices of the temporal pattern of actions and silences of persons in conversations are highly stable, and are related to such gross personality attributes as psychiatric diagnosis. Thus chronic schizophrenics compared to normals have highly irregular action lengths and do not coordinate their action with those of an interviewer.

That the frequency of the individual's contribution depends on the rates of other persons with whom he interacts has also been demonstrated.[62] Rates of communication of the individual are affected by the rates of the other persons in a group: The lower the rates of the others, the higher the individual's rate. Each person, however, appears to have an upper limit which he does not exceed. Klein, in her observation of the frequency of participation of group members, makes the following comment:

> Moreover, it seems as though each member has in mind a standard time which he feels entitled to fill, so that when he feels he has spoken too much, or too little, in the first half-hour of the meeting, he will modify his volubility during the second half in order to average on the whole his self-appointed allowance of communication.[63]

This kind of allotment reflects more than personality factors. It depends on the relation between the partners in a communicative exchange. One study of communication rates between partners who were initially unacquainted and were instructed to get to know each other found the lengths of communications to be inversely related. In other words, if one partner talked frequently, the other reduced his talking.[64] Another investigation suggests that the amounts of time each person spends communicating to the other when closely acquainted are positively related.[65] Bales and Hare compared the interaction profiles of

59. BALES & BORGATTA, 1956.   60. BERKOWITZ, 1958; SLATER, 1958; THOMAS & FINK, 1963.   61. FESTINGER, SCHACHTER, & BACK, 1950; WILNER, WALKLEY, & COOK, 1952; BYRNE & BUEHLER, 1955.   62. BORGATTA & BALES, 1953.   63. Reprinted with permission from J. KLEIN. *The study of groups.* London: Routledge and Kegan Paul, Ltd., 1956. Pp. 166-167.   64. BALES & HARE, 1965.   65. STRODTBECK & MANN, 1956.

various types of groups and found distinct differences in profiles.[66] For example, juries showed more agreement and less tension and antagonism than the average group.

The amount of communication engaged in by the various members of a group has also been related to the affect, power, and status structures. With respect to affect, Bales reports that persons who are high on initiation are also high on popularity and status—their status being reflected by the fact that they are perceived to have the best ideas and to guide the discussion effectively. This is consistent with exchange theory in that such persons move the whole group toward its goals. Another investigator reports correlations between status and frequency of participation.[67] In one study, however, the correlation between participating and being liked was considerably lower than that between participating and being chosen as most productive.[68] This is consistent with Bales' initial findings that the relation between liking and frequency of initiation is curvilinear: The highest initiator in a five-man group was less liked than the person second or third in initiating communication; he was also more disliked than all others.[69] Possibly the highest initiator is perceived as raising the costs of other members by taking too much of the time available for talking.

In Chapter 7, evidence was cited in support of the proposition that, other things being equal, an increase in interaction results in an increase in liking. Here the reverse might be noted: An increase in liking results in an increase in interaction. One investigator created two different types of two-person discussion groups.[70] In one the participants were friends, and in the other nonfriends. The discussion between friends was longer, and each member of the friend pair contributed a relatively equal amount to the discussion. Nonfriends had shorter discussions and less equal contributions. Since interaction leads to liking, and liking to further interaction, such sequential effects should, over time, increasingly restrict communication to group members who are friends. This is consistent with a discussion by Klein, who suggests that in informal friendship groups, the affect structure provides a fairly accurate picture of the communication structure.[71] A study of rumor transmission in a neighborhood group has provided empirical support for this suggestion.[72]

Power, Status, and Communication

The structural variable that has most frequently been investigated in relation to communication is status, although the situations studied often involve differences in power as well. Two studies pertaining primarily to the relation between power and communication will be cited first.

Husbands and wives were studied in a situation requiring them to reconcile

66. Bales & Hare, 1965.   *67.* Bales, 1953.   *68.* Norfleet, 1948.   *69.* Bales, 1953.   *70.* Potashin, 1946.   *71.* Klein, 1956.   *72.* Festinger, Cartwright, Barber, Fleischl, Gottsdanker, Keysen, & Leavitt, 1948.

differences of opinion.[73] This provided evidence for an association between frequency of communication and power. The spouse having the highest frequency of communication most frequently won the arguments. Further empirical support for the association between frequency of communication and power has been presented in an investigation of problem-solving groups.[74] After providing persons variously ranked high or low in talkativeness with a hint about a uniquely good solution to a problem, the investigator found that the more talkative persons were more influential in getting this solution adopted.

Two relations between communication and status may be proposed: (1) Communication is more frequently directed toward persons of high or equal status than toward those of low status, and (2) where the equality of status of two persons is in doubt, they are likely to avoid communication with each other. Evidence for each of these relations is presented below.

A number of investigations suggest that communication is likely to be directed upward in the status and power hierarchies. In each of two studies, status differences were created by telling one group of participants that their task was more important than that of the other group with whom they were working.[75] One of these studies, in addition, created the impression of differences in power by telling low-status participants that the high-status group would determine whether they would be allowed at a later time to join the high-status group. An analysis of written messages exchanged by the groups revealed a clear tendency in both studies for messages irrelevant to the task to be directed upward in the status hierarchy.

Other investigators studied communications between members of different professions attending a mental health conference.[76] Prior to meetings of discussion groups, each participant was asked to estimate how much he felt various other persons would influence him. The individuals perceived to have the greatest potential influence were classified as high-power persons, and those perceived to have little potential influence were classified as low-power persons. Later observation of the frequency and direction of communications demonstrated that subsequent communicative behavior was consistent with these perceptions. Low-power persons more frequently directed communications to high-power persons than to other low-power persons.

Kelley has suggested that one possible reward for communicating upward is that it is regarded as a substitute for moving to a higher status.[77] But the upward flow is due in part to processes inherent in the communication and status structures and to processes that make the communication and status structures interdependent, so that a person's position in one is supported by his position in the other. The mutually reinforcing relation between liking and frequency of interaction has already been commented on. Liking leads to more frequent interaction, and increasing interaction produces more liking. A similar

73. STRODTBECK, 1958.   74. RIECKEN, 1958.   75. KELLEY, 1951; COHEN, 1958.   76. HURWITZ, ZANDER, & HYMOVITCH, 1960.   77. KELLEY, 1951.

relation between frequency of interaction and status appears. Those who frequently initiate communications are more frequently judged as having the best ideas and as doing the most to guide discussion: This should contribute to the status of the high contributor.

Similarly, high-status and low-status persons differ in the content of their communications in a manner consistent with their respective statuses. High-status communicators more often give information and opinion, activities associated with high-status, whereas the responses of the low-status persons are passive, involving such responses as agreement, disagreement, and requests for information.[78] An analysis of the content of messages exchanged between high-status and low-status members also indicated that the high-status members protected their positions by not criticizing their job in messages sent to low-status persons.[79] At the same time the messages from low-status persons admitted confusion over the task, a communication content consistent with low status.

Further indirect evidence indicates that high status is associated with high rates of communication.[80] High-status persons direct their communication toward other high-status persons, while low-status persons, less at ease in interaction, inhibit their responses, and when they communicate, do so mainly to high-status persons. Since high-status persons are more often the recipients of communication, and since such communication normally requires a response, one would expect a high rate of return communication on their part. These various processes converge to account in part at least for the association between a high position in the status structure and an active position in the communication structure.

Several studies document the point that persons who are equal in status are more likely to communicate with each other than with persons having higher or lower status. One study, on the basis of replies to questions asking ninth-grade and tenth-grade girls whom in their own grade they would like most to talk with on a number of designated topics, produced the matrix shown in Table 9-2.[81] Participants were arranged in order of status on the vertical axis as initiators of communications and on the horizontal axis as recipients of communications. The figures in the cells represent the proportion of topics they would like to talk about—in other words, the desired amount of communication. The matrix provides quantitative evidence that persons are most likely to receive communications from others having a status equal to their own, and also that persons at all status levels prefer to direct communications toward others having higher status. This evidence may be observed if the matrix is examined in the following way. First, from the increasing figures in each row, it is clear that persons at all status levels prefer to communicate with those having higher status: The higher the status of the recipient, the more communications are

78. Bales, 1952.   79. Kelley, 1951.   80. Hurwitz et al., 1960.   81. Riley, Cohn, Toby, & Riley, 1954.

Table 9-2 **Status and the desire to communicate**

STATUS OF INITIATOR		STATUS OF RECIPIENT					
		Low 0	1	2	3	4	High 5
Low	0	**0.07**	0.26	0.22	0.26	0.41	0.49
	1	0.11	**0.26**	0.26	0.26	0.47	0.60
	2	0.07	0.20	**0.38**	0.42	0.54	0.69
	3	0.07	0.18	0.36	**0.62**	0.76	0.81
	4	0.05	0.19	0.33	0.52	**0.81**	0.88
High	5	0.04	0.16	0.25	0.39	0.66	**1.36**

Source: Reprinted by permission from Matilda W. Riley et al. Interpersonal orientations in small groups: A consideration of the questionnaire approach. *American Sociological Review,* 1954, **19,** 715-724.

directed to him. Second, in each column except the first, the highest figure falls on the principal diagonal of the matrix. Thus the largest number of communications is received from persons having a status equal to that of the recipient. Presumably it is least costly to communicate with persons of equal status. Communication upward is hazardous; people are never sure that the high-status person will behave in a rewarding fashion. Equals have sufficient counterpower to ensure equal exchange.

The second point—that when the equality of status of two persons is in doubt they are likely to avoid interaction—was a suggestion by Homans.[82] Interaction is potentially costly, because a person might come out of it with a demonstrably lower status. If he avoids interaction, he can at least preserve a precariously balanced subjective equality of status. One study of power relations and desire for interaction between professions provides some support for this idea.[83]

The Normative Structure and the Communication Process

A whole structure of rules or norms of conduct specify appropriate linguistic behavior. These include not only the grammatical rules of a language, but also those rules regulating the content and frequency of messages between persons which governs the flow of interaction. In part these arise in response to features of the affect, status, and power structures previously described. In part, however, they are intrinsic to the rules of the participants in a particular institutional structure. The latter is illustrated by the flow of communication in most classrooms when it is expected that the teacher will lecture and the students

82. HOMANS, 1961.   83. ZANDER, COHEN, & STOTLAND, 1959.

listen. Less obvious is the role of such normative elements in less institutionally structured gatherings, ranging from an assemblage of persons in a park or on a busy street, through persons at a cocktail party, to those participating in a ritual such as a funeral or a wedding. In such instances, the communication behavior of persons is governed by a variety of rules which dictate the degree to which each person has communicative access to others, the degree of mutual involvement permitted, the amount of attention that must be paid to the purposes of the larger gathering, etc. These rules are the subject of books on etiquette and have recently been the subject of a study by Goffman in his penetrating analysis, *Behavior in Public Places*. He describes the norms of civil inattention governing the communication and resultant organization of interaction among strangers on a street or other setting where they are in visual contact with each other.

> What seems to be involved is that one gives to another enough visual notice to demonstrate that one appreciates that the other is present (and that one admits openly to having seen him), while at the next moment withdrawing one's attention from him so as to express that he does not constitute a target of special curiosity or design.
>
> In performing this courtesy the eyes of the looker may pass over the eyes of the other, but no "recognition" is typically allowed. Where the courtesy is performed between two persons passing on the street, civil inattention may take the special form of eyeing the other up to approximately eight feet, during which time sides of the street are apportioned by gesture, and then casting the eyes down as the other passes—a kind of dimming of lights. In any case, we have here what is perhaps the slightest of inter-personal rituals, yet one that constantly regulates the social intercourse of persons in our society.[84]

Similarly he notes that norms govern the accessibility of each person to the others in a social setting. These norms provide for access, but at the same time protect each person from unwelcome intrusions and also provide for graceful disengagement. Commenting particularly on rules governing the termination of a conversation, Goffman says:

> Just as the individual is obliged not to exploit the accessibility of others (else they have to pay too large a price for their obligation to be accessible), so he is obliged to release those with whom he is engaged, should it appear, through conventional cues, that they desire to be released (else they have to pay too great a price for their tact in not openly taking leave of him). A reminder of these rules of leave-taking can be found in elementary school classrooms where leave-taking practices are still being learned, as, for exam-

84. Reprinted by permission from E. GOFFMAN. *Behavior in public places: Notes on the social organization of gatherings.* New York: The Free Press of Glencoe, 1963. P. 84.

ple, when a teacher, having called a student to her desk in order to correct his exercise book, may have to turn him around and gently propel him back to his seat in order to terminate the interview.[85]

Summary: The communication structure

Groups existing for any length of time have a definite communication structure. Individuals show consistency in the number of communications they receive, the number they initiate, and the content of the communications they initiate. Frequency of communication is associated with the status a person has in a group; the higher his status, the more likely he is to initiate and receive communications. Normally, however, individuals with the highest status are not the best liked. The larger the group, the more the disparity between the high and the low communicators.

Individual differences in communication rates are associated with variations in personality as well as the individual's place in the affect and status structure of the group. In addition, communication rates are affected by the degree of conformity to group norms.

Positive affect toward others is likely to be associated with a high amount of communication: friends communicate more with friends than with nonfriends. In informal friendship groups the affect structure closely resembles the communication structure. Two relations between communication and status have been found: (1) Communication is more frequently directed toward persons of high or equal status than toward those of low status, and (2) where the equality of status of two persons is in doubt, they are likely to avoid communication with each other. These relations follow from the processes inherent in the communication and status structures and from processes that simultaneously determine the communication, status, affect, and power structures. In part these are exchange processes. Communication occurs among equals because each has sufficient counterpower to ensure equality of exchange. Communication is often directed upward because of the greater reward-cost outcomes that may be derived from communication with a high-status group.

---

85. Reprinted by permission from E. Goffman. *Behavior in public places: Notes on the social organization of gatherings.* New York: The Free Press of Glencoe, 1963. P. 110.

10

Emerging Norms and Conformity

Members of all groups exhibit certain regularities in their patterns of interaction. A close look at these patterns reveals that they often involve behavior which is considered desirable by group members. Further, they often involve behavior in which members exert pressures upon one another to conform to some recognized standard. Such regularities in group behavior have been explained in terms of *social norms*. A social norm is an expectation shared by group members which specifies behavior that is considered appropriate for a given situation. In this context behavior is broadly conceived to include not only overt behavior, but also verbal behavior associated with an individual's perceptions, thoughts, or feelings. Small groups not only set appropriate standards for overt behavior, but also attempt to control the words, feelings, and thoughts of members. For example, a child is apt to be censured by his parents not only for hitting his brother, but also for saying that he hates him. Similarly, most groups censure expressions of disloyalty exhibited by their members.

As an illustration, norms typical of a fraternity may be described. A fraternity is likely to consider the following appropriate: making moderately good grades, dating girls from certain sororities but not others, helping on fraternity projects, having feelings of loyalty toward the fraternity, being congenial with fraternity brothers, and believing that one's own fraternity is the best on the campus. Behaviors such as being placed on probation for poor grades, dating girls from the "wrong" sorority, refusing to cooperate on fraternity projects, disliking the fraternity, and fighting with fraternity brothers are likely to be regarded as inappropriate.

Closely associated with social norms are the mechanisms through which they are enforced. Of interest in this discussion are the means by which group members communicate to others the nature of appropriate and inappropriate behavior and the ways in which they exert pressure on other members to conform to the norms. Also important are the conditions that maximize or minimize these norm-defining and norm-enforcing processes. This chapter will focus primarily on these processes and conditions, while Chapters 13 and 14 will focus upon norms as rules of conduct, in connection with the topic of social roles.

Norms and Norm Formation

The formation of a norm as a frame of reference against which one's perceptions are evaluated may be illustrated by a well-known laboratory experiment conducted by Sherif.[1] In each trial, three persons were taken into a dark laboratory room and told that a point of light would appear, move a short distance, and then disappear. Their instructions were to call out the number of inches they thought the light had moved. The light was turned on repeatedly at intervals, and the participants made a judgment each time. They were not asked to respond in any particular order; each gave his judgment as soon as he was ready.

Although individuals started out with somewhat different judgments in the experimental situation, after a number of trials the differences were narrowed down. Ultimately, judgments made by the three individuals were within an inch or two of each other. For example, on the first appearance of the light, one individual may make a judgment of 2 inches, another a judgment of 12 inches, and a third a judgment of 8 inches. But repeated presentations of the light result in a gradual shift in the judgments of all three until they stabilize around a mean, say, of 7 inches, with a range from 6 to 8 inches. Thus members of this small group eventually agree with respect to the distance that they believe the light moves on each trial.

The judgments in the experiment pertain to a well-known perceptual effect. A stationary point of light shown briefly and repeatedly in a dark room will appear to move, a phenomenon known as the *autokinetic effect*. Thus the participants have no real basis for judging the amount of movement: The light is actually stationary. In the absence of clear perceptual cues upon which they might base their judgments, participants apparently turn to each other for guidance. Many groups have been studied in this basic situation and in related ones, and the end result is nearly always consensus on some very narrow range of judgments (see Figure 10-1). This agreed-upon range has been referred to as a *social norm*.

A number of observations may be made about these laboratory norms. If an

1. SHERIF, 1948.

Figure 10-1 *Convergence of judg-ments of the autokinetic effect in a two-person group. The difference be-tween the mean judgments of two persons computed over each succes-sive block of ten trials is shown. (Data from which the figure was pre-pared were taken from an unpub-lished study by D. Schweitzer.)*

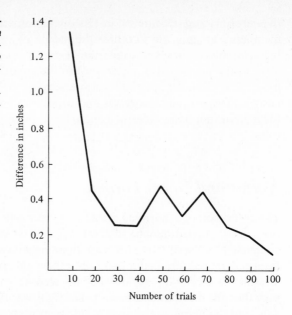

individual has formed a norm in the group situation and on a later occasion is tested alone, he still responds in terms of the norm. If participants each form their norms in individual situations, however, and are later placed together in a group, they will gradually change these individual norms to arrive at a common group norm. Another noteworthy fact is that most individuals in this labora-tory situation state that they have *not* been influenced by the judgment of the other persons. Thus, this experiment demonstrates that a small group of per-sons, faced with a novel ambiguous situation, will in a short time arrive at a normative interpretation which they share. Moreover, this occurs without the participants being aware of having influenced one another, and the norm per-sists in later situations.

That actual pressures toward consensus are present in this situation has been demonstrated in several experimental variations. In one variation, a naïve indi-vidual was paired with a high-status person who, by arrangement with the experimenter, established a norm at one point and then deliberately shifted to another. The naïve participant was observed to follow the high-status person's judgments. If norms were shifted too often and too radically, the naïve individ-ual became very uncomfortable, presumably because he experienced a conflict over whether to conform to his subjective experience or to the judgments of the high-status person. Finally, the amount of change in this situation as well as in other situations where a person is exposed to the opinions of others appears to be related to the size of the discrepancy between the two opinions. A small discrepancy between two or more participants appears to have little or no effect on subsequent judgments, moderate discrepancies have significantly greater effects, large discrepancies have little or no effects again, and extremely large discrepancies have large negative or boomerang effects.[2]

Forces toward Norm Formation

That individuals in the laboratory who are confronted with the autokinetic situation will arrive at consensus has been clearly demonstrated. Moreover, consensus is arrived at in many other situations where individuals interact with each other, both in the laboratory and outside. A major aim of this chapter is to explain *why* persons in interaction gradually acquire certain uniformities in their behavior.

Pressures toward conformity in the behavior of group members arise whenever reward-cost outcomes are likely to be adversely affected by nonconformity. Such pressures are likely to arise for behavior relevant to the achievement of group goals. For example, rules against all members of a committee talking at once are obviously needed. Or in a squadron of military planes, strict conformity to carefully defined maneuvers is essential if accidents are to be avoided. These examples involving goal-relevant behavior are obvious, but we have already noted that there are pressures toward conformity of one's thoughts and feelings. We may ask, for example, why one's *opinions* or *beliefs* tend toward conformity.

Physical versus Social Reality

Festinger has postulated a drive within human organisms to evaluate their opinions.[3] He notes that having incorrect opinions can be punishing or even fatal. An example of punishing consequences would be the false belief that the girl you are dating is in love with you. This may lead to highly embarrassing, inappropriate behavior on your part. Fatal consequences are illustrated by the occasionally encountered opinion, "I didn't think the gun was loaded."

There are two sources that we rely on to determine the validity of our opinions: physical reality and social reality. We use our senses to obtain a good deal of information about the physical environment; to some extent, our opinions are validated by such information. But a second source of information is other persons. To a large extent, they interpret the world for us. When we are children, our parents warn us of dangers in the environment and explain away our unfounded fears. They also direct us toward rewarding aspects of the environment. Ultimately we learn to lean heavily on the opinions of others to validate our own. An important difference between physical and social sources of information is that social reality is often less certain: Frequently there is little consensus among the opinions of other persons.

The relative weights of these sources of information vary with different cir-

2. WHITTAKER, 1964*b*.   3. FESTINGER, 1950, 1954.

cumstances. Experimental research, discussed below, indicates the factors that account for variation in the extent to which a person may depend upon physical or social reality. In general, if clear stimulus cues are provided for a perceptual judgment, or if information is provided leading to an obviously correct answer, the individual is not much influenced by the judgments of other persons. When the stimulus material is difficult, however, or is structured so that the correct answer is not very clear, as in the autokinetic situation, the individual is more prone to rely upon judgments by other persons. However, social pressure may vary in different circumstances. Unanimous opinion is especially powerful and may be shown to shape an individual's responses even where his senses indicate that he is making an error. This is demonstrated in the classic study by Asch.[4]

A college student entered the laboratory along with seven other students and was seated at the end of the row. The experimenter explained that the investigation concerned the ability to make certain perceptual discriminations. Sets of lines of varying length were presented and compared with a "standard" line. In each set the particular line that equaled the standard line was to be chosen. Individuals called out their judgments by identifying the correct line. A series of eighteen different sets were shown and judged.

During the first few trials, the student found the judgments to be simple and obvious—any dolt could see which line was equal to the standard. To his great dismay, however, he discovered that on the next trial, the line that he saw as obviously correct was not chosen by the other students; they unanimously agreed on a line that was unquestionably longer than the standard line. In fact, as the experiment continued, he found that the rest of the group agreed with his perceptions on only one-third of the trials.

Most persons placed in these circumstances felt great pressure to disregard their own perceptions and to conform to the rest of the group by choosing answers that seemed obviously wrong. About one-half of them yielded somewhat to this pressure, conforming to the group on two or more of the trials. One-fourth of the participants conformed on four or more trials. Others resisted the pressure, although not without great discomfort. What the participant did not know is that the other seven students were in the confidence of the experimenter, who had previously arranged with them to make wrong judgments. In this experiment, the powerful social pressure from the unanimous consensus of the seven other students frequently led an individual to conform even though the stimulus situation was clear and unambiguous.

A variant of this experiment was designed to test the point made earlier: that judgments easily made from clear and unambiguous information would be less susceptible to conformity pressures than judgments having a basis only in social reality.[5] Also, more difficult judgments should exhibit more conformity than easy judgments. In this study, each individual heard the responses of four

4. Asch, 1956.   5. Blake, Helson, & Mouton, 1956.

other persons by means of earphones. He was under the impression that the other four were in adjoining rooms, although actually all their responses were tape-recorded. Since his judgments were made after he heard theirs, he was subject to their influence. Each individual (1) responded to a simple task (the number of clicks of a metronome), (2) expressed attitudes having a basis only in *social reality* (answers to questions about war and peace), and (3) solved arithmetic problems varying in difficulty. The experimenter arranged matters so that the simulated group responses concerning the metronome and arithmetic items were frequently wrong, and so that the attitude items were frequently unpopular (unpopularity was determined by the answers of a standardization group like the experimental subjects).

As might be expected, when presented with the metronome and arithmetic items, participants were less prone to conform to the wrong responses given by the group than they were when presented with attitude items. On the trials where the simulated group gave the wrong answer, 57 percent of the individuals nevertheless made the correct choice of metronome clicks, and 63 percent gave the correct answer to the arithmetic problems. But in the expression of attitudes, only 20 percent chose the answers preferred by the control group. A large proportion of the remainder chose the response unanimously presented by the simulated group on the tape recording. Similarly, greater conformity to simulated group responses occurred for the more difficult arithmetic items than for the easier ones. Many other experiments, with different materials and situations, have yielded similar results.[6] There is some doubt whether matters of taste or preference, such as esthetic judgments of drawings, are subject to conformity pressures. One experiment[7] failed to find conformity on such judgments; however, another investigation requiring judgments of beauty did demonstrate conformity tendencies.[8]

It may be concluded that the greater the anchorage of a judgmental situation in unambiguous stimulus information, the greater the resistance to conformity pressures will be. This resistance will be lower the more difficult the information is. Judgmental situations anchored only in social reality will exhibit considerable conformity behavior.

Mechanisms Underlying Conformity

Of special interest are the mechanisms underlying conformity in laboratory situations such as those discussed. Deutsch and Gerard have pointed out that in the typical laboratory experiment on social influence, such as those of Sherif and Asch, two quite different processes might operate.[9] One is *normative influence*, which occurs when an individual conforms to an expectation of another

6. CRUTCHFIELD, 1955; WEINER, CARPENTER, & CARPENTER, 1956; KELLEY & LAMB, 1957; COLEMAN, BLAKE, & MOUTON, 1958; PATEL & GORDON, 1960; RADLOFF, 1961.　　7. CRUTCHFIELD, 1955.　　8. MADDEN, 1960. 9. DEUTSCH & GERARD, 1955.

person or group because of the satisfying feelings it generates. But they note that participants in these experiments did not form a group in the sense that they faced a common task requiring cooperative effort. Rather they were individuals merely in the presence of one another, each making his own judgments "independently."

This suggests that another form of influence might well have been important in bringing about conformity: *informational influence.* This occurs when information from an outside source is accepted as evidence about reality. These two kinds of influence can be thought of as separate: An individual may conform to another person's judgment because he finds it satisfying or avoids embarrassment, or he may conform because he thinks the other chose the correct answer. Our previous discussion suggests that informational influence will be maximized to the extent that the judgmental situation is anchored only in social reality—a situation where there are no objective facts to contradict the information provided. Clearly, this condition is met in Sherif's experiment on the autokinetic effect, but not in Asch's experiment on the judgment of lengths of lines.

An experiment conducted by Deutsch and Gerard partly succeeded in creating situations where only one form of influence was allowed to operate.[10] A comparison of these situations made it very clear that the tendency of the participants to conform was in large part due to informational influence. Normative influence also played a part, of course, since it is difficult to eliminate this source completely. This experiment contrasted a public condition with an anonymous one. More conformity to the judgments of the other group members occurred under the public condition in part because of the participant's unwillingness to publicly disagree, and in part because the other's judgments were used as a guide to the correct answers.

Also apparent from this investigation were processes leading to resistance to influence, called *counternorm effects.** One process producing resistance was *self-commitment.* Before being exposed to the judgments of other persons, participants wrote their judgments either on a paper which was to be handed in to the experimenter or on a magic pad which they erased after each judgment. Both of these forms of commitment reduced conformity to the judgments of other participants.

In another report, Gerard points to a more subtle form of self-commitment taking place in the presence of the group: Once having made a decision, a participant feels constrained to persist in choices consistent with it. He concludes as follows:

Once having made a decision, and having acted on the basis of it, any change or reversal by the subject during subsequent trials would be inconsis-

---

* Deutsch and Gerard refer to an individual's own expectation as a source of influence, and call it *normative influence.* A far less confusing term is *counternorm effect.*

10. Deutsch & Gerard, 1955.

tent with his initial decision, and perforce with the considerations that generated that decision in the first place, since the basic conditions from trial to trial remain relatively unchanged. A change in behavior would also necessarily rearouse the original conflict, forcing the subject to again work through the same doubts and misgivings. The initial decision, then, commits the subject, although not irrevocably, to yield to the group or to be independent whenever the same two alternatives present themselves on succeeding trials.[11]

The individual supports his stand by generating appropriate evaluations of himself, the other person, and the latter's evaluation of him. If he chooses to be independent, he tends in time to view his own performance favorably, that of others whose judgments disagree with his unfavorably and perceive that they evaluate his performance unfavorably.

Though in the initial studies by Asch it was assumed that normative influence stemmed from the group, one investigator has shown that individuals appear also to be subject to unintentional normative influence from the experimenter. Such an effect decreases conformity to the groups since individuals expect that the experimenter will evaluate them relative to their making a correct or an incorrect response.[12] Finally, we might note that an individual who behaves independently is not necessarily following his own evaluation of the information. Instead, he might be deliberately taking an anticonformist stand.[13]

Opinions are especially subject to strong conformity pressures when they conflict with behavior that is highly relevant to maintaining the group or achieving its goals. A group member's pessimism concerning ultimate achievement of the group goal may interfere with active efforts of the group to achieve its goal. On the other hand, opinions that have little relevance to maintenance of the group or achievement of its goals are likely to arouse only weak conformity pressures.

While norms often lead to punishment of deviant behavior, norms may under certain conditions reduce costs. Thibaut and Kelley have pointed out a subtle advantage of establishing norms to guide interaction.[14] Consider two persons who cannot simultaneously achieve their best outcomes; for example, a husband who wants to go to the movies and a wife who wants to go dancing. This situation requires the use of power by one party to extract desired behavior from the other. But the constant use of personal power, which is costly, is not necessary if they can agree on a rule for trading, so that on one occasion they go dancing and on another to the movies. Ultimately agreement on this trade manifests itself in a regular sequence of behavior. If the sequence is interrupted, the injured party appeals to the rule to restore the appropriate sequence.

11. Reprinted with permission from H. B. GERARD. Deviation, conformity and commitment. In I. D. STEINER & M. FISHBEIN (Eds.), *Current studies in social psychology.* New York: Holt, Rinehart and Winston, Inc., 1965. P. 264.   *12.* SCHULMAN, 1967.   *13.* THIBAUT & KELLEY, 1959.   *14.* THIBAUT & KELLEY, 1959.

As Thibaut and Kelley note, such norms are excellent substitutes for personal influence.[15] A good example is found in the recent trend toward formal or informal marriage contracts, favored by the woman's liberation movement. The argument is that, in an ordinary marriage, where the rights and obligations of each party are not spelled out, much conflict is generated by the partners' different conceptions of their obligations and rights. This conflict leads to repeated maneuvering in attempts to influence the partner to behave in the desired fashion. The recommended contracts would consist of a list of the obligations and rights of each partner, jointly and explicitly agreed upon by both partners. These essentially constitute norms for the dyad in question.

The advantage of such norms is that they would eliminate the continual power struggle that would otherwise prevail. Instead of attempting to influence the partner through the exercise of power, an appeal need only be made to the prevailing norm. The appeal to enforce an action is to an impersonal norm rather than to another person. Since exercises of power are always based on exchanges, they typically engender obligations. That is, each exercise of power may gain compliance from the other party, but it leaves the wielder of power open to some form of exchange. An appeal to a norm does not have this consequence, and so both parties reduce their costs by establishing a norm.

Some norms serve the purpose of identifying group membership. The satisfactions that persons experience when conforming to such norms stem from the feeling that one belongs to a group whose membership is valued. Conformity to rules of etiquette and to those governing correct speech signifies membership in polite, middle-class society, just as conforming to the norms of toughness may signify one's status in a lower-class boys' gang.

Norm-sending Processes

According to Thibaut and Kelley, norms typically develop in a situation where persons would not ordinarily adopt the attitudes or behavior in question.[16] There is no need for group controls when persons spontaneously produce certain behaviors of their own accord. But where the environment provides little structure, or where individuals have some resistance to performing particular actions that are necessary to group functioning, normative processes emerge to provide structure or to ensure that the behavior will be carried out. The operations by which norms are communicated and enforced have been termed *norm-sending processes*.[17] Norm sending has three essential components: (1) defining the attitudes or behavior in question, (2) monitoring the extent to which a person conforms to the norm, and (3) applying sanctions (reward or punishment) for conformity or nonconformity.

Norm sending may occur in many different ways. One example is that of direct, explicit norm sending. The instructor in a class may indicate exactly

15. Thibaut & Kelley, 1959.   *16.* Thibaut & Kelley, 1959.   *17.* Rommetveit, 1955.

what reading is expected of the class members, what kinds of examination questions must be prepared for, and what attendance is expected. Similarly, the parent in part transmits certain norms to his child in explicit verbal terms. He is not to tell lies, to make faces, or to break household furnishings. Much norm sending, however, involves *indirect* communication. Norms for appropriate behavior on the part of a graduate student illustrate this process.

The graduate student is expected to be highly responsible and capable of independent study and work. Absence from seminars and failure to perform assigned tasks are violations of the norm. He is also expected to have a serious attitude toward his work and the profession for which he is preparing. If certain incidental behaviors on his part do not seem consistent with these expectations, faculty members are likely to have a low opinion of him. For the most part, however, these expectations are not conveyed to the new graduate student in so many words. Aside from evaluating the student's task performance through assignment of grades, the faculty communicates the norm by example and through various subtle sanctions.

In the first place, the professor who is enthusiastic about his research and who spends a lot of time at it sets an example for the graduate student. By giving heavy assignments, he makes clear that he expects a great deal of work from the student. In particular, he watches for signs of resistance to such tasks and ridicules typical objections or excuses commonly used by undergraduates. For example, the graduate student who asks how many pages an assigned paper should consist of is likely to be met with a raised eyebrow.

In the second place, most graduate students participate in some sort of professional employment under the supervision of professors. Under many professors, the assistant soon finds that his personal life is to be subordinated to his job. He is on call at any time, including weekends or holidays, should the work require it. He is likely to be given a brief period and a firm deadline for completing an arduous task. No questions are asked about other commitments that he might have; they are automatically assumed to be subordinate.

Thus, while normative expectations held by faculty members toward graduate students are not usually expressed in so many words, the "norms are sent" to the student through example, through assignment of tasks, and through indirect sanctions applied to inappropriate conduct. Incidentally, this illustration is not meant to imply that the faculty member is the only norm sender. Other graduate students also serve an important function in this respect.

Summary: Norms and Norm Formation

A *social norm* is an expectation shared by group members which specifies behavior that is considered appropriate for a given situation. Social norm is broadly conceived to include not only overt behavior, but also verbal behavior associated with an individual's perceptions, thoughts, or feelings. Pressures toward conformity in the behavior of group members arise whenever reward-cost outcomes are likely to be adversely affected by nonconformity. Such pressures are likely to arise for behavior relevant to the achievement of group goals.

Norms also control opinions and beliefs, especially where they are relevant to maintenance of the group or achievement of its goals. A basic human requirement appears to be the need for validation of one's opinions. Although clear information from the physical environment contributes to the satisfaction of this need, the behavior of other persons also provides a source of validation. Particularly in situations where he is uncertain or confused—where he does not know how to react—a person can turn to the behavior of other persons to observe a stable world. This social reality provides him with a reference point for his own behavior. The more ambiguous the nonsocial stimulus situation, the more likely he is to depend on social reality for orientation.

Operations by which norms are communicated and enforced have been termed norm-sending processes. Norm sending has three essential components: (1) defining the attitudes or behavior in question, (2) monitoring the extent to which the person conforms to the norm, and (3) applying sanctions (reward or punishment) for conformity or nonconformity. Norms may be communicated and enforced in a considerable variety of direct or subtle ways. Two forms of influence operating in small groups are (1) informational influence, where an individual accepts some information about reality from another person, and (2) normative influence, where an individual conforms to the expectations of another person.

A Theory of Normative Behavior

Any theory that attempts to account for the normative character of social interaction must answer three questions about the focus, extent, and distribution of conformity in a group.

1. What determines the kinds of behavior or attitudes that become targets of norm sending? This question is dramatized by observations of the tremendous variability from group to group in the areas for which conformity is demanded. This is especially apparent for groups with widely different cultures; in fact, the fascination of the study of other societies lies largely in the differences between their norms and ours. But illustrations from our own society also make the point. In some areas, individual variability is little constrained by norms. It matters little which shoe we put on first in the morning; no one cares what color pajamas we wear or which side of the street we walk on; and we may assemble our meals from a wide variety of foods without being censured. In other areas, individual variability is severely curtailed. In certain occupations, men must wear suits, shirts, and ties. When eating in the company of others, people are expected to observe certain rules of etiquette. An adequate theory must explain why some behaviors and attitudes are subjected to normative control and others are not.

2. Why is much greater conformity to norms found in some groups than in others? To illustrate, some religious groups conform much more strictly to the tenets of their faith than others. Similarly, the amount of discipline and obedience to orders is greater in some military units than in others. An adequate theory must explain these differences.

3. What determines the distribution of conformity *within* a group? To illustrate again with religious behavior, some members of the same church practice their religion more faithfully than others. Some college students carry out assignments and attend classes more regularly than others. In any social group such as a fraternity chapter, certain members conform more closely to normative demands than others. Thus, some members do more than their share of committee and project work.

These three questions, then, deal respectively with the focus, extent, and distribution of conformity to norms. Again relying extensively on concepts from exchange theory, we can answer them in terms of the effects of four conditions: (1) the degree to which group members find the behaviors or attitudes of other persons rewarding or costly, (2) the power structure of the group, as determined by the distribution of resources, dependencies, and alternatives, (3) the degree to which behavior in accordance with the norm is intrinsically rewarding or costly, and (4) the degree to which behavior is open to surveillance and to imposition of sanctions.

The next three sections discuss the focus, extent, and distribution of conformity in terms of the four conditions outlined above.

Areas in Which Norms Emerge

Norms have a variety of *indirect* reward-cost outcomes, such as making the continued exercise of interpersonal power unnecessary, or helping to affirm a person's group membership. A more extended discussion of conformity theory would include a consideration of these indirect outcomes, but the present treatment will emphasize the more direct outcomes related to needs arising in the process of group formation and development.

REWARDS AND COSTS OF CONFORMITY   Persons form groups to satisfy a variety of needs. Normative controls arise in the areas of behavior where members have become dependent upon the group for need satisfaction. These norms encourage behavior that maximizes member satisfaction and discourage behavior that might interfere with satisfaction. The prevalence and strength of the norms depend in part upon the extent to which members rely on the group for satisfaction of the particular needs aroused, and in part upon the strength of these needs.

Groups generally serve one or both of two types of needs: task-related needs and social-emotional needs. Behaviors that contribute to accomplishment of a group task are likely to be subjected to normative control, for they lead to achievement of the group goals and satisfaction of the members, as well as to avoidance of failure. Thus norms develop to ensure cooperative action and to establish consensus on attitudes relevant to group goals. For example, members of a group must be required to attend meetings fairly regularly if the group is to survive. Members elected to office must be willing to serve; others must be willing to work as committee members. Consequently norms develop to encourage regular attendance and acceptance of service to the group, and sanctions are applied for failure to meet these task needs.

That the necessity for successfully achieving group goals leads to norm development is dramatized by Sutherland's classic study of the professional thief.[18] Behaviors that would result in failure and arrest have strong negative sanctions, while those that are essential for success are mandatory. For example, when thieves collaborate on a job, strict punctuality is a must. Failure to appear at the appointed time and place endangers the success of the enterprise and might even lead to arrest. Thus there is no waiting among thieves, and sanctions are likely to be applied to the person who fails to show. Similarly, professional criminals require each other to remain aloof from acquaintance with strangers or neighbors. A growing acquaintance with noncriminals lessens the anonymity of the criminal and might ultimately lead to detection and arrest of him and his associates.

Quite different needs are satisfied in groups formed largely for social-emotional satisfaction. These groups strongly emphasize individual needs, such as needs for friendship and love, for opportunities to share one's triumphs and defeats, and for belonging, acceptance, and support. Examples of this type of group are fraternities and sororities, which emphasize social needs like friendship and shared activities, and the family, which emphasizes emotional support. In such groups, norms arise to encourage fair treatment and to prohibit competition and aggression. Thus fraternity brothers are not supposed to compete with each other for the affection of the same girl. In the family, strong sanctions are applied against aggressive actions of the children toward each other or toward their parents.

The distinction between task-related and social-emotional needs should not be thought of as absolute; most groups in part satisfy both needs. For example, it has been shown that industrial work groups provide some emotional support to the individual workers that counteracts various anxiety-producing aspects of their work environment.[19]

POWER STRUCTURE OF THE GROUP   The attitudes and behaviors that are necessary to the satisfactions of the most powerful persons in the group are most likely to be subjected to normative control. For example, in a family with small

18. SUTHERLAND, 1937.   19. SEASHORE, 1954; ROETHLISBERGER & DICKSON, 1939.

children, norms develop in directions desired by the parents rather than the children, because of the great discrepancy in power between them. As the children reach adolescence and young adulthood, however, the norms change as a result of a shift in the balance of power towards more equality. This occurs because of the increase in alternative satisfactions available to the young person, who finds increasing emotional satisfactions in his peer groups, and because of his reduced economic dependence on his parents when he obtains a job. These norm shifts are illustrated by the adolescent's criticism of some of the parents' behaviors and by the greater freedom he has in the hours he keeps and the activities he participates in which are not supervised by his parents.

INTRINSIC COSTS AND REWARDS   Certain behaviors are less susceptible to control than others by virtue of the fact that they are intrinsically associated with very high rewards or costs other than those derived from conformity. Thus, these behaviors produce rewards or costs that, compared with positive or negative sanctions from other members, have a relatively large effect on the total satisfaction experienced by the person. Any behavior associated with powerful biological or social motives may fall into the high-reward class. Thus, smoking, which becomes a persistent habit difficult to break and which probably receives support from physiological drives, is unlikely to be successfully prohibited through legislative or other normative controls. Costly behaviors, too, are often exempt from normative control; other persons cannot reasonably *require* an individual to perform the behavior. For example, a commando mission behind enemy lines is not regarded as a normative requirement, and only volunteers are assigned.

When behavior is very costly, norms are likely to arise to reduce cost. For example, the medical student finds himself burdened with far more to do than he can possibly accomplish. Under these circumstances, he has to make decisions about what shall have priority. But this is a common problem for all medical students. In this instance, to avoid excessive competition from brilliant students, the group members are likely to develop norms concerning how much work they will perform and what aspects of their work shall have priority, as well as norms ensuring cooperation with each other in sharing the work burden.[20]

Similarly, where present normative behavior leads to unsatisfactory reward-cost outcomes, old norms may fade and new norms providing more satisfactory outcomes may arise. A number of students of deviant subcultures have elaborated the process by which old norms are supplanted by new ones.[21] Fundamental to the initiation of this process is a lack of integration between the normatively approved means and goals in a group: Behaving in the approved

20. BECKER, GEER, HUGHES, & STRAUSS, 1961.   *21.* COHEN, 1955; MERTON, 1957*b;* CLOWARD & OHLIN, 1960.

manner does not result in effective goal achievement. For example, the young, relatively untrained worker who adopts the middle-class norm that one should strive to move up the economic ladder through hard work may not find anyone willing to employ him. Where many individuals find themselves in this situation, they may in interaction with each other develop new normatively approved means of their own that do lead to goal achievement, or perhaps they may collectively develop new normatively approved goals that they can achieve with the means available to them.

Patterns of gang delinquency have been explained in this fashion. Lower-class boys or members of minority groups blocked in attempts to achieve the success goals of the dominant middle-class culture collectively fashion a set of normative expectations, a way of life containing means and goals that are functionally compatible. Such means as stealing and such goals as obtaining kicks from drugs, while disapproved by the larger society, become approved means and goals within this delinquent subgroup.

SURVEILLANCE AND SANCTIONS   Obviously, attitudes and behaviors that are difficult to monitor are less likely to be subjected to normative control. Sanctions cannot be applied unless transgressions are noted. Thus one's public or overt behavior is controlled by norms to a greater extent than one's private behavior or beliefs. The importance of surveillance may be illustrated by comparing open hostility with the indirect expression of aggression. The latter occurs much more frequently. Open hostility toward another person, such as physical violence, is easily observed and sanctions are readily applied; but various subtle forms of aggression, such as criticism in a context of pretended well-meaning, are difficult to detect and to punish.

SUMMARY: THE FOCUS OF CONFORMITY   Persons form groups to satisfy a variety of needs. Normative controls arise in the areas of behavior where members have become dependent upon the group for need satisfaction. In groups that have primarily a task function, for example, norms develop to ensure cooperative action and to establish consensus on attitudes relevant to goals. In groups that have predominantly a social-emotional orientation, behaviors providing emotional support, friendship, or love are more likely to be subjected to normative control. Attitudes and behaviors that are necessary to the satisfactions of the most powerful persons in the group are apt to be supported by norms.

Behaviors that are associated with powerful physiological drives or that are very costly are difficult to subject to normative pressures. In situations where costly behavior is necessary to achieve group goals, norms are likely to arise to minimize costs for members. Where present normative behavior has relatively unsatisfactory outcomes, norms are likely to be modified to produce more acceptable reward-cost outcomes. Finally, behaviors that are difficult to monitor are less likely to be subjected to normative control.

Degrees of Conformity in Different Groups

The second question which any theory of normative behavior must answer is why much greater conformity is found in some groups than in others. Why, for example, are discipline and obedience to orders greater in a military unit than in a classroom group? The answers to this question are again found in the four conditions previously enumerated. The first is the degree to which members find the behavior of other persons in the group rewarding or costly.

REWARDS AND COSTS OF CONFORMITY   Festinger, Schachter, and Back have suggested that the extent to which a group can exert pressure on its members to conform to some norm is limited by the cohesiveness of the group.[22] In Chapter 7 cohesiveness was defined in terms of forces acting on a member to remain in the group. Several bases of attraction to the group were noted: (1) high reward-cost outcomes stemming directly from interaction between members, (2) group activities that are rewarding for their own sake, and (3) membership in the group as a means to attaining other ends. Attraction is also relative to the comparison levels of group members. The total force operating on group members to remain in the group is a function not only of these outcomes internal to the group, but also of the outcomes available in alternative relations outside the group.

Since the strength of the negative sanctions that a group can exert on its members is limited by the strength of the forces that hold members in the group, we might expect that the severity of the negative sanctions that a group can impose on a recalcitrant member would vary with the strength of cohesive forces. Cohesion, in turn, depends on the degree to which the reward-cost outcomes of members exceed their comparison levels. Casual observation of groups that are able to impose severe negative sanctions on their members supports this formulation. In such groups, members have high outcomes, or very low comparison levels and comparison levels for alternatives, either because they can command little in alternative relations or because alternatives are blocked.

Most adolescent groups have high outcomes for individual members, since they often provide satisfaction for powerful needs and are highly cohesive. Military units, religious sects, and prisoner groups have members with low comparison levels and comparison levels for alternatives. The alternative to conformity in a military situation is often a court martial and imprisonment, or a dishonorable discharge. Members of religious sects often have low alternative sources of satisfaction.[23] This may be true because their distinctive values and behavior patterns make interaction with outsiders more costly or because they are rejected by other groups. Consequently the sect may very effectively control

---

22. FESTINGER, SCHACHTER, & BACK, 1950.   23. POPE, 1942.

its members through such techniques as ostracism should they attempt to deviate from sect norms. Similar considerations apply to prisoner groups, since a prisoner is forced by assignment to prison blocks to associate with certain other prisoners, and he has no alternative associations.

A closely related point is that membership in groups other than the one in question may make conformity in that group costly. This is the case where the groups have conflicting norms. For example, if a person belongs to a fraternity which subscribes to the notion that the proper grade for a gentleman is a C, and if he also belongs to a campus group which stresses scholarship, he may find conformity to the norms of the latter group costly. From this line of reasoning it would seem that to the extent which a group discourages its members from association with other groups that have conflicting norms, it elicits a higher degree of conformity from its members because of reduced cost.

Various empirical studies have presented systematic evidence that pressures toward conformity behavior are stronger in a more cohesive group. One investigation determined the uniformity of attitudes and behaviors in campus housing groups which had various degrees of cohesiveness.[24] It was found that the more cohesive the group, the more uniform the attitudes and behavior of the members. Moreover, in the more cohesive groups, those who deviated from the norm were less likely to be accepted as friends.

Exchange theory suggests that the reason why conformity to the opinions of group members is greater in a group with high cohesiveness than in a group with low cohesiveness is that, in the former, conformity is more rewarding and deviation, more costly. Where cohesiveness is high, members place more value on such rewards as being liked. And if conforming to a given norm is required for being liked, members of a very cohesive group may be expected to conform.

An experiment supports this interpretation.[25] In one condition, members of two groups, one high and one low in cohesiveness, were led to believe that agreeing with the opinions of other members was important for being liked. In another condition, members of groups high and low in cohesiveness were led to believe that agreement was irrelevant to being liked. Under the condition where agreeing with other members' opinions was important for being liked, the great majority of members in the group with high cohesion conformed to tape-recorded opinions represented as coming from participants like themselves. But under the same condition in the group with low cohesion, whose members did not care whether they were liked or not, there was no such tendency toward conformity. Moreover, in the other highly cohesive group, which had been led to believe that agreeing with opinions was unimportant to being liked, members showed no tendency to conform. Thus, we may conclude that conformity to a group norm is a function of the extent to which conformity to that norm is thought to be rewarding.

24. FESTINGER et al., 1950.   25. WALKER & HEYNS, 1962.

POWER STRUCTURE OF THE GROUP   Since the degree to which persons in a group are able to influence each other is dependent on the basis of power that exists between members, group conformity might be expected to vary with such bases. Some empirical studies support this expectation, as discussed below. To the extent that the power structure of the group is based on forms of power that increase over time, the conformity level of group members may be expected to be high. Where the prevailing modes of control have bases that lose effectiveness over time, the level of conformity may be expected to be low.

Extensive use of coercive power initially increases the likelihood of conformity—particularly public compliance—but used repeatedly, arouses resistance to conformity. At the same time, the exercise of coercive power reduces the level of attraction. One laboratory investigation relates the use of coercive and legitimate power to conformity.[26] To establish a basis for the legitimate and illegitimate exercise of power, participants who had agreed to serve in an experiment were informed what fines would be levied for working too slowly. When the supervisor levied fines outside this legitimate range, resistance to conforming to the norm increased. We might infer from these findings that an important condition for minimizing resistance to conformity to the norm is that sanctions perceived as illegitimate be avoided. Another study suggests that reward is more effective than punishment in bringing about conformity, mainly because of the resistance aroused by the use of punishment.[27]

Coercion in a laboratory situation is rather mild. An exception to our generalization about the ineffectiveness of coercive power for normative control may occur under extreme conditions of coercion: The basis of power may be converted to referent power. Some individuals imprisoned for a long time in Nazi concentration camps in World War II strongly *identified* with their captors: they adopted some of their attitudes and behaviors, and even incorporated pieces of Gestapo uniforms into their dress. In large part this probably occurred because the tremendous coercive power possessed by camp guards could be used as reward power. In the terminology of reinforcement theory, *avoidance of a punishing contingency* is rewarding. Thus, by easing up various constraints, sometimes in exchange for informing or other cooperative behavior, captors exercise powerful reinforcements. Where this continues over a period of years, it is not surprising that this coercive power is converted into referent power.

In those instances where normative controls are based primarily on referent power from the start, groups are likely to exercise strong conformity pressures over a long period of time. This accounts for the durability of parental control in most families and the relative permanence of an individual's religion. Referent power also controls a broader range of behavior compared with expert or coercive power.

26. FRENCH, MORRISON, & LEVINGER, 1960.   27. ZIPF, 1960.

INTRINSIC COSTS AND REWARDS   In groups where behavior that happens to be in conformity with group norms is rewarding for its own sake, conformity is likely to be high. This is often characteristic of groups where satisfaction of social-emotional needs is dominant, or in task groups where the tasks themselves are enjoyable. Examples of the former are fraternities and sororities; of the latter, sports clubs. Where conformity involves behavior that is costly, however, as where tasks are boring, fatiguing, or dangerous, conformity is likely to be at a lower level, unless the costs of nonconformity are correspondingly increased. In work situations where sanctions for nonconformity are weak, the level of conformity to official norms concerning production may be low. This line of reasoning is often used as an argument against seniority, tenure, and civil service systems, which protect the worker against severe sanctions.

SURVEILLANCE AND SANCTIONS   Where conforming behavior is not intrinsically satisfying or is costly in terms of time, fatigue, or tedium, surveillance becomes necessary. Unless behavior is monitored in some way and sanctions are imposed for failure to conform, such behavior is unlikely to occur. An obvious example is the military group, where many activities are not satisfying for their own sake. Similarly, most work situations have organized systems of surveillance and sanctions. Factory workers punch time clocks to provide a check on their working hours, whistles are blown to indicate the start and end of work shifts, and foremen and supervisors monitor the work operations to ensure a minimum interruption of work activities.

As the type of work becomes more intrinsically satisfying, surveillance and sanctions are much less evident. Various skilled crafts and professional work activities illustrate the point. For example, the skilled craftsman works with a minimum of supervision and control, and there is little monitoring of the teaching activities of the professor. If these people are not intrinsically motivated, they are unlikely to do a good job.

Research suggests that another type of condition may make surveillance unnecessary. In a study where individuals felt that they were moderately accepted by other members of the group and that they had a possibility of becoming completely accepted, a high degree of conformity to the norms in *both* public and private behavior was found.[28] On the other hand, persons who had a very low degree of acceptance and who perceived the likelihood of being rejected by the group conformed very closely to the norm in their public behavior, but deviated markedly in private. Thus it appears that it is possible to create certain types of motivating conditions that will lead a person to conform both publicly and privately, without the necessity for surveillance. Where the major motive for conformity is insecurity over status, public conformity is likely to be high, but conformity in private behavior is unlikely to occur.

Two other conditions that require careful surveillance if conformity is to

28. DITTES & KELLEY, 1956.

occur are the exercise of coercive power and the exercise of nonlegitimate power. Under conditions of surveillance, these processes are likely to create public compliance accompanied by marked resistance which expresses itself in sharp dissension in private attitudes. Several experiments support this conclusion.[29]

SUMMARY: CONFORMITY IN DIFFERENT GROUPS   To the extent that conformity is costly, forces exerted toward it cannot exceed forces to remain in the group. Chapter 7 established that the latter forces are a function of the cohesiveness of a group. Several forms of attraction may contribute to cohesiveness: (1) high reward-cost outcomes stemming directly from interaction between members, (2) group activities that are rewarding for their own sake, and (3) membership in the group as a means to attaining other ends. Cohesiveness is also based on the comparison levels of group members, and the total force operating on group members to remain in the group is a function not only of attraction to the group, but also of the outcomes available in alternative relations outside the group. It is clear that the extent to which groups may exert negative sanctions for nonconformity depends upon their cohesiveness. Both casual observations and more formal investigations are consistent with this view.

Conformity also varies markedly with the power structure of the group and with the bases of power. Referent power is more likely to lead to relatively enduring conformity, while coercive power is likely to produce temporary conformity under conditions of surveillance only. Extreme coercion, however, may be converted to referent power. The exercise of coercive power leads to the accrual of resistance to conformity. Possibly the resistance arising to coercive power is essentially a weakening of other forms of power, such as referent power. Finally, the continued exercise of power may produce shifts in reward-cost outcomes that strengthen or weaken the power relation.

Groups vary markedly in the extent to which the behavior relevant to their functions and goals is intrinsically satisfying. In groups where behavior that happens to be in conformity to group norms is rewarding for its own sake, conformity is likely to be high. This is often characteristic of groups where satisfaction of social-emotional needs is dominant, or in task groups where the tasks themselves are enjoyable. Where conformity involves behavior that is costly, conformity is likely to be at a lower level. Finally, where conforming behavior is not intrinsically satisfying, surveillance becomes necessary.

Distribution of Conformity in the Group

The third question which must be answered by a theory of normative behavior is why there is variation among group members in the extent to which they conform to norms. While answers to the first two questions resided largely in

---

29. RAVEN & FRENCH, 1958*a;* FRENCH, MORRISON, & LEVINGER, 1960.

group processes, the question of individual differences in conformity within different groups requires attention to both group processes and personality factors. Certain group conditions, such as the power structure of the group, may increase or decrease variation among members. But personality factors also play an important part in variation through their relation to structures or processes that characterize a particular group. This section considers both group and individual factors in explaining the distribution of conformity.

REWARDS AND COSTS OF BEHAVIOR   As already shown, where outcomes experienced in the group are high and those available in alternative relations are low, uniformity occurs in the behavior and attitudes of the members. Thus, all members conform to approximately the same degree. Where cohesiveness is low, however, a much wider variation in conformity is likely to occur. Those members who have important satisfactions outside the group will frequently deviate from the norm, as will members who do not find much satisfaction in the group. This is illustrated by a study of books on psychology written by ministers and books on religion written on psychiatrists.[30] The study showed how each person developed attitudes *deviant from the norms of his group*. For the ministers, psychology or psychiatry was an important nonmembership reference group; for the psychiatrists, religious groups were important reference groups. Thus allegiance to outside groups is likely to produce deviation from the norms of one's group. Another illustration is the previously cited study of pressures toward conformity in housing groups: The occupants showing least conformity to norms were found to have more affiliations with outside groups.[31]

Another factor making for individual differences in conformity is the varying pressure exerted upon different persons in the group. When a member of a group begins to deviate from normative behavior, other members place increasing pressure on him to conform.[32] In terms of exchange theory, this occurs because his deviant behavior has reduced the rewards and increased the costs of other members. If, however, he behaves in an increasingly deviant fashion, a certain point on a continuum of deviance is reached where pressures toward conformity are reduced, and he is rejected.[33] In part, this may be a function of another principle for which there is fragmentary evidence, namely, that pressures on a person toward conformity are associated with the perception of the likelihood that he will conform.[34] If a person is thought of as a "hopeless" deviant, pressures to conform are rather light; attempts to elicit conformity from him are too costly in time, energy, and frustration. Such a person, if he remains in the group, has a very low status and at the same time experiences very little pressure toward conformity.

Individuals also vary in their susceptibility to conformity pressures. The research literature on this topic indicates that susceptible individuals are sub-

30. KLAUSNER, 1961.   31. FESTINGER et al., 1950.   32. FESTINGER, 1950.   33. SCHACHTER, 1951.
34. FESTINGER, 1950.

missive, not very self-confident, little inclined to nervous tension, authoritarian, not highly intelligent, not very original, low in need achievement, high in need for social approval, conventional in values, and high in need for conformity.[35] To the extent that a group has members who vary markedly in these characteristics, it is likely to have a greater variability in conformity.

Personality or other individual differences, however, are not always associated in the same way with conformity; their effect varies with the situation. Thus, a study of individual conformity dealt with three different tasks: a perceptual judgment task, self-reports of agreement with peer-group norms, and self-estimates of acceptance of pressures from authority. A small but consistent trend was found for persons who conform in one situation to conform in the other two.[36] A similar investigation of conformity in a variety of situations suggests that the small correlations typically observed in studies of this sort are accounted for by those persons who are at the extremes of the conformity-nonconformity distribution, and that the conformity of most people who lie between these two extremes is greatly influenced by situational variables.[37]

Finally, the more important the norm, the less deviance from it will be permitted. Where norms concern less crucial values, we may expect more people to deviate, creating more variability in conformity by group members. This idea is indirectly supported by data on opinions discussed in Chapter 4 showing that the amount of deviant opinion on crucial issues is comparatively small.

POWER STRUCTURE OF THE GROUP   Various studies support the view that the higher the status of a person, the more likely he is to conform to group norms. For example, high school students who are best liked are seen as having the greatest proportion of conforming traits,[38] campus leaders reflect most closely the values of the college community,[39] high-status workers in an industrial work group conform most closely to the output norms of the group,[40] and politicians reflect the values of the voters.[41] Verba suggests that this demand for greater conformity on the part of leaders arises from their central role in the group, especially their function as representatives and spokesmen for the group.[42] In this role they must represent group opinion, not their own desires.

Another facet of the role of the leader, however, requires him to break away from the norms at times. He has the greatest contact with parts of the social system external to the group. Under some circumstances, the group must change if it is to function efficiently. Then it is the role of the leader to introduce changes in the norms. Hollander has pointed out that although the leader must deviate from group norms in order to bring about changes, he is at the same time *conforming* to the expectations the group has about his role.[43] Hollander has made some further progress toward resolving the apparent paradox

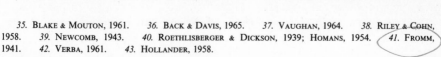

35. BLAKE & MOUTON, 1961.   *36.* BACK & DAVIS, 1965.   *37.* VAUGHAN, 1964.   *38.* RILEY & COHN, 1958.   *39.* NEWCOMB, 1943.   *40.* ROETHLISBERGER & DICKSON, 1939; HOMANS, 1954.   *41.* FROMM, 1941.   *42.* VERBA, 1961.   *43.* HOLLANDER, 1958.

in findings that a leader is often both a conformist and a deviate. In the early phases of interaction, a leader is likely to conform in order to build up status and power. In this process, he builds up credit—a preponderance of attitudes toward him on the favorable side. In later stages of interaction he can engage in some deviant behavior, using some of his favorable credit balance in the process.

This idea might also be expressed in terms of the "security" of the leader. One study has shown that when the security of the leader of a delinquent gang is threatened, he conforms closely to the group norms.[44] On the other hand, a leader whose position cannot be shaken may engage in deviant behavior at little cost. To a large extent, the security of the leader is a function of the basis and amount of power he has. For example, where he exercises leadership because he has expert knowledge or because his power is legitimate, he is freer to depart from the norms of the group. Also, he is less free to deviate if his status is based on the ability to satisfy the social-emotional needs of members, and more free if his status is based only on task competence.[45]

The degree to which high-status persons are pressured to conform also depends on the behavior in question. High-status persons are apt to be punished less than others in the group for minor infractions, but more than others where their behavior prevents achievement of important groups goals.[46] Homans has discussed at some length the amount of conformity exhibited at various status levels.[47] He concludes from a number of studies that both high-status and low-status people conform less than those intermediate in status. In these studies, persons with varying degrees of acceptance from the group had to choose between: (1) an answer which appeared to be correct but which differed from reported group judgments and (2) an apparently wrong answer, favored by group members. For persons at each status level (level of acceptance by the other members), Homans enumerates rewards that they might anticipate and costs that they risk incurring.

Whether he goes along with the group or whether he acts independently, a high-status person has little to lose if his choice is later shown to be wrong; he can spend some of his credit. But if he acts independently and his choice turns out to be correct, he validates his high status. Thus the balance of potential outcomes for high-status persons favors nonconformity in this situation.

Similarly, whether he goes along with the group or acts independently, a low-status person has little to lose if he turns out to be wrong. Since he is already at the bottom of the status hierarchy, he cannot be lowered further; moreover, wrong behavior on his part might even be ignored. If he conforms to the group and turns out to be right, little is gained; he has only behaved like other members. If he acts independently and is proved correct, he has the

---

44. Short, 1961.   45. Back & Davis, 1965.   46. Wiggins, Dill, & Schwartz, 1965.   47. Homans, 1961.

satisfaction of showing up the rest of the group. For him, the balance of outcomes favors nonconformity.

For the person of intermediate status, aspiring to move toward the top level, rewards and costs are otherwise. If he goes along with the group and turns out to be right, he adds a slight increment to his status. If he is wrong, he loses little in company with other members. But if acts independently and is proved wrong, he suffers an appreciable loss of status; he does not possess the credit standing of the high-status member, and unlike the low-status person, he has plenty of room to move downward. This risk outweighs any benefits he might achieve through an independent, correct decision. The balance of outcomes in his case favors conformity.

A study of the relation between conformity and sociometric status in cliques of delinquent boys yields further evidence in support of this association between status and conformity. When persons in first, second, and last positions in cliques of four or five boys were compared, nonconformity was found to be greatest for the highest-status boy, next greatest for the lowest-status boy, and least for the second-highest boy.[48]

So far, then, this discussion has favored Homans's view that persons of moderate status conform more than persons of high or low status. The relation between one's status and the degree to which he conforms, however, is also influenced by the source of status: Does it come from inside the groups, from outside the group, or from both sources? Source is important because the rewards and costs are different depending on source.

The importance of source of status has been demonstrated by Emerson in a study of conformity in which individuals were asked to judge the distance between lights in a dark room before and after exposure to a fictitious group norm.[49] The participants were Boy Scouts who knew each other and who belonged to patrol groups. The status of each boy was determined by the number of times he was chosen by boys in his own patrol and boys from other patrols. Low-status boys (who received few choices from either source) were strong conformers. Moderate-status boys (who received many choices from one but not both sources) did not conform, and high-status boys (who received frequent choices from both sources) did conform. Thus, high conformity was associated with high and low status, but not with moderate status. This is just the opposite of Homans's view, supported by a study of delinquent boys.

Emerson explained these findings in terms of his power dependence theory, described in Chapter 8. Persons who were valued in their own group and also desired by the members of other groups had maximum power. One way by which group members can reduce such a person's power relative to their own is to accord him status. To the degree that the powerful person becomes dependent on the esteem of the others in his group, he will be subject to conformity

48. HARVEY & CONSALVI, 1960.   49. EMERSON, 1964.

pressure. But those not valued by both these sources have less power and less status to protect, and so are freer to deviate. These processes would only be expected to operate in established groups, and not in briefly joined laboratory groups of strangers. Further, the study of delinquent boys mentioned earlier differs from the Boy Scout study in that the delinquent boys did not have status outside their own group.

INTRINSIC COSTS AND REWARDS   Some group members gain intrinsic satisfaction from the performance of normative behavior, not only because conforming brings rewards from other group members and leads to accomplishment of group goals, but also because the behavior satisfies certain needs that the person has. In a social-emotional group which has norms of friendly, cooperative behavior, persons with high needs for affiliation enjoy behavior that happens to conform to the norm. For some other members, normative behavior may be singularly unrewarding. For example, persons with marked hostility feelings may find it difficult to conform because of the need to express their hostility. In task groups, persons who have strong achievement needs and who are skilled in the appropriate group activities may experience pleasure in carrying out the tasks. But unskilled persons may experience too much difficulty and frustration in the task group.

Essentially, what we have described is an interaction between group processes and personality characteristics that produces different reward-cost outcomes for conforming behavior on the part of various group members. A number of studies support this exchange-theory interpretation of conformity in terms of intrinsic motivation. For example, one investigation has shown that persons made to feel accepted by a group are more attracted to it if they have low self-esteem, and they conform to a greater extent.[50] Presumably these members have a greater need for acceptance, possibly because they perceive fewer alternatives. Two other studies have shown that persons with strong needs for social approval conform to a greater extent than those with less strong needs for approval.[51] Similarly, more self-confident persons in a task group are less dependent on the judgment of others and conform to a lesser extent.[52]

Another study has identified two patterns of reaction leading to conformity.[53] One represents a process of *social accommodation*, where a drive to maintain positive relations with people who are liked contributes to conformity. The other process is one of *self-correction*. The individual perceives a discrepancy between the opinions of others and his own as a piece of information that can be used to arrive at a "correct" opinion. These processes of social accommodation and self-correction resemble another suggestion: Conformity may be primarily a reaction to the source of the communication (a person) or to the communication itself.[54] Persons reacting to the source are thought to be

50. DITTES, 1959.   *51.* MOELLER & APPLEZWEIG, 1957; STRICKLAND & CROWNE, 1962.   *52.* BRAY, 1950; HOCHBAUM, 1954; SMITH, 1961.   *53.* WILSON, 1960.   *54.* McDAVID, 1959.

motivated by a need for acceptance, those reacting to the communication, by a need for success.

These distinctions parallel those already drawn between what Deutsch and Gerard have called *normative influence* and *information influence,* and may well explain other differences among persons in conformity.[55] Thus, the finding that first-born males who are more achievement-oriented conform to a greater degree is understandable.[56] Males with a higher need for achievement are likely to perceive a testing situation as a test of achievement. This is apt to make them more subject to informational influence, particularly if the situation is sufficiently ambiguous for them to doubt their own judgment. While in this study first-born males were not found to be higher on affiliative needs, other studies[57] have found this to be the case. Thus, it could be argued that first-borns might also be more subject to normative influence as well.

The concept of alienation is relevant to this discussion. One author suggests that alienation has three components: powerlessness, social isolation, and normlessness.[58] He found that scales measuring these components are highly correlated, indicating that deviation (normlessness) may frequently be a function of powerlessness and social isolation. Another investigation indicates that the extent to which a person conforms is a joint function of the strength of his need for affiliation with other persons and various conditions of social support.[59] Thus, when a person has a strong need for affiliation and is unanimously opposed in attitude by other members, he changes his attitude to join with the other members. When group members are divided, however, there is little change in his attitude. Or if the high-affiliation member has a single partner who supports his position in opposition to the majority, he does not shift toward conformity. Individuals low in the need for affiliation do not conform to the attitudes of a unanimous majority opposed to them. These findings are consistent with exchange theory, especially if the reasonable assumption is made that individuals with low needs for affiliation with other persons find satisfactions alternative to the feeling of being accepted. In some cases, such persons may even obtain some perverse satisfaction from *not* being accepted by others.

SURVEILLANCE AND SANCTIONS   The extent to which the position of a group member exposes him to public view would appear to be important in determining conformity. Certain kinds of high-status positions are subject to monitoring and punitive action. For example, school principals and civic or governmental officials feel strong pressures to conform to certain norms. Only in the sense that the position itself calls for behavior deviant from that of other persons are they relatively free not to conform. Certain other types of leadership positions,

---

55. DEUTSCH & GERARD, 1955.   56. SAMPSON & HANCOCK, 1967.   57. WRIGHTSMAN, 1960.   58. DEAN, 1961.   59. HARDY, 1957.

however, are less public in nature; hence the incumbent is less constrained by surveillance.

Whether or not persons having low status in a group are likely to be affected by surveillance and sanctions depends upon certain conditions. The behavior of a person with low status is likely to receive less attention than that of a high-status person, and he is less likely to be punished for norm violation. On the other hand, certain personal factors or characteristics of the group structure may expose him to public view. If he is especially interested in moving upward in the group, if he is anxious over the possibility that he may be rejected by the group, or if group conditions create feelings of insecurity, he may take pains to make his behavior public, hoping that conformity will promote upward mobility. A commonplace example is the relatively low-status executive who goes out of his way to agree with senior executives at committee meetings.

SUMMARY: DISTRIBUTION OF CONFORMITY IN THE GROUP   Where cohesiveness is high, conformity in the behavior and attitudes of members is likely to occur. Where cohesiveness is low, a much wider variation in conformity will be present. Members who have important satisfactions outside the group will frequently deviate from the norm, as will members who do not find much satisfaction in the group. The varying pressure exerted toward different persons in the group also creates individual differences in conformity. The person who engages in moderate deviation from the norm is at first likely to experience strong pressures toward conformity. If he rarely conforms, however, pressures toward conformity may diminish; in a sense he may be regarded as a hopeless deviant.

The person high in the power structure who occupies a position of leadership has two contrary demands placed upon him. One is to conform more closely to the norms of his group than the average member, and the other is to deviate from group norms by introducing changes in group goals and activities. Empirical evidence is consistent in demonstrating that leaders may be both more conforming and less conforming, in appropriate circumstances. In a general sense, conformity and status are associated. The most conforming are those with moderate status, and the next most conforming are those with the lowest status. Those with the highest status conform least. With respect to persons having low status, this finding applies mainly where the low status is relatively permanent and there is little opportunity or hope of increasing status.

There is an interaction between group processes and personality characteristics that produces different reward-cost outcomes for conforming behavior on the part of various group members. In social-emotional groups, persons with high needs for affiliation are most likely to conform because conformity is compatible with their needs. Persons who are hostile or lacking in social skills, however, are likely to exhibit minimum conformity. In a task group, the need for achievement and the possession of skills relevant to group goals are likely to produce high conformity for some members. For members lacking these qualities, conformity is likely to be low. These ideas are well supported by empirical research.

Finally, conformity depends upon the extent to which a person's position is exposed to public view. Also, conditions or personal characteristics that cause a person to make his behavior relatively public are likely to encourage conformity.

Conformity to Norms of Social Responsibility

In the 1960s, a young girl named Kitty Genovese was attacked in a residential section of New York City by a man with a knife who stabbed her repeatedly: she screamed for help and tried to fight him off until she died of numerous stab wounds. During this time thirty-eight persons remained in the safety of their apartments, many of them watching from their windows, and none came to her aid.[60] This crime received widespread publicity in the news media, along with much speculation about why people do not come to the aid of other persons in such situations. In response to this incident, a number of social psychologists devoted their attention to discovering the conditions under which individuals do or do not come to the aid of other persons in distress.

Underlying the idea that such situations require people to aid the person in distress is a *norm of social responsibility*. People are expected to aid those who are helplessly dependent upon them, who are defenseless in a dangerous situation, or who are in strong need of assistance in some way. A corollary of this norm is that people are not supposed to harm others intentionally. As we will see shortly, situational factors play an important role in conformity to the norm of social responsibility. These factors appear to operate through their effect on the rewards and costs for conformity or through the individual's definition of the norm as relevant or irrelevant to the situation.

Typically, heroic or altruistic behavior involves costs to the individual that are not adequately compensated by the rewards in the situation. Persons conform to such norms because not to do so would result in lowered self-esteem and guilt. Such costs, however, can be avoided if a situation is defined as one in which the norm does not apply. Schwartz, in his analysis of situations in which moral choices arise, suggests two conditions that must be satisfied before an individual will feel compelled to behave in accordance with a moral norm.[61] First, the person must define the situation as one in which his acts have consequences for the welfare of others, and second, the situation must be defined as one in which he ascribes to himself responsibility for those acts and their consequences. To the degree that either one or the other of these conditions is absent or minimized, a person's behavior will be unaffected by the appropriate norm irrespective of how strongly he believes in it.

60. ROSENTHAL, 1964.   61. SCHWARTZ, 1968a.

Schwartz assessed these two conditions as relatively enduring characteristics of an individual, by means of a self-report and a projective test. Then he put these individuals in hypothetical situations where they had an opportunity to behave altruistically. He found that participants who generally saw themselves as willing to assume responsibility and who were sensitive to the consequences of their behavior did tend to conform to altruistic norms.[62] In a later study, asking volunteers to donate bone marrow for transplantation to a dying patient, he created situations varying in the consequences of the participants' behavior for that patient and in the extent to which they felt responsible for saving the patient's life.[63] He found again that maximizing these two conditions produced altruistic behavior.

Studies of bystander intervention in contrived emergencies are consistent with this formulation. In one experiment, participants heard over an intercom what appeared to be an epileptic seizure by a fellow participant.[64] More than eight out of ten of those individuals who thought that they alone were aware of their fellow participant's plight reported the emergency before the end of the seizure when the intercom was cut off. However, fewer than one in three of those participants who believed that four other participants also were aware of the incident did so. These investigators, Darley and Latané, concluded from their observations that the possibility of *diffusing responsibility to other persons* altered their perception of the costs in the situation. They suggested that the seizure created a conflict situation of the *avoidance-avoidance* type. (Avoidance-avoidance is a standard concept in learning theory, and is depicted by a spatially arranged situation where an individual wishes to avoid two objects or states of affairs, but is faced with a dilemma: If he moves away from either one, he gets closer to the other.)

Individuals could avoid guilt over not helping the victim by making a move to help. On the other hand, only by not helping could they avoid making fools of themselves (by overreacting, ruining the experiment by leaving their intercom and destroying the anonymous nature of the situation). When an individual was alone, the obvious distress of the victim and his need for help was so important that his conflict was easily resolved in favor of helping the sufferer. For the participants who knew other bystanders were present, the cost of not helping was lessened, and the conflict they were in was more acute. Trapped between the two negative alternatives of allowing the victim to suffer and disrupting the experiment to help, these individuals vacillated rather than making a decision to act.[65]

In other situations, bystanders' failure to act appeared to be related to defining the situation as one that did not require action. Thus, inaction was not thought to have adverse consequences for the welfare of another person. Here again, the presence of other persons was associated with a failure to act. In one

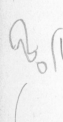

62. SCHWARTZ, 1968*b*.   63. SCHWARTZ, 1970.   64. DARLEY & LATANÉ, 1968.   65. DARLEY & LA-TANÉ, 1968, p. 382.

situation, individuals found themselves in a room where smoke began to flow from the ventilator.[66] Some participants were alone, some were with two experimenter accomplices who ignored the smoke, and some were with two other naïve participants. Three-quarters of the individuals who were alone reported the smoke. But in only one-third of the groups of three naïve participants did at least one person report the smoke. When in the presence of two nonreacting confederates of the experimenter, only one person in ten reported the smoke.

Somewhat similar results were reported for another situation.[67] In this instance, persons were led to believe that they heard a woman fall and cry out in pain in the next room. They encountered this emergency under four conditions: (1) waiting alone, (2) waiting with another person who was an accomplice of the experimenter and who was instructed to remain as passive as possible, (3) waiting with a stranger who was a naïve participant, and (4) waiting with a friend.

Here again, the presence of another person who did not react to the emergency markedly inhibited action. Three-quarters of the persons who experienced this emergency alone responded with aid to the victim. Only one in fourteen of those individuals in the presence of a confederate intervened. In fewer than half of the groups composed of two strangers did at least one person offer assistance. This figure was higher for groups composed of friends, but less than one would expect if the presence of another person did not have an inhibiting effect. In addition to the idea that the presence of other persons leads to a diffusion of responsibility and less pressure to conform to the normative demands of the situation, Latané and Rodin suggest a second process at work that leads the person to *misperceive the situation,* so as not to regard it as one requiring him to act.

> A bystander to an emergency must first come to some general interpretation of the situation, and then, on the basis of this interpretation, he may choose what to do. Many emergencies are rather ambiguous: it is unclear whether anything is really wrong or whether anything can be done about it. In a previous experiment, smoke might have represented fire, but it might have been nothing more than steam from a radiator. In the present experiment, a crash and the sounds of sobbing might have indicated a girl with a badly injured leg, but it might have meant nothing more than a slight sprain and a good deal of chagrin. In deciding what interpretation to put on a particular configuration of emergency symptoms, a bystander will be influenced by his experience and his desires as well as by what he sees. In addition, if other people are present, he will be guided by their apparent reactions in formulating his own impressions. Unfortunately, their apparent reactions may not be a good indication of their true feelings. Apparent passivity and lack of concern on the part of other bystanders may indicate that they feel the emer-

66. Latané & Darley, 1968.   67. Latané & Rodin, 1969.

gency is not serious, but it may simply mean that they have not yet had time to work out their own interpretation or even that they are assuming a bland exterior to hide their inner uncertainty and concern. The presence of other bystanders provides models for each individual to observe, but it also provides an audience to any action he may undertake. In public, Americans generally wish to appear poised and in control of themselves. Thus it is possible for a state of "pluralistic ignorance" to develop, in which each bystander is led by the apparent lack of concern of the others to interpret the situation as being less serious than he would if he were alone. To the extent that he does not feel the situation is an emergency, of course, he will be unlikely to take any helpful action.[68]

The difference in the reactions of strangers and friends in this situation may be accounted for in part, the investigators suggest, by the tendency for friends to be less concerned about possible embarrassment and to be less likely to misinterpret the others' inaction. Friends also may be less prone than strangers to pass off responsibility to the other party.

While these investigators conclude that these results cast doubt on the old adage that there is safety in numbers in an emergency situation, a related study in a field setting suggests that this may not always be the case.[69] Four teams of investigators, each made up of a victim, sometimes a model helper, and two observers, staged collapses on express trains of the New York City Eighth Avenue Independent Subway. In these incidents, which involved over 4,000 subway riders unknowingly as participants, they used victims "who appeared to be either drunk or ill, and who were Negro or white." In some situations no model helper was used, and in others, a model intervened either early or late in the incident. Unlike the behavior of participants in the laboratory, bystanders in this setting responded with aid in a much higher proportion of instances. In sixty-two out of sixty-five instances, the victim who appeared ill received spontaneous help before the model intervened. Even the "drunk" received spontaneous aid half the time.

These investigators suggest two possible explanations for the disparity between their results and those described earlier. First, the conditions of these emergency situations were markedly different. Bystanders could actually observe the victim and this may well have constrained any tendency to conclude that an emergency did not exist, and also may have overwhelmed other considerations underlying any tendency to diffuse responsibility. Second, even if there was a tendency for diffusion of responsibility to occur, it was simply outweighed by the increase in the probability that *someone* in a subway car averaging forty-five passengers would eventually intervene. Drunken victims were

68. Reprinted by permission from Academic Press, Inc., and B. LATANÉ and J. RODIN. A lady in distress: Inhibiting effects of friends and strangers on bystander intervention. *Journal of Experimental Social Psychology,* 1969, **5**, 198–199.   69. PILIAVIN, RODIN, & PILIAVIN, 1969.

presumably helped less often because the costs of helping were perceived as greater, because the victim was considered partly responsible for his plight, and because his situation was considered less serious.

A number of other investigations demonstrate conditions that contributed to the assumption of responsibility and awareness of consequences, and which in turn affected the degree to which persons conformed to moral norms. One study varied the degree to which participants were physically close to the victim, ranging from a condition where the victim who presumably received the shocks was in a separate room and could only be heard pounding on the wall in protest to a condition in which he was in physical contact with the participants, and where it was necessary to force the victim's hand onto the plate for shocks beyond the 150-volt level.[70] Presumably having the victim immediately present and forcing him to submit to the shock heightens both responsibility and awareness of consequences.

Where the victim was not present, only one in three participants defied the experimenter in favor of a norm against inflicting severe pain on other persons. Where the victim was in close contact, more than two in three participants refused to shock the victim. Clearly, where a person can directly observe his own involvement and the victim's responses, it is more difficult to deny responsibility or to fail to perceive the consequences of actions.

A further factor in this series of studies concerns the experimenter's role. The stronger the norms governing the relation of experimenter to participant and the greater the transfer of responsibility from the participant to the experimenter the more willing the participant will be to deliver a painful shock to the victim. Consistent with this premise is the fact that when the experimenter was physically close and able to exercise surveillance, obedience to his demand that the participant shock their partners was maximal.[71]

Other studies are also consistent with the notion that aiding another person is related to both the degree to which the helper is aware of the consequences of his behavior and the degree to which he ascribes responsibility to himself for such consequences. To the degree that an individual perceives that his partner's success is dependent on him, he will exert himself on the partner's behalf.[72] Experimental manipulations that make individuals aware of the consequences of their behavior for other persons increase the degree to which they conform to the norm of social responsibility. To the degree, however, that participants feel less responsible in the situation, such conformity is reduced.

These conclusions have been borne out by two other studies of response to the dependency of another person on the participant.[73] In both instances, less aid was given to the dependent person if the giver perceived the dependence of the other person as due to his own choice rather than beyond his control. In

70. MILGRAM, 1965.   71. MILGRAM, 1965.   72. BERKOWITZ & DANIELS, 1963; GORANSON & BERKOWITZ, 1966; BERKOWITZ, KLANDERMAN, & HARRIS, 1964.   73. SCHOPLER & MATHEWS, 1965; HOROWITZ, 1968.

addition, the greater the freedom to choose to help or not to help, the more help was extended. In terms of the previous argument, freedom of choice would increase the effects of responsibility. The costs of helping, which have been shown to affect the amount of aid given to others,[74] may also in part be related to conformity to norms because of the effects of these costs on responsibility. Those persons who can most bear the burden of aid have the least cost, and thus have the greatest responsibility to help.

As we have seen, conditions bring about conformity through their effects on an individual's feelings of responsibility and awareness of consequences. Other conditions appear to affect conformity by raising the salience of the norms in a given situation. For example, *seeing another person engage in helping behavior* increases the likelihood that one will offer aid to persons in need. Thus, in one study, seeing a lady being helped with a flat tire on a freeway increased the frequency with which motorists stopped and offered aid to another car deliberately placed in similar straits farther down the way.[75] Similarly, observing a model contribute to a Salvation Army kettle increased the frequency of donations on the part of bystanders.[76]

In another study, midtown Manhattan pedestrians encountered an open envelope with a wallet protruding from it. With it was a letter addressed to the owner making it appear that a previous finder was in the process of mailing it back and had lost it. The letter also contained the previous finder's feelings about returning the wallet. Finders of the envelope and wallet most often mailed it back when they perceived themselves as similar to the previous finder and when his feelings about returning it were positively expressed in the letter. When the previous finder was seen as dissimilar, his feelings (positive or negative) had no effect on the number of intact wallets returned.[77] This is consistent with modeling theory as discussed later in Chapter 15.

The Norm of Reciprocity

A variety of other conditions appear to increase the likelihood of helping behavior because they increase the salience of a corollary to the social responsibility norm—the norm of reciprocity.[78] The norm of reciprocity suggests that receiving prior help from another person, whether or not he is later in need, would increase helping behavior. This is supported by experiments.[79]

Blocking or hindering someone instead of helping also follows a reciprocity norm. Prior interference from another person will lead to hindering a victim if he is similar and to helping if he is dissimilar to the person originally blocking the individual. The heightened tendency toward aiding the dissimilar other person in response to having been hindered is due to the heightened awareness

74. MIDLARSKY, 1968; WAGNER & WHEELER, 1969.   75. BRYAN & TEST, 1967.   76. BRYAN & TEST, 1967.   77. HORNSTEIN, FISCH, & HOLMES, 1968.   78. GOULDNER, 1960.   79. GORANSON & BERKOWITZ, 1966; GREENGLASS, 1969.

of the norm of responsibility. Possibly, a heightened sense of justice also operates in some of these situations, as demonstrated by an experiment where individuals who had been betrayed by their earlier partners exerted greater efforts on behalf of a later partner who had been similarly betrayed than on behalf of one who had previously been rewarded.[80] Here it seems that altruistic behavior arises to establish social justice.

Norms and Harming Another Person

Not only are people expected to help other persons in distress, but some norms require that people under most circumstances refrain from harming others. The fact that harming another person appears justified under certain circumstances, (e.g., in self-defense or instances of justified retaliation) suggests that norms against harm doing are related to more general norms of equity or fairness in human exchanges. Walster and Berscheid, who have reviewed the research on harm doing within an equity framework, suggest that when an individual harms another person, he experiences discomfort arising from two sources.[81] One is anxiety over possible retaliation, and the other is distress over having behaved in a manner which violates one's ethical principles and self-expectations. People may relieve such distress by restoring equity through an actual exchange—by compensating the victim or punishing oneself—or through certain psychological processes.

These processes include the same mechanisms previously noted in the discussion of reactions to the failure to go to a victim's aid. Thus the harm doer may derogate his victim, somehow making him responsible for his own fate. The harm doer may minimize the harm done by his acts or deny responsibility for them. Whether persons restore equity through an actual exchange or by psychological means depends on a number of conditions. First, increasing the outcomes of the victim through compensation appears much more commonly than reducing the outcomes of the harm doer by self-punishment. This is consistent with the general principle that people will select that technique which is in the long run least costly.

Compensation appears favored when it can be done without excessive costs and without creating further inequities. Thus two experiments suggest that where persons are limited to either overcompensating or undercompensating a victim as well as other means of restoring equity, they are less apt to use compensation than when the available compensation is adequate. One experiment which was later replicated is summarized as follows:

Women from various church groups were led to cheat fellow parishioners out of trading stamps in a vain attempt to win additional stamps for themselves. When the women were subsequently given an opportunity to com-

80. SIMMONS & LERNER, 1968.   81. WALSTER, BERSCHEID & WALSTER, 1973.

pensate the victim (at no cost to themselves), it was found that adequacy of compensation was crucial in determining whether or not the women chose to compensate. Women who could compensate (exactly restoring the number of books the partner had lost) were much more likely to make restitution than were women limited to insufficient compensation (a few stamps) or to excessive compensation (a great many stamp books).[82]

When available modes of compensation are inappropriate or too costly, an individual often resorts to cognitive distortions which restore psychological equity by justifying his behavior in a manner that appears plausible to himself as well as others. The type of justification employed and the degree to which psychological equity is successfully achieved will depend on the credibility of available justifications. Credibility in turn depends on the degree to which the justifications require a distortion of reality. Particularly where persons have had considerable contact with each other in the past or anticipate considerable contact in the future, maintaining distortions will be difficult. Thus, people are more apt to derogate a stranger than a friend who has been victimized by their acts. Persons who are "out of sight" can be kept "out of mind." Members of a dominant group can believe that members of a disadvantaged minority are shiftless, lazy, or happy with what little they have as long as they maintain adequate social distance through various forms of segregation. To the extent that such justifications are effective, people can persist in behavior which runs counter to norms specifying that one should help or at least not harm others.

More will be said about maintaining behavior deviant from norms in Chapter 17, where the mechanisms that people employ to maintain a favorable view of themselves when engaging in behavior contrary to norms they have accepted will be discussed. These mechanisms involving the self-concept reduce the costs of lowered self esteem and guilt, and help to explain why people frequently fail to conform to norms.

Summary: Norms of Social Responsibility

The idea that people should aid persons in distress or who are in strong need of assistance is widely shared, and amounts to a norm of social responsibility. A corollary norm is that one should not intentionally harm other persons. Situational factors play an important role in conformity to the norm of social responsibility. These factors appear to operate through their effect on the rewards and costs for conformity or through the individual's definition of the norm as relevant or irrelevant to the situation. Typically, altruistic behavior involves costs that are not adequately compensated by the rewards in the situation. Helping behavior occurs because, otherwise, lowered self-esteem and guilt would be costly.

82. Reprinted by permission from E. WALSTER, E. BERSCHEID, G. W. WALSTER. New directions in equity research. *Journal of Personality and Social Psychology,* 1973, 25, 159.

Two crucial aspects of an individual's definition of the situation appear to determine whether or not he helps a person in trouble. He is more likely to act if he ascribes to himself some responsibility for offering assistance, and if he assumes that his acts have consequences for the welfare of the other person. Thus, individuals who believe they alone are in a position to help are more likely to render aid. When other persons are also present, the individual is less likely to assume responsibility, and he diffuses it to the others. When it is not clear to the individual that his actions will do any good, he less often tries to help.

The norm that people should not harm other persons if they can help it appears to be not only a derivative of the norm of social responsibility, but also to involve equity or fairness in human exchanges. For example, other persons can be harmed if it is justified by self-defense. Discomfort at harming another person appears to arise from two sources: (1) anxiety over possible retaliation and (2) distress over having behaved in a manner which violates one's ethical principles or self-expectations. People may relieve such distress by compensating the victim, punishing themselves, or through such psychological mechanisms as derogating the victim, blaming him, or denying harm or responsibility.

Norms and Deviance in Society

The discussion has for the most part been concerned with norms and conformity in small groups; however, a considerable amount of work has been done on conformity in the larger society. Generally the emphasis in this research has been on the other side of the coin, on deviation rather than conformity, but many of the principles outlined for small groups apply to this larger context and are part of contemporary theories of deviation.

Two general themes are found in contemporary theories of deviancy. The first is that pressures toward deviancy and resultant breakdown in conformity arise as a result of a disjunction between the normatively approved means and the culturally prescribed values in a society. The second theme emphasizes the reaction of society in labeling acts and persons as deviant.

Deviation from Norms as a Disjunction between Means and Values

The first theme was noted briefly in the discussion of the forces leading to the emergence of new group norms. Where persons cannot achieve satisfactory reward-cost outcomes by conforming to the norms specifying how these are to be achieved, pressures emerge that result in a breakdown in consensus or agreement about what is appropriate behavior; this constitutes a state of relative normlessness.

This state of relative normlessness has been termed *anomie.* Merton, the principal proponent of this thesis, has argued that the widely diffused values of material success in a democratic society coupled with barriers to access via legitimate channels for many groups (e.g., low-income groups, racial and ethnic minorities) explains the high rates of deviance in such groups.[83] Cloward has added another element to this thesis.[84] He argues that deviancy is not only high in these groups because they lack access to legitimate means but also because they have more immediate access to illegitimate means than many groups with lower rates of deviance. Thus, the poor living in the inner city have more access to prostitution, drug peddling, and other forms of criminal activities.

A state of anomie at the societal level may be experienced at the level of the individual by a psychological state called alienation. Seeman has delineated a number of dimensions of this feeling state including powerlessness, meaninglessness, normlessness, isolation, and self-estrangement.[85] The dimension of powerlessness involves the expectancy held by the individual that his own behavior cannot determine his outcomes. Meaninglessness involves low expectancy that satisfactory predictions about future outcomes can be made. Normlessness encompasses the feeling or expectancy that socially disapproved behaviors are necessary to achieve goals. The term *isolation* does not refer to lack of warmth of social relations but to a kind of detachment in which the person assigns low reward value to goals and beliefs that typically are valued highly in a society. Finally, *self-estrangement* also has a somewhat different meaning than the obvious one in that it involves a feeling of lack of intrinsic satisfaction in one's activities. One's work, for instance, is perceived as a means toward an end, making a living, rather than as an intrinsically satisfying end in itself.

The notion that anomie at the subcultural level is accompanied by alienation at the level of the personality and the idea that both are related to deviant behavior has received careful examination in a community study.[86] An attempt was made to account both for the differential rates of deviancy between three ethnic groups that made up the population of a small Western community and for individual differences in deviancy within each group. The sharp differences in rates of deviance, with American Indians having most deviants, Spanish-Americans next, and then Anglo-Americans, were found to be related to three conditions. First, the groups differed with respect to the degree to which they had access to goals via legitimate or socially approved means. By virtue of their socio-economic status, Anglo-Americans had considerably greater access than Spanish-Americans or American Indians, with the American Indians favored somewhat over the Spanish-Americans. Second, the groups differed in the degree to which their members agreed on norms, with much less anomie for the Anglo-American group than for the American Indians and Spanish-Americans. Third, the groups differed in the degree to which they had access to illegitimate means to goal achievement in terms of exposure to deviant role

83. Merton, 1957b.   84. Cloward, 1959.   85. Seeman, 1959.   86. Jessor, Graves, Hanson, & Jessor, 1968.

models, opportunities to engage in deviant behavior, and protection against possible punishment for such behavior. Again, the Anglo-American group was favored, having less access to illegitimate means than the American Indians or the Spanish-Americans, and the Spanish-Americans having less than the American Indians.

The persons in this study were classified on the basis of individual measures that paralleled these group measures, and the relation of each of these measures to individual differences in deviant behavior was investigated. These included a measure of the degree to which they expected to achieve valued goals, a measure of alienation based on the dimensions delineated by Seeman, and measures of internal control including attitudes against deviancy, the tendency to think and plan ahead, and the tendency to defer gratification.

With the exception of the last two measures of internal control these individual characteristics were found to be related to deviancy in terms of both excessive use of alcohol and a variety of other forms of deviancy, ranging from being stopped for speeding to stealing. This supports the idea that deviancy may occur as a result of pressures toward deviance stemming from a disjunction between culturally approved goals and means and weak social and personal controls. (Additional evidence in support of this idea comes from a study showing that the greater the pressure toward success exerted by parents, the higher the rate of cheating of their children on an experimental task.[87]) That a condition of anomie at the sociocultural level may produce alienation at the personality level was supported in part by the finding of a much higher rate of alienation among American Indians and Spanish-Americans than among Anglo-Americans, who as a group were found to be lowest in anomie. Also consistent with the theory that groups experience alienation where their access to culturally valued goals is limited is the finding that, in a Southern community, a higher rate of alienation prevails among blacks and among the poorly educated than among whites and among the well educated.[88]

Components of alienation appear also to be related to the breakdown of normative restraints that characterize riots. Thus a study of the riot-torn areas of Watts found that those blacks who scored high on measures of isolation, powerlessness, and racial dissatisfaction were more prone to participate in violence.[89]

Labeling Theory and Deviance as Normative Process

A second approach to the explanation of deviant behavior, called *labeling theory,* is found in the recent writings of Becker, Lemert, and Matza, who all emphasized the reaction of society to the deviant.[90] Numerous studies have provided evidence that most people at some time or other engage in deviant

87. PEARLIN, YARROW, & SCARR, 1967.   88. MIDDLETON, 1963.   89. RANSFORD, 1969.   90. BECKER, 1963; LEMERT, 1967; MATZA, 1969.

behavior which is of sufficient seriousness to warrant legal action.[91] For most people, such behavior does not become persistent, but the deviancy of some individuals becomes known and they become targets for punishment or treatment by society. It is these individuals who persist in deviancy. We may ask whether society's reaction to the deviant accentuates deviant behavior and accounts for its persistence.

Social control or labeling theories of deviation emphasize two ways in which the reaction of other persons may contribute to the initiation and persistence of deviant behavior. First, as Lemert has emphasized, a given act must be *defined* as deviant.[92] Behavior which is different or even harmful may be defined as normal and acceptable in a given group or context and the person behaving in this manner will not be defined as deviant. In another context, a person behaving in exactly the same way might be defined as deviant. In intimate groups such as the family, behavior which might be defined as neurotic is defined by family members as normal. In business firms, practices which are technically instances of stealing such as the appropriation of company supplies by employees, may be normalized by defining such losses as "inventory shrinkage."

Whether the behavior in question is defined as normal or deviant will depend on the costs involved, particularly to those in power who have access to the machinery of social control.[93] Thus societal reaction is inherently a part of what constitutes deviancy. Deviance is not a property of an act per se but of the definition that others make of it.

This becomes apparent when one considers a variety of acts which may or may not be different or harmful and may or may not be defined as deviant. There is considerable evidence that smoking cigarettes is harmful; yet a person who smokes is not classified as deviant. The practice of witchcraft which today we would regard as harmless was at one time regarded as extremely serious deviant behavior punishable by death. Thus labeling theorists would argue that the explanation of deviant behavior must include an account of how such behavior becomes successfully labeled as deviant. This explanation is essentially the same as that previously advanced in the discussion of factors related to the emergence of norms. Those forms of behavior which adversely affect the outcomes of the more powerful group members are apt to be defined as deviant.

A second way in which the reaction of society is involved in the explanation of deviant behavior is that *being labeled* a deviant is a crucial step in the process of becoming deviant. Becker has described the process of becoming a deviant in terms of the concepts of *career* and *career contingency* used in the study of occupations.[94] Career refers to the sequence of movements which persons normally make from one position to another in an occupational system. Career contingency refers to those factors on which movement from one position to

91. Porterfield, 1946; Wallerstein & Wyle, 1947; Kinsey, Pomeroy, & Martin, 1949.   92. Lemert, 1967.   93. Lemert, 1967.   94. Becker, 1963.

another depends. These include not only the objective facts of the social structure, the steps required for movements, etc., but also the changes in the perspectives and motivations of the individual that accompany such movement. The obvious first step in the career of a deviant is committing an act that potentially can be classified as deviant. Such a step may be unintentional, as where someone breaks a rule in ignorance or because of stress created by inability to achieve goals by legitimate means. With respect to the role of motivation generally emphasized in both popular and scientific explanations of deviancy, Becker argues that it is crucial to explain why some persons act in response to impulses toward deviant behavior and others do not. One set of contingencies at this point is the person's *commitment* to conventional institutions and behavior.

In speaking of commitment, I refer to the process through which several kinds of interests become bound up with carrying out certain lines of behavior to which they seem formally extraneous. What happens is that the individual, as a consequence of actions he has taken in the past or the operation of various institutional routines, finds he must adhere to certain lines of behavior, because many other activities than the one he is immediately engaged in will be adversely affected if he does not. The middle-class youth must not quit school, because his occupational future depends on receiving a certain amount of schooling. The conventional person must not indulge his interests in narcotics, for example, because much more than the pursuit of immediate pleasure is involved; his job, his family, and his reputation in his neighborhood may seem to him to depend on his continuing to avoid temptation.[95]

From childhood on, most persons become increasingly committed to conventional norms. The investment in normative behavior is so heavy that it is too costly to be swayed by one's own impulses. Thus, adolescents who were concerned about maintaining parental and teacher respect and who were dependent on direction from these adults were found less frequently to have engaged in delinquency or to have been apprehended by police than those adolescents who were unconcerned.[96] These concerns also led to less cheating in a situation where they were given an opportunity to defraud the experimenter.

Other persons, however, have avoided such commitments, either because in the course of growing up they have not become tied to conventional commitments or because they have learned to neutralize conventional codes of conduct by generating extensive justifications for deviating from them. Sykes and Matza have described some of the techniques employed by delinquents to neutralize the effects of norms and to provide justification for their violation.[97] These

95. Reprinted by permission from H. S. Becker. *Outsiders: Studies in the sociology of deviance.* New York: The Free Press, 1963. P. 27.   96. Piliavin, Hardyck, & Vadum, 1968.   97. Sykes & Matza, 1957.

include blaming other persons for their behavior, denying that their behavior has really hurt anyone, viewing their behavior as justified by the character of the victim, and denouncing as hypocrites those who condemn them.

Once a person commits a deviant act he may continue, depending in part on whether he develops a taste for such activity. A crucial contingency frequently is the availability of more experienced deviates who help the neophyte to learn new kinds of experiences and to define these as pleasurable. Becker has documented this in his classical study of marijuana users, who typically must be taught by other users how to handle some of the initially unpleasant reactions to marijuana and at the same time to recognize and define other effects as pleasurable. He quotes an experienced user describing how he handles a newcomer to marijuana use.

> Well, they get pretty high sometimes. The average person isn't ready for that, and it is a little frightening to them sometimes. I mean, they've been high on lush [alcohol], and they get higher that way than they've ever been before, and they don't know what's happening to them. Because they think they're going to keep going up, up, up till they lose their minds or begin doing weird things or something. You have to like reassure them, explain to them that they're gonna be all right. You have to just talk them out of being afraid. Keep talking to them, reassuring, telling them it's all right. And come on with your own story, you know: "The same thing happened to me. You'll get to like that after awhile." Keep coming on like that; pretty soon you talk them out of being scared. And besides they see you doing it and nothing horrible is happening to you, so that gives them more confidence.[98]

A vital step in the process of becoming a deviant is the experience of being caught and publicly labeled a deviant. The contingencies here depend not so much on what the deviant does but on what other persons do. The consequences of discovery have implications for the deviant's further social participation and his self-image. He acquires a new public identity. Depending on the nature of his behavior, he is labeled a fag, a hippie, a mugger, a rapist.

Becker argues that the assignment of the status of deviant has powerful effects because it leads others to assign to the person other undesirable traits as well. Further, the status of deviant is a *master status,* as is race in our society. A person is treated in terms of this status first, and in terms of other subordinate statuses second. Thus, once an individual is classified as a criminal, a homosexual, or an addict, for instance, this characterization overrides all others and leads other persons to view him as different and deviant in general. Such treatment sets in motion a self-fulfilling prophecy. Regarded as different, the deviant is often shut off from participation in more conventional groups and from the routines associated with conventional living. One need only consider immediate

---

98. Reprinted by permission from H. S. BECKER. *Outsiders: Studies in the sociology of deviance.* New York: The Free Press, 1963. P. 55.

constraints placed on the social interactions of the homosexual, alcoholic, or addict. Once identified they are apt to lose their jobs and most of their friends, and to be unwelcome in many of their former haunts.

While labeling does not inevitably lead to further deviancy, it is frequently difficult, if not impossible, to reverse the trend, because even though the addict may break his habit or the criminal may go straight, other persons may still continue to treat him as a deviant.

The final step in the process frequently involves movement into an organized deviant group. This has a powerful affect on the deviant's self-concept and his way of life. Such groups provide the deviant with a self-justifying rationale for his deviancy. While not all deviant groups have as well organized ideology as the homosexual community, theirs is a case in point, as Becker observes:

> Magazines and books by homosexuals and for homosexuals include historical articles about famous homosexuals in history. They contain articles on the biology and physiology of sex, designed to show that homosexuality is a "normal" sexual response. They contain legal articles, pleading for civil liberties for homosexuals. Taken together, this material provides a working philosophy for the active homosexual, explaining to him why he is the way he is, that other people have also been that way, and why it is all right for him to be that way.[99]

Such groups provide the deviant with group-developed solutions to many of the problems they face in common as deviants. The young thief, for example, learns from older, more experienced members how to dispose of stolen goods with a minimum of danger of arrest. Thus, the deviant is even more apt to continue in his ways. He has learned both how to avoid trouble and also the rationale for continuing as a deviant. Finally, he may well have learned to effectively repudiate the conventional world.

Summary: Norms and Deviance in Society

Conformity in total societies has received considerable attention, usually with the emphasis on deviation from norms. Two general themes are found in contemporary theories of deviance. The first is that pressures toward deviant behavior and the resultant breakdown in conformity arise as a result of a disjunction between normatively approved means and culturally prescribed values in a society. Some persons cannot achieve satisfactory reward-cost outcomes by conforming to the norms. This leads to a breakdown in the normative structure. Such persons also have access to and develop illegitimate means to achievement of their personal goals. The individual state of mind corresponding to this state of anomie in the society has been termed alienation, which includes feel-

---

99. Reprinted by permission from H. S. BECKER. *Outsiders: Studies in the sociology of deviance.* New York: The Free Press, 1963. P. 38.

ings of powerlessness, meaninglessness, normlessness, isolation, and self-estrangement.

The second theme used to explain deviance is labeling theory, which emphasizes the reaction of society to the person committing a deviant act. Labeling theory stresses two ways in which the reaction of other persons may contribute to the creation and persistence of deviant behavior. First, certain acts must be defined as deviant. A person behaving exactly the same way may be defined as deviant in one context and as normal in another. Second, being labeled a deviant is a crucial step in the process of becoming deviant. Being labeled a deviant helps create a new public identity which is reinforced by the consistent attributions of other undesirable characteristics by others and results in a dramatic change in patterns of association with others. A person goes through a series of actions which lead him progressively toward deviant behavior. Those individuals who have not developed strong commitments to conventional norms are especially susceptible to this progressive movement toward deviance. During this process the perceptions and motivations of the person may undergo profound change to make his actions more compatible with the movement toward deviance. Another factor playing an important part in this movement toward deviance is interaction with individuals like himself who exert pressures to conform to *their* norms, which are at variance with those of the larger society.

11

Leadership

Leadership has played a vital role in the affairs of men since earliest recorded history. Historians give considerable attention to the role of politicians and statesmen in the development of empires, territories, and nations. In modern society, organizational and informal activities alike are characterized by a difference in the contributions of the participants. Some individuals contribute more of their energies or skills than others, and they vary in the extent to which they exert influence over each other. Business organizations, government, political parties, and nonprofit institutions illustrate this emphasis on leadership by providing unusually high rewards for their leaders, by conducting a continual search for men with leadership ability, and by stressing human relations or leadership training.

This widespread interest in leadership documents the point that it is of considerable concern. But both the popular view of leadership and the early research of behavioral scientists overestimate the importance of the contribution of the individual leader. Current formulations of the problem take a quite different form, focusing on the nature of leadership behavior and its relation to individual personality, to the composition and function of the group, to the situation, and to the group structure.

The history of research on leadership reflects in capsule form the gradual evolution of social psychology into an increasingly complex and sophisticated structure. Like much early research in the behavioral sciences, the initial approach to leadership was to compare individuals, in this case to explore how leaders differ from nonleaders. This tactic is generally acknowledged to have been premature: Few stable differences were found. A later approach focused on leadership *behavior*, emphasizing those acts leading either to goal achievement or to the maintenance and strengthening of the group. In this approach all members of the group were seen as performing leadership acts in varying degrees. Subsequently, the identification of different kinds of leader behaviors made it possible to identify some individual characteristics associated with these behaviors.

The focus on leadership behavior was accompanied by an interest in the effects of the situation and of the composition of the group on leadership behavior. Also of concern was the effects of various kinds or styles of leadership behavior on the productivity and satisfaction of group members. Out of this line of investigation, interest turned toward the structural determinants of leadership: It was believed that relatively permanent patternings of group interaction developed and provided a context within which leadership was exercised. An evolving view of leadership placed stress on the *leader-follower relation,* recognizing that the behavior of the leader depends upon the complementary behavior of followers. Also, it has become increasingly apparent that a type or style of leader behavior that is effective in one situation may not be effective in another. Finally, many present-day students of the topic regard leadership as the allocation of leadership roles to certain individual members of a group. Such role allocation may be readily interpreted by exchange theory, which analyzes the leadership process in terms of the reward-cost outcomes of leaders and followers. This chapter will review the various approaches to leadership, placing emphasis upon the more current research strategies. In Chapter 12, the relation between the leadership structure (including leadership style) and group productivity will be dealt with.

Nature of Leadership

Early research on leadership shared with the average man a fundamental bias referred to in Chapter 2: the tendency to see persons as origins of actions. Leadership behavior was believed to originate from the personal qualities of the leader, and insufficient attention was given to the contribution of the group structure and situation to such behavior. The extreme form of this bias is reflected in such statements as "A military officer is a leader of men," which implies that his personal qualities enable him to lead enlisted men in any and all situations.

Empirical studies compared leaders with nonleaders, focusing on personality traits in the hope of uncovering the bases of leadership. Unfortunately, the relation between personality traits and leadership proved more complex than originally assumed. After a review of the research on this topic conducted before 1952, Gibb concluded that attempts to find a consistent pattern of traits that characterize leaders had failed.[1] He pointed out that the attributes of

1. GIBB, 1954.

leadership are any or all of those personality characteristics that, in any *particular situation,* make it possible for a person either to contribute to achievement of a group goal or to be seen as doing so by other group members.

As Cartwright and Zander noted, dissatisfaction with the trait approach led to a new tactic focusing on leadership *behavior.*

> Dissatisfaction with the trait approach has, then, given rise to a view of leadership which stresses the characteristics of the group and the situation in which it exists. Research conducted within this orientation does not attempt to find certain invariant traits of leaders. Rather, it seeks to discover what actions are required by groups under various conditions if they are to achieve their goals or other valued states, and how different group members take part in these group actions: Leadership is viewed as the performance of those acts which help the group achieve its preferred outcomes. Such acts may be termed *group functions.* More specifically, leadership consists of such actions by group members as those which aid in setting group goals, moving the group towards its goals, improving the quality of the interactions among the members, building the cohesiveness of the group, or making resources available to the group. In principle, leadership may be performed by one or many members of the group.[2]

As the above quotation suggests, a wide variety of acts, depending on the situation and the character of the group, could be classified as leadership behavior. There is growing empirical[3] and theoretical convergence[4] on considering as leadership behavior those acts that are functionally related either to goal achievement or to the maintenance and strengthening of the group. Acts in the former category, instrumental to achieving the goals of the group, include making suggestions for action, evaluating movement toward the goal, preventing activities irrelevant to the goal, and offering solutions for goal achievement. Acts serving to maintain the group through meeting the social-emotional needs of the group members include encouraging other members, releasing tension that builds up, and giving everyone a chance to express himself.

In short, the attributes of leadership are any or all of those personality characteristics that, in any particular situation, make it possible for a person to contribute to achievement of a group goal, to help hold the group together, or to be seen as doing so by other members. The latter qualification concerning the perceptions of group members should be underscored. Certain characteristics of an individual or his behavior may not in fact be functionally related either to goal achievement or to the maintenance and strengthening of the group. But to the degree that they are perceived as related, other members will accord leadership status to persons possessing the characteristics or performing the behavior. The emphasis, then, is placed on leadership behavior: those actions that actu-

2. Reprinted by permission from D. CARTWRIGHT and A. ZANDER (Eds.), *Group dynamics: Research and theory.* (2d ed.) New York: Harper & Row Publishers, Incorporated, 1960. Pp. 492-493.   3. HALPIN & WINER, 1952.   4. PARSONS & BALES, 1955; THIBAUT & KELLEY, 1959; CARTWRIGHT & ZANDER, 1960.

ally are or perceived to be functionally related either to goal achievement or to the maintenance and strengthening of the group. Such behavior is engaged in to varying degree by all group members. At the same time, some individual personality or other characteristics are associated with those persons who take the lead in performing these functions, but these characteristics will vary depending upon the type of group and the task situation.

Role Differentiation

The behavioral or functional approach to leadership emphasizes that leadership behavior may be performed by any group member; yet relatively early in the life of a group, certain persons engage in such behavior to a much greater degree than others. This specialization has been conceptualized as *role differentiation*.[5] Since role differentiation is most readily observed in groups with a minimum of structure, most of the relevant research has been done on newly formed laboratory groups. While many of the findings have implications for leadership behavior in well-established groups, some caution should be exercised in generalizing to such groups.

Nature of Role Differentiation

As noted in Chapter 9 in the discussion of the communication structure, at a relatively early point in the development of newly formed, initially leaderless groups, the frequency, direction, and content of communication became established at different levels for different members. The individual who talked the most also received the most communication from others. He directed a larger proportion of his comments to the group as a whole rather than to individual members, and these comments were more often in the positive task-oriented categories—giving suggestions, information, and opinion. Other group members were more apt to consider the person most frequently initiating actions as having the best ideas and as doing the most to guide the discussion effectively. Such specialization of behavior and the development of consensus in recognition of the specialization are the substance of role differentiation.

Heinicke and Bales, who observed the development of such consensus in groups over a series of sessions, describe it in terms of an early struggle between men with top status from which the victor ultimately emerges as the agreed-upon leader.[6] Although the groups studied had developed a high degree of status consensus by the end of the first session, during the second session this consensus declined, and a somewhat different hierarchy emerged. The second session was characterized by a status struggle, particularly between the two top men. Subsequently, however, the struggle was resolved, and consensus on the

---

5. Bales & Slater, 1955.   6. Heinicke & Bales, 1953.

old structure reappeared, along with a more positive social-emotional atmosphere.

The roles of the two top-status individuals were critical. During the first two sessions, the number one man played a very active part, apparently in order to establish his position and defend it. He initiated many suggestions, and received many agreements and disagreements. His activity in the second session appeared to be a defense of his top position, challenged by the number two man. Since he was secure by the third and fourth sessions, however, he was able to permit other persons to play more active roles. Although he continued to receive the most responses, especially agreement, he no longer had to exert himself unduly to win his point.

Some of the groups studied by these investigators, however, did not show this trend toward consensus. For these groups, member agreement on the statuses of other members fluctuated in an erratic fashion. This appeared to be a function of the extent to which agreement was reached at the end of the first session. The high-consensus groups were characterized by high agreement among members on their relative ranking at the end of the first session. Those groups who failed to obtain any stability in agreement even in later sessions were characterized by low agreement from the beginning. This suggests the underlying reason for their failure to reach consensus: The groups reaching agreement early were high in initial value consensus, and the groups failing to agree contained members holding divergent values. Bales and Slater suggest that this initial agreement made it possible for members to agree on who was producing the best ideas for solving the group task, and that these individuals were allowed and encouraged to specialize in this task actively.

Recently, differentiation in rates of participation has been shown to occur immediately in some groups.[7] In about half of the discussion groups studied, the rates of participation for members gradually diverged during the forty-five-minute session, as in the groups studied in successive sessions by Heinicke and Bales, with a similar type of explanation. For the remainder, however, such differentiation appeared full-blown as early as the first minute of interaction. A possible explanation for both initial consensus and early differentiation is that members were similar in background and personality characteristics, as well as in shared interpersonal perceptions.

Task and Social-Emotional Specialization

Role differentiation between leader and nonleader is not the only kind of differentiation that may occur. Under certain circumstances, both a task leader and a social-emotional leader may emerge. The *task leader* is a person who supplies ideas and guides the group toward a solution. The *social-emotional leader* helps to boost group morale and to release tension when things are difficult. Such a

7. FISEK & OFSHE, 1970.

differentiation was observed in the groups studied by Bales and Slater.[8] In their investigation, the task specialist was ranked high on initiation, receiving, and guidance, but was not ranked high on liking. The social-emotional leader was usually the best liked among the members. Increasing specialization in these two functions appeared in successive sessions. In the first session, in slightly over half the groups, the man who ranked first on ideas was liked best, but by the fourth session this held true for only 9 percent of the groups.

ROLE DIFFERENTIATION AND EQUILIBRIUM   Such role differentiation has been related theoretically and empirically to certain basic tendencies toward a state of equilibrium in groups.[9] The equilibrium problem will be treated in greater detail in Chapter 12, but it may be briefly noted here that movement toward task accomplishment in groups frustrates needs and incurs other costs. Forces then arise to direct group activities away from the task and toward dealing with the needs and reducing or compensating for the costs. These diversionary activities, since they interfere with task accomplishment, eventually in turn give rise to forces directing the group back to task activities.

The effect of the two sets of forces is to maintain a balance or equilibrium between meeting both the task and the social-emotional functions of groups. One manifestation of the forces toward equilibrium is the development of hostility toward the task leader, who is pushing the group toward task accomplishment. Bales and Slater describe this process for groups high on status consensus which have a clear-cut differentiation between task and social-emotional roles.[10] According to these investigators, the task leader initially generates liking because he satisfies needs of members for completing the task. But he arouses hostility because of his prestige, because he talks a large proportion of the time, and because he requires other members to focus on the task. The more he talks, the more ambivalent other members become toward him. Eventually they transfer some liking from him to another person who is less active and who contributes to the release of tensions in the group by joking or by diverting the group momentarily at peak tensions. This social-emotional leader reasserts the desirable values and attitudes that have been disturbed, deemphasized, threatened, or repressed by the requirements of the task.

Apparently, to the degree that hostility toward the task leader occurs, differentiation between the two roles takes place. There are two grounds for this expectation. First, such hostility makes performance of both roles incompatible, and second, the personalities of the members attracted to and capable of playing the two roles are likely to be different.[11] The social-emotional specialist must like and be liked if he is to meet the social-emotional needs of others. In contrast, the task specialist must be emotionally detached. If he is to lead the group to accomplish its goals, he cannot become so emotionally dependent upon other members that he is unable to exercise power over them.

8. BALES & SLATER, 1955.   9. LEWIN, LIPPITT, & WHITE, 1939; PARSONS & BALES, 1955; COCH & FRENCH, 1958.   10. BALES & SLATER, 1955.   11. BALES & SLATER, 1955.

Data on differences between the idea specialist and the best-liked person are consistent with this supposition.[12] Best-liked persons like other group members strongly and about equally. The idea specialist differentiates his liking to a much greater extent: He likes some members much more than others. Other research indicates that effective leaders differentiate between followers to a greater extent than ineffective leaders: They see the personalities of the members they like best and least as more dissimilar.[13] Bales and Slater suggest that these differences reflect personality differences between those persons who become social-emotional specialists and those who function as task leaders. Liking everyone strongly and to an equal degree may reflect a strong need to be liked on the part of those who become social-emotional leaders. Because of this need, they may have developed considerable skill in making other people like them. The task leader, on the other hand, may well be one who is able to accept negative reactions from others.

CONDITIONS FAVORING MAXIMUM ROLE DIFFERENTIATION   The reasoning to this point suggests that the degree of role differentiation varies directly with the extent to which task functions are unrewarding or costly. The less satisfaction experienced in working toward a goal and the more costs incurred, the more likely task and social-emotional functions are to be centered in different persons. Rewards are low where task success is unrelated to member needs. Costs are high where members disagree on both the importance of the task and how it is to be accomplished. Similarly, costs are apt to be high to the degree that influence attempts among group members must be largely personal in nature. These conditions prevail in groups where the affect, status, power, and communication structures are relatively undeveloped and where there is little consensus on values, on the appropriateness of activities, or on the facts of the situation and how facts are to be assessed. As we noted in Chapter 10, where members agree on and appeal to norms, conformity is attained without the high costs incurred through the use of personal influence.

These suppositions may be tested by examining cases both where role differentiation has occurred to the greatest degree and where it has not. Verba has argued that the temporary small experimental groups studied by Bales and his colleagues provided conditions especially conducive to role differentiation.[14] Having to arrive at a joint solution to a hypothetical problem in human relations could be expected to stimulate differences of opinion because of value differences. At the same time, the patently experimental atmosphere would not prompt high involvement in the task, and thus task efforts by a leader would not be well appreciated. Moreover, these initially leaderless groups were composed of university undergraduates who, with few exceptions, were strangers whose status characteristics (age, sex, etc.) provided little basis for differentiation, and hence attempts to assume leadership had little support from established status characteristics or from an established group structure. Experimen-

12. FIEDLER, 1960.   *13.* BALES & SLATER, 1955.   *14.* VERBA, 1961.

tal studies of emergent leaders and of leaders in groups with an established structure suggest that established leaders are less directive and evoke less resistance on the part of followers than emergent leaders. Verba draws the following conclusions:

> In the experiments, therefore, individuals who do not value highly interpersonal control by others are brought together in groups where the exercise of such control has no external backing from some extra-group hierarchy. The members are unknown to each other and have no apparent status differences such that one member would be expected to exert more influence in the group than another. Under these circumstances it is no wonder that the most active group member, even if he contributes the most to group performance, will tend to be rejected by the group on socio-emotional criteria. His control attempts are viewed as arbitrary and as direct personal challenges. And such directives are likely to arouse negative reactions. As Frank has put it, "Resistance to an activity is readily aroused if it involves submitting to an arbitrary personal demand of someone else, and it is thereby equivalent to a personal defeat."[15]

These comments should not be interpreted to mean that role differentiation will not occur in established groups outside the peculiar culture of the laboratory. Everyday experience, as well as empirical studies, shows that role differentiation does occur in some established groups under many circumstances.[16] Evidence of such differentiation in the structure of families in many societies has been found,[17] but other studies arouse some doubt about whether such differentiation occurs uniformly in family interaction in American society.[18] In established groups in natural settings, bifurcation of roles might be expected where the leader and other group members differ sharply in task involvement and in their views or orientation to the task. In industrial groups, by virtue of his position in the managerial hierarchy, the supervisor is likely to be more involved in task accomplishment than the worker, and to see the work situation differently from him. Under these circumstances it is not surprising that informal leaders emerge to perform a social-emotional function. In fact, a wide range of circumstances can create differences in attitudes and values between a task leader and his followers, thus encouraging the emergence of a social-emotional leader.

On the other hand, any set of circumstances that reduces these differences increases the probability that one person will be able to carry on both functions, and this seems to be the general case. Several studies indicate that where conditions make either task accomplishment or solving emotional problems highly salient for all members of the group, the person who leads the way in

---

15. Reprinted by permission from S. VERBA. *Small groups and political behavior: A study of leadership.* Princeton, N.J.: Princeton University Press, 1961. Pp. 169–170.   16. ZELDITCH, 1955; GRUSKY, 1957.   17. ZELDITCH, 1955.   18. LEIK, 1963; LEVINGER, 1964b.

solving the salient problem will be liked, and bifurcation of the two roles will be minimized.[19] It would seem that the task leader is especially apt also to perform a social-emotional function where highly skilled, closely coordinated teamwork is required, in a situation involving risk. Such conditions rouse much tension that must be repeatedly dissipated if the group is to function well as a team. Goffman discusses this function of the chief surgeon supervising his team during an operation. Some tension-relieving examples are:

> *(Intern holds retractor at wrong end of incision and goes "away," being uninterested in the operation.)*
>
> Chief Surgeon *(in mock English accent):* You don't have to hold that up there, old chap, perhaps down here. Going to sleep, old boy?
>
> Chief Surgeon *(on being accidentally stabbed in the finger by the assistant surgeon, who is using the electric scalpel):* If I get syphalis (sic) I'll know where I got it from, and I'll have witnesses.[20]

Hostility toward the leader and role differentiation are also reduced where the style of leadership encourages a wide distribution of directive acts so that no one person becomes the sole target of hostility for reward-cost outcomes reduced by such acts. Thus, the democratic leader who encourages division of responsibility and participation in decisions may well be able, as Thibaut and Kelley suggest, to carry on both a social-emotional and a task role.[21] Hostility generated by the activities of a task leader may also be expressed by scapegoating, or by the displacement of hostility toward the low-status member of a group. In groups where task motivation and interest were low, a moderately strong relationship was observed between the degree to which the task leader stood out above the others in task-related activity and the amount of hostility directed toward the person with the lowest score in task participation.[22] Where the legitimacy of task activity was high, as measured by the members' task motivation and interest, there was little relation between these indicators of role differentiation and scapegoating.

LEGITIMACY OF LEADERSHIP   The laboratory groups in which the bifurcation of leadership was first studied differed in another respect which is important to an understanding of why this phenomenon is less evident in groups that have existed over a period of time. As previously noted, where costs incurred by group members are perceived to be due to the personal acts of the task leader, hostility is likely to be directed toward him. Thibaut and Kelley point out, however, that where group members perceive the directive attempts of the

19. MARCUS, 1960; TURK, 1961; MEILE, 1962; BURKE, 1967, 1968.   *20.* Reprinted by permission from E. GOFFMAN. *Encounters: Two studies in the sociology of interaction.* Indianapolis: The Bobbs-Merrill Company, Inc., 1961. P. 122.   *21.* THIBAUT & KELLEY, 1959.   *22.* BURKE, 1969.

leader as *legitimate,* hostile reactions are not apt to occur. Verba makes the following comment on this point:

> One of the most effective ways in which the instrumental directives of a group leader acquire legitimacy and avoid being received as personal, arbitrary challenges to the group members is for the leader to be perceived as acting not as an individual but as the agent of some impersonal force, such as the "demands of the situation" or the group traditions and norms. The invocation of some external authority by the group leader relieves the follower of the burden of accepting the control of another individual. Thibaut and Kelley, in a study of power relations in the dyad, conclude that group norms have the effect of reducing the tension between the more powerful and the less powerful member of the group. The impersonalization of expectations of behavior through the adoption of norms makes the influence relationship between the more and the less powerful group member more stable and palatable for both of them. For the less powerful member, the use of controls without a normative base would make those controls arbitrary and unpredictable, and lead to resistance on his part. For the more powerful member of a dyad, the use of purely personal power would also be unpleasant. He must either reduce his attempted control (and thereby perhaps endanger the accomplishment of the group goal) or risk the negative reactions of the other member. Thus the exercise of control in the name of a set of norms that legitimizes the control is to the advantage of both leader and follower.[23]

One way in which the leader's actions acquire legitimacy is through formal recognition of his leadership role. This is demonstrated in an experiment where one supervisor was elected and the other was assigned by the experimenter.[24] Under these circumstances, the elected supervisor, who is likely to be perceived as having more legitimate power, was shown to exert a greater influence over his work group than the nonelected supervisor.

Another investigation, conducted in a classroom situation, indicated that the arousal of hostility toward the instructor was a direct function of the extent to which he violated the legitimate expectations of the student by following his own inclinations rather than the student's desires.[25] In ROTC classes, instructions for making paper objects were given somewhat too rapidly to be grasped thoroughly. Votes were then taken to determine whether the procedure should be repeated or not, under the following two conditions: In the *teacher-centered condition,* students were led to expect that the instructor's vote would have twice the weight of the group. In the *student-centered condition,* students were

---

23. Reprinted by permission from S. Verba. *Small groups and political behavior: A study of leadership,* Princeton, N.J.: Princeton University Press, 1961. Pp. 172–173.   24. Raven & French, 1958.   25. Horwitz, 1963.

led to expect that the instructor's vote would be weighted only one-fourth as heavily as that of the group.

Actual votes, which took the form of ratings of the desire for continuing or for going back over the instructions, were disregarded. Votes were announced by arrangement so that the instructor moderately favored going on to the next topic, but the group moderately favored repeating the instructions for making the paper objects. With these ratings, continuing was legitimate in the teacher-centered group because of the extra weight given to the instructor's rating. In the student-centered group, however, going on meant that the instructor was arbitrarily reducing the weight given to the students' desires relative to the weight given his own, and this action was perceived as illegitimate. Considerably more hostility toward the instructor was expressed in this condition, as determined by student evaluations of him collected by the experimenter.

Another type of social norm protects the task leader from the damaging psychological effects of withdrawal of positive affect. In time, norms develop to encourage a degree of social distance between the leader and most of his followers, preventing the development of emotional dependence of the leader on all but a few of his followers. This allows him to carry out his task functions without experiencing too painfully the emotional rejections that he encounters.

As Homans notes, a distinction should be made between liking and esteem.[26] Leaders are often respected, particularly if they have earned respect through skillful leadership; but they are less often liked. To the degree that a task leader is successful in providing the group with many rewards, he may be liked. In the long run, however, his control over the rewards and costs received by the members of the group and his superior status are likely to produce ambivalent feelings toward him. Thus, in most groups outside the special conditions of the laboratory, a full-blown distinction between task and social-emotional leadership does not occur. The tendency for these functions to be incompatible when lodged in the same person results in a certain ambivalence toward the leader, and undoubtedly contributes to the costs that a leader experiences.

SUMMARY: ROLE DIFFERENTIATION   Under certain circumstances, a task leader and a social-emotional leader emerge to lead the group. The task specialist organizes and directs the activities of members so that they are focused on achieving group goals with maximum efficiency. The social-emotional specialist boosts morale and releases tensions arising from the group's work activities. These two specialists help to maintain the group in a state of equilibrium. Movement toward task accomplishment in groups frustrates needs and incurs other costs, so that forces arise to direct group activities away from the task and toward dealing with the needs and reducing or compensating for the costs. The social-emotional specialist, through joking or encouragement, or through generating esprit de corps, helps to dissipate these diversionary forces.

26. HOMANS, 1961.

The task specialist is seldom the best-liked member of the group. His role in focusing the efforts of other members on achievement precludes this and occasionally generates some hostility toward him. For adequate functioning, moreover, he cannot become so emotionally dependent on other members that he is unable to exercise power over them. This is reflected in his highly selective liking for other members, as compared with the social-emotional leader, who likes others strongly and equally well.

Role differentiation varies directly with the extent to which task functions are unrewarding or costly. It is likely to be maximized in groups where the affect, status, power, and communication structures are relatively undeveloped and where there is little consensus on values, on the appropriateness of activities, or on the facts of the situation and how these facts are to be assessed. In established groups, where the power of the leader has mainly a legitimate basis, hostile feelings and reactions toward him are somewhat reduced. His requests are seen not as stemming from some personal or arbitrary need, but from the demands of the situation or from the group norms. In most groups outside the laboratory, a full-blown distinction between task and social-emotional leadership does not occur. These functions, when lodged in the same person, generate feelings of ambivalence toward him, and contribute to the costs he experiences.

Leadership is also less likely to be divided when, for all members of the group, conditions make either task accomplishment or solving emotional problems dominant and the other function becomes minimal. In that case the one person contributing to the salient function will probably be liked. Another factor reducing hostility toward the task leader is the distribution of responsibility for and participation in decisions, so that no one person becomes the sole target of hostility.

Role Allocation and Exchange Theory

Exchange theory suggests that whether a person assumes a leadership function depends upon the reward-cost outcomes experienced by him and his followers. The rewards and costs would be a function of the requirements of the situation, such as the nature of the task confronting the group; the characteristics, needs, and skills of the person and his followers; his position in the power and communication structures; and in some instances, his position in the affect structure. These rewards and costs are considered in more detail below.

Rewards and Costs of the Leader

The rewards of leadership are twofold: first the satisfactions to be gained from successful task accomplishment, and second, the rewards gained from leadership activity in itself. These include satisfaction of needs for achievement and dominance, as well as other social-emotional needs.

Persons who assume leadership incur a number of costs. In addition to the effort directly expended in goal-related activities, the leader experiences costs in the form of strains stemming from the necessity of serving as a model for group behavior. Other costs include anxiety imposed by the ever-present possibility of failure; rebuffs in his attempts to lead, with consequent loss of status; and blame as well as guilt when his direction is accepted but results in group failure. Finally, since his behavior is apt to affect adversely the reward-cost outcomes of other members, he faces the costs of losing their friendship. He risks not only his status but also his popularity. Closely related is the cost of loneliness. The leader is often avoided, not only because he may have incurred hostility, but also because of his power: others regard interaction with him as risky in terms of possible adverse reward-cost outcomes.

Rewards and Costs of Followers

Following a leader has several rewards. First among these is goal achievement. Often followers are willing to be led because they recognize that without leadership, the goals of the group would not be achieved. Second, just as certain personality needs are met by leadership behavior, others are met by followership. Dependency needs are directly met by following a leader. If the leader has highly valued characteristics, other needs may be met vicariously through identification with him. Similarly, through identification with the leader, followers may be provided with a sense of shared outlook that provides support for their view of social reality.[27] Both of these consequences of identification with the leader may underlie the phenomenon of leader charisma, a special quality thought to characterize many leaders.[28] The suggestion, in other words, is that charisma is a function of the extent to which followers can identify with a leader—can take him as a model to which they aspire either in fantasy or in reality. Finally, one of the rewards gained by the follower is a cost foregone. By accepting a follower role he escapes anxiety over the risk of failure in a leadership role and also escapes blame when failure occurs.

Among the costs of being a follower is low status. In some groups—for example, work groups—the worker-follower receives less pay as well. The follower also has less control over the activities of the group and of specific other members. Thus these activities may be less rewarding and more costly to him than they would be if he had a greater degree of control. He also foregoes the intrinsic satisfaction that might be gained from engaging in leadership tasks: He is more likely to be assigned the duller routine jobs.

Situational Determinants of Leadership

Rewards and costs associated with various leader and follower behaviors are in part a function of situationally imposed requirements. A number of studies suggest that if the costs of inaction in the face of situational demands are great

27. HOLLANDER & JULIAN, 1969. 28. WEBER, 1968.

enough, group members will respond with appropriate behavior. Thus, in initially leaderless groups studied in the laboratory, or in groups studied in a natural setting where established leaders fail to carry out leadership functions, certain members will rise to the occasion.[29] What kinds of behaviors will occur and who will perform them are in part dictated by the demands of the situation. One investigator finds that the social-emotional specialist in a mental hospital group is more apt to exercise leadership when conflict develops between patients.[30] Others have shown that as a group proceeds through the problem-solving process, members respond with behavior appropriate to the problem that the group faces at that particular phase of the process.[31]

Who will respond depends on the rewards and costs arising out of the interplay between the demands of the situation and the characteristics of individuals. The distribution of skills affects the costs of members; those who have the required skills to a high degree can respond at less cost to themselves than those less skilled. Studies that show a shift in leadership with a change in the nature of the task document this point. For example, in one study, the same group was observed while performing six different tasks, and leadership ratings for each member in each task situation were obtained.[32] These were statistically analyzed to determine the basic task functions underlying the specific tasks. The analysis suggested that there were two families of tasks underlying leadership in the group. One was characterized by ability to lead in task situations that call for *intellectual* solutions and the other by ability to lead in task situations that call for *manipulation of objects*.

Situations calling for different interests also yield varying reward-cost outcomes for members assuming leadership. Persons other than the designated leader emerge to perform a leadership function in connection with a specific problem in which they are especially interested.[33]

Personality Characteristics and Leadership Behavior

At the beginning of the chapter we noted that the study of individual differences between leaders and nonleaders has not proved very fruitful. This conclusion should not be interpreted to mean that the distribution of leadership among members has no relation to their personality. While no personality trait guarantees leadership in all situations, studies of the relative frequency of various characteristics of both leaders and followers, and studies of the generality or specificity of leadership from situation to situation and group to group, suggest that certain personality characteristics increase the likelihood of a person's adopting a leader or follower role in a wide variety of situations. This is

---

29. BALES & SLATER, 1955.   30. PARKER, 1958.   31. BALES & STRODTBECK, 1951.   32. CARTER, HAYTHORN, & HOWELL, 1950.   33. CROCKETT, 1955.

especially true if leadership *behaviors* are compared, in contrast to fixed traits thought to be relatively permanent characteristics of the person.

Several studies illustrate that leadership has some generality across different tasks.[34] The greatest amount of generality across tasks occurs when the tasks have a related content. This was demonstrated in the previously described study when the tasks employed required the ability to lead in intellectual task situations or in situations calling for the manipulation of objects.[35] Within either class of tasks, the same persons usually served as leaders. In another study, the composition of three-man groups working on the same task was varied.[36] Those who were high on task ability, individual assertiveness, and sociometric popularity in the first group ranked high in these respects in three subsequent group sessions where they interacted with different persons.

Some characteristics, such as intelligence, or some general skills, such as verbal fluency, may be associated with leadership in a wide range of situations because persons high in these can successfully perform leadership activities at low cost. Leader or follower roles may be related to personality because the activities called for by these roles lead to the satisfaction of dominant personality needs. This is consistent with evidence that leaders are generally high in such traits as ascendance[37] and dominance,[38] and it is consistent with the argument that those who readily take the follower role find in it satisfaction for strong dependency needs.[39]

Studies of a wide variety of groups in natural settings show that task leaders of more effective groups are able to differentiate to a greater degree among their followers than are leaders of less effective groups.[40] They see their best and poorest workers as more dissimilar than do less effective leaders. Since this perceptual characteristic relates to effective functioning of the group, it will be discussed in more detail in the next chapter. In those instances where a division of the leadership role takes place, a closely related finding mentioned earlier is the more selective liking for members expressed by the task leader in contrast to the social-emotional leader. Comparison of each type of leader by Bales and Slater indicates that the social-emotional leader likes everyone strongly and equally, while the task leader likes others more selectively. Bales and Slater interpret this difference, as well as the greater rigidity and absolutism implied by the social-emotional specialist's high F-scale scores (see Chapter 2), as indicating a strong need to be liked on the part of the person who is a social-emotional specialist:

> These best liked men, then, say in effect, "I like everyone." In connection with their high F-score, this suggests the possibility of a certain rigidity in the attitudes of many best liked men toward interpersonal relationships.

34. CARTER & NIXON, 1949; GIBB, 1954; KATZ, MCCLINTOCK, & SARNOFF, 1957.   35. CARTER, HAYTHORN, & HOWELL, 1950.   36. BORGATTA, COUCH, & BALES, 1954.   37. GUETZKOW, 1960.   38. HUNTER & JORDAN, 1939; RICHARDSON & HANAWALT, 1943.   39. FROMM, 1941.   40. FIEDLER, 1960.

They may "have to be liked" and may achieve prominence in this respect because of the ingratiating skills they have acquired during their lives in bringing this desired situation about. Their avoidance of differentiation in ratings may be an expression of the compulsive and indiscriminate nature of this striving.[41]

Bales and Slater interpret the task specialist's *~~power~~ poorer* F scores and more selective liking for other group members as indicating ability to face a certain amount of negative feeling:

> It would seem to be important for the task specialist to be able to face a certain amount of negative feeling toward him without abandoning his role, and his apparent willingness to make differentiated liking choices may be indicative of at least a minimal ability of this kind. Not to have to like everyone implies an awareness and acceptance of the fact that everyone may not have to like him.[42]

Finally, some characteristics may be associated with leaders because their possession leads others to allow them to assume leadership. The nature of these characteristics depends upon the reward-cost outcomes they provide for followers. Sanford's study of the types of leadership preferred by authoritarian and equalitarian individuals provides an illustration.[43] He found that authoritarians and equalitarians differ in the kind of leadership they require and also in their reactions to leader behavior. Authoritarians prefer leaders with status and strength who exercise firm direction. They do not like weak leaders, and are hostile toward them. Equalitarians, in contrast, while able to accept strong leadership if the situation demands it, do not find it more satisfying. Equalitarians evaluate leaders in terms of their consideration for group members and for the group's welfare, while authoritarians are goal-oriented.

Summary: Personality and Leadership

Leadership has some generality across different tasks, especially if the tasks are similar in content. Also, when the composition of groups performing the same task is varied, the same persons are likely to assume leadership in the different groups. Certain personality characteristics, such as intelligence or verbal fluency, may be associated with leadership in a wide variety of tasks because these skills are relevant to successful performance. A characteristic apparently possessed by many task leaders is the ability to maintain emotional distance between themselves and many of their followers. The social-emotional leader, on the other hand, apparently has a strong desire to be liked by all group mem-

41. Reprinted by permission from R. F. BALES and P. E. SLATER. Role differentiation in small decision-making groups. In T. PARSONS and R. F. BALES (Eds.), *Family, socialization and interaction process.* Chicago: The Free Press of Glencoe, Ill., 1955. Pp. 294–295.   *42.* Reprinted by permission from R. F. BALES and P. E. SLATER. Role differentiation in small decision-making groups. In T. PARSONS and R. F. BALES (Eds.), *Family, socialization and interaction process.* Chicago: The Free Press of Glencoe, Ill., 1955. P. 295.   *43.* SANFORD, 1952.

bers. Finally, certain characteristics of followers favor those persons as leaders who can best provide high reward-cost outcomes for persons with these characteristics.

Effects of Group Structures on Leadership

The discussion so far has emphasized several points: (1) Persons exercise leadership behavior to the extent that such behavior provides favorable reward-cost outcomes to both leader and follower; (2) depending on the requirements of the situation, those with appropriate abilities, interests, and needs assume leadership functions to a greater degree than others; and (3) where leadership is stable, the stability is owing to the leader's possession of characteristics with similar implications in a wide variety of situations. In laboratory groups, whose existence is normally of very short duration, these several factors might adequately explain why some persons manage to retain leadership over a period of time. In groups that have functioned long enough to develop stable structures and a certain routine, however, much of the stability in leader personnel can be explained in other terms. Perhaps this is best understood if we ask ourselves why the leader-follower relation that emerges in one situation continues into a new one.

In part the answer lies in the fact that the mutually rewarding pattern in the previous situation has created certain stabilities in the communication, power, and status structures that reinforce initially established leadership patterns. These stabilities of structure are established in several ways. With respect to the communication structure, Klein suggests that habits of communication used to solve a series of similar problems carry over into a situation characterized by new problems:

> Suppose now that in the history of the group the same problem has frequently arisen. In that case the sequence in which contributions to the task are made will tend to become habitual. It will become habitual for certain members to speak before others do, for Jack to wait until Joe has spoken. In this way, restrictions in free communication are brought about. The need for orderliness and predictability of behavior will further accentuate this tendency toward restricted communication. Once such a routine has become established, it tends to remain whether the task is a routine one or not. Thus the communication structure may become independent of the problem to be solved. . . .[44]

As some investigators have noted, successful performance of an activity contributing to the group's goal achievement raises a person's status.[45] Once a status structure is established, with high status ascribed to those exercising

---

44. Reprinted by permission from J. Klein. *The Study of Groups.* London: Routledge & Kegan Paul, Ltd., 1956. P. 25.   45. Parsons, Bales, & Shils, 1953.

leadership, it is likely to be perpetuated. Berger, Cohen, and Zelditch have argued that, particularly in the absence of other information, status gained as a result of task proficiency in one area generalizes to other areas.[46] Similarly, Hollander notes that early task competence and conformity to group norms earn a leader status credits, as seen in Chapter 9. Later the leader can "spend" these credits to increase his influence in those situations where he must depart from expectations to function innovatively as a leader.[47]

The communication and status structures mutually reinforce each other and are in turn related to power, in a rather complex fashion. Status is often a resource adding to the power of the high-status person, but at the same time status may serve as a brake on power: Status is endangered if power is used too freely (see Chapter 9). The relation among power, leadership, and *communication centrality* (see Chapter 12) is also relevant. Klein has argued that the most central person in a communication network has greater direct and indirect access to the information others possess, and since many others must exert influence on the group through him, he can control the flow of such information to his advantage. In addition, his very centrality makes the group highly dependent on him for the performance of leadership functions.[48] Both he and others are apt to define him as the leader. That he is so defined is supported by a number of investigations discussed in more detail in the next chapter. In these experiments the channels of communication open to members of problem-solving groups were arranged so that some persons held much more central positions than others. When the participants were asked to indicate who was the leader in their groups, the person with the most central position was most frequently named.

Finally, occupying a particular status, either as a leader or as a follower, affects the skills and motives of each status occupant so as to maintain the existing structure. In discussing the tendency of leaders in the labor movement to perpetuate themselves, Michels notes that leaders develop skills in the exercise of leadership functions, an opportunity largely denied to followers.[49] At the same time their greater investment in time and energy, as well as the integration of this role into the self, results in strong motivation on the part of leaders to maintain their position. The corresponding lesser involvement of a follower, often accompanied by a sense of obligation to the leader, further maintains each in his respective role.

Leadership, Authority, and the Normative Structure

Stability in leadership is also a product of the normative structure. In time the expectations that members share for each other's conduct are such that the leader is expected to lead and the followers to comply with his direction. Ex-

46. BERGER, COHEN, & ZELDITCH, 1966.   47. HOLLANDER, 1960.   48. KLEIN, 1956.   49. MICHELS, 1949.

pectations which are enforced by group-imposed sanctions are the basis for the leader's authority. Blau has described the emergence of authority in both informal and formal groups.[50] In informal groups, the initial influence of the leader over a follower rests on an exchange of outcomes in which the follower, in return for his compliance with his leader's requests, obtains task-related rewards at low cost as a result of the task competence provided by the leader. The followers come to respect the leader's guidance and competence, his fairness, and his concern for group achievement. They exchange views concerning his leadership and arrive at consensus. At that point, social pressures arise to provide continued support and recognition to the leader: His position is *legitimized*. These social pressures prevent individual members who might otherwise oppose the leader from expressing their resistance. Once recognized as the legitimate leader of the group, most members willingly comply with his requests at little cost to him or to themselves.

Blau's analysis, however, points up a basic dilemma of leadership.[51] To become a leader, one must have power and the group must approve the use of that power. But attaining power and attaining social approval are somewhat incompatible. The demands that a leader has to make on members may lower their outcomes and interfere with obtaining their positive regard. Power is attained by providing others with resources that raise their outcomes and make them dependent, but also requires that the leader remain independent of any resources they might offer in return. Thus, he cannot accept favors which they tender to reduce their debt to him, and his refusals are apt to be seen as rejections. So it is not easy for him to gain their approval of him as their legitimate leader.

The solution to this dilemma is a temporal one. In the early phase of a group's existence, the leader mobilizes his power in ways that do not lead to follower approval beyond that necessary to gain leadership, but in later phases, he uses his power in a fashion that leads to approval and legitimation. Thus, in the early phases he does not hesitate to compete with group members for power. He attempts to demonstrate his competence as the best man for the job of leading the group. For example, the potential leader of a gang uses his physical strength first against the other members to assert his dominance over them. Only then can he organize their activities and lead them in street activities. Similarly, the man who uses his intelligence, skill, and experience in problem-solving groups first demonstrates his competence to lead. Once established, the leader may then use his augmented resources to keep group members happy, to gain their approval and their recognition of him as the group's legitimate leader.

In the case of formal authority, this first phase of power mobilization is bypassed. The initial power of a formal leader, such as a manager in a business establishment, rests on the conditions of the employment contract, where ac-

---

50. BLAU, 1964a.   51. BLAU, 1964a.

tions contrary to his orders allow him to impose on recalcitrant employees sanctions such as dismissal or demotion. In time, however, he too, through the manner in which he exercises his power based on formal sanctions, may acquire legitimate authority.

The official position and power of the manager give him various opportunities to furnish important services to subordinates that obligate them to him. His superior knowledge and skill, on the basis of which he presumably was selected for his position, enable him to train newcomers and advise oldtimers. His formal status gives him access to top echelons and staff specialists in the organization, making it possible for him to channel needed information to subordinates and to represent their interests with the higher administration. While his official duties as manager *require* him to perform a minimum of these services for subordinates the extra effort he devotes to benefit them beyond this minimum creates social obligations. Of special significance in this connection are the manager's status prerogatives and formal powers, for he can win the appreciation of his subordinates merely by not exercising these: by not insisting on the deference due his rank, by not enforcing an unpopular housekeeping rule, by ignoring how much time subordinates take for lunch as long as they perform their duties. Every privilege the manager is granted and every rule he is empowered to enforce increase the capital on which he can draw to make subordinates indebted to him. By not using some of his power, he invests it in social obligations. The advantages subordinates derive from his pattern of supervision obligate them to reciprocate by complying with his directives and requests.[52]

Complying with the requests of a superior is certainly not always satisfying, and this leads to a further development and strengthening of the leader's legitimate power. Blau suggests that doubts arise from time to time about the value of complying in exchange for the resources provided by the leader, generating cognitive dissonance.[53] As noted in Chapter 3, engaging in behavior contrary to one's attitude arouses cognitive dissonance. Such dissonance, Blau suggests, is resolved when the members enhance the value of the benefits that they receive from the leader and depreciate the costs of compliance. They come to see compliance as something they give freely, and the manager's directives as his duty or responsibility rather than an expression of his will. In this way, cognitive dissonance is resolved, and the leader's position is legitimated.

Thus, to the extent that a manager's power to enforce compliance is legitimated by the norms of a group and thus transformed into authority, compliance rests on a new level of exchange, that between the followers where compliance to the directives of the manager is exchanged for approval from their fellow followers.

In many instances of course, the authority that a leader exercises over a

52. BLAU, 1964, p. 206.   53. BLAU, 1964.

follower does not arise out of the interaction between the two, but through the socialization process. Both parties have internalized the cultural standards that dictate that one will comply with the demands of another person occupying a particular position. Blau refers to this as institutionalized authority.[54] This form of influence was discussed in Chapter 8 as legitimate power.

Summary: Group Structure and Leadership

In established groups, the formation of stable structures has much to do with maintaining certain persons as leaders over a long period of time. The mutual rewards experienced by members of a successful group create stabilities in the communication, power, and status structures that reinforce initially established leadership patterns. This occurs as a result of established habits of communication and the linkage among the communication, status, and power structures. Occupying a central position in the communication structures gives the leader an advantage over others in continuing to initiate, direct, and maintain activities. Established leaders also have the best opportunity to develop leadership skills as well as the strongest motivation, stemming from their desire to maintain their status. The lack of opportunity for followers to develop leadership skills, their lesser involvement, and their sense of obligation to leaders also stabilize the leadership structure.

Finally, normative expectations emerge that specify the right of the leader to lead and the followers to comply which are enforced by group-imposed sanctions and serve to legitimate the leader-follower relation.

---

54. BLAU, 1964.

12

Group Productivity and Satisfaction

Motivation
Satis

One important group process has not yet been discussed: the ongoing work activity of the group aimed at accomplishing a task or solving a problem. Various names applied to this process include *group decision, group problem solving,* and *group productivity.* This aspect of group behavior pervades every part of daily life. Probably most important decisions in human societies are made in group settings. Primitive societies have their tribal councils, and modern societies abound with such decision-making groups as legislatures, cabinets, supreme courts, juries, parole boards, corporate boards, school boards, commissions, and more informal, idiosyncratic groups such as committees, work groups, individual families, and friendship groups. Moreover, almost all the output of goods and services of human society is produced in group situations. Departments or sections of factories, offices, and institutions consist of small groups of workers who influence each other with respect to the quality and quantity of the product or service they produce.

The process by which such groups arrive at decisions concerning the various problems that confront them is an interesting one. Two kinds of problems face all task groups. One set of problems arises from the task and its setting. Typically, the focus here is on utilizing available group resources in a manner that maximizes productivity. A second set revolves around the maintenance of internal relations that promote satisfaction, leading members to remain in the group and to contribute to the group efforts. The distribution of rewards among group members so as to maintain optimum levels of motivation and satisfaction is especially important in this context.

Early laboratory studies usually assigned to a group a problem having a single correct solution. In everyday situations, however, groups often arrive at consensus on issues that have no single answer. Many recent studies have assigned this kind of task to laboratory groups; illustrations are simulated committee decisions, jury decisions, and case conferences. In addition, many types of groups have been studied in actual field situations, including juries, committees, conference groups, and all kinds of work groups. Productivity in problem-solving laboratory groups has usually been defined in terms of the quality and speed of solutions to problems provided by the experimenter. In field situations, productivity is usually defined in terms of the quality and quantity of the daily work task.

Individuals versus Groups

Often behavioral scientists investigate problems that have some relation to commonsense or lay beliefs. One such belief relative to thinking or problem solving is expressed in the saying "Two heads are better than one." Much early research on group problem solving was addressed to the question: Are individuals or groups better at solving problems? As research findings accumulated, it became apparent that the answer was more complicated than originally assumed. Conflicting results obtained by numerous investigators suggest that the answer varies depending on the kind of task confronting the group, the manner in which effectiveness is assessed, and the nature of the group, including the resources and abilities of its members.

In order to compare individual efforts with those of the group, one must conceptualize a baseline measure that represents individual performance. Typically, this baseline is some function of the level of performance that would be attained if individuals were to work alone (i.e., without influencing each other's performance). Group performances that depart from this baseline are *true group effects*.

Various models have been invented for obtaining a baseline. The performances of actual groups are compared to see whether they perform better or worse than what might be expected from these models. An analysis of the departures from these models helps clarify the ways in which group factors either facilitate or interfere with task accomplishment.

These models differ depending largely on which of three general types of tasks are employed: group learning tasks, problem-solving tasks, and group-decision tasks. The latter two types of tasks have been used most frequently, with most attention given to problem solving. Steiner has provided a taxonomy of models for assessing the potential productivity of problem-solving groups.[1] One such model originally independently developed by Taylor and by Lorge

1. STEINER, 1966.

and Solomon suggests that the potential performance of a group equals that of its best member.[2] Sometimes a task is such that if any one person in the group solves the problem then the solution is apparent to all. In that case the chances that a group will be successful is a function of the size of the group and the probability that persons characterizing the group will be able to solve the problem.

A somewhat more complicated model was advanced by Lorge and Solomon to handle problems requiring a pooling of abilities.[3] In this model a problem must be solved in two or more stages; no one in the group can solve all parts, but one or more persons can solve each step alone. This model does not require that members be able to influence each other, and yet it successfully predicted the results of a previous investigation which purported to show that the group was superior to the individual.[4] A number of other models have been advanced to account for group superiority which similarly do not require the assumption of true group effects.

When predictions from these models are compared with results from real groups, the supposed advantages of groups have been called into question. Frequently, the performance of groups has been inferior, but in some instances, real groups have performed at a level superior to that expected. These results have led investigators to examine the ways in which group processes add to or detract from effective problem solving. In a review of this literature Kelley and Thibaut suggest that how a group performs in comparison with its most proficient member depends on the type of problem.[5]

When a problem is relatively simple and its solution easily verifiable, the chances are that the solution of its best members will become the group solution; i.e., the group will perform at the level of its most proficient member. Where a problem consists of a number of parts and the members of a group differ in their capabilities with respect to the parts, group performance may exceed that of the most proficient member. Thus, it could well be that no one in the group has sufficient talent to solve all parts of the problem, but the group contains members who can solve all the parts. Thus, by pooling abilities, the group can solve a problem that the most proficient member cannot.

Where a problem is such that the activities of group members distract or otherwise interfere with each other, and where the solution is not obvious so that resistance to the acceptance of the best answer occurs, groups can be expected to perform worse than their most proficient members working alone. Crucial to whether group or individual performance is superior is the difficulty of the problem relative to the capabilities of group members. As Thibaut and Kelley note:

> It appears that, with an easy set of problems, the more capable individuals can master most of the items alone and can contribute little to one another

---

2. Taylor, 1954; Lorge & Solomon, 1955.   3. Lorge & Solomon, 1955.   4. Shaw, 1932.
5. Kelley & Thibaut, 1969.

in group discussion. With more difficult items, each capable person is likely to be able to solve some but not other items; thus, a pair of such persons can gain from pooling their complementary resources. The situation is reversed for persons of low abilities. With difficult items, they do very poorly alone and can contribute little to each other (or to a person from any other ability level) in the course of joint problem solving. With easier items, each person is able to master certain ones alone and pairs will show a pooling effect. In sum, the pooling effect seems to require that group members confront tasks of *moderate* difficulty to them, neither too easy nor too difficult.[6]

That groups are not as proficient in solving problems as one might expect from their greater resources has led to the study of the manner in which group settings limit the potentials of groups. For the most part, these factors are related to features of the group structure and task situation.

Group Structure and the Task Situation

The outcome of a task situation is affected by group factors if they bring about changes in any of the following: (1) the resources available to the group, (2) the application of these resources to the task, and (3) the likelihood that the task will be carried out, or at least the likelihood that agreement about the proper approach will be achieved.

Phases in Group Task Performance

If task groups are observed in action, the process is seen to follow a fairly uniform sequence. Group members exchange information relevant to the problem, one or more solutions based on such information are proposed, and finally agreement is reached. In everyday situations the agreed-upon solution in most instances carries implications for change in the future behavior of the group members: They subsequently carry out the task in some manner. For example, the decisions of a work group concerning new production methods are implemented by a change in their work activities. In laboratory studies this phase of the task process is sometimes ignored or considered a part of the preceding agreement phase. All four phases should, however, be kept in mind in discussing the relation between a particular factor and the quality of the group product. This is necessary because the effects of a condition may be conducive to high quality with respect to one phase of the task but may work in the opposite direction in another phase. A particular factor affects the quality of the group product through its effects on group structures and such emergents of interaction as group frames of reference and cohesion.

6. Reprinted by permission from H. H. KELLEY & J. W. THIBAUT, Group problem solving. In G. LINDZEY & E. ARONSON (Eds.), *The handbook of social psychology.* (2nd ed.) Vol. 4. Reading, Mass.: Addison-Wesley Publishing Company, Inc., 1969. P. 71.

With respect to a given problem-solving phase, certain structures or emotional or cognitive states are more crucial than others. In large part, the communication structure determines how effectively a group marshals resources; the power structure determines the particular combination of elements that becomes the group solution; and group cohesiveness determines how quickly a group reaches agreement and the extent to which it is motivated to carry out the solution.

Structural Effects on Early Phases

Since the importance of various features of the affect, status, communication, and power structures vary depending on the phase of the problem-solving sequence, early and late phases will be discussed separately. The early phases, discussed in this section, include the amassing of such resources as the relevant information about the problem and the environment, and the later phases, discussed in the subsequent section, refer to combining resources into some proposed course of action and implementing it by group members. Since the effects of the leadership structure have been dealt with in the research literature somewhat independently of other structural features, these will be discussed later in the chapter.

EFFECTS OF GROUP SIZE   The effects of the size of the group provide an excellent illustration of how a condition may have a rather complex relation to the task process. One might expect that as the size of a group increased, its effectiveness would rise as a function of accumulation of resources such as ideas and information. Yet idea productivity is not linearly related to size. As Gibb has suggested, idea productivity is a negatively accelerated increasing function of the size of a group.[7] This means that with each increment in size there is a progressively smaller increment in the number of ideas. In large part this appears to result from the effects of size on the *communication structure*. It is noted in Chapter 9 that as size increases stronger restraints against communicating appear—restraints which only a few persons seem able to overcome. Everyone has observed such effects. In small groups the rate of participation is fairly equal among members, but in large groups the bulk of the talking is done by relatively few persons, with most remaining comparatively silent.[8]

Thus, an increase in group size will result in an increasing fund of information, an advantage counteracted by increasing restrictions on communication. Some additional disadvantages experienced by large problem-solving groups will be noted later.

COMMUNICATION STRUCTURE   A major feature of communication networks is the extent to which each person has direct access to other members of the

7. GIBB, 1951.   8. KELLEY & THIBAUT, 1954.

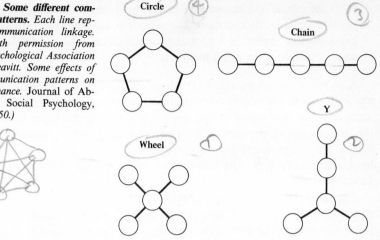

Figure 12-1 Some different communication patterns. *Each line represents a communication linkage. (Adapted with permission from American Psychological Association and H. J. Leavitt. Some effects of certain communication patterns on group performance.* Journal of Abnormal and Social Psychology, *1951,* **46,** *38–50.)*

group. A person may occupy a central position, where he is able to communicate directly with many other members, or he may be in a peripheral position, where he can communicate only indirectly through a third person with most members. Most experimental studies of the effects of communication structure on task behavior have used communication nets varying in this property of *centrality-peripherality.*

In one experiment, five-man groups solved a simple problem under conditions where communication was restricted in accordance with one of the four communication nets reproduced in Figure 12-1.[9] Each person was given a card containing five different symbols. The problem consisted of finding the symbol that was common to everyone's card. Group members agreed on the leader and established a stable structure most rapidly when they were organized according to the wheel, and did so progressively less rapidly when organized according to the Y, the chain, and the circle, with the circle never obtaining a stable organization. Similarly, performance was best with the wheel and poorest with the circle. Subjects performing in a circle network wrote more messages and made and corrected more errors than the other groups. All members of a circle network enjoyed their task to a greater extent than those occupying positions of low centrality in other networks. In the other networks, persons occupying a central position were apt to enjoy their task to a great degree, while those in a peripheral position were apt to be rather dissatisfied. Leavitt presents a succinct summary:

> Patternwise, the picture formed by the results is of differences almost always in the order *circle, chain, Y, wheel.*

We may grossly characterize the kinds of differences that occur in this

9. Leavitt, 1951.

way: the circle, one extreme, is active, leaderless, unorganized, erratic, and yet is enjoyed by its members. The wheel, at the other extreme, is less active, has a distinct leader, is well and stably organized, is less erratic, and yet is unsatisfying to most of its members.[10]

A series of studies by other investigators helps to explain why performance and satisfaction are related to centrality. Leavitt had suggested that the relative independence of action of the person occupying a central position in contrast to the dependence of persons at the periphery leads other members to perceive him as the leader, leads him to perceive himself as a leader, and accounts for his higher satisfaction. The last part of this suggestion has received some empirical support.[11]

The conditions underlying the relative effectiveness of groups with different communication structures have not yet been clearly delineated. Most investigations indicate that the effects of communication networks on performance vary with the task.[12] A number of different explanations for this have been suggested. It is difficult to choose from among these, since each has some empirical support. Christie, Luce, and Macy have suggested that network characteristics are increasingly important when individuals follow *the rule of communicating to the member who will benefit most* (will gain the most pieces of new information).[13] Communication is most efficient *when the exchanges of information are at a minimum.*

Where individuals follow this rule (and Christie and his colleagues show that they increasingly do as the number of trials increases), the probability is higher in some networks than in others of hitting on an optimum solution involving the minimum of information exchanges. If we compare the chain with the circle, for instance, the restrictions on the end men in the chain—they can send only to one other person—begin a process in which following the rule of optimum transfer of information leads to optimum performance. But in the circle, where all participants must make their first choice at random, and only one combination of choices will lead to a solution involving the minimum number of exchanges, the chances of this optimum outcome are much less.

The network that is most restricted, of course, is the wheel. In this network, four out of five persons must send to one man, the person at the hub. Each sends information to one person each time an exchange is allowed, and participants who proceed on the basis of the rule of optimum information transfer will communicate with the person at the hub and are bound to end up with a sequence of exchanges involving the minimum number, which in this case is five. In this instance the characteristics of the network force optimum organization on the group.

10. Reprinted by permission from H. J. Leavitt. Some effects of certain communication patterns on group performance. *Journal of Abnormal and Social Psychology,* 1951, **46,** 46.   *11.* Trow, 1957; Shaw, 1954.   *12.* Shaw, 1964.   *13.* Christie, Luce, & Macy, 1952.

In their experiments, Guetzkow and Simon also find that networks having a centralized structure allow the best performance.[14] But they have a different explanation—that such networks favor optimum exchange of information thus helping members to develop *the most efficient organization.* Networks restricting information exchange appear to have two negative effects.[15] First, they reduce both the volume of specific suggestions made for organizing the group and the spread of the planning ideas through the group. Second, they reduce the readiness with which the most effective members may be adequately placed.

These two explanations (maximum information transfer and optimal organization) both favor centralized structures. The principle of maximum information transfer best fits the Christie, Luce, and Macy experiments because their participants were not allowed to exchange information about the organization of the group, while the principle of optimal organization fits the Guetzkow and Simon studies because participants were allowed to communicate about organization.

Shaw has objected on two grounds to the conclusions of Guetzkow concerning the mediating effects of organization.[16] He feels, first, that this explanation is not in accordance with some further empirical evidence, and second, that a theory which he proposed not only predicts the same effects of organization but in addition is a more economical approach since it explains many other findings.

He suggests that the effects of varying communication nets can be explained in terms of the concepts of independence and saturation. *Independence* refers to the freedom with which an individual may function in a group. A person's independence is influenced by the access to information provided through his network position and by other conditions, such as the type of task faced by the group. Independence is thought to primarily affect member satisfaction. Persons whose positions allow for a high degree of independence are well satisfied, since they can fulfill such needs as those for autonomy, recognition, and achievement. Thus, the findings that participants in more central positions are more satisfied than those in peripheral positions are as expected. Further, independence affects performance by bringing about an increased willingness to perform under the more autonomous conditions.

Shaw defines *saturation* broadly to include the requirements placed upon a position (by any source) in a communication structure that call for action by the participant in that position.[17] These requirements are a function of the number of incoming and outgoing channels connected to the position and the nature of the task.

Saturation relates primarily to performance. A consideration of how the type of organization affects saturation suggests that the various results obtained are consistent with the concepts of independence and saturation. Initially the effect of a centralized structure is to increase saturation for those individuals in

14. GUETZKOW & SIMON, 1955.   *15.* GUETZKOW & DILL, 1957.   *16.* SHAW, 1964.   *17.* SHAW, 1964.

central positions—particularly on complex tasks, where much information must at first be exchanged in order for members to orient to the task. As problem solving becomes routinized and members learn their roles, saturation decreases.

This formulation is consistent with the results reported.[18] Moreover, it resolves what appeared to be a conflict with experimental data demonstrating that, on a complex task under the centralized wheel, performance was poorer in the beginning and superior to that of the circle on later trials.[19] That groups learn to organize their functioning more efficiently in time is also consistent with a study reporting that differences in the production of correct solutions in a simple task for groups run under the condition of the circle and the wheel disappeared after a large number of trials involving reinforcement for speed and accuracy of solutions.[20]

Shaw has suggested that the effects of a wide variety of other variables in network studies are understandable in terms of how these variables affect independence and saturation.[21] Studies of the effects of network change on performance and satisfaction of participants indicate that, when possible, groups continue the type of organization developed under the conditions of one network even though *changed to a new one.*[22] But if the initial network is relatively inefficient and the new one is superior, some shift toward the new one occurs. Thus, groups that shift from a completely connected network to a more centralized one (e.g., the wheel) change more, a result consistent with a decrease in saturation and an increase in independence.

Other findings suggest that some caution should be exercised in generalizing from these studies of isolated networks to situations where the networks are a part of a larger organization.[23] Four laboratory organizations were formed consisting of five-man subgroups organized either in the wheel network or a totally connected network (one in which members had direct access to every other member). Members were restricted to networks when communicating within their subgroups, but could communicate with other persons in the larger organization. The four organizations differed in the degree to which their subnetworks were of the centralized or decentralized type. Contrary to the case for isolated networks, decentralized subgroups with completely connected networks were just as likely as the centralized subgroups to develop a centralized problem-solving procedure. Decentralized organizations performed better, and while differences in satisfaction were not associated with network position, higher satisfaction occurred in a predominantly decentralized network. The investigators suggest that the presence of alternative communication channels in the larger organization accounted for these differences.

That such extra-network factors operate is supported by abundant evidence.

18. Leavitt, 1951; Shaw, 1954.   19. Mulder, 1960.   20. Burgess, 1968.   21. Shaw, 1964.
22. Lawson, 1965; Cohen, 1962; Cohen, Bennis, & Wolkon, 1962.   23. Cohen, Robinson, & Edwards, 1969.

For example, one study demonstrates that rate of participation is determined in part by the feedback persons receive.[24] In this study the number of contributions of certain arbitrarily chosen members was increased by telling them that their contributions were insightful. Similarly, contributions by other members were decreased by labeling their contribution as not insightful. Moreover, the member's position in structures other than communication, such as the affect, status, and power structures, will greatly affect the reactions of others to his contribution. If he has high status, for example, he may receive approval for mediocre contributions. Under such circumstances, the input of ideas in the early phase of problem solving is apt to be adversely affected.

At times, communication patterns in groups outside the laboratory may roughly approximate laboratory networks. Virtually all nonlaboratory situations involve restrictions of some kind. And nearly always, some members of the group play a more centralized role in communication. Even when group members function in a face-to-face situation where it is theoretically possible for all to hear the contributions of others, the flow of ideas is often restricted by status or other considerations, and often takes a hierarchical structure. For instance, the contributions of lower-status individuals may only gain general consideration if they are attended to and relayed by certain others. In his classic study of a street-corner gang, Whyte observed that the suggestions of low-status boys rarely obtained a hearing in a discussion unless they were picked up and repeated by the higher-status members of the group.[25]

AFFECT, POWER, AND STATUS STRUCTURES   The affect, status, and power structures discussed in previous chapters affect the forms of communication that occur in groups and, thus, relate to effective performance. Sociometric choices are rarely equally distributed. Most commonly, a minority of group members receive many choices. Also, some subgroups are often partially or completely isolated from other group members. Consequently some persons occupy a central position in the friendship structure, and they are apt to possess and provide more information than others. Their ideas will have greater circulation and receive more attention. A quite different effect on communication arises from the fact that people often communicate in social-emotional areas unrelated to the task. Since such communication actively diverts time and energy from the task, we can conclude that strong affect is apt to interfere with task communication.

The status and power structures partly reinforce the effects of liking on the communication structure. Differences in status both facilitate and inhibit communication among group members. Because power is usually associated with status, it appears to have similar effects; however, the effects of power need to be investigated with status held constant. So far as can be determined, no one has performed such a study.

24. OAKES, DRUGE, & AUGUST, 1960.   25. WHYTE, 1943.

These facilitating or interfering effects of status and power differences interact further with the content of the communication. In particular, ideas of individuals that are perceived as contrary to those of high-status persons are apt not to be communicated, at least to these persons, even though they might be ideas of high quality. A low-status person is unlikely to make a suggestion if he thinks it will be resisted by a high-status person.

Like certain conditions of affect, status and power differences may result in behaviors that divert time and energy from the task. As discussed in Chapter 9, individuals may engage in communication irrelevant to the task as a substitute for upward mobility in the status hierarchy or in an attempt to improve their status via status contagion. Similarly there is evidence to suggest that a certain amount of energy of group members will be expended in a struggle for positions of power and status. This is consistent with the previously discussed point that stability of structure is a necessary condition for speed and quality in group problem solving.

Status incongruency (see Chapter 9) might be expected to have adverse effects on communication similar to those of strong affect. It might, for example, generate anxiety about one's statuses and lead to defensive behavior that interferes with effective functioning. This seems not to be the case, however. While one study shows that status congruency in Air Force crews is associated with individual satisfaction, poor performance is also related to it.[26] A possible explanation for this is found in industrial work groups, where status congruency slowed productivity by changing the amount of interaction and the orientation to the task.[27] Status congruency facilitates interaction—people are sure of where they stand with respect to each other. Thus, it increases general satisfaction in the group, encouraging a good deal of *nontask activity*. It also increases conformity to group production norms—norms that frequently place limits on productivity. (In those instances where group norms specify high productivity, status congruency may be expected to lead to high output.) Sometimes status congruency results in dissatisfaction because such a state violates one of the norms of justice—the idea that all members should be treated equally. Where status congruency prevails, those with higher status receive much greater outcomes than those with low status and, in terms of the equal treatment ethic, this may seem unfair to the low-status members.[28]

BRAINSTORMING   Throughout the problem-solving process groups move toward premature closure. Before the dimensions of the problem are adequately examined, solutions may be offered and before many possible solutions are advanced, the process of evaluation occurs leading to a decision which ignores many potentially good alternatives. The technique of *brainstorming* has been suggested by Osborn as a way of preventing the evaluation process from short-

26. ADAMS, 1953.   27. ZALEZNIK, CHRISTENSEN, & ROETHLISBERGER, 1958.   28. BRANDON, 1965.

circuiting the earlier phase of idea generation.[29] Brainstorming instructions encourage group members to list all the ideas that come to mind—even the most harebrained—and to resist initially any attempts to evaluate their quality. While some investigators utilizing this technique have demonstrated its usefulness,[30] others make clear that brainstorming groups still do not generate as many ideas as the same number of persons working alone.[31] Another approach has shown that instructions which direct group members to focus on getting the problem clear before considering possible solutions produce solutions that are superior.[32]

SUMMARY: STRUCTURE AND EARLY PHASES   Early phases in task solution include the exchange of information and the presentation of a variety of solutions or plans of action. The relation of size of group, communication, affect, status, and power structures to these phases has been discussed. Idea productivity is a negatively accelerated increasing function of the size of a group, a function resulting largely from the effects of size on the communication structure. Larger-sized groups produce restraints against communicating which only a few persons overcome.

Problem-solving situations have been studied in groups having a variety of experimentally contrived communication nets. The primary feature of these nets is that individuals vary in the direct access they have to communication with other members and the access other members have to them. Some members occupy central positions; they can give communications directly to and receive communications directly from others. Other members occupy peripheral positions; they can communicate with most other group members only indirectly through a third person or a chain of persons. A given communication network may be relatively undifferentiated with respect to centrality-peripherality; all members may occupy a similar position. Or it may be quite differentiated, with some members occupying central positions and others peripheral ones. Empirical studies consistently support the conclusion that the relatively undifferentiated structure yields greater member satisfaction. For simple problems, the differentiated structure is most effective, but for complex problems, the undifferentiated structure is more effective in some instances. The differentiated structure loses its superiority for a complex problem because the persons occupying central positions become overloaded in serving as communication links.

The affect structure has important consequences for the performance of task groups, particularly through its connection to the communication structure. Unless special restrictive conditions prevail, communication is likely to follow friendship links. A high degree of liking is apt to facilitate communication. If,

29. OSBORN, 1957.   *30.* PARNES & MEADOW, 1959.   *31.* TAYLOR, BERRY, & BLOCK, 1958; DUNNETTE, CAMPBELL, & JAASTAD, 1963.   *32.* DAVIS & RESTLE, 1963.

however, communications occur in the social-emotional area rather than the task area, task performance is likely to be interfered with.

Status and power structures are likely to interfere with communication in a similar way. Ideas perceived as contrary to the opinions of high-status or high-power individuals are unlikely to be communicated. Instead, low-status persons may engage in communication irrelevant to the task to compensate for their low position. Some energy may be expended in a struggle for power and status that might otherwise be spent on the task. Status congruency facilitates interaction among group members, but much of this interaction may be irrelevant to the task. Where group norms specify low productivity, status congruency will lower production through increasing conformity to these norms. Groups tend to move prematurely to the evaluation of solutions before many possible solutions have been developed. Brainstorming as well as instructions designed to create a problem-centered rather than a solution-centered orientation have been suggested as methods of counteracting this tendency.

Factors Affecting Later Phases

In the later phases of the problem-solving task, a tendency toward premature closure sometimes occurs, as it does also in the information-gathering phase. The group may decide in favor of a poorer solution than might have been obtained had the group been slower in reaching a decision. Even a unanimous decision by a majority is no guarantee of the best solution.[33] Thus, techniques which slow the group down as they move toward problem solution,[34] which protect minority opinions,[35] or which require the group to retrace their steps and arrive at a second solution[36] have all been shown to improve the quality of group problem solving.

A major reason why premature closure results in poorer solutions is that the group's acceptance of a solution is not necessarily associated with its quality. Personal characteristics and structural features, both unrelated to the quality of a person's contributions, often determine acceptance. For example, the sheer talkativeness of a member has been shown to influence the final group decision.[37] To the extent that talk is unrelated to cognitive ability, such influence is unlikely to be beneficial.[38] Similarly, persons who have been successful in past group activities may by virtue of their reputations exert undue influence. Where their past experience does not aid the current effort, their influence may thwart potentially valuable contributions by other members.

A variety of structural features of groups often interfere with effective resource utilization, which further explains why groups are not as effective as they might be. These features are discussed below.

33. Bass, 1963.   *34.* Maier & Maier, 1957.   *35.* Maier & Solem, 1952.   *36.* Maier & Hoffman, 1960.   *37.* Riecken, 1958; Hoffman & Maier, 1964.   *38.* Mann, 1959.

COHESIVENESS   Though a high degree of attraction among members may facilitate the exchange of information, it may reduce the quality of the solution. Maximum attempts to influence others and to be influenced in turn may be expected in a highly cohesive group. If it were assumed that each person is equally likely to come up with a necessary element in the solution and that it is unlikely that any member will have all the necessary elements, then high mutual attraction should maximize the communication of information as well as receptivity to the communications of others, facilitating the joint production of an optimum solution.

Yet an important objection to this reasoning must be raised. High cohesiveness is associated with a marked degree of symmetry in the influence process.[39] Pressures toward agreement in highly cohesive groups are so strong that persons avoid the costs of resistance; they give in to keep peace. The result may be loss of valuable elements necessary to a solution. Because of mutual acceptance of everyone's ideas, cohesiveness should facilitate problem solving only when all members are capable of contributions of equal value. In the typical experimental situation, where problems are selected that minimize individual differences in resources and where the participants (generally college students) are relatively homogenous, this condition may be approximated. But it is unlikely to prevail in many situations outside the laboratory. If the group is highly cohesive but heterogeneous in ability, qualitatively poor elements are likely to be included in a solution. Even members of laboratory groups, which have a relatively low degree of cohesiveness due to the temporary nature of the group, often allow each other an equal amount of time even though contributions are quite unequal.[40]

STATUS AND POWER   Not only will differences in power and status affect the frequency with which various members contribute information and make suggestions, but these differences will also affect the weights assigned to contributions from different members. For two reasons, the contributions of those with high power and status will carry more weight in arriving at a final solution. The first is their relatively greater control over the reward-cost outcomes of members. The second derives from their central location in the communication structure. They have more information about the task, the setting, and the opinions and suggestions of others, and this provides them with an opportunity consciously or unconsciously to filter such information in a manner that supports their particular solution.

Whether differences in power or status improve or impair the quality of a solution depends on the degree of concentration of power and the basis of the power. One might expect that, to the degree that power in the group is a function of expertness, concentration of power would improve quality if other

39. BACK, 1951.   *40.* DAVIS & RESTLE, 1963.

things affecting quality were equal. But where power is inversely associated with the quality of individual contributions, it has a detrimental effect. Instances where a group flounders because the persons with greatest power had the poorest contributions to make should be familiar to everyone. A study of Air Force crews undergoing the rigors of survival training illustrates the point: Crews relied more heavily on the aircraft commander, whose power was highest in the group but whose knowledge regarding survival techniques was meager compared to that of the survival-training instructor.[41]

The implementation of a solution is also important. Marked differences among members in the degree to which they participate in development of a solution may later seriously interfere with implementation of the solution. If persons are constrained from actively participating in the development of a solution because of power or status considerations, their resistance to implementation is increased. The second-best solution that is put into practice by group members is in most instances preferable to the best possible solution that is not adopted or is inadequately implemented.

FEEDBACK   It is well-established that individual learning is facilitated if a person is informed how well he is doing. Feedback of information in a group problem-solving situation should also affect performance of the group. Several experiments have investigated this hypothesis.[42] In one investigation,[43] seven-man groups were provided with *confounded feedback*[44] or *direct feedback* pertaining to the success or failure of their speed of reaction to a stimulus. *Confounded feedback* was a condition in which individual members were informed only whether the *group* had failed to react within a prescribed limit, and *direct feedback* was a condition in which *each member* was informed of his own failures, those of each other member, and those of the group as a whole. The effect of these conditions on performance was that direct feedback brought about the most improvement in performance; confounded feedback resulted in only a slight improvement.

These laboratory experiments set up artificial restrictions on communication, but they nevertheless are analogous to conditions in problem-solving groups outside the laboratory. For example, in some small-group settings, the criterion of good performance is not always clear, a condition analogous to not receiving adequate feedback. In larger organizational settings, the fragmentation and division of work tasks among a large number of individuals and the inherent difficulties in communication may create a similar condition analogous to confounded feedback.

Berkowitz and Levy have noted that groups having high pride in their performance are generally productive.[45] They suggested that this condition may derive from the members' perception of the high level of their performance; in

---

41. Torrance, 1955.   42. Rosenberg & Hall, 1958; Pryer & Bass, 1959; Zajonc, 1962.   43. Zajonc, 1962.   44. Rosenberg & Hall, 1958.   45. Berkowitz & Levy, 1956.

other words, members have pride where feedback on a good performance is available. Berkowitz and Levy conducted an experiment in a simulated air defense maneuver. Groups of airmen were given favorable or unfavorable evaluations of the performance of their group as a whole or of the individual members. Groups receiving favorable evaluations of the group as a whole were found to have higher pride in their performance and to be more motivated than groups receiving unfavorable group evaluations and than groups receiving only individual evaluations.

Thus, in one study, feedback on the performance of the group as a whole was relatively ineffective in improving performance; in the other, it was especially effective. Feedback on performance is apparently important to problem-solving groups, but further study is needed in order to identify the kind of feedback which is most effective for various kinds of tasks and situations.

SUMMARY: LATER PHASES   Although a high degree of cohesiveness among group members may facilitate the exchange of information, it may also reduce the quality of the solution. Cohesiveness equalizes the weight given to the contributions of each member. Chances of a high-quality solution to a group problem are lessened by heterogeneity in the ability of the group members. On the other hand, cohesiveness may contribute to effective implementation of the solution if group members are relatively homogeneous in ability.

Contributions from individuals of high power and status are weighted heavily because of these people's relatively greater control over the reward-cost outcomes of members and because of their central location in the communication structure. Whether or not this condition is detrimental depends upon the competence of the high-status and high-power persons. If they are especially competent, the group is effective; if they are less competent than the average member, the power and status structures inhibit effective performance.

Neither feedback on overall group performance nor feedback on individual performance is consistently superior. Further research is needed to identify the conditions under which each type of feedback is beneficial.

Individual versus Group Risk Taking

A study by Stoner over a decade ago indicated that decisions made by the group after discussion are more risky than decisions made by individuals before discussion.[46] This finding is of interest not only because it is contrary to the widely held expectation that groups will be more cautious and conservative than individuals, but also because many decisions in businesses, universities, and governments are made by groups. Many studies have been conducted since then to test the generality of these findings and the validity of explanations that have been offered to account for them. Consideration of these studies and the

46. STONER, 1961.

(Risky Shift)

ideas developed to explain the findings is quite instructive in demonstrating the complexity and the multifaceted character of group process and in showing the limitations of simple conceptualizations of such processes.

Typically, individuals are asked to make a decision concerning action in a risk-taking situation (e.g., taking a higher-paying but less secure job than held at present). Then an experimental treatment is introduced which most often consists of a group discussion in which members arrive at a consensus about what should be done. The difference in the degree of risk taking between the average position of group members before discussion and the decision eventually made typically defines the magnitude of the *risky shift* (the shift toward a greater risk after discussion).

Three general types of risk situations have been employed. One, and by far the most frequently used type of situation, is administered in a paper-and-pencil test, *the choice-dilemma questionnaire.* This instrument has been described as follows:

> It consists of twelve hypothetical, "real life" situations in which a fictitious person must choose between a risky or a conservative course of action. Of these two alternatives, the risky option was constructed to be more desirable, but also to have less chance of succeeding. For example, a sample item describes an electrical engineer who has a choice between: (a) remaining at his present, secure job—one with a modest salary but little hope of improvement—or (b) joining a new firm which has a highly uncertain future but offers the possibility of sharing in the ownership. The respondent's task is to indicate what the odds for success would have to be before he would advise the fictitious person to attempt the risky alternative. On this task the respondent can choose among 1, 3, 5, 7, or 9 chances in 10 that the risky alternative will be successful. There is an additional category for each item which allows respondents to indicate whether they feel that the risky course of action should not be attempted no matter what the odds.[47]

A second type of risk-taking situation requires individuals to choose the level of difficulty they wish to attempt on items of old college board exams. The levels of difficulty are represented in terms of the percentage of a national sample of students failing the item. The more difficult the item, the greater the risk of failure, should items at that level be chosen. A third type of situation consists of experimental gaming situations where participants must choose between wagers with a relatively low payoff with a good chance of occurring and more risky large payoffs, with a low probability of occurring.

The risky-shift phenomenon has been observed under a variety of treatment conditions, with or without requiring the group to achieve consensus,[48] and

47. Reprinted by permission from K. L. DION, R. S. BARON, & N. MILLER. Why do groups make riskier decisions than individuals? In L. BERKOWITZ (Ed.), *Advances in experimental social psychology.* Vol. 5. New York: Academic Press, Inc., 1970. P. 308.   48. WALLACH & KOGAN, 1965.

with or without face-to-face communications.[49] It has also occurred in experimental conditions without group discussion but where participants were made aware of the risk preferences of other group members[50] or where they were asked to restudy the choice-dilemma items and respond again.[51] The risky shift, as well as its opposite, a shift in the direction of caution, has in some instances been observed among different types of people and types of tasks, although Dion, Baron, and Miller note that the evidence is equivocal on betting or gambling tasks.[52] At the same time, these reviewers comment that the tasks studied generally lack any real consequences for the participants.

Four major explanations and some minor variations of these have been offered to explain the risky shift. One of the earliest proposed was that of diffusion of responsibility.[53] Initially this explanation emphasized that a group decision produced a reduction in fear of failure by diffusing responsibility to all who shared in the decision. Subsequent findings showing that the risky shift was present even where no group decision was made have led to a modification of this explanation. As Dion and his colleagues suggest, current formulations suggest the following causal chain:

> (1) group discussion creates affective bonds; (2) affective bonds permit diffusion of responsibility; (3) diffusion of responsibility reduces fear of failure; (4) reduced fear of failure produces the risky shift.[54]

Research relevant to these conceptual links has produced generally conflicting results. As noted previously, a risky shift has occurred without group decision or without discussion, where individuals were instead informed of the choices of other group members,[55] or listened to,[56] or allowed to observe the discussion of another group.[57] The evidence concerning the conceptual linkage between group discussion and the increase in bonds of attraction with consequent reduction of fear of failure is conflicting, and it is not clear from current theory and research concerning the effects of fear of failure on motivation that reduced fear of failure would lead to an average increase in the willingness to take risks.[58] Nevertheless it is possible, as Dion and his colleagues note, that increased risk taking may result from a diffusion of responsibility that does not depend on these mediating variables, thus accounting for at least some of the observed effects of group participation on risk taking.

A second explanation argues that persons who are more persuasive take a more risky position. This might be so either because they are more self-confident or because they have available to them a more potent rhetoric with which to argue their case. Kelley and Thibaut have suggested that such advocates

49. KOGAN & WALLACH, 1967*a;* LAMM, 1967; KOGAN & WALLACH, 1967*b.*   *50.* TEGER & PRUITT, 1967. *51.* BATESON, 1966; FLANDERS & THISTLETHWAITE, 1967.   *52.* DION et al., 1970.   *53.* KOGAN & WALLACH, 1967*c.*   *54.* Reprinted by permission from K. L. DION, R. S. BARON, & N. MILLER. Why do groups make riskier decisions than individuals? In L. BERKOWITZ (Ed.) *Advances in experimental social psychology.* Vol. 5. New York: Academic Press, Inc., 1970. P. 312.   *55.* TEGER & PRUITT, 1967; BLANK, 1968.   *56.* KOGAN & WALLACH, 1967*d.*   *57.* LAMM, 1967.   *58.* ATKINSON, 1964.

have a command of the English language that provides them with a more dramatic rhetoric than that of less persuasive people, and further, that the conflicts and uncertainties involved in the more risky alternative lead them to state their arguments with heightened intensity and amplitude.[59] Individuals perceived to be influential are in fact more likely to take risky positions.[60]

A third explanation is that the risky shift is due simply to increased familiarization.[61] Initial unfamiliarity with a choice situation requires caution at first, which is reduced after participants have gained a greater familiarity and understanding. The effect of discussion is to increase familiarity and understanding of the situation. This idea was tested by having participants merely restudy the choice-dilemma situations in preparation for a later discussion (which was not held). Although positive findings were obtained, other investigators have failed to replicate these results.[62] Further, this explanation fails to account for cautious shifts typically observed with two of the choice-dilemma items.

A fourth explanation, proposed by Brown, which appears to handle most adequately the facts concerning the risky shift, is based on *value* and *relevance*.[63] When individuals encounter situations of risk one of two values is engaged—risk or caution. In some situations (like most of those in the choice-dilemma questionnaire), taking a risk is valued in American society. For example, people are encouraged to risk current assets for the sake of future profits. In other situations, such as those possibly involving the welfare of innocent other persons, caution is valued. Making one of these values salient increases the frequency of arguments favorable to that value during the group discussion, and increases the weight of those arguments in determining the group decision.

The second part of Brown's explanation is that members assimilate their position to the value that is relevant to the situation. Before group discussion individuals see themselves at or above the average in possessing the valued attribute. Thus, in a situation where the value of risk becomes salient, an individual is willing to take as great a risk as (or a greater risk than) the average group member. In the absence of knowledge about the risk preference of other persons, individuals must guess at this. Some, at least, guess wrong. When, during the discussion they hear the actual risk preferences of other persons or when they learn of them in other ways, as we have seen, those who are closer to the average change their choice in the risky direction, thus shifting the mean of the group and accounting for the risky-shift effect.

The value explanation has advantages over the other explanations. The most important is that it can account for cautious shifts as well as risky ones, and also for the occurrence of the shift in the absence of group discussion (either where persons learn their relative standings on the value in question through listening to the discussion of another group or where the experimenter supplies the relevant information).

59. Kelley & Thibaut, 1969.   60. Wallach, Kogan, & Bem, 1962; Wallach, Kogan, & Burt, 1965; Flanders & Thistlethwaite, 1967.   61. Bateson, 1966; Flanders & Thistlethwaite, 1967.   62. Dion et al., 1970.   63. Brown, 1965.

That Brown's theory is better able to handle the facts does not mean that the mechanisms suggested by some of the other theories cannot account for some of the observed results as well. Further, the situations employed have generally involved hypothetical or relatively inconsequential losses, and thus some caution should be observed in generalizing to real-life situations of risk. Finally, as Brown noted, the theory is still incomplete, and thus it is difficult to predict whether a cautious or a risky shift will occur in a given situation.[64] This depends on the unknown characteristics that evoke either caution or risk as a value.

Leadership Structure and Task Performance

The style of leadership may also have significant effects on group satisfaction and productivity. Few studies in the behavioral sciences have had greater impact than the initial studies of leadership style. Kelley and Thibaut have provided the following succinct description of the 1939 investigations by Lewin, Lippitt, and White:

> Four clubs of 11-year-old boys were formed in such a way that they were equated with respect to certain personal and sociometric characteristics of their members. Four adults performed a sequence of planned leadership roles ("authoritarian," "democratic," and "laissez-faire") so that, with minor exceptions, each adult played each leadership role and each club was exposed to each style of leader. Activities were held relatively constant between the various clubs by the device of permitting democratic and laissez-faire clubs to select an activity and then imposing the same activity on the club(s) concurrently being led by an authoritarian leader.
>
> The results that bear most directly on problem solving can be summarized briefly. *Authoritarian* leadership appeared to induce the following characteristic reactions in the clubs: great dependency on the leader, marked intermember "irritability and aggressiveness," low frequencies of "suggestions for group action and group policy," dissatisfaction with club activities, and high quantity and low quality of productivity. . . . Under *laissez-faire* leadership, the clubs showed little dependency on the leader, great "irritability and aggressiveness" among members, high frequencies of "suggestions for group action and group policy" accompanied by great discontent about progress and achievement, considerable dissatisfaction with club activities, and apparently intermediate productivity. *Democratic* leadership produced low dependency on the leader, low incidence of intermember "irritability and aggressiveness," high frequencies of "suggestions for group action and group policy," great satisfaction with club activities, and an intermediate quantity of productivity of high quality.[65]

64. Brown, 1965.   *65.* Reprinted by permission from H. H. Kelley & J. W. Thibaut. Experimental studies of group problem solving and process. In G. Lindzey (Ed.), *Handbook of social psychology.* Vol. 2. Reading, Mass.: Addison-Wesley Publishing Company, Inc., 1954. P. 776.

Later investigations have in the main confirmed the findings. These include further experimental studies[66] comparing participatory (democratic) and supervisory (laissez-faire) leaders, as well as studies in such settings as the classroom[67] and a variety of work situations.[68] Some of the conclusions drawn from the initial studies, however, require qualification. In a study of decision-making groups in government and industry, a high level of member participation was associated with *low* satisfaction.[69] Presumably, in such groups the members expected and desired strong leadership, and these expectations were not met. Personality characteristics also determine the degree to which authoritarian or democratic leadership is associated with satisfaction, as noted in Chapter 11. Finally, reactions to leadership styles are related in a rather complex way to such characteristics as age, marital status, and educational status.[70]

In spite of these qualifications of the original studies, when the vagueness of variables in the initial studies is considered, it is surprising that such confirmation has been obtained. A more systematic conceptual analysis based on the discussion of leadership in Chapter 11 and a closer look at some of these studies should provide further understanding. The following analysis will be divided into two parts, the first discussing satisfaction and the second, productivity.

LEADERSHIP AND SATISFACTION   Satisfaction may be thought of as resulting from need gratification. In the course of problem solving, individual needs may be satisfied through task accomplishment, through the work activity itself, or through the interactions with other persons on the job. Studies such as those carried on by the Survey Research Center of the University of Michigan have shown that the groups that were most satisfied with their jobs had supervisors who did not supervise closely but allowed their subordinates a certain degree of self-determination in carrying out their activities.[71] Presumably this situation allowed workers to satisfy needs for self-determination and self-realization.

Another study seemingly contradicts the negative effects of close supervision.[72] Among a group of white-collar employees, freedom from close supervision was associated with dissatisfaction.[73] This underscores the point that rewards must always be assessed against expectation. As Homans has suggested, these employees were less satisfied with their situation because the lack of close supervision led them to expect more rewards than they were in fact receiving; since they were carrying more responsibility, they felt they should be paid more than they were.[74]

The study of supervisors revealed other differences among supervisors suggesting that they differ in the extent to which they gratify the needs of the employees under them.[75] Thus *employee-oriented supervisors* had more satisfied groups than *production-oriented supervisors*. Employee-oriented supervisors kept

66. SELVIN, 1960.   67. ANDERSON & BREWER, 1945, 1946; ANDERSON, BREWER, & REED, 1946; ROBBINS, 1952; PRESTON & HEINTZ, 1949.   68. KATZ & KAHN, 1952.   69. BERKOWITZ, 1953.   70. SELVIN, 1960. 71. KATZ & KAHN, 1952.   72. MORSE, 1953.   73. HOMANS, 1961.   74. HOMANS, 1961.   75. KAHN & KATZ, 1953.

the needs of employees in mind. For example, they explained the reasons for changes in work routines, considered aspects of the work situation other than productivity, and set reasonable goals for performance. They also spent more time in leadership or supervision. In contrast, production-oriented supervisors focused on production, often excluding attention to other aspects of work and the personal needs of their employees. They spent less time supervising and more time doing the actual work.

In short, the supervisors whose leadership style maximizes gratification of important needs in the work situation have the most satisfied employees. This finding is consistent with the findings about leadership and group process discussed earlier.

LEADERSHIP AND PRODUCTIVITY   It was noted previously that groups are less effective in dealing with complex problems when the communication structure has only one or a few members in central positions. The central members become overloaded or saturated with communications and are unable to handle them. Shaw suggests that the independence of members and the saturation factor interact to produce the observed effects of leadership style on morale and performance:

> To summarize, it is believed that leadership type should influence group behavior not through either independence or saturation alone, but rather through the combination of these two processes. Authoritarian leadership should decrease independence for most of its members (and hence decrease morale), and should decrease saturation effects for all group members (and hence improve performance). Nonauthoritarian leadership should increase independence for all group members (and hence increase morale), and should increase saturation for all group members (and hence lower performance).[76]

These suppositions were borne out by Shaw's observations of groups with different networks and different styles of leadership. As did Lippitt and White, he found higher morale in the democratically led groups.[77] His findings on performance, while consistent with the above reasoning, did differ in one respect: For the authoritarian groups, performance was better, both quantitatively in terms of time and number of messages employed, and qualitatively in terms of errors.

Leadership style could be expected to affect the quality and quantity of production in a group since it affects the quality of solutions and the motivation to implement them. We pointed out earlier that increases in group size produce a communication structure that is highly differentiated, and that this condition is detrimental to the early phases of problem solving. There is some

76. Reprinted by permission from M. E. SHAW. A comparison of two types of leadership in various communication nets. *Journal of Abnormal and Social Psychology*, 1955, **50**, 128.   77. LIPPITT & WHITE, 1943.

evidence that by encouraging participation, a discussion leader can partially counteract this effect of increased size.

In one investigation, thirty-four groups were provided with a leader who conducted the discussion in a permissive manner, asking questions to stimulate thinking, encouraging participation of all members, and promoting the expression of various points of view, but refraining from expressing his own opinions.[78] The performance of these groups in solving a problem was compared with that of thirty-three groups who were provided not with a leader but with an observer who merely listened to group members while they discussed the problem. Group members privately recorded their answers before and after an eight-minute discussion. The groups did not differ appreciably in the proportion of correct answers before discussion, but after discussion the proportion of correct answers was significantly higher for the groups that had discussion leaders. A further analysis revealed that this improvement appeared particularly in groups where a minority initially had the correct solution. In such instances the discussion leader served to encourage the expression and consideration of the ideas of the minority (sometimes a single individual), which otherwise would often be suppressed by the majority.

Chapter 11 noted that one consequence of the group-decision process is the increased likelihood that the decision would be carried out by group members. This appears to result both from increased understanding of the solution and from the emergence of a normative structure favoring actions in accordance with the solution. Under these circumstances, a solution is gradually fashioned as group members come to see and evaluate the situation in a similar manner. Through the sharing of information and exertion of social pressures by means of giving or withholding social approval, gradual consensus is achieved.

Such consensus not only facilitates cooperative action, should the implementation of the solution require it, but also reinforces individual motivation to carry out the solution. This interpretation fits the experimental studies on the effects of group decision discussed in Chapter 5, and supports the finding that in an industrial setting changes introduced through group discussion are more successfully implemented. In the latter study, investigators varied the extent to which workers participated in the development of new work procedures. Participation ranged from no participation, through indirect participation via representatives, to direct participation.[79] Productivity of the groups varied directly with the amount of participation.

In most work situations rules regarding quality and quantity of production are set up by management, an agent *external* to the work group. It has long been known that norms very rapidly arise within the group to govern the quality and quantity of production. The degree to which these norms are affected by the standards set by management will depend in part on the attitudes that group members have toward management. To the extent that the supervi-

78. Maier & Solem, 1952.   79. Coch & French, 1958.

sor, by his style of supervision, creates favorable attitudes toward himself and management, the production rules that he represents are apt to have their effect on the group norms. This may well be an important reason why the "democratic" supervisors in the studies described earlier had groups with higher productivity.[80]

Though this discussion has for the most part emphasized the advantages of democratic as opposed to authoritarian leadership, these advantages depend upon the demands of the situation, the distribution of skills within the group, and the group's expectations, as well as other variables. Unfortunately, as Gibb has noted, these qualifications have often been ignored:

> It is common in our culture at the present time to place negative values on authoritarian leadership. Much of this attitude seems to be due to a prolonged period of ideological opposition to cultures authoritarianly organized, and a false assumption of identity between an authoritarian leadership style and authoritarian political systems. Studies of groups in action reveal that in certain circumstances authoritarian leadership is highly valued. There is in the American culture an ambivalence about leadership technique, and morale is sometimes higher and satisfactions maximized when more authoritarian techniques are employed.[81]

He further notes that there are group situations in which authoritarian form of leadership is more effective than a democratic form:

> . . . leadership is more authoritarian, more dictatorial, and more restrictive when (1) speed and efficiency are emphasized to the point of outweighing the formalities, and (2) when the novelty of the situation for each member precludes his ego-involvement with particular procedures, so that he does not interpret direction as being in any way critical of his ability. If the group is faced with a need for emergency action, then that leader behavior is most effective which is prompt and decisive and which is perceived by the members as likely to remove quickly the threats in the situation. Authoritarian leadership is practically demanded under such circumstances.[82]

Some progress has been made toward distinguishing situational and other variables that are associated with the effectiveness of leadership style. Fiedler has offered a model based on a classification of situations according to the ease with which the leader may influence performance of the group task.[83] Three situational components are (1) the leader's personal relations with members of his group, i.e., the degree to which he is liked and respected, (2) the degree of structure in the task, ranging from highly routine, clearly spelled-out tasks to

80. KATZ & KAHN, 1952; LIKERT, 1961. *81.* Reprinted by permission from C. A. GIBB. Leadership. In G. LINDZEY & E. ARONSON (Eds.), *The handbook of social psychology.* (2nd ed.) Vol. 4. Reading, Mass.: Addison-Wesley Publishing Company, Inc., 1969. P. 262. *82.* Reprinted by permission from C. A. GIBB. Leadership. In G. LINDZEY & E. ARONSON (Eds.), *The handbook of social psychology.* (2nd ed.) Vol. 4. Reading, Mass.: Addison-Wesley Publishing Company, Inc., 1969. P. 263. *83.* FIEDLER, 1964.

tasks that are vague and indefinite, and (3) the legitimate power and authority associated with the leader's position.

He suggested that the leader who is liked and respected by his group, who is faced with a highly structured task, and who wields considerable power by virtue of the authority invested in his position is in a relatively favorable position to influence the group. The leader who is disliked in a group faced by a vague, unstructured task and who has little formal power may encounter difficulty in wielding influence. In very favorable or very unfavorable situations a style of leadership involving active intervention and control is apt to be effective. In moderately unfavorable situations, however, a more democratic, permissive style focusing on human relations is more effective. A wide variety of situations studied by Fiedler and his colleagues as well as other investigators appear to fit this model.[84]

SUMMARY: LEADERSHIP   Although there are some exceptions, a democratic style of leadership appears to generate more satisfaction among group members and more effective group functioning than an autocratic or a laissez-faire style. Exceptions occur when members expect strong leadership; under these circumstances they may be dissatisfied with a democratic leader.

Satisfaction has rather complex relations to a number of group variables. In industrial settings, leaders who do not supervise too closely but permit some self-determination on the part of members appear to obtain a higher level of satisfaction. But certain circumstances may provide an exception to this generalization: Freedom from supervision led to a low degree of satisfaction in one study, apparently because the greater responsibility assumed by these employees led them to expect more rewards than they were receiving. Supervisors may also obtain high satisfaction from workers if they show a particular interest in the workers' welfare. Apparently the leaders who focus upon their leadership role instead of just being one of the workers also produce greater satisfaction.

The relation between leadership style and productivity may be explained in terms of the independence of members and the saturation or overloading of members with communications. Authoritarian leadership reduces independence and saturation; thus it is likely to produce less satisfaction but greater productivity. A discussion leader in larger groups to some extent counteracts the undesirable effects of size, increasing participation particularly on the part of the minority. This improves the quality of the group product. Participation in these circumstances and in those where the leader encourages group decisions also appears to produce a high level of motivation, increasing the likelihood that the task will be effectively carried out.

Most work situations generate informal group norms that define an appropriate production level. Leadership that fosters good attitudes toward management on the part of the workers is likely to contribute to setting a high

84. FIEDLER, 1964.

production norm. Under most circumstances this condition is likely to prevail where leadership is democratic in style. In other circumstances, however, authoritarian leadership may be highly effective. These include emergency situations requiring rapid action and situations in which wise authoritarian leadership can make the best use of the inequalities among the members in personality, temperament, and skills. Situations where the leader is either in a very strong position or a very weak one favor an authoritarian style; a situation where the leader has a modicum amount of influence favors a democratic style.

The Problem-solving Process

So far group problem solving has been considered primarily from the standpoint of factors affecting the quality of the group product, with only occasional attention to member satisfaction. Certain features of the ongoing process of problem-solving and its relation to satisfaction will now be discussed.

PHASES OF ONGOING PROCESS   Certain regularities in the interactions of members in problem-solving groups have been noted in discussing communication and leadership structures. These uniformities were observed when the behaviors of group members were analyzed in terms of Bales' categories for interaction process analysis (see Chapter 9). In these accounts, ongoing interaction was divided into three parts: first, middle, and final phases. When high points were compared for various major categories of behavior, it was found that in phase one, acts related to problems of *orientation* and *evaluation* had the highest relative frequencies. In the middle phase, acts related to evaluation increased slightly, reaching a maximum in this phase, with acts related to orientation dropping off appreciably. From phase to phase, acts related to problems of *control* and the relative frequencies of positive and negative responses steadily increased, reaching a maximum in the final phase.

The shift from problems of orientation to those of evaluation and finally to those of control appears at first to be only as expected. It seems reasonable that when a group attempts to solve a problem, its members first exchange information about the problem and the situation, then evaluate the information, and finally suggest a course of action. However, further reflection on the reasons for this sequence, along with consideration of the findings on the increase of positive and negative reactions as the group progresses from phase to phase, should uncover a number of principles previously encountered in the discussion of conformity. These principles also explain the friction frequently arising in ongoing group interaction. It has already been observed that positive and negative reactions—social approval and its withdrawal—are forms of pressure that bring about conformity in the group. Pressures toward conformity arise in a group not only because lack of conformity makes concerted action difficult, but also because the existence of conformity is gratifying in its own right. This follows from the assumption that persons have a drive to evaluate their opinions and that, in the absence of some nonsocial criterion, they do so by comparing them with other people's opinions which are close to their own.

The increased appearance of negative and positive reactions from phase one to phase two reflects the increasing pressures for conformity as the group shifts from problems of orientation to problems of evaluation. The facts of the situation are generally seen in the same way by different members. Indeed, the participants in Bales's groups were all given the same facts. In the evaluative phase, however, expressions of opinion about the task and situation are likely to vary from member to member unless the group shares the same values. In the problem-solving situation studied by these investigators, problems were chosen on which members were expected to differ. The differences ordinarily lead to an increase in positive and negative reactions until conformity is achieved. In fact, if too rapid movement occurs before value conformity is achieved, so that the participants begin making suggestions for action, the group will be forced back to the unresolved problem of lack of conformity. This will lead to an increase in behaviors falling into the evaluative categories and a decrease in responses classified in the categories of control. As these differences are resolved, suggestions for action will be increasingly accepted, and the frequencies in this category will increase. The group will then move into the final phase.

The higher rate of negative responses in the last phase appears to occur mostly in the early part of it and is probably a consequence of still unresolved value differences. Positive responses appear to dominate in the latter part of the final phase. This occurs not only because participants find agreement and successful control rewarding but also because group members attempt to restore the reservoir of positive feeling that was depleted as persons attempted to exert pressure on each other to change.

Attempts to influence or exercise power in such groups are based to a considerable extent on the exchange of social approval for conformity. If we assume, after the pattern of Homans, that each exchange of a unit of social approval between A and B for a unit of movement toward the other's opinion results in a smaller increment of profit for both, then the likelihood that each will be able to influence the other is reduced.[85] On each occasion the cost of the movement in terms of integrity as well as loss of reward from other like-minded persons is greater, and the reward is less because of increasing satiation. Such a situation, assuming that both persons expect to continue to interact, constitutes a threat which motivates an exchange of a considerable number of units of social approval to bring the profit level up so that each will again be disposed to make such exchanges in the future.

This principle appears to apply to many situations where individuals have drawn heavily on their reserve of power over another person. When a person as a result of his repeated demands has considerably lowered his power relative to another, the power balance is upset, and the threat of loss of future rewards is

85. HOMANS, 1961.

particularly likely to motivate him to lavish rewards on the more powerful person in an attempt to restore his power to a comfortable level. The resolutions, promises, and more solicitous behavior after a lovers' quarrel illustrate the point.

This discussion of process raises a problem which hitherto has been dealt with insufficiently. As Barnard noted, every human organization must solve two problems.[86] The first is the problem of effectiveness, which means achieving group purposes. The second is the problem of "efficiency," which refers to providing satisfaction to individual members. In the short-lived laboratory groups typically studied, satisfaction is of little concern. Presumably participants in these studies either receive enough satisfaction to remain in the situation or find refusing to cooperate in the study too costly. In everyday situations, unlike the laboratory, the group must solve the problem of satisfaction or it will cease to exist.

FORMS OF MEMBER SATISFACTION   As previously observed, satisfaction is generally viewed as a function of need gratification. To understand satisfaction in task groups it is useful to distinguish between needs according to the source of the rewards that lead to their satisfaction. One such source is obvious: the reward offered in exchange for task accomplishment. In industrial groups rewards for task accomplishment are largely monetary. In other groups the rewards may be status, social approval from other members, and other "psychic" rewards. A second source of rewards lies in features of task activity itself that allow for the satisfaction of such needs as those for self-expression, self-development, and self-determination.

So far, the needs and rewards we have discussed are directly or indirectly related to task performance. A third class of needs and rewards is related to features of the group; these arise out of interaction above and beyond task activity. Zaleznik, Christensen, and Roethlisberger have emphasized these needs and rewards in their investigation of worker satisfaction and productivity, and refer to them as *internal or group-controlled rewards* to distinguish them from external or management-controlled rewards. They describe them as follows:

> The internal needs or rewards include the need for belonging to a group; for associating with other human beings; for expressing and sharing in sentiments of loyalty, friendliness and affection; for giving and receiving emotional support; for receiving the marks of group approval which we include in the ordinary terms of prestige and esteem. All these needs stem from human association and interaction in a group setting. We can think of the satisfaction of these needs, consequently, as "reward by the group" in contrast to reward by management in satisfying needs for job status.[87]

86. BARNARD, 1938.   87. Reprinted by permission by A. ZALEZNIK, C. R. CHRISTENSEN, & F. J. ROETHLISBERGER. *The motivation, productivity, and satisfaction of workers: A prediction study.* Boston: Harvard University, Bureau Business Research, 1958. P. 324.

DETERMINANTS OF SATISFACTION   The satisfactions individuals receive are more than simply a function of the *amount* of reward obtained in a group. Whether the reward is in terms of dollars, intrinsic job satisfaction, or approval, an amount that satisfies one person may not satisfy another, for a number of reasons. First, individuals vary with respect to the strength of their needs. Second, they vary with respect to the number of alternatives for need gratification. The person who is receiving considerable gratification from other groups will be less dependent on a particular group for gratification, and he may be able to exact more rewards than a person who is more dependent on the group. Third, individuals differ with respect to their comparison levels—in how much they feel they can *expect* from the group.

Crucial to an understanding of the relation of rewards to both productivity and satisfaction is the recognition of expectations in mediating their effects. Whether a reward is adequate depends on what persons expect in the situation—their comparison level—what they regard as an equitable or just reward. It has been emphasized that the exchange process is greatly influenced by conceptions of justice or equity (see Chapter 9). Rewards as well as costs must be conceived of in much more complex terms than simple need gratification or deprivation. Costs such as the experience of inequity, or rewards such as the achievement of a just state of affairs must be considered a part of outcomes in work situations.

The most influential formulation of equity theory as it applies to work situations has been that of Adams.[88] Basic to equity theory is *social comparison.* Individuals compare their inputs and outcomes with those obtained by other persons. Adams's concept of inputs is similar to Homans's idea of investments (see Chapter 9). Inputs can be any set of attributes that both persons in an exchange recognize and that the possessor uses as a basis of comparison. If an attribute is relevant in a particular situation, then a just return is expected by the person possessing the attribute. In work situations, the most obvious input is effort toward task accomplishment. But depending on group norms or values, almost any attribute may be considered relevant including sex, race, and education. Outcome similarly is a broad category, including anything that both parties recognize, and which has marginal utility to the recipient. Outcomes may have either positive or negative valences; the costs may exceed the rewards, or vice versa. Comparisons occur either between two parties in a reciprocal exchange situation, such as two persons cooperating on a task, or where each is in an exchange relation with a third person, as in the case of two workmen employed by a third person or by a business firm.

According to Adams, a state of equity exists when the ratio of inputs and outcomes of an individual is equal to that of the person with whom he compares himself.[89] Thus, the *principle of equity* is that the more an individual puts into an activity, as compared with the input of another person, the more he should get in return. Two states of inequity can occur. In one, the ratio of outcomes to inputs for person *P* is smaller than that of a comparison other, *O,* and this is experienced by *P* as unjust or unfair. A second state of inequity is to *P*'s objective advantage in that his ratio of outcomes to inputs is greater. This state is apt to produce guilt feelings and embarrassment. Thus, both states of inequity are thought to be aversive or psychologically uncomfortable, although Adams suggests that discomfort in the second case where the inequity is to one's objective advantage is less apt to be experienced.

Since both departures from equity are aversive, the person will be motivated to reduce inequity. While few would be surprised if persons attempted to change a situation which is objectively to their disadvantage, that they would redress a situation which is to their advantage would be surprising. Such a reduction of inequity could throw light on some situations where productivity and satisfaction are not related in a direct fashion to the amount of rewards.

Attempts to restore equity may take a variety of forms. An individual may attempt to actually alter his inputs or his outcomes or those of other persons in such a manner as to restore equality between ratios, or he may cognitively distort them so that they have an apparent equality. He may cease to compare outcomes with a particular other person, choosing perhaps someone else, or finally he may leave the field (e.g., quit his job). Cognitively distorting inputs or outcomes or those of others may take a number of forms. He may exaggerate or minimize a given input or outcome, or he may alter the weight of a given attribute in the determination of inputs or outcomes. Thus, the older worker who is paid a lot more than a younger worker doing the same task may decide that it is only right that seniority be heavily emphasized in determining the rate of pay. Outcomes or inputs that were previously irrelevant may be invested with new relevance in an attempt to achieve equity. The executive in a branch office in San Francisco may decide that living in that city is an outcome of sufficient value to equalize his ratio of outcomes to inputs in comparison with that of his better-paid colleague living in New York City.

Adams suggests a number of conditions which will determine the choice of modes of equity reduction. Among these he notes that persons will generally try to maximize positive outcomes and avoid increasing inputs that are effortful and costly to change. In particular, an individual will resist real and cognitive change in inputs as well as outcomes that are central to his self concept and self-esteem. Since he is more aware of his own outcomes and inputs, he will find it more difficult to cognitively alter them than to alter those of other persons. Leaving the field, except perhaps temporarily as in the case of absenteeism, is apt to occur only when the magnitude of inequity is high and other means of reducing it are unavailable.

Much of the research generated by this equity theory as it applies to work situations has focused on the effects of inequitable wage payments and in particular on the somewhat unexpected prediction that overpayment may result in lower productivity and satisfaction. That this can occur was suggested by two studies in which university students were hired as interviewers and led to believe that they were overpaid (because they were paid the same as qualified interviewers).[90] In the first study, they were paid on an hourly basis and it was predicted that the overpaid students would reduce inequity through increasing their inputs by doing more interviews. This prediction was confirmed. The second experiment in part replicated the first, but in addition included groups either equitably or inequitably paid on a piecework basis. For the group inequitably paid, the prediction was somewhat more complex. Participants could not increase their inputs by increasing the number of interviews since their outcomes would be correspondingly increased. Thus, the investigators predicted that individuals overpaid on a piecework basis would complete fewer interviews. This prediction was also confirmed.

A field study illustrating the case of underpayment was made in a series of supermarkets.[91] In this investigation the productivity of cashier-bagger pairs were studied. Cashiers were of higher status on a number of dimensions. They were full-time employees who received higher pay than the part-time baggers. Furthermore, psychologically they were superior to the baggers in that the baggers were perceived as working for the cashiers. On a number of variables such as sex, age, and education, however, baggers frequently had the more valued inputs. Thus, at times a college male might find himself paired with a younger female cashier with a high school education. In these instances, the college male with higher inputs would be receiving lower outcomes in terms of pay and subordinate status. Interviews revealed that when such pairing occurred those with the superior inputs in terms of age, sex, and education worked at a slower pace, thus bringing their total inputs into line with their lower outcomes. That such an adjustment was widespread was revealed in an analysis of the financial operation of these stores. When the stores were ranked on labor efficiency and on an index which reflected the degree to which outcome and input ratios between cashiers and baggers were discrepant, the correlation was almost perfect.

In general, studies of the effects of underpayment have supported predictions from equity theory;[92] however, the earlier results concerning overpayment have been called into question on a number of grounds. First, it has been argued that the manipulation employed to create the condition of overpayment may have also threatened the self-esteem of individuals as well as their feelings of security regarding further work or the continuation of a high piece rate. Reaction to these effects might be to improve the quality of performance and reduce the quantity.[93] Further, at least one study suggested that the effects of overpayment dissipate rapidly, either because individuals gain security and prove themselves capable fairly quickly, or because they are able to convince themselves that their performance does merit the high piece rate. Another suggestion is that in everyday work situations pay inequities are created by an

90. Adams & Rosenbaum, 1962.   *91.* Clark, 1958.   *92.* Pritchard, 1969.   *93.* Lawler, 1968.

impersonal firm, so that the advantaged worker is less apt to feel that his being overpaid constitutes unfairness on his part.[94]

Studies have attempted to cope with these difficulties.[95] While the evidence is not entirely consistent, it does support the effects predicted by equity theory for overpayment. This research as well as the recent work of Leventhal suggests that some conditions will augment or in some instances eradicate the effects of inequity. The same variables that affect the degree of obligation induced by the norm of reciprocity (see Chapter 10) affect assessments of equity. Thus, the inputs of another person will be subjectively assessed in terms of the difficulties and limitations he works under,[96] the resources available to him,[97] and his intentions. Feelings of inequity and attempts to reduce them will be diminished where the inequity created is a result of chance rather than the intention of the parties, or where the greater inputs causing the inequity are provided by the person who is most capable (either because of his superior resources or situational opportunities).

SUMMARY: THE PROBLEM-SOLVING PROCESS   Certain actions occur at maximum frequency in different phases of the problem-solving sequence. In the early phase, acts related to problems of orientation and evaluation are at a maximum; in the final phase, acts related to problems of control reach their peak. An overall trend is that the relative frequencies of both positive and negative responses increase from phase to phase. The relative predominance of the various forms of action in different phases is in part related to the demands imposed by the necessity of solving a problem, but it also stems from the interaction of several other variables.

One variable underlying the relative frequencies of different acts is the need of the group to obtain conformity from its members. As the group shifts from orientation to evaluation, it reacts negatively toward those who do not conform and positively toward those who do. In the initial part of the final phase, which involves control, the high frequency of negative reactions occurs because of unresolved value differences. The later part of the final phase is characterized by many positive reactions. These reactions apparently serve to restore positive feeling in the group, which has been depleted by the many influence attempts aimed at achieving agreement.

Satisfaction in groups takes several forms. Some satisfaction lies in the reward for task accomplishment, which may be monetary or "psychic." The latter is illustrated by the status or social approval accorded members for successful achievement, and by the satisfaction of needs for self-expression, self-development, and self-determination. Another type of satisfaction is unrelated to task needs; it stems from the enjoyment of social interaction.

Satisfactions are not a simple function of the amount of rewards received in

94. PRITCHARD, DUNNETTE, & JORGENSEN, 1971.   95. ANDREWS, 1967; LAWLER, 1968; PRITCHARD et al., 1971.   96. LEVENTHAL & MICHAELS, 1969, 1971.   97. LEVENTHAL, YOUNTS, & LUND, 1970.

a group. Individuals vary with respect to the strength of their needs, the number of alternative satisfactions, and how much they expect from the group. The relation of rewards to both productivity and satisfaction can only be understood in terms of the principles of equity. Whether a reward is adequate depends on what people expect from the situation—their comparison levels—and on what they regard as equitable or just rewards. Individuals compare their inputs (or investments) and outcomes with those obtained by other persons. Thus, the more an individual puts into an activity compared to another person, the more he feels he should get in return. A state of equity exists when the ratio of inputs and outcomes of an individual is equal to that of the person with whom he compares himself. While it is obvious that an individual may feel angry or dissatisfied if he receives less than he considers fair, he may also feel uncomfortable, embarrassed, or guilty if he receives more than his due. In both instances, he may attempt to redress the imbalance, although this is less frequent when outcomes are in his favor.

Satisfaction and Productivity

This final section will discuss a most perplexing problem: the relation between group productivity and satisfaction. Personnel policies in many organizations are formulated on the assumption that satisfied workers will be productive workers; yet research does not support this assumption. Brayfield and Crockett, in a critical review of this literature, conclude:

> In summary, it appears that there is little evidence in the available literature that employee attitudes of the type usually measured in morale surveys bear any simple—or, for that matter, appreciable—relationship to performance on the job.[98]

Satisfaction or morale, however, is related to employee absences and employment stability.[99] Less satisfied workers have higher rates of absence and are more apt to quit their jobs. These findings are consistent with the general principle that individuals avoid punishing situations and seek out rewarding ones; they stay away from a job they do not like and they try to find one that they do like. A more recent review of this literature arrives at essentially the same conclusions.[100]

The failure to find a direct relation between productivity and satisfaction has prompted a closer look at the reasoning that led early investigators to expect a positive relation. One line of reasoning assumes that satisfaction and productivity are both a function of rewards, and hence they should vary together. The relation between productivity and rewards, however, bears further scrutiny.

---

98. Reprinted by permission by A. H. BRAYFIELD & W. H. CROCKETT. Employee attitudes and employee performance. *Psychological Bulletin,* 1955, 52, 408.   99. BRAYFIELD & CROCKETT, 1955.   100. VROOM, 1964.

First, productivity is a function of much more than motivation. Earlier in the chapter, a wide variety of factors were reviewed that affect both the quality and the quantity of production. There are some very good reasons why rewards, satisfaction, and productivity do not necessarily vary together in the typical work situation. As Katz and Kahn argued, not only are such rewards often removed in time and space, but instead of being administered according to a worker's productivity, they are often given out according to very broad classifications of length of service, type of work, and similar characteristics.[101]

They also note that such rewards will be obtained only if a worker remains in the system; hence, they may motivate a sufficient level of productivity to ensure continued employment, but a level that does not result in differences among workers within an organization.

Implicit in the argument of a direct relation between productivity and rewards is the assumption that rewards regarded by management as important are in fact important rewards for the worker. Brayfield and Crockett have suggested that the importance to the worker of differential monetary rewards has been greatly overestimated. While recent evidence[102] suggests that wages are not unimportant, other sources of reward in the work situation are also important in explaining differences in productivity and satisfaction. The work of Likert and his associates, as well as that of Argyris, underscores satisfaction intrinsic to job activity, particularly as it is affected by the style of supervision.[103] Rewards deriving from interaction have been emphasized by a long series of investigations (starting with the famous Hawthorne studies) under the influence of Mayo and culminating in the work of Zaleznik, Christensen, and Roethlisberger.[104] In fact, Zaleznik and his colleagues, in a study of satisfaction and productivity in an industrial setting, found no relation among satisfaction, productivity, and monetary rewards. Like their predecessors, these investigators found that productivity was greatly influenced by group norms which specified what was an appropriate level of productivity—a "fair day's work." Those who were dependent upon and rewarded by the group conformed to these norms.

These findings suggest another reason why productivity in work situations, unlike that in the laboratory, is not a simple function of rewards provided by an external agent. Internal rewards in the work situation may counteract the effects of external rewards. The worker who is given a monetary reward by management for high productivity may be deprived of the social-emotional rewards administered by the group because his level of productivity exceeds the group norm. For most workers, rewards of the latter type are far more important; hence relatively small differences in productivity between workers are found even when the system of payment is designed to encourage such differences. Where such differences do exist, they can be explained largely in terms

101. Katz & Kahn, 1952.   *102.* Lawler, 1971.   *103.* Likert, 1961; Argyris, 1960.   *104.* Zaleznik et al., 1958.

of the worker's position in the group as it affects and is affected by his adherence to the group norms.

Monetary rewards are probably important in some situations. For example, where the work setting isolates workers from each other, or where the task is dull and routine, monetary rewards should be important.

So far, discussion has been based largely on differences between the laboratory situation, where productivity and rewards are related, and the work situation, where they are not. It has been suggested that satisfaction and productivity are not necessarily related by being linked to rewards, because the relation between productivity and rewards is not what it has been assumed to be. Rewards in the work situation are more complex, and their administration is not uniformly and differentially related to differences in productivity. Vroom, on the basis of a survey of the literature, and Porter and Lawler, on the basis of a study of seven organizations, have proposed explanations to account for the relation among rewards, productivity, and satisfaction.[105] Both make use of expectancy theory.[106] Work effort is related to performance to the degree that the worker perceives that increased performance will in fact lead to increased rewards. Both also recognize that productivity is more than simply a function of motivation, that the determinants of motivation involve more than just monetary rewards, and that the effects of rewards are always relative to expectations about what is just or equitable.

SUMMARY: SATISFACTION AND PRODUCTIVITY   Two common assumptions in industry—that satisfaction and productivity are closely related and that they are a direct function of the amount of reward received by the worker—are probably both unwarranted. In the first place, rewards are seldom administered in direct proportion to the worker's productivity. Second, monetary rewards are usually less important than rewards arising out of task activity and out of group interaction. These two factors, along with style of supervision, appear to be more important than monetary rewards as determinants of both productivity and satisfaction. Moreover, the several kinds of rewards available to the worker do not add up to produce a greater total reward: Under some circumstances they interfere with one another. Finally, models based upon expectations about what rewards are just or equitable provide adequate explanations of the complex relation among rewards, productivity, and satisfaction.

---

105. VROOM, 1964; PORTER & LAWLER, 1968.   *106.* ATKINSON, 1958.

PART THREE

The Individual and the Social System

In Part Two group structure and process were illustrated in newly formed laboratory groups, in more stable units such as work groups, and in institutional settings such as the family. Emphasis was placed upon an analysis of group structures in terms of affect, power, status, and communication, and the relation of these structures to certain group processes was discussed. Using the concept of social role as the major unit of analysis, Part Three considers in more detail structure and process in institutional settings such as the family or the school.

Part Two discussed in some detail two processes that contribute to development of institutional structure. Chapter 10 described how social norms emerge. Chapter 11 described the process of role differentiation by tracing the development of the role of leader. It was seen that agreement among members about who is the leader of a group emerges in a relatively short time, a fact which signifies recognition of the role category or position of leader. This group acquiescence to the initiating behavior of the leader suggests that the differentiation is accompanied by the growth of norms specifying that the leader should direct the group's activities. These norms emerge out of a process of negotiation in which both leader and follower exchange satisfactory outcomes. Underlying this negotiation are some of the power processes discussed in Chapter 8.

The twin processes of norm formation and role differentiation result in the elaboration of a *social system, role categories,* and the corresponding *expectations* that guide interaction. Such systems constitute the *institutional structure.* Although the development of the leadership structure was observed under the highly simplified conditions of the small-group laboratory, the same processes can be observed with ease in nonlaboratory settings. As formal organizations—fraternities, social clubs, business enterprises, or churches—are created, or as they undergo marked changes, new positions and associated expectations to govern the behavior of members can be seen emerging.

The chapters in Part Three will be concerned with the consequences of such social systems for the behavior of group members. Chapter 13 will introduce the basic concepts that are used to analyze these systems. Chapter 14 will describe features of the systems that create strains interfering with individual and group functioning, and the means by which these strains are resolved.

13

Social Roles

This chapter and the next one will stress the nature of interaction from a perceptual-cognitive point of view. To some extent, certain perceptual-cognitive features of interaction have already been identified in the chapters on group structure and process. First, shared perceptions have been found to develop concerning the position occupied by each person in a group structure. For example, evidence has been presented that persons who have considerable power to influence others are perceived by group members as occupying positions of power. Similarly, group members agree on who in the group has little power. Persons who most frequently initiate and direct group action are recognized by other group members as occupying positions of leadership. Those who rarely initiate action and who generally follow the lead of others are recognized as followers.

A second feature of interaction already noted is that group members agree in holding certain expectations for the behavior of persons who occupy particular positions in the group structure. A person in a position of high power is expected to influence others readily and effectively, a leader is expected to suggest constructive actions leading to achievement of group goals, and a follower is expected to refrain from offering suggestions and to agree with the leader's ideas.

A third concept developed was that of social norm, defined as an expectation shared by group members which specifies behavior that is considered appropriate for a given situation. Social norms include not only overt behavior, but also verbal behavior associated with an individual's perceptions, thoughts, or feelings. For the most part, norms were considered as they applied to all group members, although considerable emphasis was given to the fact that different expectations are held for leaders and followers. Major attention was devoted to the mechanisms through which norms are enforced and to conditions that maximize or minimize norm-defining and norm-enforcing processes. The present series of chapters pertains to virtually all forms of human interaction, focusing upon the concept of norm as a rule of conduct and applying it to any individual who occupies a definite position in the social structure. In this sense, *social norm* is more appropriately subsumed under the concept of *social role*.

Nature of Social Roles

Two Characteristics of Expectations

Two features of expectations which are especially important for understanding the concept of social role are their anticipatory nature and their normative quality.

ANTICIPATORY NATURE OF EXPECTATIONS   An individual regularly expects that he will behave in a certain manner, and he usually has definite expectations concerning the behavior of persons with whom he interacts. The importance of this aspect of interaction may be readily appreciated if we consider situations where such expectations are at a minimum; for example, a child's homesick feeling during his first experience with a summer camp, a teenager's tension on his first date, a young person's initial experience with a new and unfamiliar job. Also illustrative are the feelings of uncertainty and the resultant tentative and shifting quality of interaction that occurs in a newly formed group. These situations in which expectations are minimal may be contrasted with others where expectations are well developed; for example, the smoothly functioning, comfortable interaction occurring between two old friends.

This anticipatory quality of interaction is important because it guides the behavior of an individual, a point spelled out by George Herbert Mead.[1] One anticipates how the other person might react to his various actions and shapes his behavior accordingly. Often these anticipations take the form of rehearsing one's social interactions before they transpire. The attitude of the other person is inferred from subtle cues provided by his appearance, expression, and posture; by his previously known and current behavior; and by the situational context within which interaction takes place. From such information, the individual draws inferences concerning what the other person feels and thinks about him and how he is likely to behave toward him. In everyday interaction, the process of anticipating the attitudes and behaviors of the other person is

1. MEAD, 1934.

greatly simplified. Through long experience, an individual classifies the behavior of other persons in various situations into categories that represent the distinctive attitudes of each class of persons-in-situations. This enables him to anticipate the attitude of the other person in each new encounter simply by placing him and the situation in the appropriate category.

These points concerning the anticipatory quality of interaction have been strikingly illustrated by Garfinkel, who arranged with his students to behave contrary to expectations in everyday situations.[2] In one such study, the students were asked to act for a time as if they were boarders in their own homes instead of as a member of the family. In most cases, family members were stupified. They struggled hard to make the strange actions intelligible and to restore the situation to normal. The following are examples:

> One student acutely embarrassed his mother in front of her friends by asking if she minded if he had a snack from the refrigerator. "Mind if you have a little snack? You've been eating little snacks around here for years without asking me. What's gotten into you?" One mother, infuriated when her daughter spoke to her only when she was spoken to, began to shriek in angry denunciation of the daughter for her disrespect and insubordination and refused to be calmed by the student's sister.[3]

NORMATIVE QUALITY OF EXPECTATIONS   Because persons anticipate the behavior of others, interaction has a contingent quality. A person's behavior is contingent upon his anticipation of how the other will react toward him. When he tells a joke, he anticipates that the other will laugh or be amused; otherwise he is unlikely to tell it. If he confides a distressing personal problem, he expects some expression of sympathy; if he does not want sympathy, he keeps the problem to himself. Since many powerful social-emotional needs are satisfied only through interaction with other persons, an individual must be able to anticipate reactions of the other to his own behavior if he is to satisfy his needs. A person desiring sociable conversation must be able to anticipate what behaviors on his part will elicit responsive conversation from the other.

Usually such anticipations are correct and well established only in situations which the individual has previously encountered, where he and the others involved have certain shared experiences in common. Each party to the interaction shares expectations concerning his own and the other's behavior. Such well-established shared expectations usually have an obligatory quality. The other person is not only expected to behave in a certain way; it is believed that he *should* behave in that way. Failure on his part to meet expectations is likely to be met with surprise, disgust, anger, or indignation, as shown above. This normative quality of expectations stems from the fact that only when one is

2. GARFINKEL, 1967.   3. Reprinted with permission from H. GARFINKEL, *Studies in ethnomethodology.* Englewood Cliffs, N.J.: Prentice-Hall, Inc., 1967. Pp. 47-48.

able to anticipate consistently the behaviors of others can one maximize one's reward-cost outcomes. The extent to which expectations are normative varies in proportion to the importance of the rewards and costs involved. Norms involve important rewards and costs to the extent that they are functionally integrated with the value structure of the group, a point to be discussed in more detail later.

Some Role Concepts

POSITION OR ROLE CATEGORY; ROLE PLAYER OR ACTOR   The terms *role category* and *position* refer to a grouping of persons whose behavior is subject to similar expectations. The person in the role category is referred to as the *role player* or *actor*. Chapter 2 referred to Schutz's notion of typification of the objects in an individual's world, including typing of people.[4] It was shown there that children and adults type the people around them, sometimes in the form of a stereotype. Some of these typifications are role categories.

There are three bases for grouping people into a role category: (1) they occupy the same position in a social relation or system, (2) they occupy a special position in a small group, and (3) their qualities constitute a type. The first of these is the most common. An illustration is that actors in the role category of mother in the system of social relations called the *family* are subject to certain broad expectations for their behavior. Only those categories of actors defined in the same way by two or more persons meet the criteria for defining a position. Role categories may be perceived in the same way by all members of a society, or by only a few individuals. An example of groupings that are widely agreed upon is age-sex position: "small boy," "small girl," "young man," "young woman," "old man," "old woman." Persons whose occupations require them to interact widely with others outside their occupation also occupy positions based on widely shared perceptions. Illustrations are surgeon, taxi driver, lawyer, professor, barber.

In the second type of role category, clearly defined categories of persons are shared by only a small number of persons. Most small groups have such positions peculiar to their own group. Perhaps a clear example is the "lunch-boy" mentioned by Homans.[5] The newest employee in a small group of men working in a factory was assigned to the position of lunch-boy, which required him to bring back from the plant restaurant the food ordered by his fellow workers. This example suggests another basis for placing persons into role categories, namely, by their group function. Thus Benne and Sheates have distinguished such small-group roles as the opinion giver, the orienter, the clown, the expert, and the director.[6]

The third basis for classification into role categories focuses primarily on qualities of the actor occupying the role. An example might be that of the "good Joe" or "yes-man." Categories of this sort have been referred to as social

4. SCHUTZ, 1964.   5. HOMANS, 1961.   6. BENNE & SHEATES, 1948.

types.[7] For the most part, this analysis will be concerned with role categories in a social relation or system.

ROLE EXPECTATIONS; SOCIAL ROLE   Expectations have been described in terms of the anticipatory and normative quality of interaction. Role expectations are expectations that are associated with a role category. As in the case of role categories, the number of persons who hold expectations with respect to a particular category may vary from two persons to virtually everyone in a society of millions. Expectations associated with age-sex positions illustrate culturewide expectations.

For example, in American society expectations traditionally associated with the role category "little girl" include the belief that she should like dolls and dresses, that she should cry more readily and be more affectionate than her brother, and that she should be well-mannered as compared with little boys. These expectations also include beliefs concerning what she should not do: She should not be able to outbox all the boys in the neighborhood, she should not be especially interested in playing cowboys and Indians, and she should not get as dirty as little boys when she plays outside. Currently, such differences in normative expectations for boys and girls—and for men and women—are under vigorous attack by the woman's liberation movement,[8] which, in essence, argues for the elimination of sex roles, allowing each individual to develop according to his own potentialities, regardless of gender.

Subgroup expectations may also be illustrated: Parents in lower socioeconomic classes have somewhat distinctive expectations toward the role category of "child." To a greater extent than parents at middle socioeconomic levels, they generally expect children to obey and respect adults and to please them.[9] Finally, some expectations associated with a position may be relatively unique, as when a particular mother and child share the expectation that she should sing him a certain lullaby when she puts him to bed.

Role expectations associated with a role category may vary with respect to consensus. Some expectations are widely agreed upon; others are unique to particular individuals. Most people in our society would agree that an actor in the role of husband should provide at least a portion of the income for his family. That the wife also should be expected to earn income by working is a belief held much less widely.

The more general term *social role* (or simply *role*) is used to refer to both a position and its associated expectations. When the role of mother is referred to, both the position in a family system and its attached expectations are being designated.

ROLE BEHAVIOR   Role behaviors are the behaviors of an actor in a role category that are relevant to expectations for that role. These behaviors may or may not conform to expectations. For example, a professor may explain some

7. KLAPP, 1962.   8. MEDNICK & TANGRI, 1972.   9. KOHN, 1963.

ideas very poorly. Explanation of ideas is relevant to his role and consequently this is role behavior, although it does not conform to the expectation that a professor should explain things clearly. While performing his role he also engages in behavior irrelevant to it. To illustrate, while lecturing he might light a cigarette, an act that has nothing to do with his role.

Role expectations and role behaviors should be clearly distinguished from each other. Expectations represent how actors in a role category are supposed to behave; particular individuals, however, may deviate markedly from these expectations in their actual behavior. The behaviors that constitute a particular role enactment are generally a result of role bargaining or negotiation between partners. The initial expectations held by role partners often allow considerable leeway in how to behave; also, the partners are rarely in perfect agreement. Often this looseness is tightened up through negotiation between the partners, who ultimately arrive at greater agreement and clearer, more definite expectations.

Summary: Nature of Social Roles

A position or role category is a category of persons occupying a place in a social relation. Some role categories are recognized on a societywide basis, and some are relatively rare, perceived by only a few people. Role expectations are expectations that are associated with a role category. Role expectations may be widely agreed upon, or there may be varying degrees of disagreement among participants in the system of relationships. Social role refers to both the role category and its associated expectations. Finally, role behaviors are the behaviors of an actor that are relevant to the role that he is performing.

The Social System

Particular social roles cannot be considered apart from their relation to other social roles. Every social role has others to which it is related. Together, related social roles make up a system or structure within which persons interact. Such interlocking social roles are commonly referred to by social psychologists as *social systems.* An example of a social system is the family—not a particular family, but the systematic relations between the positions of husband and wife, father and child, mother and child, brother and sister, etc. Other examples of social systems include the prison, the monastery, the hospital, and the school. This section introduces a number of important system concepts.

Relations among Social Roles

ROLE PARTNERS   The expectations associated with a role category specify particular behaviors toward actors in other related role categories. Actors occupying these related role categories are known as *role partners,* a term adopted from Bredemeir and Stephenson.[10] Examples are: mother and child, doctor and patient, teacher and student. An actor may have many role partners: partners of a mother are not only her children, but also her children's father, teachers, playmates, neighbors, pediatrician, dentist. These persons, when acting as her role partners, relate to her as a mother of the children with whom they are interacting.

ROLE OBLIGATIONS AND RIGHTS   The intimate connections between related role categories may be more fully appreciated by considering role relations in terms of obligations and rights. Consider two role categories such as husband and wife. Associated with the position of husband are certain expectations concerning how this actor is expected to act toward his role partner, his wife, and how she is expected to behave toward him. These relations can be described from the standpoint of the husband or from that of the wife.

From the standpoint of the role category of husband, the expectations about his behavior are referred to as *role obligations,* and the expectations about the behavior of his wife are referred to as *role rights* or *privileges.* From the standpoint of the position of wife these same expectations become privileges and obligations, respectively. For example, according to the traditional division of labor in the American family, an obligation of the husband is to provide food, shelter, clothing and the amenities of living for his wife. From her point of view that is a right or privilege she enjoys as a wife. Conversely, a husband in American society traditionally expects his wife to take care of the house and attend to such matters as shopping, cleaning, and laundry. From his point of view this is a right associated with his role; it is an obligation associated with the role of the wife. In short, the obligations of an actor are the rights of his role partner; his own rights are the obligations of his role partner.

Social Roles in Ongoing Interaction

At any time an actor may simultaneously occupy a number of positions: Both he and his role partners define him in terms of several role categories, and his behavior is influenced by the role expectations attached to these categories. Illustrations include a physician treating a member of his own family, or a teacher having her own child as a pupil in her classroom. As will be discussed in more detail in the next chapter, this simultaneous occupation of more than one role category is important because in many situations an actor occupies two positions in which expectations are contradictory, leading to role strain.

At any one time, however, a person never enacts all the role categories that he occupies in the course of his daily activities. At a given moment, some of his positions are active; they are used by him and by other persons to anticipate his behavior and to judge its appropriateness. Later, other positions become active while the former become latent; he is no longer placed in those categories. This

10. BREDEMEIER & STEPHENSON, 1962.

shifting from one role category to another, positions becoming active and latent as one goes about his daily life, has been vividly pictured by Linton in a classic passage:

> Let us suppose that a man spends the day working as clerk in a store. While he is behind the counter, his active status is that of a clerk, established by his position in our society's system of specialized occupations. The role associated with this status provides him with patterns for his relations with customers. These patterns will be well known both to him and to the customers and will enable them to transact business with a minimum of delay or misunderstanding. When he retires to the rest room for a smoke and meets other employees here, his clerk status becomes latent and he assumes another active status based upon his position in the association group composed of the store's employees as a whole. In this status his relations with other employees will be governed by a different set of culture patterns from those employed in his relations with customers. Moreover, since he probably knows most of the other employees, his exercise of these culture patterns will be modified by his personal likes and dislikes of certain individuals and by considerations of their and his own relative positions in the prestige series of the store association's members. When closing time comes, he lays aside both his clerk and store association statuses and, while on the way home, operates simply in terms of his status with respect to the society's age-sex system. Thus if he is a young man he will at least feel that he ought to get up and give his seat to a lady, while if he is an old one he will be quite comfortable about keeping it. As soon as he arrives at his house, a new set of statuses will be activated. These statuses derive from the kinship ties which relate him to various members of the family group. In pursuance of the roles associated with these family statuses he will try to be cordial to his mother-in-law, affectionate to his wife and a stern disciplinarian to Junior, whose report card marks a new low. If it happens to be lodge night, all his familial statuses will become latent at about eight o'clock. As soon as he enters the lodge room and puts on his uniform as Grand Imperial Lizzard, in the Ancient Order of Dinosaurs he assumes a new status, one which has been latent since the last lodge meeting, and performs in terms of its role until it is time for him to take off his uniform and go home.[11]

INTERACTIONAL CONTEXT   At any point in time, the *interactional context* is an important determinant of the role categories a person occupies, of the expectations applied to the role category, and of the range of permissible behavior defined by the expectations. The two features of the interactional context that determine these factors are the *characteristics of the situation* and the *characteristics of the actors*.

First, persons are placed in a role category appropriate to their characteris-

11. Reprinted with permission from R. LINTON, *The cultural background of personality.* New York: Appleton-Century-Crofts, Inc., 1945. P. 78.

tics and behavior. How they are categorized will determine what expectations will emerge. If a person enters a bank and with passbook in hand approaches a woman who is standing behind a partition with a window grill, each will use certain information to categorize the other: he defines her as a teller, and she defines him as a customer. As soon as such categorization is made and as long as it is maintained, certain expectations and certain interactions will occur. There will be a polite exchange of greetings, the passbook will exchange hands, etc. Should he suddenly produce a gun, however, he would be categorized differently by this woman and new expectations and behavior on her part would undoubtedly occur. Similarly, if the woman behind the partition behaved in a manner which indicated that she was not a teller, he would change his expectations and behavior. This example illustrates the principle that expectations are always tied to categories of persons as well as categories of situations. Before expectations emerge, categorization must take place; and if categories shift in a given interaction situation, expectations will change.

As discussed in Chapter 10, a number of features of the situation may well alter expectations or at least make them relatively ineffective in influencing behavior. The expectation that a bystander should come to the aid of a person in distress appears to be nullified where features of the situation (e.g., the presence of many other persons who might help) allow him to perceive that action on his part was not necessary or morally required.

Summary: The Social System

A social system is a group of related social roles. Each role category in a social system relates to one or more other role categories. Persons occupying these other categories are known as role partners. The obligations of an actor in a role category are the rights of his role partner; his own rights are the obligations of his partner. Individuals assume various roles at different times and on different occasions. Sometimes they simultaneously perform more than one role. When expectations associated with these multiple role categories are incompatible, role strain results. The role categories an actor occupies, the expectations applied to the role category, and the range of permissible behavior defined by the expectations are functions of the interactional context. Two features of the interactional context that determine these factors are the characteristics of the situation and the attributes of the actors.

Social Norms and Roles

Early in the chapter, two important properties of expectations were stressed: their anticipatory nature and their obligatory nature. The actor is not neutral about whether his expectations are confirmed by the behavior of the other person. He not only anticipates the person's behavior, but feels that the other is obligated to behave in accordance with his anticipations. He assumes that the

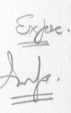

other shares with him common role expectations. Thus role expectations are normative, and in varying degrees the actor is disturbed if the other person does not conform as expected. Although group norms were discussed in Chapter 10, treatment was confined largely to pressures toward conformity and the conditions producing various degrees of conformity. This section will discuss normative expectations within the larger perspective of social roles.

Social norms have a variety of properties:

1. They shape behavior in the direction of shared values or desirable states of affairs.

2. They vary in the degree to which they are functionally related to important values.

3. They are enforced by the behavior of other persons.

4. They vary in how widely they are shared; they may be societywide, or they may belong to groups of varying sizes, even as small as a two-person group.

5. They vary in the range of permissible behavior; some norms set more stringent limits on behavior than others.

Norms and the Value Structure

Behavior which is contrary to expectations may arouse surprise, disgust, anger, or indignation. On the psychological level of analysis, such reactions can be explained in terms of social learning. A well-brought-up Moslem has learned to react with revulsion to the eating of pork, just as Americans, as members of their society, would react to the eating of caterpillars. Similarly, the typical American middle-class male would react with feelings ranging from embarrassment to indignation if a host suggested that as a guest he should sleep with the host's wife. But in societies where wife lending under such circumstances is expected, a guest might well react with similar feelings if such an offer were *not* made.

On the sociological level of analysis, these reactions are related to the value structure of the group. Just as actors in a group share expectations about one another's conduct, they share notions concerning desirable conditions or states of affairs. These conditions are called *values*. Values can be ranked in terms of how important they are to the members of a group. Prominent values among a group of conservationists, for instance, might include such conditions or states of affairs as the aesthetic qualities of the land, protection against inroads on nature by man and his machines, preservation of wildlife species, and spending time in the out-of-doors. A ranking of values would constitute the value hierarchy of that group. These value rankings may differ from group to group; for example, the conservationists' ranking of values would be different from the ranking of the same values by a group of lumbermen or miners. Norms are functionally related to values in that conforming to certain rules of conduct fosters the achievement of certain desired states. For example, good health is a value in Western society, and various hygienic rules are norms that direct behavior toward achieving this valued state.

The degree of functional dependence between values and norms varies. The violation of some norms may barely endanger a value, whereas the violation of others may greatly jeopardize the achievement of a desired condition. To illustrate, the norms governing cleanliness in the operating room of a hospital are functionally related to the value of health to a higher degree than is the expectation that a person will cover his mouth when he sneezes in the presence of others.

Enforcement of Norms

Norms are enforced by means of *sanctions*. This term refers to the actions of others or of an actor himself that have the effect of rewarding conformity and punishing nonconformity to norms by facilitating or interfering with the need gratification of the individual. *Positive sanctions* involve the use of reward or other forms of satisfaction, such as approval or praise. *Negative sanctions* involve the use of punishment or deprivation of satisfactions. Further, where the source of reward or punishment is the behavior of others, the term *external sanction* is employed. Where the source is within the actor, *internal sanction* is used. Examples of external sanctions are giving an employee a raise in pay or docking an employee who is late for work. Examples of internal sanctions are a feeling of pride for having conformed to a norm in the face of strong temptations to violate it, or a feeling of guilt for having failed to conform.

In connection with the previous example of the student who, for a time, assumed the role of boarder in his own home to the consternation of his family, Garfinkel gives a number of examples of sanctions applied by family members, including:

> Characterizing the student as mean or nasty.
> Shouting and angry denunciation.
> Mocking the student by joining in the role (e.g., a sample response: "Certainly, Mr. Herzberg!").
> Charging him with being a wise guy, and using sarcasm.
> Ostracizing him (illustrated by such comments as: "Don't bother with him, he's in one of his moods again!).
> Threatening retaliation (illustrated by such comments as: "Pay no attention but just wait until he asks me for something" and "You're cutting me, okay I'll cut you and then some").[12]

The strength of the sanction varies with the importance of the value and the extent to which the norm is instrumental to the achievement of the value.

12. GARFINKEL, 1967.

While external sanctions may be relied on almost exclusively to enforce norms that are of little importance, norms that relate to important values and that are highly instrumental in achieving those values are rarely if ever enforced by external sanctions alone. Groups socialize their members so that they develop strong internal sanctions for these norms. The processes of socialization and internalization will be discussed in more detail in Chapters 15, 16, and 17.

Variations in Sharing Normative Expectations

Expectations may be shared by any number of persons, ranging from members of a large society to a two-person group. In Western society, such behaviors as the handshake, the kiss, and the bowed head in prayer are regulated by societywide norms. Many behaviors, however, are specific to smaller groups. For example, a particular church denomination has certain ritualistic behavior which is required of its members; nonmembers do not and are not expected to participate. Small groups engaging in face-to-face interaction inevitably develop sets of social norms to guide the conduct of the members. Work groups, for example, set standards for how much work shall be done in a day, and members who violate the standards are punished. On most college campuses there are subgroups of students who maintain a norm with respect to how much time is spent in studying. Those who study too much are called such derogatory names as "grinds," "brains," and "eggheads."

Finally, the smallest unit, a pair of persons, such as a husband and wife, may engage in behavior which is essentially normative but peculiar to them. For example, the husband may take the dog out every morning, and the wife may drive the children to school.

Variations in Limits of Behavior

From personal experience people know that some rules can be honored by a rather wide range of conduct, while others are more exacting and require a specific line of behavior. Thus, norms should be thought of as specifying the limits of permissible or required behavior in a particular interactional context—limits which may be relatively wide or narrow, depending on the particular norms as well as on other components of the interactional context. The range of permissible or required behavior may be illustrated by considering arrival times at a dinner party. The host usually tells his guests that the dinner party will begin at some specific hour. Few guests arrive punctually; most arrive some time after the hour. But there is a relatively narrow range of permissible or required arrival time, and when this is violated, profuse apologies from the late guests are called for. On the other hand, the range of arrival times is much greater for an evening cocktail party.

Social Roles and Social Interaction

In the remainder of this chapter social interaction will be analyzed in terms of role concepts. The previous emphasis on the normative aspects of expectations was not meant to imply that role behavior is simple conformity to role expectations. Role expectations provide a broad script for the drama of role enactment—a tremendous leeway for ad-libbing. And from experience, people know that performances of different actors enacting the same role vary considerably. For example, even though a single set of expectations for the role of professor could be identified, not all professors behave in the same way in the classroom. Some professors are very informal, crack jokes, call students by their first names, and show a personal interest in them—that is, they play *both* leader roles: task and social-emotional (see Chapter 11). Other professors are more formal and serious and serve primarily as task leaders, seldom responding to students as individual persons.

There is much interest in identifying the sources that guide the portrayal of a role in certain directions. Three sources are *situational demands, personality,* and *intruding roles.* In addition, role performances occurring in specific interactions are worked out through a process of *role negotiation* with role partners. These four sources operate to give direction to role enactment within the wider range of expectations associated with the role category. Each of these directional sources will be discussed in turn.

Situational Demands

Sarbin and Allen have noted that many situations call for a specific kind of role performance.[13] They have termed the elements of the situation that call out this performance *role demands.* A good example is found in the discussion in Chapter 3 of the *demand characteristics* of the experiment. Certain features of experiments outside the framework of the experimenter's interest place strong pressures on participants to behave in accordance with the experimenter's hypotheses. The prestige of the institutional setting and of the experimenter together with the student's role as an individual in training make him cooperative and concerned about performing satisfactorily. The authors have chosen the term *situational demands* rather than *role demands,* however, in recognition of the fact that the demands are not associated with role categories or positions, but rather with situations. Enactment of the *same* role by different performers in many different kinds of situations is the issue. Each different situation has its own demands.

Situational demands are illustrated by an investigation in which tests of vocational interests and aesthetic preferences were given to ROTC students in two settings: (1) in the facilities of the military science department with admin-

13. SARBIN & ALLEN, 1969.

istration of the tests handled by a teacher who was a military officer, and (2) in psychological laboratories in a room decorated esthetically with art materials with a psychologist administering the test.[14] The tests given under the military conditions were labeled tests of military effectiveness; those under artistic conditions, tests of artistic ability. Large differences in performance on these identical tests were obtained, suggesting that the setting, the tester, and the test labels produced situational demands relevant to the testing situation.

Personality and Role Skills

A second source directing role enactment stems from the personality characteristics and the skills of the actor. How he enacts the role is affected by his aptitudes for it, his self concept, his attitudes, his needs, and his *role identity.* In the next chapter, many examples will be given of how a disparity between aptitude or personality and role expectations creates considerable strain in role enactment; a pacifistic, peace-loving young man may be either unable or able only at great cost to perform the role of soldier in time of war. In this chapter the concern is with the special direction that personality and role skills may give to role enactment. Two teachers with very different personalities and aptitudes might both be successful teachers, enacting this role in very different ways.

McCall and Simmons have called attention to the importance of *role identity,* defined as the character and the role that an individual devises for himself as an actor in a role category—the way he likes to think of himself being and acting.[15] A role identity is a somewhat idealized conception of one's performance. Yet it is more than simply daydreams. Such thoughts and anticipations are the primary source of plans of action. These imaginings often include vicarious performances—rehearsals of the enactment to be portrayed. The imagined reactions of other persons to one's role performance are used as criteria for evaluating and modifying these plans. These idealized conceptions of performance can also be used to evaluate how one enacted one's role—to identify mistakes, overplays, and underplays.[16]

Role identities are expressions of relevant aspects of an actor's *self concept.* The self concept may be thought of as an interlocking set of views that an individual holds about himself as a person. It serves as a core from which role identities are formulated in connection with role categories that the actor occupies.

Intruding Roles

A third source of direction lies within the system of roles itself. An actor's behavior is rarely, if ever, influenced by one role alone. He simultaneously

14. Kroger, 1967.   *15.* McCall & Simmons, 1966.   *16.* McCall & Simmons, 1966.

occupies a number of role categories. While one role usually will be more dominant in a given situation than other roles, these other roles may influence role enactment to some extent. Thus, portrayal of a particular role by men or by women, that of physician, for example, may be somewhat different because of the intrusion of their sex roles. Outside the classroom, at a fraternity beer bust, for instance, a professor might enact the role of a "good Joe," but his role as professor may nevertheless intrude to some degree. The next chapter will discuss in much greater detail the effects of system features which both facilitate and interfere with a particular role performance.

Role Negotiation

A fourth direction stems from the process of *role negotiation* or bargaining.[17] An actor and his role partners can be thought of as working out through negotiation, either direct or indirect, how each will behave in particular encounters and situations, as well as the more general features of their relationship that develop over time. The use of the term *negotiation* should not be construed to mean that this process is as deliberate as that of negotiating a sale price between salesman and customer. Role negotiation may be very subtle and indirect, with one or both parties unaware that they are vying for a particular role bargain.

The nature of the role bargain that emerges depends upon many factors, including: (1) the role identities of both parties, (2) situational demands, (3) the social power of each person in terms of resources, dependencies, and alternatives, (4) the interpersonal skills of the two parties, and finally (5) the effectiveness of third parties in influencing the outcome of the negotiation. Many of the principles of interpersonal strategy previously discussed in Chapter 8 can be applied to role negotiation.

Role negotiation occurs to some degree in every relationship, but it is an especially important determinant of role behavior under the following circumstances: (1) where the limits of the roles are so broad as to leave unspecified the particular nature of role performances, (2) where the role expectations held by actor and role partner for their respective roles are not in agreement with each other, (3) where the actor's characteristics preclude performing the role in the usual way, (4) where situational demands interfere with role enactment, (5) where other roles intrude upon performance, and (6) where the disparity of social power between actor and role partner is not so great as to preclude negotiation.

Role negotiation may be illustrated in the marriage relation where, sometimes at least, all the above circumstances prevail. The roles of husband and wife are culturally prescribed only in terms of broad limits; partners rarely agree on all aspects of their roles; often the personality, aptitudes, skills, or role

17. GOODE, 1960.

identities of one or both partners are not entirely suited to the role of husband or wife; situational demands often interfere with role performance; other roles (such as careers) often intrude; and the relative disparity in social power is not great (at least in Western societies).

The changes that are occurring in the roles of men and women in contemporary societies throughout the world, both within marriage as well as outside of it, can be explained partly by the effects of larger social changes on role bargaining between the sexes. An examination of these effects should serve to illustrate the theory of role negotiation previously presented and to show how interpersonal processes are influenced by and in turn influence social and cultural change. Two major social changes have had considerable effects on role negotiation between the sexes, particularly as they affect the roles of husband and wife. One has been a change in the economic structures of modern societies toward providing women with an economic role outside the family economy. A second has been a change in cultural belief systems concerning sex differences as well as the ideals governing relations between persons.

The belief that traditional sex differences are the result of social definitions has largely superceded the belief that they are a product of biological necessity. The norm of equality and the idea of the primacy of the status of a person as an individual over more specific statuses have become increasingly widespread. These changes in turn have influenced the content and salience of the role identities that both sexes bring to a relationship. In marriage, for instance, the identity that many women project for that of wife includes the expectation that they will be able to carry on a full-time career. This expectation has been facilitated by changes in the socialization of women that have increased their capabilities and aspirations for this new economic role and by changes in opportunities for the enactment of this role. The latter has come about as a result of mechanization in the home and by the reduction of traditional barriers to equality in employment.

These changes, as well as shifts in the functions of marriage in modern urban societies, have increased the woman's bargaining position: She now has more resources and alternatives. Women's increased employment opportunities, the decrease in family size, and the greater personal freedom accorded women along with a decline in the stigma attached to divorce have made this alternative to an unsatisfactory marital relation more palatable to women than has been the case in the past. At the same time these changes have made men more dependent on the marriage relation. Employed wives often make a significant contribution to the total resources available to family members. In a significant proportion of marriages the life style of the husband as well as that of the wife has become increasingly dependent on her economic contribution. Moreover, with high mobility and other features of urban life reducing the possibility for close emotional support in relationships outside of marriage, men are probably more psychologically dependent on the marriage relationship today than in previous times. To the degree that the husband has internalized the new values and norms emphasizing equality between the sexes, the wife is able to invoke these norms as a form of legitimate power during episodes of role negotiation within marriage.

The accumulation of countless episodes of negotiation among married couples as influenced by this alteration in the power relations within marriage has resulted in a shift toward equality, and this shift is rapidly gaining widespread cultural acceptance, particularly in those segments of Western society where those forces influencing the power relation between the sexes have had their greatest impact.

The actual process of role negotiation ranges from intelligent discussion and argument to the exercise of the many forms of interpersonal influence discussed in this book. If agreement cannot be reached through discussion then social power may be exercised in various ways. One spouse may attempt to be especially nice to the other by buying a gift or by performing special favors. This invokes the norm of reciprocity since it makes the partner feel obligated to return the treatment. (It might also make the partner feel guilty, raising further problems.) Where conflict on role performance becomes more serious, threats or deprivation may be used. Partners may refuse to speak to each other. They may stop doing the little things for each other that they ordinarily performed routinely. More powerful moves involve threats to leave home, to have an affair, to get a divorce, or in some families, the use of physical violence. But the bulk of negotiation, at least in a new marriage, probably takes the form of discovering disparities in expectations, and working them out through discussion and argument to eventually arrive at normative agreements on performances.

As Goode has emphasized, third parties may often enter into the negotiation process.[18] When other members of the primary or extended family live with the husband and wife, this is especially the case. Another factor that brings third parties into the process is continued dependence (financial or psychological) of the marital partners on their parents. While this factor varies greatly for different families, it is a very real problem for some. Many of the proverbial mother-in-law jokes are based upon an intrusion by her into the negotiating process—an event that can only occur, however, when it is permitted by the marital partners.

While research on the determinants of role portrayal is scarce, there has been some work whose findings are consistent with the above formulation. One role-playing experiment was able to show that to the degree that a particular role portrayal was inconsistent with an important dimension of the self, actors resisted the attempt on the part of another person to get him to play that role.[19] In one condition, for instance, males who regarded themselves as dominant resisted the attempts of a female confederate of the experimenter to get them to agree to play a submissive role as a price for her agreeing to go out with him.

18. GOODE, 1960.   *19.* BLUMSTEIN, 1970.

The degree of resistance varied with the attractiveness of the female confeder-ate. Male participants were more willing to take on an identity contrary to their self conception in the condition where the female confederate was attractive than in the condition where she was unattractive.

Finally, those who scored high on a test of Machiavellianism[20] (designed to measure both the motivation and abilities to manipulate others) were more apt to adopt a role opposite to their self concept when such behavior would result in a date with the girl. The fact that the behavior of the male participants in the study was influenced by whether the role-playing episode was private or was thought to be observed by others supports the previous statement that the final role bargain that emerges is often influenced by other persons as well as the two actors involved in the negotiation.

Summary: Social Roles and Social Interaction

Many kinds of role enactments are usually possible for a given social role. The direction that these performances take is guided by several forces other than the role expectations themselves: situational demands, individual personality and role skills, intruding roles, and role negotiation between partners. Elements of the current situation that call for a specific kind of role performance consti-tute situational demands. Personality and role skills include the individual's traits and other characteristics, his aptitudes, his needs, and his role identity, which is an extension of his self concept. Intruding roles are imposed by the social system, in instances where expectations from more than one role cate-gory are relevant to a given role performance.

Role negotiation arises from lack of agreement between role partners on the appropriate role performances. Situational demands and third parties to the interaction may also create the necessity for negotiation between role partners. Negotiation is not necessarily deliberate; one or both parties may be unaware that they are vying for a particular role bargain. The actual process of negotia-tion ranges from intelligent discussion and argument to the use of many other forms of interpersonal influence.

Social Role as an Integrating Concept

The concept of social role is one of the most central in the behavioral sciences. It serves to integrate the varied actions of an individual, it shows how the diverse actions of members of a group form a unity in group action, and it links the individual to the group and to society.

If one were to follow a person around, he would find that person's actions at different times to be strikingly varied. He is a "loving" father of a daughter, a

---

20. BLUMSTEIN, 1970.

less loving and more stern father of a son, a friendly companion to his wife, a physician dealing with nurses and his patients in a relatively impersonal manner, and a good sport with his bowling friends. He has a variety of role identities that are extensions of his self concept. By taking these roles together, one is able to view him as a person and thus see unity in his varied actions.

The concept of social role also serves to link three major areas of interest: social systems, personality, and culture. Sociologists, who focus on an analysis of social systems, and anthropologists, who study comparative social structure, have found it useful to conceptualize the systems of recurring interactions in a group in terms of social-role concepts. The ongoing behavior of any group can be analyzed in these terms. In a university, for instance, one may note interactions that recur from day to day. In room after room of a classroom building, certain patterned interactions take place: One person stands before a group of others; he speaks, and they write in their notebooks. The pattern can be analyzed in terms of the role behavior of those occupying the positions of teacher and student. In other buildings on campus, patterned interactions occur between actors in other role categories, such as deans and secretaries, professors and laboratory assistants, members of the board of regents, and administrative officials. All these patterns can be conceptualized in terms of position and role expectations and can be studied as a system—as a unity of interdependent parts. Certain large problems, such as what happens to the other parts of the social system when a particular position drops out of it or when the role expectations associated with a role category change, may be treated on this level of analysis.

In the past, social psychologists were chiefly interested in those types of roles toward the cultural end of the continuum, since their main concern was with societywide regularities in behavior rather than with regularities common to the members of smaller subgroups. In more recent years, as social psychologists have become concerned with smaller groups, they have expressed more interest in roles toward the unique end of the continuum.

At a somewhat different level, social psychologists are also interested in features of social systems that relate to personality formation. Certainly such features of a system as the clarity of the role expectations, the amount of consensus among actors about these expectations, and the integration of the expectations so that the actor does not encounter conflicting expectations, will have implications for problems in the areas of personality formation and social interaction. Part of the discussion of role in connection with personality formation must wait until the analysis of processes of social learning (Chapter 15).

Chapter 14 will be concerned with the ideas reviewed here in connection with the concept of role and how they add to our understanding of human interaction. The focus will be on situations in which contrary forces make role enactment difficult: first, because most of the research has concentrated on role conflict, and second, because it is easier to detect the factors underlying human interaction when its normally smooth-flowing character is disrupted.

14

Role Strain and its Resolution

This chapter will be concerned with the effects of the social system, personality variables, and cultural elements on role behavior, with primary attention to the social system. Basic to this discussion is the idea of *role strain* or the difficulties that persons experience in performing a particular role. When persons attempt to perform a role in a manner that minimizes strain, they may fail to do so either because the role partner is dissatisfied or because certain features of the role system produce difficulties. The latter source of strain will be analyzed on three levels: the social system, the personality and role skills of the individual, and the cultural system. When human behavior is viewed in terms of the social system, recurrent interactions between individuals are focused upon and conceptualized in terms of position and role. On this level, concern is not with the characteristics of the actors themselves, but with characteristics of the system of relations between actors. When the individual is focused upon, analysis takes place in terms of personality or role skills; concern is with the role skills and various conceptual components of the personality in relation to the role requirements: needs, self conceptions, and attitudes. Components of the cultural system are studied in terms of shared cognitions about the social and nonsocial world.

Sociologists as sociologists are concerned primarily with analysis on the social-system level; psychologists as psychologists are concerned with analysis at the level of the individual. Anthropologists are concerned with cultural systems. Social psychologists, however, while focusing on the individual, attempt to relate his behavior to all three levels. Those familiar with the work of Talcott

Parsons will recognize in the above distinctions an indebtedness to him.[1] In preference to direct adoption of his terminology in this book, however, many of his ideas have been recast in terms that are more commonly employed in the field, and considerable attention is given to the contributions of other sociologists. *— But is a "structure" real?*

Social System Variables and Role Strain

Throughout this discussion the importance of expectations in the interaction process has been emphasized. Such expectations make interaction possible to the extent that they are held in common and fulfilled by the members of a group. Interaction becomes difficult or impossible to the extent that group members do not hold expectations in common or behave contrary to them. Where persons have conflicting expectations, strain results both from the conflict aroused by role bargaining and from the fact that the resultant role bargain is rarely satisfactory to all concerned. On the level of the individual personality, strain involves experiencing conflicting tendencies to act and feelings of inadequacy, guilt, embarrassment, and need frustration. On the level of the social system, strain is associated with interpersonal conflict and the failure of the system to maximize the achievement of its goals. The degree of strain is reflected in the cultural system, in terms of inconsistencies among its elements.

An illustration of strain resulting from different conceptions of role held by an actor and his role partner is found in the early sessions of psychotherapy. The new patient normally comes to therapeutic sessions with the expectation that the therapist, like a physician, will provide some prescription for his problems. He expects the therapist to be extremely active—to ask him questions and to tell him how to solve his problems. The therapist, on the other hand, usually expects the patient to solve his own problems gradually through a process in which the patient is very active in reporting his feelings and thoughts and his own reactions to them, and in which he gradually arrives at a new view of himself and his place in the world. In short, the therapist expects the patient to talk a great deal and sees his own role as facilitating the patient's verbalizations, while the patient expects the therapist to do most of the talking and perceives his role as passive and dependent. How this leads to strain is illustrated by the reactions of several different patients to the inactivity of the therapist:

Patient [1]: A couple of seconds ago, uh, there was a silence in which I had nothing to say or I didn't say anything. And just before you said something I thought of this fact that, uh, I wonder *who's* going to talk first and *why*.

1. PARSONS & SHILS, 1951.

Patient [2]: I was trying to arrive at a couple of things *(sigh)*. The reaction of the analyst sitting and just staring at me, and waiting for me to say something or to think of something leads to two kinds of feelings in me. One, instead of coming forth and being able to think of things, is that I either draw a blank or, uh, have to fight to try and almost make up things to fill the void.

Patient [3]: Well, actually, I haven't found this, uh, the kind of experience that I've anticipated. It's rather frustrating. It's difficult for me to carry on a one-man conversation with myself, something I've never been able to do.

Patient [4]: I thought, uh, there would be more of a, uh, interaction, back and forth in trying to at least, get at your reactions to the kind of feeling I have.[2]

Clarity and Consensus in Role Expectations

Expectations associated with roles in a social system vary in clarity and in the degree of agreement or consensus among persons. Where expectations are unclear, strain is produced by individual uncertainty about what is expected and by the many conflicting interpretations of what role behavior is appropriate.

Newly developed roles, in particular, often lack clarity. For example, in one study, psychiatric nurses required to enact a rather vaguely defined new role complained that, unlike their earlier role, it did not provide a clear-cut basis for action.[3] The nurses had been instructed to respond to the patients as individuals, recognizing each patient's needs and attempting to satisfy them. The new role permitted extreme freedom to the patients (all of whom were chronic schizophrenics) limited only by considerations for their health and safety and the nurses' own physical and psychological comfort.

Not only did these expectations for the roles of patient and nurse conflict with the nurses' personal norms, preferences, and capabilities, with the traditional role of nurse, and with the institutional requirements of the hospital, but they also did not offer a sufficient guide to action or allow for a consistent treatment of the patients by different nurses. Schwartz comments on the lack of consensus:

The emphasis upon responding to patients in individualized ways and the consequent reduction in shared patterns of action resulted in nurses handling the same patient behavior in different ways. Nurses who wanted privacy in the nursing office while making out reports found that other nurses permitted patients free access to the office, sometimes to their great annoyance. Some nurses wanted to remove the food cart after nourishments had been served; others preferred to leave the cart on the ward for the entire

2. Reprinted with permission from H. L. Lennard & A. Bernstein. *The anatomy of psychotherapy.* New York: Columbia University Press, 1960. P. 168.   3. Schwartz, 1957.

evening, even though a patient usually played with the food and threw it around the ward.[4]

Schwartz notes further that the lack of clear-cut expectations left the nurses at a loss to know how to behave. One nurse, referring to the ward administrator who introduced the new role, made the following comments in an interview:

I don't think he recognized—or he probably recognized it and was trying to break us of it—the fact that we do need and want certain very definite lines set up which we can feel our way around. Over and above that, fine—we'll be permissive, we'll be comfortable, we'll do this, that and the other thing; but we do have to have certain anchors and guideposts. Otherwise we just feel as though the world is falling apart. . . .[5]

Other studies of emerging roles similarly document the point that lack of clarity in new roles leads to role strain. Wardwell, in a study of a relatively new occupational role, that of chiropractor, also observes that a lack of clarity is a source of strain. He comments:

In addition to the ambiguity in the definition of the role of any doctor, the chiropractor's role is ambiguous for several other reasons. There is vast ignorance on the part of the patients and potential patients as to what chiropractors do, and, more important, chiropractors themselves disagree on the question of what chiropractic treatment should be. The "straights" limit themselves to spinal manipulation alone, sometimes "adjusting" only upper cervical vertebrae, while the "mixers" also use heat, light, air, water, exercise, diet regulation, and electric modalities in their treatment. State laws differ as widely in the scope of practice they permit. In most states chiropractors are limited to spinal manipulation and simple hygienic measures, while in others they may perform minor surgery, practice obstetrics, and sign death certificates. . . .[6]

Where role expectations in a social system are unclear for whatever reason, strain in social systems leads to periodic attempts by the actors occupying positions in the system to clarify their roles. In large systems, such as business organizations, one such attempt takes the form of developing and elaborating manuals of operation that make explicit what is expected of each position occupant in the system. The same process can be observed in small systems, such as a family, or even a two-person relation like that between two lovers.

---

4. Reprinted with permission from C. G. SCHWARTZ. Problems for psychiatric nurses in playing a new role on a mental hospital ward. In M. Greenblatt, D. J. Levinson, & R. H. Williams (Eds.), *The patient and the mental hospital.* New York: The Free Press of Glencoe, Inc., 1957. P. 412.   5. Reprinted with permission from C. G. SCHWARTZ. Problems for psychiatric nurses in playing a new role on a mental hospital ward. In M. Greenblatt, D. J. Levinson, & R. H. Williams (Eds.), *The patient and the mental hospital.* New York: The Free Press of Glencoe, Inc., 1957. P. 413.   6. Reprinted with permission from the University of Chicago Press and W. A. WARDWELL. The reduction of strain in a marginal social role. *American Journal of Sociology,* 1955, **61,** p. 17.

One function of lovers' quarrels is to redefine their relations to each other—in the terminology of this discussion, to clarify their respective roles.[7]

The discussion so far has focused upon the *expectations* associated with positions in a given system. The positions or role categories themselves may also show lack of clarity, with similar consequences. In categorizing others, persons may use a wide variety of cues, such as dress, voice, and manner of behavior, as well as more explicit identifying information such as titles or uniforms. Stone has provided a penetrating analysis of the cues furnished by dress in interaction.[8] Where such categorization cannot be made with confidence and accuracy, uncertainty and inappropriate behavior with attendant role strain will occur. Further evidence comes from a study of over 1,000 embarrassing incidents reported by students and other persons.[9] Confusion of role category was a frequent source of embarrassment (e.g., incidents included a man accidentally entering the ladies' room; a boy with long hair being mistaken for a girl; a customer being mistaken for a sales clerk).

TYPES OF DISAGREEMENT ON ROLE EXPECTATIONS   Two aspects of disagreement may be discussed, one pertaining to the *way* in which actors disagree, and the other pertaining to *which* actors disagree. When either form of consensus is lacking, concerted action by the actors is hindered, and they are likely to be anxious and uncertain concerning their rights and obligations.

The way in which actors in the same role category may disagree on expectations takes at least five forms: (1) Actors may disagree on what expectations are included in a given role. (2) They may disagree on the range of permitted or prohibited behavior. (3) They may disagree on the situations to which a given expectation applies. (4) They may disagree on whether the expected behavior is mandatory or simply preferred. (5) They may disagree on which should be honored first when an expectation conflicts with another.

Lack of consensus on the role of wife in our society is a good example, especially in the case of a husband holding traditional views of inequality, since all five forms may be illustrated: (1) There may be lack of agreement on whether being a wife should require a woman to forgo employment. (2) A husband may disagree with his wife in believing that part-time employment is permissible, but full-time is not. (3) They may disagree in believing that she should only be employed in a case of economic necessity. (4) He may believe she absolutely should not work, and she may feel it simply would be better if she did not. (5) Finally, he may believe that her family obligations take precedence over her employment, and she may have the opposite opinion. Although these illustrations pertain to an actor and his role partner, the five forms of disagreement may also apply to actors in the same position.

The various role partners of an actor may also define the actor's role differently from each other. Where such conflict cannot be avoided or resolved, the

7. WALLER & HILL, 1951.   8. STONE, 1959, 1962.   9. GROSS & STONE, 1964.

individual faces negative sanctions from at least one of his partners in the form of withdrawal of affection and regard, or from the self in the form of shame or guilt. An everyday example is the child whose parents seriously disagree on what expectations are appropriate for his role.

Since sanctions for lack of conformity to a role expectation may be imposed by people other than one's role partners, conflicting expectations on the part of these significant others may also be a source of strain. A common example here is the mother-in-law who interferes with her daughter's marital relations by attempting to redefine the role expectations held by the young couple toward the positions of husband and wife.

CONDITIONS RELATED TO CONSENSUS   Although it was initially assumed that consensus on role expectations would generally be high, empirical studies have demonstrated a considerable range of disagreement for some role expectations.[10] Further systematic study has identified some of the conditions under which consensus is low. In a study of school superintendents and school boards, two types of consensus were studied.[11] The first was consensus among actors occupying the same position on their own role, and the second, consensus between an actor and his role partners on their respective roles. The following is a brief summary of this extensive study.

When actors in the same position in different school systems were compared, consensus on role expectations was found to vary with (1) the content of the role expectation, (2) the degree of similarity in social backgrounds of the actors, and (3) the extent to which the actors belonged to organizations of the same or different sizes. Within single school systems, similarity in selected attributes was associated with greater consensus among actors. Interaction among school board members was greater when they agreed on expectations, and they were also more satisfied. Consensus between school board members and their superintendents was not associated with similarity of background or amount of interaction. When there was consensus, the superintendent evaluated his board more favorably, but neither the superintendent nor the board was more satisfied.

These findings make sense in terms of the peculiarities of the system studied. Members of a school board can only act effectively as a group, and hence consensus is required. But as Gross and his colleagues point out, most of the functions of the superintendent's office involve him in interaction with actors other than school board members: teachers, principals, community leaders, etc.[12] Thus, consensus with these partners was more vital to his satisfaction than consensus with the board. But since the superintendent was dependent upon the conformity of the board to his professional expectations, he did evalu-

10. DAVIS, 1954; HALL, 1955; BORGATTA, 1955; ROMMETVEIT, 1955; GROSS, MASON, & MCEACHERN, 1958; BIDDLE, ROSENCRANZ, & RANKIN, 1961; SNYDER, 1964.   *11.* GROSS et al., 1958.   *12.* GROSS et al., 1958.

ate them more favorably when they agreed with him on role expectations. That similarity of background and amount of interaction were not related to consensus between superintendent and board is understandable if we assume that the superintendent is oriented toward other professionals in defining role expectations for his position and those of board members.

These findings support the argument that in a system involving professionals and nonprofessionals, the satisfaction of the professional is based in part on how well the nonprofessionals facilitate the achievement of professional goals. Boards within which there is agreement on educational matters and boards which conform to professional expectations on these matters would be expected to function in a manner that facilitates the achievements of goals defined by the superintendent as desirable.

Other studies are generally consistent with these findings. A study of role consensus among hospital administrators, hospital board members, and community leaders suggested that a particular role is described differently by the actor and his role partner to the extent that each has different linkages with other positions in the social system.[13] This suggestion was based on the idea that the more frequently persons interact cooperatively, the more obligated to each other they feel. To illustrate, hospital administrators are linked to and have more contact with various professional groups, including the medical staff; and board members are linked to and have more contact with community leaders. Consequently, it was found that in describing their role, administrators expressed more administrator obligations to the medical staff than did board members describing the administrator role. Similarly, hospital board members in describing their roles expressed more board-member obligations to community groups than did administrators in describing the board-member role. In another hospital study, consensus was found to be greater when training and preparation for a role were extensive and when roles were specifically defined by the organization; it was also greater for actors in positions having the most contacts and the most frequent communications with other individuals in the social system.[14]

Another investigation in a different social system tested the hypothesis that a high degree of consensus between actor and partner facilitates relations between an actor and his role partner.[15] Support for the hypothesis was found in a comparison of role conceptions of foremen and union stewards in industry. Foremen who saw the steward's role as the stewards did reported easy relations with their stewards. Similarly, stewards who defined the role of foreman in the same way as foremen did reported easy relations with their foremen.

Findings from another study that consensus on role expectations was greater in smaller than in larger organizations add support to the idea that frequency of interaction—particularly of the informal type—is related to consensus.[16]

13. Hanson, 1962.   *14.* Julian, 1969.   *15.* Jacobsen, Charters, & Lieberman, 1951.   *16.* Thomas, 1959.

Further, if it is assumed that mothers have greater interaction with children than do fathers, the greater agreement on role expectations found between mothers and children than between fathers and children further supports this idea.[17]

A study of the roles of doctor, registered nurse, practical nurse, and patient in a tuberculosis sanitarium tested three hypotheses[18]: (1) The greater the training and preparation for a role, the greater will be the agreement among actors on their role and that of their role partners. In other words, because of their more extensive training, doctors and registered nurses were expected to agree more than practical nurses and patients on their own roles as well as those of their various partners. (2) Both kinds of consensus should vary according to the specificity with which the organization defined roles. Since the patients' behavior in the sanitarium was defined in more detail than the behavior of the staff, greatest agreement was expected on the patient role. (3) The actors who have the greatest communication and contact as determined by the organization of the social system should have the highest consensus between actors and role partners. More specifically, doctors and registered nurses should agree to a greater extent on their respective roles than doctors and practical nurses, since the chain of command in the hospital requires greater contact between the former staff members than the latter. While the data were not in complete accord with these three hypotheses, they supported them for the most part.

Elsewhere the authors have suggested that lack of consensus is related to the manner in which expected behavior affects the reward-cost outcomes of persons in interaction. Thus, to the degree that a role expectation has important consequences for actors in a particular role category, consensus among them is apt to be high. In Chapter 10, it was noted that norms emerge in those areas of behavior most critically related to the reward-cost outcomes that persons experience in a relation; and further, to the degree that their outcomes are important, maximum pressures toward conformity can be expected. Some support for this has been found in a study of the role conceptions of teachers.[19] Consensus among teachers was high. They were almost unanimous in agreeing that teachers should be paid more for their services.

Consensus between actors and role partners appears also to vary with the degree to which an expectation has similar implications for the outcomes of each party. If they both stand to benefit equally by conforming to the expectation, consensus is high. Lack of consensus may frequently take the form of each partner emphasizing as important those expectations that are to his advantage. In a study where males and females were allowed to describe what type of role they preferred to play in marriage, both sexes emphasized the obligations of the other's role to the neglect of the rights of their role partners.[20] A study of consensus between actor and partner involving the expectations of teachers,

17. CONNOR, GREENE, & WALTERS, 1958.   *18.* JULIAN, 1969.   *19.* MANWILLER, 1958.   *20.* KIRKPATRICK, 1936.

parents, students, and school officials for the role of teacher provides further illustrations.[21] The greatest overall agreement on conceptions of the role of teacher was that between school teachers and school officials. The greatest disagreement was that which existed between the expectations of teachers and pupils for the role of teacher. The role conceptions of parents were intermediate—somewhat closer to that of teachers than those held by students, but further from the teachers than those of school officials. Exchange theory helps to explain these findings regarding consensus for different role partners, and makes sense of the specific areas of disagreement, as the authors noted in another book:

> Any particular action of a teacher is apt to produce similar outcomes for both teacher and school official, but an opposite outcome for the student. For example, a teacher who fails a student who has performed poorly is upholding the standards of the school and will be supported by the principal. But this action is costly to the pupil. Since the outcomes of the parent are similar in part to those of the pupil and in part to those of the teacher and school official, parents would be expected to agree with them only in part.
>
> These differences in consensus become clearer when we examine the areas of disagreement about the role of the teacher held by his role partners. Most obviously in support of this principle are findings that teachers, parents, and school officials expect and approve of more supervision of pupils by teachers than do pupils, and that teachers to a greater extent than these other groups disapprove of teachers doing menial tasks. Less obviously relevant are findings which suggest that parents expect teachers to engage in more maintenance of order, more control of deviant behavior, and more supervision outside the classroom and to speak out more frequently at PTA meetings than the teachers themselves believe is appropriate. These role items all involve additional demands on the teacher that adversely affect the rewards and costs experienced in his role.[22]

Not all expectations that make up the role of teacher have the same implications for the outcomes of teacher and school official. Here again, however, the above principle appears to operate. In a study of the relative importance attributed to facets of the teacher role, considerable disagreement was found between teachers and administrators in two high schools. A major concern of the administrator is school-community relations. This would lead him to focus on aspects of the teacher role relevant to this function. Thus, administrators ranked as most important that teachers act as a liaison between school and community, but ranked the teacher's role as "director of learning" only fifth. The teacher's main concern is his instructional function, which is reflected in

21. BIDDLE et al., 1961.   *22.* Reprinted with permission from C. W. BACKMAN & P. F. SECORD. *A social psychological view of education.* New York: Harcourt, Brace & World, Inc., 1968*b*. Pp. 120-121.

his stress on serving as a "mediator of culture" (ranked first) and "director of learning" (ranked second). Finally, 80 percent of the teachers indicated that they should have final say on doubtful cases of pass-fail, but only 40 percent of the principals and superintendents thought so.[23]

The discussion of role consensus has focused largely on lack of agreement between the various parties in a role relationship. A third area of disagreement has been ignored: that which may exist between each of the role partners and third parties. Chapter 13 noted that role bargaining frequently is influenced by the expectations of audiences or third parties. That sharp differences may exist between what a partner may expect of an actor and what various third parties expect has been demonstrated.[24] Expectations that business executives thought were held toward them by their bosses, wives, colleagues, parents, children, and the organization in relation to each of these partners were compared. Frequently, in these comparisons the expectations held by a partner for an actor's relation to a third party (e.g., the expectations a wife had for her husband's behavior toward his boss) was different from those expectations attributed to the other partner (i.e., in this instance, the boss). Moreover, frequently these actors admitted a line of conduct closer to that advocated by the third party than by his role partner in that particular relationship.

Finally, many of the studies of conformity to group norms discussed in Chapter 10 are probably applicable. It is likely that many factors which produce conformity also produce consensus on role expectations. For example, a study of the aircraft commander role showed that role consensus is related to crew cohesion, and an investigation of role conceptions in small, medium, and large organizational units in a welfare agency found greater consensus in the smaller units.[25]

SUMMARY: CLARITY AND CONSENSUS   Expectations associated with roles in a social system vary in clarity and in the degree of consensus among actors. Clarity is mainly a function of the explicitness and specificity of expectations. Newly developed roles often lack clarity and thereby lead to role strain. Lack of clarity may also result from successive changes in a role. Although most research had been devoted to the clarity of expectations, ambiguity in the role category may also produce strain.

An actor and his role partner may disagree in five ways: (1) about the expectations included in a given role, (2) about the range of permitted or prohibited behavior, (3) about the situations to which the role applies, (4) about whether the expected behavior is mandatory or simply preferred, and (5) about which expectation should be honored first. Disagreement on an actor's role may also occur between two or more of the actor's partners or among persons outside the system.

When actors in the same position in different school systems were compared,

23. FISHBURN, 1962.   *24.* KEMPER, 1966.   *25.* HALL, 1955; THOMAS, 1959.

consensus among actors on their own position was found to vary with (1) the content of the role expectation, (2) the degree of similarity in the actor's social backgrounds, and (3) the extent to which the actors belonged to organizations of the same or different sizes. Within single school systems, similarity in certain attributes was associated with greater consensus among actors, although similarity in other attributes was not.

Probably because the superintendent is oriented toward other professionals in defining role expectations for his own position and for his school board, consensus between board members and their superintendents was not associated with similarity of background or the amount of interaction they had. Studies in other contexts have provided support for a positive relation between amount of interaction and consensus. In hospital settings, consensus is greater for those roles having extensive training and preparation, for those that are specifically defined, and for those whose actors interact frequently with each other. Linkages of various positions within a social system are likely to affect the way in which role expectations are defined. One principle that is consistent with a number of research findings is that consensus varies with the degree to which expectations have important and similar consequences for those in interaction. Many of the factors that produce conformity to group norms probably increase consensus on roles. Finally, lack of consensus may involve third parties to a relation.

Satisfaction with one's role is contingent upon the type and amount of consensus, and the particular social system to which the role belongs. School board members having high consensus were more satisfied; this follows from the fact that agreement is necessary to successful performance. Consensus between the superintendent and his board was not associated with higher satisfaction for the school superintendent, who must relate to many role partners with diverse views. In a different social system, high consensus between foremen and union stewards on their roles in industry facilitated relations between these role partners. Finally, lack of consensus may also involve disagreements with third parties to a relationship who often influence the role behaviors of the partner in interaction.

Mechanisms for Increasing Consensus

Role strain often builds up to a crisis which motivates the participants to seek a clarification of rights and obligations existing between them. Such attempts may range from informal rap sessions in small systems to elaborate negotiating committees in large systems. As problems of clarity and consensus increase, either because of the growing size or complexity of the system or because of rapid changes, social machinery evolves to deal with lack of consensus and related problems.

Such machinery takes a number of forms. First, special positions and subsystems emerge to cope with the problem of lack of consensus. This is often the major function of coordinating and liaison committees in organizations. Second, more active efforts are made to formalize relations by specifying in operation manuals how each actor is to behave toward his role partners in the system. Accompanying this are techniques for ensuring the standard socialization of actors. Elaborate selection procedures, orientation and training programs, periodic refresher courses, etc., become a part of the system. Finally, rituals and ceremonies develop which function not only to increase identification with group goals, but which serve periodically to reinforce agreement on the rights and obligations of each person in the system.

Frequently such mechanisms fail and continued crisis produces confrontations between role partners that result in a change in the terms of previous role bargains. This most frequently occurs where the expectations governing a relation have sharply different implications for the outcomes of participants and where the disadvantaged role partner has recently gained greater power. Thus, the increased power of blacks in American society and of students on campuses have forced, through a series of crises, new relationships with their role partners which represent a new consensus.

Conflicting and Competing Expectations

Another source of role strain lies in conflicting or competing expectations that make up a role. Such conflict or competition may pertain to expectations regarding the same role partner; an example is a mother who knows that she should not hurt her child but who also knows that she must discipline him. Conflict or competition may also involve different role partners: A woman with a new baby may find that the baby's demands on her time interfere with her obligations to other family members.

Conflict arises when one expectation requires behavior of the actor which in some degree is incompatible with the behavior required by another expectation. The actions may be physically incompatible because one action is the opposite of the other. They may be socially incompatible because they are not expected of the same person. Finally, they may be psychologically incompatible because they require the actor to adopt opposite psychological sets.[26] To illustrate the latter, on the occasions that a mother treats some minor wound experienced by her child, when she removes a painful splinter, she may have difficulty assuming the attitude of clinical detachment necessary for performing the operation.

Competition between expectations occurs when the actor cannot adequately honor both expectations because of limitations of time or energy. Conflict and competition will be discussed below.

26. NYE, 1961.

CONFLICT AND COMPETITION IN RELATION TO THE SAME PARTNER   Several examples of conflict and competition within a role involve the relation of a professional person with patients. Three facets of the physician's role have been distinguished: (1) He is a scientist-warrior on the frontiers of knowledge, (2) he is a technician-savior of the sick, and (3) he is a small-business retailer of knowledge which he has purchased at considerable cost to himself.[27] A similar set of elements has been noted within the role of the chiropractor.[28] While aggressive bill collecting is consistent with the small-business-retailer aspects of the doctor's role, it is inconsistent with the image of the gentle healer or the altruistic scientist.

Somewhat similar conflicting elements in the nursing role have been described.[29] On the one hand, nurses themselves, as well as the general public, expect nurses to behave as mother surrogates whose obligations run the gamut from washing a patient's feet to listening sympathetically to his innermost feelings. On the other hand, they are also defined as medical specialists or healers whose duties are to perform the technical tasks specifically necessary to combat the patient's affliction and to restore him to society. The basic conflict is between a set of expectations characterized by affect, sympathy, and emotional involvement, and another set involving restriction of these feelings. Schulman summarizes his observations on the conflict between these two facets of the nurse's role as follows:

> In terms of a single broad variable—the presence or lack of affect—the roles of mother surrogate and healer are seen to be in conflict. In its developmental or historical aspect there has been a transition from behavior expectations associated with the ancient ideal of the woman and mother toward those of the technical healing specialist, a transition never easy or simple. Each of the steps leading to the dominance of the healer role is marked by opposition, especially from nursing itself, but also from associated groups and from the lay public. In its present phase this role conflict is evidenced in repeated attempts to "redefine" nursing and the great emphasis now placed on "just where the nurse fits" in her relations with other occupational groups and in the community. Even more, one sees the conflict in stark evidence when the question is repeated a thousandfold in American schools of nursing and at every meeting of nurse-educators: "Just where are we going?"[30]

Undoubtedly an examination of the elements in other treatment roles, such as those of the clinical psychologist or the social worker, would reveal a similar configuration of conflicting elements. Other roles as well have been studied. Thus, conflict has been found between two facets of the role of inspectors in manufacturing firms.[31] In part, inspectors are expected to judge the quality of

---

27. LEE, 1944.   28. WARDWELL, 1955.   29. SCHULMAN, 1958.   30. Reprinted with permission from S. SCHULMAN. Basic functional roles in nursing: Mother surrogate and healer. In E. G. Jaco (Ed.), *Patients, physicians, and illness.* New York: The Free Press of Glencoe, Inc., 1958. P. 537.   31. PUGH, 1966.

the products produced and reject products of substandard quality. At the same time they are expected to serve as production auxiliaries helping production people avoid mistakes in quality. Often behavior in the pursuance of the former objective interferes with the latter function. A study of the role of stockbroker similarly revealed a number of facets of this role that were in conflict.[32] As an investment adviser he is expected to provide customers with impartial and sound advice. As a broker, however, he is expected to consummate a sale.

CONFLICT AND COMPETITION IN RELATION TO DIFFERENT PARTNERS   In the area of conflict and competition between expectations from different partners, the role of the school superintendent is again a useful example. Gross, Mason, and McEachern note that a superintendent must interact with teachers, school board members, PTA members, civic leaders, etc.[33] Often the demands of each relation raise problems of time allocation, as well as difficulties in meeting diametrically opposed expectations. One such conflict which they investigated in some detail was the conflict between the salary demands of teachers and parents on the one hand and the economy-minded expectations of members of the city council and taxpayer associations on the other. Whereas a majority of the teachers and parents were perceived by the school superintendents as wanting them to fight for maximum salary increases, a majority of the members of the city council and the taxpayers associations were perceived as wanting them to "hold the line" or "be reasonable in their salary budget recommendations."

Another example of competition due to time allocation may be somewhat more familiar to the college student acquainted with university professors. The professor is expected not only to teach, but in addition to engage in scholarly research and to devote some time to community service. To the extent that all three of these expectations concerning the professor's duties are held by his dean, this is an example of competition within a single role sector. Actually, however, these demands arise in part from various role partners: His fellow professors and colleagues in his own discipline particularly expect him to do research, and members of the community in which the university is located also make direct demands upon his time.

Actors in Several Roles

COMPETITION BETWEEN ROLES   Normally an actor occupies a number of positions at any one time. His behavior is consequently subject to a number of sets of expectations. Some of these may be in conflict or competition. Gross and his colleagues have noted that school superintendents suffer strain over allocating time between their roles as husband and father and their role as head of a school system. Whereas a majority of the superintendents studied indicated that their wives expected them to spend most of their evenings with their family

32. EVAN & LEVIN, 1966.   33. GROSS et al., 1958.

or friends, over half of them stated that parents and PTA groups expected them to devote most of their evenings to school and community business.

Most students do not have to go beyond their own experience to observe another illustration of competing role demands. In addition to meeting the expectations associated with the position of student, they may also encounter expectations associated with such positions as husband or wife, son or daughter, employee, and sorority or fraternity member. Not only do these conflicting expectations result in strain within the individual, but they undoubtedly interfere with the effective functioning of the educational system.

CONFLICT BETWEEN ROLES   Burchard's study of role conflict for military chaplains provides an excellent illustration of conflicting expectations encountered in two especially incompatible roles, those of a religious leader and a military officer. In particular this conflict poses a problem in the chaplain's relations with the enlisted men with whom he mainly deals:

> Relations with enlisted men are of great concern to chaplains, since enlisted men form the largest single audience toward which chaplains direct their behavior. All chaplains are aware that the fact that they are officers poses a barrier to primary relations with enlisted men. By and large chaplains are probably more conscious of rank than any other group of officers in the armed forces, mainly because of their ambivalent attitude toward it. The desire to become an integral part of the military hierarchy, to become accepted as one of the fellows, is very strong. On the other hand a priest, minister, or pastor is one who is set apart from the group, a leader of the flock, not just one of them. But a good leader must be accessible; he must not be too distant from his flock; he must be on good personal relations with those he is leading. A military officer, however, must not be familiar with his men. His ability as a leader is presumed to depend, in part, on his ability to keep at a distance from his men. The chaplain, being both a military officer and a clergyman, must somehow come to grips with the problem of carrying on an effective religious ministry for enlisted personnel and at the same time of retaining his status as an officer.[34]

Similar incompatibilities between the roles performed by elected public officials have been observed.[35] Partisan behavior expected of the party official may conflict in letter as well as spirit with the impartial behavior expected of a judge or administrator. Another study has described a role conflict between attributes and expectations associated with the role of successful insurance agent and the role of friend within a group of agents.[36] Many studies have highlighted the conflict between the expectations associated with the role of professional and that of employee in bureaucratic settings.[37] Teachers in school settings, lawyers

34. Reprinted with permission from American Sociological Association and W. W. BURCHARD. Role conflicts of military chaplains. *American Sociological Review,* 1954, **19,** p. 532.   *35.* MITCHELL, 1958.   *36.* WISPÉ, 1955.   *37.* SCOTT, 1966.

working for large corporations, social workers in bureaucratically organized agencies, and physicians and scientists in government and business experience strains arising from the conflict between the expectations for autonomy associated with their role as professionals and the expectation that, like any other employee, they will submit to bureaucratic controls.

On the level of the social system, Getzels and Guba have suggested that the severity of role conflict arising from enacting several roles will vary with two factors: (1) the relative incompatibility of the expectations involved and (2) the rigor with which these expectations are defined in a given situation.[38]

For example, an examination of three roles, those of wife, mother, and employee, would disclose that the roles of wife and mother would contain many more common expectations than either would have with the role of employee. We would expect that a woman who occupied the roles of wife and mother would experience less conflict between roles than if she were to occupy, say, the roles of wife and employee. In the latter case she would be under considerably greater strain because of the greater incompatibility of these roles. Moreover, their conflict would be accentuated if her employer and her husband held traditional expectations for the role of wife and mother. Finally, the research on role strain in industry suggests that role strain will vary with both the number of people and the relationships in a worker's role set.[39]

Reduction of Conflicting Role Expectations

Social systems also have features that serve to reduce strain resulting from conflicting role expectations. These features include certain structural aspects of the system, the establishment of priorities for different role obligations, special rules that protect actors in certain positions from sanctions, and the merging of conflicting roles.

HIERARCHY OF OBLIGATIONS   Role obligations in a social system are arranged in a hierarchy. The participants in a system recognize that certain obligations take precedence over others. Where obligations have equal priorities, strain arises. But if obligations associated with one role category take precedence, little strain arises. In the case of a death in the family, for instance, obligations toward one's kin to aid the bereaved, to help in funeral arrangements, etc., take precedence over occupational role obligations.

An examination of the excuses that people use in situations of role conflict reveals how frequently this type of conflict resolution appears. The commonly heard form is "I would like to but I can't because . . . ," followed by assertion of a higher priority. Sample excuses are "I would like to go to the dance with you but I have to study for an exam," or "I can't be present for the exam next week because I have to report for an Army physical." The excuse allows the individual to resolve a conflict because both persons in these instances accept a

38. GETZELS & GUBA, 1954.   *39.* SNOEK, 1966.

given order of priority. A study of the maneuvers used in the role-conflict situations provides some evidence on this point.[40] Actors frequently employed such excuses and perceived that they would not have to conform to expectations and that they had avoided disapproval.

In part, such a hierarchy of role obligations reflects the value structure of the group. Role obligations high in the hierarchy are functionally related to values deemed important by the group. In part the hierarchy also reflects the resistance of some roles to modification in instances of conflict, because to change these roles would disrupt the system to a greater extent. To illustrate, Nye suggested in 1961 that the role of a woman as a wife and mother, which is in conflict with her role as an employee, is being modified because of the relative inflexibility of the employee role.[41] To this we might add the pressure arising from the current desire of women to achieve equality with men. Roles also vary in the extent to which they may be modified by conflict; some are most resistant to change.[42]

STRUCTURAL FEATURES THAT REDUCE STRAIN   Several structural features of systems that reduce role strain are differences in the power of various role partners to exert sanctions, restrictions on allowing actors to take more than one role, and spatial and temporal separation of situations involving conflicting role expectations.

As observed earlier, the intensity of role strain experienced by an actor may be a function of conflict in expectations between an actor and his role partner or conflict in expectations between two or more role partners. In many such instances an individual will experience relatively little strain because of a disparity in power between those who hold the conflicting expectations. If one of the partners is able to apply only very weak sanctions, his expectations are likely to be disregarded. The pervasiveness of power differences in most systems prevents much strain that would otherwise arise from role conflict.

Preventing actors from occupying more than one role category is another feature of systems that reduces role conflict which might otherwise arise. When the expectations associated with two positions are in conflict, norms may prohibit a person from occupying both positions simultaneously. For example, nepotism rules in many organizations specify that no more than one person from a family may be employed within the organization or within a particular department of the organization. This prevents possible conflict between an actor's occupational and kinship obligations.

Temporal and spatial separation of situations involving conflicting role expectations is another system feature that reduces role conflict. While he is on the job during the working day, the male is exposed to the expectations associated with his occupational position. But for most occupations, these expectations do not operate at home during the evening hours, when they might con-

40. BLOOMBAUM, 1961.   41. NYE, 1961.   42. BATES, 1956.

flict with expectations associated with such positions as husband and father. If the temporal and spatial separation of such situations breaks down, however, the individual suddenly becomes aware of the conflict arising from occupancy of several positions. This appeared to be the case in a series of disasters studied by Killian. He states:

> When catastrophe strikes a community, many individuals find that the latent conflict between ordinarily nonconflicting group loyalties suddenly becomes apparent and that they are faced with the dilemma of making an immediate choice between various roles. . . . The choice required of the greatest number of individuals was the one between the family and other groups, principally the employment group or the community. Especially in Texas City, many men were at work away from their families when disaster struck and presented a threat to both "the plant" and "the home." In all the communities there were individuals such as policemen, firemen, and public utilities workers, whose loved ones were threatened by the same disaster that demanded their services as "trouble shooters." Even persons who had no such definite roles to play in time of catastrophe were confronted with the alternatives of seeing after only their own primary groups or of assisting in the rescue and relief of any of the large number of injured persons, regardless of identity. Indeed, only the unattached person in the community was likely to be free of such a conflict.[43]

In another disaster study, however, workers who were more spatially separated from their homes appeared to experience less strain over the potential conflict between family and work obligations than workers who were closer to their homes.[44]

PROTECTION FROM SANCTIONS   An actor who is especially subject to sanctions because his position exposes him to conflicting role expectations is likely to be protected by the system. He may be insulated from observation, a special tolerance may be established for his actions, he may be protected from reprisals by those whose expectations he violates, or he may join with other actors in the same position and develop patterns of concerted action.

Merton has pointed out that where role partners have conflicting expectations concerning an actor, the actor may be protected by insulating him from observation.[45] Lawyers, physicians, ministers, and priests are often accorded the privilege of withholding from police or other authorities information given to them by their clients, patients, or parishioners. A lawyer, for instance, cannot be forced to divulge information which would indicate that his client is guilty. If he were required, as is any other citizen, to tell the court all he knows of a

43. Reprinted with permission from the University of Chicago Press and L. M. KILLIAN. The significance of multiple-group membership in disaster. *American Journal of Sociology,* 1952, **57,** pp. 310-311.   *44.* WHITE, 1962.   *45.* MERTIN, 1957*b.*

crime, he would find himself in conflict with the expectation appropriate to a lawyer that he act in the interest of his client. Not all factors that prevent observability have emerged because of role strain: they may originate for quite unrelated reasons. For example, in American society, teenagers and adults have different expectations for many areas of adolescent behavior. Although strain over these conflicting expectations is sometimes avoided by deliberate concealment, observability is also restricted by the pattern of association along age lines in our society. This is, much adolescent behavior takes place out of sight and hearing of adults.

Arrangements that result in high visibility, however, may win for the actor a special tolerance which thereby reduces strain.[46] When the actors in a system are all aware that a certain actor is subject to incompatible role expectations, they may tolerate his failure to meet either one or the other set of expectations, or perhaps both. Here, high visibility of a conflict may result in the individual being able to fashion a solution which is most satisfactory to himself without incurring negative sanctions from either side. Or he may avoid conflict by doing nothing, on the grounds that it is up to the two sides to reconcile their differences.

In a system that is so organized that certain actors are especially vulnerable to conflicting expectations, patterns often emerge to protect them from reprisals. The union steward who behaves contrary to management's expectations, for instance, is normally protected from management reprisals by contract rules guaranteeing his job security. Another illustration is the pattern of social distance which usually develops to protect the superior in an organization from emotional dependence on his subordinates. For example, when a military officer or a civilian boss is forced to decide between the expectations of his superiors and those of his subordinates, the strain which might arise from withdrawal of affection and esteem by the subordinates is minimized if he has maintained social distance from them.

Finally, actors who are subject to conflicting expectations develop various patterns of concerted action to protect themselves.[47] Such protective devices range from customary reluctance to give aid to those who attack a fellow actor, as in the reluctance of a lawyer or physician to testify against a colleague in a malpractice suit, to the development of formal associations such as bar associations or teachers' federations which function to protect their members from conflicting role obligations. These group solutions often become normative and are sometimes formalized into written codes.

MERGING OF ROLES   Turner has hypothesized two tendencies which, operating over a period of time, result in a gradual modification of role structure in the direction of reducing conflicting expectations. With both of these tendencies, a

46. MERTON, 1957b.   47. MERTON, 1957b.

single role emerges from two conflicting roles, either through one absorbing the other or through a merger. Turner states his hypotheses as follows:

> Whenever the social structure is such that many individuals characteristically act from the perspective of two given roles simultaneously, there tends to emerge a single role which encompasses the action. The single role may result from a merger process, each role absorbing the other, or from the development and recognition of a third role which is specifically the pattern viewed as consistent when both roles might be applicable. The parent and spouse roles illustrate the former tendency. In popular usage the sharp distinctions are not ordinarily made between parent and spouse behavior that sociologists invoke in the name of logical, as distinct from folk, consistency. The politician role exemplifies the second tendency, providing a distinct perspective from which the individual may act who otherwise would be acting simultaneously as a party functionary and as a government official. What would constitute a role conflict from the latter point of view is susceptible of treatment as a consistent pattern from the point of view of the politician role.[48]

Some data in support of this mode of reducing strain are available.[49] The therapist-researcher in a hospital devoted entirely to clinical research frequently experienced strain arising from conflict between expectations attached to his position as therapist and his position as researcher. In some instances this conflict was resolved by role segregation. A patient would be treated in terms of one or the other role, but not both. He would be receiving therapy from one staff member and participating in a research program of some other staff member. A second way of reducing strain was redefinition of the role, creating a unique combination of obligations and rights drawn from each set of role expectations.

Summary: Conflicting Role Expectations

Role strain may arise from the conflicting or competing expectations that make up a role. Conflict or competition may arise with respect to the behavior of the actor toward one partner, or it may arise from differences in expectations held by different role partners toward the actor's behavior. Conflict arises when one expectation requires behavior that in some degree is incompatible with another; competition occurs when an actor cannot honor two or more expectations because of limitations of time.

Role strain is greatly limited by the presence of a hierarchy of role obliga-

---

48. Reprinted with permission from R. H. TURNER. Role-taking process versus conformity. In A. Rose (Ed.), *Human behavior and social processes: An interactionist approach.* Boston: Houghton Mifflin Company, 1962. P. 26.
49. PERRY & WYNNE, 1959.

tions in a social system. Any system inevitably has many conflicting expectations, but where clear priorities are established, the actor has little difficulty in deciding on the appropriate behavior. These hierarchies reflect the value structure of the group and also indicate that some roles are more likely to disrupt the system than others. Such structural features as differences in the power of various role partners to exert sanctions, restrictions on actors occupying more than one position, and spatial and temporal separation of situations also function to reduce strain.

Actors who are especially subject to sanctions because their position exposes them to conflicting role expectations are likely to be protected by the system. They may be insulated from observation, a special tolerance may be established for their actions, they may be protected from reprisals by those whose expectations they violate, or they may join with other occupants of the same position to develop patterns of concerted action. Finally, roles may be modified by a merger of two conflicting roles; each may absorb the other, or a third role may develop that eliminates the conflicting expectations.

Discontinuities Encountered in Status Passage

As previously observed, role strain arises in a particular system in part because the positions are so organized that it is possible for an actor to occupy simultaneously two or more positions which subject him to conflicting expectations. Strain may arise if a system is so organized that the positions an actor *successively* occupies involve conflicting expectations. Two such forms of position shift or *status passage* may be identified: long-term and short-term.

Benedict, in a now classic discussion, has illustrated the problematic aspects of the former type of shift in our society by demonstrating that role expectations associated with the position of child are often diametrically opposed in certain respects to those associated with the position of adult.[50] She notes that the child is expected to be sexless, nonresponsible, and submissive, whereas the adult rule requires just the opposite traits of behavior. A person growing to maturity not only must learn new role behavior, but at the same time must unlearn opposite kinds of behavior. Certainly a great deal of strain associated with the passage from childhood to adulthood stems from such discontinuities between the two roles. A similar analysis could be made of the transition from the adult role to that of the aged, from worker to foreman, or from enlisted man to commissioned officer.

One study notes certain discontinuties experienced by the professional as he moves from the position of professional in civilian life to that of professional in the military.[51] The degree of strain experienced by the actors in changing positions is dependent on more than the degree of disparity between the expectations involved. In addition, it is a function of the certainty, clarity, and abrupt-

50. BENEDICT, 1938.   51. BIDWELL, 1961.

ness of the transition, as well as the relative desirability of the positions involved.

Shutler has called attention to short-term shifts leading to conflict.[52] Examples are found in the transition for the ten-year-old from masculine aggressiveness on the ball field to dutiful obedience in the home, or the transition from aggressive career activities during the day to warm support of children in the evening for the business executive.

REDUCTION OF STRAIN ASSOCIATED WITH CHANGES IN ROLE CATEGORIES   Little strain need be expected in systems where status passage is dependent on the possession of certain attributes rather than on the actor's performance. Such attributes as chronological age, seniority, years in grade, etc., are gained automatically; hence there is high certainty that one will pass to the next position in the system. In systems where positions are achieved on the basis of performance, however, as where competitive examinations are used, one can expect an additional source of strain: the uncertainty of achieving the transition. When this type of strain becomes acute, informal patterns frequently emerge which have the effect of guaranteeing the position change. In many organizations, a given position may technically be filled by anyone, but the informal practice is to choose the person who occupies a particular other position. The president in such an organization, for instance, can confidently expect to be elected to the board of directors at the expiration of his term of office.

Anthropologists have long emphasized the importance of ceremonies in connection with the degree of clarity of the transition. In all societies important transitions are given ceremonial recognition, termed *rites of passage,* which clarify for everyone the new position of the individual. These rites mark initiation into adulthood, marriage, and death, as well as entrance into various special groups. They often involve renaming of the actor. As a result, neither the actor in his new role nor his partners are in doubt about how each should behave.

The exotic character of such ceremonies in other cultures should not blind us to the presence of rites of passage in Western society. A few such rites are confirmation in religious systems, graduations in educational systems, parties celebrating promotion in business, and pinning in the courtship process. Many features of adolescent behavior in Western society are a consequence of the adolescent's attempt to clarify his position in the absence of such forms of ceremonial recognition.[53]

With respect to the degree of abruptness in the transition, in most instances the change of position is not so abrupt as it might appear. Strauss suggests that one can denote stages of passage within each position, with the final stages serving to prepare the individual for the next position.[54] To illustrate, most graduate students in the later stages of their training may teach a course or two, and this experience eases the transition into the professorial status which many

52. SHUTLER, 1958.   *53.* BLOCH & NIEDERHOFFER, 1958.   *54.* STRAUSS, 1959.

graduate students subsequently occupy. The early stage of role enactment often involves a certain degree of tolerance with respect to the behavior of the actor. Other people realize that he needs time to get used to his new position. Such "honeymoons" are recognized not only for newlyweds but also for presidents of various organizations and for some government leaders. In American society, parents are prepared for postparental life by the temporary absence of their children during the late phase of the child-rearing period, as when the children leave for college, for military service, or for distant employment.[55]

Strauss also discusses "coaching" which, in many systems, eases status passage.[56] He uses the term to refer to the tendency for persons who have gone through a series of transitions to guide and advise those who follow. In this process, the coach interprets the neophyte's present experience and instructs him on what lies ahead, what he should be learning at each point, what he should guard against, etc. The process should be familiar to college students who are accustomed to "wising up" the entering freshman on various phases of college life that he will encounter in his roles as student, pledge, and fraternity man. At times, the coach may conspire with others to set the stage for experiences which he feels will help his protégé to develop, as when a business executive manages to give a particularly challenging assignment to one of his junior executives whom he is grooming for advancement. This and other processes which facilitate the adoption of new roles will be discussed further in Chapter 15.

Finally, if a system is so organized that movement is normally from a position of lower desirability to one of higher, the strain is apt to be less. In some societies age-sex positions are organized in this way: the successive positions of infant, child, youth, mature adult, and elder adult are increasingly more desirable role categories. In American society, while this is the case in the early part of the sequence, it is not true for the last part. Movement from the position of mature adult to that of the aged is considered undesirable. Goffman has observed a number of devices on the levels of both the individual and the system that emerge to reduce the deleterious effects of such movement on self-esteem.[57] For instance, it is a common practice in organizations to create a new position of equal or high status for a person who is about to be demoted. Or retirement may be formally recognized by conferring a new title. With much pomp and circumstance, retiring professors at university commencements are awarded the title Professor Emeritus. In industry, employees may receive a gold watch with an appropriate inscription for faithful service, and sometimes they are given a retirement party.

System Organization and Role Strain

One additional characteristic of social systems associated with role strain might be mentioned. Systems are so organized that the actors occupying one position

55. Deutscher, 1962.   56. Strauss, 1959.   57. Goffman, 1952.

are adequately rewarded for their conformity to the expectations of their partners. This element is inherent in the previously discussed reciprocal nature of role expectations: obligations of the actors occupying a particular position are the rights of their role partners. From the standpoint of a given position, a system may be so organized that the rights associated with the position may not be sufficiently rewarding to motivate actors to carry out their obligations. In such a situation the actors feel they are being taken advantage of, being unfairly treated, etc., and this may generate ambivalence toward meeting the expectations of the role partner. This condition is generally followed by attempts to restructure the relation in such a way as to equalize the rights and obligations associated with the two positions.

Fulfillment of role obligations is most often insufficiently rewarded where role expectations are unique, since in this type of expectation the reward for conformity stems only from the partner. In the case of widely shared expectations, the general approval of others of conforming to cultural and subcultural expectations provides some reward even when the partner does not adequately reciprocate. To illustrate, even if a wife is not meeting some of the cultural expectations traditionally associated with the position of wife, such as being an adequate homemaker, a husband is not likely to develop ambivalence about his obligation to support her, because others strongly sanction this obligation. However, strain may readily arise in connection with violation of complementary expectations unique to a particular married couple, such as the mutual expectation that a visit to one spouse's parents will be followed by a visit to the other's parents.

The possibility of similar strain occurring in connection with cultural and subcultural role expectations should not be minimized by the foregoing comments. This is particularly likely at a time when role expectations are going through a process of change. Studies of the changing roles of husband and wife conducted in 1955 have shown that college men and women overemphasize the rights associated with the marital position of their own sex and underemphasize its obligations.[58] This change is doubtless even more accelerated today, in view of the strong pressures toward equality for women.

It is not always the person who receives fewer rewards in a relation who experiences role strain. Because of the operation of equity norms, including the norm of reciprocity,[59] in many situations where obligations do not match rights, actors may experience a certain amount of guilt, which contributes to role strain.[60]

The above examples of role strain have been concerned with strain arising out of inequalities in role rights and obligations. Another source of strain occurs in systems where the content of the roles leads to continuous interference on the part of the actors in one position with the goal achievement of actors in one or more other positions.[61] An example is the system of relations which provides the structure for a competitive game. In such games the expectations

58. KIRKPATRICK, 1955.   59. GOULDNER, 1960.   60. EVAN, 1962.   61. FOSKETT, 1960.

are that one actor will attempt to frustrate the goal achievement of another, as in bridge or football. Such conflict is intentionally built into the system of a game. Often, however, such conflicts develop in nongame systems. Few systems are so perfectly integrated that they entirely avoid strain arising from this source.

Finally, Martin, in a penetrating analysis of structural strain in a psychiatric hospital, has noted a system feature resulting in strain.[62] When an actor relates to two different role partners, the stage is set for the development of coalitions of two versus one in the triads so formed. To illustrate, the patient is a role partner of both the nurse and the psychiatric resident physician. Under such circumstances, two of the three parties may combine to control or block the goal achievement of the third party, or one party may play the other two off against each other to his own advantage. This maneuver is illustrated in a family system by the child who asks his father's permission to attend a movie but prefaces it with the information, "It's OK with mother if it's all right with you."

This discussion of features of social systems which lead an individual to experience role strain should serve to emphasize that many problems in interpersonal relations are a function of the social system rather than being unique features of the "personalities" of the system participants. Similarly, reduction of such strain is more than a matter of individual dynamics or processes—a point to be elaborated shortly.

Imbalance in Role Rights and Obligations

Where the source of strain arises out of inequality in the rights and obligations of reciprocal roles, tendencies develop within the system toward the development of a more equitable balance. Such pressures toward modification of existing role obligations occur either when the actors are inadequately motivated to fulfill their obligations, or when because of frustration, they engage in behaviors that interfere with the need gratification of their role partners. For example, over the past fifty years in America, the conflict between employers and employees which arose out of inequalities in rights and obligations has gradually produced a new equilibrium between these two roles.

Personality and Role Strain

So far, we have been examining the characteristics of a social system that lead to role strain and interfere with the smooth, almost automatic quality of interaction between persons. Role strain may also stem from characteristics of individual actors which interfere with role enactment or performance, or from the fact that a role which an individual has to perform is not suited to his needs.

62. MARTIN, 1961.

Individual characteristics that lead to difficulty in meeting role expectations fall into three classes. First, the actor may lack certain abilities and attributes necessary for successful enactment of the roles involved. Second, he may have a self concept contrary to the role expectations he is supposed to enact. Finally, he may have certain attitudes and needs that interfere with the enactment of a particular role.

Individual Attributes, Role Enactment, and Role Strain

Individual attributes that facilitate or interfere with successful role enactment may be either personal qualities such as the individual's physical characteristics, abilities, skills, or personality traits, or socially conferred attributes such as an academic degree, a license, or other evidence of certification.

These may be related to role enactment in two ways. The particular attribute may directly facilitate or interfere with the expected behavior, or it may merely be an attribute traditionally associated with a role. The latter is important because expectations that others have concerning actors refer not only to behavior but to attributes of the individual as well. For instance, those who "look the part" often function more effectively in a given situation than those who do not. Consider, for example, the case of a young, boyish-looking physician. It could be argued that by virtue of his youthful vigor and his up-to-date training in medical school, he can function more effectively in his role as physician than an older colleague. Yet the fact that persons think of a physician as an older, more fatherly person may well diminish the confidence he inspires in his patients and reduce his effectiveness. Although this illustration is purely speculative, a study of the academic profession indicates that those who are judged as "looking like professors" are also judged as more successful in this role.[63]

More often a given attribute may interfere directly with the role behavior itself. On this point illustrations are legion. The boy with the puny build on the football field, the student of mediocre abilities in graduate school, and the shy, retiring person in the role of a salesman are all cases in point.

There is considerable evidence that particular positions attract individuals whose personalities allow them to perform the role more readily, presumably with less strain.[64] Students high in authoritarianism are found in greater proportions in military academies and Southern colleges.[65] Hard-core Nazis have been found to be more given to projection, to extreme antisocial sadism, and to contempt for tenderness.[66] These personality traits presumably enable them to perform the Nazi role more adequately. Among Soviet Russian refugees, professional persons and administrators were found to have personality characteristics compatible with their occupations.[67] Among a sample of managers in

63. ELLIS & KEEDY, 1960.   *64.* INKELES, 1963.   *65.* STERN, STEIN, & BLOOM, 1956.   *66.* DICKS, 1950.   *67.* INKELES, HANFMANN, & BEIER, 1958.

industry, those high on personality attributes congruent with this occupational role obtained the most need satisfaction from their jobs.[68]

A number of studies, while not measuring role strain directly, do include a measure of role performance. If poor performance may be regarded as indicating role strain, these investigations provide some evidence concerning the contribution of personality to role strain. Two closely related investigations in a hospital setting may first be cited.[69] Mental hospitals long had a custodial orientation toward patients that emphasized a highly controlled setting concerned mainly with detention and safekeeping. Patients were thought of in stereotyped terms, as being categorically different from normal persons, totally irrational and unpredictable. More recently, many hospitals have abandoned this orientation for a humanistic one that conceives of the hospital as a therapeutic community rather than a custodial institution. Patients are viewed in more psychological and less moralistic terms, and the attempt is made to give them more individual freedom and responsibility.

We might anticipate that a hospital aide with an authoritarian personality would find the custodial orientation more compatible than the humanistic one. This is supported by the finding that in three hospitals, the more the staff member exhibited aspects of the *authoritarian personality,* the more he subscribed to a custodial orientation. Evidence was also presented that in a hospital with a humanistic orientation, those nurse's aides who had custodial orientations were rated by their supervisors as less able to relate constructively to patients.

Another investigation was concerned with the relation between the extent to which a student has an authoritarian orientation and how well he can perform in a university which emphasizes abstract analysis, relativity of values and judgment rather than fixed standards, and a personal, humanistic orientation rather than an impersonal one—all values rather incompatible with authoritarianism.[70] It was found that by the end of the freshman year, 20 percent of the students high in authoritarianism had withdrawn, but none of those low in authoritarianism had done so. Complaints of the dropouts indicated that their actions were taken because of the conflict between their personalities and the requirements of the particular college they had entered. As noted in Chapter 13 and discussed in greater detail in Chapter 17, an individual attempts to behave and tries to get others to behave toward him in ways that are consistent with the picture he has of himself, his self concept. Backman and Secord have demonstrated that where persons can choose a particular role or particular kind of role portrayal, they choose those congenial to their self conceptions.[71] Confronted with the choice among three different types of marital roles,[72] the wife-and-mother role, the companion role, and the partner role, college women selected that type of marital role most congruent with their self conceptions.

68. SIEGEL, 1968.   *69.* GILBERT & LEVINSON, 1957*a*, 1957*b*.   *70.* STERN et al., 1956.   *71.* BACKMAN & SECORD, 1968*a*.   *72.* KIRKPATRICK, 1955.

Similarly, college students indicated a preference for and actually chose to major in subjects leading to an occupation congruent with their self conceptions.[73] However, when such choices are not possible and actors are forced to enact a role uncongenial to their self concept, strain is apt to arise.

Attitudes Needs, Role Enactment, and Role Strain

An actor's attitudes may facilitate or hinder role enactment. A person who tends to accept the dictates of authority figures would be able to play a subordinate role without strain, while another who tends to reject authority might well suffer considerable strain in such a role.

Finally, there are instances of role strain arising not so much because the person is unable to live up to its expectations, but because the role does not allow for the expression of his needs, does not require him to make use of his skills and abilities, or is not suited to his personality and temperament. In these instances strain does not arise from inadequacies in the individual, but from his dissatisfaction with the role. For example, a person with strong achievement needs may be frustrated by an occupational role that does not provide him with attractive opportunities for advancement. Or a person in an occupational role which allows him little contact with people may be dissatisfied because he is deprived of the social conversation which he greatly enjoys.

Individual Processes Leading to the Resolution of Role Strain

When an actor is exposed to role strain, in addition to the resources available to him through participation in the social system, he has at his command certain individual processes that reduce role strain. An actor may sometimes adjust to conflicting expectations by restructuring the situation. Burchard, in his study of role conflicts among military chaplains, suggests how this is accomplished. For example, the chaplains and ex-chaplains who felt that there was no conflict between war and the Christian "turn-the-other-cheek" philosophy justified their position by such lines of reasoning as "The individual and the nation are different" and "Necessity for self-defense obviates any antiviolence teachings of Jesus."[74] The first of these quotations is a differentiation of the expectation so that it applies to one situation and not the other, and the second quotation nullifies one expectation by invoking another which is higher in the hierarchy of role obligations. Burchard notes that these devices have some resemblance to the familiar adjustment mechanisms of compartmentalization and rationalization, respectively.

Similarly a study of conflict between the role of college man and hasher revealed a variety of defenses which male student waiters and kitchen help in sorority houses use to resolve conflict.[75] These included rationalizing the job as

73. BACKMAN & SECORD, 1968*a*.　　*74.* BURCHARD, 1954, p. 34.　　*75.* ZURCHER, 1966.

just temporary, both projection and verbal aggression against the girls in the house, and withdrawal into a variety of forms of horseplay. Horseplay among seven- and eight-year olds on a merry-go-round has been used by Goffman to illustrate the phenomenon of role distance.[76] Where conflict exists between an actor's self conception and the expectations associated with a position that he occupies, he may in a variety of ways indicate that he does not seriously embrace the role, thus avoiding the attribution of role characteristics that conflict with his self conception. Boys of seven or eight may be seen establishing role distance by clowning on a merry-go-round because to take the role of serious merry-go-round rider would imply attributes associated with the role of young child, which they are attempting to abandon.

Another study explored the way in which actors resolved a dilemma engendered by choosing not to fulfill a role obligation in a conflict situation.[77] Actors were asked to imagine a situation in which as student monitors they were to enforce an overly severe curfew rule. After they made a decision about whether they could report a violation on the part of a fellow student, they were presented with six reasons for their choice of action and asked to choose three. The reasons selected by students who chose not to enforce the rule reflected a reliance on a number of adjustment techniques which allowed them to cognitively restructure the situation. These included rationalization, displacement, and wish-fulfilling fantasy.

Another mode of individual resolution takes the form of reducing dependence on the group or role partner supporting one of the expectations. The individual accomplishes this by leaving the group, by redefining its value to him, or by making it irrelevant to the conflict situation. The first mode is illustrated by the older fraternity pledge who feels too much strain and gives up his intention to join the fraternity. The second is illustrated by the man caught in a conflict between the role of husband-father and part-time community leader who redefines his community activity as less important and accepts a less demanding task. The third mode is illustrated by the military chaplain who makes his officer rank irrelevant to his religious relations to enlisted men.

Individual Determinants of Choice Resolution

UNIVERSALISTIC VERSUS PARTICULARISTIC BIAS   Where affective or cognitive adjustments fail to resolve the conflict, the individual may respond in a number of other ways.[78] He may stall or delay making a decision concerning the conflicting expectation. He may reject responsibility for the decision, either by withdrawing from the position or by shifting responsibility to someone else, including those persons who hold the conflicting expectations, those in higher authority, or occasionally, a subordinate. Everyday examples of these ways of resolving role conflict abound. Everyone has been the victim of stalling tactics on the part of another person faced with conflicting role expectations. Passing

76. GOFFMAN, 1961.   77. COUSINS, 1951.   78. GULLAHORN & GULLAHORN, 1963.

the buck up or down an organizational hierarchy is commonplace, and reliance on the authority of experts is frequent. However, most instances of role conflict cannot be solved in this manner. Individuals must decide between conflicting demands. How these decisions are made is the next topic for discussion.

The theory of role enactment outlined in Chapter 13 provides the structure for understanding those studies which have focused on how individuals resolve role conflicts. Resolution is achieved through interpersonal negotiation or role bargaining. The bargain achieved is determined by the personalities of the role partners, the demands of the situation in which the parties find themselves, their relative power with respect to each other, and their relative power with respect to third parties or audiences who may exert influence on the final decision.

The role of personality factors was demonstrated in the findings of an early investigation showing that individuals consistently resolved role conflict between obligations to a friend and that toward society as a whole in either a *particularistic* manner, favoring the friend, or a *universalistic* manner, favoring society.[79] Whether a person resolves a conflict in favor of the particularistic obligations to his friend or in terms of universalistic obligations to abstract principles or society as a whole has also been demonstrated to be affected by features of the situation.[80] Thus, in a series of hypothetical situations, individuals were asked to choose whether they would act in a manner that favored another person or in a way to uphold some general social norm. These situations were contrived so as to vary the severity of sanctions that the other person might experience if the norm was violated, to vary the degree of social distance between the individual and the other person, and to vary the privacy of the individual's acts. One situation, for example, was a student usher observing another student letting off a smoke bomb in a chapel. Respondents were asked whether they would report him if they were the usher. Under one condition the student culprit was a friend of the usher; under another, he was not. Also, under one condition, the respondent faced having others know that he had reported the culprit; under another, no one would know. The results indicated that when sanctions were weak, when the culprit was a friend, and when reporting was private, the respondent chose a particularistic response: he did not report the culprit. The opposite of these three conditions more often yielded universalistic responses.

INDIVIDUAL ROLE HIERARCHIES   Where actors are faced with conflicting expectations arising from occupying several role categories, they are likely to resolve strain by choosing certain roles over others.[81] This suggests that the individual has an established set of role hierarchies or priorities. McCall and Simmons have similarly suggested a hierarchy of role identities.[82]

Two determinants of the relative position of a role in an individual hierarchy have been suggested by Getzels and Guba.[83] One is the need structure of the

79. STOUFFER & TOBY, 1951.   80. SUTCLIFFE & HABERMAN, 1956.   81. BURCHARD, 1954; GETZELS & GUBA, 1954.   82. MCCALL & SIMMONS, 1966.   83. GETZELS & GUBA, 1954.

individual, and the other is the legitimacy of the role expectations. To illustrate the effects of need structure, a woman with strong achievement needs who is both a mother and a career woman might be expected to honor her career obligations over those associated with her role as mother, since this course will allow greater satisfaction of her achievement needs.

By the term *legitimacy,* Getzels and Guba appear to mean a feature of social systems previously noted—namely, the hierarchization of role obligations within a social system. Actors in a given system agree that certain obligations will take precedence over others in a case of conflict. In their study of conflict between the roles of teacher and military officer, Getzels and Guba make this comment on legitimacy:

> No matter what major role an actor may select, he must face the realities of the situation in which he finds himself. He cannot long ignore the legitimate expectations of others upon him without retaliation from them. None of the Air University officer-instructors, whatever his personal predilection, may with impunity overlook the fact that he is part of a Military organization. Moreover, it is clear that he will eventually (perhaps soon) be reassigned to a military command rather than to another teaching position—at most the tour of duty at the University is three years. That the situation is so ordered placed added legitimacy upon the officer role over and above the instructor role.[84]

Ultimately, then, the particular form which a role hierarchy takes in an individual results from the interaction between pressures to adopt the system of priorities prevailing in the social system and pressures of individual needs.

A Theory of Role Conflict Resolution

Gross, Mason, and McEachern have developed a systematic theory of role-conflict resolution.[85] An individual who is faced with conflicting expectations A and B may choose one of three alternatives: He may conform either to expectation A or to expectation B; he may choose to compromise by meeting both expectations in part; or finally, he may attempt to avoid conforming to either expectation. Gross and his colleagues posit that the choice an actor makes in such a situation will be a function of three variables: (1) the perceived legitimacy of the expectations, (2) the perceived strength of the sanction applied for nonconformity to each of the expectations, and (3) the orientation of the actor relative to legitimacy and sanctions.

LEGITIMACY   An expectation is perceived as a *legitimate obligation* by an actor if he believes that his role partners "have a right" to hold such an expectation. It is illegitimate if they have no right. To illustrate, an instructor would con-

84. Reprinted by permission from the AMERICAN SOCIOLOGICAL ASSOCIATION and J. W. GETZELS & E. G. GUBA. Role, role conflict, and effectiveness. *American Sociological Review*, 1954, **19**, 174.   85. GROSS, MASON & McEACHERN, 1958.

sider it legitimate for his students to expect him to grade examinations in an impartial manner. He believes they have a moral right in our school system to be treated equally. But for a student to expect that he should be given preferential treatment would be illegitimate.

Gross and his associates assume that actors are predisposed to conform to expectations which they perceive as legitimate and to avoid conforming to expectations which they perceive as illegitimate. If legitimacy is for the moment considered alone, the following predictions can be made: If one of the conflicting expectations is legitimate and the other illegitimate, the actor will choose to honor the legitimate one. If both are legitimate, he will compromise. If both are illegitimate, he will avoid meeting either.

SANCTIONS   A *sanction* consists of actions toward an actor by a role partner or by the actor himself which gratify or frustrate his needs. Actions which are gratifying are *positive sanctions;* punishing ones are *negative sanctions.* A second assumption in this theory of role conflict resolution is that actors are predisposed to act on the expectations which they believe will result in the strongest negative sanctions if they fail to comply. Considering sanctions alone, it could be expected that if one of the expectations carried strong negative sanctions and the other weak sanctions, the actor would choose to honor the former. If both carried strong negative sanctions, then a compromise would be expected to occur. If sanctions for both expectations are weak, no prediction is possible, unless they differ in legitimacy.

In everyday life, since legitimate expectations generally carry stronger sanctions for nonobservance than do illegitimate ones, sanctions and legitimacy are likely to agree on the appropriate resolution of a conflict. In fact, this marked association between sanctions and legitimacy is an important way in which social systems aid in resolving role conflicts. On occasion, however, an actor may find himself in a situation where legitimacy is balanced by sanction. Take a student in an examination situation. A legitimate expectation held by his instructor is that he will not aid another student by giving him the answers to the questions. But because of friendship, another student may expect such help, although both recognize that this is an illegitimate expectation: No student has a legitimate right to ask another to help him cheat. In this instance, the sanctions imposed for nonobservance of the illegitimate expectation, such as loss of regard from the student who expects help, may be considerably stronger than the sanctions imposed by the instructor. To handle a case like this, where sanctions and legitimacy work at cross purposes, Gross and his associates introduce a third assumption.

ORIENTATION   The third assumption is that persons may be classified according to the strength of their *orientation* to legitimacy or to sanctions. Gross and his fellow investigators posit three types of orientation toward expectations:

1. A moral orientation, which favors legitimacy

2. An expedient orientation, which favors sanctions

3. A moral-expedient orientation, which takes both legitimacy and sanctions into account

On the basis of the theory, these investigators developed predictions for the outcome of all the various combinations of legitimacy, sanctions, and orientations in instances where school superintendents were confronted with conflicting expectations. These theoretical predictions were then checked against actual data obtained from school superintendents. They were presented with four structured potential role-conflict situations concerning (1) hiring and promotion of teachers, (2) salary increases for teachers, (3) the priority given to financial or educational needs in drawing up a school budget, and (4) the superintendent's allocation of his after-office hours. For each situation, the respondent was asked to choose one of three alternatives which best expressed the expectation of each of some eighteen relevant groups and individuals, including local politicians, teachers, taxpayers associations, and wife.

The superintendents' ideas of the legitimacy of the expectation held by various groups and the strength of the sanctions was determined by a carefully structured interview. From questionnaire responses, their orientation was derived. If they frequently chose such strong categories as *absolutely should* or *absolutely should not,* they were classed as having a moral orientation. If they used such categories as *preferably should* or *preferably should not,* they were classed as expedient. Finally, those whose responses showed neither of the above patterns, i.e., were relatively inconsistent in their choice of categories, were classed as moral-expedient.

The information obtained by these operations made it possible to predict the behavior of each of the superintendents on the basis of the theory. To illustrate, a superintendent who was classified as having a moral-expedient orientation, and who perceived that two groups held legitimate but conflicting expectations for his conduct backed by strong negative sanctions, would be expected to compromise. This prediction obtained from theory could then be compared with the interview information on how the superintendent did act. Appropriate predictions were made for all superintendents. For 264 of the 291 role conflict cases (91 percent) examined in this portion of the study, the theory led to the correct prediction. Such accuracy could be expected to occur purely by chance less than 1 time in 100.

Only in the case of competing expectations involving a time-allocation situation did the proportion of correct predictions drop below 0.91. In this situation, with 48 cases, the proportion was 0.79. It was the one case involving conflict arising from being in two roles. As a husband and father, a respondent was exposed to the expectation by his family that he spend his after-office hours with them. At the same time, many groups in the community were seen by him as holding the expectation that he should devote his evenings to school and community affairs. A slight tendency on the part of the respondents to give priority to one role obligation over the other, regardless of the effects of legitimacy, sanctions, and orientation, was noted. If the theory were to include the effects of role priorities, the accuracy of prediction could probably be improved for this kind of conflict.

Since the theory was initially tested, one study has used it to predict role-conflict resolution in four different groups.[86] Two groups of business executives, a group of company training directors, and a group of labor leaders were studied. The overall accuracy of prediction was 71 percent. This percentage, while significantly above chance, was somewhat lower than that achieved by Gross and his associates. The investigators suggested that the difference might be due to the less structured measurement procedures used.

The theory has also been applied in studies of police officers and police trainees.[87] Though the accuracy of prediction attained was roughly comparable to that of the study reported immediately above, it again fell considerably below the level attained by Gross and his associates. The investigators interpreted this difference as reflecting different orientations of the actors in the populations studied. To illustrate, whereas school superintendents were considerably influenced in their resolution of conflict by the perception of the sanctions involved, patrolmen were relatively little influenced by this variable. Such differences suggest that caution should be exercised in generalizing the relative influence of legitimacy and sanctions to groups which have not been studied. In fact, Ehrlich, Rinehart, and Howell suggest that an alternative model which ignores legitimacy and sanctions and which predicts that the expectations held by an actor's most important reference group will be conformed to may provide a simpler scheme for predicting role conflict resolution.[88] For the population they studied, at least, the predictive accuracy of this simpler model was comparable to that yielded by the theory of Gross, Mason, and McEachern.

Role Bargaining

An individual may also reduce role strain through negotiation, as explained in Goode's theory of role bargaining.[89] His concepts are similar to and consistent with those of exchange theory. Since the actor cannot possibly meet all of the demands of all his role partners, he "shops around" to see where he can obtain the best reward-cost outcomes. He negotiates a series of role bargains with his partners in which the "role price," or the extent to which he will meet the expectations of his partner, will be the resultant of three factors: (1) his desire to carry out the activity because of the intrinsic gratification that he receives from it and his commitment to it in terms of his values, (2) his perception of how much the partner will reward or punish him for his role performance, and (3) the evaluation that other persons who are important to him place on the bargain struck.

86. Shull & Miller, 1960.   *87.* Ehrlich, Rinehart, & Howell, 1962.   *88.* Ehrlich, Rinehart, & Howell, 1962.   *89.* Goode, 1960.

The last-mentioned factor places limits on a "free role" bargain. To a certain degree, there is a consensus among the actors on the going role price or fair arrangement. In instances where either party drives too hard a bargain, outside parties are apt to exert pressure to change the relation back to the going role price. Our focus on institutional or organizational roles, as well as our attempt to bring out in bold relief system effects on interaction, has obscured somewhat the individual efforts of the actor to reduce strain. Goode's conception should serve as a reminder that individuals have leeway to improvise and to enact roles in a manner congenial to their tastes and personalities.

Means of Resolving Other Forms of Role Strain

The emphasis in this section has been on individual processes leading to the reduction of strain arising from a single source: exposure to competing or conflicting expectations. This treatment reflects the current research emphasis. Unfortunately, systematic research on individual mechanisms for resolving strain from other sources, such as inability to play a given role and inequities in role obligations, is largely lacking. As a result, comments in this connection must be somewhat speculative and brief. Some mention has already been made of the interpersonal strategies individuals use to alter each other's behavior in a manner which leads to a tolerable balance of role rights and obligations.

When individuals are unable to fulfill the obligations associated with the position which they occupy, they may employ the familiar adjustment mechanisms described in the clinical literature, e.g., rationalization, escape through illness. Chapter 15 will treat these mechanisms in somewhat more detail. Similarly, Chapter 15 will also show that to a great extent, the process of role learning facilitates position change because roles are always learned in pairs. When a person learns a given role he must also learn, although perhaps to a lesser degree, the behavior involved in a counterposition. Since movement from one position to the position held by a role partner often occurs, as in the transition from child to parent, worker to foreman, and enlisted man to officer, an actor entering the new role has already become somewhat familiar with it.

Summary: Individual Processes

Even though the social system is structured to minimize role strain, the multitude of expectations to which the individual is exposed inevitably creates some strain. Various mechanisms are available to him for reducing strain. He may restructure the situation, he may establish his own hierarchy of values, or he may use rationalization, displacement, or wish-fulfilling fantasy. An extreme solution is to leave the system.

Individuals appear to be oriented toward role-conflict resolution at some point on a continuum ranging from preference for the particularistic expectation to preference for the universalistic expectation. The former is illustrated by obligations to friends; the latter by obligations to society.

In a study of superintendents in a school system, some evidence was presented indicating that individuals can be classified according to whether they are oriented toward legitimate expectations, toward expectations that have strong sanctions, or toward some compromise position. An expectation is perceived as legitimate if the actor perceives that his role partners have a right to hold such an expectation. The responses of superintendents to a variety of situations were predicted with a high degree of accuracy by the use of such variables. The application of the theory to various other groups by different investigators yielded an appreciably lower degree of accuracy.

Another process that emphasizes the active contribution of the individual to resolving conflicting expectations is role bargaining. An actor establishes a series of role bargains with his partners so as to maximize his reward-cost outcomes while still obtaining favorable evaluations from other persons.

Other forms of role strain, such as inequities in role obligations, may be resolved through interpersonal strategies or alleviated by use of defense mechanisms such as rationalization. Strain resulting from inability to play a role is mitigated by processes facilitating role learning, to be discussed in Chapter 15.

Culture and Role Strain

In recent years there has been an increasing awareness that strain occurs at the points in a system where the system of beliefs or ideology shared by the actors in a situation runs counter to role expectations. It has frequently been noted that the strong emphasis on equality in the ideology of American society places strain on role relations that involve inequality.

In the military service, for instance, a certain strain has been noted in the relations between various ranks, because military protocol involves a denial of equality. A subordinate in interaction with a superior in the military hierarchy is expected to show deference in a variety of ways. He must salute first, give way to a superior who wishes to pass him on a stairway, stand when the superior enters a room, and use such deferential terms as "sir" when addressing him. Persons who have not internalized the nonequalitarian ideology of the military subculture find such role behavior uncomfortable, and the discomfort often leads to subterfuges designed to avoid acts of deference. A newly enlisted soldier may frequently avoid saluting an officer by studiously looking the other way when an officer passes. A newly commissioned officer may feel somewhat sheepish about demanding deference and thus may not "notice" this intentional slight.

Such problems are not confined to the military. Because of the pervasiveness of the equalitarian element in the American ideology, almost any superior-subordinate relation will suffer some strain. Examples are the foreman-worker relation in industry, the doctor-nurse relation in medicine, the student-teacher relation in education, and the parent-child relation in the family. Currently the inequality between the traditional husband-wife and father-mother roles is under attack by the woman's liberation movement and other groups.

When the ideology itself contains conflicting elements, some conflict between ideology and role expectations is inevitable. Individuals in occupations such as medicine, social work, the ministry, and the teaching profession are exposed to a number of ideological elements emphasizing service to humanity. Yet at the same time they share with other members of society the ideals of materialistic success. Attempts on the part of the members of such professions to bolster their economic position are consistent with the latter ideological elements, but may be in conflict with the former.

Cultural Variables and the Resolution of Role Strain

In the preceding discussion of individual adjustments to role strain, the tendency of actors to restructure the situation by means of such mechanisms as rationalization and compartmentalization was noted. Where many incumbents of the same role position find themselves subject to similar role strains, mutual support is present for finding a common means of resolution, and this often results in the development of a shared system of beliefs concerning appropriate forms of resolution. Such a situation may also lead to a gradual modification of the conflicting role expectations as each person troubled by the conflict supports the other in moving toward a modification of the expectations involved.

Myrdal's analysis of the historical development of the dogma of racial inequality provides an illustration of how a belief develops and becomes widely diffused when many persons in a population face a conflict.[90] The belief that blacks were biologically different from and inferior to whites served to resolve the conflict between the American creed with its emphasis on human equality, on the one hand, and the early practice of slavery and the later forms of racial discrimination, on the other. In terms of the role-conflict schema of this book, many persons who were both Americans and slaveholders, or later, who were Americans and members of groups which engaged in racial discrimination, could reconcile these conflicting expectations by viewing the situation in terms of this belief: "All men are created equal, but this does not include Negroes because they are biologically different from whites."

Shared belief systems may also add legitimacy to a particular role. When actors are not in agreement on the legitimacy of the expectations associated with their role, they may collectively develop a series of beliefs that rationalize the legitimacy. Wardwell, in his analysis of a marginal social role, that of chiropractor, has shown how the ideology of an oppressed minority served to reduce strain.[91] Chiropractors explained their marginal position in the healing profession as resulting from selfishly motivated persecution by the medical profession. An analysis of the belief systems of many other occupational groups would undoubtedly show that certain widely held beliefs have as a major function the reduction of role strain.

90. Myrdal, 1944.   91. Wardwell, 1955.

Albert Cohen has offered a theory to explain the emergence of subcultures.[92] While his theory is not couched in the language of role analysis, it is relevant to the discussion here because it attempts to explain how new beliefs and norms emerge in response to strain. In particular, it throws light on the way individuals with similar problems of adjustment collectively facilitate the emergence of a solution involving a modification of previous role expectations. In essence, his theory suggests that when some or all members of a group face a common problem which cannot be solved by behaving in accordance with their currently held norms, members will, through a process of mutual facilitation, arrive at a new set of expectations which will allow a solution.

Cohen uses his theory to explain the emergence of certain norms among lower-class delinquent boys, but the same theory can be applied to other groups. For instance, a shared belief system which develops to resolve role strain may be found in norms which function to restrict competition in groups. Many situations, particularly in American society, call for competition. We compete in the schoolroom, on the job, and in the courtship process, as well as in a myriad of other situations. But unlimited competition often has disastrous side effects, both for the individual and for the group. It creates feelings of inadequacy and interpersonal hostility. Because of this, groups often attempt to restrict competition by developing role expectations that control competitive output or restrict the kinds of tactics which an individual may use.

To illustrate, assume that an instructor, toward the end of the semester, assigns a term paper and indicates that grades will be determined in large part by the length of the paper. This is a problem that most students can easily imagine. The solution prescribed by the traditional norms in this situation is that each should do his best in competition with the others. This, however, is not a very comfortable solution. The pressure to prepare for finals, finish other term papers, and maintain participation in a variety of extracurricular activities is great. Under these conditions, each student may begin to tentatively explore what the other is planning to do. Such questions as "How long is your paper going to be?" and "How much time are you spending on your paper?" will be raised. Along with these questions, each may express opinions about the injustice of the assignment.

Through these exchanges the students encourage each other to move toward a reorientation of which each approves and which ultimately allow them to agree not to submit more than a certain number of pages. This solution, which originally found little support, now becomes established because it fits in with norms that have emerged from the process of mutual facilitation. If the students consistently behave in accordance with these newly formed expectations concerning their own role, their role partner, the instructor, is likely ultimately to revise his own expectations of the student role to fit the new formulation. The process illustrated here is a never-ending source of cultural innovation and often is initiated because of the presence of role strain.

92. COHEN, 1955.

PART FOUR

Socialization

The topic of socialization has been reserved for the final part because virtually all the preceding portions of the book are relevant to it. Socialization is an interactional process whereby an individual's behavior is modified to conform to expectations held by members of the group to which he belongs. Thus, it includes not only the process by which the child gradually acquires the ways of the adults around him, but also the process by which an adult takes on behaviors appropriate to the expectations associated with a new position in a group, an organization, or society at large.

Since socialization processes involve social learning in which other persons are the principal instructive agents, much of the material in Part One on social influence and attitude change is relevant. In large part, moreover, socialization takes the form of learning role expectations associated with role categories; hence, Part Three on social roles is directly relevant.

Chapter 15, the first of three chapters on socialization, discusses processes of social learning involving the effects of reward and punishment, as well as learning from models and the learning of roles. Chapter 16 examines relations between the social structure and the individual. Some attempt is made to indicate conditions that account for the formation of moral values and the conscience, and for such social motives as aggression and achievement. Finally, Chapter 17 asks broad questions concerning the social determinants of individuals behavior, with particular emphasis on the formation of the self concept. An attempt is made to explain both stability and change in individual behavior in terms of interpersonal theory. Much stability in self and behavior stems from the constancy of the interpersonal environment. Both the individual and the social structure contribute to this constancy. Potential changes in self and behavior result from fortuitous changes in the environment or from the movement of the individual through different role categories in the social structure.

15

Processes of Social Learning

One of the most significant and remarkable processes occurring in human beings is the transformation of the helpless infant into the mature adult. No other species goes through as long and as intensive a process of development, and in no other species is the contrast between infant and adult so great. As he develops, the child learns one or more languages, a wealth of empirical facts about his physical and social environment, and a variety of special skills and bodies of knowledge. He also acquires attitudes and values, some of them pertaining to moral standards and others that are ways of relating to people, such as loving or hating and helping or hurting other persons.

Social psychologists are interested in the more social aspects of this developmental process. The concern in this chapter will not be with formal learning or the acquisition of knowledge and skills, but will focus on the relation of the individual to other persons. The processes by which such relations develop are known as *socialization*.

The principal agents in socialization are other persons, most notably the child's parents, teachers, siblings, playmates, and others who are significant to him. Much of what the child learns in the process of growing up is not systematically and consciously taught. Parents do not generally define themselves as teachers, yet they serve this role. Most of what they teach is not conveyed with deliberate intent; nevertheless, the child learns effectively.

Formerly, the term *socialization* had not been applied to adult learning experiences, but had been restricted to children. This traditional usage of the term was almost synonymous with the everyday phrase "bringing up the child." More recently the concept of socialization has been broadened to include aspects of adult behavior as well. Currently, socialization is thought of as an interactional process whereby a person's behavior is modified to conform with expectations held by members of the groups to which he belongs. This more inclusive definition recognizes that socialization does not stop at a certain age, but instead, continues throughout life. Socialization processes are especially active each time a person occupies a new position, as when he joins a fraternity or sorority, gets promoted in a business organization, becomes a parent, or is inducted into military service.

Two aspects of socialization distinguish it from other processes of change. First, only the attitudinal and behavioral changes occurring through *learning* are relevant. Other changes, such as those resulting from growth, are not a part of the socialization process. Second, only the changes in behavior and attitude having their origins in *interaction with other persons* are considered products of socialization. The term *interaction* is here defined broadly, to include communication through the mass media, as when a student nurse reads a biography of Florence Nightingale.

Several illustrations may clarify these distinctions. Learning motor skills, such as running or jumping, without tutelage by other persons is not a socialization process. Learning to speak in the vernacular of one's own locality, on the other hand, is clearly a product of socialization because such learning is heavily dependent on interaction with other local inhabitants. Other illustrations of socialization include learning the folkways and customs of one's society or regional group and learning the religious beliefs and moral values of one's society and family.

Socialization should not be thought of as molding a person to a standard social pattern, however. Individuals are subjected to different combinations of socialization pressures, and they react differently to them. Consequently socialization processes can produce distinctive differences among persons as well as similarities.

Socialization processes receive considerable attention in such fields as developmental psychology, sociology of the child, portions of clinical psychology, certain aspects of group psychology, and culture and personality. Over the years, however, a certain division of labor has developed, reducing the overlap between these areas. In particular, social psychologists have usually limited their interest in socialization to the following four sets of processes:

1. Social learning mechanisms such as imitation, identification, and role learning

2. The establishment of internal or moral controls and other cognitive processes such as the self concept

3. The development of various social behavior patterns such as dependency, aggression, and achievement

4. The effects of social systems and the larger social structure on the development of social behaviors

This chapter will focus upon social learning mechanisms. The other topics will be discussed in Chapters 16 and 17.

Interaction between persons is especially crucial to learning social behavior. At the very least, other persons illustrate or model the various behaviors to be learned, and often they directly instruct and shape the behavior of the individual. The actions of these other persons are in turn affected in part by the social systems in which they participate and by the cultural values and patterns of their society. Thus, interpersonal process, social system, and cultural system all contribute to socialization.

How social learning takes place is only partly understood. Different explanations of social learning, some of them incompatible with each other, have been suggested. Research on social learning is aimed at sharpening our knowledge of the conditions that maximize it. A more complete understanding of social learning would enable us to explain, at least in part, how children become delinquent or neurotic, and why they fail in school, as well as why some children achieve at a high level of performance or turn out to be honest and trustworthy citizens.

Elementary Social Learning

Social learning will first be explained in terms of theory developed through laboratory experimentation. Next, the complexities introduced by social factors in natural situations will be treated.

Contingencies of Reinforcement

Though there are competing theories of learning based upon laboratory experiments, one of the most viable and popular theories is the *radical behaviorism* of B. F. Skinner.[1] It is currently being applied to a wide variety of learning problems under the rubric *behavior modification.* Radical behaviorism starts with an easily identifiable response, such as a rat pressing a lever, or a pigeon pecking at a marked spot on the wall of his cage. Three important elements associated with making this response are:

1. The occasion on which a response occurs
2. The response itself
3. The action of the environment on the organism after a response has been made

The relation among these three elements is referred to as *contingencies of reinforcement. Reinforcement* is defined, somewhat tautologically, as any action of the environment that changes the response (changes the probability that it

1. SKINNER, 1969.

will occur again). Contingencies that strengthen the response are referred to as *positively reinforcing;* those that weaken it, *negatively reinforcing.*

The occasion on which the response occurs is often marked by some special feature of the situation, called a *discriminative stimulus.* For example, the rat in a box that presses a lever to obtain a food pellet may learn to make this response only when a light is on. The light is the discriminative stimulus. Or a child may learn to ask for a favor when he can see by his mother's behavior that she is in a good mood (here the discriminative stimulus would be a whole complex of facial experssions, body attitude and movement, voice characteristics, etc.).

Responses are strengthened or weakened according to schedules of reinforcement, or the number of reinforcements and the manner in which they are delivered over a given period of time. In the laboratory, schedules are usually worked out in detail by the experimenter and delivered by automatic equipment. Thus, a pellet of food may be delivered for every twenty-five bar presses. Or a pellet may be delivered at arbitrary time intervals, regardless of what the rat does. Reinforcement may also be delivered on a random schedule. Such experimentation enables the experimenter to discover schedules that produce the strongest response in the most efficient manner.

In radical behaviorism, contingencies of reinforcement are *considered a sufficient explanation for the learning of a particular action.* If it can be shown that an individual will learn and unlearn a particular action as a result of alterations in the reinforcement contingencies that are present, these contingencies constitute both a *sufficient* and a *complete* explanation. There is no need to invoke cognitive processes, in which, for example, the individual's view of what took place is examined. All such attempts are superfluous to radical behaviorism.

For most social psychologists, this view is too extreme. While it is probably true that some social behaviors are learned in this way, much social behavior appears to require a more complex form of learning theory. Some social psychologists have responded to this problem by extending and elaborating radical behaviorism, apparently without recognizing that their elaborated versions have transmuted radical behaviorism into a version that is totally foreign to its basic tenets (for example, see Bandura[2]).

This section will discuss the learning of social behavior as a consequence of reinforcement contingencies, and some of the problems that arise in such forms of explanation.

Some acts are undoubtedly learned as a result of the way in which contingencies of reinforcement are arranged, either by design or through other circumstances. Certainly such learning has been repeatedly demonstrated in the laboratory, with both animals and children. Knowledge of positive reinforcement can perhaps be applied fairly readily to acts which occur spontaneously with reasonable frequency and in which a socializing agent is on hand to pro-

2. BANDURA, 1969, 1971.

vide a positive reinforcement (in the form of approval or some more tangible reward), and also when the environment itself is arranged so as to provide reinforcements for such acts (e.g., sliding down a sand hill may be reinforcing for a child because of the sensations it produces).

But another kind of learning is more interesting and more difficult to understand—learning involving negative reinforcement. Such learning results in inhibiting, suppressing, or not performing a particular act. Such learning is commonplace in childhood; parents exert themselves to eliminate undesirable behaviors from their children's repertory. Generally some form of negative reinforcement or punishment is involved in suppression of acts, although positive reinforcement may also play a role. Fortunately, more recent years have seen the beginning of research aimed at identifying the various conditions and contingencies under which punishment is effective.

Effects of Punishment

People have considerable faith in the efficacy of punishment. Children are spanked and scolded; employees are docked, fined, or criticized; and criminals are imprisoned. Used in this way, punishment is intended to eliminate undesirable behavior, not to establish some particular behavior.

A position popular with psychologists for several decades has been that, although punishment may temporarily suppress a particular behavior, it does not permanently weaken the motivation to perform that action. Reviews of the research literature by Church, by Solomon, by Aronfreed, and by Parke, however, demonstrate clearly that this position is true only under certain very limited conditions, and that in fact, under some conditions, punishment can be remarkably potent.[3]

In recent years, reinforcement contingencies using punishment have been developed in the laboratory that, under certain conditions, achieve suppression of behavior over long periods of time. The consequences of punishment vary markedly with the conditions under which it is administered. For example, in experiments with rats, cats, and dogs, an electric shock ranging from low to high intensity has been shown to produce the following effects corresponding to intensity: very low intensity *strengthened* behavior, moderately low intensity temporarily suppressed behavior, moderately high intensity produced partial lasting suppression, and high intensity produced complete suppression.[4] Studies of children also demonstrate that high intensities of punishment suppress acts more effectively than low intensities, although the entire range and quality of intensity have not been systematically explored. These studies have also demonstrated that the timing of punishment is important. Punishment that anticipates an act or that immediately follows an act is more effective than delayed punishment.[5]

3. CHURCH, 1963; SOLOMON, 1964; ARONFREED, 1968; PARKE, 1970.   4. ARONFREED, 1968.   5. PARKE & WALTERS, 1967; PARKE, 1969.

COMBINATIONS OF POSITIVE AND NEGATIVE REINFORCEMENT   Although punishment often produces only temporary suppression, it can be dramatically effective under certain circumstances, as when punishment to suppress a response is combined with reward for some alternative behavior that is incompatible with the behavior to be eliminated. For example, if puppies are swatted with a newspaper for eating horsemeat and are at the same time provided with an opportunity to eat food pellets instead, they develop such a strong inhibition toward horsemeat that they will starve to death if presented only with horsemeat.[6] Thus, the mere negation of a child's behavior by a parent is likely to be much less effective than negation of the behavior combined with specifying some incompatible behavior that is rewarded.

One important feature of punishment is that behaviors which successfully avoid the punishment are rapidly learned. Any action that will avoid the punishment normally following undesirable behavior tends to be positively reinforced. In other words, *avoidance of punishment* is positively reinforcing. Moreover, it is often powerfully reinforcing. A dog given an intense shock following a warning signal will very soon learn to leap over a barrier into a shockfree compartment as soon as he hears the warning signal.[7] When the shock apparatus is turned off by the experimenter, the dog will continue to make this response to the warning signal hundreds of times. Many other experiments show similar persistence of behavior learned through active avoidance or suppression.

Such avoidance behaviors are extremely difficult to extinguish. Some experiments have shown that even when the avoidance behavior itself is shocked in the attempt to extinguish it, and the animal given an alternative nonpunished behavior to perform, he still persists in the avoidance behavior.[8]

One may speculate on how analogous avoidance learning might operate in naturally occurring situations. Any action that will avoid the punishment that would normally follow undesirable behavior tends to be reinforced through avoidance learning. To illustrate, a child may learn to deny that he acted in a certain way, or he may misrepresent his motives for misbehaving. These denials or misrepresentations are likely to become habitual if they repeatedly lead to escape from punishment. Thus, while parental punishment may or may not inhibit undesirable behavior, it often does result in the child's learning behaviors not intended by the parent. Punishment also has other consequences, referred to in the discussion of the development of cognitive or moral controls in Chapter 16.

PUNISHMENT AND ANXIETY   An interpretation of punishment mechanisms which goes beyond radical behaviorism makes use of *anxiety,* an internal state of apprehension or anticipation of punishment. Aronfreed suggests that, in children, punishment leads to the control of behavior by a two-part condition-

6. SOLOMON, 1964.   7. SOLOMON, KAMIN, & WYNNE, 1953; SOLOMON & WYNNE, 1953, 1954.   8. ARONFREED, 1968.

ing process involving reinforcement contingencies.[9] First, anxiety is conditioned to the performance of the punished act, or to elements associated with the act, such as the anticipation of performing it, or to the situation or circumstances in which it is ordinarily performed. As the act is repeated, the various noxious or painful consequences induced by the socializing agent arouse anxiety about their occurrence. Repeated punishments for the act eventually produce conditioned associations between the anxious state and the mere idea of performing the act. The other part of this conditioning process consists of the attachment of anxiety reduction to nonpunished acts or their associated elements that may be substituted for the punished one.

Thus, the two-part process consists of conditioning anxiety to anticipation of the act and learning to associate the reduction of this anxiety with acts that substitute for the suppressed one. When these twin requirements have been met, the punished act will later be suppressed even when the socializing agent is no longer present. Note that this process achieves suppression or control even in the absence of cognitive processes—judgments of the act as wrong or immoral and other complex interpretations that will be dealt with in Chapter 16. This interpretation in terms of anxiety, an inner state, goes beyond radical behaviorism, which does not admit inner states into its system of explanation.

Aronfreed points out that positive and aversive outcomes are often highly interdependent in natural situations.[10] The behavior being punished, for example, often has its own intrinsic reinforcing properties. Further, punishment often consists in the withdrawal of affection or deprivation of pleasurable activities. In the latter case, when the child substitutes the approved behavior, this can be reinforced by restoring the previously withdrawn affection or pleasurable activity. The interweaving of positive and aversive reinforcements in everyday social behavior makes it difficult to assess their relative contribution, and frequently may create special outcomes (as when both types of reinforcement work together to enhance the effect).

REINFORCEMENT CONTINGENCIES AND COGNITIVE PROCESS   Though it is often possible to debate whether a particular act has been learned simply through reinforcement contingencies or by virtue of some cognitive process, it seems best to grant that at least some acts, and inhibition of some acts, are learned through simple reinforcement contingencies. Aronfreed has noted that much behavior is inhibited under conditions where there is no visible external surveillance, nor is there any discernible cognitive or moral control.[11] Pet dogs, for example, can be trained to inhibit a variety of undesirable behaviors, such as incontinence in the house, chewing on the furniture or other valued objects, or biting visitors. Children, likewise, even before they possess the rudimentary use of language, learn to inhibit various behaviors. Even after the child or the adult has the full use of language, some behavior is still learned through reinforce-

9. ARONFREED, 1968.   *10.* ARONFREED, 1968.   *11.* ARONFREED, 1968.

ment contingencies. Children punished for their choices of attractive toys dur-ing experiments but given no explanation or further criterion for the occurrence of punishment later show suppression of the punished behavior even when they are apparently free of any surveillance or risk.[12]

As a prelude to the discussion in Chapter 16 of cognitive and moral controls of behavior, some experiments showing how cognitive processes can serve to inhibit behavior are introduced here. In a controlled laboratory situation, chil-dren were given a training session and a test session.[13] During the training session, they were subjected to a variety of conditions intended to inhibit them from touching or picking up certain toys. They were assigned to groups involv-ing two intensities of punishment, an early and a late punishment, and two levels of cognitive structure. Children in the low-cognitive-structure treatment were told that they should not touch or play with some toys, and that if they picked them up during the training session, a buzzer would sound. For this treatment, on trials where punishment was delivered, only the buzzer was sounded—no remarks were made.

In the high-cognitive-structure treatment children received a more elaborate rationale for not playing with certain toys, as follows:

> . . . Some of these toys you should not touch or play with, because I don't have any others like them. And if they were to get broken or worn out from boys playing with them, I wouldn't be able to use them any more. So for that reason I don't want you to touch or play with some of these toys. And if you pick one of the toys you're not supposed to touch or play with, I'll tell you and you'll hear a buzzer.[14]

When the buzzer was later sounded for touching a forbidden toy, the experi-menter said, "No, that one might get broken."

Following the punishment training session, the children were left alone with the toys that they had been punished for choosing, in order to test for devi-ations from the training. The results are shown graphically in Figure 15-1. Those who had been given a rationale for not playing with some of the toys showed less disobedience than those who were simply told that they should not play with some of the toys. Moreover, the relation between the rationale and the timing of punishment is of interest. Where there was a rationale, the amount of playing with the forbidden toys was not appreciably different in the early and late punishment conditions. But in the absence of a rationale, early punishment produced fewer transgressions. The rationale apparently helps to bridge the delay between the commission of the deed and the punishment, making delayed punishment more effective than it otherwise would be.

12. Aronfreed & Reber, 1965; Aronfreed, 1966.   *13.* Parke, 1970.   *14.* Reprinted with permission from R. D. Parke. The role of punishment in the socialization process. In R. A. Hoppe, G. A. Milton, & E. C. Simmel (Eds.), *Early experiences and the processes of socialization.* New York: Academic Press, Inc., 1970. P. 92.

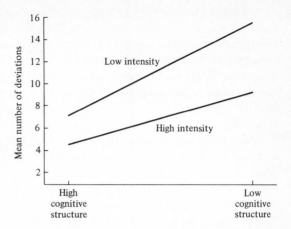

Figure 15-1 Effects on deviation produced by cognitive structure and intensity of punishment. *The minimum number of deviations (touching forbidden toys) is produced by high intensity of punishment and a strong cognitive structure. Reprinted by permission from R. D. Parke. The role of punishment in the socialization process. In R. A. Hoppe, G. A. Milton, & E. C. Simmel (Eds.),* Early experiences and the processes of socialization. *New York: Academic Press, Inc., 1970. P. 95.*

Another investigation obtained quite similar results.[15] And in still a third study, a rationale was used which focused on the child's intention rather than his deed, with the phrase, "No, you should not have *wanted* to pick up that thing." This treatment was also successful in producing inhibition.[16] It seems quite clear that cognitive processes may under certain conditions help to inhibit behavior.

Reinforcement in Natural Settings

A study of mothers' views of their own effectiveness was consistent with the previously reported experiments on cognitive processes.[17] The mothers who said that they combined physical punishment of aggressive behavior with extensive use of reasoning reported less aggressiveness in their children than did mothers who reported using physical punishment alone.

Aronfreed and Parke both point to a number of complications in using reinforcements in natural settings.[18] Frequently, where it might be desirable to substitute positive reinforcement for punishment, it is not possible to do so. Aronfreed noted that frequently the behaviors that the socializing agent wishes to control are positively reinforced through their intrinsic characteristics or by other means independent of the agent. For example, a small child may enjoy provoking a pet dog because he is entertained by the barks his behavior elicits from the dog. For this reason, the use of positive reinforcement by the agent is apt to be relatively ineffective in dealing with these behaviors because of the strength of the competing intrinsic reinforcement. For these behaviors the agent is apt to use aversive controls.

15. CHEYNE & WALTERS, 1969.   *16.* ARONFREED, 1965.   *17.* SEARS, MACCOBY, & LEVIN, 1957.   *18.* ARONFREED, 1968; PARKE, 1970.

A further problem in controlling children's behavior, identified by Aronfreed, is that many of the most socially desirable forms of conduct are very different from the undesirable but highly motivated acts they must replace (e.g., requiring an energetic, active child to cease his activity and to sit quietly).[19] Thus, a problem for the agent who desires to use positive controls is to get the child to replace his undesirable behavior by the very different desirable acts, so that the agent can reinforce them. The desired acts are unlikely to occur spontaneously, and so it is difficult to shape behavior in the desired direction.

Parke notes that there is little information concerning the use of punishment in natural situations.[20] What kinds of punishments are employed, and how often are they used relative to other techniques for control? It is not really known what kinds of punishments are most effective. Also, punishment sometimes has paradoxical effects (e.g., low-intensity punishment repeatedly following the performance of an act will often *increase* the probability that it will occur).[21] Another valid question is whether socializing agents especially favor using punishment for certain types of transgressions: Does aggressive behavior elicit punishment more frequently? How do the child's reactions to the punishment affect its future use? And especially important is the larger context in which punishment is administered. Is it applied in an overall context of acceptance of the child by the parent? Or is it done in a way which makes the child feel totally rejected? Much more research needs to be done in natural settings before questions of this kind can be answered.

Summary: Elementary Social Learning

Radical behaviorism conceives of learning as a function of contingencies of reinforcement involving: (1) the occasion on which a response occurs, (2) the response itself, and (3) the action of the environment on the organism after a response has been made. Reinforcement is any action of the environment that changes the probability of a response. The occasion on which the response occurs is often marked by some special feature of the situation, called a *discriminative stimulus*.

Although it was once thought that punishment was ineffective in inhibiting behavior, this view has been completely contradicted by more recent research. Under certain conditions, punishment has dramatic and long-lasting inhibiting effects. Especially effective is administering punishment in combination with reinforcement of an alternative or substitute acceptable response for the act that is to be inhibited. Some additional conditions determining the consequences of punishment are its intensity, the nature of the original learning, and the sequencing of reinforcement and punishment.

Behaviors which successfully avoid punishment are rapidly learned. This

19. Aronfreed, 1968.   *20.* Parke, 1970.   *21.* Aronfreed, 1968.

occurs because escape from punishment is a form of reinforcement (of the act instrumental to the escape). One view of punishment as a means of suppressing a response links punishment with anxiety by a two-part process of conditioning. This consists of conditioning anxiety to anticipation of the punished act, and learning to associate the reduction of this anxiety with acts that substitute for the suppressed one. Suppression of this kind is thought to be achieved even in the absence of such cognitive processes as moral judgments.

While some types of learning may well be adequately explained in terms of reinforcement contingencies, it also seems clear that cognitive processes are capable of facilitating learning to suppress certain acts. For example, in experiments children who are given reasons why they should not perform certain acts and who are also punished for doing them suppress these acts more thoroughly than children who are simply punished.

Learning from Models

People often model their behavior after that of another person. The modeled behavior may be directly observed, visually portrayed in the mass media, verbally described, or perhaps simply imagined. In a few instances, the observer immediately enacts the behavior that he has observed. But on most occasions, the modeled behavior is not enacted until later. This means that in some way he learns the pattern through observation alone. For this reason, conventional learning theory is not too helpful in providing a full explanation of modeling. Nearly always, learning research has used tasks in which the learner can be directly observed in the process of improving his performance, situations where he is enacting observable behavior. Only in recent years has explicit attention been given to learning through modeling. Appropriate ways of conceptualizing the observational learning that takes place through modeling are still a matter of controversy. Many different conceptualizations are available, each with some research which seems to support them. A good discussion of these different views may be found in Berger and Lambert.[22]

One relatively comprehensive view of modeling suggested by Bandura will be presented here.[23] The discussion will bring out the elements of the modeling process, but leave for future research the problem of specifying the exact nature of the learning mechanisms that underlie modeling. Bandura has suggested that modeling requires an individual to attend to the behavior of the other person, to remember what he has observed, to have the corresponding necessary skills, and to be motivated to enact the behavior. Thus, four related processes are involved in modeling. These are examined below.

22. BERGER & LAMBERT, 1968.   23. BANDURA, 1969, 1971.

Attending to the Behavior of the Model

For modeling to occur, the observer must *attend* to the behavior of a model. Factors which affect the availability of models who exhibit a given type of behavior will influence what is learned. A child growing up in a poor area in the inner city where there are frequent instances of street fighting is more apt to encounter models exhibiting aggressive behavior than a child in the affluent suburbs. Other factors affecting attention include the functional value of the behavior, the attractiveness of the model to the observer, and the intrinsic character of the mode of portrayal of the behavior. Commenting on the last factor, Bandura suggests that televised models are particularly likely to command attention. Anyone who has found himself watching a boring program just because the television set happened to be on can appreciate this. But although attention is a necessary condition for modeling to occur, it does not by itself produce modification of behavior. This displayed act may simply be noted and then forgotten. For modeling to occur, the act must be remembered or retained.

Remembering What Has Been Observed

Two representational systems are involved in observational learning, an imaginal one and a verbal one. Attending to a model may produce relatively enduring, retrievable images of the modeled sequence of behavior. This can be appreciated from experience. It is difficult to recall the name of a person without an image of how he looks, or to think of playing tennis without picturing a court and moving players. But even more powerful than such imagery is the ability to verbally code sequences of behavior. This undoubtedly accounts for the notable speed and relatively long-term retention of what is observed by humans. For example, the imagery retained from a single trip as a passenger in a car is less dependable than the verbal introduction, "Turn right at the second traffic light and left after crossing the railroad tracks."

 Studies have shown that observers who are instructed to code modeled activities into words, concise labels, or vivid imagery retain the behavior better than those who passively observe or who are mentally preoccupied while watching the performance of models.[24] Similarly, mental rehearsal will aid in retention of the modeled patterns of behavior. More complex social behavior is itself primarily verbal, and thus is presumably grasped in verbal terms when observed. The section below on role learning will discuss such behavior.

Capacity to Perform

To duplicate the behavior of a model an observer must have the component elements in his behavioral repertoire and be able to coordinate their enactment

24. BANDURA, GRUSEC, & MENLOVE, 1966; COATES & HARTUP, 1969; GERST, 1969.

in accordance with his symbolic representation of modeled behaviors. Since an individual cannot observe himself but has to rely either on the verbal reports of others or on vague proprioceptive cues, his behavior at first may totally miss the mark, or may be only a rough approximation which is subsequently refined.

Motivation to Learn and to Imitate

Traditional reinforcement-oriented theories have emphasized that learning takes place only in the presence of reinforcement. But Bandura suggests that imitative learning can occur without reinforcement.[25] People may observe, code, and retain patterns of behavior that can be reproduced at a later time even when they are not rewarded. Frequently, of course, reinforcement may occur at each of these stages. Thus, a person who anticipates a need for learning the behavior of a model may be motivated to attend more closely to the model's behavior, to code, and to rehearse the behavior more systematically and carefully. This process may involve a subtle form of reinforcement that is difficult to detect.[26]

Much of the early theorizing and research on modeling or observational learning focused on the motivation underlying the choice of a particular model. Psychoanalytic theory emphasized two types of motivation for identification with a model. According to psychoanalytic theory, a child during his first year of life experiences a nurturant relationship with an adult, usually the mother. At times she holds back this affection and support. The resulting threat of loss of love with its accompanying anxiety was thought to motivate the child to "introject" her behavior and attributes. These ideas were subsequently reformulated in learning-theory terms. One such formulation was that of Sears, who argued that as a result of a warm nurturant relation with the mother, the child acquires a dependency need.[27] When the mother, in her attempts to train the child, withdraws affection, the resulting frustration of the dependency need motivates the child to imitate or role-play the mother's behaviors. The relation among nurturance, withdrawal of love, the development of dependency, and identification or modeling was also employed to explain the development of cognitive or moral controls. The child was thought not only to incorporate the parents' behavior into his behavioral repertoire, but the parents' standards for conduct as well.

While the initial research by Sears, Maccoby, and Levin[28] supported this formulation, later work by them[29] as well as that of others casts doubt on the idea that frustration of dependency needs was a crucial determinant of identification and conscience formation. While a nurturant relationship between a model and a child has been shown to increase the child's imitation of the model, this result does not apply to all types of responses or in all situations. Thus, one study reported that aggressive responses were imitated regardless of

25. BANDURA, 1969, 1971.   26.. MICHAEL & MACCOBY, 1961.   27. SEARS, 1957.   28. SEARS, MAC-COBY, & LEVIN, 1957.   29. SEARS, RAU, & ALPERT, 1965.

the degree of a model's nurturance, and in another study, the adult's nurturance diminished the degree in which the child adopted the high standards of achievement.[30] This effect occurred because their adoption would result in negative self-evaluation and self-denial.

A second early theory of identification with a similar psychoanalytic origin emphasized anxiety reduction as the motivation underlying identification. Defensive or aggressive identification was thought to occur as a consequence of the resolution of the Oedipus complex in which the male child, fearful of castration by the father in retaliation for his incestuous desires for the mother, reduces his anxiety by identifying with the father. While there is some clinical[31] and anecdotal[32] evidence supporting the idea that aggressors may serve as models, it is not clear why copying the behavior of a threatening competitor would be anxiety-reducing. In fact, Bandura suggests that just the opposite effects might be expected.[33]

Whiting has proposed a modification of this theory which asserts that envy and vicarious gratification rather than anxiety reduction are the motives underlying identification.[34] The child models his behavior after powerful adults because they are able to obtain envied rewards. Finally, others have suggested a social power explanation: The child identifies with the controller of resources rather than the envied consumer. One experiment, in which children were exposed to models who either controlled the resources (attractive play materials, appetizing foods, or other desired objects), or were the recipients of them, supported the power theory.[35] The children modeled their behavior more after the controller than after the recipient of the resources.

Social learning theory suggests that whether a nurturant or an aggressive person or one with high power and status will be a model will depend on the consequences of such behavior for the model and the observer. Thus, in the case of models with high status and power, individuals are apt to learn that the behavior of such models is frequently rewarded, and that reproducing such behavior is likely to have favorable consequences. This is particularly true in situations in which the person lacks confidence in his choice of appropriate behaviors. Thus, modeling in a given situation is a function not only of the characteristics of the model but of the observer as well. Persons with low self-confidence are apt to be more subject to modeling influences.

Stotland has conducted a series of studies suggesting that *similarity* between model and learner is a major factor in choice of a model.[36] Identification based on similarity is quite different from other forms discussed so far. According to Stotland, there is a kind of identification based on a perceptual-cognitive process, as opposed to a learning process involving motivation. He believes that identification of this nature may be particularly useful in explaining some

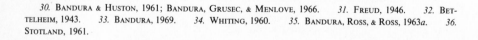

30. Bandura & Huston, 1961; Bandura, Grusec, & Menlove, 1966.   *31.* Freud, 1946.   *32.* Bettelheim, 1943.   *33.* Bandura, 1969.   *34.* Whiting, 1960.   *35.* Bandura, Ross, & Ross, 1963a.   *36.* Stotland, 1961.

forms of unintentional or incidental learning. Identification based on similarity occurs when a person conceives of himself and another individual as having some trait in common and further perceives that the other individual has some additional trait. He then believes himself to have the second trait and often behaves accordingly.

Particularly distinctive in this form of identification is that any two attributes that just happen to be found in another person may result in identification, if the observer possesses one of them. No meaningful relation between the attributes is required, nor does the observer need to have a motive for identifying. The model need not be an object of affection or fear, as in some of the previously discussed theories. One condition determining whether or not identification occurs is the congruence of the model's trait with one's self concept. Identification may not occur when the trait is particularly incongruent with the existing self concept.

In one of Stotland's experiments, involving seventy college women, each woman worked alone but was led to believe that she was a member of a three-person group.[37] She was asked to choose the musical tune she preferred in each of eight pairs of tunes. After making her choice, she heard over earphones two other women state their preferences. She then announced her own choices into a (dead) microphone. In fact, the two other women were paid participants whose voices were transcribed. The woman was led to believe that her preferences were more similar to those of one of the two paid participants than to those of the other. She was then given another task, consisting of indicating which nonsense syllable she preferred in each of ten pairs of syllables, but this time was allowed to hear the choices made by each of the paid participants before making her choice. The purpose was to determine whether she would favor the preferences of the paid participant who had made choices of musical tunes most similar to her own. It was found that the women did prefer the nonsense syllables chosen by the paid participant with whom they had agreed more often on musical preferences, especially when the musical preferences were strong.

An extensive series of other experiments conducted by Stotland and his colleagues deals with different traits and characteristics as a basis for similarity, as well as with various situational variables that might affect the process of identification.[38] While these studies generally provide support for a similarity theory of identification, in some other investigations observers preferred to emulate the behavior of dissimilar models.[39] These studies support Bandura's interpretation that it is not similarity per se and its implications for cognitive consistency that are important in learning, but whether the imitation of similar or dissimilar models has been associated with rewarding consequences in the past.

In earlier theories of modeling the emphasis on relations with parents has

37. STOTLAND, 1961.   *38.* STOTLAND, 1961.   *39.* BANDURA & KUPERS, 1964; HICKS, 1965; JAKUBCZAK & WALTERS, 1959; EPSTEIN, 1966.

ignored the importance of extrafamilial influences in identification. The social learning approach corrects this shortcoming. In American society, the child must depend considerably on models other than the parents, including age-mates and older children, as well as on a variety of models presented through the media of literature, radio, television, and the cinema. Modeling in these contexts can easily be encompassed by social learning theory. This approach also allows for a much more complex kind of response acquisition than simple mimicry of parental models. For example, innovative behavior can be explained in terms of the combination of diverse responses from a variety of models. Finally, since modeling is viewed as occurring in a wide variety of contexts with diverse actual, electronic, or verbally displayed models, Bandura suggests that the social learning approach can explain a higher-order form of modeling in which rules rather than specific behaviors are acquired.[40]

He proposes that this is accomplished by selecting a certain attribute of the model's behavior that might be displayed in a variety of contexts, and reinforcing the model for such displays, but not reinforcing irrelevant behaviors. Although this general scheme has been supported in a simplified experimental situation involving modification and use of sentence style, it remains to be demonstrated for more social forms of action.[41] Indeed, the process itself may well be considerably more complex in the case of social or moral acts, and the role of reinforcement may be less prominent than has been proposed. Only research with more complex forms of social acts can confirm or deny these suggestions.

Summary: Learning from Models

Modeling requires an individual to attend to the behavior of the other person, to remember what he has observed, to have the corresponding necessary skills, and to be motivated to enact the behavior. What behavior is modeled thus depends upon its availability and frequency, its functional and attention value, and the attractiveness of the model. When the model's behavior takes a form that can be visualized, the observer may use imagery to recall its enactment. Such behavior may also be verbally coded, and thus retained in a more abstract but also more precise form for a longer period of time. Much social behavior is itself primarily verbal and is probably directly put into linguistic form at the time of observation. When the behavior of the model consists of complex physical activities, the observer must have the necessary component elements in his behavioral repertoire, and be able to enact them in a manner coordinated with what he has observed. Often this takes much practice for a smooth performance.

Earlier theorizing and research on modeling focused on the motivation for choice of a model. Psychoanalytic theory, focusing on the infant, emphasized the development of a nurturant relation toward an adult, usually the mother,

40. Bandura, 1969, 1971.   *41.* Bandura & Harris, 1966.

and the withholding of this nurturance, producing anxiety which is reduced by incorporating her behavior and other attributes. Recast in learning-theory terms, nurturance was seen as leading to a dependency need. The frustration of this need by withdrawal of affection produced the motivation to imitate the mother, and also to incorporate her attitudes and moral values. Doubt has been cast upon research supporting this interpretation by more recent work failing to confirm the earlier findings. Another psychoanalytic theory of identification explains choice of an aggressive model. The male child was seen as fearful of castration by the father in retaliation for his incestuous desires for the mother, and as reducing this anxiety by identifying with his father. But it is not clear why such identification should be anxiety-reducing. Another variant identifies envy and vicarious gratification as motives for choosing a powerful figure as a model, a figure who is envied because of the gratification he receives. Another possible interpretation stresses the control of resources rather than their receipt in the choice of powerful figures as models. Finally, there is some evidence that models similar in some fashion to the observer are more often imitated. This may be because imitation of such models has been associated with rewarding consequences in the past.

Role Learning: Content and Process

Much of the discussion on elementary social learning applies primarily to very simple acts. Even learning through models, at least as studied in laboratory experiments, has been limited primarily to the imitation of simple acts. A great deal of what the child learns is more complex. These broader characteristics of socialization will be discussed below in terms of its content, its characteristic processes, and facilitating or interfering conditions.

The Content of Role Learning

Role learning includes learning to behave, feel, and see the world in a manner similar to that of other persons who are in the same role category. Because of the necessity for learning how to interact effectively with other persons while playing the role, the behavior, feelings, and orientations of role partners are also learned. The mother of a newborn infant not only learns how it feels to be a mother, but also gradually acquires insight into the feelings of her child. In addition, role learning is important in the development of those perceptual-cognitive responses collectively referred to as the *self*. The first two aspects of role learning will be discussed below; discussion of the self will be deferred until Chapter 17.

LEARNING NORMS AND VALUES ASSOCIATED WITH THE ROLE   Fellow actors share an overall ideology concerning their relations to role partners: They agree on appropriate attitudes and behavior toward these partners. The hospital intern, learning the role of physician, learns to view nurses, patients, and hospital orderlies as other doctors view these role partners. Similarly, the fledgling thief learns from his more professional associates appropriate ways of viewing victims and the police.[42] The role aspirant acquires other attitudes and values shared by more experienced actors that are only indirectly concerned with role partners. The medical student learns the attitudes of physicians toward life and death and toward the uncertainty of medical knowledge, as well as toward political issues affecting the practice of medicine.[43]

The role learner also acquires appropriate emotional responses to his own actions or those of others that conform to or deviate from the values and norms he has acquired. He learns to apply sanctions to himself and to others when behavior deviates from accepted norms. These reactions of pride, approval, disgust, rage, guilt, and shame effectively shape his behavior and experience in the desired directions.

Often role expectations require that the actor experience emotions or feelings quite different from those of persons who are in similar situations but do not occupy the same role category. Young boys who are being raised to play a traditional sex role, for example, gradually learn not to cry in circumstances where it may be quite appropriate for young girls to cry. Learning the role of physician provides a somewhat more complex example: The male medical student must learn to inhibit responses of sexual excitement to female nudity. The female learning the role of patient similarly learns to inhibit responses of embarrassment when examined by a physician. Another emotion inhibited by physicians is like or dislike of patients. Two studies describe how physicians learn to inhibit these feelings and note that such emotions might otherwise interfere with professional obligations to accord equal interest and care to all patients.[44]

ROLE SKILLS AND TECHNIQUES   Most roles require learning specific skills and techniques. Compare the awkward situations frequently experienced by the novice with the smoothly functioning behavior of the old hand. These skills and techniques fall into two classes: (1) those which are directly related to the accomplishment of the tasks inherent in the role and (2) those dealing with demands of role partners that might create problems, but which are only indirectly, if at all, concerned with the role tasks. For example, a teacher not only must learn the subject matter and how to present it clearly, but he must also learn how to maintain order in the classroom. The former is easier to acquire than the latter, and some teachers have difficulty with frequent classroom disruptions that interfere with the learning process.

The necessity for dealing with excessive demands of role partners is particularly strong in occupations where emergencies constantly arise.[45] The individual in such an occupation learns to play one emergency against another so as to

42. SUTHERLAND, 1937.   *43.* BECKER, GEER, HUGHES, & STRAUSS, 1961.   *44.* MARTIN, 1957; DANIELS, 1960.   *45.* HUGHES, 1958.

maintain some control over his activities. Hughes, commenting on such devices, notes in part:

> The worker thinks he knows from long experience that people exaggerate their troubles. He therefore builds up devices to protect himself, to stall people off. This is the function of the janitor's wife when a tenant phones an appeal or a demand for immediate attention to a leaky tap; it is also the function of the doctor's wife and even sometimes of the professor's wife. The physician plays one emergency off against the other; the reason he can't run right up to see Johnny who may have the measles is that he is, unfortunately, right at that moment treating a case of the black plague.[46]

LEARNING ROLE IDENTITIES   Finally, as noted in Chapter 13, people learn role identities which are somewhat idealized conceptions of their behavior and other attributes in a particular relationship. And as will be discussed in more detail in Chapter 17, these role identities become a part of the individual's self concept and are maintained or changed through interaction with other persons. To illustrate, a medical intern behaves and is seen by role partners behaving as a doctor; ultimately he comes to see himself as enacting that role.[47]

Role Learning Process

Role learning encompasses all the social learning principles discussed earlier in this chapter as well as all the principles examined in Chapters 3 to 5 on attitude change and in Chapter 10 on conformity. The only distinctive unity to role learning is that these principles combine to structure the behavior of group members in a manner appropriate for the positions they occupy. A deeper understanding of role learning may be obtained by setting up an oversimplified conception of the learning process and then noting ways in which the conception is inadequate.

One oversimplified conception of the socialization process is that the old hand teaches the novice. Such a teacher-student conception is deficient in a number of respects. First, it emphasizes the process of tuition and neglects other processes of social learning. For example, much role learning occurs through practice, in the absence of a teacher; thus, it varies according to the opportunities provided for practice. Also, learning occurs as a result of encountering and arriving at solutions to problems inherent in the role. The development of appropriate emotional detachment on the part of the medical student is learned in part by role practice and tuition, but more dramatic learning occurs following the discomfort aroused when the medical student becomes too attached to a patient. One medical student asserts that:

> As a student in medical school I tended to become more emotionally identified with the patient, or at least with those who were loved ones of the

---

46. Reprinted with permission from E. C. Hughes. *Men and their work.* New York: The Free Press of Glencoe, Inc., 1958. P. 55.   *47.* Huntington, 1957.

patient. I had to learn to restrain myself, to see that this is just another case of something that will go on and on and never end completely, as long as there is human life and death. . . .[48]

The teacher-student conception of role learning also suggests that the learner is relatively passive. In fact, however, he is active, choosing ways of playing a particular role from a permissible range of expectations. In Chapter 14 this point was emphasized by discussing at some length how an individual negotiates with his role partners to construct and play his own version of the role. A child, for example, often negotiates his role with his parents. Consider the common struggle between child and parent aiming to negotiate the child's bedtime. Another illustration is the initial negotiations for the use of the family automobile between the young person with a newly acquired driver's license and his parents.

The teacher-student conception also places too little emphasis on role partners, who contribute much to role learning. For example, the medical student's thoughts, feelings, actions, and self conceptions are modified not only through direct instruction, but also as a result of the ways in which patients, fellow medical students, nurses, and other partners behave toward him. The emphasis on the role of the teacher, similarly, blinds us to the important part played by peers in socialization. Fellow actors serve as sources of reward, as instructors, and as models.

Finally, the teacher-student paradigm suggests that socialization is a series of lessons with beginnings and ends. In fact, however, many role elements are learned long before the point in time designating the beginning of the lessons. For example, certain elements in the role of the doctor are learned in a crude form even by the child as a patient.

Role Learning: Facilitating and Interfering Factors

Further understanding of role learning can be gained by examining factors that facilitate or interfere with it. As in the case of bodily processes, we are seldom aware of role learning until something interferes with its normal functioning. For purposes of exposition, facilitating and interfering factors will be divided into three categories: those primarily related to characteristics of the social system through which the learner is moving, those related to features of the role learning situation, and finally, those stemming from relevant characteristics of the individual.

Role Learning and the Social System

In Chapter 14 features resulting in role strain and its resolution were discussed. The same features often interfere with or facilitate learning.

48. Reprinted with permission from the University of Chicago Press and M. J. Daniels. Affect and its control in the medical intern. *American Journal of Sociology,* 1960, **66,** 260.

CLARITY AND CONSENSUS   The *clarity* of role expectations affects the ease with which the role is learned. For instance, the female might be expected to have a more difficult time than the male in learning her sex role because in our society the female role is not very clear and is rapidly changing.[49] The degree of *consensus* on appropriate behavior for an actor also affects learning. Where there is consensus, rewards for appropriate behaviors are more likely to be consistently applied and thus to facilitate learning.

What has been said with reference to clarity and consensus of expectations applies with equal force to positions or role categories. If one's role partner is not clear about the position one holds, or if one's role partners do not agree on one's position, learning is more difficult. Illustrative cases are a mother who treats her grown daughter sometimes as an adult and at other times as a child, or a son who is treated by his father at an appropriate age level and by his mother as a baby.

Where cues to positions are clear, confusion is less likely. For instance, sex-role learning is undoubtedly facilitated by the obviousness of the cues to sexual identity. Because one's sex is seldom mistaken even with current unisex fashions, a person is rarely treated inappropriately for his role. Cues to age status are not as obvious. A twenty-one-year old person may be treated like an adolescent in one instance and like an adult in another, an inconsistency which interferes with his learning appropriate adult behavior.

COMPATIBILITY OF EXPECTATIONS   Compatibility between simultaneously assumed roles and between successive roles will further affect role learning. Role learning is a continuous process of learning new responses and discarding old ones. A child passing from one age category to the next, a military cadet moving from one class to the next, or a medical student becoming an intern face difficulties if there are discontinuities between expectations for each successive position. Chapter 14 dealt in some detail with these problems as well as with features of the social system, such as rites of passage, which facilitate or impair the ease of transition. A somewhat analogous problem has not been dealt with, however. Roles vary in the compatibility of expectations held by actors and role partners. This has prompted some students of occupational socialization to place major emphasis on the process by which the learner puts aside the lay conception of the occupation and learns to view his role as other actors do.[50] Simpson has described this process for student nurses.[51] The matriculating student views the nursing role largely in terms of a humanitarian, nurturant relation to patients. After a year and a half of training, however, she sees the role in terms of specific technical skills, as do professional nurses. Although direct evidence is lacking, it is plausible to assume that the greater the difference between the lay conception of the role held by the aspirants to the position and the role expectations of those persons already socialized, the more difficulty the aspirants will have in learning the new role.

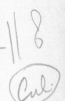

49. ROSE, 1951.   *50.* SIMPSON, 1960; HUGHES, 1958.   *51.* SIMPSON, 1960.

LEARNING BEFORE ENTERING THE ROLE   Many elements of a role are learned before the time one occupies the position. First, they can be learned by adopting the role in play or in fantasy. Before she enters nursing training, a woman has learned some of the elements in the nursing role first by playing nurse as a child and later by rehearsing this role in her daydreams. Second, learning similar roles may facilitate learning a new role. In learning and playing the role of Girl Scout, a woman has learned first-aid techniques that will later be part of her nursing repertory. Third, occupying positions that are related to a role provides an opportunity to gain some acquaintance with the roles of partners. For example, a nursing trainee has probably occupied the role of patient and as such has learned certain elements in the nursing role.

A study has provided evidence in support of the principle that through interaction with role partners one may learn elements in their role.[52] Under certain circumstances, these elements are likely to be assimilated into one's own role. Reasoning from the general principle set forth originally by Cottrell that persons incorporate elements of the role of the other into their own roles, it was hypothesized that children with siblings of the opposite sex would possess more traits appropriate to the opposite-sex role than children with same-sex siblings would.[53] The personality traits of 192 pairs of young siblings, rated by school-teachers, were classified as belonging to the masculine or feminine role. Some sibling pairs consisted of brother and sister, while others were both boys or both girls.

Two hypotheses tested with respect to sex-role traits were as follows: (1) Cross-sex siblings were expected to possess more traits appropriate to the opposite-sex role, and (2) this assimilation of traits belonging to the opposite-sex role was expected to be more noticeable for the younger sibling. The reasons for the second hypothesis are that the older sibling is more likely to be a model for identification and that, being older, he is better able to differentiate his own from his sibling's role, thus resisting the assimilation of cross-sex traits.

The data, tabulated separately for each sex, consisted of frequency counts of the number of masculine and feminine traits possessed by siblings in each of the four types of sibling pairs. Both hypotheses were supported. The older girl with a younger brother had more high-masculinity traits and fewer low-masculinity traits than her counterpart, the older girl with a younger sister. Even more striking was the number of masculine traits characterizing the younger girl with the older brother. Similar results were obtained for boys, although differences were not as pronounced. In conclusion, this study demonstrates that under certain conditions, frequent interaction with a role partner produces some assimilation of the characteristics of the partner's role.

Role learning is facilitated in social systems that are so organized that actors normally serve as role partners to actors whose roles they will later enact. When the role involves behavior contrary to that expected of the partner, however, this facilitating effect in part may be counterbalanced by the necessity of unlearning behavior incompatible with the new role.

A facilitating effect might also be expected when actors are given the opportunity to practice the role behaviors of the position they will occupy next. Such is the case for the medical student, who in his clinical year of training is allowed to perform various aspects of the physician role. If such practice is based on an inappropriate conception of the role, however, the neophyte may have to unlearn such responses when he does occupy the position.

PERVASIVENESS OF A ROLE   Roles differ in the number and variety of behaviors they encompass. Some roles include a relatively small portion of an individual's total behavior; others may be all-encompassing. Roles of latter type take more time and effort to learn. Contrast the occupational role of a priest, for example, with that of a carpenter. The priest role pervades almost all aspects of the priest's life and requires a long, arduous period of socialization, whereas the role of carpenter is segregated from other aspects of the carpenter's life and is learned in a much shorter period.

REWARDS AND COSTS OF ROLES   Finally, roles may be contrasted with respect to the rewards and costs of occupying a position. Persons may be highly motivated to learn one role but not another because of differences in their reward value. Age roles are a case in point. The child may be highly motivated to adopt the role of youth and the youth that of mature adult. In American society, however, persons are not motivated to adopt the role of the aged or even the middle-aged.

Role Learning and Situational Characteristics

Socialization by some groups effects dramatic changes in the behavior of the learner, but for other groups it results in only a few superficial changes. Contrast the changes that accompany socialization by a religious order, a military academy, or even a graduate school with those that occur as the individual becomes a member of a fraternal organization, a service club, or a similar group. In some instances, these differences reflect the nature of the role itself: Some roles are more encompassing than others. But also they reflect the fact that some groups operate under conditions that maximize the effectiveness of their attempts to socialize their members. In fact, where extensive changes must occur, the group normally commands optimum conditions for socialization. In cases of extremely effective socialization such as those in the Chinese war colleges or POW camps referred to in Chapter 3, in military academies, or in professional graduate schools, a number of features that facilitate the adoption of new behavior and identities are apparent.

why so little?

CONDITIONS PRODUCING DESOCIALIZATION   Of first importance are factors serving to divest the neophyte of his previous roles and group allegiances. In some instances the learner is physically isolated from persons who had previously gratified his needs and who had supported his previous status. Isolation is illustrated in socialization of the Coast Guard cadet.[54] For the first two months the new "swab" is not allowed to leave the base or in other ways to have contact with noncadets. All clues to previous social position are suppressed so that interaction in terms of earlier statuses is discouraged, as shown in the following quotation:

> Uniforms are issued on the first day, and discussion of wealth and family background are taboo. Although the pay of a cadet is very low, he is not permitted to receive money from home. The role of the cadet must supersede other roles the individual has been accustomed to play. There are few clues left which will reveal social status in the outside world.[55]

CONDITIONS INTENSIFYING SOCIALIZATION   Most socializing situations do not involve strict physical isolation, but the same effects may be accomplished by monopolizing the waking time of the learner through the sheer volume of demands made. The graduate student in a professional school, for example, generally finds little time for anything but study activities that restrict his interaction almost exclusively to other students and faculty. By ensuring that he will be treated according to his new position rather than his previous ones, such monopolization strengthens the new role behavior and weakens the old. Relatively exclusive interaction within the new group fosters the growth of each member's dependency on this group for satisfaction of needs, which in turn increases the cohesiveness of the group and its consequent influence on its members. The more control that socializing groups have over the total situation in which the new group member finds himself, the greater their effectiveness.

Rituals and ceremonies often facilitate initiation into a group role. The practice of hazing is an example. By emphasizing the low status of the prospective member, previous social positions are depreciated and the attractiveness of the new position is heightened. In effect, the fraternity pledge is told: "No matter who or what you were, you are nothing now but a lowly pledge; but if you successfully pass through this period you will have all the rewards of our lofty status."

The sharp contrast between the low status of the prospective member and that of the fully accepted member of the group should maximize the *status envy* experienced by the potential member, thus motivating him to identify with the accepted member. The worth of the new status may be increased by the discomforts experienced by the learner during hazing. On the basis of dissonance theory (see Chapter 3), persons would be expected to view the position as

having increased in value in order to balance the cognitions of having willingly exposed themselves to the discomforts of hazing.[56]

Hazing also appears to increase cohesion among prospective members as they form a protective ingroup against the onslaughts of the socializing agents. Such cohesion will facilitate learning, providing that the group of new candidates does not develop norms opposed to those which the socializing agents are trying to inculcate. A variety of factors work against this outcome, including a curious feature of the hazing process itself, namely, a temporary reversal of roles. For a day, fraternity pledges may revolt, capture one or more active members, and subject them to some of the indignations which they experience. Dornbusch has suggested that "Gizmo Day," a variant of this practice in the Coast Guard Academy, has the effect of reducing hostility between swab and upperclassmen by teaching the swab that hazing is not a personal matter but a feature of the social system. He describes what the swab learns:

> One is not being hazed because the upperclassman is a sadist, but because one is at the time in a junior status. Those who haze do not pretend to be superior to those who are being hazed. Since some of those who haze you will try to teach you how to stay out of trouble, it becomes impossible to attribute evil characteristics to those who injure you. The swab knows he will have his turn at hazing others. At most, individual idiosyncrasies will just affect the type of hazing done.
>
> This emphasis on the relativity of status is explicitly made on the traditional Gizmo Day on which the swabs and their hazers reverse roles. The swabs-for-a-day take their licking without flinching and do not seek revenge later, for they are aware that they are under the surveillance of the first-classmen. After the saturnalia, the swabs are increasingly conscious of their inability to blame particular persons for their trouble.[57]

More rigorous ordeals, such as rites of passage, have additional functions: emphasizing for the neophyte the features of the new role which contrast with the previous role, and proving that he is capable of performing the new behavior. This fits in with the empirical finding that the greater the changes required from one age role to the next, the more intense the ordeal.[58]

Related to hazing and sometimes a part of it is the ritualistic performance of behaviors that are inconsistent with one's previous roles. Such performances range from primitive ordeals among nonliterates to public confessions of error in modern societies. Confessions were a prominent feature of socialization in the Chinese war colleges described in Chapter 3. On the basis of dissonance theory, one would expect that the practice of condemning past behavior, such

56. ARONSON & MILLS, 1959.   57. Reprinted with permission from S. M. DORNBUSCH. The military academy as an assimilating institution. *Social Forces, 1955,* 33, 319.   58. WHITING, KLUCKHOHN, & ANTHONY, 1958.

as filial piety, would produce cognitive elements dissonant with the past behavior, and would reduce the likelihood of its recurrence.

Learning of the new role is affected by the conditions which facilitate or inhibit identification with the role model. Studies of socialization in medical school and in graduate schools have dealt with the effects of using faculty members or peers as models.[59] The role of an established group member as model has already been discussed extensively. Also important, however, are peers.

Two conditions affecting the choice of models were previously noted. First, the model often possesses something that the identifier wishes to have: love, privileges, etc. Second, similarity of the model to the identifier encourages identification. Whereas established group members might serve as models because of their control over resources, peers might be expected to serve as models because of their similarity to the learner. In fact, a near-peer, a person who is somewhat further advanced in the socialization process, should be especially effective as a model. The near-peer is similar to the learner but also has obtained some of the privileges of the established group member. A child might be expected to model his behavior after a somewhat older child. An undergraduate might similarly take a graduate student as a model, and a first-year medical student a second- or third-year student.

Role Learning and Individual Characteristics

The discussion of role strain in Chapter 14 indicated that possession of appropriate abilities and personality characteristics, as well as an appropriate self conception, facilitates role performance. These individual characteristics, as well as situational factors that affect the relative power of role partners, also influence the process by which a role is negotiated. The role of self in this context will be examined in more detail in Chapter 17.

Summary: Role Learning

A general form of social learning is role learning, which includes learning to behave, feel, and see the world in a manner similar to that of other actors occupying the same role. Underlying role learning are the processes of social learning discussed earlier. Role learning also includes acquiring an understanding of the attitudes of fellow actors and role partners, and learning certain skills and techniques associated with the role. Critical elements in the role learning process include not only direct tuition by experienced actors, but the forced learning brought about by problem situations and the behaviors of role partners.

Several conditions in the social system facilitate or interfere with role learn-

---

59. MERTON, READER, & KENDALL, 1957; GOTTLIEB, 1960; KENDALL, 1960.

ing. One factor is the clarity and consensus with which role categories are perceived by actors and partners. Consensus on expectations and the compatibility of expectations in successively occupied roles are important. To some degree role learning may be facilitated by learning that occurs before entering the role. This includes not only practicing the role in imaginative play or fantasy, but also learning elements of the role by occupying the role of a partner. The ease with which roles may be learned varies with the extent to which they pervade many or few situations in a person's life. Extremely satisfying roles may create strong motivation, facilitating learning.

Situational conditions also facilitate or interfere with role learning. Some groups operate under conditions that maximize socialization. A formal process by which the person is first desocialized is often effective. This includes his isolation from previous relations and positions, either by physical means or through monopolization of his time. The greater the control of the group over rewards and punishment and the fewer the sources of satisfaction alternative to the group, the greater the person's dependency on it and therefore the more effective the socialization process. Rituals and ceremonies such as hazing are often effective. They depreciate the current status of the prospective member and enhance the attractiveness of the position aspired to. Opportunities for identification facilitate role learning. Finally, the relative power of the socializing agent and the individual being socialized will affect the resultant role performance and the ease or difficulty with which it is learned.

16

Cognitive Controls and Social Motivation

The socialization processes discussed in Chapter 15 produce profound changes in the individual. Elementary social learning leads to the formation of certain habits and to the inhibition of others. These behaviors occur even when no socialization agent is around to supervise. But at this level these behaviors are essentially habitual and spontaneous; the individual does not think about them or have complicated feelings concerning them. Other more complex forms of social learning, such as modeling and role learning, were also discussed. Certainly thought and judgment play some part in these more complex forms.

This chapter deals more directly with cognitive processes. As they develop, children establish a set of behavior standards and acquire a wide variety of motive patterns and associated habits. Behavior standards have their origin in the expectations that other persons hold toward the child's behavior. The child gradually learns what these expectations are and eventually adopts some of them as his own. The expectations that he adopts and that have a moral element are commonly referred to as the *conscience*.

The conscience is a system of norms that a person applies to his own acts or contemplated acts to arrive at a judgment about whether they are right or wrong. Typically, acts that are wrong according to these norms produce feelings of shame and guilt, which in turn lead to various behaviors intended to reduce guilt feelings. Actions in harmony with these norms either go unnoticed or produce positive feelings toward the self. Often psychologists and sociologists refer to norms that function in this way as *internal controls* or *cognitive controls*. The entire process by which the norms of the parents are adopted by the child is known as *internalization*.

Social motives include such behavior patterns as aggression and achievement; these arise from certain socialization experiences to be described later. For example, a strong drive for achievement may be encouraged by parents who place stress on success, competition, and ways of getting ahead.

The Development of Cognitive Controls

This section identifies the factors that are important in the learning by a child of internal controls which enable him to behave according to his own standards.

Effects of Deprivation and Isolation

Attachment to and affection for one or more socializing agents in childhood seems crucial to normal development. Such attachments create incentives for the child to behave according to the expectations of these agents in order to retain their approval and affection, which is a source of great satisfaction to him. Unless acceptance by other persons is vitally important to the child, he will have little motivation to modify his behavior in directions desired by them. The first prerequisite for the development of this dependency is the presence of another person. Though children are usually born into families and cared for by them, in occasional instances a child has been relatively isolated during his early years because of parental neglect. In addition, children raised in some institutions may not experience the warm relation normally established between child and parent. These children have been studied and compared with those socialized in a typical family.

In two different cases of extreme isolation, mothers kept their infant daughters in solitude in a secluded room over a period of years, giving them only enough attention to keep them alive.[1] When discovered around the age of six, both children were extremely retarded, exhibiting behavior resembling that of infancy. Neither could talk. One of them could not even walk. They exhibited fear of strangers and appeared unable to form a relation to other persons. Ultimately, one was placed in an institution for retarded children and died at an early age before developing very far. The other girl achieved a normal level of development.

Studies of children in institutions where individual attention from adults was extremely limited also report some physical and social retardation in a less extreme form.[2] Moreover, older children who have spent their early years in an institutional environment exhibit more problem behavior, more demands for attention, and more aggression. They are retarded in speech development, mental development, and educational performance. Children of similar background

1. DAVIS, 1947.   *2.* SPITZ, 1945, 1946; SPITZ & WOLFE, 1946; DENNIS & NAJARIAN, 1957.

who spent their early years in a foster home instead of an institution do not show these forms of retardation.[3]

It has been found that the home background of children with behavior problems is often characterized by extreme parental neglect.[4] Finally, research on animals raised from infancy in an atypical environment shows that they have abnormalities of one kind or another. Such environments either severely restrict sensory stimulation or establish some specific deficiency of environment that the investigator considers important.[5] Examples of the latter include absence of the mother or lack of opportunity to interact with peers.[6] Both conditions have striking consequences for the adult behavior of the animals who have been raised in this fashion.

From such studies, it is clear that environments involving restriction of one kind or another often affect the organism adversely. It is difficult, however, to identify the exact conditions responsible for the negative effects. Several factors have been suggested as primary causes:

1. The absence of a mother or mother substitute, resulting in lack of opportunity to form a close attachment to an adult, distorts or prevents later relations to others.

2. The restricted sensory stimulation interferes with the formation of perceptual categories, symbols, and concepts.

3. The restricted environment prevents the organism from learning how to profit from experience.

4. Infancy is a critical period during which certain stimulation and experience must be available for normal maturation. For example, a chimpanzee raised in complete darkness shows deterioration of the cells of the retina.[7] Apparently, without the stimulation of light the visual mechanism does not develop properly.

These factors are not mutually exclusive; in fact, they might all be operative.

In spite of the availability of these different explanations of the effects of isolation and deprivation, the favored view has been that it is the strong attachment of the child to the mother that is crucial in producing adequate socialization. This strong attachment has been thought to make the child dependent upon the mother's approval and affection. Effects occurring as a result of isolation or deprivation have been thought to issue primarily from lack of this dependency on a mother.

Evidence against this favored view has been mounting steadily. First, the pervasiveness of the effects of deprivation and isolation have been questioned: Their effects depend on the age of the child when deprivation occurs, the length and form of the deprivation, and the age of the child when the effects are

3. GOLDFARB, 1943*a*, 1943*b*.   *4.* BOWLBY, 1952, 1960; REDL & WINEMAN, 1951; GLUECK & GLUECK, 1950.   *5.* SCOTT & MARSDON, 1950; HEBB, 1958; FULLER, 1960.   *6.* HARLOW & HARLOW, 1962.   *7.* RIESEN, 1961.

assessed. These conditions can be illustrated from the conclusions of a survey of the effects of early deprivation in mammals and humans by Bronfenbrenner.[8] Many of the effects originally attributed to maternal deprivation are more appropriately attributable to the stimulus deprivation which generally accompanied the maternal deprivation. Further, long-term effects may differ from those immediately observed. Maternal deprivation in early infancy, before age six months or so, results in few observable effects at the time but apparently interferes with the development of a dependent relation and with the ability to form close relations with others in later life. Separation from the mother in middle infancy may result in heightened dependency expressed at the time in terms of anxiety, fear, and withdrawal, but later expressed in terms of a heightened concern over attachment with others.

The short-term and long-term effects from general stimulus deprivation as well as maternal separation alone or in combination appear to differ and are related to the time of deprivation. Children institutionalized during early infancy, where they presumably suffer reduced stimulation associated with institutional life, appear to suffer fewer immediate effects than those institutionalized after six months when, according to Bronfenbrenner, strong dependency on the mother has been established, resulting in considerable trauma due to separation from the mother.[9] However, when such children are exposed to a more normal environment, those deprived in middle or late infancy recover rapidly whereas the effects associated with early separation are apt to persist for some time. How long appears to depend on the behavior in question. Though early writers viewed the effects of early deprivation as relatively longstanding or permanent, later studies suggest this not to be the case, particularly for intellectual or language abilities or serious psychopathology. Whether milder effects which interfere with optimal functioning persist is still an open question.

Finally, there is some question whether dependency is a clearly indentifiable, unified behavior pattern. Not only are correlates of dependent behavior at one point in a child's life different from those at another stage, as noted above, but also the various behaviors included under the rubric *dependency* are not always found together in the same child. For example, attention seeking and expressions of the desire to be physically near the mother, while both thought to be indicative of a dependent relation with her, have been shown to occur quite independently, and to have only a low correlation with each other.[10]

Development of Affectional Systems

Perhaps the most telling evidence against the view that attachment to the mother is the key to socialization is found in the work of the Harlows on attachment or affectional systems in monkeys. Their work suggests that a re-

8. Bronfenbrenner, 1968.   *9.* Bronfenbrenner, 1968.   *10.* Maccoby & Masters, 1970.

lated series of affectional systems that emerge in an orderly fashion must be understood in order to grasp adequately the nature of the socialization process. [11]

The Harlows have distinguished five relatively separable affectional systems in primates: the mother-infant affectional system, the reciprocal infant-mother system, the agemate or peer affectional system, the heterosexual affectional system, and the paternal affectional system. [12] The behaviors acquired in the course of the development of each system are a part of normal social growth, and development in one system facilitates development in other systems. Thus, the security provided in the infant-mother system provides a basis for exploration of the surrounding animate and inanimate environment, which facilitates the growth of the peer affectional system. In turn, this affectional system lays the ground work for the development of the heterosexual system. While it is not clear that these systems must develop in a certain order, there is evidence that all five of them are required for normal behavior.

In some studies by the Harlows, monkeys that were deprived of normal opportunities to develop a given affectional system were found to be retarded with reference to behaviors associated with other systems. Monkeys were deprived of normal interaction with a mother in one of three ways: (1) raised in total isolation, (2) brought up with dummy surrogate mothers covered with terry cloth but complete with bottle and nipple, or (3) raised with agemates only. When monkeys raised in this way were later placed with normally reared agemates, they were found to be retarded in relating to these peers. While these monkeys eventually made adequate social adjustments, it seems clear that normal mothering is important for the normal development of peer relations.

In another study by these investigators, monkeys were provided with normal mothering but deprived of opportunities to interact with peers for various periods of time starting at birth, at two weeks, at four months, and at eight months. When subsequently allowed to interact with peers, these primate youngsters developed normal play and social behaviors, but the rapidity of their development was inversely related to the age at which peer associations began. Thus the development of both the mother-infant and the peer systems is essential. The Harlows conclude:

> In designing our original studies we tended to contrast the relative importance of mother-infant relationships as opposed to infant-infant affectional relationships in the socialization process. We are now convinced that this is the wrong way to look at these social forces. Both normal mothering and normal infant-infant affectional development are extremely important variables in the socialization of rhesus monkeys and presumably of the higher primates. These variables are interactive, and either variable may not of necessity socially destroy an infant monkey if it is subsequently allowed to lead a normal or more or less normal life, but there can be no doubt that the

11. Harlow & Harlow, 1965, 1966.   *12.* Harlow & Harlow, 1965, 1966.

easier and safer way to become a normal monkey is to learn to love and live with both mothers and age-mates.[13]

Formation of Moral Controls

A young child's behavior is largely subject to external controls—the rewards and punishments administered by those about him. Gradually, however, his behavior becomes subject to internal controls in that he appears to be able to conform to the expectations of other persons even under circumstances where they are not present or are unable to reward or punish him. This change has been most systematically described as moral development, in terms of cognitive developmental theory. Initially Piaget and later Kohlberg saw the child as moving through a series of stages as a result of the unfolding of the child's cognitive capacities, partly due to maturation or biological growth, and partly due to the kinds of experiences with the environment that normally accompany growing up.[14]

Piaget conceptualized this process as a series of transitions from a state of moral absolutism to a morality based upon reciprocal agreement. In the first stage, behaviors are totally right or wrong and rules are sacred and unalterable. Acts are judged right or wrong on the basis of the magnitude of their consequences, the extent of conformity to the rules, and whether or not they are punished. The child believes in *immanent justice:* Rule violations are followed by accidents or misfortunes willed by God or by some inanimate object.

In the more advanced state of reciprocity, rules are established through social agreement and may be modified for good reason. Diverse views of right and wrong are acknowledged, and a major consideration is whether the deed was performed intentionally or not. Punishment is not ordained by some impersonal entity. Moreover, it is fitted to the magnitude of the misdeed and may involve restitution or retaliation.

The transition from the first to the second stage is facilitated by the growth of cognitive capacities that move the child away from: (1) a state of egocentrism in which he assumes that others view events in the same way that he does and (2) a state with respect to realism in which the child confuses objective and subjective reality (e.g., he thinks of his dreams as actually occurring). Basic to such a shift is the development of the conception of one's self as a distinct person with one's own views and feelings that may be different from those of others. Piaget emphasizes the contribution of interaction with peers to this development.

Hoffman notes that in Piaget's discussion, two processes appear to emerge and account for these effects.[15] The first pertains to the child's increasing share in decision making and how it affects his view of rules and authority. As the

13. Reprinted by permission from H. F. HARLOW and M. K. HARLOW. The affectional systems. In A. M. Schrier, H. F. Harlow, & T. Stollnitz (Eds.), *Behavior of nonhuman primates.* Vol. 2. New York: Academic Press, Inc., 1965. P. 272.   14. PIAGET, 1932; KOHLBERG, 1969.   15. HOFFMAN, 1967.

child grows older, he attains more equality with parents and older children, thus reducing their authority. His respect for himself and his peers is enhanced. He is better able to interact with other persons to arrive at cooperative agreement about rules. He sees rules as a product of mutual consent instead of as coming from absolute authority.

The second, more complex process involves interacting with other persons in terms of roles, including taking the role of the other person. This role taking enables the child to see similarities and differences between himself and others, and to understand the perspectives and the feelings of others. His moral judgments can now be based not just on the overt behavior of another person, but on his intentions and other facets of his inner state.

Kohlberg has advanced a more elaborate conception of moral development, consisting of six stages.[16] The first stage is an *obedience or punishment orientation:* Conduct is controlled by commands or pressures from other persons that are complied with to avoid punishment and to obtain rewards. The second stage is a *naïvely egoistic orientation:* The right action is that which satisfies one's needs. A *good-boy orientation* constitutes the third stage: Pleasing other persons and obtaining their approval is what is important. Stage four stresses *authority and maintaining social order.* Stage five is a *contractual legalistic orientation:* There is recognition of an arbitrary element in moral rules, and a contract which involves the rights of other persons. Finally, stage six stresses *individual conscience:* Moral rules are self-defined and accepted, although usually shared by others.

At any one age, an individual may make a moral judgment falling into any one of the six stages. But about 50 percent of his moral judgments fall into one stage, with frequency dropping off rapidly in the adjacent and especially the more remote stages.[17]

These stages are thought of as distinct and successive, as different patterns of moral thought. Consistent with this is the point that while a child at one stage can comprehend moral conceptions at a lower stage, he cannot follow most of those at a higher stage.[18] Kohlberg also reasons that if these stages depend upon certain basic cognitive or thought structures, there should be a relation between moral development and cognitive development of a nonmoral kind. That is, certain basic cognitive patterns should underlie both kinds of development. And so he views the correlations between moral development on the one hand and age and IQ on the other as support for the idea of stages of moral development. It is important to remember, however, that IQ tests correlate with virtually all other measures that require verbal skills for a good score; hence, this evidence for stages must be regarded as quite weak.

Cross-cultural studies of moral development in United States, Taiwan, and Mexican urban middle-class boys show similar development from country to country at ages ten, thirteen, and sixteen. Moreover, studies from two isolated

16. KOHLBERG, 1969.   *17.* KOHLBERG, 1969.   *18.* REST, TURIEL, & KOHLBERG, 1969.

Self-int. the key; w/ so emotion in learned ways of advancing self-int.

villages, one in Turkey and the other in Yucatan, reveal similar development.[19] Perhaps the strongest data come from a longitudinal study of middle-class and working-class boys convering a period of twelve years; at the beginning of the study the boys ranged in age from ten to sixteen, and at the conclusion they were from twenty-two to twenty-eight. Except for some regression in level of moral development in about one-fifth of the boys at the period between high school and college, the findings show progressive movement up the hierarchy of stages in moral thinking.[20]

In sum, the current interpretation of the formation of the conscience—a set of controls associated with anxiety, guilt, and moral values—is that it results from the unfolding of the child's cognitive capacities. This unfolding occurs partly through maturation or biological growth, and partly through experiences with the environment that normally accompany growing up. Piaget conceptualized this as occurring through a series of stages ranging from a state of moral absolutism to a morality based upon reciprocal agreement. This transition moves from egocentrism, where the child assumes that others have the same view of the world that he does, to the full recognition of individuality, where other persons have different views from his own. These changes reflect the growing status of the child vis-à-vis others and his activities in taking roles that other persons often enact. Kohlberg identifies six stages of moral development: (1) an obedience or punishment orientation, (2) a naïvely egoistic orientation, (3) a good-boy orientation, (4) an orientation toward authority and social order, (5) a contractual legalistic orientation, and (6) an orientation toward individual conscience.[21] Chiefly supporting this notion of stages are cross-cultural studies and a twelve-year longitudinal study of moral development. The main limitation of this view at present is that it is based on children's judgments of the moral conduct of hypothetical other persons rather than on observations of the children's own behavior, and indices of moral behavior have only modest correlations with cognitive stages of moral development.

Learning Explanations of Cognitive Controls

Chapter 15 explained how some internal controls are acquired through elementary social learning processes, based mainly on reinforcement contingencies. These internal controls largely do not involve cognitive processes, but are essentially habitual and spontaneous. A sense of right and wrong is not involved. A different explanation is that learning takes place through imitation and modeling. This explanation has been widely used to explain the development of internal controls, but this explanation now seems less consistent with accumulated evidence.

A key factor in this explanation was the strength of dependency and its role in leading the child to identify with his parents. According to this view both

19. KOHLBERG, 1969.   *20.* KOHLBERG, 1969.   *21.* KOHLBERG, 1969.

dependency and internalization are strengthened by a combination of a highly nurturant relationship between parent and child and the use of disciplinary techniques involving temporary withdrawal of love. Identification was postulated as one possible intervening process in which the child experiencing anxiety over the loss of love was motivated to reproduce the parents' behavior and adopt his standards of conduct. This process was not only thought to underlie the development of internalized control, but also to account for the incorporation of appropriate adult forms of behavior (e.g., sex-role learning). This overly simplified view of the basic mechanism of identification, while consistent with the findings of a number of earlier investigations, has been called into question by the lack of consistent correlation found in later studies between the postulated child-rearing antecedents of identification and their consequences—resistance to temptation, indicators of guilt, and sex-typed behaviors.[22]

Recent experimental studies mostly within the framework of the more complex conception of identification and modeling behavior outlined in Chapter 15 fail to support the conclusion that learning from models plays a major role in the development of internalized control. These studies include the effects of observing a model's behavior on resistance to temptation,[23] on the inhibition of aggression,[24] on self-imposed performance standards resulting in self-denial,[25] and on the deferment of gratification.[26] Hoffman, in a review of these findings, concludes that while learning from models can readily lead to the expression of previously inhibited impulses, such observation does not often produce the reverse effect. In other words, internal controls do not seem to be acquired through models, although learning from models can weaken or lift controls.[27] These laboratory findings are generally in keeping with the few naturalistic findings on modeling, which also provide little support for the view that identification is a significant factor in the development of an internal moral orientation.

As Hoffman is careful to note, it is possible that the relative weakness of internalized inhibitions in these studies may result from the inability to create sufficiently strong identification motives in the laboratory, where the model is typically a stranger rather than the parent or someone with a close relationship with the child. At any rate, these findings from laboratory studies along with more naturalistic studies cast some doubt on the validity of utilizing the concept of identification in attempting to understand the development of internal controls.

Child-rearing Practices and Moral Development

Much of the nonexperimental literature concerned with internalization has focused on the relation between child-rearing practices and various indices of

22. BANDURA & WALTERS, 1963; SEARS, RAU, & ALPERT, 1965.   23. WALTERS, LEAT, & MEZEI, 1963; WALTERS & PARKE, 1964; Stein, 1967.   24. BANDURA, ROSS, & ROSS, 1963b; BANDURA, 1965.   25. BANDURA & KUPERS, 1964; BANDURA & WHALEN, 1966; MISCHEL & LIEBERT, 1966; BANDURA, GRUSEC, & MENLOVE, 1967.   26. MISCHEL, 1965; BANDURA & MISCHEL, 1965.   27. HOFFMAN, 1967.

internalization. Hoffman and Saltzstein, in a study of the effects of parental discipline,[28] proposed a threefold classification of disciplinary techniques: (1) power assertion techniques, in which the parent, by virtue of his power over the child, punishes the child either physically or by depriving him; (2) withdrawal of love, in which the parent explicitly or implicitly implies dislike for the child; and (3) induction, in which the parent gives explanations or reasons why he wants the child to change his behavior, particularly in terms of the consequences of the child's behavior for the parent or for other persons.

Hoffman has reviewed various studies in an attempt to determine how these forms of discipline relate to internalization or moral development. Internalization measures include resistance to temptation, degree of guilt feeling, independence from external sanctions, and the acceptance of responsibility for one's conduct. He found power assertion by the mother to be negatively related to moral development. Less consistently, induction by the mother and the expression of affection were positively related to moral development. Withdrawal of love and affection related only infrequently to internalization, contrary to earlier views on this topic. Few relationships appeared between moral development and the father's style of discipline and his affection toward the child, although boys from homes without fathers showed lower moral development than boys from intact homes.

Finally, Hoffman and Saltzstein did a separate analysis for lower-class and middle-class children.[29] For lower-class children, few significant relations between maternal child-rearing practices and indices of moral development were observed. One common explanation for this is that the behavior of lower-class children is more oriented toward external sanctions, but Hoffman notes that data from his study with Saltzstein do not support this interpretation.[30] He suggests two other possibilities. One is that lower-class parents frequently use power assertion, an element that appears to be negatively related to moral development; use of power assertion cancels out positive effects that would otherwise occur and which are typically observed in middle-class samples. Finally, he notes that a number of features of lower-class family life may reduce the impact of maternal discipline. The mother is frequently employed and thus away from home; the home is more crowded and thus the child's behavior is more influenced by others, particularly siblings; the mother may rely more on the father to do the disciplining; and the child may be encouraged to spend more time out of the house.

Hoffman has offered the following explanation of the superiority of induction compared to love withdrawal and power assertion.[31] His explanation is based primarily on the idea that there is an optimal level of arousal of the child's need for approval: Too little arousal leaves the parent's control weak, but too much arousal may create anxiety or anger which interferes with learning the appropriate behavior.

28. HOFFMAN & SALTZSTEIN, 1967.   29. HOFFMAN & SALTZSTEIN, 1967.   30. HOFFMAN & SALTZSTEIN, 1967.   31. HOFFMAN, 1967.

Hoffman's reasoning is that any disciplinary action contains all three types of discipline: induction, withdrawal of love, and power assertion. In such an encounter a variety of motives are aroused. Where power assertion predominates, anger is apt to be at a maximum; not only does the child experience frustration over being blocked from completing the forbidden act but his need for autonomy is also frustrated. Further, he is provided with a model for the direct discharge of his anger as well as an object, the parent, against which to express his anger. In addition, his attention is directed largely to the consequences of his behavior for himself rather than in the case of induction, where frequently the child's attention is directed to the consequences of his behavior for others. No matter what the predominant technique employed, a disciplinary encounter is apt to arouse the child's need for approval, especially if he has been accustomed to a high level of affection. Where withdrawal of love or power assertion techniques predominate, arousal may be too great, thus interfering with effective learning in the situation. Induction, less threatening to the need for approval, is more apt to provide an optimum level of arousal. In addition, it provides cues to the child about what is wrong with his behavior and how he might behave in order to restore parental approval.

One emotional resource which is particularly apt to be capitalized on in instances of induction is the child's ability to empathize. Particularly where induction takes the form of pointing out to the child consequences of his behavior for others, his attention is directed to the reaction of others and he is apt to experience their discomfort vicariously and at the same time to connect this experience to the fact that his behavior was responsible for the other's discomfort. In fact, through being exposed to the content of parental inductions he is able to learn acceptable patterns of moral assessment in various situations. It was noted above in the discussion of the situational determinants of conformity that for persons to define a situation as involving a moral choice they must perceive that their behavior has consequences for the welfare of others and that they are responsible for their behavior. Parents who frequently employ induction provide opportunities for the child to learn to assess situations in this manner.

The infrequent and inconsistent relations between withdrawal of love and moral development contradict much of the earlier thinking about moral development, particularly the view that it results from dependency and identification. The Hoffman and Saltzstein study suggests that while withdrawal of love may not be related to the strength of internal controls, it may account in part for variations in the manner in which these controls operate. Hoffman was able to distinguish two groups of internalizers on the basis of story-completion tests designed to tap qualities of their moral judgments. These two types were described as follows:

To summarize, the humanistic-flexible and conventional-rigid groups appear to be two variants of an internalized conscience which differ not only in the manifest content but also in the hierarchical arrangement and motivational basis of their moral standards. Thus, in making moral judgments about other people's violations, the humanistic-flexible subjects tend to stress the consequences for others and are more likely to take extenuating circumstances into account. Their story completions suggest they are more tolerant and accepting of their own impulses. That is, though high on guilt and other indices of internalization, they give evidence of being able to contemplate or consider in fantasy behaving in violation of their standards. They also appear to experience guilt primarily as a direct result of harmful consequences of their behavior for others, rather than unacceptable impulses in themselves. The conventional-rigid subjects, on the other hand, are more likely to give a religious or legal basis for their moral judgments and to ignore extenuating circumstances. Their story-completions suggest that they may, to a relatively great extent, operate in accord with the Freudian notion that guilt stems less from the amount of harm actually done than from awareness of unacceptable impulses, and they tend to avoid expressing these impulses even in fantasy. This pattern, together with the sentence completion findings, suggests that repression may be an underlying mechanism in these subjects. Perhaps impulse intolerance is a way of avoiding moral conflict, i.e., one experiences no conflict if unaware of temptation. Thus, although the two groups were selected on the basis of conscious moral judgments, they appear to reflect moral syndromes which differ beyond the conscious and rational aspects of moral orientations.[32]

Compared to the humanistic-flexible group, parents of the conventional-rigid group were more apt to use withdrawal of love as a disciplining technique. Hoffman suggests that this technique, combined with the lower power assertion and high induction and affection which characterized both groups of internalizers, may lead to intensified inhibition of hostility and of impulses associated with other behaviors frowned upon by parents. On the other hand, parents whose children were characterized as having a humanistic-flexible conscience were reported to use power assertion more often than parents of conventional-rigid children. Finally, the parents of the humanistic-flexible children appeared to model this orientation in their own behaviors.

These findings on withdrawal of love suggest that some earlier concern with the growing use of this technique in middle-class American families[33] and its possible consequence—producing persons who are overly rigid and guilt-ridden—may be well founded despite the lack of support in later studies for some of the earlier formulations which emphasized the effects of withdrawal of love on dependency and conscience formation.

In sum, disciplinary techniques include the following: (1) power assertion

32. Reprinted by permission from M. L. HOFFMAN. Moral development. In P. H. Mussen (Ed.), Carmichael's manual of child psychology. (3d ed.) Vol. 2. New York: John Wiley & Sons, Inc., 1970. P. 339.   33. BRONFENBRENNER, 1958.

techniques, in which the parent, by virtue of his power over the child, punishes him either physically or by depriving him; (2) withdrawal of love, in which the parent explicitly or implicitly dislikes or threatens not to like the child; and (3) induction, in which the parent gives explanations or reasons for the child to change his behavior. Power assertion by the mother is negatively related to moral development. Induction and the expression of affection by the mother were positively related. Some class differences have been found.

In general, induction appears to have the best results. Disciplinary encounters arouse the need for approval, so that power assertion or withdrawal of love may be so upsetting that they interfere with effective learning. Induction may also improve the child's ability to empathize with others, since it involves pointing out the consequences of his actions. Persons with different types of internal controls have been identified: humanistic-flexible and conventional-rigid. The former individuals stress consequences for others and take extenuating circumstances into account. They are more accepting of their own impulses; guilt arises largely from consideration of the harmful consequences of their behavior to others. Conventional-rigid individuals provide a religious or legal basis for their moral judgments and ignore extenuating circumstances. Guilt appears to be based upon their own impulses rather than upon harm done to others. Withdrawal of love combined with low power assertion and high induction is especially apt to produce conventional-rigid individuals.

Summary: *The Development of Cognitive Controls*

A prerequisite to adequate socialization appears to be the dependency of the infant on another person. In the typical family, the development of dependency is assured by the nature of family interaction, which necessarily produces strong dependencies as well as occasional frustration and conflict. In extremely atypical families, or in the case of institutionalized children, only a weak dependency may develop. That various forms of deprivation, such as an impoverished environment, interfere with normal socialization is clear, but identifying the precise determining factor is difficult. Multiple interpretations are possible. Moreover, such effects depend upon the particular factor, the age of the child when deprivation occurs, the length and form of the deprivation, and the age of the child when the effects are assessed.

Studies of both monkeys and humans suggest that the idea of dependency as a unified motive system is an oversimplification. The behaviors and other elements related to dependency do not seem to constitute a single system. Their occurrence is often highly contingent, requiring certain conditions to prevail which vary in many ways. Research with monkeys, for example, has distinguished five relatively separate systems of affection, each having their own development (e.g., infant-mother system; agemate system).

The conscience—a set of controls associated with anxiety, guilt, and moral values—is thought to result from the unfolding of the child's capacities, occurring partly through biological growth and partly through experience. Somewhat different stages have been proposed by Piaget and by Kohlberg. Piaget's system ranges from a state of moral absolutism viewed egocentrically to a relative morality based upon reciprocal agreement. Kohlberg's system ranges from a premoral stage in which external controls prevail to a stage in which behavior is in accord with self-accepted moral principles.

The earlier view that identification with a model played a major role in conscience formation is not consistent with recent evidence. Though learning from models frequently results in the expression of a previously inhibited impulse, it does not seem to be effective in producing inhibition of various behaviors. Some disciplinary techniques are more effective than others in producing internal controls. Power assertion by the mother is negatively related to moral development, while induction and affectionate behavior are positively related to moral development. Induction—giving explanations or reasons why the child should change his behavior—appears to obtain the best results. Often power assertion and withdrawal of love are so upsetting that they interfere with effective learning.

Social Motives

One way of looking at sets of behaviors, both in everyday language and in social psychology, focuses upon the direction common to members of a set. What seems to be its directional quality? What is accomplished in common by the members of the set? A set of behaviors that have a common goal of this nature usually can be identified as a *social motive*. Examples of such motives are aggression and achievement. Aggressive behaviors and achievement behaviors are widespread in modern societies. The former range from various forms of physical violence to malicious gossip, and have in common the desire to injure or harm another person. The latter range from striving for success in a lifelong career to playing to win a hand of bridge. Because aggressive behaviors often create social problems, and because the motivation to achieve is considered important to success, the ways in which these motives are socialized will be discussed below.

Aggression

A behavioral act which has an intent to harm or injure someone, either physically or otherwise, may usually be labeled *aggressive*. Aggression may be so disguised that the perpetrator of an aggressive act may not be consciously aware of his intent. Sears, Maccoby, and Levin note:

> Aggression, as the term is commonly used, means behavior that is intended to hurt or injure someone. Most human adults have quite a repertory of acts

that fit this definition. Some of these are bold and violent, others sly and attenuated. Some are accompanied by rage or annoyance; others are done coldly and seemingly, to the perpetrator, without emotion. The complexity and subtlety of adult aggression is the end product of two or three decades of socialization by the individual's parents and peers, however, and bears little resemblance to the primitive quality of the infant's action patterns, from which it developed.[34]

Although the primitive rage that accompanies aggression in the infant may be unlearned, the intent and the form of aggression in the socialized individual are learned. Sears, Maccoby, and Levin have suggested that this learning falls into a pattern: The child experiences discomfort which initially leads to rage and to behaviors that evoke discomfort in other persons. These behaviors also frequently lead others unintentionally to reward him by relieving his discomfort. In time, the infant learns that the experience of aggression is likely to bring about rewarding behavior from other persons.

Eventually, these investigators suggest, aggressive acts become satisfying in themselves as a result of two processes. First, as a result of punishment for aggression, the child experiences tension in connection with aggressive impulses. This tension is relieved, at least momentarily, when the aggressive act occurs. Such release of tension, subjectively experienced as "letting off steam," is rewarding. Second, since aggression frequently results in reward, either as a result of the child's tension release or because others act to relieve his frustration, and since such cues as the signs of distress in the other person are followed by reward, the infliction of discomfort on others becomes rewarding in itself. In other words, seeing distress in others has become a rewarding experience; hence the individual produces it through aggressive actions.

Early research on the determinants of aggression was guided by the notion that the strength of aggression was a function of the degree of frustration experienced. The first studies appeared to provide support for this notion.[35] More recent evidence, however, suggests that the relation between these variables is not so simple.

First, it has become clear that frustration does not always lead to aggression. While there is evidence that in animals other than man such a linkage may be innate, if it exists in man it is greatly modifiable by learning. Berkowitz, in a recent assessment of the status of the frustration-aggression hypothesis, has provided an analysis of the nature of frustration and has identified some of the conditions under which frustration leads to aggression.[36] Frustration is thought to arise as a result of the blocking or nonconsummation of an anticipated, desired state of affairs. The anticipatory state is important in understanding the conditions under which a situation is experienced as frustrating and thus liable

---

34. Reprinted by permission from R. R. Sears, E. E. Maccoby, & H. Levin. *Patterns of child rearing.* New York: Harper & Row, Publishers, Incorporated, 1957. P. 218.   35. Dollard, Doob, Miller, Mowrer, & Sears, 1939.   36. Berkowitz, 1969.

to result in aggression. If blocking of an act leading to a goal is nonarbitrary, frustration may not occur since success was not necessarily expected. On the other hand, where success is expected but arbitrarily blocked, frustration occurs.

Pigeons were taught to peck a key by reinforcing them with food; they became aggressive and attacked other pigeons when the experimenter ceased giving them food for their pecking responses.[37] Humans similarly led to anticipate a given level of reward react with aggression when it is not achieved, even if the level of reward received is actually greater than it has been in the past. Students of revolution, as Berkowitz notes, have long been aware that revolutionary outbreaks are apt to occur during periods of rising expectations (frequently stimulated by an increase in the level of experienced rewards). A study applying the frustration-aggression hypothesis to the phenomenon of political instability accompanying modernization indicated that as people experienced rising levels of education and food consumption, political instability increased.[38]

Aggression may not occur in response to frustration in situations where inhibitions to aggression are strong or where the individual has learned nonaggressive responses to a frustrating event. The latter might be illustrated by a child who learns to persist in a task rather than explode in helpless rage when thwarted in some task activity.

In contrast, the lowering of inhibitions against aggression may produce more hostile acts, as demonstrated by Geen and Berkowitz.[39] Male college students were given one of several arousal treatments: (1) were presented with an insoluble jigsaw puzzle, (2) were insulted by the experimenter after failing the insoluble puzzle, and (3) were neither frustrated nor insulted. Subsequently, each student viewed either a violent prize-fight movie or a film of an exciting but nonviolent track race. The prize-fight scene was introduced in a way that lowered inhibitions against aggression. When the film was over the participant was given an opportunity to give an electric shock to a person he had met earlier (a confederate of the experimenter). The opportunity was presented in the guise of a learning experiment, with electric shocks used as punishment for mistakes. The intensity of shocks administered by a participant were taken as a measure of his aggressiveness.

Those who saw the violent fight film gave significantly more intense shocks than the nonaroused individuals in both frustrating conditions (one in which they were insulted and the other in which they were not), whereas those who saw the racetrack film gave significantly more intense shocks only in the insulted conditions. These results are interpreted by Berkowitz as indicating the effect of the fight film on lowering inhibitions to aggression.

Further research by Berkowitz and his associates has illustrated a further

37. Azrin, Hutchinson, & Hake, 1966.   38. Feierabend & Feierabend, 1966.   39. Geen & Berkowitz, 1967.

condition that affects the probability of aggression occurring in response to frustration—the presence of aggressive cues. Stimuli which have become associated with aggression or with frustration elicit aggression in frustrating situations. While retreating somewhat from an earlier position[40] which asserted that aggression-eliciting external stimuli were necessary for aggression to occur, Berkowitz now maintains that such cues somehow facilitate or increase the probability of an aggressive response, but that aggression can occur in their absence as well.[41]

The notion that stimuli associated with aggression can elicit aggressive responses to frustration was demonstrated in a study in which, after frustration, individuals were given the opportunity to administer shock to the person who had been the source of their frustration. Those participants who administered the shock from a room in which a pistol and rifle were displayed on a table nearby administered significantly stronger shocks than those who administered the shocks in the presence of a neutral or irrelevant object.[42] The effect of stimuli associated with aggression and with the person who is a source of frustration was demonstrated in another study in which participants, some of whom had been angered by the experimenter's accomplice posing as another participant, observed a violent fight movie whose main character had a first name either the same as or different from the name of the experimenter's confederate. When given a subsequent opportunity to administer shock to the instigator of their anger, participants who had been exposed to the film character with the same name as the confederate administered more shocks than did participants exposed to the film character having a different name.

Not only can frustration occur without aggression, but the frustration-aggression hypothesis has had to be modified in the direction of allowing for aggression without prior frustration. Aggressive behavior can be learned in a variety of situations in the same manner and by the same processes of social learning as previously described. The child may learn aggression when the contingencies of reinforcement are suitably arranged. It is not the intention of the mother to reward such behavior; nevertheless, by continuing to be the source of frustration, and by giving such positive rewards as picking the child up and soothing him in response to aggressive behavior, she fosters the continuance of aggression. As the child grows older, tolerant or permissive attitudes toward aggression will allow the continued expression of aggression, which by now has become self-rewarding.

Direct tuition may also foster aggression. A number of studies suggest that where parents approve of aggression against agemates, it will occur.[43] Finally, the processes of role learning and identification are consistent with the findings that parental aggression in the form of punishment of the child, particularly physical punishment, is associated with high aggression. This point is made

40. Berkowitz, 1965.   *41.* Berkowitz, 1970.   *42.* Berkowitz & LePage, 1967.   *43.* Davis & Dollard, 1940; Lesser, 1952.

clear by Sears, Maccoby, and Levin in summarizing their research on aggression and its control:

> When the parents punish—particularly when they employ physical punishment—they are providing a living example of the use of aggression at the very moment they are trying to teach the child not to be aggressive.
>
> The child, who copies his parents in many ways, is likely to learn as much from this example of successful aggression on his parents' part as he is from the pain of punishment. Thus, the most peaceful home is one in which the mother believes aggression is not desirable and under no circumstances is ever to be expressed toward her, but who relies mainly on non-punitive forms of control. The homes where the children show angry, aggressive outbursts frequently are likely to be homes in which the mother has a relatively tolerant (or careless!) attitude toward such behavior, or where she administers severe punishment for it, or both.[44]

Thus, the two factors contributing to aggression stressed by these investigators are high permissiveness for aggression and much punishment of aggressive acts. Several other studies have reported similar familial antecedents of aggression.[45] In sum, one basic condition for aggression to occur seems to be the arbitrary interruption of a sequence leading to a goal. When inhibitions to aggression are strong or when nonaggressive responses to a frustrating event have been learned, aggression may not occur. But when a situation lowers inhibitions against aggression, hostile acts occur more frequently. Some experiments have shown that when a frustrating event has occurred, the presentation of aggressive cues (e.g., aggressive behavior by a model or situational props such as a gun) will facilitate aggressive behavior. Frustration is not a necessary condition for aggression. Aggression may be learned directly, as in the case of any behavior—through modeling or suitable contingencies or reinforcement.

Achievement

Individuals respond differently to situations in which some standard of excellence might be applied to their behavior. At one extreme, persons set high standards for themselves, strive very hard to achieve them, and respond with considerable feeling to their success or failure in meeting them. At the other extreme, persons are unlikely to set such standards, exert little effort, and feel relatively indifferent about achieving the standards. These two kinds of persons are said to differ in *achievement motivation.* This behavior has been extensively investigated in recent years. Generally it has been measured either in terms of some behavioral index of overachievement or underachievement or in terms of

44. Reprinted by permission from R. R. SEARS, E. E. MACCOBY, & H. LEVIN, *Patterns of child rearing.* New York: Harper & Row, Publishers, Incorporated, 1957. P. 266.   *45.* BANDURA & WALTERS, 1959; LYNN, 1961; MCCORD, MCCORD, & HOWARD, 1961.

achievement themes in stories elicited by a series of pictures taken from the Thematic Apperception Test.[46]

MATHEMATICAL MODEL FOR ACHIEVEMENT   The extensive research on achievement motivation has led to one of the few examples of a fairly precise mathematical formulation of motivational phenomena. Atkinson has suggested that in situations calling for behavior which is to be evaluated against some standard of excellence, behavior is influenced by the following[47]:

1. The strength of motives to approach success (M_s) and to avoid failure (M_{af}).
2. The probabilities that a given act will result in success (P_s) or failure (P_f).
3. The incentive value in that activity of success (I_s) or failure (I_f).

These variables are thought to combine in a *multiplicative* fashion so that the tendency to approach success (I_s) is equal to $(M_s \times P_s \times I_s)$, and the tendency to avoid failure (T_f) is equal to $(M_{af} \times P_f \times I_f)$. The theory assumes that the incentive value of success in a given activity is proportionate to the difficulty of the task (i.e., $I_s = 1 - P_s$). Thus, success at a difficult task is valued more than accomplishment of an easy task. Similarly the negative incentive value of failure is greater when a task is easy than when it is difficult (i.e., $I_f = - P_s$). Thus, it is more distressing to fail an easy task than a more difficult one.

This formulation may be illustrated by assigning some arbitrary values to the motivation to succeed (M_s) for several individuals.[48] The tendency to achieve success can then be calculated for them, for tasks of different difficulty. These values are shown in Table 16-1. For example, for easy task *A,* the probability of success is assumed to be 0.90. The incentive value of success is then only 0.10 (obtained by $1.00 - 0.90$). If M_s is 1, then the tendency to achieve success is equal to $0.90 \times 0.10 \times 1 = 0.09$, as shown in the fourth column. Other values are similarly calculated.

Table 16-1 provides an understanding of how to make predictions of the

46. McClelland, Atkinson, Clark, & Lowell, 1953.   *47.* Atkinson, 1964; Atkinson & Feather, 1966.   *48.* Atkinson & Feather, 1966, p. 330.

Table 16-1   Calculation of tendency to achieve success

TASK	PROBABILITY OF SUCCESS	INCENTIVE VALUE	$M_s = 1$	MOTIVE TO SUCCEED $M_s = 2$	$M_s = 3$
A	0.90	0.10	0.09	0.18	0.27
B	0.70	0.30	0.21	0.42	0.63
C	0.50	0.50	0.25	0.50	0.75
D	0.30	0.70	0.21	0.42	0.63
E	0.10	0.90	0.09	0.18	0.27

Source: Reprinted with permission from J. W. Atkinson & N. T. Feather. *A theory of achievement motivation.* New York: John Wiley & Sons, Inc., 1966, p. 330.

tendency to achieve success given tasks of varying difficulty, different incentive values, and the manner in which persons react to success or failure. In Table 16-1 we see that *the tendency to achieve success is strongest on tasks of intermediate difficulty, especially where the motive to achieve (M_s) is strong.*

A similar table may be constructed for the tendency to avoid failure. Such a table would show that this motive will also be maximized at intermediate levels of difficulty, especially where the motive to avoid failure is strong. Thus, where the tendency to achieve success is strong, tasks of intermediate difficulty are favored; where the tendency to avoid failure is strong, such tasks are least favored. Here tasks that are either very easy or very difficult are preferred. Since actual behaviors in a given situation will be influenced by both these tendencies, the resultant achievement-oriented tendency will reflect the predominance of one or the other.

Weinstein reports that in eighteen studies using different types of groups and situations, the predicted relation between a strong motive to achieve and the preference for an intermediate risk—risking neither too much nor too little—was confirmed with remarkable consistency.[49] He notes, however, that these studies used different measures of need achievement and different risk-taking situations. To examine what these measures have in common, his own study used eight different measures of need achievement and twelve measures reflecting risk-taking preference in a variety of contexts such as problem solving, athletic tasks, choice of potential dates, betting preferences, and vocational preferences. Surprisingly, he found little correlation among the different measures of achievement, and factor analyses suggested that these measures belonged to different dimensions having little in common. A similar result was obtained for the measures of risk taking. These findings raise the question whether need achievement represents a single dimension or characteristic and further suggest that risk taking varies markedly depending upon the situation in which it is studied.

The effects of achievement-oriented tendencies on the level of performance in an achievement situation are also thought to vary with the relative strength of M_s. When the motive to avoid failure is greater than the motive to achieve, an inhibiting or dampening effect on performance is predicted by achievement theory. Thus, better performance can be expected when the motive to achieve is the stronger. This prediction has received support from a number of studies.[50] Finally, the theory predicts different reactions to the experiences of success and failure by the two motive groups. Those persons whose motive to achieve success is greater than their motive to avoid failure will persist in the face of failure to a greater degree when their initial expectation of success is high than when it is low. However, those in whom the motive to avoid failure predominates will persist to a greater extent in the face of failure when they initially perceive that the probability of success is low than when they perceive it is high. These are

49. WEINSTEIN, 1969.   *50.* ATKINSON & LITWIN, 1960; ATKINSON & O'CONNOR, 1966; KARABENICK & YOUSSEF, 1968.

nonobvious predictions and can only be understood by substituting values in the formulas and calculating the resulting motives.

Reactions to success or failure in terms of lowering or raising one's level of aspiration are also expected to be different. One would typically expect that a person would raise his level of aspiration after success by choosing a more difficult task and lower his level following failure by choosing a less difficult task. Instead, the model predicts that those whose motive to avoid failure is greater than their motive to approach success would choose an easier task after success and a more difficult task after failure.

Moulton has explained this in the following way. Success or failure on a task changes its attractiveness because the subjective probability of success is altered. For the individual oriented toward avoidance of failure, success on an easy task increases the subjective probability of success. But such success also increases the strength of the motive to avoid failure, because this motive is a function of the probability of success on the task and the incentive value of failure (which remains constant). Thus, this stronger motive to avoid failure leads him to choose a still easier task. On the other hand, if he fails a task, he lowers his estimate of probable success in subsequent trials. Since the incentive value of failure remains constant, a lower expectation of success lowers his motive to avoid failure, and he chooses a more difficult task. Similar deductions may be made for other cases. Predictions based on this reasoning were for the most part supported in several investigations.[51]

Achievement theory has also been applied to more everyday situations, including vocational aspirations, occupational mobility, and differences in achievement motivation among class, ethnic, and national groups. Consistent with the theory, students who were unrealistic in their vocational aspirations, aspiring to occupations requiring abilities either greater or less than their own, were found to be low in achievement motivation and high in achievement-related anxiety.[52] The hypothesis that achievement motivation plays a part in explaining upward social mobility has received some support. For the lower two levels of occupational status but not in the top two levels, achievement motivation is associated with upward mobility.[53] Achievement motivation is also stronger among middle-class than working-class children,[54] and stronger among Jewish than Italian children.[55] A cross-cultural study found Brazilians to be lower than Americans.[56]

CHILDHOOD ANTECEDENTS OF THE MOTIVATION TO ACHIEVE   Eight-year-old to ten-year-old children with strong motivation to achieve had parents who expected independent accomplishment at an earlier age, and who gave more frequent and stronger rewards for independent accomplishments.[57] These find-

51. FEATHER, 1961, 1965; MOULTON, 1965.   52. MAHONE, 1960.   53. CROCKETT, 1962.   54. DOUVAN, 1956; ROSEN, 1956, 1959; MILSTEIN, 1956.   55. ROSEN, 1959.   56. ROSEN, 1964.   57. WINTERBOTTOM, 1958.

ings were supported further in a study in which interaction between parents and their child in a problem-solving situation was observed.[58] Parents of children with strong achievement motivation set high standards of excellence for the child, gave approval for progress toward those standards, and showed disappointment for poor performance. A longitudinal investigation provides some suggestive evidence concerning the degree to which achievement motivation and parental practices are consistent over time, as well as the comparative importance of early and late child-rearing practices.[59] Moderate stability in achievement motivation over time was observed. But the attitudes of mothers concerning independent accomplishment during childhood and adolescence were opposite. The earlier a mother encouraged independent accomplishment from her grade school son, the less she encouraged such behavior in adolescence. Independence and achievement training in early childhood and in later adolescence had little relation to one another. Also, achievement motivation in adolescence and maternal practices at that time were not much related, in contrast to the findings of an early study of achievement motivation and maternal practices during childhood.[60] The motivation to avoid failure in adolescence, however, was related to early childhood practices. And the later the maternal demands for independent accomplishment, the higher the adolescent anxiety in achievement situations.

SITUATIONAL DETERMINANTS   As in the case of aggression, recent research focusing on achievement motivation has shifted away from concern with child-rearing antecedents to situational determinants. How the person defines a situation affects the expression of achievement motivation in behavior. Important in this definition are the values and goals that the person perceives in the situation.[61] For example, the relation between achievement motivation and grades in college holds only for those students who perceive that grades are instrumental for future career success.[62] Further, strong achievement motivation affects occupational choice only for those persons who are knowledgeable about potential rewards and who view occupations as intrinsically satisfying.[63]

Features of the situation that affect a person's attribution of success or failure to his own efforts and abilities rather than to chance or luck also appear to be crucial in determining whether predictions from the theory will be borne out.[64] Individuals differ in seeing the causation of events and their reinforcing consequences as either internal (under their own control) or external (beyond their own control).[65] Weiner and Kukla have noted a number of ways in which views of success and failure affect behavior: Since strongly motivated individuals generally ascribe success to their efforts, they experience more reward, and thus are more active in attempting to achieve. They also persist longer because

58. ROSEN & D'ANDRADE, 1959.   *59.* FELD, 1967.   *60.* WINTERBOTTOM, 1958.   *61.* KAHL, 1965.
62. RAYNOR, 1970.   *63.* LEUPTOW, 1968.   *64.* FEATHER, 1967; WEINER & KUKLA, 1970; CRANDALL, KATOVSKY, & CRANDALL, 1965; COLEMAN, CAMPBELL, HOBSON, ET AL., 1966.   *65.* ROTTER, 1966.

they are more likely to ascribe failure to lack of effort than to a lack of ability. Finally, they prefer tasks of intermediate difficulty, since these yield the most information about their own capabilities.[66]

In sum, achievement motivation has been conceptualized as a multiplicative function of the following: (1) the strength of the motive to approach success and to avoid failure, (2) the probabilities that a given act will result in success or failure, (3) the incentive value of success or failure in that activity. One prediction that follows from this conceptualization is the relation between a strong motive to achieve and a preference for intermediate risks. A large number of studies have confirmed the predicted relations, with only a few exceptions. Some support has been obtained for another prediction: that the stronger the achievement motive, the better the performance. Specific predictions for motives to succeed and to avoid failure have also been made for persistence at the task. Parents who expect independent accomplishment at an early age and who strongly reward such accomplishments raise independent children. Parental behavior, however, is not consistent from early childhood to adolescence. Recent research has shown the importance of situational determinants in achievement behavior, particularly the definition of the situation by the actor.

Gaps in Knowledge of Social Motives

Available research on social motives has serious limitations. Almost all of it has been cross-sectional; groups of children are studied at a certain age, but rarely is the same child studied longitudinally (over a period of many years). Consequently knowledge of the continuity or discontinuity in the behavior of individual children is lacking. Generally the assumption has been made that the child acquires certain traits or characteristics which persist into adulthood.[67]

Moreover, although parental behavior toward children of a particular age is undoubtedly dependent upon the relationship between child and parent at an earlier age, their relationship is not necessarily a consistent one. For example, a father who initially shows great enthusiasm and warmth toward his small son may be quite frustrated in his attempts to make a companion out of his son at that age. Early warmth and enthusiasm may then be replaced by a more indifferent attitude that is quite inconsistent with his earlier feelings. Some studies suggest that these qualifications concerning presently available research are justified. With respect to aggression, one study has shown that although strong punishment of preschool children produced more aggressive behavior in them at preschool age, at age twelve the same children were relatively low in antisocial aggression.[68] At this age, however, the children exhibited more indirect forms of aggression and showed more anxiety concerning aggression. Permissiveness presented a similar problem with respect to continuity. High permissiveness toward children at preschool age, also associated with high aggression

66. WEINER & KUKLA, 1970.   67. MISCHEL, 1968.   68. SEARS, 1961.

at that age, continued to be associated with high aggression at age twelve. But children whose parents were permissive exhibited less aggression in indirect forms and less anxiety over aggression at age twelve.

Some caution is necessary in interpreting these results, because at preschool age aggression was assessed by interviews with mothers, and at age twelve it was evaluated by having the children fill out a questionnaire. Also, the correlations were quite low in both studies. An independent study shows that ratings of aggressiveness in children by their parents do not correlate with ratings made by their classmates in school.[69] This lack of correlation suggests that self-ratings and parental ratings might also not be comparable.

A number of other investigations in which the same children were studied over a period of many years indicate that some characteristics prominent at one age often disappear at another. One study finds considerable stability in dependence and passivity at different ages for females but not for males.[70] Another reports that overdependence and seriousness were moderately correlated in early childhood and preadolescence, while selfishness, quarrelsomeness, and attention-demanding behavior had markedly different frequences in the same children at different ages.[71]

Another problem which deserves more study than it has received is the consistency of maternal behavior toward children. One study compares observational data collected during the first three years of life with interview data on the same children collected between the ages of nine and fourteen.[72] Considerable maternal consistency on a dimension of love versus hostility was found between the two periods. In other words, mothers who were loving toward their small children were likely to be loving at later ages, while those who were less loving or were hostile toward them as infants were likely to have a similar attitude later. Consistency was not perfect, of course, and in many individual cases, mothers had markedly different attitudes toward their children at the two age levels.

The same investigators found little consistency on another dimension, the extent to which mothers controlled their children or allowed them independence. Maccoby has noted that one reason why very different behaviors toward the child are manifested at different ages is that a particular behavior may be more compatible with the personality and capacity of the mother at one age than at another.[73] For example, maternal warmth toward an infant may be equated with considerable body contact, such as holding, carrying, rocking, and nursing; but toward a child of school age, warmth may mean an expression of interest in his accomplishments and pride in his independence. A mother who enjoys infants may be unable to be equally warm toward the same child when he is older.

We have already mentioned a longitudinal study which showed at least

69. WALDER, 1961.   *70.* KAGAN & MOSS, 1960.   *71.* McFARLANE, ALLEN, & HONZIK, 1954.   *72.* SCHAEFER & BAYLEY, 1960.   *73.* MACCOBY, 1961.

Infl. on Trait ⊖.

moderate stability for achievement motivation between childhood and adolescence but a reversal of maternal attitudes concerning independent accomplishment between these two age periods.[74] Moreover, in that same study the relation between early-childhood maternal practices and achievement motivation disappeared by adolescence and was only modestly related to maternal practices at that time. Further, the failure to find consistent relations between achievement-oriented tendencies and risk preferences[75] as well as the effect of situational factors on achievement-related behavior suggest caution in concluding that such a motive constitutes a stable and pervasive trait of personality.

Murphy has called attention to marked changes that take place in children and has suggested that the conception of a fixed personality structure persisting throughout life has been overstressed:

> The concept of character in the sense of a fixed core-structure persisting through the lifetime of an individual has been so reified that it has become virtually a part of our mythology . . . it makes us regard the surprises, the dramatic changes as somehow exceptions to the rule. . . .
>
> Among the children we have observed, new interactions contribute to change at times of transition due to internal changes in the child, external changes such as a new school, neighborhood, or major changes in the pattern of family relationships and the interactions of these inner and external changes. . . .
>
> Longitudinal studies generally show tendencies to constriction preceding the adolescent blossoming, but in some individuals this phase becomes fixed into a lasting character-rigidity while with others it is outgrown. Observations in adolescence, college and post-college stages also show dramatic changes in some individuals in relations between drive, expression, control, and defense. . . .[76]

Finally, most research on social motives has focused largely on parent-child interaction to the neglect of interaction with other family members and the peer group. These other sources are important in childhood socialization. Harlow's work on monkeys demonstrates the importance of sibling and peer interaction for the development of dependency and attachment motives and associated behavior.[77] Undoubtedly much aggression is learned from peer and sibling models. The authors' review of school achievement in another publication emphasizes the importance of the peer group for achievement.[78] Probably the most striking and significant finding of a national study of equality of educational opportunity was that the most influential characteristic of the school environment in affecting the performance of students, particularly from disadvantaged homes, was the educational background and aspirations of the other

74. FELD, 1967.   75. WEINSTEIN, 1969.   76. Reprinted by permission from an unpublished manuscript by L. MURPHY, 1961.   77. HARLOW & HARLOW, 1965, 1966.   78. BACKMAN & SECORD, 1968b; BACKMAN, 1971.

students in the school.[79] In other societies, such as the Soviet Union, other children are an even more potent source of influence in the socialization process.[80]

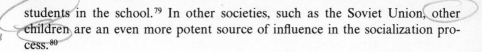

Socialization and Family Structure

That two children from the same family turn out so differently is often surprising to many people. To queries of why this is so, the behavior scientist points out that among other things no child has the same family environment as his siblings. Each, by virtue of his age, sex, and order of birth, has a unique position in the family structure, and encounters quite different interpersonal influences. An older brother may be treated quite differently than a younger sister, both by the parents and by other children in the family.

Birth Order

Of the many aspects of family structure, birth order has been singled out in recent years for special attention, perhaps because of the ease with which it may be identified. Stimulated by the work of Schachter[81] more than a decade ago but with a history that goes back considerably before that,[82] a steady stream of investigations has attempted to relate birth order to a wide variety of characteristics: social eminence and other indicators of achievement, intelligence, delinquency, mental illness, alcoholism, and such personality characteristics as affiliation, dependency, and conformity.

Sampson has sketched in eloquent language the drama inherent in birth order and has suggested outcomes that might be expected from its enactment:

> The child firstborn occupies the center stage in a drama whose participants include two rather inconsistent, somewhat anxious and confused actors, who nevertheless are proud of their product and wish him to obtain the skill and attributes which they lack and to attain heights which they long for but find themselves frustrated in reaching. They wish him to progress with lightning pace, yet often act in ways which only serve to increase his dependence on them. And the child himself, alone in this most confusing world, turns toward his parents, looming so large, so powerful, so distant, and uses them as his model for coping with the complexities he daily encounters.
>
> One day, another is born. The stage now holds four; the play has suddenly been changed. More experienced parents, less confused by opening night jitters, more set in their stage movements, now work upon the second. From stardom on center stage to a lesser role . . . the fate of the child firstborn. Soon the second finds himself cast in more prominent parts, and

79. COLEMAN ET AL., 1966.   *80.* BRONFENBRENNER, 1970.   *81.* SCHACHTER, 1959.   *82.* JONES, 1931.

learns rapidly to manipulate the stronger first by playing upon his own relatively less powerful position. And he, the second, finds a model, closer, manipulable, less powerful to use to grasp the complexities of his own world. He has a ready antagonist and target, and thus suffers less from the pains of withholding aggressive attacks when his paths are thwarted. He finds himself less caught up in the future of his parents and less the victim of their oversolicitous actions, and thus finds a lesser conflict over dependency.

The second child grows up looking outward upon a world of peers and learns those skills required for coping with similars. The first child grows up looking inward, for without there lies a world of still powerful adults, a more difficult breed to handle, a breed requiring a different set of skills.

Together they grow up, each moving forward, but down a different path. For the first, still driven by the now internalized desires of his parents, education and intellectual achievement become important. He turns toward the world of thought, leaving the world of people, and sociability, and play to the younger member of his family.

What seems like a reversal emerges at this point. The inner-oriented first-born turns outward to seek union and agreement with others when his world becomes difficult to handle or issues of choice arise. The outer-oriented secondborn turns inward to seek isolation within himself when difficulties and decisions arise. The power and distance of his parents not only give the first a reduced sense of personal autonomy, but also direct him more toward others as useful figures for providing structure, setting directions, and handling problems. On the other hand, the closer model which exists for the second not only permits him to develop a stronger sense of self-confidence, but also instructs him in the more autonomous manipulation of others; these turn him back upon his own skills when problems and issues of choice arise.[83]

Sampson's review of the literature, published in 1965, found some support for this general picture. In his 1966 review, Warren found fewer relations between birth order and behavior indices.[84] Firstborn of both sexes attended college in relatively greater numbers than later-born, and were more susceptible to social pressure and more dependent than later-born. Firstborn women, when anxious, desired the company of others more strongly than later-born women. But even these positive results dwindled away in a 1972 review of the research literature conducted by Schooler.[85] The disproportional college attendance of firstborns was found to be a reflection of differences among social class in family size during the postwar baby boom.[86] And more recent studies

83. Reprinted by permission from E. E. SAMPSON. The study of ordinal position: Antecedents and outcomes. In B. A. Maher (Ed.), *Progress in Experimental Personality Research.* New York: Academic Press, Inc., 1965. Pp. 220-222.   84. WARREN, 1966.   85. SCHOOLER, 1972.   86. GRABILL, KISER, & WHELPTON, 1958; PRICE & HARE, 1969.

reviewed by Schooler yielded a preponderance of negative evidence for birth-order effects on conformity and affiliative behavior.

Why does such a promising feature of family structure yield such a dismal research picture? Are Sampson's logic and reasoning wrong, or are there serious limitations to the research conducted? Sampson and others have offered some cogent criticisms of the research on birth order.[87] Family members have been categorized somewhat differently from study to study, and often other structural differences have not been taken into account. Some investigators have grouped together firstborns and only children in their comparison with later-born children. Others have excluded only children from this comparison. Some have controlled for the effects of social class; others have not. Other family structure characteristics have similarly varied from study to study, including the sex of the children compared, family size, the sex of the siblings, and the spacing of children. Finally, the behavior thought to be affected by birth order has been measured in many different ways. These include measures of overt behavior, responses to objective personality instruments, and projective measures, all of which have frequently been shown to be poorly correlated. Thus, for all of these reasons the lack of consistent results is not surprising, and it is perhaps premature to conclude that birth order has no effect. More research, more adequately designed to take into account the operation of other features of family structure, is necessary in order to obtain a clear picture of these phenomena.

Other Family Structure Variables

Toman, on the basis of his clinical experience, has suggested that age and sex are the minimum characteristics that must be taken into account in considering family structure.[88] Thus, instead of placing all firstborn children in one category and later-born in another, he identifies four relations as quite distinct from each other. These are (1) older brother versus younger sister, (2) older brother versus younger brother, (3) older sister versus younger brother, and (4) older sister versus younger sister. In the discussion of role learning (see Chapter 15), a study was cited suggesting that consideration of these dyads might be important.[89] The relevant finding was that cross-sex siblings acquire through identification more of the traits of the opposite sex than do like-sex siblings.

Toman stresses a quite different point. He believes that the patterns of relation developed in these family dyads generalize to later relations with persons of the same and the opposite sex. For example, the person who has been an older brother might as an adult be expected to assume considerable responsibility, to be authority-oriented, to be a hard worker, and to relate well to other

87. Sampson, 1965; Warren, 1966; Kammeyer, 1967.   88. Toman, 1969.   89. Brim, 1958.

men. If he has had only a younger brother but not a younger sister, he might well expect his wife to have some of the qualities of his younger brother.

But family structure is more complicated than we have indicated. Toman suggests that the four dyads take one form when the age difference is approximately three to six years, another form when there is only one year's difference between the siblings, and still another when the age difference is great. A further complicating factor is the manner in which the parents relate to the sibling combinations. The sheer amount of interaction between parents and siblings will markedly affect the relation between siblings, according to Toman. If the parents assume all responsibilities themselves, an older brother is unlikely to take on responsibility as part of his role. The effects of sibling relations are likely to be optimal when parents have a laissez-faire attitude toward the children or when they reinforce the particular roles suited to the sibling configuration.

The manner in which parents relate to only children similarly makes quite a difference. The stereotype of the spoiled only child would be likely to apply where parents centered their life on the one child. But this need not occur; for example, some families may have a single child because the parents, particularly the mother, feel inadequate with children, do not wish to be "bothered" with additional children, etc.

Toman is most interested in the implications of family structure during socialization for the new adult family formed by the children when they marry. He suggests that, other things being equal, perpetuation of a role similar to that played during socialization leads to the best adjustment. Thus, an older brother of a younger sister would most readily adjust to a marriage with a woman who had been the younger sister of an older brother. Of course, if either of these earlier relations had been particularly unsatisfactory ones, the prediction would not hold.

Research by Stotland and his associates provides some tentative empirical support for Toman's idea that the pattern of relations developed in the family is carried over into other relations.[90] This, they suggest, occurs because the child learns distinctive social schemata as a result of early family experience. The only child, for instance, confronted with the marked difference in power and status between himself and his parents, will adopt this difference as a basic schemata and perceive all human relations in terms of hierarchical relations.

This brief discussion of family structure illustrates some of the directions that might be taken in research attempting to relate family structure during socialization to later behavior. It also illustrates the paucity of present knowledge, for the discussion has been based largely upon clinical literature rather than research studies.

90. Stotland, Sherman, & Shaver, 1971.

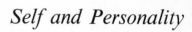

17

Self and Personality

It has been shown that the behavior of an individual is a product of many different factors. Sometimes these have been classified into just two categories: individual and situational. If this is done, an important and troublesome question arises: What is the relative importance of individual factors in comparison with situational factors? This question has received widely varying answers. Their range may be illustrated by presenting two views that are at opposite extremes.

Individual versus Situational Determinants of Behavior

One view is that behavior springs fully from structured dispositions within the individual; the other is that an individual's behavior is determined by the situation he is in. As social psychologists, the authors have for the most part emphasized social conditions under which people in general behave. More attention has been given to situations than to individual characteristics. Yet, social psychologists also have much to contribute to the understanding of individuals. The form which these contributions take depends in part how the difference between the two extreme views is resolved. Below is a description of these views.

Behavior as Individual Dispositions

The lay view of personality is well expressed in Heider's observation that persons are seen as the origins of actions.[1] As noted in Chapter 2, it is much

1. HEIDER, 1944.

simpler to interpret a hostile act as a natural expression of a malevolent person than to understand the situational and circumstantial factors that led him to commit the act. The average man exaggerates the role of the person as causal agent. He fails to see the social forces that make persons act as they do in various situations. But this lay view is also held, in more sophisticated and more qualified form, by many clinical psychologists, personality theorists, and other students of individual behavior. Essentially this conception of individual behavior assumes that the behavior patterns which characterize a person reflect intraindividual structures or mechanisms such as habits, needs, cognitive structures, or, most frequently, personality traits. Miller has described the approach as follows:

> Psychologists have traditionally limited themselves to the individual, engaging in a quest for "genotypic" traits which provide the basis for predicting the subject's behavior with many kinds of people in many situations. For example, the predisposition to anxiety has been considered a general trait. Scores on anxiety tests have been used to predict the capacities for achievement in school, for getting along socially, and for controlling physical movements.[2]

Behavior as a Function of the Situation

Sociologists, anthropologists, and many social psychologists have taken an opposite view. They have argued that a person's behavior is mostly a reflection of the situation he happens to be in. Inherent in the situation are the social forces that shape and determine his behavior at any given moment, although it is recognized that his previous experience with such situations has predisposed him to react in certain ways in the particular circumstances. Their view has been eloquently expressed by Brim:

> When one looks at what is actually going on around him, he finds striking the great variation in the individual's behavior from one situation to another during the course of the day: as the individual moves, for example, from his occupational role, to his various family roles, to his roles with the neighbors in the community, and so on. Recall the familiar example of the German adult male who is meek and subservient to his superiors in his occupational role, but who changes into a domineering, hostile, and aggressive father upon returning to his home. Consider the modern executive who in his occupational role is autonomous, creative, and decisive but who upon going home and taking up his status as husband may become docile and dependent in family matters. What should capture the interest of the student of

2. Reprinted with permission from D. R. MILLER. The study of social relationships: Situation, identity, and social interaction. In S. Koch (Ed.), *Psychology: A study of a science.* Vol. 5. *The process areas, the person, and some applied fields: Their place in psychology and in science.* New York: McGraw-Hill Book Company, 1963. P. 641.

personality, therefore, is not the consistency of individual differences as he looks upon behavior. Rather it is the great adaptability, the truly impressive variation in response to situational demands, which characterizes man as he moves from one situation to another.[3]

Dispositional and Situational Factors in Moral Behavior

Chapter 16 took a kind of middle position between these two extreme views. The attempt to identify conditions that lead to differences in development for different individuals implied that certain persistent individual differences could be found. But it was also found that the same individuals behaved differently in different situations. A child may be dependent at one time and independent at a later stage, and dependency is expressed differently in different relational systems (between mother and child, between peers or siblings, etc.). Acts of aggression and achievement as well as the operation of internal controls appeared to be greatly influenced by features of the situation and by how these were defined by people in interaction.

It might be instructive to look at an intensive study of the role of dispositional and situational factors in moral behavior, conducted almost a half century ago.[4] Chapter 16 discussed the development of cognitive controls in children, based on the assumption that such controls are more fully developed in some children than in others. If that is true, it would seem that honesty, to take one example, would be a general trait or broad disposition. An honest person would behave honestly in many different situations; a dishonest one would behave dishonestly on many occasions.

In this classic study, large numbers of children were exposed to a variety of situations in which they could lie, steal, and cheat. They were also asked to describe their feelings about moral issues in several different settings. The investigators found that, by and large, children responded very differently in different situations and settings. Moreover, the greater the difference in the situations compared, the less consistently the children responded in the different situations.

Moral behavior was surprisingly specific to the particular situation. For example, cheating on one speed test was only moderately associated with cheating on another speed test. Moreover, cheating on different kinds of tests had only a low association, and if the tests were given in different settings (e.g., one in the classroom and the other outside) correlations were even lower. A later analysis of these extensive data, using more modern statistical techniques such as factor analysis, did not change the essential conclusions drawn by the original investigators.[5] Thus, the correct conclusion from this study is that

3. Reprinted with permission from O. G. Brim, Jr. Personality development as role-learning. In I. Iscoe & H. W. Stevenson (Eds.), *Personality development in children.* Austin: University of Texas Press, 1960. P. 137.   4. Hartshorne & May, 1928; Hartshorne, May, & Shuttleworth, 1930.   5. Burton, 1963.

children are only partially consistent from situation to situation in lying, cheating, or stealing, and that the more different the situation, the less likely they are to be consistent.

Mischel points out that these findings anticipate later work on cognitive controls and moral behavior.[6] Relatively little consistency has been found between expressed willingness to postpone smaller rewards for the sake of receiving larger ones later and the actual postponement when given the opportunity.[7] Another study found moral judgments made in different situations to be highly specific with little consistency in the judgments made by the same individual.[8] A review of research in three areas of moral behavior—judgments of standards of right and wrong, resistance to temptation in the absence of external restraint, and indices of remorse and guilt following the performance of a guilt-arousing act—suggested that these areas were almost completely independent of each other.[9] Thus, persons apparently cannot be characterized according to their degree of morality except in a rather ambiguous, unspecified sense.

Individual-in-Situation

These findings do not settle the issue of individual dispositions versus situational determinants. But it turns out that questions about the relative importance of individual and situational determinants are misguided. We know that people behave consistently at times and on some occasions, but we also know that they behave inconsistently at other times and on other occasions. What we need to do is to conceptualize the problem of behavior determinants in a different way. Suppose we start with the assumption that *in virtually every action both the individual and the situation are contributors.* This would lead us to think in terms of *individual-in-situation units.* But this does not take us far enough, because if we consider every individual to be unique and every situation to be specific, we would have too enormous a number of units to deal with. The solution to this problem would be to think of *types* of individuals and *categories* of situations. Our units would then become *type-category* units. Simple examples of types are already at hand from the earlier discussion of social roles: mother, child, teacher, husband, doctor. While these roles do serve as crude illustrations, they leave something out, for role categories are not types of individuals; they are a category of persons who occupy a place in a social relation. In our discussion of social roles, we noted that actors in the same role category may develop different role identities. It is certainly possible, however, to conceive of other more suitable ways of classifying people for purposes of type-category units. Later we will suggest one way of looking at these units.

A partial way of looking at a category of situations which emphasizes *interpersonal* behavior would be to think of the situation category as a type of

6. MISCHEL, 1968.   7. MISCHEL, 1968.   8. JOHNSON, 1962.   9. MISCHEL, 1968.

person. Thus, an interaction unit would be characterized as type-type. Examples would be mother-child, teacher-pupil, doctor-patient. Other ways of characterizing situations will be discussed later. At this point let us recapitulate what we have been saying. We have suggested that individual attributes and categories of situations must be looked at simultaneously—that the joint unit representing some attribute of an individual and a situation must become the focus of attention.

Before moving on to consider some possible conceptualizations, let us look at some more data relevant to this idea. In considering sets of descriptions of behavior in various settings made by oneself, by observers, or by means of tests or other instruments, it is possible to analyze the amount of variation in these descriptions which can be attributed to individuals, to situations, and to individuals-in-situations. The last of these three sources of variance is termed *interaction,* and will be explained as the data are presented.

Argyle and Little discuss a study in which individuals made quantitative estimates of their own behavior when in interaction with various other persons known to them: liked coworker, female friend, boss, etc.[10] They made these ratings in terms of eighteen types of behavior: gossip and chatting, discussing personal problems, relaxed—tense, swearing, expressing love and admiration, looking the other person in the eye, etc. From this information it was possible to estimate the amount of variation in the ratings that could be attributed to the individual raters, to the different interaction situations (the different persons with whom individuals interacted), and the individuals-in-situation interaction.

These estimates of variance are given in Table 17-1. To get some idea of what these figures mean, consider the first row. Close to one-quarter of the variance in gossiping and chatting is explained by the situation—by whom the individual is talking to. As a group, for example, presumably individuals talk more to their spouses or girl friends than to their bosses. Only 10 percent of the variance in gossiping or chatting is attributable to individual differences. Apparently gossiping or chatting is not a trait of individuals that manifests itself across a broad selection of person situations.

Fully two-thirds of the variation in gossiping and chatting is attributed to the individual-in-situation interaction. This means that individuals differ in the amount of talking they do, depending upon which class of person they are talking to: One individual talks most to his wife and least to his boss, another individual talks most to a male friend and least to a disliked coworker, etc. *The amount of talking depends primarily upon who the talker is and to whom he is talking.*

In general, though the amount of individual variance is greater for some actions, an examination of the mean estimates at the bottom of the table shows

10. ARGYLE & LITTLE, 1972.

that individual actions account for only 16 percent of the variance, while situation variance and individual-in-situation variance each account for about 40 percent.

Table 17-1   *Variance attributable to individuals, situations, and individuals-in-situations*

	PERCENT VARIANCE		
NATURE OF INTERACTION	INDIVIDUALS	SITUATIONS	INDIVIDUAL-IN-SITUATION
1. Gossip and chat versus little gossip and chat	10	23	67
2. Discussion of personal problems versus no such discussion	12	53	35
3. Formal and rule-governed behavior versus informal behavior	4	62	34
4. Relaxes versus is tense	12	56	32
5. Swears versus never swears	16	34	50
6. Often refers to sex versus never refers to sex	7	56	37
7. Takes great care with personal appearance, etc., versus takes less care	38	19	43
8. Is concerned about whether the other thinks well of him versus is unconcerned	13	52	35
9. Openly shows emotional states versus conceals emotional states	17	35	48
10. Conceals anger and irritation versus shows them freely	36	13	51
11. Freely expresses love, admiration, etc., versus conceals them	15	46	39
12. Openly reveals ambitions and financial situation versus does not reveal them	6	62	32
13. Doing things for the other depends on reciprocity	19	37	44
14. Looks the other person in the eye versus avoids looking him in the eye	30	27	43
15. Sits or stands very close versus stays at a distance	15	52	33
16. Has a relaxed posture versus has a rather tense posture	19	38	43
17. Enjoys being with the other person versus does not enjoy it	6	68	26
18. Is very much at ease versus is very ill at ease	15	52	33
Mean percent variation	16	44	40

Source: Adapted with permission from Basil Blackwell, Ltd., Oxford, and Argyle, M., & B. R. Little. Do personality traits apply to social behavior? *Journal for the Theory of Social Behavior,* 1972, 2, 1–36.

This study is not presented to prove that individual variance is unimportant or to provide firm quantitative estimates of each type of variance. Considered as evidence, it is of limited value in that estimates of behavior are made by self-ratings, which may be considerably different from observational ratings. Rather it is discussed in order to suggest alternative conceptualizations to the idea that individuals are the source of most of the variation in behavior, and to alert us to the importance of situations and to the concept of individuals-in-situations. It may be added, however, that reviews of a variety of evidence on this issue by Mischel and by Argyle and Little strongly favor situations and individuals-in-situations as sources of variance in behavior.[11]

Finally, there is one way in which this conception of individual-situation or type-category units may be too narrow. Situations have been represented in this example by "other persons." Yet situations can be readily conceived of in another sense; for example, a mother and child can be thought of as interacting in church, in the privacy of their home, in their neighbor's house, and so on. Besides these interaction settings, there are situations that partly determine the types of interaction. A mother and child may be playing a game, or the mother may be feeding, teaching, or punishing the child, and so on. Ultimately what is needed is a unit that is classified in terms of four categories: individual type, person category interacted with, setting in which interaction occurs, and type of situation (game, entertainment, work, love, etc.). Curiously, neither psychologists nor sociologists have given much attention to conceptualizing situations in the sense meant here, and they will not be dealt with further here. Some exceptions to this generalization are the discussions of *behavior settings* by Barker and his colleagues, preliminary attempts at classification by Krause and by Frederiksen, and a classification of *episodes* by Harré and Secord.[12] As shown throughout this book, social psychologists have looked at "structures," such as the affect, power, and status structures, and these have some relevance to situations. But these structures represent too high a level of abstraction to aid in resolving the present issue; they leave out too much of the situation.

Later in this chapter a variation of the individual-in-situation unit will be discussed, the idea of an *interpersonal system* comprising a characteristic that an individual attributes to himself, his interpretation of his own behavior in relation to that attribute, and his idea of another person's view of that attribute in him. This concept has been discussed elsewhere by the authors under the rubric of *interpersonal congruency theory.*[13]

Interpersonal systems are a product of a creative synthesis arising out of the interaction of the individual with other persons in various situations and set-

11. MISCHEL, 1968; ARGYLE & LITTLE, 1972.   *12.* BARKER, 1968; KRAUSE, 1970; FREDERIKSEN, 1972; HARRÉ & SECORD, 1972.   *13.* SECORD & BACKMAN, 1961, 1965.

tings. Entering into this synthesis are individual attributes, the individual's position in a system of interpersonal relations, the constraints and possibilities in the moment-to-moment situations in which he finds himself, and the constraints imposed by cultural forces. Prior to discussing these interpersonal systems in detail, the concept of the self and how it develops and functions will be explained.

Nature of the Self Concept

One consequence of being human is that a person becomes an object to himself. Because of his possession of language and a superior intelligence, man has a unique capacity for thinking about his body, his behavior, and his appearance to other persons. Each of us has a set of cognitions and feelings toward himself. The terms most commonly applied to this set of elements are *self* and *self concept*.

It is convenient to think of a person's attitudes toward himself as having three aspects: the cognitive, the affective, and the behavioral. The *cognitive* component represents the content of the self, illustrated by such thoughts as, "I am intelligent, honest, sincere, ambitious, tall, strong, overweight, etc." The *affective* component represents one's feelings about oneself and is more difficult to illustrate, because feelings about oneself are usually not expressed in words. It would include a rather general feeling of self-worth, as well as evaluations of more specific cognitive aspects or other aspects of self. For example, a woman may dislike her nose, which is slightly crooked. The *behavioral* component is the tendency to act toward oneself in various ways: A person may behave in a self-deprecating or a self-indulgent manner, or he may show oversensitivity to certain of his characteristics.

Social Nature of the Self

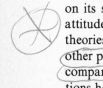

A tradition going back to the earliest formulations on the self is the emphasis on its social nature. While *all* attitudes are rooted in social experience, self-attitudes are thought to be a product of interaction in a special sense. First, theories of self-development emphasize the individual's perception of how other persons see him. Second, they focus attention on the process by which he compares his ideas about himself with social norms, that is, with the expectations he believes other persons have concerning what he should be like. These features were stressed in one of the earliest treatments of the self by Cooley, who likened our perceptions of how others see us to the reflections of a looking glass. Referring to this "looking-glass self," Cooley noted:

> As we see our face, figure, and dress in the glass, and are interested in them because they are ours, and pleased or otherwise with them according as they do or do not answer to what we should like them to be; so in imagination we

perceive in another's mind some thought of our appearance, manners, aims, deeds, character, friends, and so on, and are variously affected by it.

A self-ideal of this sort seems to have three principal elements: the imagination of our appearance to the other person, the imagination of his judgment of that appearance, and some sort of self-feeling, such as pride or motification. The comparison with a looking-glass hardly suggests the second element, the imagined judgment, which is quite essential. The thing that moves us to pride or shame is not the mere mechanical reflection of ourselves, but an imputed sentiment, the imagined effect of this reflection upon another's mind.[14]

SELF AND ROLE   Cooley's idea of self as emerging out of reflected views held by other persons was elaborated further by Mead, by Goffman, and by others.[15] The process by which the self concept is developed through social interaction may in part be seen as the assignment of the person to a series of social roles. As an individual moves through the social structure, he is placed in various role categories. He is first a baby, later a small boy. He is a dull pupil, John's little brother, and Tommy's best friend. As he performs these roles, his self concept is influenced by the ways in which his role partners see him and by the manner in which he enacts these roles. For each role, he learns the expectations that other persons associate with the category, and he forms a role identity corresponding to each. In a sense, the picture he has of himself is one with many facets or aspects, each corresponding to a particular identity. As shown later, however, they do not remain entirely independent; certain processes modify these aspects of self. Goffman has vividly described the impact of role expectations on the individual:

> It is important to note that in performing a role the individual must see to it that the impressions of him that are conveyed in the situation are compatible with role-appropriate personal qualities effectively imputed to him: a judge is supposed to be deliberate and sober; a pilot, in a cockpit, to be cool; a bookkeeper to be accurate and neat in doing his work. These personal qualities, effectively imputed and effectively claimed, combine with a position's title, when there is one, to provide a basis of self-image for the incumbent and a basis for the image that his role others will have for him. A self, then, virtually awaits the individual entering a position; he need only conform to the pressures on him and he will find a *me* ready-made for him.[16]

When children are asked to describe themselves, the impact of their parent's definitions of them often are readily seen in the results. They have formed a rudimentary self out of the images that these significant other persons have of

14. Reprinted with permission from C. H. COOLEY. *Human nature and the social order.* New York: Charles Scribner's Sons, 1902. Reprinted: New York: The Free Press of Glencoe, Inc., 1956. P. 152.   *15.* MEAD, 1934; GOFFMAN, 1959, 1961.   16. Reprinted with permission from E. GOFFMAN. *Encounters: Two studies in the sociology of interaction.* Indianapolis: The Bobbs-Merrill Company, Inc., 1961. Pp. 87-88.

them. Adults, however, are likely to make a greater use of various socially defined categories. These differences are well illustrated by the work of Kuhn and his associates. They administered the Twenty Statements Test, an unstructured self-measurement instrument which asked subjects to make twenty statements in answer to the question "Who Am I?" Reproduced below are the responses of a fourth-grade girl and a university senior.[17] Kuhn and his associates found an increasing use of social categories with age. At seven years of age, only one-fourth of the twenty statements were so classified, but at age twenty-four, about half were social categories.

RESPONSES OF A 4TH GRADE GIRL (ORIGINAL SPELLING RETAINED)	RESPONSES OF A UNIVERSITY SENIOR
I boss to much.	I am of the female sex.
I get mad a my sisters.	My age is 20.
I am a show off.	I am from [city and state].
I interupt to much.	I have two parents.
I talk to much.	My home is happy.
I wast time.	I am happy.
Sometimes I am a bad sport.	I have been to 4 colleges.
I fiddle around.	I will graduate in [month and year].
I am careless at times.	I have a brother.
I forget.	I am a [sorority name].
Sometimes I don't do what mother tells me to.	I am in the Waves Officer School.
I tattle on my sisters.	I attend church.
Sometimes I am unkind.	I live a normal life.
	I am interested in sports.
	I am a [department major].
	I am attractive.
	I have high moral standards.
	I am an adjusted person.
	I am of the middle class.

This corresponds to the increasing number of role categories occupied as the child grows up.

A more subtle learning than that just illustrated also occurs as the individual assumes various roles: His self-regard is shaped by the feelings which other persons have toward him. As a baby and small child, he is likely to be loved, an experience that plants the rudiments of a positive self-regard. (The above example of the fourth-grade girl is rather atypical of the frequent use of negative self-attributes.) Attitudes expressed toward him by successive role partners as he proceeds through life's stages add to and develop further the affective elements in his self-image.

That an individual's view of himself is influenced by the reflected impres-

17. KUHN, 1960.

sions of other persons has been extensively documented by correlational, longitudinal, and experimental studies.[18] These studies generally show a relation between an individual's perceptions of how others judge him and his self conception. Also related to his self conception is how others actually judge him. Often, however, the observed relations are small, and suggest that the lookingglass conception of the self is a greatly oversimplified notion of the process through which the self develops. Some of the reasons why these studies show only a modest or in some instances only a slight relation between a person's self conception and that of other persons studied will be briefly suggested below.

First, it should be clear that people are influenced by many groups other than the particular group included in a given study. Some groups may exert influence on the person's self concept even though he is not a member of the group.[19] Frequently, such reference groups are those which the individual aspires to belong to but as yet is not a member. In fact, one study suggests that people systematically shift their choice of *significant others* (a term for a person whose reflected views of an individual have an impact on his self concept) to those persons who will be of greater importance at the next stage of the life cycle.[20] This study also suggests that the significance of another's view of self will depend in part on the aspect of self in question. The opinions of some significant others are relevant largely to the performance of a specific role, while others have a more pervasive influence. For example, a baseball coach's opinion of one's ball-playing ability may be respected, but not his view of one's intellectual capacities. Whether a particular other person will have influence depends on the many conditions discussed earlier under the topic of social influence (see Chapters 3, 4, and 5).[21]

ROLE IDENTITIES   Most persons develop positive self-esteem because they are favorably regarded and loved by others. This positive evaluation accounts for the somewhat ideal character of role identities. The discussion of role performance in Chapter 13 emphasized that a person's role portrayal is strongly influenced by his idealized conception of himself in that role, i.e., how he likes to think of himself being or acting in that role. In part, these identities are shaped by the culturally prescribed expectations and attributes which other persons hold for any individual occupying a particular social position. In part, however, role identity consists of unique elaborations that an individual has been able to work out in his interactions with others during the course of his life. Thus, the individual actively enters into the creation and maintenance of the self. His self conceptions are not by any means entirely a reflection of the definitions of him by other persons.

18. Manis, 1955; Miyamoto & Dornbusch, 1956; Videbeck, 1960; Reeder, Donohue, & Biblarz, 1960; Maehr, Mansing, & Nafzger, 1962; Backman & Secord, 1962; Backman, Secord, & Peirce, 1963; Mannheim, 1966; Kemper, 1966; Quarantelli & Cooper, 1966; Doherty & Secord, 1971.   *19.* Mannheim, 1966. *20.* Denzin, 1966.   *21.* Sherwood, 1965.

Summary: The Nature of the Self

The self is acquired from the views that other persons have toward an individual, and from his active reconstructions of their views occurring in the process of interaction. Cooley, in his concept of the looking-glass self, suggests that an individual forms an opinion of how he appears to the other person, guesses how that person judges his appearance, and reacts with a positive or negative self-feeling to the imagined judgment. The process by which the self concept is developed through social interaction may in part be seen as the assignment of the person to a series of social roles as he moves through the social structure. As he performs these roles, he learns the expectations that other persons associate with the category, and he forms a role identity corresponding to each. These role identities are somewhat idealized conceptions of role performance. They are not simply reflections of the cultural prescriptions held by other persons, but reflect unique elaborations which the individual has fashioned in his interaction with others throughout his life. Thus, the self is not simply a reflection of the definitions of other persons, but is a creative synthesis arising out of the interaction process, and it is repeatedly resynthesized as a result of critical new experiences.

Stability of Self and Individual Behavior

It has been emphasized that the individual being socialized is not a passive object molded and shaped by persons who are older, more powerful, wiser, and more experienced. Even casual observation of small children reveals that they are not so easily molded in this fashion: They often stubbornly resist parental influence. In part, such resistance is due to biological characteristics of the organism, including such factors as energy level and temperament. In addition, once the self concept is established and certain behavior patterns are adopted, conditions arise that cause the individual to be less readily influenced and to resist change activity. The present section will show how the *person may be immersed in a social environment of interacting forces and still behave in a distinctive manner that at many points is opposed to these forces.*

This view recognizes stability over time in an individual's behavior but attempts to explain it in terms of stabilities in his relations to other persons. In part, constancies in a person's behavior result from his participation in various social systems; in part, however, they are due to individual mechanisms that stabilize his interpersonal environment. This section will present the mechanisms and show how they maintain behavior unchanged. A later section will show how forces in the social system create stability and maintain behavior, and also how they lead to changes in self and behavior.

An Interpersonal Theory of the Self

The individual is not passive, but is an *active agent* in maintaining a stable interpersonal environment. To elaborate on this point, elements from a theory published elsewhere by the authors will be introduced.[22] The attempt here will be to show that circumstances may put pressure on the individual to change, but active efforts on his part maintain stability of self and behavior. Certain of his characteristics contribute to this process, such as his concept of himself, his individual ways of perceiving other persons, and his learned behavior patterns.

The unit of analysis has three components, consisting of (1) an aspect of *P*'s self, (2) *P*'s interpretation of his behavior relevant to that aspect, and (3) his beliefs about how another person *(O)* behaves toward him and feels toward him with regard to that aspect. The assumption is made that *P attempts to maintain a state of congruency between these three components. A state of congruency exists when the behaviors of P and O imply definitions of self congruent with relevant aspects of his self concept.*

Three forms of congruency may be illustrated: congruency by implication, congruency by validation, and congruency by comparison. In congruency by implication, *P* may perceive that *O* sees him as possessing a particular characteristic corresponding to an aspect of his self concept. A girl who regards herself as beautiful may perceive that another person also thinks she is beautiful. In congruency by validation, the behavior or other characteristics of *O* allow or call for behavior on the part of *P* that confirms a component of self. For example, an individual who regards himself as strong and protective is especially able to behave in this fashion when he interacts with a person who is dependent. In congruency by comparison, the behavior or attributes of *O* suggest by comparison that *P* possesses a particular self-component. Thus a *P* who regards himself as highly intelligent may choose to interact with those of lesser intelligence.

Stabilizing Mechanisms in Interaction

According to interpersonal congruency theory, the individual actively uses techniques or mechanisms for maintaining his interpersonal environment so as to maximize congruency. These include cognitive restructuring, selective evaluation, selective interaction, evocation of congruent responses, and congruency by comparison.

COGNITIVE RESTRUCTURING   The interpersonal environment enters into congruency only as it is seen by the individual. In instances where the actual expectations of other persons are not congruent with the person's self concept

22. SECORD & BACKMAN, 1961, 1965.

or behavior, it is sometimes possible for him simply to *misperceive how the others see him* in order to achieve congruency without a change in self or behavior. The individual may also *misinterpret his own behavior* so as to achieve maximum congruency with an aspect of his self concept and his perception of the other. Finally, he may *restructure the situation* in order to change the evaluation of his behavior.

A number of correlational studies have found that the correspondence between self as seen by the individual and as he thinks others see him is greater than the actual correspondence between the self concept and the views held by other persons.

The results of an experimental study illustrate some of the forms that restructuring takes.[23] College students rated themselves and another person in their class on a variety of traits. They were then exposed to fictitious ratings of themselves which in varying degrees involved unfavorable evaluations. In different instances, they were led to believe that the ratings came from an authoritative source, from a friend, or from a stranger. Some shifts in the direction of evaluating the self more negatively occurred, but in addition, students distorted the evaluations in a favorable direction when asked to recall them. When given the opportunity, they also dissociated the devaluations from the source by denying that those evaluations were actually made by the other persons. By and large, their reactions were more marked when the degree of devaluation was the greatest and when the ratings were perceived as coming from an authoritative source or from a friend rather than from a stranger. Studies cited in the above discussion of the looking-glass self as well as several others support the general principle that individuals process information about the self in a manner to support congruency.[24]

Restructuring is frequently involved in achieving congruency between self and behavior. Most persons view themselves favorably, as good and moral persons. When they perform a wrong or questionable act, creating incongruency, they are apt to restructure the situation cognitively so that the act in question is no longer incongruent. Typically, cognitive restructuring involves either defining the situation so that the act is no longer viewed as bad or perceiving the situation as one in which a person can feel that he is not fully responsible for his behavior and its consequences.[25] In terms of congruency theory this may involve misperceiving the attributes of the other or the nature of the act, or it may involve misinterpreting one's own behavior.

Examples of this kind of restructuring are found in Matza's suggestion that delinquents learn a variety of techniques of neutralization that allow them to behave in a delinquent fashion without suffering guilt.[26] These include cognitive restructuring of one's own behavior and attributing certain characteristics to the other person. Examples are denial of responsibility for the act; denial

23. HARVEY, KELLEY, & SHAPIRO, 1957.   24. HARVEY, 1962; VAN OSTRAND, 1963.   25. SCOTT & LYMAN, 1968.   26. MATZA, 1964.

that the act is injurious; perceiving the victim as not a victim but the object of rightful retaliation; perceiving that other persons are as bad as oneself and are hypocritical when they condemn him; and finally, perceiving that the act, though wrong, was in accordance with some higher loyalty such as helping out a friend. Other social psychologists have offered typologies of accounts that individuals give to explain their behavior when it is incongruent with their self concepts.[27] Many of these accounts take the form of restoring interpersonal congruency.

Experiments in which individuals were led to believe that they had hurt another person similarly demonstrate restoration of congruency through cognitive restructuring.[28] Participants who delivered electric shocks to a victim as part of an experiment minimized their estimates of the pain experienced by him, especially if they were allowed to make their own decision whether to deliver the shock or not. When it was difficult to minimize the pain, they often restructured the situation by increasing their feeling of obligation to administer shocks, placing the responsibility on the experimenter instead of themselves.

Experimental studies such as these generally introduce conditions which block some ways of achieving congruency and allow others. In everyday situations, a variety of factors operate to favor one or the other resolution of the dilemma of having behaved contrary to one's self conception. While some of these factors have been suggested by the discussion of laboratory studies, the evidence for other factors is absent or at best indirect.

How an actor perceives a situation so as to maximize congruency will depend on characteristics of the actor, the act, and the victim, as well as features of the situation that affect the opportunity to misperceive in a fashion leading to congruency. Characteristics of the actor are important largely as they affect the opportunity to legitimately feel not responsible. These include not only personality characteristics but also constraints and possibilities inherent in the role expectations and role identities that become salient in a given situation. Thus, males may claim nonresponsibility because they were intoxicated. For a female such a claim is less acceptable, in traditional circles at least; however, she may plead illness or irrationality and find her claims accepted by herself and others more readily than if she were a male.

One's position in the power and status structure may provide opportunities or barriers to the claim of nonresponsibility. A lower-echelon employee can escape responsibility with the claim, "I only work here," but a chief executive in an organization realizes that "The buck stops here." A recent analysis of reactions to the trial of Lt. William Calley, convicted of participating in the My Lai massacre in Vietnam, found that many persons were critical of the trial on the grounds that Lieutenant Calley was simply following orders and thus was not responsible.[29] This reasoning was particularly found among persons from

27. Scott & Lyman, 1968; Lofland, 1969.   *28.* Brock & Buss, 1962.   *29.* Kelman, 1971.

lower socioeconomic groups, whose low position in the power structure would make it easy for them to view the My Lai incident in these terms.

A number of personality characteristics may influence the degree to which an individual will feel not responsible. Persons differ in the degree to which they characteristically attribute the causes of events to fate, luck, or other external forces or to their own efforts. Personality characteristics may also affect the degree to which the person achieves congruency in ways other than the attribution of nonresponsibility. When an act is performed on behalf of a friend, individuals with a particularistic orientation may be more prone than individuals with a universalistic orientation to justify conduct contrary to a favorable self-image. Similarly individuals at different stages of moral development may be expected to use different ways of handling inconsistencies between self and behavior.

A number of characteristics of an act may be systematically related to the use of various cognitive devices to resolve incongruency. If an act has unknown or disputed consequences, one may engage in it without viewing it as contrary to one's self-image. Many individuals may persist in smoking, contrary to their image of themselves as rational persons who would not do something to injure their health, if they believe that the adverse affects attributed to smoking have not been conclusively established. Similarly, the degree to which the frequency of a specific behavior is unknown makes it relatively easy for persons to convince themselves that engaging in such behavior is not inconsistent with a favorable self-image since "everybody" probably does the same thing (congruency by comparison). Finally, the degree to which an act is seen as under voluntary control will influence acceptance of responsibility for the act and resultant feelings of incongruity.

SELECTIVE EVALUATION   In the process of selective evaluation, an individual maximizes congruency or minimizes incongruency by altering the evaluation of self, behavior, or the other person in a positive or negative direction. For example, behaviors or attitudes of persons who are of no importance to the individual are not considered incongruent even though they are at variance with his self concept or his behavior. Thus, an individual may maximize congruency by favorably evaluating those who behave congruently toward him and devaluating those who behave incongruently. Similarly, where an individual's behavior toward another person is incongruent with his self concept, he may sometimes minimize incongruency by devaluing the other person (as in devaluing a victim to whom he has done harm).

Some correlational support for selective evaluation was found in a study of a sorority, where girls who were liked most by a member were those whom she perceived as having the most congruent views of her and who actually had the most congruent views.[30] A number of experimental studies provide more direct

30. BACKMAN & SECORD, 1962.

support.[31] They demonstrate that when an individual is negatively evaluated by another person, he reduces his liking for him. In a sense, he discredits the source of the negative evaluation, thus eliminating the incongruency.

It has been demonstrated several times that individuals may reduce incongruency between their self conception as a good person and doing harm to another person by perceiving the victim less favorably and thus perhaps more deserving of the harm-doer's action.[32] One study is of particular interest for congruency theory because self concepts were experimentally varied.[33] Some participants received personality evaluations designed to enhance their self esteem while others received evaluations that (temporarily) lowered their self-esteem. Some were given the choice of delivering or not delivering a series of electric shocks to another person, while others were given no choice. Having choice would increase responsibility for this incongruent behavior and increase the pressure to resolve the incongruency. Where individuals had a choice, those with the more positive self conception felt *less* friendly toward the victim after they had administered the shocks. Thus, devaluing him is one of the ways of resolving the incongruency. Those having no choice did not modify their feeling of friendliness after delivering the shock, presumably because they did not feel responsible for their behavior. Similarly, those with low self-esteem did not change their friendship rating.

Characteristics of the victim and the situation set limits on restructuring. Some experimental evidence suggests that individuals are less apt to misperceive if they expect to be confronted with evidence contrary to their perceptions.[34] When the victim is generally disliked by other persons, an individual is more likely to devalue him because the group supports it. Finally, where barriers to empathy with the victim exist (as where he is categorized as highly dissimilar), devaluation of the victim and misperception of the consequences of devaluation are maximized.[35]

Congruency is also a function of the importance of the aspect of self relevant to behavior or to interaction with another person. If an *insignificant* aspect of self is at variance with a person's perception of his behavior or that of another, incongruency is minimized. Consequently, an individual may maximize congruency by altering the values placed on various aspects of self so that the aspects which are in agreement with his perceptions of his behavior and that of others are most highly valued. Similarly, he may devalue aspects of self which are not congruent with components of his behavior and the behavior of others. An example from McCandless illustrates the process with respect to self and behavior:

Let us take, for example, a boy who has entered junior high school, when for the first time clear choices of activity must be made, some being sacrificed so that others may be pursued. He has equally strong and equally valued con-

31. HARVEY, KELLEY, & SHAPIRO, 1957; HOWARD & BERKOWITZ, 1958; HARVEY, 1962.   *32.* DAVIS & JONES, 1960; GLASS, 1964.   *33.* GLASS, 1964.   *34.* DAVIS & JONES, 1960.   *35.* DAVIS & JONES, 1960.

ceptions of himself as an athlete and as a scholar, but must choose between two activities: debate and basketball. He chooses debate. It might be predicted that he will sharply devalue the importance of basketball, and possibly of all sports; but will sharply upgrade the importance of debate and other types of intellectual activity. The actual *direction* of his conception of himself as an athlete may not shift, but the *value* to him of this facet of his self-concept will change in a negative direction. Conversely, the value of intellectual activities will become greater, and the importance of the intellectual facet of his self-concept will increase.[36]

SELECTIVE INTERACTION   Another important but easily overlooked means by which an individual may maintain interpersonal congruency is through selectively interacting with certain persons and not others. More precisely he elects to interact with those persons with whom he can most readily establish a congruent state. For example, if he regards himself as especially intelligent, he interacts frequently with persons who respect his intelligence or who allow him to exercise it. In this manner he avoids a good deal of strain which might be placed on his self concept if he were to interact indiscriminately. By making friends of such persons, he creates an important and durable source of support for congruent interactions. In a study of a sorority, girls interacted most frequently with those whom they perceived as confirming their self concepts to the greatest extent.[37]

In the discussion of role strain in Chapter 14, a number of studies were cited indicating that strain arises when a role category is incompatible with an individual's characteristics. This suggests that he is likely to avoid entering such positions and to seek more compatible role categories. Several additional studies indicating that selective interaction contributes to congruency may be cited.

One study demonstrates that teachers who have been teaching for many years have smaller discrepancies between their self concept and their perception of the teacher role than do inexperienced teachers.[38] This did not appear to be a function of change in self or in perception of the teacher role, but was apparently owing to the tendency of those with larger discrepancies between self and the teacher role to become dissatisfied and drop out.

Studies of occupational socialization also support this notion of selective interaction. They suggest that selection of a particular occupation is affected by the individual's conception of himself in relation to the characteristics of these occupational roles. A study of specialty choice among medical students illustrates this phenomenon.[39] The personality of the student who picked out a particular specialty was found to be similar to the personality of practitioners in that specialty. To illustrate, among the five specialties studied, pediatricians

---

36. Reprinted with permission from B. R. McCANDLESS. *Children and adolescents.* New York: Holt, Rinehart and Winston, Inc., 1961. P. 201.   *37.* BACKMAN & SECORD, 1962.   *38.* HOE, 1962.   *39.* STERN & SCANLON, 1958.

were socially aggressive, assertive, and demonstrative, whereas obstetricians and gynecologists were more restrained, self-conscious, and diffident. If we assume that these occupational roles create conditions congenial to the prevailing personality characteristics of people found in the role, then the selection of the role by those having similar personalities creates conditions requiring little change in self. In another investigation, college students majoring in art, education, engineering, and nursing were shown to have self concepts resembling the attributes composing the occupational image associated with each of the majors.[40] For example, attributes distinguishing the image of artist included the following: disorderly, dissatisfied, dramatic, hostile, imaginative, rebellious, self-indulgent, unconventional. Compared with nonart majors, art majors saw themselves as more like the artist image on most of these traits. Presumably this congruency contributed to their choice of art as a major.

A longitudinal study of college roommates provides further support for selective interaction.[41] Views of self, reflected self, and actual views held by one's roommate were obtained in October and again in May of the following year. More initial and subsequent congruency between self and reflected self was found for those roommates who stayed together when given a choice. For the satisfied roommates, there was also more consensus between the self-rating and the roommate's rating. The possibility that these findings might be due to a greater similarity between satisfied pairs of roommates than between dissatisfied pairs was ruled out by an analysis demonstrating that similarity did not relate to satisfaction with or selection of a roomate. Earlier studies, while not conducted in the context of congruency theory, are nevertheless consistent with the principle of selective interaction.[42]

Finally, individuals choose to interact with persons whose behavior permits them to behave in a congruent way. In one study, the needs of pairs of friends were compared.[43] Individuals who perceived themselves as high on a particular need perceived their friends to be high on a need that would require them to behave in a congruent way. For example, individuals who saw themselves as high on the *need for succorance* (a need for emotional support and help) viewed their close friends as high on the *need for nurturance* (a need to give help and support to others).

RESPONSE EVOCATION AND SELF-PRESENTATION   An individual also maintains congruency by developing techniques that evoke congruent responses from other persons. Goffman has suggested that in everyday interaction a man presents himself and his activities so as to guide and control the impressions others form of him.[44] These actions may represent deliberate calculations or the actor may be quite unaware of the effects he produces.

A number of clinical, field, and experimental studies have focused on these

40. BACKMAN & SECORD, 1968*b*.   *41.* DOHERTY & SECORD, 1971.   *42.* NEWCOMB, 1961; BROXTON, 1963.   *43.* SECORD & BACKMAN, 1964*b*.   *44.* GOFFMAN, 1959.

forms of response evocation. Thus Berne describes a patient who frequently attempted in group therapy to elicit from others support for her view as a person who was unjustly criticized and misunderstood:

> The point was that this sort of thing happened regularly to Camellia. As she saw it, people were always misunderstanding her and criticizing her. In reality, it was she who made a practice of misunderstanding people and criticizing them. Rosita perceived correctly that she herself hadn't criticized Camellia and that on the contrary Camellia had implicitly criticized her by weeping. She retained . . . control of the situation by not allowing herself to be drawn unfairly into the parental role of comforting and apologizing to Camellia. . . . Camellia had demonstrated more than once that she was adroit in eliciting pity and apologies. The educated members were now becoming aware that they were being manipulated into giving her something she did not deserve, and the purpose of this segment of the group at that moment was to make Camellia aware of what she was doing.[45]

Weinstein has suggested a number of strategies that individuals may use to elicit or block responses from others that provide or disrupt congruency.[46] Thus, an individual may prevent another from questioning his accuracy or expertise by using a *preapology*, "Off the top of my head, I'd say. . . ." He may also employ an *icon*, a linguistic device for confirming a preferred identity. The use of name dropping, place dropping, or experience dropping, as in, "As I told the boss . . ." or "Back at Harvard . . ." illustrate this form of self-presentation. Finally, Weinstein has noted that an individual may cast the other person in a role that calls for certain desired behaviors. A child may say, "You're my big brother so you should help me fix my bicycle."

A number of lines of research have been concerned with the determinants of self-presentation. One line involves studies of embarrassment.[47] This psychological state has been conceptualized as a reaction to loss of self-esteem resulting from the perception of negative reactions from others. Behavior designed to avoid or restore loss of self-esteem has been termed *facework*.[48] These studies, along with those concerned with reactions to failure or anticipated failure,[49] as well as to unfavorable evaluation from others,[50] indicate that people react to such situations by attempting to restore a favorable impression of themselves through favorable self-presentation.[51]

CONGRUENCY BY COMPARISON   Incongruency may be partially resolved through a comparison process. An individual possessing an undesirable trait, for example, may exaggerate the extent to which other persons have the same

45. Reprinted with permission from E. BERNE, *Transactional analysis in psychotherapy: A systematic individual and social psychiatry.* New York: Grove Press, Inc., 1961. P. 95.   46. WEINSTEIN, 1966, 1969.   47. GROSS & STONE, 1964; MODIGLIANI, 1968.   48. GOFFMAN, 1955; ARCHIBALD & COHEN, 1971; BROWN, 1970.   49. JONES, GERGEN, GUMPERT, & THIBAUT, 1965.   50. HARDYCK, 1968.   51. MARACEK & METTEE, 1972.

trait, thus minimizing its importance in himself by comparing himself with them. In one investigation, participants in an experiment were led to believe that they were high on a trait that they had previously indicated as undesirable.[52] They had previously ranked both themselves and their friends on a series of traits including the manipulated one, which had been ranked low. When given an opportunity to rank themselves and their friends again, they saw the objectionable trait as more characteristic not only of themselves but of their friends as well. By misperceiving this trait as prominent in their friends, they could reason that they did not have the trait to an undue degree. Similar results were obtained in another study.[53]

Individuals may also reduce incongruency by selecting certain persons as objects of comparison. In an experiment, participants were given information leading them to believe they were quite hostile, and were allowed to select one person whose score they might see.[54] They chose a person from the most hostile group, thus making themselves appear less hostile by comparison. That individuals may not necessarily choose others worse off than themselves for comparison under all conditions, however, has also been shown. Participants were induced to have high or low motivation to score favorably on a personality test.[55] Compared to those less strongly motivated, those highly motivated chose to a greater degree to compare themselves with someone who scored above them. This appears to contradict the immediately preceding findings and common sense as well. Why would those most motivated to achieve subjective feelings of success compare themselves with a person who could be expected to provide a failure experience? Wheeler suggests one possible answer:

> One explanation of the paradox is as follows: When an individual is highly motivated, he assumes similarity with someone who appears to be slightly superior in the ability in question. By comparing his ability with that of the slightly superior individual, the comparer is attempting to confirm the similarity he has assumed. The comparer is attempting to prove to himself that he is almost as good as the very good ones; he would experience subjective feelings of failure only if he found a greater ability difference than expected.[56]

In sum, in his interactions with other persons the individual strives to achieve congruency by a variety of methods or processes. They are as follows:

1. Cognitive restructuring. An individual may misperceive another person's behavior so as to achieve congruency with aspects of his behavior and self concept. He may also misinterpret his own behavior so as to achieve maximum congruency with an aspect of his self concept and his perception of the other person.

52. Secord, Backman, & Eachus, 1964.   *53.* Bramel, 1962.   *54.* Hakmiller, 1966.   *55.* Wheeler, 1966.   *56.* Wheeler, 1966, p. 30.

2. *Selective evaluation.* An individual may maximize congruency by evaluating more favorably those components that are congruent; he may minimize incongruency by devaluating those components that are incongruent.

3. *Selective interaction.* An individual may maximize engagement in congruent patterns of interpersonal behavior by selecting and interacting with those persons whose behavior requires a minimum change from previously congruent interpersonal situations in which he has engaged.

4. *Response evocation and self-presentation.* An individual may behave so as to evoke congruent responses from other persons.

5. *Congruency by comparison.* When a person is confronted with an incongruent evaluation, he may accept the evaluation but minimize the effect of incongruency by attributing the trait to significant others. Thus, its presence in himself is lessened by comparison; he has no more of it and no less of it than other people.

Affective Congruency versus Self-enhancement

As noted earlier, the concept of congruency may be applied to feelings as well as to cognitive elements. A state of affective congruency exists when P believes that O feels toward him as P feels toward himself, either in regard to himself as a whole or in regard to some aspect of self. Especially relevant here is the positive or negative quality of the feeling: Is it approval, liking, admiration, or love? Or is it disapproval, hatred, or contempt? In another form of affective congruency, P has comparable feelings toward an aspect of self and his corresponding behavior. Affective congruency is maintained by the same mechanisms as those previously described for cognitive congruency. Persons may misperceive how others feel about them. They may selectively associate with and selectively evaluate other persons. They may attempt to evoke congruent feelings from other persons.

One of the most interesting forms of affective congruency occurs when P negatively evaluates some aspect of himself or his behavior and seeks congruent behavior from other persons which, in this case, would be a *negative evaluation.* This runs counter to the common observation, supported by research, that people generally react with satisfaction to positive evaluations and with hostility or resentment to negative ones. The general preference for positive evaluation—the desire for self-enhancement—can, however, be explained in terms of affective congruency. The only assumption necessary is that most people have positive feelings about themselves.

Various studies that demonstrate the desire for self-enhancement are consistent with the principle of affective congruency, if it is assumed that the great majority of participants had positive feelings toward themselves. In several investigations, participants used a variety of mechanisms to protect themselves from a person who evaluated them unfavorably. For example, the person was not believed, he was disliked and discredited, his attitude was distorted in a favorable direction, or he was avoided.[57] Or, when persons knew that evaluations of them on the basis of tests were going to be made public, they were more likely to distort their self-evaluations in favorable directions as a protective device.[58] The use of selective evaluation of other persons to maintain affective congruency has also been demonstrated.[59] Students who were initially strangers in several ten-man groups engaging in face-to-face interaction were led to believe that certain others in the group liked them. They subsequently reported liking these particular persons more than they liked other members of the group.

None of the experiments cited provides a comparative test of the principles of self-enhancement and affective congruency. That is, they do not furnish positive evidence for one concept and negative evidence for the other. A really adequate experiment has yet to be conducted, although several experiments provide some tentative support for affective congruency as opposed to self-enhancement. One investigation involving failure in a group situation indicated that under one experimental condition, subjects with high self-esteem protected themselves from unfavorable evaluations by other persons better than did those with low self-esteem.[60] This result is predicted by the principle of affective congruency, but not by a postulated need for self-enhancement. A self-enhancement principle would predict that protective mechanisms would be used by persons with low self-esteem as well as those with high self-esteem.

Another investigation is somewhat relevant, since it concerns congruency between *O*'s evaluation and *P*'s behavior although it does not pertain to *P*'s self concept.[61] As noted earlier, if another person behaves congruently toward an individual, the individual should like him. A group task was manipulated so that participants perceived their performance as good or poor. After completion of the task, each participant was exposed to positive and negative evaluations of their work in the form of a note, presumably from another group member. These evaluations were either congruent or incongruent with the individuals' performances. The congruency effect did occur even in instances where the evaluation was unfavorable: Persons were liked if they evaluated the participant's performance as he himself did.

This result was accompanied by another effect. Persons were also liked if they evaluated an individual's performance favorably—even if he himself evaluated it poorly. Although apparently contradictory to congruency theory, this finding can be reconciled if it is assumed that when another person evaluates an individual's performance, some of his evaluation is perceived as applying to aspects of self that are positively valued. To the extent that individuals

57. Harvey, Kelley, & Shapiro, 1957; Dittes, 1959; Harvey, 1962; Johnson, 1966; Eagly, 1967.   58. Gerard, 1961.   59. Backman & Secord, 1959.   60. Stotland, Thorley, Thomas, Cohen, & Zander, 1957.   61. Deutsch & Solomon, 1959.

interpreted the favorable reaction of another person as applying to some aspects of self as well as to performance, they would be led to like the other person because *this* aspect of his behavior *is* congruent.

Another study reported that individuals who had chosen not to attempt a test for which they had been led to believe they did not have the ability to pass were more attracted to a person who evaluated this ability unfavorably than to another who evaluated them favorably in this respect.[62] On the other hand, in another investigation even individuals who had been led to believe that they were low on a particular ability responded more favorably to positive evaluators than to negative ones.[63]

Two experiments appear to support the desire for self-enhancement rather than affective congruency as a response to lowered self-esteem. One experiment introduced female participants to a handsome male who behaved in an accepting manner, engaged them in a conversation, and asked them for a dinner date.[64] Some of the women were subsequently given a personality assessment, followed by false feedback that, momentarily at least, increased their self-esteem. Others had their self-esteem lowered by similar means. When later given an opportunity to express their feelings toward the male confederate whom they had earlier interacted with, those with the lower self-esteem liked him better. In the other study, individuals who were led to believe that they were accepted by other group members were more attracted to the group than those led to believe that they were poorly accepted.[65] This tendency was greater for those low in self-esteem than for those high in self-esteem. Walster[66] has suggested a reason why results from the latter investigation as well as those from her own dating experiment differ from those of other investigators,[67] who report positive relations between liking for others and self-esteem. In these other experiments, participants were certain of the degree of acceptance by other persons, but in these two experiments genuine acceptance was not clear.

Of crucial importance is the identification of the means by which people handle unfavorable evaluations of themselves so as to preclude change. What conditions are associated with different reactions to the receipt of such information? The above comments suggest that one variable is the overall self-esteem of the individual. In one study, identical unfavorable information about oneself and about another person led to less change in perception of self than of the other, and the information about oneself was viewed as less accurate.[68] Further, participants high in self-esteem resisted change in the unfavorable direction to a greater degree than did those whose self-esteem was low. On the other hand, positive information about themselves led to greater change for individuals high in self-esteem than for those low in self-esteem. Further, participants with high self-esteem used unfavorable information to change their self concept in a favorable direction whereas those low in self-esteem responded to favorable

62. WILSON, 1965.   63. JONES, 1966.   64. WALSTER, 1965.   65. DITTES, 1959.   66. WALSTER, 1965.   67. MASLOW, 1942; STOCK, 1949; BERGER, 1952; OMWAKE, 1954.   68. EAGLY, 1967.

information by changing in the unfavorable direction. Evidently in this study the processing of information was influenced in a direction favoring congruency.

A number of situational variables, including characteristics of the information available in the situation, have similarly been related to whether persons respond in the positive direction of increasing congruency or in the negative direction of decreasing congruency. A study of change in the self concept during a two-week T-group session found that where peers were in high agreement concerning the characteristics of another person, correspondence between the self and the average judgment of others was strong. Where agreement was low, however, the correspondence was weaker. Moreover, those persons about whom there was low agreement perceived themselves in a more favorable light than warranted by the average ratings of their peers.[69]

As might be expected from the discussion of the effects of communication characteristics on attitude change, the degree of discrepancy between the individual's self conception and his idea of how others see him influences not only the effects of such information on his self conception but also the frequency and degree to which he employs a variety of congruency-producing devices. Thus, when individuals were given test information falsified in an unfavorable direction, moderate discrepancies rather than large or small ones had the greatest effect on their self conceptions. Participants who received small discrepancies recalled the information as more favorable than did those who received intermediate or large discrepancies. On the other hand, participants who received large discrepancies were more likely to reject the source of information by questioning the competence of the investigators and were also more likely to devalue the information by questioning the validity of the test and the care with which the results had been prepared.[70] Similarly the credibility of the source has been related to a person's reactions to negative evaluations. In agreement with other studies of source credibility, evaluations from others considered low in credibility are not accepted.[71]

Definitional leeway allowing the individual to distort information in a direction which for most people results in affective congruency is not only affected by characteristics of the message, but by features of the situation itself.[72] Greater certainty in a negative self-appraisal produces a favorable evaluation of the performance of a person who negatively evaluates one. But no matter how large a degree of certainty the individuals studied felt about their negative self-evaluation, they liked the persons who evaluated them positively more than those who evaluated them negatively. Evidently both the tendency to achieve congruency and the desire to maximize self-esteem were operating in the situation and differentially affected the measures employed. Interestingly, those individuals who scored high on a measure of the need for approval in the

69. SHERWOOD, 1967.   *70.* JOHNSON, 1966.   *71.* JOHNSON & STEINER, 1968.   *72.* JONES & SCHNEIDER, 1968.

uncertain condition responded more positively when evaluating the performance of the positive evaluator. Evidently such individuals were particularly prone to accept favorable evaluations where uncertainty might be expected to reduce the strength of the tendency toward cognitive congruency.

Jones has demonstrated that to the degree that individuals anticipate challenges to their self conceptions in the future, they favor accurate evaluations of themselves over unduly favorable ones.[73] Similarly, another investigation suggests that reactions to negative evaluations may be influenced by the desire to protect oneself from being blamed for failure.[74] Participants in an experiment were led to believe that they were low in a particular ability. They either were allowed to commit themselves to a level of task performance commensurate with their perceived level of ability or were not allowed to make a choice at that time but led to believe that they would be able to do so later. Under these circumstances, committed participants responded more positively to a peer who evaluated their performance positively than to one who evaluated them in a negative but congruent fashion. Those participants who did not have the opportunity to commit themselves evaluated the negative evaluator more favorably. These investigators interpreted their results as indicating that those having made a commitment to any easy task could accept positive evaluations from others without incurring the obligation to take on a more difficult task with the probability of failure. Those who had not yet committed themselves, however, could be expected to find a positive evaluation uncomfortable because it might carry the unwanted obligation to choose a difficult task. Finally, another study suggests that individuals are hesitant to accept favorable information about the self and that they change their self-assessment if it appears possible that as a result of further evaluation they may be judged as having overestimated themselves.[75]

SUCCESS AND FAILURE IN THE INTERPERSONAL SYSTEM   The discussion of interpersonal congruency theory has emphasized mechanisms by which the individual achieves or maintains congruency between self and others. But cognitive and affective congruency prevails between one's own behavior and the two other elements in the interpersonal system. Recent investigations, while employing somewhat different methodologies and theoretical orientations, all support the notion that successful or unsuccessful behavior as fostered and defined by significant others is closely linked with equivalent definitions of self.[76] Success experiences lead to positive self-regard and favorable evaluations from others, and these reactions maintain successful performance. As Rosenberg succinctly notes in comparing adolescents of high self-esteem with those of low self-esteem (termed *egophobes*):

What the future holds in store for these youngsters is impossible to say. Yet if one speculates on their prospects, one can easily envision the possibility of

73. JONES, 1968.   74. JONES & RATNER, 1967.   75. EAGLY & ACKSEN, 1971.   76. ROSENBERG, 1965; DIGGORY, 1966; COOPERSMITH, 1967.

a self-fulfilling prophecy. The young man who is confident of himself and not afraid of failure is likely to throw himself wholeheartedly into his work and to make full use of his creative potentialities. The insecure youngster, on the other hand, is likely to be inhibited by his fear that he will make mistakes, etc. Similarly, the former would probably enjoy competition with others, would willingly assume responsibility, and would seek out positions of leadership, whereas the latter would tend to avoid competition, responsibility, and leadership. Furthermore, it is possible that, broadly speaking, other people tend, more or less unconsciously, to accept the opinions we hold of ourselves. If we communicate, through our manner and action, the view that we are good, they are likely to think we are good; if we show that we consider ourselves unworthy, they may be disposed to agree that we are right. Finally, of course, the egophobe's anxiety, depression, interference with concentration, and interpersonal difficulties are in fact likely to interfere with his quest for occupational success. Ability aside, then, there are a number of powerful reasons for expecting the egophobe's dire predictions about his occupational future to be true. The very thing that makes him so strongly desire success, viz., his low self-esteem also makes him anticipate failure and very likely helps to produce failure. This vicious circle is calculated to reduce his potential occupational contributions at the same time that it enhances his emotional distress.[77]

Stabilizing Effects of the Social Structure

This chapter has emphasized that the stability and consistency over time of an individual's self and behavior rests on constancies in his interpersonal environment. But, as has been stressed, the individual contributes much to these environmental constancies, mainly through the operation of a variety of interpersonal processes. Another source of stability lies in the social structure, which helps to maintain a constant interpersonal environment in several ways. Factors in the social structure that affect behavior have been identified in earlier chapters of the book; here it will be shown how they contribute to stability and consistency in the individual's behavior.

CONSISTENCY IN THE INTERPERSONAL ENVIRONMENT   So far, the discussion of congruency has been limited largely to interaction between an individual and one other person with regard to a single aspect of self and behavior. It would be unrealistic, of course, to consider that all such aspects of self and relations to different persons are independent of each other. In that case the person, chameleonlike, would change his self and behavior each time he interacted with a different person or each time a different aspect of self was involved. While some variability from situation to situation does occur, most students of personality

---

77. Reprinted with permission from M. ROSENBERG. *Society and the adolescent self-image.* Princeton, N.J.: Princeton University Press, 1965. Pp. 238-239.

believe that there is also much consistency in a person's behavior in different situations.

To the extent that different situations support similar aspects of self and behavior, these aspects may be said to support each other. Consequently, resistance to change in such components of self or behavior is apt to be especially great, and change is unlikely to be accomplished by shifts in single relations that may be fortuitously encountered. Much further theorizing and research is needed on the relations among different dyadic interactions. For the present, one experimental illustration may suffice.

An experiment was conducted to test the hypothesis that the greater the number of significant persons supporting an aspect of self, the more resistant to change is that aspect.[78] College students were asked to rank themselves on a series of fifteen characteristics and also to estimate how they thought each of five persons important to them would rank them on these characteristics. They were given several personality tests for the ostensible purpose of determining how much insight they had into their own personalities. For each individual, the experimenter selected two traits for special analysis and treatment. Both traits were ranked among the highest five applying to self by each person, but one represented high perceived agreement among the five significant other persons, and the other represented low perceived agreement. The specific hypothesis was that the trait having the greater consensus would be more resistant to change than the trait having the lower consensus.

On a later occasion, a false report purportedly based upon the personality tests was presented to each individual. Actually, the report was based upon initial self-rankings. It contained descriptive statements very similar to those on which the individual had previously ranked himself. The rank order of traits on this report as arranged by the experimenter was the same as the individual's previous ranking, except that the two traits selected for special treatment were reported as being eight rank steps lower than he had ranked them.

After the participant had had time to study this report, and presumably to note the discrepancies between it and his rankings of himself, he was asked to rank himself again. On the second self-ranking, most participants were influenced by the false report to lower the ranking of these two traits; however, *the trait having low consensus was lowered to a greater extent than the trait having high consensus.* Thus, the study demonstrates that the greater the number of significant other persons who are seen as defining oneself in a manner compatible with one's own definition, the more resistant to change is that self-definition.

A further study using high school students as participants and obtaining measures of actual as well as perceived consensus found a similar relation between both actual and perceived consensus and resistance to change.[79] Two

78. BACKMAN, SECORD, & PEIRCE, 1963.   79. MCCONNELL, 1966.

investigations in a field setting where changes over time were related to consensus provides further support for the above conclusions.[80]

CONTINUITY IN THE ENVIRONMENT   Many factors help to stabilize the interpersonal environment. First are the processes that give rise to subinstitutional regularities. Belonging to a group and holding particular positions in its affect, status, power, and leadership structures ensures that other members will treat one in a regular fashion. Behaviors on his part or those of other persons which are inconsistent with his position are apt to be countered with sanctions from the members. Second, the institutional structure as reflected in the system of culturally constrained role expectations that guide interaction similarly help to stabilize both the personnel and the behavior of the individual and his partners in interaction. With respect to this second source, a person is seen by others and sees himself in ways dictated by the various role categories he occupies. Persons learn not only the behavioral expectations belonging to a position or role category, but also the personal attributes associated with it. By occupying certain positions they are consistently defined by others and consequently define themselves in terms of traits associated with the role category. Perhaps age-sex roles are the most obvious example. Various personality characteristics typical of maleness or femaleness in a given group are learned and maintained because males and females are consistently defined as possessing them.

The previous discussion of the ways in which the individual contributes to stabilizing his interpersonal environment included the point that he is likely to enter groups and participate in social systems if the probability of establishing congruent relations is high. Once he has entered such groups, his participation in congruent relations is in part determined by the conditions and processes that control the groups. For long periods of his life, a person is surrounded by the same other individuals, who include family members, playmates, and friends. Even when actual individuals change, those who replace earlier associates have certain similarities to the previous ones because of the constraining effects of the social structure (a person stays in a certain socioeconomic class, in a certain occupation, etc.).

It has been emphasized that the person is not a passive product of social forces but an active agent in creating, maintaining, and on occasion changing drastically his interpersonal environment. Yet under certain circumstances he may be relatively helpless in avoiding certain identities. This was illustrated in the discussion of the labeling approach to deviant behavior in Chapter 14. Deviant labels such as thief, homosexual, drug addict, and mental patient have powerful constraining affects on self-definitions and the definitions and behaviors of others. The works of Goffman, Becker, Lofland, and others suggest reasons why this is true.[81]

80. BOHNSTEDT, 1970; DOHERTY & SECORD, 1971.   81. GOFFMAN, 1963; BECKER, 1963; LOFLAND, 1969.

First, as *master statuses,* categories of deviance dominate the attributions that others make to a person, bringing other attributes into line with the pejorative character of the deviant status. Once an individual is known as a thief or as a drug addict, persons attribute other socially undesirable characteristics to him and avoid seeing him in desirable ways, such as a good father, a helpful friend, etc. Many of his behaviors which might be defined in a favorable or neutral fashion are now viewed in a way that confirms his deviancy. The mental patient who tries to escape the boredom of the hospital routine by daydreaming may be defined as withdrawn and out of contact. Even past behaviors once considered normal may be reinterpreted to fit his deviant status. A fall from a tree, an early childhood disease, or some harmless escapade may be interpreted as early causes or signs of deviance. The very pervasiveness in Western society of the idea that a deviant is a sick person illustrates this point further.

Nor are his present or future behaviors likely to bring about a totally new definition of the deviant's characteristics and behaviors. Once treated and pronounced cured or rehabilitated, the deviant is still not completely returned to the status of normal. His deviant label remains; he is an ex-felon, an ex-addict, or an ex-mental patient. Since the degree of consensus among significant others appears to be an important factor in ensuring stability, being labeled a deviant by almost everyone has a powerful impact on the deviant's identity. He finds it difficult to define himself in any other way.

Consensus is also fostered by certain conditions of total institutions in which many deviants are detained or treated. The elaborate observation and record-keeping activities and periodic case conferences in which information is exchanged among the staff in the wards of mental hospitals provides an excellent example. Further, attributions of deviancy are made by others whose views are highly credible. In Western society attribution specialists have emerged who are widely thought to have the professional skills and knowledge necessary to make scientifically sound diagnoses of deviancy. Few will side with the mental patient who asserts, contrary to his diagnosis, that he is as sane as his psychiatrist, clinical psychologist, or social worker. Thus the behavior and definitions of other persons are powerfully constrained by the deviant label attached to the individual. The high recidivism rate of ex-prison inmates is undoubtedly in part explained by the fact that once they are labeled felons it is difficult to secure satisfactory employment, and they gravitate back into former criminal pursuits.

The various processes contributing to stability in individual behavior are presented in a single perspective in Figure 17-1. Starting from the left, contributions of the social structure are indicated: (1) It determines the frequencies of interaction between a person S and various other persons; (2) it places S in various role categories; and (3) it influences the behaviors of other persons toward S and his toward them. Each process in turn serves to establish a certain interpersonal environment in which S moves. In interaction with this

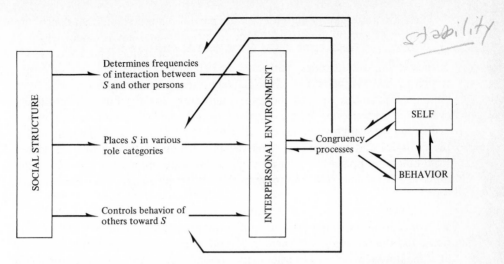

Figure 17-1 *Relations among social structure, interpersonal environment, self, and behavior.*

environment, *S* strives to establish relations that are congruent with self and behavior. The various congruency processes discussed in the previous section are employed by *S* to achieve congruency. Note, however, that these processes in turn act on the interpersonal environment. To a certain degree, *S* is able to determine the frequency with which he interacts with various other persons, the role categories he is placed in, the manner in which he enacts those roles, and the behavior that others display toward him; thus he shapes the interpersonal environment to a limited extent.

Summary: Stability of Self and Behavior

Much consistency in behavior occurs because the individual responds actively to situational factors in a manner that maintains the distinctive character of his behavior. This activity was discussed in terms of interpersonal congruency theory, in which the unit of analysis consists of three components: an aspect of *P*'s self, his interpretation of his behavior relevant to that aspect, and his beliefs about how another person *(O)* behaves toward him and feels toward him with regard to that aspect. A person attempts to maintain a state of congruency among the three components. Congruency exists when the behaviors of *P* and *O* imply definitions of self compatible with relevant aspects of his self concept. In congruency by implication, *P* may perceive that *O* sees him as possessing a particular characteristic corresponding to an aspect of his self concept. In congruency by validation, the behavior or other characteristics of *O* allow or call for behavior on the part of *P* that confirms a component of self. In congruency by comparison the behavior or attributes of *O* suggest by comparison that *P* possesses a particular self component. Congruency may also be affective, as when *P* has the same feelings toward himself that *O* has toward him.

There are a number of activities on the part of the individual that contribute to stability of self by creating for him an interpersonal environment which is likely to be congruent with his self concept and behavior. These include (1) misperceiving the attitudes, attributes, or behavior of other persons, or misinterpreting his own behavior, (2) selectively interacting with persons who have congruent attitudes or who behave congruently toward him, (3) positively evaluating persons who have congruent attitudes or behavior toward him, (4) evaluating most highly the aspects of self that he perceives as congruent with the attitudes and behavior of other persons, (5) evoking congruent responses from others by presenting himself in an appropriate manner or by casting the other in a congruent role, and (6) maintaining affective-cognitive consistency in self.

Both institutional and subinstitutional forces help to maintain the person's self conception and his behavior and to maintain the personnel, the attributions, and the behaviors of others in his interpersonal environment. Stability is at a maximum where consensus exists among significant others, particularly consensus on those statuses that exert a powerful organizing influence on the perception and attributions of others as well as the person himself.

Changes in Self and Individual Behavior

Not only is the social structure a source of stability, but under certain conditions it also induces changes in the interpersonal environment. As a person moves through the social structure, systematic changes occur in the ways he is categorized and the ways other persons behave toward him. Features of the social structure also induce changes in the personnel of his environment. In addition, various fortuitous events can produce changes. To illustrate changes arising from the social structure, the discussion below will treat the positional changes which occur with increasing age and with occupational socialization.

Life-Cycle Changes

Each society has laid out for the individual a series of role categories that he will occupy at various stages of his life. Thus, every male will occupy such categories as infant, small boy, big boy, adolescent, young man, middle-aged man, and elderly man. In addition, each person will have a certain place in his family, depending upon its structure and composition. He will have a certain birth order as the youngest, the oldest, or in some middle position. He will have either no siblings, or one or more siblings. Family activities may frequently or infrequently include contacts with other relatives such as grandparents, uncles and aunts, and cousins.

Outside the family, the male will occupy certain roles in his peer groups. At adulthood he will sometimes enter military service, and usually he will marry, acquiring the roles of husband, father, etc. His occupational role will play an important part in his life. All these roles contribute to his self concept. To the extent that they are sequential and discontinuous, with movement from one to the next requiring behavior changes, they are instrumental in bringing about certain changes in the self. Cavan provides a vivid description of the discontinuity of the role category forced upon a man at retirement showing how, at this point in life, a new and less valued self-image is thrust upon the person:

At the point of retirement, we may make a generalized picture of the male. He has a well-ingrained self-image as competent, successful at some level of work, usefully productive, self-supporting, and able to provide for his family. This image has been built up over years of time by the favorable reactions of his family, friends, co-workers, and those segments of society whose opinion he values. He has, moreover, found a kind of work—a social role—that permits him to express his self-image satisfactorily, and he is firmly incorporated into a physical environment and a group of co-workers which make it possible for him to carry out his role.

Using the concepts employed above, let us consider what happens at the point of compulsory retirement. First, the means of carrying out the social role disappears: the man is a lawyer without a case, a bookkeeper without books, a machinist without tools. Second, he is excluded from his group of former co-workers; as an isolated person he may be completely unable to function in his former role. Third, as a retired person, he begins to find a different evaluation of himself in the minds of others from the evaluation he had as an employed person. He no longer sees respect in the eyes of former subordinates, praise in the faces of former superiors, and approval in the manner of former co-workers. The looking glass composed of his former important groups throws back a changed image: he is done for, an old-timer, old-fashioned, on the shelf.[82]

Several studies of occupational socialization document formative effects on the self concept as an individual passes through the social structure. These effects have been traced by comparing the frequency and the rank order in which nursing students in various stages of professional training designated themselves by an occupational self-reference.[83] Only a third of those near the end of their freshman year identified themselves as nurses in one of the first three statements on the Twenty Statements Test, but more than seven out of ten students did so by the end of their junior year. This demonstrates the incorporation of the image of "nurse" into the self.

A similar trend has been noted in medical students.[84] Thirty-one percent of the first-year medical students reported that they felt more like a doctor than a

---

82. Reprinted by permission from R. S. CAVAN. Self and role in adjustment during old age. In A. M. Rose (Ed.), *Human behavior and social processes: An interactionist approach.* Boston: Houghton Mifflin Company, 1962. P. 80.   83. KUHN, 1960.   84. HUNTINGTON, 1957.

student when dealing with patients. This figure rose to 85 percent for students finishing their fourth year of training. Whether or not students primarily saw themselves as doctors also depended on which role partner they were interacting with. When they were interacting with fellow students, faculty members, or nurses, the percentage of those who saw themselves as physicians was considerably less than when they were dealing with patients.

This finding is consistent with the theoretical position that the expectations of role partners are an important determinant of how the actor sees his role. More students see themselves as physicians when they are interacting with patients, who are more likely than other role partners to see them as doctors. Further support stems from the finding that 39 percent of the 117 first-year students who thought their patients regarded them as doctors defined themselves as such, whereas only 6 percent of the 35 students who believed their patients defined them as students saw themselves as doctors.

Finally, one would expect students to have a rather unstable image of themselves as doctors because of the lack of consensus among their role partners. Presumably, when the student physician graduates, and his partners actually see him and are believed by him to see him as a doctor, this occupational role will become a stable part of his self-image. When the cues associated with a role category are clear and unambiguous, consensus may be expected to occur eventually and the role expectations to be ultimately associated with self. Where the cues to a role category are vague or ambiguous, as they are in the interim position of medical student, agreement among role partners and consequent stability of the self concept would seldom be obtained.

Learning to view oneself in a new manner involves considerably more than applying a new self-referent to oneself. One learns to see oneself in terms of the range of physical, social, and personality attributes which are characteristic of fellow actors, even including those attributes that are not directly concerned with the performance of the role. Recent studies showing differences between occupational groups in self-decriptions provide ample documentation of this point.[85] Typically, such studies of occupational socialization show a gradual shift in personality characteristics in the direction of the appropriate professional image as the neophyte proceeds through training.

Occupying a new position in the social structure may also involve radical changes in the personnel in one's environment. New persons become significant, old associates drop out or fade in significance. The person who is inducted into the service or who takes a position in a strange community is suddenly surrounded by new associates. To the degree that these persons define him in an unfamiliar way, and to the extent that the effects of the new definitions are not countered by the various means of maintaining congruency previously discussed, strong forces are created toward a change in self and behavior.

85. SCANLON, HUNTER, & SUN, 1961.

Changes in Group Structures

This treatment of the effects of social structure has emphasized changes related to passage through the institutional structure. Changes of a subinstitutional character must also be considered. An abrupt change in one's group position in the status, power, or leadership structure may change his self conception, his behavior, and the behaviors and attribution of others. The transformations that accompany abrupt elevation in status and power of individuals are often commented upon. In fact, these comments are often prefaced by the phrase, "I knew him when . . ." which serves to signify that the person was at one time quite different.

Changes in one's affective relations with other persons that accompany the growth of a new and close friendship, a love relationship, or the development of a relationship with a therapist are often accompanied by drastic change. These changes may work on affective or cognitive components, or both. If one component is changed, the other is likely to be modified to reestablish affective-cognitive consistency. Cognitive changes in self that have been observed to occur after a period of psychotherapy provide an example.[86] Psychotherapy is a very intense emotional experience, and in client-centered therapy, where cognitive changes have been clearly documented, the therapist is warm and accepting toward the patient. The therapist's attitude may lead the patient gradually to increase the amount of positive affect toward himself, which in turn is followed by the adoption of more positive self-cognitions to achieve consistency.

The powerful effects of consensus and credibility on the development of a person's self conception as a deviant have already been noted. Lofland has drawn attention to the importance of persons who do not react in the conventional manner to evidence of deviance.[87] They, unlike the average person, see good in everyone. If religious, they emphasize that all are sinners and all capable of redemption. These persons, whom he calls *normal-smiths,* often play a crucial role in returning persons to the status of normality and thus breaking the vicious circle that supports a deviant identity. Frequently because they are ex-deviants themselves, reformed alcoholics, drug addicts, or felons, their definitions and examples carry additional credibility. Their power to change may be further amplified through organization into groups, such as Alcoholics Anonymous or Synanon (an organization of ex–drug addicts, whose functioning was described in Chapter 3). In one sense, psychotherapists, too, are normal-smiths, because they believe the patient can change.

Often highly significant others become the source and support for elements of the ideal self which in turn exert pressure to change one's self conception and role identities. Through this kind of pressure the individual can be viewed as actively creating new dimensions of the self.

86. Rogers & Dymond, 1954.   *87.* Lofland, 1969.

Once a component of an interpersonal system changes, other components in the system are apt to change in the direction of obtaining congruency. This can be illustrated by a number of research findings. One experiment temporarily lowered the self-esteem of one group of participants.[88] Compared to another group whose self-esteem had not been lowered, the former group, when given an opportunity to cheat on an exam, did so to a greater extent. Presumably cheating behavior was more frequent for this group since it was not incongruent with their lowered self conception. The results of another study suggest the conditions under which stability in behavior is obtained in response to congruency and illustrates the tendency toward congruency between the self concept and task performance.[89] Participants with low self-esteem who were certain of their low self-appraisal and who were led to believe they were personally responsible for having done well in early trials of a task failed to improve in response to feedback concerning success. Others who were either unsure of their low self-appraisal or were led to attribute their success to luck did improve in line with their perceived success. This is consistent with somewhat indirect evidence that a person's conception of his abilities may produce corresponding changes in his performance.

The manner in which the views of other persons may lead to a *self-fulfilling prophecy* has been demonstrated by showing the effects of teachers' expectations on the performance of schoolchildren. Although there has been controversy concerning the methodology of these studies, some substance to the idea of a self-fulfilling prophecy remains.[90]

In this study, a nonverbal IQ test was administered in eighteen classrooms ranging from the first to the sixth grade, and represented to the teachers as a measure that could predict academic blooming. Names of 20 percent of the children were chosen *at random*, and reported to the teachers as likely to make considerable gains during the coming year. Some eight months later, they were found to have made greater gains than children not named, especially those children in the lower grades. A reasonable assumption is that the expectations of the teachers toward these designated children shaped their self concepts so as to produce a performance congruent with it.

While no measures of self concept were taken for these children, the work of Brookover and his associates as well as the experimental studies described earlier lend support to this interpretation.[91] In a study of over 500 children during their seventh-grade through twelfth-grade years the student's self conception of his ability was found to mediate between the definitions of significant others (especially the parents, and to lesser degree the peers) and his performance in school.

88. ARONSON & METTEE, 1968.   89. MARACEK & METTEE, 1972.   90. ROSENTHAL & JACOBSON, 1968; BARBER & SILVER, 1968; ROSENTHAL, 1968.   91. BROOKOVER et al., 1967.

Summary: Changes in Self and Behavior

As an individual moves through the social structure, systematic changes occur in the ways he is categorized and the ways that other persons behave toward him. Features of the social structure also induce changes in the personnel of his environment. In addition, fortuitous events can produce changes. Each society has laid out for the individual a series of role categories that he will occupy at various stages of his life. Moreover, as the individual occupies new role categories, he sometimes encounters a whole new set of persons who will treat him differently from his earlier companions. The self-fulfilling prophecy illustrates the force that expectations of other persons may have for shaping one's behavior in a new direction. If some event leads significant others to predict a new direction for an individual's life, they may help to create such changes by their treatment of him.

Changes in group structure also occur, as when an individual acquires a new position in the group. New friendships and loves will sometimes create significant changes in an individual, which have ramifications throughout his life. Sometimes a change in an affective component of self will lead to comparable cognitive changes in order to maintain consistency between these two facets of self. And often a fortuitous event may have profound ramifications. Commission of a deviant act, for example, may catapult the individual into a new deviant category in which he is systematically labeled by others as deviant, and from which it becomes difficult for him to return to a former status. In fact, systematic labeling processes may fix him more firmly in the category of deviant.

Glossary

ABX theory of attraction An explanation of liking proposed by Theodore Newcomb based on the relations among persons *A* and *B* and a mutual attitude object, *X*. (*X* may be another person.)

achievement motivation The degree to which an individual sets high standards, strives to achieve them, and responds with feeling to failures or successes in such efforts.

action instructions Information given to the recipient of a fear-arousing communication about ways of coping with the danger.

actor (See *role player*.)

advocating a contrary position A way of changing attitudes; an individual is induced to advocate a position contrary to that which he believes, which often leads him to move toward the position advocated.

affect display A category of movement in which feelings or emotions are conveyed by facial expressions.

affective congruency A state of consistency between the actor's feelings about an element of his self concept, his related behavior, and the feelings toward these system components held by other persons.

affect structure The pattern of attraction and repulsion of a group of individuals to each other.

affectional system A set of patterned behaviors displaying liking between two organisms.

aggression Action which has an intent to harm or injure someone either physically or mentally.

alienation A condition in which an individual feels relatively powerless and socially isolated, and does not share the prevailing social norms and values.

altercasting The process by which another person (an alter) is placed in an identity or a role that requires him to behave in a manner advantageous to the manipulator.

anomie A condition of society in which the use of normatively approved means does not result in obtaining culturally valued goals for all or a portion of the population, giving rise to pressures toward norm violation and social change. This state is experienced at the individual level by a condition called *alienation*.

anxiety An internal state of apprehension or anticipation of punishment.

assimilation effect Perceiving the attitude of a communicator whose position is relatively close to that of the respondent as even closer than it is.

attraction to an ego ideal A form of need complementarity in which an individual is attracted to another person who has characteristics that the individual had once aspired to but never developed and which are conspicuously absent in him.

authoritarian personality A pattern of traits with an important relation to prejudice.

The individual with such a personality has unrecognized hostility toward authority figures and strong repressive measures for controlling his own impulses, is rigid in interactions with others, and emphasizes power, status, and dominance in relating to other persons.

autokinetic effect The phenomenon that a stationary point of light shown briefly and repeatedly in a dark room will appear to move.

background expectations Those aspects of interactions that are taken for granted by everyone, and are so well accepted that their violation often produces incredulity and bewilderment.

balance theory A set of propositions that specify combinations of positive and negative elements that are in a state of balance or imbalance.

balanced state In balance theory, a condition in which all elements are consistent with each other (usually in terms of their positive or negative values).

bargaining In exchange theory, a process in which each of two or more persons attempts to negotiate a definition of the situation and of the resultant relationship that will maximize his outcomes.

behavior modification The form of psychotherapy that makes use of behavioristic learning principles.

behavior setting A unit of analysis describing a way of acting in a particular situation (e.g., church behavior).

behaviorism An approach to psychology emphasizing the observation and manipulation of overt behavior under laboratory conditions and the restriction of concepts and theory to what can be inferred from such procedures.

belief component One of the two parts of an attitude, consisting of the content of the attitude, typically expressed in verbal statements. (See *evaluative components.*)

belief dilemma An attitude or opinion that has an imbalance of positive and negative elements.

bolstering In balance theory, supporting an attitude object by relating it to other cognitive objects in a balanced way. Typically the additional support is added to an attitudinal element that is opposed to the persuasive communication, so that the respondent can resist the communication.

boomerang effect A change of attitude by the recipient of a persuasive communication in a direction opposite to that intended by the communicator.

brainstorming A process in which group members are encouraged to list all the ideas which come to mind, even the most ridiculous, and to avoid evaluating their quality.

career The sequence of movements which persons normally make from one position to another as in an occupation or any other way of life, including becoming a deviant.

career contingencies Those factors on which sequential movement from one position to another depend.

cathartic effect A supposed reduction in the tendency of a viewer to perform aggressive behavior, brought about by a vicarious release of aggressions through viewing the aggressive behavior of other persons in fictional media or other events.

centrality-peripherality The location of an individual in a communication structure. Central positions allow direct access to a maximum number of other members; peripheral positions allow minimum access to other members.

chronic personality characteristics Characteristics of an individual that are relatively enduring—present at different times and in different situations.

clique A subgroup whose members have many mutual choices and few choices of persons outside of the clique.

coalition formation Development of a pair and a third party in three-person groups.

coercive persuasion Use by communicators of complete control over respondents, with respect to both communication and sanctions, to bring about desired attitudes or behaviors.

coercive power The ability to punish another person.

cognitive balancing, as a defense process Resisting a communication by making some element of it consistent with attitudes one already holds and which are inconsistent with accepting the persuasive attempt. (See *bolstering, denial,* and *differentiation,* which are specific forms of cognitive balancing.)

cognitive controls Constraints on behavior resulting from an individual's acceptance of norms or standards as guides.

cognitive element A single unit of knowledge, a single belief, or an evaluation held by a person about some object in his environment, about his behavior, or about himself.

cognitive restructuring Restoring a state of congruency by misperceiving how other persons see one, by misinterpreting one's own behavior, or by restructuring the situation to change the evaluation of the relevant behavior.

cognitively complex Using many dimensions in evaluating people.

cohesiveness The net force

acting on the members of a group to keep them in it. It is a product of (1) the attractiveness of the interaction with group members, (2) the inherent value to the individual of the group activities themselves, (3) the extent to which membership achieves other ends, and (4) the extent to which attractive outcomes are available in alternative relations outside the group.

commitment A personal decision to engage in a line of behavior.

commitment A process in which the actor adheres to normative behaviors because the disruptive consequences of not conforming would interfere with the achievement of his ends or values.

commitment In interpersonal attraction, a tacit agreement to give priority to and maintain an intimate relationship with a particular individual.

common fate A situation in which individuals or groups will win or lose together; it encourages working together and often increases attraction or reduces prejudice.

common relevance In the *ABX* theory of attraction, *X,* or the attitude object has to be of interest (or relevant to) both person *A* and person *B*.

communication centrality A location in a group providing maximum access for transmission and receipt of information.

communication structure The pattern of information access and transmission characterizing a set of positions in a group.

comparative function The use by an individual of a reference group as a standard by which to evaluate his condition or fate.

comparison level In exchange theory, a plane of expectation or expected outcome which is influenced by an individual's past experiences in a relationship, his past experiences in comparable relationships, his judgment of what outcomes others like himself are receiving, and his perception of outcomes available to him in alternative relations.

competition In role expectations, a condition in which the actor cannot adequately honor conflicting expectations because of limitations of time or energy.

complementary needs A state in which each member of a dyad has a need which is expressed in behavior that is rewarding to the other member.

compromise process In forming attractions, a process in which a group moves toward an equilibrium in which each individual's position in the affect structure is the best that he can obtain in terms of reward-cost outcomes.

concreteness-abstractness A pervasive quality on which individuals may be characterized. Concrete individuals make extreme distinctions, depend on authority and other extrapersonal sources, and have a low capacity to act "as if." Abstract persons behave in the opposite of these ways.

conflict In role expectations, a condition which arises when one expectation requires behavior of the actor which in some degree is incompatible with the behavior required by another expectation.

confounded feedback A condition in which individual members of a group are informed only whether the group as a whole has failed to react within a prescribed limit. (Contrast with *direct feedback.*)

congruency (See *interpersonal congruency.*)

congruency by comparison A condition that occurs when the behavior or attributes of *O* suggest that *P* possesses a particular self-component.

congruency by implication A condition that occurs when *P* perceives that *O* sees him as possessing a particular characteristic corresponding to an aspect of his self concept.

congruency by validation A condition that occurs when the behavior or other characteristics of *O* allow or call for behavior on the part of *P* that confirms a component of *P*'s self.

conscience A system of norms that an individual applies to his own acts or contemplated acts to arrive at a judgment about whether they are right or wrong.

consensual validation A process by which an individual checks his ideas or beliefs against those of other people in order to determine their validity. (See also *social reality.*)

contingencies of reinforcement In behaviorism, a relation among the following three elements: (1) the occasion on which a response occurs, (2) the response itself, and (3) the action of the environment on the organism after a response has been made.

contrast effect Perceiving the attitude of a communicator whose position is relatively distant from that of the respondent as even more distant than it is.

coping with danger Overcoming a problem—one way of reacting to a fear-arousing communication (e.g., stopping smoking after being warned of the hazard of lung cancer).

cost In exchange theory, the undesirable consequences of carrying out an activity or taking an action.

counternorm effects Those aspects of the influence process which produce resistance to the influence attempt.

credibility The degree to which a communicator is believable. One's credibility is a function of his personal characteristics, his position or status, the nature of the communication, the context in which it is delivered, his relation to the listener, and the listener's characteristics.

cue trait A quality of a stimulus person which is used as a basis for making further judgments about the person.

debt management In a social sense, the process by which an individual keeps his social debts to a minimum. The social debt depends not only on the rewards and costs experienced by both donor and recipient but also on the degree to which the donor's acts are perceived by the recipient as voluntary, intentional, and without ulterior or sinister motives.

defensive attribution Placing blame for a serious and frightening accident on the victim, in order to avoid thinking that a similar accident might happen to oneself (e.g., a responsible person would not have such an accident).

degree of involvement The strength of an individual's feeling about an attitude issue. The degree of involvement partially determines the effect on a recipient of a discrepancy between the positions of the communicator and the respondent.

demand characteristics The features of an experiment or of an experimenter's behavior that convey to the participant the desired outcome of the experiment.

denial In balance theory, declaring the value of the attitudinal element to be opposite to what the communicator has said. Denial is a form of resistance to attitude change.

deintensification An attempt to underplay an emotion, as when a fearful person attempts to look less afraid.

dependency A determinant of social power by virtue of an individual's need for *resources* that another person possesses.

descriptiveness The degree to which an item yields information about the person as an individual.

desocialization The process of removing a person from the role categories which he has previously occupied.

differentiating item In the description of persons, a word, phrase, or statement about the abilities, interests, or beliefs of persons.

differentiation In balance theory, the splitting of an attitudinal element into two parts, positive and negative, in order to resolve an inconsistency created by a persuasive communication. In this way an individual restores consistency among his attitudes and thus avoids the pressure to change his attitude.

direct feedback A condition in which each member of a group is informed of his own performance, those of other members, and those of the group considered as a whole. (Contrast with *confounded feedback*.)

discrimination The inequitable treatment of individuals considered to belong to a particular social group.

discriminative stimulus In behaviorism, a special feature of a situation which has been associated with making a particular response.

display rules Various movements by which an emotion differing from the real feelings of the individual is presented. There are four kinds: *deintensification, overintensification, masking,* and *neutralization.*

disposition The tendency of an individual to behave in a particular way across a wide variety of situations.

dispositional item In the description of persons, a word, phrase, or statement that labels how the person behaves in a broad class of situations.

dissonance An inconsistency between two or more elements. Two elements are in a dissonant relation if, considering these two alone, the opposite of one would follow from the other.

distributive justice A condition in which the outcomes of each individual—his rewards minus his costs—are directly proportional to his investments.

dyad A two-person group.

dyadic Of or pertaining to two persons.

egocentrism A form of personal involvement in which the other person is described in subjective, self-oriented terms representing the observer's personal frame of reference.

egophobe An individual with low self-esteem.

emotional inoculation Repeated exposure to an anxiety-arousing series of communications which leads to development of resistance to attitude change. (Same as *immunization.*)

emotional role playing A situation intended to bring about attitude change by placing an individual in a position that arouses his fears and concerns so that he will change a disturbing behavior (e.g., smoking).

environmental supports (for prejudice) Social conditions and individual characteristics that support negative attitudes toward members of minority groups.

evaluative component One of the two parts of an attitude, which refers to the positive or negative character of an individual's orientation toward an aspect of his world. (See *belief component.*)

exchange theory A set of propositions relating interaction of persons to the level of satisfying outcomes they experience and specifying the consequences of these outcomes for maintenance or change of the interaction.

expectations An individual's anticipations that he and other people will behave in certain definite ways. In entertaining such expectations, the individual anticipates the nature of interaction in particular situations. Further, his expectations and those of the other party are generally shared.

expert power A form of potential influence over another person by virtue of the special knowledge that an individual possesses.

external sanction A form of social control in which the environment or other persons punish an individual for an act.

facework Behavior designed to avoid or restore loss of self-esteem.

factor analysis A statistical procedure that groups psychologically related attributes together so that the groups or clusters may be identified as basic dimensions underlying the mathematical ratings.

forewarning Informing the recipient of a communication of the communicator's intent in delivering the communication. One line of attitude-change research has attempted to determine the effects of forewarning on attitude change.

forming alternative relations Establishing a satisfying relation with a person other than *P*, resulting in reduced dependency on *P* and a shift toward

equalization of the relative social power of *P* and *O*.

galvanic skin response A measure of emotional response taken by attaching electrodes to the skin and using instrumentation that will detect slight changes in the electrical resistance of the skin that usually accompany emotional responses.

group-decision process A procedure in which a group is exposed to a persuasive communication or presented with a problem, followed by discussion and a decision on whether to adopt the recommended behavior.

hierarchy of role obligations An arrangement of role obligations according to priorities. Those with the highest priority represent the strongest obligations, and should be enacted in preference to those lower in the hierarchy whenever there is a problem of enacting the role. (See *role obligations.*)

icon In interpersonal strategy, a linguistic device for confirming a preferred identity; in an attempt to impress others, the individual mentions names of important persons he has known or places that he has been or refers to significant experiences.

identification Choosing a person as a model for one's own behavior.

illegitimate In reference to influence attempts, not in accord with the types of requests that the individual has the right to make.

illustrators Movements which illustrate what is being communicated verbally.

immanent justice The idea that rule violations are followed by accidents or misfortunes willed by God or by some inanimate object.

immunization (See *emotional inoculation.*)

implication model A means of studying the inferences that individuals make from cue traits provided as information about the stimulus persons. Individuals make judgments of the probability of inferring a particular trait from a cue trait.

implicit personality theory The system of terms that an individual uses in thinking about and describing other persons.

independence The freedom with which an individual may function in a group, derived from his position in the communication structure, from the actions of other members, from situational factors, and from the individual's own perceptions and cognitions of the situation.

index of uniformity A numerical figure which represents the definiteness or strength of a stereotype.

individual-in-situation A unit of analysis in which a particular person's behavior under particular conditions is the focus of study.

induced-compliance paradigm An experimental setting in which a participant is caused to behave in a manner contrary to his attitude.

induction A form of parental discipline in which the parent gives explanations or reasons why he wants the child to change his behavior, particularly in terms of the consequences of the child's behavior for the parent or other persons.

informational influence A process in which an individual accepts information from an outside source as evidence about reality. (Contrasted with *normative influence.*)

ingratiation tactics A set of behaviors for obtaining the support or approval of other persons. Such tactics include giving compliments, behaving in a pleasing manner, and agreeing with or conforming to the expressed opinions of the other person.

ingroup A group of persons who experience a sense of belonging, a sense of having a like identity. (See also *outgroup*.)

institutionalization A relationship which has become socially recognized and approved. Shared expectations have emerged recognizing the rightness or legitimacy of the relation. The rights and obligations are shared and enforced not only by the participants but by other parties as well.

interaction process analysis A method designed by Robert Bales for observing communication among members of a group in a systematic, quantitative fashion.

interactional context A function of the characteristics of the situation and the actors which determines the role categories to be enacted, the role expectations to be applied, and the range of permissible behavior.

internal controls Norms or standards of conduct that an individual accepts as his own and which place limits on the expression of various behaviors.

internal sanction A form of social control in which the individual experiences anxiety, guilt, or shame as a consequence of an act.

internalization The process by which a child acquires norms or standards of conduct from his parents or other sources and makes them his own.

interpersonal congruency A system state prevailing when the behaviors of *P* and *O* imply definitions of self consis-

tent with relevant aspects of *P*'s self concept.

interpersonal system A set of elements consisting of: (1) an aspect of S's self, (2) S's interpretation of his behavior relevant to that aspect, and (3) his beliefs about how another person behaves toward him and feels toward him with regard to that aspect.

intruding role A position that generates expectations which are superimposed upon the main role being enacted.

investments Characteristics of an individual or features of his past history or background that have become associated with the expectation of a certain level of outcomes. For example, seniority on a job becomes associated with the expectation of additional pay.

isolate In sociometry, a group member who is rarely chosen by other members.

isolation In *alienation*, a kind of detachment in which the individual assigns a low value to goals and beliefs that typically are highly valued in society.

justifiability Excusability; may be interpreted in terms of loci of cause. An action performed because of powerful external pressures is likely to be seen as justifiable.

justification The act of thinking of cognitive elements that reduce the uncomfortable dissonance felt after making a decision and engaging in a contrary behavior.

kinetic information Gestures, expressive movements, posture, observable tension or relaxation, and similar items which are used to make judgments about persons.

labeling theory An explanation of deviant behavior

which emphasizes the reaction of other persons to the individual labeled deviant.

latitude of acceptance The range of attitude positions differing in both directions from that of the individual but which are nevertheless accepted by him or favorably evaluated by him. (See also *latitude of rejection*.)

latitude of rejection The range of attitude positions that are sufficiently different from the individual's own so that he unfavorably evaluates them or rejects them. (See also *latitude of acceptance*.)

law of primacy In learning theory, the principle that material presented first will be better learned and better remembered than material presented last.

leader-follower relation Complementary behavior occurring between a leader and his followers.

legitimacy (in a relationship) The recognition by the parties to a relationship and by outside parties that a relationship based on shared agreement concerning patterns of exchange has been developed. (See also *institutionalization*.)

legitimacy (of a role expectation) The recognition by an actor that his role partners are justified in holding a particular expectation.

legitimacy of leadership A condition in which group members accept an individual as their leader and share this acceptance with each other.

legitimate power The ability to modify another person's behavior by virtue of the fact that both accept certain norms and values which prescribe behaving in a particular fashion.

locus of cause Where an act originates. The locus of cause is viewed as internal if the act seems to originate in the actor and as external if it seems to originate in compelling circumstances.

Machiavellianism The degree to which an individual is motivated to manipulate and does manipulate other persons to gain his own ends. A personality test for measuring this trait is called the Mach V.

marginal persons (in voting) Individuals who are not firmly decided on how they are going to vote, who often change their minds during a campaign or make up their minds late in the campaign.

masking Giving the appearance of experiencing a certain feeling in order to conceal one's true feelings.

master status A classification which dominates the evaluation of a person. Each individual has many statuses, but master statuses (e.g., status as a criminal or a mental patient) have a compelling effect on how he is evaluated.

mixed-motive situation A gamelike situation in which both cooperation and competition are part of the process of negotiation.

model The concepts used to describe a process and an explication of the way in which the process works.

modeling Learning to perform the behavior of a person whom one has observed.

mutual need gratification A form of complementarity in which each member of a dyad has an inner urge which is expressed in behavior that is rewarding to the other member.

need for nurturance An inner urge to give help and support to other persons.

need for succorance An inner urge to receive emotional support and help from other persons.

negative reference group A group used by an individual as a standard to deviate from.

negative referent power A condition where an individual is influenced to behave in a manner opposite to that of the power figure.

negative reinforcement The reinforcement of a response that successfully avoids an aversive or punishing stimulus.

negative sanctions Actions by other persons that negatively reinforce or punish an individual.

neutralization Behavior by which an agitated person tries to appear unperturbed.

norm of altruism The widely shared idea that a person in need is entitled to receive help. (Compare *norm of social responsibility*.)

norm of fairness or justice The idea that in a social exchange where each party receives something from the other, the amount received by each party should be in accord with his contribution.

norm of reciprocity The idea that when an individual does a favor for another person, the other person is obligated to do something in return.

norm of social responsibility The generally accepted idea that an individual should help other persons in need. (Compare *norm of altruism*.)

norm-sending processes The operations by which norms are communicated and enforced.

normal-smith A type of individual who sees good in everyone and believes that all sinners are capable of redemption. The term comes from the function of the normal-smith in eliminating deviant behavior.

normative function (of a reference group) The use of a group as a source of standards of conduct and belief by the individual.

normative influence A process in which an individual conforms to the expectation of another person or a group because of the satisfying feelings such behavior generates. (Contrasted with *informational influence*.)

normative judgments Judgments shared by a group which are believed by members of the group to be appropriate or expected.

opinion leader An individual whose views are more influential than others in leading to the adoption of new attitudes or behaviors. Often such leaders are limited to certain topic areas (e.g., fashion or marketing).

orientation (toward role obligations) An actor's preferred attitude toward certain expectations, particularly when he is faced with role strain. Three possible orientations are: (1) a moral orientation, which favors doing the legitimate thing, (2) an expedient orientation, which favors doing what will be rewarded and not punished, and (3) a moral-expedient orientation, a compromise attitude which takes both morality and expediency into account.

other-oriented In personal involvement, seeing the other person as an entity separate from the self.

outcome In exchange theory, the net effect of carrying out an activity, expressed in terms of rewards less costs.

outgroup Considered from the point of view of ingroup members, a group with distinctive characteristics that set them apart from the ingroup. (See also *ingroup*.)

overintensification Expression of more emotion than one feels.

panel technique A method of studying the effects of political campaigns or other mass communications by making repeated studies of a select group of persons.

paradigm A particular method of research based upon a specific set of concepts.

parallel model explanation An attempt by Leventhal to explain the persuasive effects of communications which arouse fear. The model proposes two parallel and independent reactions: (1) to control the fears aroused by the threat and (2) to cope with the danger. The two reactions have different consequences for attitude change.

partial withdrawal Activity reducing O's dependence on P and resulting in a shift toward equalization of the relative social power of P and O.

particularistic orientation The tendency to behave toward another person in terms of his unique characteristics or his special relationship to oneself rather than in terms of some abstract category (e.g., honesty or morality). (See also *universalistic orientation.)*

personal involvement The way in which an observer brings himself into a description of another person.

personal stereotype A single individual's opinions.

personality The set of attributes which represent an individual's nature and characteristic behavior.

physical reality That which is believed to be true based on the direct evidence of one's senses. (Contrasted with *social reality.)*

position A form of *role category* designating a class of persons in a social system.

positive sanctions Actions by other persons that gratify or reinforce an individual's behavior.

power assertion A form of parental discipline in which the parent, by virtue of his power over the child, punishes him either physically or by depriving him.

preapology A preface to remarks, designed to prevent other persons from questioning one's expertise or accuracy.

prejudice An attitude that predisposes a person to think, perceive, feel, and act in favorable or unfavorable ways toward a group or its members.

primacy-recency Refers to the effects of the order in which persuasive material is presented. From principles of learning theory (and other theories) certain deductions can be made about whether material presented first or last will be more effective in particular circumstances.

primary group Any small, intimate group in which members are highly dependent on each other for the satisfaction of their emotional needs (e.g., nuclear family, friendship groups, small groups dealing with enduring stresses and problems).

principle of equity The idea that the more an individual puts into an activity, as compared with the input of another person, the more he should get in return.

prisoner's dilemma A game situation in which each party has a cooperative choice or a competitive choice but in which the outcome is dependent on the choice made by the other party. The competitive choice will yield either the best outcome or the worst outcome, depending on the other party's choice.

private stereotype The attributes an individual personally believes belong to a category.

proprioceptive cues Information from sensory receptors in the body which react to position or movement.

psychegroup In sociometry, a group structure characterized by a social or emotional criterion of sociometric choice (e.g., individuals may be asked to choose whom they like most in the group).

public commitment In coercive persuasion settings, the confession of wrong thinking and profession of "proper" attitudes.

public stereotype The adjectives an individual thinks would be attributed to a person category by the general public.

radical behaviorism An extreme form of behaviorism, identified with B. F. Skinner, in which all behavior change is accounted for in terms of contingencies of reinforcement.

reciprocal In personal involvement, seeing a mutual, two-way relationship between oneself and another person.

reference group A group that the individual takes as a standard for self-evaluation and attitude formation.

referent power The influence which an individual has over another person who uses him as a model for identification. Often the prolonged use of reward power transforms it into referent power. (See also *reward power.)*

reinforcement In radical behaviorism, any action of the environment that changes the response (changes the probability that it will occur again).

resource In social power, a property or conditional state of an individual—a possession, an attribute of appearance or personality, a position he holds, or a certain way of behaving—which enables him to modify the rewards and costs experienced by another person.

response evocation In congruency theory, behaving so as to evoke congruent responses from other persons.

responsibility The amount of personal volition involved in a particular act. When the cause of an act is seen as external, the individual is seen as having minimal responsibility for it. When the cause

role learning Learning to behave, feel, and see the world in a manner similar to that of other persons who are in the same role category.

role negotiation The process by which an actor and his role partners work out to their mutual satisfaction how each ⸻ ⸻ behave in particular en⸻ situations, and ⸻ at the general ⸻ eir relationship ⸻ ly this process is ⸻ nd more subtle ⸻ han ordinary ne⸻ ⸻ partners may ⸻ hat they are ne⸻ ⸻ so known as *role*

⸻ **ns** Behavior ex⸻ ⸻ le partners be⸻ ⸻ ositions they oc⸻ ⸻ on to each other. ⸻ *rights,* which are ⸻ ⸻ ent of role obli⸻

⸻ The individual in ⸻ gory or position. ⸻ d to as an *actor.*) ⸻ An actor occupy⸻ ⸻ category which ⸻ rticular behaviors ⸻ rs in related role

⸻ Privileges expected ⸻ ners because of the ⸻ ey occupy in rela⸻ ⸻ h other. (See also ⸻ *ons,* which are the ⸻ t of role rights.) ⸻ Difficulties in at⸻ ⸻ ⸻ enact a role. ⸻ Vays of behaving ⸻ ace another person ⸻ e parties being es⸻ ⸻ vare of the influ⸻ ⸻ ss.

⸻ **f a reference group)** ⸻ inant of the effec⸻ ⸻ a reference group. ⸻ s rarely behave in ⸻ e with a reference ⸻ all occasions; they ⸻ when the reference ⸻ alient (e.g., an indi⸻ ⸻ more apt to behave

religiously when he is in church or in the temple.

sanctions Rewards for conforming to social norms or punishments for not conforming.

saturation The requirements placed upon a position in a communication structure that call for action by the individual in that position.

scapegoating The venting of hostility felt accumulated toward some inviolable figure upon an innocent victim who will not retaliate.

selective avoidance A process by which an individual refrains from exposing himself to communications that are dissonant with his attitudes.

selective evaluation A process in which an individual maximizes congruency or minimizes incongruency by altering his estimation of self, behavior, or the other person in a positive or negative direction.

selective exposure The process by which an individual chooses to notice communications that are consonant with his attitudes and chooses not to notice communications that are dissonant with them.

selective interaction A process in which an individual chooses to be involved with those persons who behave congruently toward him and avoids involvement with those who behave incongruently toward him.

self (See *self concept.*)

self commitment Making a judgment or decision in a manner that makes one feel obligated to stand by the act.

self concept The set of cognitions and feelings that an individual has about himself.

self correction Correcting one's own discrepant opinion to agree with that of other persons whose opinion is seen as valid.

self-enhancement, need for

Christmas Wishes

The idea that individuals have an urge to behave so as to receive positive evaluations from others and to evaluate themselves positively.

self estrangement In *alienation*, a lack of intrinsic satisfaction in one's activities.

self-fulfilling prophecy The idea that strong expectations concerning an individual's behavior will eventually lead him to fulfill those expectations by behaving in accord with them.

self presentation Acting so as to guide and control the impressions that other persons form of oneself.

significant other A term for a person whose opinions are especially important to an individual, particularly with respect to his self concept.

simple differentiating item In the description of persons, a level of descriptiveness that refers to the individual described but does not provide much information about him as a person. Simple differentiating items include appearance items, behavior items denoting specific acts but not implying a disposition or trait, global dispositions or categories, expressions of liking or disliking, and role category items.

situational demands The expectations imposed upon an actor by the nature of the circumstances. These include not only role expectations, but also any special features of the situation that generate expectations.

situational personality characteristics Traits of an individual which are temporary or which occur only under certain conditions (e.g., anxiety about failing at the time of taking a test). Often such characteristics are created experimentally to determine their effects on individuals in

combination with other conditions.

social accomodation A normative process consisting of conforming behavior resulting from a desire to maintain positive relations with liked people.

social comparison The process of evaluating one's inputs and outcomes in relation to those obtained by other persons in order to see whether they are equitable.

social contract An unwritten pact which takes the form of a rule or norm on which both parties have agreed.

social-emotional leader An individual who helps to boost group morale and to release tension when things are difficult.

social motive A set of behaviors that have a common goal as their object.

social norm An expectation shared by group members which specifies behavior that is considered appropriate for a given situation.

social power A property of a relationship between two or more persons such that the power of person *P* over person *O* is a joint function of his capacity for affecting the outcomes of person *O* relative to his own outcomes.

social reality Perception of the attitudes and opinions of other people as a major resource for checking opinions or beliefs. (Contrast with *physical reality.*)

social role A social role consists of a category of persons and the expectations for their behavior. (Also referred to as *role.*)

social stereotype (See *stereotyping.*)

social system A set of interlocking social roles (e.g., the roles in a nuclear family).

socialization A process of change occurring throughout

the life career of an individual as a result of his interactions with other persons.

sociogram A plotting in graphic form of sociometric data. Each member of the group is represented by a circle or point. Choices made by each member are drawn in the form of arrows running toward the object of the choice. If rejections are included, they are usually represented in the form of broken arrows.

sociogroup In sociometry, a group structure emerging from choices based upon a working or living type of criterion (e.g., individuals may be asked whom would they most like to work with or live with).

sociometric measurement A method of studying structures based on affection or attraction. The basic data collected consist of choices of the most preferred (and sometimes the least preferred) members of the group made by each individual member. The choices are then tallied and patterns discernable in them are identified.

star In sociometry, a frequently chosen member of a group.

state of congruency A condition in which the behaviors of *P* and *O* imply a definition of self that is consistent with relevant aspects of *P*'s self concept.

state of egocentrism The assumption by a child that other persons view events in the same way that he does.

state of equity A condition in which the ratio of inputs and outcomes of an individual is equal to that of the person with whom he compares himself.

state of realism A condition in which the child confuses objective and subjective reality (e.g., he thinks of his dreams as actually occurring).

status The worth of a person as estimated by a group or class of persons. (See *status*.)

status congruence A condition in which all the status attributes of a person rank higher than, equal to, or lower than the corresponding attributes of another person. (See *status*.)

status conversion processes A series of changes that lead to status congruence. The individual behaves so that other persons will judge him similarly on the various dimensions of status. (See *status*.)

status envy Jealousy of a person who occupies a powerful and coveted position. Status envy has been proposed as one of the sources of identification with a role.

status passage Change from one role category to another during the course of an individual's life.

status structure The set of prestige categories recognized by members of a group. (See *status*.)

status symbol An attribute which initially has no intrinsic value but which through regular association with a particular level of worth comes to be seen as indicative of that level.

stereotyping A sociocultural phenomenon in which people identify a category of persons, agree in attributing sets of traits or characteristics to the category of persons, and attribute the characteristics to any person belonging to the category.

stimulus or target person The individual who is the object of a persuasive attempt.

structural information Relatively unmodifiable elements, such as physiognomy and body build or type, which are used to make judgments about persons.

synanon A group session aimed at changing the attitudes and behavior of group members and characterized by extreme candor and honesty. Such sessions involve considerable attack and criticism, but also are conducted in a larger supportive context. Emphasis is placed on getting members to admit their faults and weaknesses. These sessions are usually held in Synanon houses, residences of an organization of former drug addicts who live together in a communal style.

T group A group of persons who are led through a series of experiences intended to increase their sensitivity to their own feelings and those of other members and to how these feelings relate to their actions.

tactics Strategies deliberately adopted to influence another person.

target act The deed (e.g., a confession, a purchase, a favor, an opinion change) which is to be performed by the recipient of an influence attempt.

target person The recipient of an influence attempt.

task leader An individual who supplies ideas and guides the group toward a solution.

true group effects Group performances that deviate from a baseline performance produced by individuals working alone without influencing each other's performance.

trust An attitude reflected in behavior that would allow another person to take advantage of an individual.

two-step flow of communications The process in which many mass communications are spread to individuals indirectly, through other persons.

type-category unit A unit of analysis in which one class of individuals in one class of situations is the focus of study.

Type I complementarity Attraction and mutual need satisfaction within a dyad in which one member is high on a need and the other is low on the same need.

Type II complementarity Attraction and mutual need satisfaction within a dyad in which each member expresses his need in behavior that satisfies a different need of the other member.

typification A process of organizing the elements of one's world into types or classes.

undifferentiating item In the description of persons, the lowest level of descriptiveness; refers to an individual's material possessions or to his social setting.

universalistic orientation A tendency to behave toward other persons in terms of some abstract category rather than as particular persons (e.g., kindness or honesty). (See also *particularistic orientation*.)

utility of information The usefulness of data to an individual.

values Ideas about desirable states of affairs shared by members of a group or culture.

withdrawal of love A form of parental discipline in which the parent explicitly or implicitly implies dislike for the child because of a specific action performed by the child.

Bibliography

ABELSON, R. P. Modes of resolution of belief dilemmas. *Journal of Conflict Resolution,* 1959, **3,** 343-352.

ABELSON, R. P. Psychological implication. In R. P. Abelson et al. (Eds.), *Theories of cognitive consistency: A sourcebook.* Chicago: Rand McNally & Company, 1968. Pp. 112-139.

ABELSON, R. P., E. ARONSON, W. J. MCGUIRE, T. M. NEWCOMB, M. J. ROSENBERG, & P. H. TANNENBAUM (Eds.). *Theories of cognitive consistency: A sourcebook.* Chicago: Rand McNally & Company, 1968.

ABELSON, R. P., & G. S. LESSER. The measurement of persuasibility in children. In C. I. Hovland & I. L. Janis (Eds.), *Personality and persuasibility.* New Haven, Conn.: Yale University Press, 1959. Pp. 141-166.

ABELSON, R. P., & J. C. MILLER. Negative persuasion via personal insult. *Journal of Experimental Social Psychology,* 1967, **3,** 321-333.

ADAMS, J. S. Reduction of cognitive dissonance by seeking consonant information. *Journal of Abnormal and Social Psychology,* 1961, **62,** 74-78.

ADAMS, J. S. Inequity in social exchange. In L. Berkowitz (Ed.), *Advances in experimental social psychology.* Vol. 2. New York: Academic Press, Inc., 1965, Pp. 267-299.

ADAMS, J. S., & W. B. ROSENBAUM. The relationship of worker productivity to cognitive dissonance about wage inequities. *Journal of Applied Psychology,* 1962, **46,** 161-164.

ADAMS, S. Status congruency as a variable in small group performance. *Social Forces,* 1953, **32,** 16-22.

ADDINGTON, D. W. The relationship of selected vocal characteristics to personality perception. *Speech Monographs,* 1968, **35,** 492-503.

ADORNO, T. W., E. FRENKEL-BRUNSWIK, D. J. LEVINSON, & R. N. SANFORD. *The authoritarian personality.* New York: Harper & Row, Publishers, Inc., 1950.

AJZEN, I., & M. FISHBEIN. The prediction of behavior from attitudinal and normative variables. *Journal of Experimental Social Psychology,* 1970, **6,** 466-487.

ALEXANDER, C. H., JR., & J. EP-STEIN. Problems of dispositional inference in person perception. *Sociometry,* 1969, **32,** 381-395.

ALEXANDER, H. E. Broadcasting and politics. In M. K. Jennings & L. H. Zeigler (Eds.), *The Electoral Process.* Englewood Cliffs, N. J.: Prentice-Hall, Inc., 1966. Pp. 81-104.

ALEXANDER, N. C. A method for processing sociometric data. *Sociometry,* 1963, **26,** 268-269.

ALLEN, V. L., & R. S. CRUTCHFIELD. Generalization of experimentally reinforced conformity. *Journal of Abnormal and Social Psychology,* 1963, **67,** 326-333.

ALLPORT, G. W. *The nature of prejudice.* Garden City, N.Y.: Doubleday & Company, Inc., 1958.

ALLPORT, G. W., & B. M. KRAMER. Some roots of prejudice. *Journal of Psychology,* 1946, **22,** 9-39.

ALTMAN, I., & W. W. HAYTHORN. Interpersonal exchange in isolation. *Sociometry,* 1965, **28,** 411-426.

ANDERSON, H. H., & H. M. BREWER. Studies of teachers' classroom personalities. I.

Dominative and socially integrative behavior of kindergarten teachers. *Journal of Applied Psychology Monograph,* No. 6. Stanford, Calif.: Stanford University Press, 1945.

ANDERSON, H. H., & J. E. BREWER. Studies of teachers' classroom personalities. II. Effects of teachers' dominative and integrative contacts on children's classroom behavior. *Journal of Applied Psychology Monograph,* No. 8. Stanford, Calif.: Stanford University Press, 1946.

ANDERSON, H. H., J. E. BREWER, & M. F. REED. Studies of teachers' classroom personalities. III. Follow-up studies of the effects of dominative and integrative contacts on children's behavior. *Journal of Applied Psychology Monograph,* No. 11. Stanford, Calif.: Stanford University Press, 1946.

ANDERSON, N. H. Test of a model for opinion change. *Journal of Abnormal and Social Psychology,* 1959, **59,** 371-381.

ANDERSON, N. H. Integration theory and attitude change. *Psychological Review,* 1971, **78,** 171-206.

ANDERSON, N. H. Information integration theory: A brief survey. Technical Report No. 24. La Jolla: University of California, Center for Human Information Processing, April 1972.

ANDERSON, N. H., & S. HUBERT. Effects of concomitant verbal recall on order effects in personality impression formation. *Journal of Verbal Learning and Verbal Behavior,* 1963, **2,** 379-391.

ANDREWS, I. R. Wage inequity and job performance: An experimental study. *Journal of Applied Psychology,* 1967, **51,** 39-45.

ARCHIBALD, W. P., & R. L. COHEN. Self-presentation, embarrassment, and facework as a function of self-evaluation, conditions of self-presentation, and feedback from others. *Journal of Personality and Social Psychology,* 1971, **20,** 287-297.

ARGYLE, M. Non-verbal communication in human social interaction. In R. Hinde (Ed.), *Non-verbal communication.* New York: Cambridge University Press, 1972.

ARGYLE, M., & J. DEAN. Eye contact, distance, and affiliation. *Sociometry,* 1965, **28,** 289-304.

ARGYLE, M., & B. R. LITTLE. Do personality traits apply to social behavior? *Journal for the Theory of Social Behavior,* 1972, **2,** 1-35.

ARGYLE, M., V. SALTER, H. NICHOLSON, M. WILLIAMS, & P. BURGESS. The communication of inferior and superior attitudes by verbal and non-verbal signals. *British Journal of Social and Clinical Psychology,* 1970, **9,** 222-231.

ARGYRIS, C. *Understanding organizational behavior.* Homewood, Ill.: The Dorsey Press, 1960.

ARONFREED, J. Punishment learning and internalization: Some parameters of reinforcement and cognition. Paper presented at the biennial meeting of the Society for Research in Child Development, Minneapolis, March 1965.

ARONFREED, J. The internalization of social control through punishment: Experimental studies of the role of conditioning and the second signal system in the development of conscience. *Proceedings of the 18th International Congress of Psychology, Moscow,* 1966.

ARONFREED, J. *Conduct and conscience: The socialization of internalized control over behavior.* New York: Academic Press, Inc., 1968.

ARONFREED, J., & A. REBER. Internalized behavioral suppression and the timing of social punishment. *Journal of Personality and Social Psychology,* 1965, **1,** 3-16.

ARONSON, E. Dissonance theory: Progress and problems. In R. P. Abelson et al. (Eds.), *Theories of cognitive consistency: A sourcebook.* Chicago: Rand McNally & Company, 1968. Pp. 5-27.

ARONSON, E. The theory of cognitive dissonance: A current perspective. In L. Berkowitz (Ed.), *Advances in experimental social psychology.* Vol. 4. New York: Academic Press, Inc., 1969. Pp. 1-34.

ARONSON, E., & V. COPE. My enemy's enemy is my friend. *Journal of Personality and Social Psychology,* 1968, **8,** 8-12.

ARONSON, E., & D. LINDER. Gain and loss of esteem as determinants of interpersonal attractiveness. *Journal of Experimental Social Psychology,* 1965, **1**(2), 156-171.

ARONSON, E., & D. R. METTEE. Dishonest behavior as a function of differential levels of induced self-esteem. *Journal of Personality and Social Psychology,* June, 1968, **9,** 121-127.

ARONSON, E., & J. MILLS. The effects of severity of initiation on liking for a group. *Journal of Abnormal and Social Psychology,* 1959, **59,** 177-181.

ARONSON, E., J. A. TURNER, & J. M. CARLSMITH. Communicator credibility and communication discrepancy as determinants of opinion change. *Journal of Abnormal and Social Psychology,* 1963, **67,** 31-36.

ARONSON, E., & P. WORCHEL. Similarity versus liking as determinants of interpersonal attractiveness. *Psychonomic Science,* 1966, **5,** 157-158.

ASCH, S. E. Studies of independence and conformity. A minority of one against a unanimous majority. *Psychological Monographs,* 1956, **70** (9, Whole No. 416).

ASHMORE, R. D. Intergroup contact as a prejudice-reduction technique: An experimental examination of the shared-coping approach and four alternative explanations. Unpublished Ph.D. dissertation, Los Angeles: University of California, 1969.

ATKINSON, J. W. Toward experimental analysis of human motivation in terms of motives, expectancies and incentives. In J. W. Atkinson (Ed.), *Motives in fantasy, action, and society.* Princeton, N.J.: D. Van Nostrand Company, Inc., 1958. Pp. 288-305.

ATKINSON, J. W. *An introduction*

to motivation. Princeton, N.J.: D. Van Nostrand Company, Inc., 1964.

ATKINSON, J. W., & N. T. FEATHER. *A theory of achievement motivation.* New York: John Wiley & Sons, Inc., 1966.

ATKINSON, J. W., & G. H. LITWIN. Achievement motive and test anxiety conceived as motive to approach success and motive to avoid failure. *Journal of Abnormal and Social Psychology,* 1960, **60**, 52-63.

ATKINSON, J. W., & P. O'CONNOR. Neglected factors in studies of achievement-oriented performance: Social approval as an incentive and performance decrement. In J. W. Atkinson & N. F. Feather (Eds.), *A theory of achievement motivation.* New York: John Wiley & Sons, Inc., 1966.

AZRIN, M. H., R. R. HUTCHINSON, & D. F. HAKE. Extinction-induced aggression. *Journal of the Experimental Analysis of Behavior,* 1966, **9**, 191-204.

BACK, K. W. Influence through social communication. *Journal of Abnormal and Social Psychology,* 1951, **46**, 9-23.

BACK, K. W. *Beyond words: The story of sensitivity training and the encounter movement.* New York: Russell Sage Foundation, 1972.

BACK, K. W., & K. E. DAVIS. Some personal and situational factors relevant to the consistency and prediction of conforming behavior. *Sociometry,* 1965, **28**, 227-240.

BACKMAN, C. W. Social psychology and innovations in education. In M. C. Reynolds (Ed.), *Proceedings of the conference on psychology and the process of schooling in the next decade: Alternative conceptions.* Minneapolis, Minn.: Leadership Training Institute, Special Education, 1971. Pp. 81-93.

BACKMAN, C. W., & P. F. SECORD. The effect of perceived liking on interpersonal attraction. *Human Relations,* 1959, **12**, 379-384.

BACKMAN, C. W., & P. F. SECORD. Liking, selective interaction, and misperception in congruent interpersonal relations. *Sociometry,* 1962, **25**, 321-335.

BACKMAN, C. W., & P. F. SECORD. The compromise process and the affect structure of groups. *Human Relations,* 1964, **17**(1), 19-22.

BACKMAN, C. W., & P. F. SECORD. The self and role selection. In C. Gordon & K. J. Gergen (Eds.), *The self in social interaction.* New York: John Wiley & Sons, Inc., 1968. *(a)*

BACKMAN, C. W., & P. F. SECORD. *A social psychological view of education.* New York: Harcourt Brace & World, Inc., 1968. *(b)*

BACKMAN, C. W., P. F. SECORD, & J. R. PEIRCE. Resistance to change in the self concept as a function of perceived consensus among significant others. *Sociometry,* 1963, **26**, 102-111.

BALES, R. F. A set of categories for the analysis of small group interaction. *American Sociological Review,* 1950, **15**, 146-159.

BALES, R. F. Some uniformities of behavior in small social systems. In G. E. Swanson, T. M. Newcomb, & E. L. Hartley (Eds.), *Readings in social psychology.* (Rev. ed.) New York: Holt, Rinehart and Winston, Inc., 1952. Pp. 146-159.

BALES, R. F. The equilibrium problem in small groups. In T. Parsons, R. F. Bales, & E. A. Shils, *Working papers in the theory of action.* Glencoe, Ill.: The Free Press, 1953. Pp. 111-161.

BALES, R. F. *Personality and interpersonal behavior.* New York: Holt, Rinehart and Winston, Inc., 1970.

BALES, R. F., & E. F. BORGATTA. Size of group as a factor in the interaction profile. In A. P. Hare, E. F. Borgatta, & R. F. Bales (Eds.), *Small groups.* New York: Alfred A. Knopf, Inc., 1956. Pp. 369-413.

BALES, R. F., & A. P. HARE. Diagnostic use of the interaction profile. *Journal of Social Psychology,* 1965, **67**, 239-258.

BALES, R. F., & P. E. SLATER. Role differentiation in small decision-making groups. In T. Parsons & R. F. Bales (Eds.), *Family, socialization and interaction process.* Chicago: The Free Press of Glencoe, Ill., 1955. Pp. 259-306.

BALES, R. F., & F. L. STRODTBECK. Phases in group problem solving. *Journal of Abnormal and Social Psychology,* 1951, **46**, 485-495.

BALES, R. F., F. L. STRODTBECK, T. M. MILLS, & M. E. ROSEBOROUGH. Channels of communication in small groups. *American Sociological Review,* 1951, **16**, 461-468.

BANDURA, A. Influence of models' reinforcement contingencies on the acquisition of imitative responses. *Journal of Personality and Social Psychology,* 1965, **1**, 589-595.

BANDURA, A. Social learning theory of identificatory processes. In D. A. Goslin (Ed.), *The handbook of socialization theory and research.* Chicago: Rand McNally & Company, 1969.

BANDURA, A. *Social learning theory.* New York: McCaleb-Seiler, 1971.

BANDURA, A., J. E. GRUSEC, & F. L. MENLOVE. Observational learning as a function of symbolization and incentive set. *Child Development,* 1966, **37**, 499-506.

BANDURA, A., J. E. GRUSEC, & F. L. MENLOVE. Some determinants of self-monitoring reinforcement systems. *Journal of Personality and Social Psychology,* 1967, **5**, 449-455.

BANDURA, A., & M. B. HARRIS. Modification of syntactic style. *Journal of Experimental Child Psychology,* 1966, **4**, 341-352.

BANDURA, A., & A. C. HUSTON. Identification as a process of incidental learning. *Journal of Abnormal and Social Psychology,* 1961, **63**, 311-318.

BANDURA, A., & C. J. KUPERS. Transmission of patterns of self-reinforcement through modeling. *Journal of Abnormal and Social Psychology,* 1964, **69**, 1-9.

BANDURA, A., & W. MISCHEL. Modification and self-imposed delay of reward through exposure to live and symbolic models. *Journal of*

Personality and Social Psychology, 1965, **2**, 698-705.

BANDURA, A., D. ROSS, & S. A. ROSS. Transmission of aggression through imitation of aggressive models. Journal of Abnormal and Social Psychology, 1961, **63**, 575-582.

BANDURA, A., D. ROSS, & S. A. ROSS. A comparative test of the status envy, social power, and secondary reinforcement theories of identificatory learning. Journal of Abnormal and Social Psychology, 1963, **67**, 527-534. (a)

BANDURA, A., D. ROSS, & S. A. ROSS. Vicarious reinforcement and imitative learning. Journal of Abnormal and Social Psychology, 1963, **67**, 601-607. (b)

BANDURA, A., & R. H. WALTERS. Adolescent aggression. New York: The Ronald Press Company, 1959.

BANDURA, A., & R. H. WALTERS. Social learning and personality development. New York: Holt, Rinehart and Winston, Inc., 1963.

BANDURA, A., & C. WHALEN. The influence of antecedent reinforcement and divergent modeling cues on patterns of self-reward. Journal of Personality and Social Psychology, 1966, **3**, 373-382.

BARBER, T. X., & M. J. SILVER. Fact, fiction and the experimenter bias effect. Psychological Bulletin Monograph, 1968, **70**(6, Pt. 2).

BARKER, R. G. Ecological psychology: Concepts and methods for studying the environment of human behavior. Stanford, Calif.: Stanford University Press, 1968.

BARNARD, C. I. The functions of the executive. Cambridge, Mass.: Harvard University Press, 1938.

BARTOS, O. J. Concession making in experimental negotiations. In J. Berger, M. Zelditch, & B. Anderson (Eds.), Sociological theories in progress. Boston: Houghton Mifflin Company, 1965.

BASS, B. M. An analysis of the leaderless group discussion. Journal of Applied Psychology, 1949, **33**, 527-533.

BASS, B. M. Amount of participation, coalescence, and profitability of decision making discussions. Journal of Abnormal and Social Psychology, 1963, **67**, 92-94.

BATEMAN, R. M., & H. H. REMMERS. A study of the shifting attitude of high school students when subjected to favorable and unfavorable propaganda. Journal of Social Psychology, 1941, **13**, 395-406.

BATES, F. L. Position, role, and status: A reformulation of concepts. Social Forces, 1956, **34**, 313-321.

BATESON, N. Familiarization, group discussion, and risk taking. Journal of Experimental Social Psychology, 1966, **2**, 119-129.

BAYTON, J. A., L. B. MCALISTER, & J. HAMER. Section B: Race-class stereotypes. Journal of Negro Education, Winter, 1956, **25**, 75-78.

BEACH, L., & M. WERTHEIMER. A free response approach to the study of person cognition. Journal of Abnormal and Social Psychology, 1961, **62**, 367-374.

BECHTEL, R. B., & H. M. ROSENFELD. Expectations of social acceptance and compatibility as related to status discrepancy and social motives. Journal of Personality and Social Psychology, 1966, **3**, 344-349.

BECKER, H. S. Inference and proof in participant observation. American Sociological Review, 1958, **23**, 652-660.

BECKER, H. S. Outsiders: Studies in the sociology of deviance. New York: The Free Press, 1963.

BECKER, H. S., B. GEER, E. C. HUGHES, & A. L. STRAUSS. Boys in white. Chicago: The University of Chicago Press, 1961.

BECKER, M. H. Sociometric location and innovativeness: Reformulation and extension of the diffusion model. American Sociological Review, 1970, **35**, 267-282.

BEIGHLEY, K. C. An experimental study of the effect of four speech variables on listener comprehension. Speech

Monographs, 1952, **19**, 249-258.

BELTH, N. C. Discrimination and the power structure. In N. C. Belth (Ed.), Barriers: Patterns of discrimination against Jews. New York: Anti-Defamation League of B'nai B'rith, 1958. Pp. 10-15.

BEM, D. J. Self-perception: An alternative interpretation of cognitive dissonance phenomena. Psychological Review, 1967, **74**, 183-200.

BENEDICT, R. Continuities and discontinuities in cultural conditioning. Psychiatry, 1938, **1**, 161-167.

BENNE, K. D., & P. SHEATS. Functional roles of group members. Journal of Social Issues, 1948, **4**, 41-50.

BENNETT, E. Discussion, decision, commitment and consensus in "group decision." Human Relations, 1955, **8**, 251-274.

BENOIT-SMULLYAN, E. Status, status types and status interrelations. American Sociological Review, 1944, **9**, 151-161.

BERELSON, B. R., P. F. LAZARSFELD, & W. N. MCPHEE. Voting: A study of opinion formation in a presidential campaign. Chicago: The University of Chicago Press, 1954.

BERELSON, B. R., & P. J. SALTER. Majority and minority Americans: An analysis of magazine fiction. Public Opinion Quarterly, 1946, **10**, 168-190.

BERGER, E. M. The relations between expressed acceptance of self and expressed acceptance of others. Journal of Abnormal and Social Psychology, 1952, **47**, 778-782.

BERGER, J. B., P. COHEN, & M. ZELDITCH, JR. Status characteristics and expectation states. In J. Berger, M. Zelditch, & B. Anderson (Eds.), Sociological theories in progress. Vol. 1. Boston: Houghton Mifflin Company, 1966.

BERGER, S., & W. W. LAMBERT. Stimulus-response theory in contemporary social psychology. In G. Lindzey & E. Aronson (Eds.), The Handbook of Social Psychology. (2nd ed.) Vol. I. Reading, Mass.: Addison-Wesley Publishing Company, Inc., 1968.

BERGIN, A. E. The effect of dissonant persuasive communications on changes in a self-referring attitude. *Journal of Personality,* 1962, **30,** 423-438.

BERKOWITZ, L. Sharing leadership in small, decision-making groups. *Journal of Abnormal and Social Psychology,* 1953, **48,** 231-238.

BERKOWITZ, L. Anti-semitism and the displacement of aggression. *Journal of Abnormal and Social Psychology,* 1959, **59,** 182-188.

BERKOWITZ, L. Anti-semitism, judgmental processes, and displacement of hostility. *Journal of Abnormal and Social Psychology,* 1961, **62,** 210-215.

BERKOWITZ, L. The concept of aggressive drive: Some additional considerations. In L. Berkowitz (Ed.), *Advances in experimental social psychology.* Vol. 2. New York: Academic Press, Inc., 1965.

BERKOWITZ, L. The frustration-aggression hypothesis revisited. In L. Berkowitz (Ed.), *Roots of aggression.* New York: Atherton Press, Inc., 1969.

BERKOWITZ, L. The contagion of violence: An S-R mediational analysis of some effects of observed aggression. In W. J. Arnold & M. M. Page (Eds.), *Nebraska Symposium on Motivation.* Lincoln: University of Nebraska Press, 1970. Pp. 95-136.

BERKOWITZ, L., & D. R. COTTINGHAM. The interest value and relevance of fear arousing communications. *Journal of Abnormal and Social Psychology,* 1960, **60,** 37-43.

BERKOWITZ, L., & L. R. DANIELS. Responsibility and dependency. *Journal of Abnormal and Social Psychology,* 1963, **66,** 429-436.

BERKOWITZ, L., & L. R. DANIELS. Affecting the salience of the social responsibility norm: Effects of past help on the response to dependency relationships. *Journal of Abnor-*

mal and Social Psychology, 1964, **68,** 275-281.

BERKOWITZ, L., & R. GEEN. The stimulus qualities of the target of aggression. A further study. *Journal of Personality and Social Psychology,* 1967, **5,** 364-368.

BERKOWITZ, L., & J. A. GREEN. The stimulus qualities of the scapegoat. *Journal of Abnormal and Social Psychology,* 1962, **64,** 293-301.

BERKOWITZ, L., S. B. KLANDERMAN, & R. HARRIS. Effects of experimenter awareness and sex of subject and experimenter on reactions to dependency relationship. *Sociometry,* 1964, **27,** 327-337.

BERKOWITZ, L., & A. LE PAGE. Weapons as aggression-eliciting stimuli. *Journal of Personality and Social Psychology,* 1967, **7,** 202-207.

BERKOWITZ, L., & B. I. LEVY. Pride in group performance and group-task motivation. *Journal of Abnormal and Social Psychology,* 1956, **53,** 300-306.

BERKOWITZ, M. I. An experimental study of the relation between group size and social organization. Unpublished doctoral dissertation, Yale University, 1958.

BERLO, D. K., J. B. LEMERT, & R. J. MERTZ. Dimensions for evaluating the acceptability of message sources. *Public Opinion Quarterly,* 1969-1970, **33,** 563-576.

BERMANN, E. A. Compatibility and stability in the dyad. Paper presented at the meeting of the American Psychological Association, New York, September 1966.

BERNE, E. *Transactional analysis in psychotherapy: A systematic individual and social psychiatry.* New York: Grove Press, Inc., 1961.

BERSCHEID, E., D. BOYE, & J. M. DARLEY. Effect of forced association upon voluntary choice to associate. *Journal of Personality and Social Psychology,* 1968, **8,** 13-19.

BERSCHEID, E., & E. WALSTER. Beauty and the best. *Psychology Today,* 1972, **5**(10), 42-46, 74.

BERSCHEID, E., & E. WALSTER. Physical attractiveness. In L. Berkowitz (Ed.), *Advances in experimental social psychology.* Vol. 7. New York: Academic Press, Inc., 1973, in press.

BETTELHEIM, B. Individual and mass behavior in extreme situations. *Journal of Abnormal and Social Psychology,* 1943, **38,** 417-452.

BETTINGHAUS, E. P. Operation of congruity in an oral communication setting. *Speech Monographs,* 1961, **28,** 131-142.

BIDDLE, B. J., H. A. ROSENCRANZ, & E. T. RANKIN. *Studies in the role of the public school teacher.* Columbia: University of Missouri Press, 1961.

BIDWELL, C. E. The young professional in the army: A study of occupational identity. *American Sociological Review,* 1961, **26,** 360-372.

BIERI, J. Cognitive complexity-simplicity and predictive behavior. *Journal of Abnormal and Social Psychology,* 1955, **51,** 263-268.

BIESANZ, J., & L. M. SMITH. Race relations in Panama and the Canal Zone. *American Journal of Sociology,* 1951, **57,** 7-14.

BIRDWHISTELL, R. L. *Introduction to kinesics.* Louisville, Ky.: University of Louisville Press, Foreign Services Institute, 1952.

BLAKE, R. R., H. HELSON, & J. S. MOUTON. The generality of conformity behavior as a function of factual anchorage, difficulty of task, and amount of social pressure. *Journal of Personality,* 1956, **25,** 294-305.

BLAKE, R. R., & J. S. MOUTON. Conformity, resistance, and conversion. In I. A. Berg & B. M. Bass (Eds.), *Conformity and deviation.* New York: Harper & Brothers, 1961. Pp. 1-37.

BLANK, A. Effects of group and individual conditions on choice behavior. *Journal of Personality and Social Psychology,* 1968, **8,** 294-298.

BLAU, P. M. *The dynamics of bureaucracy.* Chicago: The University of Chicago Press, 1955.

BLAU, P. M. *Exchange and power in social life.* New York: John Wiley & Sons, Inc., 1964. *(a)*

BLAU, P. M. Justice in social exchange. *Sociological Inquiry,* 1964, **34,** 193-206. *(b)*

BLAU, P. M., & W. R. SCOTT. *Formal organizations.* San Francisco: Chandler Publishing Company, Inc., 1962. Pp. 107-108.

BLOCH, H. A., & A. NIEDERHOFFER. *The gang: A study in adolescent behavior.* New York: Philosophical Library, Inc., 1958.

BLOOD, R. O., JR., & D. M. WOLFE. *Husbands and wives: The dynamics of married living.* New York: The Free Press of Glencoe, Inc., 1960.

BLOOMBAUM, M. Factors in the resolution of role conflict. Paper presented at the meeting of the American Sociological Association, St. Louis, Mo., September 1961.

BLUMER, H. *Symbolic interactionism: Perspective and method.* Englewood Cliffs, N.J.: Prentice-Hall, Inc., 1969.

BLUMLER, J. G., & D. MCQUAIL. *Television in politics.* Chicago: The University of Chicago Press, 1969.

BLUMSTEIN, P. W. An experiment in identity bargaining. Unpublished doctoral dissertation. Nashville, Tenn.: Vanderbilt University, 1970.

BOCHNER, S., & C. A. INSKO. Communicator discrepancy, source credibility and opinion change. *Journal of Personality and Social Psychology,* 1966, **4,** 614-621.

BOHNSTEDT, M. A. Stability and change of self conception. Unpublished doctoral dissertation, University of Nevada, 1970.

BONNEY, M. E., R. E. HOBLIT, & A. H. DREYER. A study of some factors related to sociometric status in a men's dormitory. *Sociometry,* 1953, **16,** 287-301.

BORGATTA, E. F. Attitudinal concomitants to military sta-

tuses. *Social Forces,* 1955, **33,** 342-347.

BORGATTA, E. F., & R. F. BALES. Interaction of individuals in reconstituted groups. *Sociometry,* 1953, **16,** 302-320.

BORGATTA, E. F., A. S. COUCH, & R. F. BALES. Some findings relevant to the great man theory of leadership. *American Sociological Review,* 1954, **19,** 755-759.

BOWERS, J. W. Language intensity, social introversion and attitude change. *Speech Monographs,* 1963, **30,** 345-352.

BOWERS, J. W. The influence of delivery on attitudes toward concepts and speakers. *Speech Monographs,* 1965, **32,** 154-158.

BOWERS, J. W., & M. M. OSBORN. Attitudinal effects of selected types of concluding metaphors in persuasive speech. *Speech Monographs,* 1966, **33,** 147-155.

BOWERMAN, C., & B. DAY. A test of the theory of complementary needs as applied to couples during courtship. *American Sociological Review,* 1956, **21,** 227-232.

BOWLBY, J. *Maternal care and mental health.* Geneva, Switzerland: World Health Organization, 1952.

BOWLBY, J. Separation anxiety. *International Journal of Psychoanalysis,* 1960, **41,** 89-113.

BRAMEL, D. A dissonance theory approach to defensive projection. *Journal of Abnormal and Social Psychology,* 1962, **64,** 121-129.

BRAMEL, D. Dissonance, expectation, and the self. In R. P. Abelson et al. (Eds.), *Theories of cognitive consistency: A sourcebook.* Chicago: Rand McNally & Company, 1968. Pp. 355-365.

BRANDON, A. C. The relevance of expectation as an underlying factor in status incongruence. *Sociometry,* 1965, **28,** 272-288.

BRAY, D. W. The prediction of behavior from two attitude scales. *Journal of Abnormal and Social Psychology,* 1950, **45,** 64-84.

BRAYFIELD, A. H., & W. H. CROCK-

ETT. Employee attitudes and employee performance. *Psychological Bulletin,* 1955, **52,** 396-424.

BREDEMEIER, H. C., & R. M. STEPHENSON. *The analysis of social systems.* New York: Holt, Rinehart and Winston, Inc., 1962.

BREHM, J. W., & A. H. COLE. Effect of a favor which reduces freedom. *Journal of Personality and Social Psychology,* 1966, **3,** 420-426.

BRIGANTE, T. R. Adolescent evaluations of rewarding, neutral, and punishing power figures. *Journal of Personality,* 1958, **26,** 435-450.

BRIM, O. G., JR. Family structure and sex role learning by children: A further analysis of Helen Koch's data. *Sociometry,* 1958, **21,** 1-16.

BRIM, O. G., JR. Personality development as role learning. In I. Iscoe and H. W. Stevenson (Eds.), *Personality development in children.* Austin: University of Texas Press, 1960.

BROCK, T. C., S. M. ALBERT, & L. A. BECKER. Familiarity, utility, and supportiveness as determinants of information receptivity. *Journal of Personality and Social Psychology,* 1970, **14,** 292-301.

BROCK, T. C., & J. L. BALLOUN. Behavioral receptivity to dissonant information. *Journal of Personality and Social Psychology,* 1967, **6,** 413-428.

BROCK, T. C., & A. H. BUSS. Dissonance, aggression, and evaluation of pain. *Journal of Abnormal and Social Psychology,* 1962, **65,** 197-202.

BRODBECK, M. The role of small groups in mediating the effects of propaganda. *Journal of Abnormal and Social Psychology,* 1956, **52,** 166-170.

BRODBECK, M. The influence of propaganda without social support. In D. Willner (Ed.), *Decisions, values and groups.* New York: Pergamon Press, 1960. Pp. 241-245.

BRONFENBRENNER, U. Socialization and social class through time and space. In E. Maccoby, T. M. Newcomb, & E. L. Hartley (Eds.), *Readings in social psychology.*

New York: Holt, Rinehart and Winston, Inc., 1958. Pp. 400-425.

BRONFENBRENNER, U. Early development in mammals: A cross species analysis. In G. Newton, & S. Levine (Eds.), *Early experience and behavior.* Springfield, Ill.: Charles C Thomas, Publisher, 1968.

BRONFENBRENNER, U. *Two worlds of childhood: U.S. and U.S.S.R.* New York: Russell Sage Foundation, 1970.

BROOKOVER, W. B., S. THOMAS, & A. PATERSON. Self concept of ability and school achievement. *Sociology of Education,* 1964, **37,** 271-278.

BROOKOVER, W. B., ET AL. Self concept ability and school achievement. III. Third report on the continuing study of the relations of self concept and achievement. Educational Research Series 36, Cooperative Research Project 2831, February 1967.

BROPHY, I. N. The luxury of anti-Negro prejudice. *Public Opinion Quarterly,* 1946, **9,** 456-466.

BROWN, B. R. The effects of need to maintain face on interpersonal bargaining. *Journal of Experimental Social Psychology,* 1968, **4,** 107-122.

BROWN, B. R. Face-saving following experimentally induced embarrassment. *Journal of Experimental Social Psychology,* 1970, **6,** 255-271.

BROWN, R. W. *Social psychology.* New York: The Free Press, 1965.

BROXTON, J. A. A test of interpersonal attraction predictions derived from balance theory. *Journal of Abnormal and Social Psychology,* 1963, **66,** 394-397.

BRUNER, J. S., & H. V. PERLMUTTER. Compatriot and foreigner: A study of impression formation in three countries. *Journal of Abnormal and Social Psychology,* 1957, **55,** 253-260.

BRUNER, J. S., D. SHAPIRO, & R. TAGIURI. The meaning of traits in isolation and in combination. In R. Tagiuri & L. Petrullo (Eds.), *Person per-* ception and interpersonal behavior. Stanford, Calif.: Stanford University Press, 1958. Pp. 277-288.

BRUNER, J. S., & R. TAGIURI. The perception of people. In G. Lindzey (Ed.), *Handbook of social psychology.* Vol. I. Cambridge, Mass.: Addison-Wesley Publishing Company, Inc., 1954. Pp. 601-633.

BRYAN, J. H., & M. A. TEST. Models and helping: Naturalistic studies in aiding behavior. *Journal of Personality and Social Psychology,* 1967, **6,** 400-407.

BUCHANAN, W. Stereotypes and tensions as revealed by the UNESCO international poll. *International Social Science Journal,* 1951, **3,** 515-528.

BURCHARD, W. W. Role conflicts of military chaplains. *American Sociological Review,* 1954, **19,** 528-535.

BURGESS, R. L. Communication networks: An experimental re-evaluation. *Journal of Experimental Social Psychology,* 1968, **4,** 324-337.

BURKE, P. J. The development of task and social-emotional role differentiation. *Sociometry,* 1967, **30,** 379-392.

BURKE, P. J. Role differentiation and the legitimation of task activity. *Sociometry,* 1968, **31,** 404-411.

BURKE, P. J. Scapegoating: An alternative to role differentiation. *Sociometry,* 1969, **32,** 159-168.

BURNSTEIN, E., & A. V. MCRAE. Some effects of shared threat and prejudice in racially mixed groups. *Journal of Abnormal and Social Psychology,* 1962, **64,** 257-263.

BURTON, R. V. Generality of honesty reconsidered. *Psychological Review,* 1963, **70,** 481-499.

BYRNE, D., & J. A. BUEHLER. A note on the influence of propinquity upon acquaintanceships. *Journal of Abnormal and Social Psychology,* 1955, **51,** 147-148.

BYRNE, D., & G. L. CLORE, JR. Predicting interpersonal attraction toward strangers presented in three different stimulus modes. *Psychonomic Science,* 1966, **4**(6), 239-240.

BYRNE, D., & G. L. CLORE, JR. Effectance arousal and attraction. *Journal of Personality and Social Psychology Monograph,* 1967, Vol. 6, No. 4 (Whole No. 638).

BYRNE, D., G. L. CLORE, JR., & P. WORCHEL. Effect of economic similarity-dissimilarity on interpersonal attraction. *Journal of Personality and Social Psychology,* 1966, **4,** 220-224.

BYRNE, D., & A. GRIFFITT. Developmental investigation of the law of attraction. *Journal of Personality and Social Psychology,* 1966, **4,** 699-702.

BYRNE, D., W. GRIFFITT, W. HUDGINS, & K. REEVES. Attitude similarity-dissimilarity and attraction: Generality beyond the college sophomore. *Journal of Social Psychology,* 1969, **79,** 155-161.

BYRNE, D., W. GRIFFITT, & D. STEFANIAK. Attraction and similarity of personality characteristics. *Journal of Personality and Social Psychology,* 1967, **5,** 89-90.

BYRNE, D., O. LENDON, & K. REEVES. The effects of physical attractiveness, sex and attitude similarity on interpersonal attraction. *Journal of Personality,* 1968, **36,** 259-271.

BYRNE, D., & D. A. NELSON. Attraction as a linear function of proportion of positive reinforcements. *Journal of Personality and Social Psychology,* 1965, **1,** 659-663.

BYRNE, D., & R. RHAMEY. Magnitude of positive and negative reinforcements as determinant of attraction. *Journal of Personality and Social Psychology,* 1965, **2,** 884-889.

BYRNE, D., R. K. YOUNG, & W. GRIFFITT. The reinforcement properties of attitude statements. *Journal of Experimental Research in Personality,* 1966, **1,** 266-276.

BYRNE, D., & T. J. WONG. Racial prejudice, interpersonal attraction, and assumed dissimilarity of attitudes. *Journal of Abnormal and Social Psychology,* 1962, **65,** 246-253.

CAMPBELL, A., P. E. CONVERSE,

W. E. MILLER, & D. E. STOKES. *The American voter.* New York: John Wiley & Sons, Inc., 1960.

CAMPBELL, D. T. Stereotypes and the perception of group differences. *American Psychologist,* 1967, **22**, 817–829.

CAMPBELL, E. Q., & T. F. PETTIGREW. Racial and moral crisis: The role of Little Rock ministers. *American Journal of Sociology,* 1959, **64**, 509–516.

CAMPBELL, J. D., & M. R. YARROW. Personal and situational variables in adaptation to change. *Journal of Social Issues,* 1958, **14**(1), 29–46.

CANON, L. Self-confidence and selective exposure to information. In L. Festinger, *Conflict, decision, and dissonance.* Stanford, Calif.: Stanford University Press, 1964, Pp. 83–96.

CAPLAN, N. The new ghetto man: A review of recent empirical studies. *Journal of Social Issues,* 1970, **26**(1), 59–73.

CAPLOW. T. A theory of coalitions in the triad. *American Sociological Review,* 1956, **21**, 489–493.

CARITHERS, M. W. School desegregation and racial cleavage, 1954–1970: A review of the literature. *Journal of Social Issues,* 1970, **26**(4), 25–47.

CARLSMITH, J. M., B. E. COLLINS, & R. HELMREICH. Studies in forced compliance: I. Attitude change produced by face-to-face role playing and anonymous essay writing. *Journal of Personality and Social Psychology,* 1966, **4**, 1–13.

CARMICHAEL, C. W., & G. L. CRONKHITE. Frustration and language intensity. *Speech Monographs,* 1965, **32**, 107–111.

CARTER, L. F., W. W. HAYTHORN, & M. HOWELL. A further investigation of the criteria of leadership. *Journal of Abnormal and Social Psychology,* 1950, **45**, 350–358.

CARTER, L. F., & M. NIXON. An investigation of the relationship between four criteria of leadership ability for three different tasks. *Journal of Psychology,* 1949, **27**, 245–261.

CARTER, R. F. Some effects of the debates. In S. Kraus (Ed.), *The great debates.* Bloomington: Indiana University Press, 1962, Pp. 253–270.

CARTWRIGHT, D. The nature of group cohesiveness. In D. Cartwright and A. Zander (Eds.), *Group dynamics: Research and theory.* (3rd ed.) New York: Harper & Row, Publishers, Incorporated, 1968.

CARTWRIGHT, D., & A. ZANDER (Eds.). *Group dynamics: Research and theory.* (2nd ed.) Evanston, Ill.: Row Peterson, 1960.

CAVAN, R. S. Self and role in adjustment during old age. In A. M. Rose (Ed.), *Human behavior and social processes: An interactionist approach.* Boston: Houghton Mifflin Company, 1962.

CHADWICK-JONES, J. K. Intergroup attitudes: A stage in attitude formation. *British Journal of Sociology,* 1962, **13**, 57–63.

CHARTERS, W. W., JR., & T. M. NEWCOMB. Some attitudinal effects of experimentally increased salience of a membership group. In E. Maccoby, T. M. Newcomb, & E. L. Hartley (Eds.), *Readings in social psychology.* New York: Holt, Rinehart and Winston, Inc., 1958. Pp. 276–280.

CHEN, T. H. E. *Thought reform of the Chinese intellectuals.* Fair Lawn, N.J.: Oxford University Press, 1960.

CHEYNE, J. A., & R. H. WALTERS. Intensity of punishment, timing of punishment, and cognitive structure as determinants of response inhibition. *Journal of Experimental Child Psychology,* 1969, **7**, 231–244.

CHRISTIE, L. S., R. D. LUCE, & J. MACY, JR. *Communication and learning in task-oriented groups.* Technical Report No. 231. Cambridge, Mass.: Research Laboratory of Electronics, Massachusetts Institute of Technology. 1952.

CHU, G. C. Culture, personality, and persuasibility. *Sociometry,* 1966, **29**, 169–174.

CHURCH, R. M. The varied effects of punishment on behavior. *Psychological Review,* 1963, **70**, 369–402.

CLARK, J. W. A preliminary investigation of some unconscious assumptions affecting labor efficiency in eight supermarkets. Unpublished doctoral dissertation, Harvard University, 1958.

CLARKE, P., & J. JAMES. The effects of situation, attitude intensity and personality on information-seeking. *Sociometry,* 1967, **30**, 235–245.

CLOWARD, R. A. Illegitimate means, anomie, and deviant behavior. *American Sociological Review,* 1959, **24**, 164–176.

CLOWARD, R. A., & L. E. OHLIN. *Delinquency and opportunity: A theory of delinquent gangs.* New York: The Free Press of Glencoe, Inc., 1960.

COATES, B., & W. W. HARTUP. Age and verbalization in observational learning. *Developmental Psychology,* 1969, **1**, 556–562.

COCH, L., & J. R. P. FRENCH, JR. Overcoming resistance to change. In E. E. Maccoby, T. M. Newcomb, & E. L. Hartley (Eds.), *Readings in social psychology.* (3rd ed.) New York: Holt, Rinehart and Winston, Inc., 1958. Pp. 233–250.

COHEN, A. K. *Delinquent boys, the culture of the gang.* Chicago: The Free Press of Glencoe, Ill., 1955.

COHEN, A. M., & W. G. BENNIS. Continuity of leadership in communication networks. *Human Relations,* 1961, **14**, 351–368.

COHEN, A. M., W. G. BENNIS, & G. H. WOLKON. The effects of changes in communication networks on the behaviors of problem-solving groups. *Sociometry,* 1962, **25**, 177–196.

COHEN, A. M., E. L. ROBINSON, & J. L. EDWARDS. Experiments in organizational embeddedness. *Administrative Science Quarterly,* 1969, **14**, 208–221.

COHEN, A. R. Upward communication in experimentally created hierarchies. *Human Relations,* 1958, **11**, 41–53.

COLEMAN, J. F., R. R. BLAKE, & J. S. MOUTON. Task difficulty and conformity pressures.

Journal of Abnormal and Social Psychology, 1958, **57**, 120-122.

COLEMAN, J. S. *The adolescent society.* New York: The Free Press of Glencoe, Inc., 1961.

COLEMAN, J. S., E. Q. CAMPBELL, C. J. HOBSON, ET AL. *Equality of educational opportunity.* Washington: U.S. Office of Education, 1966.

COLEMAN, J. S., E. KATZ, & H. MENZEL. The diffusion of an innovation among physicians. *Sociometry,* 1957, **20**, 253-270.

COLEMAN, J. S., & D. MCRAE. Electronic processing of sociometric data for groups up to 1,000 in size. *American Sociological Review,* 1960, **25**, 722-727.

COLLINS, B. E. The effect of monetary inducements on the amount of attitude change produced by forced compliance. In A. C. Elms (Ed.), *Role playing, reward, and attitude change.* New York: D. Van Nostrand Company, Inc., 1969. Pp. 209-223.

COLLINS, B. E., R. D. ASHMORE, F. W. HORNBECK, & R. WHITNEY. Studies in forced compliance: XIII and XV. In search of a dissonance-producing forced compliance paradigm. *Representative Research in Social Psychology,* 1970, **1**, 11-23.

COLLINS, B. E., & R. HELMREICH. Studies in forced compliance: II. Contrasting mechanisms of attitude change produced by public-persuasive and private-true essays. *Journal of Social Psychology,* 1970, **81**, 253-264.

COLLINS, B. E., & M. G. HOYT. Personal responsibility-for-consequences: An integration and extension of the "forced-compliance" literature. *Journal of Experimental Social Psychology,* 1972, **8**, 558-593.

COLLINS, B. E., & B. H. RAVEN. Psychological aspects of structure in small groups: Interpersonal attraction, coalitions, communication and power. In G. Lindsey & E. Aronsen (Eds.), *Handbook of social psychology.* Vol. 4. Reading, Mass.: Addison-Wesley Publishing Company, Inc., 1969. Pp. 102-204.

COMMITTEE ON GOVERNMENT OPERATIONS, U.S. SENATE, EIGHTY-FOURTH CONGRESS, SECOND SESSION. Hearings on "Communist interrogation, indoctrination and exploitation of American military and civilian prisoners." June 19, 20, 26, 27, 1956.

CONNOR, R., H. F. GREENE, & J. WALTERS. Agreement of family members' conceptions of "good" parent and child roles. *Social Forces,* 1958, **36**, 353-358.

CONVERSE, P. E. Information flow and the stability of political attitudes. Paper presented at the meeting of the American Psychological Association, New York, September 1961.

COOK, T. D. Competence, counterarguing, and attitude change. *Journal of Personality,* 1969, **37**, 342-358.

COOLEY, C. H. *Human nature and the social order.* New York: Charles Scribner's Sons, 1902. Reprinted: New York: The Free Press of Glencoe, Inc., 1956.

COOPER, J., & E. E. JONES. Opinion divergence as a strategy to avoid being miscast. *Journal of Personality and Social Psychology,* 1969, **13**, 23-30.

COOPER, J., & S. WORCHEL. Role of undesired consequences in arousing cognitive dissonance. *Journal of Personality and Social Psychology,* 1970, **16**, 199-206.

COOPER, J. B. Emotion in prejudice. *Science,* 1959, **130**, 314-318.

COOPER, J. B., & D. POLLOCK. The identification of prejudicial attitudes by the galvanic skin response. *Journal of Social Psychology,* 1959, **50**, 241-245.

COOPER, J. B., & H. E. SIEGEL. The galvanic skin response as a measure of emotion in prejudice. *Journal of Social Psychology,* 1956, **42**, 149-155.

COOPER, J. B., & D. N. SINGER. The role of emotion in prejudice. *Journal of Social Psychology,* 1956, **44**, 241-247.

COOPER, L. (Trans.) *The rhetoric of Aristotle.* New York: Appleton-Century-Crofts, 1932.

COOPERSMITH, S. *The antecedents of self-esteem.* San Francisco: W. H. Freeman and Company, 1967.

COSER, L. *The functions of social conflict.* Chicago: The Free Press of Glencoe, Ill., 1956.

COSER, R. L. Role distance, sociological ambivalence, and transitional status systems. *American Journal of Sociology,* 1966, **72**, 173-187.

COTTRELL, L. S., JR. The analysis of situational fields in social psychology. *American Sociological Review,* 1942, **7**, 370-382.

COUSINS, A. N. Social equilibrium and the psychodynamic mechanism. *Social Forces,* 1951, **30**, 202-209.

COWEN, E. L., J. LANDES, & D. E. SCHAET. The effects of mild frustration on the expression of prejudiced attitudes. *Journal of Abnormal Social Psychology,* 1958, **58**, 33-38.

COX, K. K. Changes in stereotyping of Negroes and whites in magazine advertisements. *Public Opinion Quarterly,* 1969, **33**, 603-606.

CRANDALL, V. C., W. KATKOVSKY, & U. J. CRANDALL. Children's beliefs in their own control of reinforcements in intellectual-academic achievement situations. *Child Development,* 1965, **36**, 91-109.

CRISWELL, J. H. Racial cleavage in Negro-white groups. *Sociometry,* 1937, **1**, 81-89.

CROCKETT, H. J., JR. The achievement motive and differential occupational mobility in the United States. *American Sociological Review,* 1962, **27**, 191-204.

CROCKETT, W. H. Emergent leadership in small, decision-making groups. *Journal of Abnormal and Social Psychology,* 1955, **51**, 378-383.

CROCKETT, W. H., & T. MEIDINGER. Authoritarianism and interpersonal perception. *Journal of Abnormal and Social Psychology,* 1956, **53**, 378-380.

CRONBACH, L. J. Processes affecting scores on "understanding of others" and "assumed similarity." *Psychological Bulletin*, 1955, **52**, 177-193.

CRONBACH, L. J. Proposals leading to analytic treatment of social perception scores. In R. Tagiuri & L. Petrullo (Eds.), *Person perception and interpersonal behavior.* Stanford, Calif.: Stanford University Press, 1958. Pp. 353-380.

CRUTCHFIELD, R. S. Conformity and character. *American Psychologist*, 1955, **10**, 191-198.

CURRY, T. J., & R. M. EMERSON. Balance theory: A theory of interpersonal attraction? *Sociometry*, 1970, **33**, 216-238.

CUTLIP, S. M. Content and flow of AP news: From trunk to TTS to Reader. *Journalism Quarterly*, 1954, **31**, 434-446.

DABBS, J. M., JR. Self-esteem, communicator characteristics, and attitude change. *Journal of Abnormal and Social Psychology*, 1964, **69**, 173-181.

DABBS, J. M., JR., & H. LEVENTHAL. Effects of varying the recommendations in a fear-arousing communication. *Journal of Personality and Social Psychology*, 1966, **4**, 525-531.

DANIELS, M. J. Affect and its control in the medical intern. *American Journal of Sociology*, 1960, **66**, 259-267.

DANIELSON, W. A. Eisenhower's February decision: A study of news impact. *Journalism Quarterly*, 1956, **33**, 433-441.

DARLEY, J. M., & B. LATANÉ. Bystander intervention in emergencies: Diffusion of responsibility. *Journal of Personality and Social Psychology*, 1968, **8**, 377-383.

DAVIS, A., & J. DOLLARD. *Children of bondage.* Washington: American Council on Education, 1940.

DAVIS, F. J. Conceptions of official leader roles in the air force. *Social Forces*, 1954, **32**, 253-258.

DAVIS, J. H., & F. RESTLE. The analysis of problems and prediction of group problem solving. *Journal of Abnormal*

and Social Psychology, 1963, **66**, 103-116.

DAVIS, K. Final note on a case of extreme isolation. *American Journal of Sociology*, 1947, **52**, 432-437.

DAVIS, K., & W. E. MOORE. Some principles of stratification. *American Sociological Review*, 1945, **10**, 242-249.

DAVIS, K. E., & E. E. JONES. Changes in interpersonal perception as a means of reducing cognitive dissonance. *Journal of Abnormal and Social Psychology*, 1960, **61**, 402-410.

DAVITZ, J. R. *The communication of emotional meaning.* New York: McGraw-Hill Book Company, 1964.

DAVOL, S. H. An empirical test of structural balance in sociometric triads. *Journal of Abnormal and Social Psychology*, 1959, **59**, 393-398.

DAWSON, P. A., & J. E. ZINSER. Broadcast expenditures and electoral outcomes in the 1970 congressional elections. *Public Opinion Quarterly*, 1971, **35**, 398-402.

DEAN, D. G. Alienation: Its meaning and measurement. *American Sociological Review*, 1961, **26**, 753-758.

DE FLEUR, M. L., & O. N. LARSEN. *The flow of information: An experiment in mass communication.* New York: Harper & Row, Publishers, Incorporated, 1958.

DE FLEUR, M. L., & F. R. WESTIE. Verbal attitudes and overt acts: An experiment on the salience of attitudes. *American Sociological Review*, 1958, **23**, 667-673.

DENNIS, W., & P. NAJARIAN. Infant development under environmental handicaps. *Psychological Monographs*, 1957, **71**(7, Whole No. 436).

DENZIN, N. K. The significant others of a college population. *Sociological Quarterly*, 1966, **7**, 298-319.

DEUTSCH, M., & H. B. GERARD. A study of normative and informational influence upon individual judgement. *Journal of Abnormal and Social Psychology*, 1955, **51**, 629-636.

DEUTSCH, M., & R. M. KRAUSS.

The effect of threat upon interpersonal bargaining. *Journal of Abnormal and Social Psychology*, 1960, **61**, 181-189.

DEUTSCH, M., & R. M. KRAUSS. Studies of interpersonal bargaining. *Journal of Conflict Resolutions*, 1962, **6**, 52-76.

DEUTSCH, M., Y. EPSTEIN, D. CANAVAN, & P. GUMPERT. Strategies of inducing cooperation: An empirical study. *Journal of Conflict Resolution*, 1967, **11**, 345-360.

DEUTSCH, M., & L. SOLOMON. Reactions to evaluations by others as influenced by self evaluations. *Sociometry*, 1959, **22**, 93-112.

DEUTSCHER, A. Socialization for post-parental life. In A. Rose (Ed.), *Human behavior and social processes: An interactionist approach.* Boston: Houghton Mifflin Company, 1962.

DEUTSCHMANN, P. J., & W. A. DANIELSON. Diffusion of knowledge of a major news story. *Journalism Quarterly*, 1960, **37**, 345-355.

DICKS, H. V. German personality traits and Nazi ideology. *Human Relations*, 1950, **3**, 111-154.

DIENSTBIER, R. A modified belief theory of prejudice emphasizing the mutual causality of racial prejudice and anticipated belief differences. *Psychological Review*, 1972, **79**, 146-160.

DIETRICH, J. E. The relative effectiveness of two modes of radio delivery in influencing attitudes. *Speech Monographs*, 1946, **13**, 58-65.

DIGGORY, J. C. *Self evaluation: Concepts and studies.* New York: John Wiley & Sons, Inc., 1966.

DINNERSTEIN, D. A study of the development of certain cognitive structures. Unpublished doctoral dissertation, Graduate Faculty of Political and Social Science, New School for Social Research, 1951.

DION, K., E. BERSCHEID, & E. WALSTER. What is beautiful is good. *Journal of Personality and Social Psychology*, 1972, **24**, 285-290.

DION, K. L., R. S. BARON, & N. MILLER. Why do groups make riskier decisions than individuals? In L. Berkowitz (Ed.), *Advances in experimental social psychology.* Vol. 5. New York: Academic Press, Inc., 1970. Pp. 306-377.

DITTES, J. E. Attractiveness of group as a function of self-esteem and acceptance by group. *Journal of Abnormal and Social Psychology,* 1959, **59,** 77-82.

DITTES, J. E., & H. H. KELLEY. Effects of different conditions of acceptance on conformity to group norms. *Journal of Abnormal and Social Psychology,* 1956, **53,** 100-107.

DODD, S. C. A social distance test in the Near East. *American Journal of Sociology,* 1935, **41,** 194-204.

DOHERTY, E. G., & P. F. SECORD. Change of roommate and interpersonal congruency. *Representative Research in Social Psychology,* 1971, **2**(2), 70-75.

DOLLARD, J., L. W. DOOB, N. E. MILLER, JR., O. H. MOWRER, & R. R. SEARS. *Frustration and aggression.* New Haven, Conn.: Yale University Press, 1939.

DORNBUSCH, S. M. The military academy as an assimilating institution. *Social Forces,* 1955, **33,** 316-321.

DOUVAN, E. M. Social status and success strivings. *Journal of Abnormal and Social Psychology,* 1956, **52,** 219-223.

DUDYCHA, G. J. The attitudes of college students toward war and the Germans before and during the Second World War. *Journal of Social Psychology,* 1942, **15,** 317-324.

DUNCAN, S. Nonverbal communication. *Psychological Bulletin,* 1969, **72,** 118-137.

DUNCAN, S. D., JR. Some signals and rules for taking speaking turns in conversations. *Journal of Personality and Social Psychology,* 1972, **23,** 283-292.

DUNCAN, S. D., JR. Toward a grammar for dyadic conversations. *Semiotica,* 1973, in press.

DUNCAN, S. D., JR., & R. ROSENTHAL. Vocal emphasis on experimenters' instruction reading as unintended determinant of subjects' responses. *Language and Speech,* 1968, **11,** 20-26.

DUNNETTE, M. D., J. D. CAMPBELL, & K. JAASTAD. The effect of group participation on brainstorming effectiveness for two industrial samples. *Journal of Applied Psychology,* 1963, **47,** 30-37.

EAGLY, A. H. Involvement as a determinant of response to favorable and unfavorable information. *Journal of Personality and Social Psychology Monograph,* 1967, 7(3, Whole No. 643), 1-15.

EAGLY, A. H., & B. ACKSEN. The effect of expecting to be evaluated on change toward favorable and unfavorable information about oneself. *Sociometry,* 1971, **34,** 411-422.

EAPEN, K. E. Daily newspapers in India: Their status and problems. *Journalism Quarterly,* 1967, **44,** 520-532.

EDWARDS, A. L. *Techniques of attitude scale construction.* New York: Appleton Century Crofts, 1957.

EHRLICH, H. J., J. W. RINEHART, & J. C. HOWELL. The study of role conflict: Explorations in methodology. *Sociometry,* 1962, **25,** 85-97.

EISENSTADT, S. N. The place of elites and primary groups in the process of absorption of new immigrants in Israel. *American Journal of Sociology,* 1951, **57,** 222-231.

EISENSTADT, S. N. Processes of communication among new immigrants. *Public Opinion Quarterly,* 1952, **16,** 42-58.

EKMAN, P. Body position, facial expression, and verbal behavior during interviews. *Journal of Abnormal and Social Psychology,* 1964, **68**(3), 295-301.

EKMAN, P. Communication through nonverbal behavior: A source of information about an interpersonal relationship. In Sylvan S. Tompkins & Carol E. Izard (Eds.), *Affect, cognition, and personality.* New York: Springer Publishing Co., Inc., 1965.

EKMAN, P. Differential communication of affect by head and body cues. *Journal of Personality and Social Psychology,* 1965, **2,** 726-735.

EKMAN, P., & W. V. FRIESEN. Personality, pathology, affect, and nonverbal behavior. Paper presented at the meeting of the Western Psychological Association, Honolulu, Hawaii, September 1965.

EKMAN, P., & W. V. FRIESEN. Head and body cues in the judgment of emotion: A reformulation. *Perceptual and Motor Skills,* 1967, **24,** 711-724.

EKMAN, P., & W. V. FRIESEN. Nonverbal leakage and clues to deception. *Psychiatry,* 1969, **32,** 88-106.

EKMAN, P., & W. V. FRIESEN. The repertoire of nonverbal behavior: Categories, origins, usage, and coding. *Semiotica,* 1969, **1,** 49-98.

EKMAN, P., R. M. LIEBERT, W. V. FRIESEN, R. HARRISON, C. ZLATCHIN, E. J. MALMSTROM, & R. A. BARON. Facial expressions of emotion while watching televised violence as predictors of subsequent aggression. In G. A. Comstock, E. A. Rubenstein, & J. P. Murray (Eds.), *Television and social behavior.* Vol. 5. *Television's effects: Further explorations.* Government Printing Office, 1971.

ELDRED, S. H., & D. B. PRICE. Linguistic evaluation of feeling states in psychotherapy. *Psychiatry,* 1958, **21,** 115-121.

ELLIS, R. A., & T. C. KEEDY, JR. Three dimensions of status: A study of academic prestige. *Pacific Sociological Review,* 1960, **3,** 23-28.

ELMS, A. C. Role playing, incentive, and dissonance. *Psychological Bulletin,* 1967, **68,** 132-148.

ELMS, A. C., & I. L. JANIS. Counter-norm attitudes induced by consonant versus dissonant conditions of role-playing. *Journal of Experimental Research in Personality,* 1965, **1,** 50-60.

EMERSON, R. M. Power-dependence relations. *American Sociological Review,* 1962, **27,** 31-41.

EMERSON, R. M. Power-dependence relations: Two experiments. *Sociometry*, 1964, **27**, 282-298.

EPSTEIN, R. Aggression toward outgroups as a function of authoritarianism and imitation of aggressive models. *Journal of Personality and Social Psychology*, 1966, **3**, 574-579.

EPSTEIN, B. R., & A. FORSTER. Barriers in higher education. In N. C. Belth (Ed.), *Barriers: Patterns of discrimination against Jews.* New York: Anti-Defamation League of B'nai B'rith, 1958. Pp. 60-73.

EVAN, W. M. Role strain and the norm of reciprocity in research organizations. *American Journal of Sociology*, 1962, **68**, 346-354.

EVAN, W. M., & E. G. LEVIN. Status-set and role-set conflicts of the stockbroker: A problem in the sociology of law. *Social Forces*, 1966, **45**, 73-83.

EXLINE, R. V., D. GRAY, & D. SCHUETTE. Visual behavior in a dyad as affected by interview content and sex of respondent. *Journal of Personality and Social Psychology*, 1965, **1**, 201-209.

EXLINE, R. V., & L. C. WINTERS. Affective relations and mutual glances. In S. S. Tompkins, & C. E. Izard (Eds.), *Affect, cognition, and personality.* New York: Springer Publishing Co., Inc., 1965.

EXLINE, R. V., & R. C. ZILLER. Status congruency and interpersonal conflict in decision-making groups. *Human Relations,* 1959, **12**, 147-162.

FAISON, E. W. J. Experimental comparison of the effectiveness of one-sided and two-sided mass communications on the influence of economic attitudes. Paper presented at the meeting of the American Association of Public Opinion Research, Berkeley, Calif., May 1961.

FEATHER, N. T. The relationship of persistence at a task to expectation of success and achievement related motives. *Journal of Abnormal and Social Psychology*, 1961, **63**, 552-561.

FEATHER, N. T. Performance at a difficult task in relation to initial expectation of success, test anxiety, and need achievement. *Journal of Personality*, 1965, **33**, 200-217.

FEATHER, N. T. Valence of outcome and expectation of success in relation to task difficulty and perceived locus of control. *Journal of Personality and Social Psychology*, 1967, **7**, 372-386.

FEIERABEND, I. K., & R. L. FEIERABEND. Aggressive behaviors within politics, 1948-1962: A cross-national study. *Journal of Conflict Resolution*, 1966, **10**, 249-271.

FELD, S. C. Longitudinal study of the origins of achievement strivings. *Journal of Personality and Social Psychology*, 1967, **7**, 408-414.

FELIPE, A. I. Evaluative versus descriptive consistency in trait inferences. *Journal of Personality and Social Psychology*, 1970, **16**, 627-638.

FESHBACH, S. The catharsis effect: Research and another view. In R. K. Baker & S. J. Ball (Eds.), *Mass media and violence: A staff report to the national commission on the causes and prevention.* Government Printing Office, 1969. Pp. 461-486.

FESHBACH, S., & R. P. SINGER. The effects of personal and shared threat upon social prejudice. *Journal of Abnormal and Social Psychology*, 1957, **54**, 411-416.

FESTINGER, L. The analysis of sociograms using matrix algebra. *Human Relations,* 1949, **2**, 153-158.

FESTINGER, L. Laboratory experiments: The role of group belongingness. In J. G. Miller (Ed.), *Experiments in social process.* New York: McGraw-Hill Book Company, 1950. Pp. 31-46.

FESTINGER, L. A theory of social comparison processes. *Human Relations,* 1954, **7**, 117-140.

FESTINGER, L. *A theory of cognitive dissonance.* Evanston, Ill.: Row, Peterson & Company, 1957.

FESTINGER, L. *Conflict, decision, and dissonance.* Stanford, Calif.: Stanford University Press, 1964.

FESTINGER, L., & J. M. CARLSMITH. Cognitive consequences of forced compliance. *Journal of Abnormal and Social Psychology*, 1959, **58**, 203-210.

FESTINGER, L., D. CARTWRIGHT, K. BARBER, J. FLEISCHL, J. GOTTSDANKER, A. KEYSEN, & G. LEAVITT. A study of rumor: Its origin and spread. *Human Relations,* 1948, **1**, 464-486.

FESTINGER, L., & H. H. KELLEY. *Changing attitudes through social contacts.* Ann Arbor, Mich.: Research Center for Group Dynamics, 1951.

FESTINGER, L., S. SCHACHTER, & K. W. BACK. *Social pressures in informal groups: A study of human factors in housing.* New York: Harper & Brothers, 1950.

FIEDLER, F. E. The leader's psychological distance and group effectiveness. In D. Cartwright & A. Zander (Eds.), *Group dynamics: Research and theory.* Second edition. Evanston, Ill.: Row, Peterson & Company, 1960. Pp. 586-606.

FIEDLER, F. E. A contingency model of leadership effectiveness. In L. Berkowitz (Ed.), *Advances in experimental social psychology.* Vol. 1. New York: Academic Press, Inc., 1964. Pp. 149-190.

FIEDLER, F. E., & E. L. HOFFMAN. Age, sex, and religious background as determinants of interpersonal perception among Dutch children: A cross-cultural validation. *Acta Psychologica*, 1962, **20**, 185-195.

FISEK, M. H., & R. OFSHE. The process of status evolution. *Sociometry*, 1970, **33**, 327-346.

FISHBEIN, M. (ED.). *Readings in attitude theory and measurement.* New York: John Wiley & Sons, Inc., 1967.

FISHBEIN, M., & I. AJZEN. Attitudes and opinions. In P. H. Mussen & M. R. Rosenzweig (Eds.), *Annual review of psychology.* Vol. 23. Palo Alto, Calif.: Annual Reviews, Inc., 1972. Pp. 487-544.

FISHBURN, C. E. Teacher role perception in the secondary

school. *Journal of Teacher Education,* 1962, **13,** 55–59.

FISHER, S., & A. LUBIN. Distance as a determinant of influence in a two-person serial interaction situation. *Journal of Abnormal and Social Psychology,* 1958, **56,** 230–238.

FLANDERS, J. P., & D. L. THISTLE-THWAITE. Effects of familiarization and group discussion upon risk taking. *Journal of Personality and Social Psychology,* 1967, **5,** 91–97.

FORSYTH, E., & L. KATZ. A matrix approach to the analysis of sociometric data: Preliminary report. *Sociometry,* 1946, **9,** 340–349.

FOSKETT, J. M. Role conflict: The concept. Paper presented at the meeting of the Pacific Sociological Society, Spokane, Wash., April 1960.

FREDERIKSEN, N. Toward a taxonomy of situations. *American Psychologist,* 1972, **27,** 114–123.

FREEDMAN, J. L. Involvement, discrepancy, and change. *Journal of Abnormal and Social Psychology,* 1964, **69,** 290–295.

FREEDMAN, J. L. Preference for dissonant information. *Journal of Personality and Social Psychology,* 1965, **2,** 287–289.

FREEDMAN, J. L., & S. C. FRASER. Compliance without pressure: The foot-in-the-door technique. *Journal of Personality and Social Psychology,* 1966, **4,** 195–202.

FREEDMAN, J. L., & D. O. SEARS. Selective exposure. In L. Berkowitz (Ed.), *Advances in experimental social psychology.* Vol. 2. New York: Academic Press, Inc., 1965. Pp. 58–98.

FREEDMAN, J. L., & D. O. SEARS. Warning, distraction, and resistance to influence. *Journal of Personality and Social Psychology,* 1965, **1,** 262–266.

FRENCH, J. R. P., JR., H. W. MORRISON, & G. LEVINGER. Coercive power and forces affecting conformity. *Journal of Abnormal and Social Psychology,* 1960, **61,** 93–101.

FRENCH, J. R. P., JR., & B. H. RAVEN. The basis of social power. In D. Cartwright (Ed.), *Studies in social power.*

Ann Arbor, Mich.: University of Michigan Press, 1959.

FRENCH, J. R. P., JR., & R. SNYDER. Leadership and interpersonal power. In D. Cartwright (Ed.), *Studies in social power.* Ann Arbor: The University of Michigan Press, 1959. Pp. 150–165.

FREUD, A. *The ego and mechanisms of defense.* New York: International Universities Press, Inc., 1946.

FREUD, S. Instincts and their vicissitudes. 1915. In *Collected papers.* Vol. 4. London: The Hogarth Press, Ltd., 1925. Pp. 60–83. (First published in German, 1915.)

FRIEDMAN, N. *The social nature of psychological research.* New York: Basic Books, Inc., Publishers, 1967.

FRISCH, D. M., & M. S. GREENBERG. Reciprocity and intentionality in the giving of help. Paper presented at the American Psychological Association Convention, San Francisco, August 1968.

FROMM, E. *Escape from freedom.* New York: Farrar & Rinehart, 1941.

FULLER, D. L. Programmed life histories and socialization of the dog. Paper presented at the meeting of the American Psychological Association, Chicago, September 1960.

GAGE, N. L., & L. J. CRONBACH. Conceptual and methodological problems in interpersonal perception. *Psychological Review,* 1955, **62,** 411–422.

GALLO, P. S., JR. Effects of increased incentives upon the use of threat in bargaining. *Journal of Personality and Social Psychology,* 1966, **4,** 14–20.

GAMSON, W. A. Experimental studies of coalition formation. In L. Berkowitz (Ed.), *Advances in experimental social psychology.* Vol. 1. New York: Academic Press, Inc., 1964. Pp. 81–110.

GARFINKEL, H. *Studies in ethnomethodology.* Englewood Cliffs, N.J.: Prentice-Hall, Inc., 1967.

GEEN, R. G., & L. BERKOWITZ. Some conditions facilitating

the occurrence of aggression after the observation of violence. *Journal of Personality,* 1967, **35,** 666–667.

GEIVITZ, J. P. The effects of threats on prisoner's dilemma. *Behavioral Science,* 1967, **12,** 232–233.

GERARD, H. B. Some determinants of self-evaluation. *Journal of Abnormal and Social Psychology,* 1961, **62,** 288–293.

GERARD, H. B. Deviation, conformity, and commitment. In I. D. Steiner & M. Fishbein (Eds.), *Current studies in social psychology.* New York: Holt, Rinehart and Winston, Inc., 1965.

GERARD, H. B., & G. C. MATHEWSON. The effect of severity of initiation on liking for a group: A replication. *Journal of Experimental and Social Psychology,* 1966, **2,** 278–287.

GERBNER, G. The structure and process of television program content regulation in the United States. In G. A. Comstock & E. A. Rubinstein (Eds.), *Television and Social Behavior.* Vol. 1. *Content and Control.* Government Printing Office, 1971.

GERST, M. S. Symbolic coding operations in observational learning. Unpublished doctoral dissertation, Stanford University, 1969.

GETZELS, J. W., & E. G. GUBA. Role, role conflict, and effectiveness. *American Sociological Review,* 1954, **19,** 164–175.

GIBB, C. A. Leadership. In G. Lindzey (Ed.), *Handbook of social psychology.* Vol. 2. Cambridge, Mass.: Addison-Wesley Press, Inc., 1954.

GIBB, C. A. Leadership. In G. Lindzey, & E. Aronson (Eds.), *The handbook of social psychology.* (2nd ed.) Vol. 4. Reading, Mass.: Addison-Wesley Publishing Company, Inc., 1969. Pp. 205–282.

GIBB, J. R. The effects of group size and of threat reduction upon creativity in a problem solving situation. *American Psychologist,* 1951, **6,** 324. (Abstract)

GIFFIN, K. The contribution of studies of source credibility to a theory of interpersonal trust in the communication process. *Psychological Bulletin,* 1967, **68**, 104-120.

GILBERT, D. C., & D. J. LEVINSON. "Custodialism" and "humanism" in staff ideology. In M. Greenblatt, D. J. Levinson, & R. H. Williams (Eds.), *The patient and the mental hospital.* Chicago: The Free Press of Glencoe, Ill., 1957. *(a)*

GILBERT, D. C., & D. J. LEVINSON. Role performance, ideology, and personality in mental hospital aides. In M. Greenblatt, D. J. Levinson, & R. H. Williams (Eds.), *The patient and the mental hospital.* Chicago: The Free Press of Glencoe, Ill., 1957. *(b)*

GILBERT, G. M. Stereotype persistance and change among college students. *Journal of Abnormal and Social Psychology,* 1951, **46**, 245-254.

GLASS, D. C. Changes in liking as a means of reducing cognitive discrepancies between self-esteem and aggression. *Journal of Personality,* 1964, **32**, 531-549.

GLUECK, S., & E. GLUECK. *Unraveling juvenile delinquency.* New York: The Commonwealth Fund, 1950.

GOEKE, J. R. The two-step flow of mass communication: The theory re-examined. Personal communication, 1961.

GOFFMAN, E. On cooling the mark out: Some aspects of adaptation to failure. *Psychiatry,* 1952, **15**, 451-463.

GOFFMAN, E. On face-work: An analysis of ritual elements in social interaction. *Psychiatry,* 1955, **18**, 213-231.

GOFFMAN, E. The moral career of the mental patient. *Psychiatry,* 1959, **22**, 123-142.

GOFFMAN, E. *Encounters: Two studies in the sociology of interaction.* Indianapolis: The Bobbs-Merrill Company, Inc., 1961.

GOFFMAN, E. *Stigma: Notes on the management of spoiled identity.* Englewood Cliffs, N.J.: Prentice-Hall, Inc., 1963.

GOFFMAN, E. *Behavior in public places.* New York: The Free Press, 1963.

GOFFMAN, I. W. Status consistency and preference for change in power distribution. *American Sociological Review,* 1957, **22**, 275-281.

GOLD, M. Power in the classroom. *Sociometry,* 1958, **21**, 50-60.

GOLDFARB, W. The effects of early institutional care on adolescent personalities. *Journal of Experimental Education,* 1943, **12**, 106-129. *(a)*

GOLDFARB, W. Infant rearing and problem behavior. *American Journal of Orthopsychiatry,* 1943, **13**, 249-265. *(b)*

GOLDSTEIN, M. The relationship between coping and avoiding behavior and response to fear arousing propaganda. *Journal of Abnormal and Social Psychology,* 1959, **58**, 247-252.

GOLLIN, E. S. Organizational characteristics of social judgment: A developmental investigation. *Journal of Personality,* 1958, **26**, 139-154.

GOODE, W. J. Norm commitment and conformity to role-status obligations. *American Journal of Sociology,* 1960, **66**, 246-258.

GORANSON, R. E. Media violence and aggressive behavior: A review of experimental research. In L. Berkowitz (Ed.), *Advances in experimental social psychology.* Vol. 5. New York: Academic Press, Inc., 1970. Pp. 1-31.

GORANSON, R. E., & L. BERKOWITZ. Reciprocity and responsibility reactions to prior help. *Journal of Personality and Social Psychology,* 1966, **3**(2), 227-232.

GOTTLIEB, D. The socialization process in American graduate schools. Paper presented at meetings of the American Sociological Association, New York, August 1960.

GOULDNER, A. W. The norm of reciprocity: A preliminary statement. *American Sociological Review,* 1960, **25**, 161-178.

GRABILL, W. H., C. V. KISER, & P. K. WHELPTON. *The fertility of American women.* New York: John Wiley & Sons, Inc., 1958.

GREENBERG, B. S., & G. R. MILLER. The effect of low credibility sources on message acceptance. *Speech Monographs,* 1966, **33**, 127-136.

GREENBERG, M. S. A preliminary statement on a theory of indebtedness. Paper presented at the meeting of the Western Psychological Association, San Diego, Calif., March 1968.

GREENGLASS, E. R. Effects of prior help and hindrance on willingness to help another: Reciprocity or social responsibility. *Journal of Personality and Social Psychology,* 1969, **11**, 224-231.

GREENWALD, A. G. When does role playing produce attitude change? Toward an answer. *Journal of Personality and Social Psychology,* 1970, **16**, 214-219.

GROSS, E., & G. P. STONE. Embarrassment and the analysis of role requirements. *American Journal of Sociology,* 1964, **70**, 1-15.

GROSS, N., W. S. MASON, & A. W. MCEACHERN. *Explorations in role analysis.* New York: John Wiley & Sons, Inc., 1958.

GRUSKY, O. A case for the theory of familial role differentiation in small groups. *Social Forces,* 1957, **35**, 209-217.

GUETZKOW, H. Differentiation of roles in task-oriented groups. In D. Cartwright & A. Zander (Eds.), *Group dynamics: Research and theory.* (2nd ed.) Evanston, Ill.: Row, Peterson & Company, 1960. Pp. 683-704.

GUETZKOW, H., & W. R. DILL. Factors in organizational development of task oriented groups. *Sociometry,* 1957, **20**, 175-204.

GUETZKOW, H., & H. A. SIMON. The impact of certain communication nets upon organization and performance in task-oriented groups. *Management Science,* 1955, **1**, 233-250.

GULLAHORN, J. T., & J. E. GULLAHORN. Role conflict and its resolution. *Sociological Quarterly,* 1963, **4**, 32-48.

GUNDLACH, R. H. Effects of on-the-job experiences with Negroes upon racial attitudes of white workers in union shops. *Psychological Reports*, 1956, **2**, 67-77.

GUTTENTAG, M. Group cohesiveness, ethnic organization, and poverty. *Journal of Social Issues*, 1970, **26**(2), 105-132.

HAEFNER, D. Arousing fear in dental health education. *Journal of Public Health Dentistry*, 1965, **25**, 140-146.

HAKMILLER, K. Need for self-evaluation, perceived similarity and comparison choice. *Journal of Experimental Social Psychology*, September 1966, **1** (Suppl. 1), 49-54.

HALEY, J. *Strategies of psychotherapy*. New York: Grune & Stratton, Inc., 1963.

HALL, R. L. Social influence on the aircraft commander's role. *American Sociological Review*, 1955, **20**, 292-299.

HALPIN, A. W., & B. J. WINER. *The leadership behavior of the airplane commander*. Columbus: Ohio State University Research Foundation, 1952.

HANSON, R. C. The systemic linkage hypothesis and role consensus patterns in hospital-community relations. *American Sociological Review*, 1962, **27**, 304-313.

HARDING, J., & R. HOGREFE. Attitudes of white department store employees toward Negro co-workers. *Journal of Social Issues*, 1952, **8**(1), 18-28.

HARDY, K. R. Determinants of conformity and attitude change. *Journal of Abnormal and Social Psychology*, 1957, **54**, 289-294.

HARDYCK, J. A. Predicting response to a negative evaluation. *Journal of Personality and Social Psychology*, 1968, **9**, 128-132.

HARE, A. P. *Handbook of small group research*. New York: The Free Press of Glencoe, Inc., 1962.

HARGREAVES, W. A., J. A. STARKWEATHER, & K. H. BLACKER. Voice quality in depression. *Journal of Abnormal and Social Psychology*, 1965, **70**, 218-220.

HARLOW, H. F., & M. K. HARLOW. Social deprivation in monkeys. *Scientific American*, 1962, **207**, 136-146.

HARLOW, H. F., & M. K. HARLOW. The affectional systems. In A. M. Schrier, H. F. Harlow, & T. Stollnitz (Eds.), *Behavior of nonhuman primates*. Vol. 2. New York: Academic Press, Inc., 1965. Pp. 287-334.

HARLOW, H. F., & M. K. HARLOW. Learning to love. *American Scientist*, 1966, **54**(3), 244-272.

HARRÉ, R., & P. F. SECORD. *The explanation of social behavior*. Totowa, N.J.: Rowman & Littlefield, 1972. Copyright: Basil Blackwell & Mott, Ltd., Oxford.

HARSANYI, J. C. Measurement of social power, opportunity costs, and the theory of two-person bargaining games. *Behavioral Science*, 1962, **7**, 67-80.

HARTLEY, E. L. *Problems in prejudice*. New York: King's Crown Press, 1946.

HARTLEY, E. L., & R. E. HARTLEY. *Fundamentals of social psychology*. New York: Alfred A. Knopf, Inc., 1952.

HARTMANN, G. W. A field experiment on the comparative effectiveness of "emotional" and "rational" political leaflets in determining election results. *Journal of Abnormal and Social Psychology*, 1936, **31**, 99-114.

HARTSHORNE, H., & M. A. MAY. *Studies in the nature of character*. Vol. 1. *Studies in deceit*. New York: The Macmillan Company, 1928.

HARTSHORNE, H., M. A. MAY, & F. K. SHUTTLEWORTH. *Studies in the nature of character*. Vol. 3. *Studies in the organization of character*. New York: The Macmillan Company, 1930.

HARVEY, O. J. An experimental approach to the study of status relations in informal groups. *American Sociological Review*, 1953, **18**, 357-367.

HARVEY, O. J. Personality factors in resolution of conceptual incongruities. *Sociometry*, 1962, **25**, 336-352.

HARVEY, O. J., & C. CONSALVI. Status and conformity to pressures in informal groups. *Journal of Abnormal and Social Psychology*, 1960, **60**, 182-187.

HARVEY, O. J., D. E. HUNT, & H. M. SCHRODER. *Conceptual systems and personality organization*. New York: John Wiley & Sons, Inc., 1961.

HARVEY, O. J., H. H. KELLEY, & M. M. SHAPIRO. Reactions to unfavorable evaluations of the self made by other persons. *Journal of Personality*, 1957, **25**, 398-411.

HARVEY, O. J., & H. M. SCHRODER. Cognitive aspects of self and motivation. In O. J. Harvey (Ed.), *Motivation and social interaction: Cognitive determinants*. New York: The Ronald Press Company, 1963. Pp. 95-133.

HASTORF, A. H., W. R. KITE, A. E. GROSS, & L. J. WOLFE. The perception and evaluation of behavior change. *Sociometry*, 1965, **48**, 400-410.

HASTORF, A. H., D. J. SCHNEIDER, & J. POLEFKA. *Person perception*. Reading, Mass.: Addison-Wesley Publishing Company, Inc., 1970.

HEBB, D. O. The socialization of the child. In E. E. Maccoby, T. M. Newcomb, & E. L. Hartley (Eds.), *Readings in social psychology*. (3rd ed.) New York: Holt, Rinehart and Winston, Inc., 1958. Pp. 335-340.

HEER, D. M. The sentiment of white supremacy: An ecological study. *American Journal of Sociology*, 1959, **64**, 592-598.

HEIDER, F. Social perception and phenomenal causality. *Psychological Review*, 1944, **51**, 358-374.

HEIDER, F. *The psychology of interpersonal relations*. New York: John Wiley & Sons, Inc., 1958.

HEINICKE, C., & R. F. BALES. Developmental trends in the structure of small groups. *Sociometry*, 1953, **16**, 35-36.

HERZ, M. F. Some psychological lessons from leaflet propaganda in World War II. In D. Katz, D. Cartwright, S. Eldersveld, & A. M. Lee (Eds.), *Public opinion and propaganda*. New York: The Dryden Press, Inc., 1954. Pp. 543-552.

HICKS, D. J. Imitation and retention of film-mediated aggressive peer and adult models. *Journal of Personality and Social Psychology*, 1965, **2**, 97-100.

HIGBEE, K. L. Fifteen years of fear arousal: Research on threat appeals: 1953-1968. *Psychological Bulletin*, 1969, **72**, 426-444.

HIMMELWEIT, H., A. N. OPPENHEIM, & P. VINCE. *Television and the child.* New York: Oxford University Press, 1958.

HOBART, C. W., & L. LINDHOLM. The theory of complementary needs: A re-examination. *Pacific Sociological Review*, 1963, **6**, 73-79.

HOCHBAUM, G. H. The relation between group members' self confidence and their reactions to group pressures to uniformity. *American Sociological Review*, 1954, **19**, 678-687.

HOE, B. H. Occupational satisfaction as a function of self-role congruency. Unpublished master's thesis, University of Nevada, June, 1962.

HOFFMAN, L. R., & N. R. F. MAIER. Valence in the adoption of solutions by problem-solving groups: Concept, method and results. *Journal of Abnormal and Social Psychology*, 1964, **69**, 264-271.

HOFFMAN, M. L. Moral development. In P. H. Mussen (Ed.), *Carmichael's manual of child psychology.* (3rd ed.) Vol. 2. New York: John Wiley & Sons, Inc., 1970. Pp. 261-360.

HOFFMAN, M. L., & H. D. SALTZSTEIN. Parent discipline and the child's moral development. *Journal of Personality and Social Psychology*, 1967, **5**, 45-57.

HOLLANDER, E. P. Conformity, status, and idiosyncrasy credit. *Psychological Review*, 1958, **65**, 117-127.

HOLLANDER, E. P. Competence and conformity in the acceptance of influence. *Journal of Abnormal and Social Psychology*, 1960, **61**, 365-369.

HOLLANDER, E. P., & J. W. JULIAN. Contemporary trends in the analysis of leadership processes. *Psychological Bulletin*, 1969, **71**, 387-397.

HOLLANDER, E. P., & R. H. WILLIS. Some current issues in the psychology of conformity and nonconformity. *Psychological Bulletin*, 1967, **68**, 62-76.

HOLZ, R. F. Similarity versus complementarity of needs in mate selection. *Dissertation abstracts*, 1969, **29**(7-B), 2618.

HOMANS, G. C. *The human group.* New York: Harcourt, Brace & World, Inc., 1950.

HOMANS, G. C. The cash posters: A study of a group of working girls. *American Sociological Review*, 1954, **19**, 724-733.

HOMANS, G. C. *Social behavior: Its elementary forms.* New York: Harcourt, Brace & World, Inc., 1961.

HORN, D. Factors affecting cessation of cigarette smoking: A prospective study. Paper presented at the meeting of the Eastern Psychological Association, Washington, April 1968.

HORNSTEIN, H. A. The effects of different magnitudes of threat upon inter-personal bargaining. *Journal of Experimental Social Psychology*, 1965, **1**, 282-293.

HORNSTEIN, H. A., E. FISCH, & M. HOLMES. Influence of a model's feeling about his behavior and his relevance as a comparison other on observers' helping behavior. *Journal of Personality and Social Psychology*, 1968, **10**, 222-227.

HOROWITZ, E. L. The development of attitude toward the Negro. *Archives of Psychology*, 1936, No. 194.

HOROWITZ, I. A. Effect of choice and locus of dependence on helping behavior. *Journal of Personality and Social Psychology*, 1968, **8**, 373-377.

HORWITZ, M. Hostility and its management in classroom groups. In W. W. Charters, Jr., & N. L. Gage (Eds.), *Readings in the social psychology of education.* Boston: Allyn and Bacon, Inc., 1963. Pp. 196-211.

HOVLAND, C. I. (Ed.). *The order of presentation in persuasion.* New Haven, Conn.: Yale University Press, 1957.

HOVLAND, C. I. Reconciling conflicting results derived from experimental and survey studies of attitude change. *American Psychologist*, 1959, **14**, 8-17.

HOVLAND, C. I., E. H. CAMPBELL, & T. C. BROCK. The effects of "commitment" on opinion change following communication. In C. I. Hovland (Ed.), *The order of presentation in persuasion.* New Haven, Conn.: Yale University Press, 1957. Pp. 23-32.

HOVLAND, C. I., O. J. HARVEY, & M. SHERIF. Assimilation and contrast effects in reactions to communication and attitude change. *Journal of Abnormal and Social Psychology*, 1957, **55**, 244-252.

HOVLAND, C. I., & I. L. JANIS. *Personality and persuasability.* New Haven, Conn.: Yale University Press, 1959.

HOVLAND, C. I., I. L. JANIS, & H. H. KELLEY. *Communication and persuasion.* New Haven, Conn.: Yale University Press, 1953.

HOVLAND, C. I., A. A. LUMSDAINE, & F. D. SHEFFIELD. *Experiments on mass communication.* Princeton, N.J.: Princeton University Press, 1949.

HOVLAND, C. I., & W. MANDELL. Is there a "law of primacy in persuasion"? In C. I. Hovland (Ed.), *The order of presentation in persuasion.* New Haven, Conn.: Yale University Press, 1957. Pp. 13-22.

HOVLAND, C. I., & H. A. PRITZKER. Extent of opinion change as a function of amount of change advocated. *Journal of Abnormal and Social Psychology*, 1957, **54**, 257-261.

HOWARD, R. C., & L. BERKOWITZ. Reactions to the evaluations of one's performance. *Journal of Personality*, 1958, **26**, 494-507.

HOYT, M. F., HENLEY, M. D., & COLLINS, B. E. Studies in forced compliance: The confluence of choice and consequences on attitude change. *Journal of Personality and Social Psychology*, 1972, **23**, 205-210.

HUGHES, E. C. *Men and their*

work. New York: The Free Press of Glencoe, Inc., 1958.

HUNT, W. A., & J. D. MATARAZZO. Three years later: Recent developments in the experimental modification of smoking behavior. *Journal of Abnormal and Social Psychology,* 1973, **81,** 107–114.

HUNTER, E. C., & A. M. JORDAN. An analysis of qualities associated with leadership among college students. *Journal of Educational Psychology,* 1939, **30,** 497–509.

HUNTINGTON, M. J. The development of a professional self-image. In R. K. Merton, G. G. Reader, & P. Kendall (Eds.), *The student-physician.* Cambridge, Mass.: Harvard University Press, 1957. Pp. 179–187.

HURWITZ, J. I., A. ZANDER, & B. HYMOVITCH. Some effects of power on the relations among group members. In D. Cartwright and A. Zander (Eds.), *Group dynamics: Research and theory.* (2nd ed.) New York: Harper and Row, Publishers, Incorporated, 1960. Pp. 800–809.

HYMAN, H. H. The psychology of status. *Archives of Psychology,* 1942, No. 269.

HYMAN, H. H. Reflections on reference groups. *Public Opinion Quarterly,* 1960, **24,** 383–396.

HYMAN, H. H., & P. B. SHEATS-LEY. The authoritarian personality: A methodological critique. In R. Christie & M. Jahoda (Eds.), *Studies in the scope and method of the authoritarian personality.* Glencoe, Ill.: The Free Press, 1954. Pp. 50–122.

INKELES, A., E. HANFMANN, & H. BEIER. Modal personality and adjustment to the Soviet socio-political system. *Human Relations,* 1958, **11,** 3–22.

INKELES, A., & D. J. LEVINSON. The personal system and the sociocultural system in large-scale organizations. *Sociometry,* 1963, **26,** 217–229.

INSKO, C. A. Primacy versus recency in persuasion as a function of the timing of arguments and measures. *Journal*

of *Abnormal and Social Psychology,* 1964, **69,** 381–391.

INSKO, C. A., F. MURASHIMA, & M. SAIYADAIN. Communicator discrepancy, stimulus ambiguity and influence. *Journal of Personality,* 1966, **34,** 262–274.

IRISH, D. P. Reactions of Caucasian residents to Japanese-American neighbors. *Journal of Social Issues,* 1952, **8**(1), 10–17.

IRWIN, J. V., & H. H. BROCKHAUS. The "teletalk project": A study of the effectiveness of two public relations speeches. *Speech Monographs,* 1963, **30,** 359–368.

IVERSON, M. A. Attraction toward flatterers of different statuses. *Journal of Social Psychology,* 1968, **74,** 181–187.

IZARD, C. E. Personality similarity and friendship: A follow-up study. *Journal of Abnormal and Social Psychology,* 1963, **66,** 598–600.

JACKSON, D. N., & S. MESSICK. Individual differences in social perception. *British Journal of Social and Clinical Psychology,* 1963, **2,** 1–10.

JACKSON, E. F. Status inconsistency and symptoms of stress. *American Sociological Review,* 1962, **27,** 469–479.

JACKSON, E. F., & R. F. CURTIS. Conceptualization and measurement in the study of social stratification. In H. M. Blalock, Jr. (Ed.), *Methodology in social research,* New York: McGraw-Hill Book Company, 1968. Pp. 112–149.

JACOBSEN, E. W., W. W. CHAR-TERS, JR., & S. LIEBERMAN. The use of the role concept in the study of complex organizations. *Journal of Social Issues,* 1951, 7(2), 18–27.

JAHODA, M., M. DEUTSCH, & S. W. COOK (Eds.). *Research methods in social relations.* Vol. 2. New York: Holt, Rinehart and Winston, Inc., 1951.

JAKUBCZAK, L. F., & R. H. WAL-TERS. Suggestibility as dependency behavior. *Journal of Abnormal and Social Psychology,* 1959, **59,** 102–107.

JAMES, G., & A. LOTT. Reward frequency and the formation

of positive attitudes toward group members. *Journal of Social Psychology,* 1964, **62,** 111–115.

JANIS, I. L. *Air war and emotional stress.* New York: McGraw-Hill Book Company, 1951.

JANIS, I. L. Stages in the decision-making process. In R. P. Abelson et al. (Eds.), *Theories of cognitive consistency: A sourcebook.* Chicago: Rand McNally and Company, 1968. Pp. 577–588.

JANIS, I. L., & S. FESHBACH. Effects of fear-arousing communications. *Journal of Abnormal and Social Psychology,* 1953, **48,** 78–92.

JANIS, I. L., & P. B. FIELD. A behavioral assessment of persuasibility: Consistency of individual differences. *Sociometry,* 1956, **19,** 241–259.

JANIS, I. L., & J. B. GILMORE. The influence of incentive conditions on the success of role playing in modifying attitudes. *Journal of Personality and Social Psychology,* 1965, **1,** 17–27.

JANIS, I. L., & C. I. HOVLAND. An overview of persuasibility research. In C. I. Hovland & I. L. Janis (Eds.), *Personality and persuasibility.* New Haven, Conn.: Yale University Press, 1959. Pp. 1–28.

JANIS, I. L., & B. T. KING. The influence of role playing on opinion change. *Journal of Abnormal and Social Psychology,* 1954, **48,** 211–218.

JANIS, I. L., A. A. LUMSDAINE, & A. I. GLADSTONE. Effects of preparatory communications on reactions to a subsequent news event. *Public Opinion Quarterly,* 1951, **15,** 487–518.

JANIS, I. L., & L. MANN. Effectiveness of emotional role-playing in modifying smoking habits and attitudes. *Journal of Experimental Research in Personality,* 1965, **1,** 84–90.

JANIS, I. L., & C. N. RAUSCH. Selective interest in communications that could arouse decisional conflict: A field study of participants in the draft-resistance movement. *Journal of Personality and Social Psychology,* 1970, **14,** 46–54.

JANIS, I. L., & D. RIFE. Persuasibility and emotional disorder. In C. I. Hovland & I. L. Janis (Eds.), *Personality and persuasibility.* New Haven, Conn.: Yale University Press, 1959. Pp. 121-137.

JENNINGS, H. H. *Leadership and isolation.* (2nd ed.) New York: Longmans, Green, and Company, Inc., 1950.

JESSOR, R., T. D. GRAVES, R. C. HANSON, & S. L. JESSOR. *Society, personality and deviant behavior: A study of a tri-ethnic community.* New York: Holt, Rinehart and Winston, Inc., 1968.

JOHNSON, H. H. Some effects of discrepancy level on responses to negative information about one's self. *Sociometry,* 1966, **29,** 52-66.

JOHNSON, H. H., & J. A. SCILEPPI. Effects of ego-involvement conditions on attitude change to high and low credibility communicators. *Journal of Personality and Social Psychology,* 1969, **13,** 31-36.

JOHNSON, H. H., & I. D. STEINER. The effects of source on responses to negative information about one's self. *Journal of Social Psychology,* 1968, **74,** 215-224.

JOHNSON, R. C. A study of children's moral judgments. *Child Development,* 1962, **33,** 327-354.

JONES, E. E. Authoritarianism and first impressions. *Journal of Personality,* 1954, **23,** 107-127.

JONES, E. E. *Ingratiation: A social psychological analysis.* New York: Appleton Century Crofts, 1964.

JONES, E. E., & K. E. DAVIS. From acts to dispositions. In L. Berkowitz (Ed.), *Advances in experimental social psychology.* Vol. 2. New York: Academic Press, Inc., 1965. Pp. 219-266.

JONES, E. E., K. E. DAVIS, & K. J. GERGEN. Role playing variations and their informational value for person perception. *Journal of Abnormal and Social Psychology,* 1961, **63,** 302-310.

JONES, E. E., & R. DECHARMS. The organizing function of interaction roles in person perception. *Journal of Abnormal and Social Psychology,* 1958, **57,** 155-164.

JONES, E. E., K. J. GERGEN, P. GUMPERT, & J. W. THIBAUT. Some conditions affecting the use of ingratiation to influence performance evaluation. *Journal of Personality and Social Psychology,* 1965, **1,** 613-625.

JONES, E. E., R. G. JONES, & K. J. GERGEN. Some conditions affecting the evaluation of a conformist. *Journal of Personality,* 1963, **31,** 270-288.

JONES, H. E. Order of birth in relation to the development of the child. In C. Murchison (Ed.), *Handbook of child psychology.* Worcester, Mass.: Clark University Press, 1931.

JONES, S. C. Some determinants of interpersonal evaluating behavior. *Journal of Personality and Social Psychology,* 1966, **3,** 397-403.

JONES, S. C. Expectation, performance and the anticipation of self-revealing events. *Journal of Social Psychology,* 1968, **74,** 189-197.

JONES, S. C., & C. RATNER. The handling of unfavorable information by self. *Journal of Personality and Social Psychology,* 1967, **6,** 442-447.

JONES, S. C., & D. J. SCHNEIDER. Certainty of self-appraisal and reactions to evaluations from others. *Sociometry,* 1968, **31,** 395-403.

JULIAN, J. Some determinants of dissensus on role prescriptions within and between four organizational positions. *Sociological Quarterly,* Spring 1969, **10**(2), 177.

KAGAN, J., & H. MOSS. The stability of passive and dependent behavior from childhood through adulthood. *Child Development,* 1960, **31,** 577-591.

KAHL, J. A. Some measures of achievement orientation. *American Journal of Sociology,* 1965, **70,** 669-681.

KAHN, R. L., & D. KATZ. Leadership practices in relation to productivity and morale. In D. Cartwright and A. Zander (Eds.), *Group dynamics: Research and theory.* Evanston,

Ill.: Row, Peterson & Company, 1953. Pp. 612-628.

KAMMEYER, K. Birth order as a research variable. *Social Forces,* 1967, **46,** 71-80.

KAPLAN, N. Reference groups and interest group theories of voting. In H. H. Hyman and E. Singer (Eds.), *Readings in reference group theory and research.* New York: The Free Press, 1968. Pp. 461-472.

KARABENICK, S. A., & Z. I. YOUSSEF. Performance as a function of achievement motive level and perceived difficulty. *Journal of Personality and Social Psychology,* December 1968, **10,** 414-419.

KARLINS, M., T. L. COFFMAN, & G. WALTERS. On the fading of social stereotypes: Studies in three generations of college students. *Journal of Personality and Social Psychology,* 1969, **13,** 1-16.

KATES, S. L. First-impression formation and authoritarianism. *Human Relations,* 1959, **12,** 277-285.

KATZ, D., & K. W. BRALY. Racial prejudice and racial stereotypes. *Journal of Abnormal and Social Psychology,* 1933, **30,** 175-193.

KATZ, D., & R. L. KAHN. Some recent findings in human relations research in industry. In G. E. Swanson, T. M. Newcomb, & E. L. Hartley (Eds.), *Readings in social psychology.* (Rev. ed.) New York: Holt, Rinehart and Winston, Inc., 1952. Pp. 650-665.

KATZ, D., C. G. MCCLINTOCK, & I. SARNOFF. Measurement of ego-defense related to attitude change. *Journal of Personality,* 1957, **25,** 465-474.

KATZ, E. The two-step flow of communication: An up-to-date report on an hypothesis. *Public Opinion Quarterly,* 1957, **21,** 61-78.

KATZ, E. The social itinerary of technical change: Two studies on the diffusion of innovation. *Human Organization,* 1961, **20,** 70-82.

KATZ, E. On reopening the question of selectivity in exposure to mass communications. In R. P. Abelson et al. (Eds.), *Theories of cognitive consistency: A sourcebook.* Chicago: Rand McNally and Company, 1968. Pp. 788-796.

KATZ, E., & B. DANET. Petitions and persuasive appeals: A study of official-client relations. *American Sociological Review,* 1966, **31,** 811-822.

KATZ, E., & J. J. FELDMAN. The debates in the light of research: A survey of surveys. In S. Kraus (Ed.), *The great debates.* Bloomington: Indiana University Press, 1962. Pp. 173-223.

KATZ, E., & P. F. LAZARSFELD. *Personal influence.* Chicago: The Free Press of Glencoe, Ill., 1955.

KATZ, I. Experimental studies of Negro-white relationships. In L. Berkowitz (Ed.), *Advances in experimental social psychology.* Vol. 5. New York: Academic Press, Inc., 1970. Pp. 71-117.

KATZ, L., M. COHEN, & L. CASTIGLIONE. Effects of one type of need complementarity on marriage partners' conformity to one another's judgments. *Journal of Abnormal and Social Psychology,* 1963, **67,** 8-14.

KELLEY, H. H. The warm-cold variable in first impressions of persons. *Journal of Personality,* 1950, **18,** 431-439.

KELLEY, H. H. Communication in experimentally created hierarchies. *Human Relations,* 1951, **4,** 39-56.

KELLEY, H. H. Two functions of reference groups. In G. E. Swanson, T. M. Newcomb, & E. L. Hartley (Eds.), *Readings in social psychology.* (Rev. ed.) New York: Henry Holt and Company, Inc., 1952.

KELLEY, H. H. Salience of membership and resistance to change of group-anchored attitudes. *Human Relations,* 1955, **8,** 275-290.

KELLEY, H. H. Attribution theory in social psychology. In D. Levine (Ed.), *Nebraska symposium on motivation.* Vol. 15. Lincoln, Nebraska: University of Nebraska Press, 1967. Pp. 192-240.

KELLEY, H. H., & T. W. LAMB. Certainty of judgment and resistance to social influence.

Journal of Abnormal and Social Psychology, 1957, **55,** 137-139.

KELLEY, H. H., & A. J. STAHELSKI. Social interaction basis of cooperators' and competitors' beliefs about others. *Journal of Personality and Social Psychology,* 1970, **16,** 66-91.

KELLEY, H. H., & J. W. THIBAUT. Experimental studies of group problem solving and process. In G. Lindzey (Ed.), *Handbook of social psychology.* Vol. 2. Cambridge, Mass.: Addison-Wesley Publishing Company, Inc., 1954. Pp. 735-785.

KELLEY, H. H., & J. W. THIBAUT. Group problem solving. In G. Lindzey & E. Aronson (Eds.), *The handbook of social psychology.* (2nd ed.) Vol. 4. Reading, Mass.: Addison-Wesley Publishing Company, Inc., 1969. Pp. 1-101.

KELLEY, H. H., J. W. THIBAUT, R. RADLOFF, & D. MUNDY. The development of cooperation in the "minimal social situation." *Psychological Monograph,* 1962, **76,** (19, Whole No. 538).

KELLEY, H. H., & E. H. VOLKART. The resistance to change of group-anchored attitudes. *American Sociological Review,* 1952, **17,** 453-465.

KELLEY, H. H., & C. L. WOODRUFF. Members reactions to apparent group approval of a counter-norm communication. *Journal of Abnormal and Social Psychology,* 1956, **52,** 67-74.

KELLEY, K. D., & W. J. CHAMBLISS. Status consistency and political attitudes. *American Sociological Review,* 1966, **31,** 375-381.

KELMAN, H. C. The induction of action and attitude change. In S. Coopersmith (Ed.), *Personality research.* Copenhagen: Munksgaard, 1962. Pp. 81-110.

KELMAN, H. C. Assignment of responsibility in the case of Lt. Calley: Preliminary report on a national survey. Paper presented at the meeting of the Society of Experimental Social Psychology, Ohio State University, Columbus, 1971.

KEMPER, T. D. Self-conceptions and the expectations of significant others. *Sociological Quarterly,* 1966, **7,** 323-343.

KENDALL, P. L. Medical education as social process. Paper presented at the meeting of the American Sociological Association, New York, August 1960.

KENDON, A. Some functions of gaze direction in social interaction. *Acta Psychologica,* 1967, **26,** 22-63.

KENKEL, W. F. The relationship between status consistency and politico-economic attitudes. *American Sociological Review,* 1956, **21,** 365-368.

KERCKHOFF, A., & K. E. DAVIS. Value consensus and need complementarity in mate selection. *American Sociological Review,* 1962, **27,** 295-303.

KIDD, J. W. An analysis of social rejection in a college men's residence hall. *Sociometry,* 1951, **14,** 226-234.

KIESLER, C. A., & S. B. KIESLER. Role of forewarning in persuasive communications. *Journal of Abnormal and Social Psychology,* 1964, **68,** 547-549.

KIESLER, S. B. The effect of perceived role requirements on reactions to favor-doing. *Journal of Experimental Social Psychology,* 1966, **2,** 198-210.

KILLIAN, L. M. The significance of multiple-group membership in disaster. *American Journal of Sociology,* 1952, **57,** 309-313.

KIMBERLY, J. C., & P. V. CROSBIE. An experimental test of a reward-cost formulation of status inconsistency. Paper presented at the meeting of the Pacific Sociological Association, Long Beach, Calif., March 1967.

KINSEY, A. C., W. B. POMEROY, & C. E. MARTIN. *Sexual behavior in the human male.* Philadelphia: W. B. Saunders Company, 1949.

KIPNIS, D. The effects of leadership style and leadership power upon the inducement of an attitude change. *Journal of Abnormal and Social Psychology,* 1958, **57,** 173-180.

KIRKPATRICK, C. The measurement of ethical consistency in marriage. *International Journal of Ethics*, 1936, **46**, 444-460.

KIRKPATRICK, C. *The family as process and institution.* New York: The Ronald Press Company, 1955.

KLAPP, O. E. *Heroes, villains, and fools.* Englewood Cliffs, N.J.: Prentice-Hall, Inc., 1962.

KLAPPER, J. T. *The effects of mass media.* New York: The Free Press of Glencoe, Inc., 1961.

KLAUSNER, S. Z. Choosing a new reference group. Paper presented at the meeting of the American Sociological Association, St. Louis, Mo., September 1961.

KLEIN, J. *The study of groups.* London: Routledge & Kegan Paul, Ltd., 1956.

KOGAN, N. K., & M. A. WALLACH. Effects of physical separation of group members upon group risk-taking. *Human Relations*, 1967, **20**, 41-48. *(a)*

KOGAN, N. K., & M. A. WALLACH. Risky-shift phenomenon in small decision-making groups: A test of the information exchange hypothesis. *Journal of Experimental Social Psychology*, 1967, **3**, 75-84. *(b)*

KOGAN, N. K., & M. A. WALLACH. Group risk taking as a function of members' anxiety and defensiveness levels. *Journal of Personality*, 1967, **35**, 50-63. *(c)*

KOGAN, N. K., & M. A. WALLACH. Risk taking as a function of the situation, the person and the group. *New directions in psychology III.* New York: Holt, Rinehart and Winston, Inc., 1967. Pp. 111-278. *(d)*

KOHLBERG, L. Stage and sequence: The cognitive-developmental approach to socialization. In D. A. Goslin (Ed.), *Handbook of socialization theory and research.* Chicago: Rand McNally & Company, 1969. Pp. 347-480.

KOHN, A. R., & F. E. FIEDLER. Age and sex differences in the perception of persons. *Sociometry*, 1961, **24**, 157-164.

KOHN, M. L. Social class and parent-child relationships. *American Journal of Sociology*, 1963, **68**, 471-480.

KOMORITA, S. S., & A. R. BRENNER. Bargaining and concession making under bilateral monopoly. *Journal of Personality and Social Psychology*, 1968, **9**, 15-20.

KORNZWEIG, N. D. Behavior change as a function of fear arousal and personality. Unpublished doctoral dissertation, Yale University, 1967. Cited in H. Leventhal, Findings and theory in the study of fear communications. In L. Berkowitz (Ed.), *Advances in experimental social psychology.* Vol. 5. New York: Academic Press, Inc., 1970. Pp. 119-186.

KRAUSE, M. S. Use of social situations for research purposes. *American Psychologist*, 1970, **25**, 748-753.

KRECH, D., & R. W. CRUTCHFIELD. *Theory and problems of social psychology.* New York: McGraw-Hill Book Company, 1948.

KRETSCHMER, E. *Physique and character.* New York: Harcourt, Brace and Company, Inc., 1925.

KROGER, R. O. The effects of role demands and test-cue properties upon personality test performance. *Journal of Consulting Psychology*, 1967, **31**, 304-312.

KRUGLANSKI, A. W. Attributing trustworthiness in supervisor-worker relations. *Journal of Experimental Social Psychology*, 1970, **6**, 214-232.

KUHN, M. H. Self attitudes by age, sex, and professional training. *Sociological Quarterly*, 1960, **1**(1), 39-55.

KUUSINEN, J. Affective and denotative structures of personality ratings. *Journal of Personality and Social Psychology*, 1969, **12**, 181-188.

LANA, R. E. Three theoretical interpretations of order effects in persuasive communications. *Psychological Bulletin*, 1964, **61**, 314-320.

LAMM, H. Will an observer advise high risk taking after hearing a discussion of the decision problem? *Journal of Personality and Social Psychology*, 1967, **6**, 467-471.

LARSEN, O. N., & R. HILL. Mass media and interpersonal communication in the diffusion of a news event. *American Sociological Review*, 1954, **19**, 426-443.

LATANÉ, B., & J. M. DARLEY. Group inhibition of bystander intervention in emergencies. *Journal of Personality and Social Psychology*, 1968, **10**, 215-221.

LATANÉ, B., J. ECKMAN, & V. JOY. Shared stress and interpersonal attraction. *Journal of Experimental Social Psychology*, September 1966, **1** (Suppl. 1), 80-94.

LATANÉ, B., & J. RODIN. A lady in distress: Inhibiting effects of friends and strangers on bystander intervention. *Journal of Experimental Social Psychology*, 1969, **5**, 189-202.

LAUMANN, E. O. Friends of urban men: An assessment of accuracy in reporting their socioeconomic attributes, mutual choice, and attitude agreement. *Sociometry*, 1969, **32**, 54-69.

LAWLER, E. E. Equity theory as a predictor of productivity and work quality. *Psychological Bulletin*, 1968, **70**, 596-610.

LAWLER, E. E. *Pay and organizational effectiveness: A psychological view.* New York: McGraw-Hill Book Company, 1971.

LAWSON, E. D. Change in communication nets, performance, and morale. *Human Relations*, 1965, **18**, 139-147.

LAZARSFELD, P. F., B. R. BERELSON, & H. GAUDET. *The people's choice.* New York: Columbia University Press, 1948.

LAZARSFELD, P. F., & R. K. MERTON. Friendship as social process: A substantive and methodological analysis. In M. Beiger, T. Abel, & C. H. Page (Eds.), *Freedom and control in modern society.* New York: D. Van Nostrand Company, Inc., 1954.

LEAVITT, H. J. Some effects of certain communication patterns on group performance.

Journal of Abnormal and Social Psychology, 1951, **46**, 38–50.

LEE, A. M. The social dynamics of the physician's status. *Psychiatry,* 1944, **7**, 371–377.

LEIFER, A. D., & D. F. ROBERTS. Children's responses to television violence. In J. P. Murray, E. A. Rubenstein, & G. A. Comstock (Eds.), *Television and social behavior.* Vol. 2. *Television and social learning.* Government Printing Office, 1971.

LEIK, R. K. Instrumentality and emotionality in family interaction. *Sociometry,* 1963, **26**, 131–145.

LEMERT, E. *Human deviation, social problems and social control.* Englewood Cliffs, N. J.: Prentice Hall, Inc., 1967.

LENNARD, H. L., & A. BERNSTEIN. *The anatomy of psychotherapy.* New York: Columbia University Press, 1960.

LENNARD, H. L., M. JARVIK, & H. O. ABRAMSEN. Lysergic acid diethylamide (LSD 25): XII. A preliminary statement of its effects upon interpersonal communication. *Journal of Psychology,* 1956, **41**, 185–198.

LENSKI, G. E. Status crystallization: A nonvertical dimension of social status. *American Sociological Review,* 1954, **19**, 405–413.

LENSKI, G. E. Social participation and status crystallization. *American Sociological Review,* 1956, **21**, 469–480.

LERNER, M. J., & G. MATTHEWS. Reactions to suffering of others under conditions of indirect responsibility. *Journal of Personality and Social Psychology,* 1967, **5**, 319–325.

LESSER, G. S. Maternal attitudes and practices and the aggressive behavior of children. Unpublished doctoral dissertation, Yale University, 1952.

LESTER, J. T. Acquaintance and compatibility. Technical Report No. 2. Berkeley Institute of Psychological Research, 1965.

LEUPTOW, L. B. Need for achievement and occupational preferences: Some op-

erations with value-orientations as intervening variables in need-goal relationships. *Sociometry,* 1968, **31**, 304–312.

LEVENTHAL, G. S. Self-deprivation as a response to unprofitable inequity. Research proposal (renewal) #S7 0474 R submitted from North Carolina State University to the National Science Foundation. Proposed renewal date: Sept. 1, 1967.

LEVENTHAL, G. S. Influence of brothers and sisters on sex-role behavior. *Journal of Personality and Social Psychology,* 1970, **16**, 452–465.

LEVENTHAL, G. S., & J. W. MICHAELS. Extending the equity model: Perception of inputs and allocation of reward as a function of duration and quantity of performance. *Journal of Personality and Social Psychology,* 1969, **12**, 303–309.

LEVENTHAL, G. S., & J. W. MICHAELS. Focus of cause and equity and motivation as determinants of reward allocation. *Journal of Personality and Social Psychology,* 1971, **17**, 229–235.

LEVENTHAL, G. S., C. M. YOUNTS, & A. K. LUND. Tolerance for inequity in buyer-seller relationships. Paper presented at meetings of the Eastern Psychological Association, Atlantic City, N.J., 1970.

LEVENTHAL, H. Findings and theory in the study of fear communications. In L. Berkowitz (Ed.), *Advances in experimental social psychology.* Vol. 5. New York: Academic Press, Inc., 1970. Pp. 120–186.

LEVENTHAL, H., S. JONES, & G. TREMBLY. Sex differences in attitude and behavior change under conditions of fear and specific instructions. *Journal of Experimental Social Psychology,* 1966, **2**, 387–399.

LEVENTHAL, H., & P. NILES. A field experiment of fear arousal with data on the validity of questionnaire measures. *Journal of Personality,* 1964, **32**, 459–479.

LEVENTHAL, H., & P. NILES. Persistence of influence for vary-

ing durations of exposure to threat stimuli. *Psychological Reports,* 1965, **16**, 223–233.

LEVENTHAL, H., R. P. SINGER, & S. JONES. Effects of fear and specificity of recommendation upon attitudes and behavior. *Journal of Personality and Social Psychology,* 1965, **2**, 20–29.

LEVENTHAL, H., & G. TREMBLY. Negative emotions and persuasion. *Journal of Personality,* 1968, **36**, 154–168.

LEVENTHAL, H., & J. C. WATTS. Sources of resistance to fear-arousing communications on smoking and lung cancer. *Journal of Personality,* 1966, **34**(2), 155–175.

LEVENTHAL, H., J. C. WATTS, & F. PAGANO. Effects of fear and instructions on how to cope with danger. *Journal of Personality and Social Psychology,* 1967, **6**, 313–321.

LEVINGER, G. The development of perceptions and behavior in newly formed social power relationships. In D. Cartwright (Ed.), *Studies in social power.* Ann Arbor: The University of Michigan Press, 1959. Pp. 83–98.

LEVINGER, G. Note on need complementarity in marriage. *Psychological Bulletin,* 1964, **61**, 153–157. *(a)*

LEVINGER, G. Task and social behavior in marriage. *Sociometry,* 1964, **27**, 433–448. *(b)*

LEVINGER, G. Little sand box and big quarry: Comment on Byrne's paradigmatic spade for research on interpersonal attraction. *Representative Research in Social Psychology,* 1972, **3**(1), 3–19.

LEVINGER, G., D. J. SENN, & B. W. JORGENSEN. Progress toward permanence in courtship: A test of the Kerckhoff-Davis hypothesis. *Sociometry,* 1970, **33**, 427–443.

LEWIN, K. *Resolving social conflicts: Selected papers on group dynamics.* New York: Harper & Brothers, 1948.

LEWIN, K. Group decision and social change. In E. Maccoby, T. M. Newcomb, & E. L. Hartley (Eds.), *Readings in social psychology.* (3rd ed.) New York: Holt, Rinehart, and

Winston, Inc., 1958. Pp. 197-211.

LEWIN, K., R. LIPPITT, & R. K. WHITE. Patterns of aggressive behavior in experimentally created social climates. *Journal of Social Psychology*, 1939, **10**, 271-299.

LEWIS, L. D., J. M. DARLEY, & S. GLUCKSBERG. Stereotype persistence and change among college students: One more time. Unpublished manuscript, 1972.

LEWIS, W. H. Feuding and social change in Morocco. *Journal of Conflict Resolution*, 1961, **5**, 43-54.

LIBO, L. *Measuring group cohesiveness*. Ann Arbor, Mich.: Institute for Social Research, 1953.

LIEBERT, R. M., & R. A. BARON. Short-term effects of televised aggression on children's aggressive behavior. In J. P. Murray, E. A. Rubinstein, & G. A. Comstock (Eds.), *Television and social behavior*. Vol. 2. *Television and social learning*. Government Printing Office, 1971.

LIFTON, R. J. Thought reform of Chinese intellectuals. A psychiatric evaluation. *Journal of Social Issues*, 1957, **13**(3), 5-20.

LIFTON, R. J. *Thought reform and the psychology of totalism: A study of "brainwashing" in China*. New York: W. W. Norton & Company, Inc., 1961.

LIKERT, R. *New patterns of management*. New York: McGraw-Hill Book Company, 1961.

LINDZEY, G. An experimental examination of the scapegoat theory of prejudice. *Journal of Abnormal and Social Psychology*, 1950, **45**, 296-309.

LINDZEY, G., & E. F. BORGATTA. In G. Lindzey (Ed.), *Handbook of social psychology*. Vol. 1. Cambridge, Mass.: Addison-Wesley Press, Inc., 1954. Pp. 405-448.

LINDZEY, G., & D. BYRNE. Measurement of social choice and interpersonal attractiveness. In G. Lindzey & E. Aronson (Eds.), *The handbook of social psychology*. (2nd ed.) Vol. 2.

Reading, Mass.: Addison-Wesley Publishing Company, Inc., 1968. Pp. 452-525.

LINTON, H., & E. GRAHAM. Personality correlates of persuasibility. In C. I. Hovland & I. L. Janis (Eds.), *Personality and persuasibility*. New Haven, Conn.: Yale University Press, 1959. Pp. 69-101.

LINTON, R. *The cultural background of personality*. New York: Appleton-Century-Crofts, Inc., 1945.

LIPETZ, M. E. The effects of information on the assessment of attitudes by authoritarians and nonauthoritarians. *Journal of Abnormal and Social Psychology*, 1960, **60**, 95-99.

LIPPITT, R., N. POLANSKY, F. REDL, & S. ROSEN. The dynamics of power. *Human Relations*, 1952, **5**, 37-64.

LIPPITT, R., & R. K. WHITE. The "social climate" of children's groups. In R. G. Barker, J. S. Kounin, & H. F. Wright (Eds.), *Child behavior and development*. New York: McGraw-Hill Book Company, 1943. Pp. 485-508.

LISKA, G. *The new statecraft*. Chicago: Chicago University Press, 1960.

LOFLAND, J. *Deviance and identity*. Englewood Cliffs, N.J.: Prentice-Hall, Inc., 1969.

LONG, H. B. Relationships of selected personal and social variables in conforming judgment. *Journal of Social Psychology*, 1970, **81**, 177-182.

LOOMIS, J. L. Communication, the development of trust and cooperative behavior. *Human Relations*, 1959, **12**, 305-315.

LORGE, I., & H. SOLOMON. Two models of group behavior in the solution of eurek-type problems. *Psychometrika*, 1955, **20**, 139-148.

LORGE, I., & H. SOLOMON. Group and individual performance in problem solving related to previous exposure to problem, level of aspiration, and group size. *Behavioral Science*, 1960, **5**(1), 28-38.

LOTT, A. J., J. F. APONTE, B. E. LOTT, & W. H. MCGENLEY. The effect of delayed reward on the development of positive attitudes toward persons.

Journal of Experimental Social Psychology, 1969, **5**, 101-113.

LOTT, A. J., & B. E. LOTT. A learning theory approach to interpersonal attitudes. In A. G. Greenwald, T. C. Brock, & T. McOstrom (Eds.), *Psychological foundations of attitudes*. New York: Academic Press, Inc., 1968.

LOTT, A. J., B. E. LOTT, & F. M. MATTHEWS. Interpersonal attraction among children as a function of vicarious reward. *Journal of Educational Psychology*, 1969, **60**(4, Pt. I), 274-283.

LOTT, B. E., & A. J. LOTT. The formation of positive attitudes toward group members. *Journal of Abnormal and Social Psychology*, 1960, **61**, 297-300.

LOWE, R. H., & I. D. STEINER. Some effects of the reversibility and consequences of decisions on postdecision information preferences. *Journal of Personality and Social Psychology*, 1968, **8**, 172-179.

LOY, J. W., JR. Social psychological characteristics of innovators. *American Sociological Review*, 1969, **34**, 73-82.

LUCE, R.D., & H. RAIFFA. *Games and decisions*. New York: John Wiley & Sons, Inc., 1957.

LUCHINS, A. S. Forming impressions of personality: A critique. *Journal of Abnormal and Social Psychology*, 1948, **43**, 318-325.

LUCHINS, A. S. Experimental attempts to minimize the impact of first impressions. In C. I. Hovland (Ed.), *The order of presentation in persuasion*. New Haven, Conn.: Yale University Press, 1957. Pp. 62-75. *(a)*

LUCHINS, A. S. Primacy-recency in impression formation. In C. I. Hovland (Ed.), *The order of presentation in persuasion*. New Haven, Conn.: Yale University Press, 1957. Pp. 33-61. *(b)*

LUDLUM, T. S. Effects of certain techniques of credibility upon audience attitude. *Speech Monographs*, 1958, **25**, 278-284.

LUEPTOW, L. B. Need for achievement and occupational preferences: Some operations with value-orientations as intervening variables in need-goal relationships. *Sociometry,* 1968, **31,** 304-312.

LUMSDAINE, A. A., & I. L. JANIS. Resistance to "counterpropaganda" produced by one-sided and two-sided "propaganda" presentations. *Public Opinion Quarterly,* 1953, **17,** 311-318.

LYNN, R. Personality characteristics of the mothers of aggressive and unaggressive children. *Journal of Genetic Psychology,* 1961, **99,** 159-164.

MCCALL, G. J., & J. L. SIMMONS. *Identities and interactions.* New York: The Free Press, 1966.

MCCANDLESS, B. R. *Children and adolescents.* New York: Holt, Rinehart & Winston, Inc., 1961.

MCCLELLAND, D., J. W. ATKINSON, R. A. CLARK, & E. L. LOWELL. *The achievement motive.* New York: Appleton Century Crofts, 1953.

MCCLINTOCK, C. G., & S. P. MCNEEL. Reward and score feedback as determinants of cooperative and competitive game behavior. *Journal of Personality and Social Psychology,* 1966, **4,** 606-615.

MCCONNELL, M. L. B. Stability of the self concept as a function of consensus among significant others. Unpublished master's thesis, University of Nevada, 1966.

MACCOBY, E. E. Youth and political change. *Public Opinion Quarterly,* 1954, **18,** 23-29.

MACCOBY, E. E. The choice of variables in the study of socialization. *Sociometry,* 1961, **24,** 357-371.

MACCOBY, E. E., N. MACCOBY, A. K. ROMNEY, & J. S. ADAMS. Social reinforcement in attitude change. *Journal of Abnormal and Social Psychology,* 1961, **63,** 109-115.

MACCOBY, E. E., & J. C. MASTERS. Attachment and dependency. In P. H. Mussen (Ed.), *Carmichael's manual of child psychology.* (3rd ed.) Vol. 2. New York: John Wiley & Sons, Inc., 1970.

MCCORD, W., J. MCCORD, & A. HOWARD. Familial correlates of aggression in nondelinquent male children. *Journal of Abnormal and Social Psychology,* 1961, **62,** 79-93.

MCDAVID, J., JR. Personality and situational determinants of conformity. *Journal of Abnormal and Social Psychology,* 1959, **58,** 241-246.

MACFARLANE, J., L. ALLEN, & M. HONZIK. A developmental study of the behavior problems of normal children between 21 months and 14 years. Berkeley: University of California Press, 1954.

MCGUIRE, W. J. The relative efficacy of active and passive prior defense in immunizing beliefs against persuasion. *Journal of Abnormal and Social Psychology,* 1961, **63,** 326-332.

MCGUIRE, W. J. Persistence of the resistance to persuasion induced by various types of prior belief defenses. *Journal of Abnormal and Social Psychology,* 1962, **64,** 241-248.

MCGUIRE, W. J. Personality and susceptibility to social influence. In E. F. Borgatta & W. W. Lambert (Eds.), *Handbook of personality theory and research.* Chicago: Rand McNally & Company, 1968. Pp. 1130-1187.

MCGUIRE, W. J. The nature of attitudes and attitude change. In G. Lindzey & E. Aronson (Eds.), *The handbook of social psychology.* (2nd ed.) Vol. 3. Reading, Mass.: Addison-Wesley Publishing Company, Inc., 1969. Pp. 136-314.

MCGUIRE, W. J., & D. PAPAGEORGIS. The relative efficacy of various types of prior belief-defense in producing immunity against persuasion. *Journal of Abnormal and Social Psychology,* 1961, **62(2),** 327-337.

MCHENRY, R. New methods of assessing the accuracy of interpersonal perception. *Journal for the Theory of Social Behavior,* 1971, **1,** 109-119.

MCNEMAR, Q. Opinion-attitude methodology. *Psychological Bulletin,* 1946, **43,** 289-374.

MCRAE, D. Direct factor analysis of sociometric data. *Sociometry,* 1960, **23,** 360-371.

MCWHIRTER, R. M., & J. D. JECKER. Attitude similarity and inferred attraction. *Psychonomic Science,* 1967, 7(6), 225-226.

MADDEN, J. M. Personal preferences and conformity. *Journal of Social Psychology,* 1960, **52,** 269-277.

MAEHR, M. L., J. MENSING, & S. NAFZGER. Concept of self and the reaction of others. *Sociometry,* 1962, **25,** 353-357.

MAHANNAH, L. Influence of clothing color on the perception of personality. Unpublished master's thesis. Reno: University of Nevada, January 1968.

MAHONE, C. H. Fear of failure and unrealistic vocational aspiration. *Journal of Abnormal and Social Psychology,* 1960, **60,** 253-261.

MAIER, N. R. F., & L. R. HOFFMAN. Quality of first and second solutions in group problem solving. *Journal of Applied Psychology,* 1960, **44,** 278-283.

MAIER, N. R. F., & R. A. MAIER. An experimental test of the effects of "developmental" vs. "free" discussions on the quality of group decisions. *Journal of Applied Psychology,* 1957, **41,** 320-323.

MAIER, N. R. F., & A. R. SOLEM. The contribution of a discussion leader to the quality of group thinking: The effective use of minority opinions. *Human Relations,* 1952, **5,** 277-288.

MANIS, M. M. Social interaction and the self concept. *Journal of Abnormal and Social Psychology,* 1955, **51,** 362-370.

MANN, L., & I. L. JANIS. A follow-up study on the long-term effects of emotional role-playing. *Journal of Personality and Social Psychology,* 1968, **8,** 339-342.

MANN, R. D. A review of the relationships between personality and performance in small groups. *Psychological Bulletin,* 1959, **56,** 241-270.

MANNHEIM, B. F. Reference groups, membership groups

and the self image. *Sociometry*, 1966, **29**, 265-279.

MANWILLER, L. V. Expectations regarding teachers. *Journal of Experimental Education*, 1958, **26**, 315-354.

MARACEK, J., & D. R. METTEE. Avoidance of continued success as a function of self esteem, level of esteem, certainty, and responsibility for success. *Journal of Personality and Social Psychology*, 1972, **22**, 98-107.

MARCUS, P. M. Expressive and instrumental groups: Toward a theory of group structure. *American Journal of Sociology*, 1960, **66**, 54-59.

MARSH, R. C., & A. L. COLEMAN. Group influences and agricultural innovation: Some tentative findings and hypotheses. *American Journal of Sociology*, 1956, **61**, 588-594.

MARTIN, H. W. Preferences for types of patients. In R. K. Merton, G. G. Reader, & P. Kendall (Eds.), *The student-physician.* Cambridge, Mass.: Harvard University Press, 1957. Pp. 189-205.

MARTIN, H. W. Structural sources of strain in a small psychiatric hospital. Paper presented at the meeting of the American Sociological Association, St. Louis, Mo., September 1961.

MARTIN, J. D. Suspicion and the experimental confederate: A study of role and credibility. *Sociometry*, 1970, **33**, 178-192.

MARWELL, G., & D. R. SCHMITT. Dimensions of compliance-gaining behavior: An empirical analysis. *Sociometry*, 1967, **30**, 350-364.

MASLOW, A. H. Self esteem (dominance feeling) and sexuality in women. *Journal of Social Psychology*, 1942, **16**, 259-294.

MATZA, D. *Delinquency and drift.* New York: John Wiley & Sons, Inc., 1964.

MATZA D. *Becoming deviant.* Englewood Cliffs, N.J.: Prentice-Hall, Inc., 1969.

MAUSNER, B., & E. S. PLATT. Role playing as a technique for changing cigarette smoking behavior. Paper presented at the meeting of the Eastern Psychological Association, Washington, D.C., April 1968. Cited in H. Leventhal, Findings and theory in the study of fear communications. In L. Berkowitz (Ed.), *Advances in experimental social psychology.* Vol. 5. New York: Academic Press, Inc., 1970. Pp. 119-186.

MAYO, C. W., & W. H. CROCKETT. Cognitive complexity and primacy-recency effects in impression formation. *Journal of Abnormal and Social Psychology*, 1964, **68**, 335-338.

MEAD, G. H. *Mind, self and society.* Chicago: The University of Chicago Press, 1934.

MEDNICK, M. S., & S. S. TANGRI (EDS.). New perspectives on women. *Journal of Social Issues*, 1972, **28**(2), 1-250.

MEEKER, R. J., G. H. SHURE, & W. H. MOORE, JR. Realtime computer studies of bargaining behavior: The effects of threat upon bargaining. *American Federation of Information Processing Societies Conference Proceedings*, 1964, **24**, 115-123.

MEER, B., & E. FREEDMAN. The impact of Negro neighbors on white house owners. *Social Forces*, 1966, **45**, 11-19.

MEILE, R. L. Perceptions of threat and group leadership. Paper presented at the annual meeting of the American Sociological Association, Washington, D.C., 1962.

MENSH, I. M., & J. WISHNER. Asch on "Forming impressions of personality": Further evidence. *Journal of Personality*, 1947, **16**, 188-191.

MENZEL, H., & E. KATZ. Social relations and innovation in the medical profession: The epidemiology of a new drug. *Public Opinion Quarterly*, 1956, **19**, 337-352.

MERTON, R. K. Patterns of influence: A study of interpersonal influence and communications behavior in a local community. In P. F. Lazarsfeld & F. N. Stanton (Eds.), *Communications research, 1948-1949.* New York: Harper & Brothers, 1949. Pp. 180-219.

MERTON, R. K. The role set. *British Journal of Sociology*, 1957, **8**, 106-120. *(a)*

MERTON, R. K. *Social theory and social structure.* New York: The Free Press of Glencoe, Inc., 1957. *(b)*

MERTON, R. K., & A. S. KITT. Contributions to the theory of reference group behavior. In R. K. Merton & P. F. Lazarsfeld (Eds.), *Continuities in social research: Studies in the scope and method of "The American Soldier."* Glencoe, Ill.: The Free Press, 1950. Pp. 40-105.

MERTON, R. K., G. G. READER, & P. L. KENDALL (EDS.). *The student-physician.* Cambridge, Mass.: Harvard University Press, 1957.

MEZEI, L. Perceived social pressure as an explanation of shifts in the relative influence of race and belief on prejudice across social interactions. *Journal of Personality and Social Psychology*, 1971, **19**, 69-118.

MICHAEL, D. N., & N. MACCOBY. Factors influencing the effects of student participation on verbal learning from films: Motivating practice effects, "feedback," and overt versus covert responding. In A. A. Lumsdaine (Ed.), *Student Response in Programmed Instruction: A Symposium.* Washington: National Academy of Sciences—National Research Council, 1961. Pp. 271-293.

MICHELS, R. *A summary and interpretation of political parties: A sociological study of the oligarchical tendencies of modern democracy.* Glencoe, Ill.: The Free Press, 1949.

MIDDLETON, R. Alienation, race, and education. *American Sociological Review*, 1963, **28**, 973-976.

MIDLARSKY, E. Some antecedents of aiding under stress. *Proceedings of the 76th Annual Convention of the American Psychological Association*, 1968.

MILGRAM, S. Behavioral study of obedience. *Journal of Abnormal and Social Psychology*, 1963, **67**, 371-378.

MILGRAM, S. Some conditions

of obedience and disobedience to authority. *Human Relations,* 1965, **18**, 57-76.

MILLER, D. R. The study of social relationships: Situation, identity, and social interaction. In S. Koch (Ed.), *Psychology: A study of a science.* Vol. 5. *The process areas, the person, and some applied fields: Their place in psychology and in science.* New York: McGraw-Hill Book Company, 1963. Pp. 639-737.

MILLER, G. R., & M. A. HEWGILL. The effects of variations in non-fluency on audience ratings of source credibility. *Quarterly Journal of Speech,* 1964, **50**, 36-44.

MILLER, N., & R. S. BARON. On measuring couterarguing. *Journal for the Theory of Social Behaviour,* 1973, in press.

MILLER, N., & D. T. CAMPBELL. Recency and primacy in persuasion as a function of the timing of speeches and measurements. *Journal of Abnormal and Social Psychology,* 1959, **59**, 1-9.

MILLER, N. E., JR. The effect of group size on decision-making discussions. Unpublished doctoral dissertation, University of Michigan, 1951.

MILLER, N. E., JR., & R. BUGELSKI. Minor studies in aggression: The influence of frustrations imposed by the in-group on attitudes expressed toward out-groups. *Journal of Psychology,* 1948, **25**, 437-442.

MILLS, J. Interest in supporting and discrepant information. In R. P. Abelson et al. (Eds.), *Theories of cognitive consistency: A sourcebook.* Chicago: Rand McNally & Company, 1968. Pp. 771-776.

MILLS, T. M. Power relations in three person groups. *American Sociological Review,* 1953, **18**, 351-357.

MILLS, T. M. The coalition pattern in three person groups. *American Sociological Review,* 1954, **19**, 657-667.

MILLS, T. M. Developmental processes in three-person groups. *Human Relations,* 1956, **9**, 343-354.

MILSTEIN, F. A. Ambition and defense against threat of failure. Unpublished doctoral dissertation, University of Michigan, 1956.

MINARD, R. D. Race relationships in the Pocahontas coal field. *Journal of Social Issues,* 1952, **8**(1), 29-44.

MISCHEL, W. Theory and research on the antecedents of self-imposed delay of reward. In B. A. Maher (Ed.), *Progress in experimental personality research.* Vol. 2. New York: Academic Press, Inc., 1965.

MISCHEL, W. *Personality and assessment.* New York: John Wiley & Sons, Inc., 1968.

MISCHEL, W., & R. M. LIEBERT. Effects of discrepancies between observed and imposed reward criteria on their acquisition and transmission. *Journal of Personality and Social Psychology,* 1966, **3**, 45-53.

MITCHELL, W. C. Occupational role strains: The American elective public official. *Administrative Science Quarterly,* 1958, **3**, 210-228.

MIXON, D. Instead of deception. *Journal for the Theory of Social Behaviour,* October 1972, **2**, 145-177.

MIYAMOTO, S. F., & S. M. DORNBUSCH. A test of the interactionist hypothesis of self-conception. *American Journal of Sociology,* 1956, **61**, 399-403.

MODIGLIANI, A. Embarrassment and embarrassability. *Sociometry,* 1968, **31**, 313-326.

MOELLER, G., & M. H. APPLEZWEIG. A motivational factor in conformity. *Journal of Abnormal and Social Psychology,* 1957, **55**, 114-120.

MORAN, G. Dyadic attraction and orientational consensus. *Journal of Personality and Social Psychology,* 1966, **4**, 94-99.

MORENO, J. L. *Who shall survive?* (2nd ed.) Beacon, N.Y.: Beacon House, Inc., 1953.

MORGAN, W. R., & J. SAWYER. Bargaining, expectations, and the preference for equality over equity. *Journal of Personality and Social Psychology,* 1967, **6**, 139-149.

MORSE, N. *Satisfactions in the white-collar job.* Ann Arbor, Mich.: University of Michigan, Survey Research Center, 1953.

MOULTON, R. W. Effects of success and failure on level of aspirations as related to achievement motives. *Journal of Personality and Social Psychology,* 1965, **1**, 399-406.

MULDER, M. Communication structure, decision structure, and group performance. *Sociometry,* 1960, **23**, 1-14.

MURPHY, G., L. B. MURPHY, & T. M. NEWCOMB. *Experimental social psychology.* New York: Harper & Brothers, 1937.

MURPHY, L. B. Character development in normal children: Sources of flexibility. Paper presented at the meeting of the American Psychological Association, New York, September 1961.

MURSTEIN, B. L. The complementary need hypothesis in newlyweds and middle-aged married couples. *Journal of Abnormal and Social Psychology,* 1961, **63**, 194-197.

MYRDAL, G. *An American dilemma.* New York: Harper & Brothers, 1944.

NEL, E., R. HELMREICH, & E. ARONSON. Opinion change in the advocate as a function of the persuasibility of his audience: A clarification of the meaning of dissonance. *Journal of Personality and Social Psychology,* 1969, **12**, 117-124.

NELSON, D. A. The effect of differential magnitude of reinforcement on interpersonal attraction. *Dissertation Abstracts,* 1966, **27**(1-A), 253-254.

NEWCOMB, T. M. *Personality and social change: Attitude formation in a student community.* New York: The Dryden Press, Inc., 1943.

NEWCOMB, T. M. The prediction of interpersonal attraction. *American Psychologist,* 1956, **11**, 575-586.

NEWCOMB, T. M. *The acquaintance process.* New York: Holt, Rinehart and Winston, Inc., 1961.

NORFLEET, B. Interpersonal relations and group productivity. *Journal of Social Issues,* 1948, **4**(2), 66-69.

NORMAN, W. T., & L. R. GOLD-BERG. Raters, ratees, and randomness in personality structure. *Journal of Personality and Social Psychology,* 1966, **6**, 681-691.

NUNNALLY, J. C., & H. M. BOB-REN. Variables governing the willingness to receive communications on mental health. *Journal of Personality,* 1959, **27**, 38-46.

NYE, I. F. The employed mother: Basic changes in family structure. Paper presented at the meeting of the American Sociological Association, St. Louis, Mo., 1961.

OAKES, W. F., A. E. DRUGE, & B. AUGUST. Reinforcement effects on participation in group discussion. *Psychological Reports,* 1960, **7**, 503-514.

OFSHE, L., & R. OFSHE. *Utility and choice in social interaction.* Englewood Cliffs, N.J.: Prentice-Hall, Inc., 1970.

OMWAKE, K. The relationship between acceptance of self and acceptance of others shown by three personality inventories. *Journal of Consulting Psychology,* 1954, **18**, 443-446.

ORNE, M. T. On the social psychology of the psychological experiment: With particular reference to demand characteristics and their implications. *American Psychologist,* 1962, **17**, 776-783.

OSBORN, A. F. *Applied imagination.* New York: Charles Scribner's Sons, 1957.

OSGOOD, C. E. Suggestions for winning the real war with communism. *Journal of Conflict Resolution,* 1959, **3**, 295-325.

OSGOOD, C. E. *An alternative to war or surrender.* Urbana: The University of Illinois Press, 1962.

OSGOOD, C. E., & P. H. TANNEN-BAUM. The principle of congruity in the prediction of attitude change. *Psychological Review,* 1955, **62**, 42-55. Also in E. E. Sampson (Ed.), *Approaches, contexts, and problems of social psychology.* En-

glewood Cliffs, N.J.: Prentice-Hall, Inc., 1964. Pp. 237-248.

PALMORE, E. B. The introduction of Negroes into white departments. *Human Organization,* 1955, **14**, 27-28.

PAPAGEORGIS, D., & W. J. MCGUIRE. The generality of immunity to persuasion produced by pre-exposure to weakened counterarguments. *Journal of Abnormal and Social Psychology,* 1961, **62**, 475-481.

PARKE, R. D. Effectiveness of punishment as an interaction of intensity, timing, agent nurturance and cognitive structuring. *Child Development,* 1969, **40**, 213-235.

PARKE, R. D. The role of punishment in the socialization process. In R. A. Hoppe, G. A. Milton, & E. C. Simmel (Eds.), *Early experiences and the processes of socialization.* New York: Academic Press, Inc., 1970. Pp. 81-108.

PARKE, R. D., & R. H. WALTERS. Some factors determining the efficacy of punishment for inducing response inhibition. *Monographs of the Society for Research in Child Development,* 1967, **32**(109).

PARKER, S. Leadership patterns in a psychiatric ward. *Human Relations,* 1958, **11**, 287-301.

PARNES, S. F., & A. MEADOW. Effects of "brainstorming" instructions on creative problem solving by trained and untrained subjects. *Journal of Educational Psychology,* 1959, **50**, 171-176.

PARSONS, T. *The social system.* Glencoe, Ill.: The Free Press, 1951.

PARSONS, T., & R. F. BALES. *Family, socialization and interaction process.* Chicago: The Free Press of Glencoe, Ill., 1955.

PARSONS, T., R. F. BALES, & E. A. SHILS. *Working papers in the theory of action.* Glencoe, Ill.: The Free Press, 1953.

PARSONS, T., & E. A. SHILS (EDS.). *Toward a general theory of action.* Cambridge, Mass.: Harvard University Press, 1951.

PASSINI, F. T., & W. T. NORMAN. A universal conception of

personality structure. *Journal of Personality and Social Psychology,* 1966, **4**, 44-49.

PATCHEN, M. A conceptual framework and some empirical data regarding comparisons of social rewards. *Sociometry,* 1961, **24**, 136-156.

PATEL, A. S., & J. E. GORDON. Some personal and situational determinants of yielding to influence. *Journal of Abnormal and Social Psychology,* 1960, **61**, 411-418.

PAULSON, S. F. The effects of prestige of the speaker and acknowledgement of opposing arguments on audience retention and shift of opinion. *Speech Monographs,* 1954, **21**, 267-271.

PEABODY, D. Trait inferences: Evaluative and descriptive aspects. *Journal of Personality and Social Psychology Monograph,* 1967, **7**(4, Whole No. 644).

PEABODY, D. Evaluative and descriptive aspects in personality perception. *Journal of Personality and Social Psychology,* 1970, **16**, 639-646.

PEARLIN, L. I., M. R. YARROW, & H. A. SCARR. Unintended effects of parental aspirations: The case of children's cheating. *American Journal of Sociology,* 1967, **73**, 73-83.

PEEVERS, B. H., & P. F. SECORD. Developmental changes in attribution of descriptive concepts to persons. *Journal of Personality and Social Psychology,* 1973, in press.

PENNINGTON, D. F., JR., F. HARAVEY, & B. M. BASS. Some effects of decision and discussion on coalescence, change, and effectiveness. *Journal of Applied Psychology,* 1958, **42**, 404-408.

PEPITONE, A. Attributions of causality, social attitudes, and cognitive matching processes. In R. Tagiuri & L. Petrullo (Eds.), *Person perception and interpersonal behavior.* Stanford, Calif.: Stanford University Press, 1958. Pp. 258-276.

PEPITONE, A., & J. SHERBERG. Cognitive factors in interpersonal attraction. *Journal of Personality,* 1957, **25**, 757-766.

PERRY, S. E., & L. C. WYNNE. Role conflict, role redefinition, and social change in a clinical research organization. *Social Forces,* 1959, **38,** 62–65.

PETTIGREW, T. F. Personality and sociocultural factors in intergroup attitudes: A cross-national comparison. *Journal of Conflict Resolution,* 1958, **2,** 29–42.

PETTIGREW, T. F. Social psychology and desegregation research. *American Psychologist,* 1961, **16,** 105–112.

PETTIGREW, T. F. Racially separate or together? *Journal of Social Issues,* 1969, **25**(1), 43–69.

PETTIGREW, T. F., & E. Q. CAMPBELL. Faubus and segregation: An analysis of Arkansas voting. *Public Opinion Quarterly,* 1960, **24,** 436–447.

PIAGET, J. *The moral judgment of the child.* New York: Harcourt, Brace and Company, Inc., 1932.

PILIAVIN, I. M., J. A. HARDYCK, & A. C. VADUM. Constraining effects of personal costs on the transgressions of juveniles. *Journal of Personality and Social Psychology,* 1968, **10,** 227–232.

PILIAVIN, I. M., J. RODIN, & J. A. PILIAVIN. Good Samaritanism: An underground phenomenon? *Journal of Personality and Social Psychology,* 1969, **13,** 289–299.

POPE, L. *Millhands and preachers.* New Haven, Conn.: Yale University Press, 1942.

PORTER, L. W., & E. E. LAWLER, III. *Managerial attitudes and performance.* Homewood, Ill.: Richard D. Irwin, Inc., 1968.

PORTERFIELD, A. L. *Youth in trouble.* Fort Worth, Tex.: The Leo Patishman Foundation, 1946.

POTASHIN, A. A sociometric study of children's friendships. *Sociometry,* 1946, **9,** 48–70.

PRESTON, M. G., & R. K. HEINTZ. Effects of participatory *versus* supervisory leadership on group judgment. *Journal of Abnormal and Social Psychology,* 1949, **44,** 345–355.

PRICE, J. S., & E. H. HARE. Birth order studies: Some sources of bias. *British Journal of Psychiatry,* 1969, **115,** 633–646.

PRITCHARD, R. D. Equity theory: A review and critique. *Organizational Behavior and Human Performance,* 1969, **4,** 176–211.

PRITCHARD, R. D., M. D. DUNNETTE, & D. A. JORGENSEN. Effects of perceptions of equity and inequity on worker performance and satisfaction. *Journal of Applied Psychology Monograph,* 1972, **56**(1), 75–94.

PROCTOR, C. H., & C. P. LOOMIS. Analysis of sociometric data. In M. Jahoda, M. Deutsch, & S. W. Cook (Eds.), *Research methods in social relations.* Vol. 2. New York: Holt, Rinehart and Winston, Inc., 1951. Pp. 561–585.

PRUITT, D. G. Reciprocity and credit building in a laboratory dyad. *Journal of Personality and Social Psychology,* 1968, **8,** 143–147.

PRYER, M. W., & B. M. BASS. Some effects of feedback on behavior in groups. *Sociometry,* 1959, **22,** 56–63.

PUGH, D. Role activation conflict: A study of industrial inspection. *American Sociological Review,* 1966, **31,** 835–842.

QUARANTELLI, E. L., & J. COOPER. Self-conceptions and others: A further test of median hypotheses. *Sociological Quarterly,* 1966, **7,** 281–297.

RABINOWITZ, W. A note on the social perceptions of authoritarians and nonauthoritarians. *Journal of Abnormal and Social Psychology,* 1956, **53,** 384–386.

RADLOFF, R. Opinion evaluation and affiliation. *Journal of Abnormal and Social Psychology,* 1961, **62,** 578–585.

RANSFORD, H. E. Isolation, powerlessness, and violence: A study of attitudes and participation in the Watts riot. In E. F. Borgatta (Ed.), *Social Psychology: Readings and perspectives.* Chicago: Rand McNally & Company, 1969. Pp. 592–601.

RAVEN, B. H., & J. R. P. FRENCH, JR. Legitimate power, coercive power, and observability in social influence. *Sociometry,* 1958, **21,** 83–97. *(a)*

RAVEN, B. H., & J. R. P. FRENCH, JR. Group support, legitimate power, and social influence. *Journal of Personality,* 1958, **26,** 400–409. *(b)*

RAYNOR, J. O. Relationships between achievement-related motives, future orientation, and academic performance. *Journal of Personality and Social Psychology,* 1970, **15,** 28–33.

REDL, F., & D. WINEMAN. *Children who hate.* Glencoe, Ill.: The Free Press, 1951.

REEDER, L. G., G. A. DONOHUE, & A. BIBLARZ. Conceptions of self and others. *American Journal of Sociology,* 1960, **66,** 153–159.

REST, J., E. TURIEL, & L. KOHLBERG. Relations between level of moral judgment and preference and comprehension of the moral judgment of others. *Journal of Personality,* June 1969, **37,** 225–252.

RHINE, R. J. Some problems in dissonance theory research on information selectivity. *Psychological Bulletin,* 1967, **68,** 21–28.

RHINE, R. J., & L. J. SEVERANCE. Ego-involvement, discrepancy, source credibility, and attitude change. *Journal of Personality and Social Psychology,* 1970, **16,** 175–190.

RICHARDSON, H. M., & N. G. HANAWALT. Leadership as related to the Bernreuter personality measures: V. Leadership among adult women in social activities. *Journal of Social Psychology,* 1943, **36,** 141–154.

RIECKEN, H. W. The effect of talkativeness on ability to influence group solutions to problems. *Sociometry,* 1958, **21,** 309–321.

RIESEN, A. H. Critical stimulation and optimum period. Paper presented at the meeting of the American Psychological Association, New York, September 1961.

RILEY, J. W., JR., W. SCHRAMM, & F. W. WILLIAMS. Flight from Communism: A report on Korean refugees. *Public Opin-*

ion Quarterly, 1951, **15,** 274–286.

RILEY, M. W., & R. COHN. Control networks in informal groups. *Sociometry,* 1958, **21,** 30–49.

RILEY, M. W., & J. W. RILEY, JR. A sociological approach to communications research. *Public Opinion Quarterly,* 1951, **15,** 445–460.

RILEY, M. W., R. COHN, J. TOBY, & J. W. RILEY, JR. Interpersonal orientations in small groups: A consideration of the questionnaire approach. *American Sociological Review,* 1954, **19,** 715–724.

ROBBINS, F. G. The impact of social climates upon a college class. *School Review,* 1952, **60,** 275–284.

ROETHLISBERGER, F. J., & W. J. DICKSON. *Management and the worker.* Cambridge, Mass.: Harvard University Press, 1939.

ROGERS, C. R., & R. F. DYMOND (EDS.). *Psychotherapy and personality change: Coordinated studies in the client-centered approach.* Chicago: The University of Chicago Press, 1954.

ROGERS, E. M., & G. M. BEAL. The importance of personal influence in the adoption of technological changes. *Social Forces,* 1958, **36,** 329–335.

ROKEACH, M. Belief versus race as determinants of social distance: Comment on Triandis' paper. *Journal of Abnormal and Social Psychology,* 1961, **62,** 187–188.

ROKEACH, M., P. W. SMITH, & R. I. EVANS. Two kinds of prejudice or one? In M. Rokeach (Ed.), *The open and closed mind.* New York: Basic Books, Inc., Publishers, 1960. Pp. 132–168.

ROMMETVEIT, R. *Social norms and roles: Explorations in the psychology of enduring social pressures.* Minneapolis: The University of Minnesota Press, 1955.

ROMMETVEIT, R. *Selectivity, intuition and halo effects in social perception.* Oslo, Norway: Oslo University Press, 1960.

ROSE, A. M. The adequacy of

women's expectations for adult roles. *Social Forces,* 1951, **30,** 69–77.

ROSE, R. *Influencing voters: A study of campaign rationality.* New York: St. Martin's Press, Inc., 1967.

ROSEN, B. C. The achievement syndrome. *American Sociological Review,* 1956, **21,** 203–211.

ROSEN, B. C. Race, ethnicity, and the achievement syndrome. *American Sociological Review,* 1959, **24,** 47–60.

ROSEN, B. C. The achievement syndrome and economic growth in Brazil. *Social Forces,* 1964, **42,** 341–354.

ROSEN, B. C., & R. D'ANDRADE. The psycho-social origin of achievement motivation. *Sociometry,* 1959, **22,** 185–217.

ROSEN, S., G. LEVINGER, & R. LIPPITT. Perceived sources of social power. *Journal of Abnormal and Social Psychology,* 1961, **62,** 439–441.

ROSENBERG, M. *Society and the adolescent self-image.* Princeton, N.J.: Princeton University Press, 1965.

ROSENBERG, M. J. The experimental parable of inauthenticity: Consequences of attitudinal performance. In J. S. Antrobus (Ed.), *Cognition and affect.* Boston: Little, Brown and Company, 1970. Pp. 179–201.

ROSENBERG, M. J., & R. P. ABELSON. An analysis of cognitive balancing. In C. I. Hovland & I. L. Janis (Eds.), *Attitude organization and change.* New Haven, Conn.: Yale University Press, 1960. Pp. 112–163.

ROSENBERG, S., & R. L. HALL. The effects of different social feedback conditions upon performance in dyadic teams. *Journal of Abnormal and Social Psychology,* 1958, **57,** 271–277.

ROSENBERG, S., & R. JONES. A method for investigating and representing a person's implicit theory of personality: Theodore Dreiser's view of people. *Journal of Personality and Social Psychology,* 1972, **22,** 372–386.

ROSENBERG, S., & K. OLSHAN.

Evaluative and descriptive aspects in personality perception. *Journal of Personality and Social Psychology,* 1970, **16,** 619–626.

ROSENBERG, S., & A. SEDLAK. Structural representations of implicit personality theory. In L. Berkowitz (Ed.), *Advances in experimental social psychology.* Vol. 6. New York: Academic Press, Inc., 1972. Pp. 235–297.

ROSENBLITH, J. F. A replication of "Some roots of prejudice." *Journal of Abnormal and Social Psychology,* 1949, **44,** 470–489.

ROSENFELD, H. Social choice conceived as a level of aspirations. *Journal of Abnormal and Social Psychology,* 1964, **68,** 491–499.

ROSENTHAL, A. M. *Thiry-eight witnesses.* New York: McGraw-Hill Book Company, 1964.

ROSENTHAL, R. *Experimenter effects in behavioral research.* New York: Appleton-Century-Crofts, Inc., 1966.

ROSENTHAL, R. Experimenter expectancy and the reassuring nature of the null hypothesis decision procedure. *Psychological Bulletin Monograph Supplement,* 1968, **70** (6, Pt. 2).

ROSENTHAL, R., & L. JACOBSON. Pygmalion in the classroom: Teacher expectation and pupils' intellectual development. New York: Holt, Rinehart and Winston, Inc., 1968.

ROSNOW, R. L., A. G. GITTER, & R. F. HOLZ. Some determinants of post-decisional information preferences. *Journal of Social Psychology,* 1969, **79,** 235–245.

ROSOW, I. Issues in the concept of need-complementarity. *Sociometry,* 1957, **20,** 216–233.

ROSS, A. Modes of guilt reduction. Unpublished doctoral dissertation, University of Minnesota, 1965.

ROTTER, J. B. Generalized expectancies for internal versus external control of reinforcement. *Psychological Monographs,* 1966, **80**(1, Whole No. 609).

RUBIN, Z. Measurement of romantic love. *Journal of Personality and Social Psychology,* 1970, **16**, 263-273.

RUECHELLE, R. C. An experimental study of audience recognition of emotional and intellectual appeals in persuasion. *Speech Monographs.* 1958, **25**, 49-58.

RUSH, G. B. Status consistency and right-wing extremism. *American Sociological Review,* 1967, **32**, 86-92.

RYCHLAK, J. F. The similarity, compatibility, or incompatibility of needs in interpersonal selection. *Journal of Personality and Social Psychology,* 1965, **2**, 334-340.

SAMPSON, E. E. Status congruence and cognitive consistency. *Sociometry,* 1963, **26**, 146-162.

SAMPSON, E. E. The study of ordinal position: Antecedents and outcomes. In B. A. Maher (Ed.), *Progress in experimental personality research.* New York: Academic Press, Inc., 1965. Pp. 175-228.

SAMPSON, E. E. Studies of status congruence. In L. Berkowitz (Ed.), *Advances in experimental social psychology.* Vol. 4. New York: Academic Press, Inc., 1969. Pp. 225-268.

SAMPSON, E. E., & G. L. BUNKER. The effects of power and congruity on small group behavior. Unpublished report, Berkeley, University of California, 1966.

SAMPSON, E. E., & F. T. HANCOCK. An examination of the relationship between ordinal position, personality, and conformity. *Journal of Personality and Social Psychology,* 1967, **5**, 398-407.

SAMPSON, E. E., & C. A. INSKO. Cognitive consistency and performance in the autokinetic situation. *Journal of Abnormal and Social Psychology,* 1964, **68**, 184-192.

SANFORD, F. H. The follower's role in leadership phenomena. In G. E. Swanson, T. M. Newcomb, & E. L. Hartley (Eds.), *Readings in social psychology.* (Rev. ed.) New York: Holt, Rinehart and Winston, Inc., 1952. Pp. 328-340.

SARBIN, T. R., & V. L. ALLEN. Role theory. In G. Lindzey & E. Aronson (Eds.), *The handbook of social psychology.* (2nd ed.) Vol. 1. Reading, Mass.: Addison-Wesley Publishing Company, Inc., 1968. Pp. 488-567.

SAWYER, J., & H. GUETZKOW. Bargaining and negotiation in international relations. In H. C. Kelman (Ed.), *International behavior.* New York: Holt, Rinehart and Winston, Inc., 1965.

SCANLON, J. C., B. HUNTER, & G. SUN. Sources of professional identity in medicine. Personal communication, 1961.

SCHACHTER, S. Deviation, rejection, and communication. *Journal of Abnormal and Social Psychology,* 1951, **46**, 190-207.

SCHACHTER, S. *The psychology of affiliation.* Stanford, Calif.: Stanford University Press, 1959. P. 62.

SCHACHTER, S. The interaction of cognitive and physiological determinants of emotional state. In L. Berkowitz (Ed.), *Advances in experimental social psychology.* Vol. 1. New York: Academic Press, Inc., 1964. Pp. 49-81.

SCHACHTER, S., & R. L. HALL. Group-derived restraints and audience persuasion. *Human Relations,* 1952, **5**, 397-406.

SCHAEFER, E. S., & N. BAYLEY. Consistency of maternal behavior. *Journal of Abnormal and Social Psychology,* 1960, **61**, 1-6.

SCHEFF, T. J. A theory of social coordination applicable to mixed motive games. *Sociometry,* 1967, **30**, 215-234.

SCHEFF, T. J., & J. L. CHEWNING. Identity and communication in prisoner's dilemma: A theory. Unpublished report, Social Science Research Institute, University of Hawaii, Mar. 21, 1968.

SCHEFLEN, A. E. Quasi-courtship behavior in psychotherapy. *Psychiatry,* 1965, **28**, 245-257.

SCHEIN, E. H. The Chinese indoctrination program for prisoners of war: A study of attempted "brainwashing." In E. E. Maccoby, T. M. Newcomb, & E. L. Hartley (Eds.), *Readings in social psychology.* (3rd ed.) New York: Holt, Rinehart and Winston, Inc., 1958. Pp. 311-334.

SCHEIN, E. H., I. SCHNEIER, & C. H. BARKER. *Coercive persuasion.* New York: W. W. Norton & Company, Inc., 1961.

SCHELLENBERG, J. A., & L. S. BEE. A re-examination of the theory of complementary needs in mate selection. *Marriage and Family Living,* 1960, **22**, 227-232.

SCHELLING, T. C. *The strategy of conflict.* Cambridge, Mass.: Harvard University Press, 1960.

SCHILD, E. O. The foreign student, as stranger, learning the norms of the host culture. *Journal of Social Issues,* 1962, **18**(1), 41-54.

SCHOMER, R. W., A. H. DAVIS, & H. H. KELLEY. Threats and the development of coordination: Further studies of the Deutsch and Krauss trucking game. *Journal of Personality and Social Psychology,* 1966, **4**, 119-126.

SCHOOLER, C. Birth order effects: Not here, not now! *Psychological Bulletin,* 1972, **78**, 161-175.

SCHOPLER, J., & N. BATESON. The power of dependence. *Journal of Personality and Social Psychology,* 1965, **2**, 247-254.

SCHOPLER, J., & M. W. MATTHEWS. The influence of the perceived casual locus of partner's dependence on the use of interpersonal power. *Journal of Personality and Social Psychology,* 1965, **2**, 609-612.

SCHOPLER, J., & V. D. THOMPSON. Role of attribution processes in mediating amount of reciprocity for a favor. *Journal of Personality and Social Psychology,* 1968, **10**, 243-250.

SCHRAMM, W., & W. DANIELSON. Anticipated audiences as determinants of recall. *Journal of Abnormal and Social Psychology,* 1958, **56**, 282-283.

SCHRAMM, W., J. LYLE, & E. B. PARKER. *Television in the lives of our children.* Stanford, Calif.: Stanford University Press, 1961.

SCHULMAN, G. I. Asch conformity studies: Conformity to the experimenter and/or to the group? *Sociometry,* 1967, **30,** 26–40.

SCHULMAN, S. Basic functional roles in nursing: Mother surrogate and healer. In E. G. Jaco (Ed.), *Patients, physicians, and illness.* New York: The Free Press of Glencoe, Inc., 1958. Pp. 528–537.

SCHULTZ, D. P. Time, awareness, and order of presentation in opinion change. *Journal of Applied Psychology,* 1963, **47,** 280–283.

SCHUTZ, A. Equality and the meaning structure of the social world. In A. Schutz. (Collected papers) A. Broderson (Ed.), *Collected papers II: Studies in social theory.* The Hague: Martinus Nijhoff, 1964. Pp. 226–273.

SCHWARTZ, C. G. Problems for psychiatric nurses in playing a new role on a mental hospital ward. In M. Greenblatt, D. J. Levinson, & R. H. Williams (Eds.), *The patient and the mental hospital.* Glencoe, Ill.: The Free Press, 1957. Pp. 402–426.

SCHWARTZ, S. H. Words, deeds, and the perception of consequences and responsibility in action situations. *Journal of Personality and Social Psychology,* 1968, **10,** 232–242. *(a)*

SCHWARTZ, S. H. Awareness of consequences and the influence of moral norms on interpersonal behavior. *Sociometry,* 1968, **31,** 355–369. *(b)*

SCHWARTZ, S. H. Elicitation of moral obligation and self-sacrificing behavior: An experimental study of volunteering to be a bone marrow donor. *Journal of Personality and Social Psychology,* 1970, **15,** 283–293.

SCHWEITZER, D. Style of presentation as a credibility variable. Unpublished doctoral dissertation, Reno, Nevada: University of Nevada, 1967.

SCHWEITZER, D., & G. P. GINSBURG. Factors of communicator credibility. In C. W. Back-

man & P. F. Secord (Eds.), *Problems in social psychology: Selected readings.* New York: McGraw-Hill Book Company, 1966. Pp. 94–102.

SCODEL, A., & M. L. FREEDMAN. Additional observations on the social perceptions of authoritarians and nonauthoritarians. *Journal of Abnormal and Social Psychology,* 1956, **52,** 92–95.

SCODEL, A., & P. MUSSEN. Social perceptions of authoritarians and nonauthoritarians. *Journal of Abnormal and Social Psychology,* 1953, **48,** 181–184.

SCOTT, J. P., & M. MARSDON. Critical periods affecting the development of normal and maladjusted social behavior of puppies. *Journal of Genetic Psychology,* 1950, **77,** 25–60.

SCOTT, M. B., & S. M. LYMAN. Accounts. *American Sociological Review,* 1968, **33,** 46–62.

SCOTT, W. A. Professionals in bureaucracies—areas of conflict. In H. M. Volmer & D. L. Mills (eds.), *Professionalization.* Englewood Cliffs, N.J.: Prentice-Hall, Inc., 1966.

SCOTT, W.A. Attitude measurement. In E. Aronson & G. Lindzey (Eds.), *The handbook of social psychology.* (2nd ed.) Vol. 2. Reading, Mass.: Addison-Wesley Publishing Company, Inc., 1968. Pp. 204–273.

SCOTT, W. R. Rationality and non-rationality of international attitudes. *Journal of Conflict Resolution,* 1958, **2,** 8–16.

SEAGO, D. W. Stereotypes: Before Pearl Harbor and after. *Journal of Psychology,* 1947, **23,** 55–63.

SEARS, D. O. Biased indoctrination and selectivity of exposure to new information. *Sociometry,* 1965, **28,** 363–376.

SEARS, D. O. Opinion formation and information preferences in an adversary situation. *Journal of Experimental and Social Psychology,* 1966, **2,** 130–142.

SEARS, D. O. The paradox of de facto selective exposure without preferences for supportive information. In R. P. Abelson

et al. (Eds.), *Theories of cognitive consistency: A sourcebook.* Chicago: Rand McNally & Company, 1968. Pp. 777–787.

SEARS, D. O., & R. P. ABELES. Attitudes and opinions. In P. H. Mussen & M. R. Rosenzweig (Eds.), *Annual review of psychology.* Vol. 20. Palo Alto, Calif.: Annual Reviews, Inc., 1969. Pp. 253–288.

SEARS, D. O., & J. L. FREEDMAN. Effects of expected familiarity with arguments upon opinion change and selective exposure. *Journal of Personality and Social Psychology,* 1965, **2,** 420–426.

SEARS, R. R. Identification as a form of behavioral development. In D. B. Harris (Ed.), *The concept of development.* Minneapolis: The University of Minnesota Press, 1957. Pp. 147–161.

SEARS, R. R. Relations of early socialization experience to aggression in middle childhood. *Journal of Abnormal and Social Psychology,* 1961, **63,** 466–493.

SEARS, R. R., E. E. MACCOBY, & H. LEVIN. *Patterns of child rearing.* New York: Harper & Row, Publishers, Inc., 1957.

SEARS, R. R., L. RAU, & R. ALPERT. *Identification and child rearing.* Stanford, Calif.: Stanford University Press, 1965.

SEASHORE, S. E. *Group cohesiveness in the industrial work group.* Ann Arbor, Mich.: University of Michigan, Survey Research Center, 1954.

SECORD, P. F. The role of facial features in interpersonal perception. In R. Tagiuri & L. Petrullo (Eds.), *Person perception and interpersonal behavior.* Stanford, Calif.: Stanford University Press, 1958. Pp. 300–315.

SECORD, P. F. Stereotyping and favorableness in the perception of Negro faces. *Journal of Abnormal and Social Psychology,* 1959, **59,** 309–315.

SECORD, P. F., & C. W. BACKMAN. Personality theory and the problem of stability and change in individual behavior: An interpersonal approach. *Psychological Review,* 1961, **68,** 21–32.

SECORD, P. F., & C. W. BACKMAN. *Social Psychology.* (1st ed.) New York: McGraw-Hill Book Company, 1964. *(a)*

SECORD, P. F., & C. W. BACKMAN. Interpersonal congruency, perceived similarity, and friendship. *Sociometry,* 1964, **27,** 115-127. *(b)*

SECORD, P. F., & C. W. BACKMAN. Interpersonal approach to personality. In B. H. Maher (Ed.), *Progress in experimental personality research.* Vol. 2. New York: Academic Press, Inc., 1965. Pp. 91-125.

SECORD, P. F., C. W. BACKMAN, & H. T. EACHUS. Effects of imbalance in the self concept on the perception of persons. *Journal of Abnormal and Social Psychology,* 1964, **68,** 442-446.

SECORD, P. F., & E. S. BERSCHEID. Stereotyping and the generality of implicit personality theory. *Journal of Personality,* 1963, **31,** 65-78.

SECORD, P. F., W. BEVAN, & W. F. DUKES. Occupational and physiognomic stereotypes in the perception of photographs. *Journal of Social Psychology,* 1953, **37,** 261-270.

SECORD, P. F., W. BEVAN, & B. KATZ. The Negro stereotype and perceptual accentuation. *Journal of Abnormal and Social Psychology,* 1956, **53,** 78-83.

SECORD, P. F., W. F. DUKES, & W. BEVAN. Personalities in faces: I. An experiment in social perceiving. *Genetics Psychology Monographs,* 1954, **49,** 231-279.

SECORD, P. F., & J. E. MUTHARD. Personalities in faces: II. Individual differences in the perception of women's faces. *Journal of Abnormal and Social Psychology,* 1955, **50,** 238-242.

SEEMAN, M. On the meaning of alienation. *American Sociological Review,* 1959, **24,** 783-791.

SELVIN, H. C. *The effects of leadership.* Chicago: The Free Press of Glencoe, Ill., 1960.

SHAVER, K. G. Defensive attribution: Effects of severity and relevance on the responsibility assigned for an accident. *Journal of Personality and So-*

cial Psychology, 1970, **14,** 101-113.

SHAW, M. E. A comparison of individuals and small groups in the rational solution of complex problems. *American Journal of Psychology,* 1932, **44,** 491-504.

SHAW, M. E. Some effects of problem complexity upon problem solution efficiency in different communication nets. *Journal of Experimental Psychology,* 1954, **48,** 211-217.

SHAW, M. E. A comparison of two types of leadership in various communication nets. *Journal of Abnormal and Social Psychology,* 1955, **50,** 127-134.

SHAW, M. E. Communication networks. In L. Berkowitz (Ed.), *Advances in experimental social psychology.* New York: Academic Press, Inc., 1964.

SHAW, M. E., & J. L. SULZER. An empirical test of Heider's levels in attribution of responsibility. *Journal of Abnormal and Social Psychology,* 1964, **69,** 39-46.

SHELDON, W. H., & S. S. STEVENS. *The varieties of temperament: A psychology of constitutional differences.* New York: Harper & Brothers, 1942.

SHELDON, W. H., S. S. STEVENS, & W. B. TUCKER. *The varieties of human physique: An introduction to constitutional psychology.* New York: Harper & Brothers, 1940.

SHERIF, C. W., & M. SHERIF. (EDS.). *Attitude, ego-involvement, and change.* New York: John Wiley & Sons, Inc., 1967.

SHERIF, C. W., M. SHERIF, & R. E. NEBERGALL. *Attitude and attitude change: The social judgment-involvement approach.* Philadelphia: W. B. Saunders Company, 1965.

SHERIF, M. *An outline of social psychology.* New York: Harper & Brothers, 1948.

SHERIF, M., B. J. WHITE, & O. J. HARVEY. Status in experimentally produced groups. *American Journal of Sociology,* 1955, **60,** 370-379.

SHERIF, M., O. J. HARVEY, B. J.

WHITE, W. R. HOOD, & C. W. SHERIF. *Intergroup conflict and cooperation: The robbers cave experiment.* Norman, Okla.: University Book Exchange, 1961.

SHERIF, M., & C. I. HOVLAND. *Social judgment: Assimilation and contrast effects in communication and attitude change.* New Haven, Conn.: Yale University Press, 1961.

SHERWOOD, J. J. Self identity and referent others. *Sociometry,* 1965, **28,** 66-81.

SHERWOOD, J. J. Increased self-evaluation as a function of ambiguous evaluations by referent others. *Sociometry,* 1967, **30,** 404-409.

SHILS, E. A. Primary groups in the American Army. In R. K. Merton & P. F. Lazarsfeld (Eds.), *Continuities in social research: Studies in the scope and method of "The American soldier."* Glencoe, Ill.: The Free Press, 1950. Pp. 16-39.

SHILS, E. A., & M. JANOWITZ. Cohesion and disintegration in the Wehrmacht in World War II. *Public Opinion Quarterly,* 1948, **12,** 280-315.

SHOMER, R. W., A. H. DAVIS, & H. H. KELLEY. Threats and the development of coordination: Further studies of the Deutsch and Krauss trucking game. *Journal of Personality and Social Psychology,* 1966, **4,** 119-126.

SHORT, J. F., JR. Aggressive behavior in response to status threats. Paper presented at the meeting of the American Sociological Association, St. Louis, Mo., August 1961.

SHRAUGER, S., & J. ALTROCCHI. The personality of the perceiver as a factor in person perception. *Psychological Bulletin,* 1964, **62,** 289-308.

SHULL, F. A., JR., & D. C. MILLER. Role conflict behavior in administration: A study in the validation of a theory of role-conflict resolution. Paper presented at the meeting of the American Sociological Association, New York, 1960.

SHUTLER, M. E. A reexamination of Benedict's hypothesis on the effects of discontinuous cultural conditioning.

Unpublished master's thesis, University of Arizona, 1958.

SHUVAL, J. T. The micro-neighborhood: An approach to ecological patterns of ethnic groups. *Social Problems,* 1962, **9,** 272–280.

SIDOWSKI, J. B. Reward and punishment in a minimal social situation. *Journal of Experimental Psychology,* 1957, **54,** 318–326.

SIDOWSKI, J. B., L. B. WYCOFF, & L. TABORY. The influence of reinforcement and punishment in a minimal social situation. *Journal of Abnormal and Social Psychology,* 1956, **52,** 115–119.

SIEGEL, A. E., & S. SIEGEL. Reference groups, membership groups, and attitude change. *Journal of Abnormal and Social Psychology,* 1957, **55,** 360–364.

SIEGEL, J. P. Managerial personality traits and need satisfaction: The effects of role incongruity and conflict. Reprinted from the *Proceedings of the 76th Annual Convention of the American Psychological Association,* 1968.

SIEGEL, S., & L. E. FOURAKER. *Bargaining and group decision making: Experiments in bilateral monopoly.* New York: McGraw-Hill Book Company, 1960.

SIMMEL, G. *The sociology of Georg Simmel.* Translated by Kurt H. Wolff. Glencoe, Ill.: The Free Press, 1950.

SIMMONS, C. H., & M. J. LERNER. Altruism as a search for justice. *Journal of Personality and Social Psychology,* 1968, **9,** 216–225.

SIMPSON, G. E., & J. M. YINGER. *Racial and cultural minorities.* New York: Harper & Row, Publishers, Incorporated, 1958.

SIMPSON, G. E., & J. M. YINGER. *Racial and cultural minorities.* (3rd ed.) New York: Harper & Row, Publishers, Incorporated, 1965.

SIMPSON, I. H. Patterns of socialization into professions: The case of student nurses. Paper presented at the meeting of the American Socio-

logical Association, New York, August 1960.

SINGER, R. P. The effects of fear-arousing communications on attitude change and behavior. Unpublished doctoral dissertation, University of Connecticut, 1965. Cited in H. Leventhal, Findings and theory in the study of fear communications. In L. Berkowitz (Ed.), *Advances in experimental social psychology.* Vol. 5. New York: Academic Press, Inc., 1970. Pp. 119–186.

SINHA, A. K. P., & O. P. UPADHYAYA. Change and persistence in the stereotype of university students toward different ethnic groups during Sino-Indian border dispute. *Journal of Social Psychology,* 1960, **52,** 31–39.

SKINNER, B. F. *Contingencies of reinforcement: A theoretical analysis.* New York: Appleton Century Crofts, Educational Division, Meredith Corporation, 1969.

SLATER, P. E. Contrasting correlates of group size. *Sociometry,* 1958, **21,** 129–139.

SLATER, P. E., K. MORIMOTO, & P. W. HYDE. Social interaction in experimentally induced psychotic-like states. Paper presented at the meetings of the American Sociological Society, Seattle, Wash., 1958.

SMITH, K. H. Ego strength and perceived competence as conformity variables. *Journal of Abnormal and Social Psychology,* 1961, **62,** 169–171.

SNOEK, J. D. Role strain in diversified role sets. *American Journal of Sociology,* 1966, **71,** 363–372.

SNYDER, C. General and specific role expectations for teachers. Unpublished manuscript, Michigan State University. Cited in W. B. Brookover & D. Gottlieb, *A sociology of education.* New York: American Book Company, 1964.

SOEN, D., & I. TISHLER. *Urban renewal: Social surveys.* Tel-Aviv: Institute for Planning and Development, 1968. Described in Y. Amir, Contact hypothesis in ethnic relations. *Psychological Bulletin,* 1969, **71,** 319–342.

SOLOMON, R. L. Punishment. *American Psychologist,* 1964, **19,** 239–253.

SOLOMON, R. L., L. J. KAMIN, & L. C. WYNNE. Traumatic avoidance learning: The outcomes of several extinction procedures with dogs. *Journal of Abnormal and Social Psychology,* 1953, **48,** 291–302.

SOLOMON, R. L., & L. C. WYNNE. Traumatic avoidance learning: Acquisition in normal dogs. *Psychological Monographs,* 1953, **67**(4), (Whole No. 354).

SOLOMON, R. L., & L. C. WYNNE. Traumatic avoidance learning: The principles of anxiety conservation and partial irreversibility. *Psychological Review,* 1954, **61,** 353–385.

SPITZ, R. A. Hospitalism: An inquiry into the genesis of psychiatric conditions in early childhood. *The psychoanalytic study of the child.* Vol. 1. New York: International University Press, Inc., 1945. Pp. 53–74.

SPITZ, R. A. Hospitalism: A follow-up report. *The psychoanalytic study of the child.* Vol. 2. New York: International University Press, Inc., 1946. Pp. 113–117.

SPITZ, R. A., & K. M. WOLFE. Anaclitic depression: An inquiry into the genesis of psychiatric conditions in early childhood. *The psychoanalytic study of the child.* Vol. 2. New York: International University Press, Inc., 1946. Pp. 313–342.

STAGNER, R., & C. S. CONGDON. Another failure to demonstrate displacement of aggression. *Journal of Abnormal and Social Psychology,* 1955, **51,** 695–696.

STALLING, R. B. Personality similarity and evaluative meaning as conditioners of attraction. *Journal of Personality and Social Psychology,* 1970, **14,** 77–82.

STAR, S. A., & H. M. HUGHES. Report on an educational campaign: The Cincinnati plan for the United Nations. *American Journal of Sociology,* 1950, **55,** 1–12.

STAR, S. A., R. M. WILLIAMS, JR.,

& S. A. STOUFFER. Negro infantry platoons in white companies. In E. Maccoby, T. M. Newcomb, & E. L. Hartley (Eds.), *Readings in social psychology.* (3rd ed.) New York: Holt, Rinehart and Winston, Inc., 1958. Pp. 596–601.

STEIN, A., & L. K. FRIEDRICH. Television content and young children's behavior. In J. P. Murray, E. A. Rubinstein, & G. A. Comstock (Eds.), *Television and social behavior.* Vol. 2. *Television and social learning.* Government Printing Office, 1971.

STEIN, A. H. Imitation of resistance to temptation. *Child Development,* 1967, **38,** 157–169.

STEINER, I. D. Primary group influences on public opinion. *American Sociological Review,* 1954, **19,** 260–267.

STEINER, I. D. Receptivity to supportive versus nonsupportive communications. *Journal of Abnormal and Social Psychology,* 1962, **65,** 266–267.

STEINER, I. D. Models for inferring relationships between group size and potential group productivity. *Behavioral Science,* 1966, **11,** 273–283.

STEPHAN, F. F., & E. C. MISHLER. The distribution of participation in small groups: An exponential approximation. *American Sociological Review,* 1952, **17,** 599–608.

STERN, G. G., & J. C. SCANLON. Pediatric lions and gynecological lambs. *Journal of Medical Education,* 1958, **33**(Pt. 2), 12–18.

STERN, G. G., M. I. STEIN, & B. S. BLOOM. *Methods in personality assessment: Human behavior in complex social situations.* Chicago: The Free Press of Glencoe, Ill., 1956.

STOCK, D. An investigation into the intercorrelations between the self concept and feelings directed toward other persons and groups. *Journal of Consulting Psychology,* 1949, **13,** 176–180.

STONE, G. P. Clothing and social relations: A study of appearance in the context of

community life. Unpublished doctoral dissertation, University of Chicago, Department of Sociology, 1959.

STONE, G. P. Appearance and the self. In A. M. Rose (Ed.), *Human behavior and social processes.* Boston: Houghton Mifflin Company, 1962. Pp. 86–118.

STONER, J. A. F. A comparison of individual and group decisions involving risk. Unpublished master's thesis, Massachusetts Institute of Technology, School of Industrial Management, 1961.

STOTLAND, E. Identification with persons and groups. Final report on Grant M-2423 to National Institute of Mental Health, U.S. Public Health Service, October 1961.

STOTLAND, E., S. E. SHERMAN, & K. Y. SHAVER. *Empathy and birth order: Some experimental explorations.* Lincoln: University of Nebraska Press, 1971.

STOTLAND, E., S. THORLEY, E. J. THOMAS, A. R. COHEN, & A. ZANDER. The effects of group expectations and self-esteem on self-evaluations. *Journal of Abnormal and Social Psychology,* 1957, **54,** 55–63.

STOUFFER, S. A., E. A. SUCHMAN, L. C. DEVINNEY, S. A. STAR, & R. M. WILLIAMS, JR. *The American soldier.* Vol. 1. *Adjustment during army life.* Princeton, N.J.: Princeton University Press, 1949.

STOUFFER, S. A., & J. TOBY. Role conflict and personality. *American Journal of Sociology,* 1951, **56,** 395–406.

STRAUSS, A. L. *Mirrors and masks.* New York: The Free Press of Glencoe, Ill., 1959.

STRICKLAND, B. R., & D. P. CROWNE. Conformity under conditions of simulated group pressure as a function of the need for social approval. *Journal of Social Psychology,* 1962, **58,** 171–181.

STRICKLAND, L. H. Surveillance and trust. *Journal of Personality,* 1958, **26,** 200–215.

STRITCH, T. M., & P. F. SECORD. Personality in faces: VI. Interaction effects in the perception of faces. *Journal of Personality,* 1956, **24,** 270–284.

STROEBE, W., C. A. INSKO, V. D. THOMPSON, & B. D. LAYTON. Effects of physical attractiveness, attitude similarity, and sex on various aspects of interpersonal attraction. *Journal of Personality and Social Psychology,* 1971, **18,** 79–91.

STRODTBECK, F. L. Family interaction, values, and achievement. In D. C. McClelland, A. L. Baldwin, U. Bronfenbrenner, & F. L. Strodtbeck (Eds.), *Talent and society.* New York: D. Van Nostrand Company, Inc., 1958. Pp. 135–194.

STRODTBECK, F. L., & R. D. MANN. Sex role differentiation in jury deliberations. *Sociometry,* 1956, **19,** 3–11.

STRODTBECK, F. L., R. M. JAMES, & C. HAWKINS. Social status in jury deliberations. In E. Maccoby, T. M. Newcomb, & E. L. Hartley (Eds.), *Readings in social psychology.* New York: Holt, Rinehart and Winston, Inc., 1958. Pp. 379–388.

STRYKER, S. Social structure and prejudice. *Social Problems,* 1959, **6,** 340–354.

STYCOS, J. M. Patterns of communication in a rural Greek village. *Public Opinion Quarterly,* 1952, **16,** 59–70.

SURGEON GENERAL'S SCIENTIFIC ADVISORY COMMITTEE ON TELEVISION AND SOCIAL BEHAVIOR. *Television and growing up: The impact of televised violence.* Report to the Surgeon General, U.S. Department of Health, Education, and Welfare. Rockville, Md.: National Institute of Mental Health, 1971.

SUTCLIFFE, J. P., & M. HABERMAN. Factors influencing choice in role conflict situations. *American Sociological Review,* 1956, **21,** 695–703.

SUTHERLAND, E. H. *The professional thief.* Chicago: The University of Chicago Press, 1937.

SWINGLI, P. G. The effects of the win-loss difference upon cooperative responding in a "dangerous" game. *Journal of Conflict Resolution,* 1967, **11,** 214–222.

SYKES, G. M., & D. MATZA. Techniques of neutralization: A theory of delinquency. *American Sociological Review,* 1957, **22,** 667–669.

TAGIURI, R. Person perception. In G. Lindzey & E. Aronson (Eds.), *The handbook of social psychology.* (2nd ed.) Vol. 3. Reading, Mass.: Addison-Wesley Publishing Company, 1969. Pp. 395–449.

TAGIURI, R., N. KOGAN, & L. M. K. LONG. Differentiation of sociometric choice and status relations in a group. *Psychological Reports,* 1958, **4,** 523–526.

TAJFEL, H. Social and cultural factors in perception. In G. Lindzey & E. Aronson (Eds.), *The handbook of social psychology.* (2nd ed.) Vol. 3. Reading, Mass.: Addison-Wesley Publishing Company, Inc., 1969. Pp. 315–394.

TAJFEL, H., & A. L. WILKES. Salience of attributes and commitment to extreme judgments in the perception of people. *British Journal of Social and Clinical Psychology,* 1964, **3,** 40–49.

TAN, A. L., & G. DE VERA. A test of the belief congruence theory of prejudice. *Cornell Journal of Social Relations,* 1970, **5,** 166–171.

TANNENBAUM, P. H., & B. S. GREENBERG. Mass communication. *Annual Review of Psychology,* 1968, **19,** 351–386.

TAYLOR, D. W. Problem solving by groups. *Proceedings of the 14th International Congress of Psychology,* 1954.

TAYLOR, D. W., P. C. BERRY, & C. H. BLOCK. Does group participation when using brainstorming facilitate or inhibit creative thinking? *Administrative Science Quarterly,* 1958, **3,** 23–47.

TEDESCHI, J. T., B. R. SCHLENKER, & T. V. BONOMA. Cognitive dissonance: Private ratiocination or public spectacle? *American Psychologist,* 1971, **26,** 685–695.

TEGER, A. I., & D. G. PRUITT. Components of group risk taking. *Journal of Experimental Social Psychology,* 1967, **3,** 189–205.

TESSER, A., R. GATEWOOD, & M. RIVER. Some determinants of gratitude. *Journal of Personality and Social Psychology,* 1968, **9,** 233–236.

THARP, R. G. Psychological patterning in marriage. *Psychological Bulletin,* 1963, **60,** 91–117.

THARP, R. G. Reply to Levinger's note. *Psychological Bulletin,* 1964, **61,** 158–160.

THIBAUT, J. W. An experimental study of the cohesiveness of underprivileged groups. *Human Relations,* 1950, **3,** 251–278.

THIBAUT, J. W., & H. H. KELLEY. *The social psychology of groups.* New York: John Wiley & Sons, Inc., 1959.

THIBAUT, J. W., & H. W. RIECKEN. Authoritarianism, status, and the communication of aggression. *Human Relations,* 1955, **8,** 95–120.

THISTLETHWAITE, D. L., H. DE HAAN, & J. KAMENETZKY. The effects of "directive" and "nondirective" communication procedures on attitudes. *Journal of Abnormal and Social Psychology,* 1955, **51,** 107–113.

THISTLETHWAITE, D. L., & J. KAMENETZKY. Attitude change through refutation and elaboration of audience counterarguments. *Journal of Abnormal and Social Psychology,* 1955, **51,** 3–12.

THISTLETHWAITE, D. L., J. KAMENETZKY, & H. SCHMIDT. Factors influencing attitude change through refutative communication. *Speech Monographs,* 1956, **23,** 14–25.

THOMAS, E. J. Role conceptions and organizational size. *American Sociological Review,* 1959, **24,** 30–37.

THOMAS, E. J., & C. F. FINK. Effects of group size. *Psychological Bulletin,* 1963, **60,** 371–384.

TOBY, J. Some variables in role conflict analysis. *Social Forces,* 1952, **30,** 323–327.

TOMAN, W. *Family constellation: Its effects on personality and social behavior.* (2nd ed.) New York: Springer Publishing Company, Inc., 1969.

TORRANCE, E. P. Some consequences of power differences on decision making in permanent and temporary three-man groups. In A. P. Hare, E. F. Borgatta, & R. F. Bales (Eds.), *Small groups: Studies in social interaction.* New York: Alfred A. Knopf, Inc., 1955. Pp. 482–491.

TREIMAN, D. J. Status discrepancy and prejudice. *American Journal of Sociology,* 1966, **71,** 651–664.

TRENAMAN, J., & D. MCQUAIL. *Television and the political image.* London: Methuen & Co., Ltd., 1961.

TROW, D. B. Autonomy and job satisfaction in task-oriented groups. *Journal of Abnormal and Social Psychology,* 1957, **54,** 204–209.

TRIANDIS, H. C. A note on Rokeach's theory of prejudice. *Journal of Abnormal and Social Psychology,* 1961, **62,** 184–186.

TRIANDIS, H. C., V. VASSILIOU, & E. K. THOMANEK. Social status as a determinant of respect and friendship acceptance. *Sociometry,* 1966, **29,** 396–405.

TUMIN, M. M. Readiness and resistance to desegregation: A social portrait of the hard core. *Social Forces,* 1958, **36,** 256–263.

TURK, H. Instrumental and expressive ratings reconsidered. *Sociometry,* 1961, **24,** 76–81.

TURNER, R. H. Role-taking process versus conformity. In A. Rose (Ed.), *Human behavior and social processes: An interactionist approach.* Boston: Houghton Mifflin Company, 1962.

UPSHAW, H. Comparison level as a function of reward cost orientation. *Journal of Personality,* 1967, **35,** 290–296.

VAN OSTRAND, D. C. Reactions to positive and negative information as a function of certain personality characteristics of the recipient. Unpublished master's thesis, University of Colorado, 1963.

VAUGHAN, G. M. The transsituational aspects of conformity behavior. *Journal of Personality,* 1964, **32,** 335–354.

VENESS, T., & D. W. BRIERLEY. Forming impressions of personality: Two experiments. *British Journal of Social and Clinical Psychology*, 1963, **2**, 11-19.

VERBA, S. *Small groups and political behavior: A study of leadership.* Princeton, N.J.: Princeton University Press, 1961.

VIDEBECK, R. Self-conception and the reaction of others. *Sociometry*, 1960, **23**, 351-359.

VINACKE, W. E. Variables in experimental games: Toward a field theory. *Psychological Bulletin*, 1969, **71**, 293-318.

VINACKE, W. E., & A. ARKOFF. An experimental study of coalitions in the triad. *American Sociological Review*, 1957, **22**, 406-414.

VINE, I. Communication by facial-visual signals. In J. H. Crook (Ed.), *Social behavior in birds and mammals.* London: Academic Press, Ltd., 1970. Pp. 279-354.

VROOM, V. H. *Work and motivation.* New York: John Wiley & Sons, Inc., 1964.

WAGER, W. L. Interpersonal and mass communication in an organizational setting. *Sociological Inquiry*, 1962, **32**, 88-107.

WAGNER, C., & L. WHEELER. Model, need, and cost effects in helping behavior. *Journal of Personality and Social Psychology*, 1969, **12**, 111-116.

WALDER, L. O. Application of role and learning theories to the study of the development of aggression in children: III. An attempt at an empirical test of a theory. *Psychological Reports*, 1961, **9**, 306-312.

WALKER, E. L., & R. W. HEYNS. *An anatomy for conformity.* Englewood Cliffs, N.J.: Prentice-Hall, Inc., 1962.

WALLACH, M. A., & N. K. KOGAN. The roles of information, discussion and consensus in group risk taking. *Journal of Experimental Social Psychology*, 1965, **1**, 1-9.

WALLACH, M. A., N. K. KOGAN, & D. J. BEM. Group influence on individual risk taking. *Journal of Abnormal and Social Psychology*, 1962, **65**, 75-86.

WALLACH, M. A., N. K. KOGAN, &

R. B. BURT. Can group members recognize the effects of group discussion upon risk taking? *Journal of Experimental and Social Psychology*, 1965, **1**, 379-395.

WALLER, W., & R. HILL. *The family.* New York: The Dryden Press, Inc., 1951. Pp. 186-187.

WALLERSTEIN, J. L., & C. J. WYLE. Our law-abiding law breakers. *Federal Probation*, 1947, **25**, 107-112.

WALSTER, E. The effects of self-esteem on romantic liking. *Journal of Experimental Social Psychology*, 1965, **1**, 184-197.

WALSTER, E. Assignment of responsibility for an accident. *Journal of Personality and Social Psychology*, 1966, **3**, 73-79.

WALSTER, E. "Second-guessing" important events. *Human Relations*, 1967, **20**, 239-250.

WALSTER, E. Passionate love. In B. I. Murstein (Ed.), *Theories of attraction and love.* New York: Springer Publishing Co., Inc., 1971. Pp. 85-99.

WALSTER, E., E. ARONSON, & D. ABRAHAMS. On increasing the persuasiveness of a low prestige communicator. *Journal of Experimental Social Psychology*, 1966, **2**, 325-342.

WALSTER, E., V. ARONSON, D. ABRAHAMS, & L. POTTMAN. Importance of physical attractiveness in dating behavior. *Journal of Personality and Social Psychology*, 1966, **4**, 508-516.

WALSTER, E., & E. BERSCHEID. New directions in equity research. Unpublished manuscript, 1970.

WALSTER, E., & P. PRESTHOLDT. The effect of misjudging another: Over-compensation or dissonance reduction. *Journal of Experimental Social Psychology*, 1966, **2**, 85-97.

WALSTER, E., & B. WALSTER. Effect of expecting to be liked on choice of associates. *Journal of Abnormal and Social Psychology*, 1963, **67**, 402-404.

WALTERS, R. H., M. LEAT, & L. MEZEI. Inhibition and disinhibition of responses through

empathetic learning. *Canadian Journal of Psychology*, 1963, **17**, 235-240.

WALTERS, R. H., & R. D. PARKE. Influence of response consequences to a social model on resistance to deviation. *Journal of Experimental Child Psychology*, 1964, **1**, 269-280.

WARDWELL, E. Children's reactions to being watched during success and failure. Unpublished doctoral dissertation, Cornell University, 1960. Cited by J. J. Gibson & A. D. Pick, Perception of another person's looking behavior. *American Journal of Psychology*, 1963, **76**, 86-94.

WARDWELL, W. A. The reduction of strain in a marginal social role. *American Journal of Sociology*, 1955, **61**, 16-25.

WARE, R., & O. J. HARVEY. A cognitive determinant of impression formation. *Journal of Personality and Social Psychology*, 1967, **5**, 38-44.

WARR, P. B., & C. KNAPPER. *The perception of people and events.* London: John Wiley & Sons, Inc., 1968.

WARR, P. B., & J. S. SMITH. Combining information about people: Comparisons between six models. *Journal of Personality and Social Psychology*, 1970, **16**, 55-65.

WARREN, J. R. Birth order and social behavior. *Psychological Bulletin*, 1966, **65**, 38-49.

WATTS, J. C. The role of vulnerability in resistance to fear-arousing communications. Unpublished doctoral dissertation, Bryn Mawr College, 1966. Cited in H. Leventhal, Findings and theory in the study of fear communications. In L. Berkowitz (Ed.), *Advances in experimental social psychology.* Vol. 5. New York: Academic Press, Inc., 1970. Pp. 119-186.

WATTS, W. A. Relative persistence of opinion change induced by active compared to passive participation. *Journal of Personality and Social Psychology*, 1967, **5**, 4-15.

WATZLOWICH, P., J. BEAVIN, & D. D. JACKSON. *Pragmatics of human communication: A study of interactional patterns, path-*

ologies and paradoxes. New York: W. W. Norton & Company, Inc., 1967.

WEATHERLEY, D. Anti-semitism and the expression of fantasy aggression. *Journal of Abnormal and Social Psychology,* 1961, **62,** 454–457.

WEBER, M. (Collected writings) In H. Gerth and C. W. Mills (Eds. and Translators), New York: Oxford University Press, 1946.

WEBER, M. (Collected writings) In S. N. Eisenstadt (Ed.), *Max Weber on charisma and institution building: Selected papers.* Chicago: The University of Chicago Press, 1968.

WEINER, B., & A. KUKLA. An attributional analysis of achievement motivation. *Journal of Personality and Social Psychology,* 1970, **15,** 1–20.

WEINER, M., J. T. CARPENTER, & B. CARPENTER. External validation of a measure of conformity behavior. *Journal of Abnormal and Social Psychology,* 1956, **52,** 421–422.

WEINSTEIN, E. A. Toward a theory of interpersonal tactics. In C. W. Backman & P. F. Secord (Eds.), *Problems in social psychology.* New York: McGraw-Hill Book Company, 1966. Pp. 394–398.

WEINSTEIN, E. A. The development of interpersonal competence. In D. A. Goslin (Ed.), *Handbook of Socialization Theory and Research.* Chicago: Rand McNally & Company, 1969. Pp. 753–778.

WEINSTEIN, E. A., & P. DEUTSCHBERGER. Some dimensions of altercasting. *Sociometry,* 1963, **26,** 454–466.

WEINSTEIN, M. S. Achievement motivation and risk preference. *Journal of Personality and Social Psychology,* 1969, **13,** 153–172.

WEISS, W. Effects of the mass media on communication. In G. Lindzey & E. Aronson (Eds.), *The handbook of social psychology.* (2nd ed.) Vol. 5. Reading, Mass.: Addison-Wesley Publishing Company, Inc., 1969. Pp. 77–195.

WEISS, W. Mass communication. In P. H. Mussen, & M. R. Rosenzweig (Eds.), *An-*

nual review of psychology. Vol. 22. Palo Alto, Calif.: Annual Reviews, Inc., 1971. Pp. 309–336.

WELLS. Unpublished study cited in G. A. Comstock & E. A. Rubinstein (Eds.), *Television and social behavior.* Vol. 1. *Content and control.* Washington, D.C.: U.S. Government Printing Office, 1971.

WERTHEIMER, M. Values in person cognition. In *Decisions, values, and groups.* New York: Pergamon Press, 1960. Pp. 135–153.

WESTIE, F. R. Negro-white status differentials and social distance. *American Sociological Review,* 1952, **17,** 550–558.

WESTIE, F. R., & M. L. DE FLEUR. Autonomic responses and their relationship to race attitudes. *Journal of Abnormal and Social Psychology,* 1959, **58,** 340–347.

WHEELER, L. Motivation as a determinant of upward comparison. *Journal of Experimental Social Psychology,* 1966, **1,** 27–31.

WHITE, M. M. Role conflict in disasters: Not family but familiarity first. Research report. Washington: Disaster Study Group, National Academy of Sciences, National Research Council, August 1962.

WHITING, J. W. M. Resource mediation and learning by identification. In I. Iscoe & H. W. Stevenson (Eds.), *Personality development in children.* Austin: University of Texas Press, 1960. Pp. 112–126.

WHITING, J. W. M., R. KLUCKHOHN, & A. ANTHONY. The function of male initiation ceremonies at puberty. In E. Maccoby, T. M. Newcomb, & E. L. Hartley (Eds.), *Readings in social psychology.* (3rd ed.) New York: Holt, Rinehart and Winston, Inc., 1958. Pp. 359–370.

WHITTAKER, J. O. Cognitive dissonance and the effectiveness of persuasive communications. *Public Opinion Quarterly,* 1964, **28,** 547–555. *(a)*

WHITTAKER, J. O. Parameters of social influence in the autokinetic situation. *Sociometry,* 1964, **27,** 88–95. *(b)*

WHYTE, W. F. *Street corner society: The social structure of an Italian slum.* Chicago: The University of Chicago Press, 1943.

WIGGINS, J. A., E. DILL, & R. D. SCHWARTZ. On "status liability." *Sociometry,* 1965, **28,** 197–209.

WIGGINS, N., & P. J. HOFFMAN. Types of judges and cue utilization in judgments of intelligence. *Journal of Personality and Social Psychology,* 1969, **12,** 52–59.

WILLIAMS, R. M., JR. *The reduction of intergroup tensions.* New York: Social Science Research Council, 1947.

WILLIAMS, R. M., JR. Friendship and social values in a suburban community: An exploratory study. *Pacific Sociological Review,* 1959, **2,** 3–10.

WILNER, D. M., R. P. WALKLEY, & S. W. COOK. Residential proximity and intergroup relations in public housing projects. *Journal of Social Issues,* 1952, **8,** 45–69.

WILNER, D. M., R. P. WALKLEY, & S. W. COOK. *Human relations in interracial housing.* Minneapolis: The University of Minnesota Press, 1955.

WILSON, D. T. Ability evaluation, postdecision dissonance, and co-worker attractiveness. Unpublished doctoral dissertation, University of Minnesota, 1962.

WILSON, D. T. Ability evaluation, postdecision dissonance, and co-worker attractiveness. *Journal of Personality and Social Psychology,* 1965, **1,** 486–489.

WILSON, R. S. Personality patterns, source attractiveness, and conformity. *Journal of Personality,* 1960, **28,** 186–199.

WINCH, R. F. *Mate-selection: A study of complementary needs.* New York: Harper & Brothers, 1958.

WINDER, A. E. White attitudes towards Negro-white interaction in an area of changing racial composition. *Journal of Social Psychology,* 1955, **41,** 85–102.

WINTERBOTTOM, M. R. The relation of need for achievement to learning experiences in independence and mastery. In J. W. Atkinson (Ed.), *Motives in fantasy, action, and society.* Princeton, N.J.: D. Van Nostrand Company, Inc., 1958. Pp. 453-478.

WISPÉ, L. G. A sociometric analysis of conflicting role expectancies. *American Journal of Sociology,* 1955, **61,** 134-137.

WORKS, E. The prejudice-interaction hypothesis from the point of view of the Negro minority group. *American Journal of Sociology,* 1961, **67,** 47-52.

WRIGHT, P. H., & A. C. CRAWFORD. Agreement and friendship: A close look and some second thoughts. *Representative Research in Social Psychology,* 1971, **2,** 52-69.

WRIGHTSMAN, L. Effects of waiting with others on changes in level of felt anxiety. *Journal of Abnormal and Social Psychology,* 1960, **61,** 216-222.

YABLONSKY, L. *Synanon: The tunnel back.* New York: The Macmillan Company, 1965.

ZAJONC, R. B. The effects of feedback and probability of group success on individual and group performance. *Human Relations,* 1962, **15,** 149-161.

ZALEZNIK, A., C. R. CHRISTENSEN, & F. J. ROETHLISBERGER. *Worker satisfaction and development.* Boston: Harvard University Bureau of Business Research, 1956.

ZALEZNIK, A., C. R. CHRISTENSEN, & F. J. ROETHLISBERGER. *The motivation, productivity, and satisfaction of workers: A prediction study.* Boston: Harvard University, Bureau of Business Research, 1958.

ZANDER, A., A. R. COHEN, & E. STOTLAND. Power and the relations among professions. In D. Cartwright (Ed.), *Studies in social power.* Ann Arbor: University of Michigan, Research Center for Group Dynamics, 1959. Pp. 15-34.

ZAWADSKI, B. Limitations of the scapegoat theory of prejudice. *Journal of Abnormal and Social Psychology,* 1948, **43,** 127-141.

ZELDITCH, M., JR. Role differentiation in the nuclear family: A comparative study. In T. Parsons & R. F. Bales (Eds.), *Family socialization and interaction process.* Chicago: The Free Press of Glencoe, Ill., 1955. Pp. 307-351.

ZIMBARDO, P. G. Involvement and communication discrepancy as determinants of opinion conformity. *Journal of Abnormal and Social Psychology,* 1960, **60,** 86-94.

ZIMBARDO, P. G., M. WEISENBERG, I. FIRESTONE, & B. LEVY. Communicator effectiveness in producing public conformity and private attitude change. *Journal of Personality,* 1965, **33,** 233-255.

ZIMMERMAN, C., & R. A. BAUER. The influence of an audience on what is remembered. *Public Opinion Quarterly,* 1956, **20,** 238-248.

ZIPF, S. G. Resistance and conformity under reward and punishment. *Journal of Abnormal and Social Psychology,* 1960, **61,** 102-109.

ZURCHER, L. A., JR., D. W. SONENSCHEIN, & E. L. METZNER. The hasher: A study of role conflict. *Social Forces,* 1966, **44,** 505-514.

Indexes

Name Index

Page numbers in *italic* indicate illustrations.

Subject Index

Conflict:
  in nursing role, 432
  in role expectations, 431–433
  between roles, 434–435
Conformity:
  alienation and, 325
  in a cohesive group, 316
  costs of, 311–312, 315–316,
    320–321
  counternorm effects, 306
  degrees of conformity in different
    groups, 315–319
  demands by leaders for, 321
  distribution of group, 310, 311,
    319–327
  exchange of social approval for,
    390
  extent of, in group, 310, 311
  focus of group, 310
  group leaders and, 321–322
  informational influence and, 306,
    325
  intrinsic costs and rewards of,
    313–314, 318, 324–325
  mechanisms underlying, 305–308
  negative sanctions of groups, 315
  normative influence and, 305–306,
    325
  to norms of social responsibility,
    327–334
  of opinions, 303
  perceived costs of, 173
  pressures toward, 303, 316
  resistance to, 317
  reward-cost outcomes of, 172
  rewards of, 311–312, 315–316,
    320–321
  sanctions and, 314, 318–319,
    325–326
  "security" of group leaders and, 322
  self-commitment and, 306
  self-correction and, 324
  social accommodation and, 324
  social-emotional needs and, 311
  status and degree of, 322
  surveillance and, 314, 318–319,
    325–326

Conformity:
  task-related needs and, 311
  unambiguous information and,
    304–305
  unanimous opinion and, 304
  use of coercive power and, 317
  (*See also* Norms)
Confrontation, 74–75
Congruency (*see* Interpersonal
  congruency)
Conscience, 488
Conscience formation, dependency
  needs and, 473
  (*See also* Moral development)
Consensual validation, 210, 215
  dyadic attraction and, 227
  social power and, 249
Consensus:
  pressures toward, 302
  in role expectations, 422–430
Consistency, as contributor to
  influence, 62
Consistency theory, 92
Contract, social, 68
Contrast effect, 114
Control, problem-solving and, 389
Coping with danger, 96–97
  effect of fear on, 97
  factors affecting, 99–100
  feeling invulnerable and, 101
  (*See also* Fear)
Coping reactions, 97
Cost, definition of, 220
Counternorm effects, 306
Counterpropaganda, immunization
  against, 124–127
  (*See also* Persuasion)
Crime in mass communications,
  159–162
Cultural ideology:
  definition of, 183
  prejudice as part of, 183
Culture, 3
  cultural variables and resolution of
    role strain, 456–457
  emergence of subcultures, 457

Hawthorne, p. 397

Cap'sm: Economic equilibrium, w/ actors
inside it, & the whole engine
moves "forward."

Max: Series of stages, & econ. is a
function of politics (struggle).

Holism: that "factors" don't exist
apart & Analysis is not
zone or existence or explanation.

Sci. Researchers see themselves
"out of time," except as
one insight leads to another
"sequential" insight
"chain of sequences" — "program
model

Hist'ns are time-bound, or see
themselves as time bound:
"Past explains now," or
"Past as experience on its
own terms."

(cf
Kuhn,
but
w/ more
relations
connecting
— all in past
was sufficient,
but was it
necessary to
now?

Hist to reader of ASR:

1. Someone citing something does not "support" the view. (e.g. p. 508, #51.)

Opposition
Rejected

2. Ethical dim:
   Hist'n has special responsibility in his interps. (But is wh. of 4 nr. not the case?)

H: nothing is stable !
Q = How + where will it change ? not if.

3. need the longitudinal view !

4. Cul'l differences. (cf. Puritans)

5. Self-interest + its role in soc. 4.
   (p. 495, 505 = achievement, 510 - "interest")

6. Role θ = Eastern 4 ?
   or Western 4 ?
   (thinking of Ⓑ & role apart.)

7. marxian view ?
   — longitudinal relr's)

(marxian)
not
marxist

— Stanton
Dyad.
—Toward a
new Past

8. Burke, Connections : how one
   structure leads to another; + non-
   predictable; + non-stable !!
   S₁ → reward of A₁; failure of A₂; A₂ → S₂ !, etc., etc.

8. How present interp. is a
   function of present view !

S = structure
A = action
(p. 510)

4a. class diff's;
   social diff's;
   cul'l diff's;
   sequential experience !
   — Environment is a part
   of a sequence !!
   (e.g. 1942-1963
   or 1963-1976
   or 1933-1945 !)